THE
PRICE of
FREEDOM

SLAVERY *and the*
CIVIL WAR

VOLUME ONE

The Demise of Slavery

Edited by Martin H. Greenberg & Charles G. Waugh

with an introduction by Edna Greene Medford

CUMBERLAND HOUSE
Nashville, Tennessee

Published by

CUMBERLAND HOUSE PUBLISHING
431 Harding Industrial Drive
Nashville, Tennessee 37211
www.CumberlandHouse.com

The acknowledgments on pages xiii–xv constitute an extension of this page.

Cover design by Bateman Design, Nashville, Tennessee.

Library of Congress Cataloging-in-Publication Data

The price of freedom : slavery and the Civil War / edited by Martin H. Greenberg
and Charles G. Waugh ; introduction by Edna Greene Medford.
    p.   cm.
Includes bibliographical references and index.
Contents: v. 1. The demise of slavery — v. 2. The preservation of liberty
ISBN 1-58182-085-2 (v. 1 : pbk. : alk. paper)
1. United States—History—Civil War, 1861–1865—Afro-Americans.
2. Slaves—Emancipation—United States. 3. Slavery—United States—History.
I. Greenberg, Martin Harry. II. Waugh, Charles.
E540.N3 P75 2000
973.7'08996073—dc21   00-056045
                                                    CIP

Printed in the United States of America
1 2 3 4 5 6 7 8 9 10—04 03 02 01 00

*To the men and women who fought for the
integrity of our nation, the ideals it was founded
on, and the liberty of all its citizens*

Contents

Introduction

> At last our proud Republic is overtaken. Our National Sin has
> found us out. . . . Slavery has done it all. . . . We have sown the
> wind, only to reap the whirlwind. (Frederick Douglass, May, 1861)

A S AMERICANS EMBARKED ON a four-year civil war, few could have imagined (including Frederick Douglass) the enormity of the destruction
to human life and property or the irrevocable changes that the conflict
would thrust upon the nation. White men, North and South, marched
off to war confident in the justness of their cause and secure in the knowledge that God's grace would assure the victory. Their stated motivations—for Northerners, preservation of the Union and for white
Southerners, defense of their homeland and their way of life—hid the
true cause of the conflict and ensured to both sides unstinting support
from their respective populations. But while Americans denied any connection between the war and the South's peculiar institution, men like
Douglass pressed for slavery's demise, recognizing that it indeed had
been the instrument that severed the bonds of national kinship. In time,
Northern men and women and their leaders would acknowledge the
legitimacy of Douglass's assertion and would embrace both union and
abolition as twin goals of the war.

Although the North had implemented plans to end slavery in the
aftermath of the American Revolution, abolitionists had become notorious in that region by the antebellum period. Considered dangerous radicals for their often fiery rhetoric and occasional disregard of the law, the
men who opposed slavery often found themselves on the receiving end of
well-placed punches and expertly wielded clubs. While the tumultuous
decade preceding the war between the states had witnessed intense
debate over the extension of slavery, few embraced the idea of immediate
universal emancipation. Fear of a deluge of former bondsmen and women
descending on them in search of opportunity fed the racism of Northern
men and women as much as a dependence on black labor and centuries
of being able to force their will on enslaved and free African Americans

shaped the racial attitudes of Southerners. Many Northerners deemed white lives too valuable to sacrifice in a war to liberate blacks.

Abraham Lincoln's own reluctance to touch slavery grew out of a concern over the limited constitutional powers of the presidency, fear that the Border States would secede, and a desire to remain within the bounds of public opinion. In an effort to stop the rush of Southern states into the newly formed Confederacy, he tried mightily to dispel the notion that there was any association between preservation of the Union and freedom for enslaved people. As abolitionists pressed for a dual aim to the war, the president and most of the Union resisted their efforts.

The reluctance of Northerners to embrace their cause, however, did not deter African Americans from waging their own war of liberation. Soon after the conflict commenced, the enslaved absconded from the plantations and made their way to Union-occupied territory. There they received a mixed reception. Some commanders, citing their obligation to enforce the Fugitive Slave Act of 1850, returned runaways to their Rebel owners. Others followed the example of Gen. Benjamin F. Butler at Fort Monroe, Virginia, who accepted the fugitives as contrabands of war or property that was confiscatable because it had been used to wage war against the Union. Eventually, Congress codified the actions of commanders such as Butler by passage of the Confiscation Acts. The first legalized the seizure of all property—including slaves—used to assist the Confederacy. The second liberated all fugitives who, in fleeing their Rebel masters, entered Union-occupied territory. But when two Northern generals sought to move beyond this narrow definition of freedom and declared universal emancipation in the areas under their jurisdiction, a cautious Lincoln rescinded their orders and embraced a plan of his own making. Guided by the recognition of the centrality of slavery in bringing about disunion, he appealed to the Border States to implement a plan of voluntary, compensated emancipation. When no state availed itself of this opportunity, Lincoln issued his preliminary proclamation of freedom, which became final on January 1, 1863. This admittedly military measure was aimed only at the areas of the South still in rebellion, and hence was meant to deprive the Confederacy of its servile labor force while keeping foreign nations (France and England specifically) from entering the war on the side of the Rebel forces. Despite its narrowly defined goals, the proclamation gave hope to those men and women of color who had already escaped their bondage as well as those who remained behind and whose actions helped to destroy the institution of slavery from within.

In addition to its promise of freedom, the Emancipation Proclamation authorized the enlistment of black men into the Union army. At the very beginning of the war, black offers to fight (with the exception of those serving in the navy) had been refused by the commander in chief who feared that arming men of color (enslaved or free) would incite the Border States to secede and join the Confederacy. Once the ban was lifted and black men gained the right to wear Union blue, recruitment began in earnest. The majority of black fighting men—more than 90,000—hailed from the states in rebellion. Another 40,000 came from the nonseceding Border States, and more than 50,000 had resided in the free North. Eventually designated United States Colored Troops, approximately 186,000 served in the army. At least another 19,000 men of color enlisted in the Union navy.

Contrary to the supposition of some whites that African Americans would fail to meet the demands of war, black fighting men served valiantly despite the disadvantages they suffered and the prejudices they faced. Many whites found it difficult to consider black soldiers as anything but an inferior lot whose position in the military should involve performance of those duties white soldiers found repugnant. Hence, fatigue duty, digging trenches, and building fortifications often took the place of real soldiering. The sting of racial prejudice and discrimination was exacerbated by pay inequities that permitted white enlisted men to earn nearly twice that of a black man of the same rank. And if captured by Confederate forces, black Union soldiers were treated as if they were slaves in rebellion and liable to be shot or sold into slavery, regardless of prewar status.

Black troops faced these disabilities with the strength and conviction that theirs was a holy cause. As they engaged the enemy, they understood that the struggle they waged was for more than Union; it represented their best chance to win freedom for the enslaved and an extension of liberties for blacks who had been free before the war. In the assault on Fort Wagner in South Carolina, at Port Hudson and Milliken's Bend in Louisiana, at the battle of the Crater at Petersburg, Virginia, and at Chapin's Farm (where their bravery under fire earned them thirteen Medals of Honor), black men showed their resolve to struggle for freedom and liberty.

As black men went off to war, African-American women sought to make a contribution to the cause as well. A few offered direct assistance by serving on navy vessels as nurses, laundresses, and chambermaids. Harriet Tubman, whose one-woman war against slavery via the Underground Railroad had led to the freeing of many from bondage, used her skills at stealth and deception to aid the Union military. Serving as a spy and scout, the stalwart former slave trekked through coastal South Carolina where she gleaned information critical to the conducting of the war in that area. In one instance, she led Union forces on a raiding expedition up the Combahee River that resulted in the liberation of nearly eight hundred enslaved people. When not participating in such forays, Tubman provided nursing care to the fallen troops. Similarly, the black abolitionist and newspaper woman Mary Ann Shadd Cary aided the war effort by assisting in the recruitment of black troops after having received an official commission to do so. Still other women such as former patriot Sarah Parker Remond worked to keep public opinion abroad favorable to the Union cause.

Although black sentiment rested overwhelmingly with the Union effort, significant numbers of men and women involuntarily aided the Confederate cause. Enslaved African Americans provided the agricultural labor that kept the Southern army fed. Others labored in the industrial establishments of the region, especially at the various ironworks. Still others—both enslaved and free—found themselves impressed into service as military laborers who drove wagons, threw up breastworks, felled trees, manned hospitals, and performed other tasks scorned by white soldiers. A heated debate continues over the willingness of and the extent to which African Americans fought for the cause championed by their Rebel owners and neighbors. If a few actually took up arms by choice in defense of the South, thousands more either eluded the impressment raiders, ran away at the first opportunity, or clandestinely assisted the Union forces even as they feigned loyalty to the Confederacy.

With America's national sin swept away by the whirlwind of war, the newly reforged Union paused to assess the conflict's cost. Almost 620,000 lives had been lost to the nation, including nearly 38,000 men of color. Families had been torn asunder, relationships between neighbors irrevocably altered, and a way of life modified. Most Americans would judge the Civil War a tragic episode in the nation's history, but for the black men and women whose efforts aided the destruction of slavery, the cost had been an acceptable one. Given the proscriptions under which they lived before the war expanded their possibilities, African Americans judged freedom to be priceless.

Edna Greene Medford

Acknowledgments

THE SOURCES for the selections in this volume are listed below. The original spelling and punctuation have been followed throughout with only minor typographical variations for the sake of consistency. Reference notes have been combined in a separate section following the text.

Introduction by Edna Greene Medford. Copyright © 2000 by Edna Greene Medford.

African Americans, the British Working Class, and the American Civil War by R. J. M. Blackett. Copyright © 1996 by Frank Cass & Company, Ltd. Reprinted by permission of *Slavery and Abolition*, vol. 15, no. 3 published by Frank Cass & Company, 900 Eastern Avenue, Ilford, Essex, England.

Frederick Douglass and the American Apocalypse by David W. Blight. Copyright © 1985 by the Kent State University Press. First published in *Civil War History*, vol. 31, no. 4, 1985. Reprinted by permission of the Kent State University.

Massachusetts and the Recruitment of Southern Negroes by Richard H. Abbott. Copyright © 1968 by the Kent State University Press. First published in *Civil War History*, vol. 31, no. 4, 1985. Reprinted by permission of the Kent State University.

The Hard Fight Was Getting into the Fight at All by Jack Fincher. Copyright © 1990 by Jack Fincher. First published in *Smithsonian*, vol. 20, no. 7, 1990. Reprinted by permission of the author.

Abraham Lincoln and the Recruitment of Black Soldiers by John T. Hubbell. Copyright © 1983 by the Board of Trustees of the University of Illinois. First published in *Papers of the Abraham Lincoln Association*, no. 2, 1980. Reprinted by permission of the University of Illinois Press.

Terrible Dilemmas: Black Enlistment in the Union Army During the American Civil War by Gary Kynoch. Copyright © 1997 by Frank Cass & Company, Ltd. Reprinted by permission of *Slavery and Abolition*, vol. 18, no. 2 published by Frank Cass & Company, 900 Eastern Avenue, Ilford, Essex, England.

Raising the African Brigade: Early Black Recruitment in North Carolina by Richard Reid. Copyright © 1993 by *North Carolina Historical Review*. First published in *North Carolina Historical Review*, vol. 70, no. 3, 1993. Reprinted by permission of the Historical Publications Section.

Review of American Studies, vol. 21, no. 2, 1990. Reprinted by permission of the University of Calgary Press.

"We Cannot Treat Negros . . . As Prisoners of War": Racial Atrocities and Reprisals in Civil War Arkansas by Gregory J. W. Urwin. Copyright © 1996 by the Kent State University Press. First published in *Civil War History,* vol. 42, no. 3, 1996. Reprinted by permission of the Kent State University.

Captive Black Union Soldiers in Charleston—What to Do? by Howard C. Westwood. Copyright © 1982 by the Kent State University Press. First published in *Civil War History,* vol. 28, no. 1, 1982. Reprinted by permission of the Kent State University.

The Southern Side of "Glory": African American Women during the Civil War by Noralee Frankel. Copyright © 1990 by Noralee Frankel. Reprinted by permission of the author.

The New England Quarterly, vol. 24, March 1951 for "Sojourner Truth and President Lincoln" by Carleton Mabee. Copyright held by *New England Quarterly.* Reproduced by permission of the publisher and the author.

Presence and Precedents: The USS *Red Rover* during the American Civil War by Steven Louis Roca. Copyright © 1998 by the Kent State University Press. First published in *Civil War History,* vol. 44, no. 1, 1998. Reprinted by permission of the Kent State University.

Free Men of Color in Gray by Arthur W. Bergeron Jr. Copyright © 1986 by the Kent State University Press. First published in *Civil War History,* vol. 32, no. 3, 1986. Reprinted by permission of the Kent State University.

Black Southerners in Gray by Richard Rollins. Copyright © 1994 by Rank and File Publications. First published in *Black Southerners in Gray.* Reprinted by permission of Rank and File Publications.

General Patrick Cleburne's Proposal to Arm Southern Slaves by Barbara Ruby. Copyright © 1971 by the Arkansas Historical Association. First published in the *Arkansas Historical Quarterly,* vol. 30, 1971. Reprinted by permission of the Arkansas Historical Association.

THE
PRICE *of*
FREEDOM

SLAVERY *and the*
CIVIL WAR

Part 1

ABOLITIONIST SENTIMENT AND THE CIVIL WAR

CHAPTER 1

Frederick Douglass and the
American Apocalypse

David W. Blight

We can yet see in the Civil War an image of the powerful, painful,
grinding process by which an ideal emerges out of history. That
should teach us humility beyond the Great Alibi and the Treasury
of Virtue, but at the same time it draws us to the glory of the
human effort to win meaning from the complex and confused
motives of men and the blind ruck of event.

ROBERT PENN WARREN,
1961[1]

Zion shall be redeemed with judgment, and her converts with
righteousness.

ISAIAH 1:27

IN 1862–63, THE PROSPECT of emancipation gave a new purpose to the
Civil War and a new meaning to American history. For the slaves and
for abolitionists, both black and white, emancipation was initially something more easily felt than explained. For Frederick Douglass, the former
fugitive slave turned orator-editor and the leading black spokesman in
America, a most important moment had been reached in a long struggle. One year into the conflict, Douglass spoke of the inexorable way
emancipation had become the war's central question: "It is really wonderful . . . how all efforts to evade, postpone, and prevent its coming,
have been mocked and defied by the stupendous sweep of evens."[2]
Douglass searched for ways to understand and affect the turn of events.

5

In large measure, his wartime thought reflects a spiritual interpretation of the war that fits squarely into several intellectual and theological traditions: millennialism, apocalypticism, civil religion, the providential view of history, and the jeremiad. This paper will examine Douglass's place in these traditions as demonstrated in his search for the meaning of the Civil War.

For Douglass and so many of his contemporaries, God's presence in the crucible of the Civil War was an irresistible notion; the desperate nature of the conflict and the totality of its aims invoked the spiritual side of the American character. In Protestant America, North and South seemed to be contending for the future beyond the Apocalypse. Examples of the millennialist response to the Civil War are numerous. Abraham Lincoln's second inaugural address provides a famous illustration. Searching for the meaning of emancipation, Lincoln declared that the "Almighty has his own purposes," and gave the country "this terrible war, as the woe due to those by whom the offence came." But perhaps the clearest apocalyptic statement about the Civil War resounded from Julia Ward Howe's "The Battle Hymn of the Republic." Howe captured in poetry one of the central ideological and spiritual traditions of her age. In her opening line—"Mine eyes have seen the glory of the coming of the Lord"—Howe struck the essential chord of millennialism: God's second coming. She envisioned God's presence in the soldier's "watch-fires" and his imminent judgment by a "terrible swift sword." Written in 1862, the "Battle Hymn" was a millennialist paean, which for many Northern Protestants, expressed the meaning of the Civil War.[3]

In nineteenth-century America, millennialism was a cluster of religious and secular ideas inherited from the Puritans, refashioned through the Revolutionary era, nurtured through numerous waves of revivalism, and forged into a national creed during the antebellum period. It taught that Christ would have a second coming in the new Israel of America. Moreover, millennialism helped foster an American sense of mission, a belief that the United States was the redeemer nation destined to perform a special role in history. Since John Winthrop's vision of a city upon a hill, Americans had believed that their new world—and later their new nation—was a place where mankind had been offered a second chance. A new Adam could flourish in a new garden full of hope. A nation of Protestants came to interpret events, at least in part, as steps in their providential destiny. But it was believed that nations, like individuals, must suffer and be tested before they could fulfill their appointed destinies. Following biblical prophecy of the Apocalypse, many Northern Protestants had come to believe by the 1850s that their country was on the brink of such a rending, an apocalyptic war that would usher in a new era of peace and freedom.[4] Hence, as the war came and as the level of death and suffering reached shocking proportions, Douglass joined the many Americans who believed they were in the midst of a conflict for God's purposes.

Millennialism has always been a concept fraught with ambiguity, and Douglass's espousal of this tradition is no exception. It seems never to be without eschatological symbolism, whether in a purely religious or secular context. But men cannot contemplate the end of the world nor the creation of a new one through any means other than belief or illusion. The millennial vision has never been an empirical matter; the world has yet to experience the end of time or the end of history. And yet, it represents a hope of a better world without which some men have not seemed capable of living. Millennialism can be viewed as dreadful calamity as it is in many biblical uses of the concept, or it can reflect an optimistic, perfectionist view of history. Hence, the paradox and vagueness of the belief in millennialism. But the distinctions between an activistic and a pessimistic millennialism must not be too rigidly drawn. For mid-nineteenth-century American Protestants, both positions combined to form an apocalyptic outlook, the expectation of God's extraordinary intervention in history to destroy an evil age and replace it with a new, eternal creation.[5] The only certainty in millennial thought seems to have been its capacity to sustain dichotomies of belief and emotion. Prophecies of gloom and doom coexisted with ideas of national mission. Unbounded promise mixed with dreadful threat; anxiety marched with hope. When we find ambiguity in the spiritual perception of the Civil War held by Frederick Douglass, or anyone else, we should not be surprised. Such ambiguity had always characterized millennialism and apocalypticism, and helped them flourish in America.[6] Indeed, apocalypticism was often a response to or an escape from the ambiguity in millennial expectation. The reaction to the outbreak of the Civil War among Northern Protestants may illustrate this fact. Apocalypticism had always reflected the special hope of the persecuted, the dispossessed, and the enslaved; it could be cathartic, and had always been the child of crisis.[7]

Douglass's spiritual interpretation of the Civil War must also be assessed as part of the tradition of civil religion. Though the term hardly caught on in the mid-nineteenth century, the influence of the ideas it represented did. The contours of America's civil religion were forged by the actions and rhetoric of the founding fathers during the Revolutionary era. America's mission as a chosen people formed the core idea of a national faith. Indeed, this concept of mission became the central unifying myth of nineteenth-century America. Politicians and the clergy found a common creed. In the Revolution Americans experienced their "exodus"; in the Declaration of

Independence they possessed "sacred scriptures"; in Washington they found a Moses, and in Jefferson a high priest. But like the children of Israel, the Americans had to be tested. Answers to the deepest questions about national meaning and self-definition awaited in the Civil War, a conflict in which the sacred trust of the founders would be challenged and reborn. These were the myths essential to a civil religion.[8]

The literacy and oratorical tradition of the jeremiad is one of the oldest in American thought. No longer considered simply a form of lamentation about waning zeal, recent studies have deepened our understanding and broadened the definition of the jeremiad. It is a national ritual not only of self-condemnation, but also an appeal to the most optimistic aspects of the American mythology of mission. The Civil War reinvigorated the jeremiad, and Douglass made prolific use of it in ways unique to black intellectuals.[9]

Although he came by his education in a much less formal way than most of his abolitionist peers, Douglass shared with them the inheritance of the religious and ideological traditions previously mentioned. Although not a strong adherent of organized religion and openly contemptuous of the clergy throughout much of his life, Douglass nevertheless accepted and contributed to the Christian interpretation of the Civil War. Douglass found in the Civil War the fulfillment of prophecy, both biblical and his own.

On emancipation day, January 1, 1863, Douglass was in Boston to participate in what was expected to be a massive celebration at Tremont Temple. Speech followed speech throughout the day and into the evening, with Douglass providing his usual share of the oratory. Tension mounted as the large gathering waited impatiently for the news of Lincoln's proclamation. When the news finally arrived, great jubilation engulfed the crowd. Not surprisingly, this celebration was a deeply spiritual response to the most important moment in the history of black Americans. When a semblance of order was restored following the initial tears and shouting, Douglass led the throng in a chorus of his favorite hymn: "Blow ye the Trumpet Blow." Next, an old black preacher named Rue led the group in "Sound the loud timbel o'er Egypt's dark sea, Jehovah has triumphed, his people are free!"[10] These reactions were, of course, natural. But eighteen years later, while writing his third autobiography, Douglass captured the meaning of that day for his people in words that more generally reflect his vision of the war:

> It was not logic, but the trump of jubilee, which everybody wanted to hear. We were waiting and listening as for a bolt from the sky, which

should rend the fetters of four millions of slaves; we were watching as it were, by the dim light of stars, for the dawn of a new day; we were longing for the answer to the agonizing prayers of centuries. Remembering those in bonds as bound with them, we wanted to join in the shout for freedom, and in the anthem of the redeemed.[11]

The cruel and apocalyptic war had become holy.

The goal of this study is not a systematic analysis of Douglass's religion; rather it is to demonstrate how the black leader's spiritual outlook shaped his interpretation of the Civil War. In general terms Douglass was clearly a Christian. As a fugitive slave in New Bedford, Massachusetts, in 1839, Douglass became a licensed preacher in the African Methodist Episcopal Zion Church.[12] He gave ample testimony to the significance of religion in his early life as a slave. In *My Bondage and My Freedom,* he states that his "religious nature was awakened" at the age of thirteen. "I cannot say that I had a very distinct notion of what was required of me," wrote Douglass, "but one thing I knew very well—I was wretched, and had no means of making myself otherwise." He turned to prayer and to a personal faith, as he put it, "in Jesus Christ, as the Redeemer, Friend, and Savior of those who diligently seek him." Here was Christian doctrine expressed in its simplest terms.[13]

Douglass also turned to an intensely religious old black man in Baltimore named Uncle Lawson. The impressionable slave boy became "deeply attached" to the drayman, describing him in the autobiographies as his "spiritual father." Douglass spent countless hours in Uncle Lawson's shack reading the Bible aloud. The old man seems to have inspired young Frederick with a sense of hope and self-confidence. Lawson informed Douglass that God had great plans for him, that a special destiny lay ahead. It is difficult to measure the influence of Uncle Lawson on the young boy's developing mind; his autobiographies are the only source for this episode. But Douglass did develop a sense of special destiny. Indeed, he wrote the three autobiographies, in part, as a means of authenticating and recreating this conception of self. Uncle Lawson was at least one influential source of the idea of a benevolent and millennial God, a God who had the welfare of the downtrodden at heart, and who would one day intervene on their behalf. Uncle Lawson's instructions, wrote Douglass, "were not without their influence upon my character and destiny. He threw my thoughts into a channel from which they have never entirely diverged." Moreover, Douglass felt "assured, and cheered on . . . believing that my life was under the guidance of a wisdom higher than my own."[14]

Though written many years after the fact, these autobiographical statements reflect a religious outlook which Douglass sustained throughout his life. Douglass's God was the God of black Christianity: benevolent and loving, but also a deliverer. He was a God of action who would act "in His own good time," as Uncle Lawson had taught the impatient slave boy. Just as there were turning points in his own life that he could not fully explain in rational terms, Douglass came to see history in the same way. The message of a "better day coming"—the millennial tone—so prevalent in mid-nineteenth-century black thought found one of its greatest exhorters in Douglass. This was, of course, a message of hope for an oppressed people, and therefore, a struggle to sustain. By 1861, Douglass was well conditioned to the burdens of a millennial outlook and well practiced in capitalizing on the spiritual potential of major events.

The belief that history is governed by a "divine providence" can be expressed in many forms: in allusions to natural law, by faith in the doctrine of progress, and in various other modes of moral determinism. Douglass often did it very effectively in metaphor. The Civil War especially brought out this aspect of Douglass's thought. In a speech at Cooper Institute in New York in February 1863 Douglass declared not only his faith in progress, but his belief that Southerners were destined to fail because their cause violated natural law. Douglass used the phrases "laws of God" and "laws of nature" interchangeably to define history. "The world," announced Douglass, "like the fish preached to in the stream, moves on in obedience to the laws of its being bearing away all excrescences and imperfections in its progress. It has its periods of illumination as well as of darkness, and often bounds forward a greater distance in a single year than in an age before."[15] This view of history bounding forward exhibits Douglass's state of mind in the wake of emancipation. It also illuminates an essential element in the apocalyptic mentality: God was the engine of history, and his interventions kept it on a course of progress.

One of the most common ways in which Douglass expressed his providential view of history was in the phrase the "logic of events." A reformer's cause is always to some extent at the mercy of events. But Douglass often imbued this notion with a spiritual meaning. Suffering from impatience with the Union war effort in the summer of 1861, Douglass declared in a letter to a friend that his confidence rested more in the "stern of logic of events" than in the "disposition of the Federal army." As had long been his habit, Douglass's disposition fluctuated between hope and despair. In the fall of 1861, in response to a "sick and disheartened" correspondent who had challenged the black editor's optimism,

Douglass argued that the prospects for emancipation did not lie in the government at Washington, D.C. "There are powers above those of the Government and the army," he contended, "a power behind the throne, greater than the throne itself." In time, the government would be "borne along on the broad current of events." Though seemingly vague, Douglass rooted this hope in the long war theory. He maintained that if the war lasted long enough, and became desperate enough, emancipation would become an "iron necessity" of the Union cause. Keeping faith in jubilee, Douglass seemed to be telling his frustrated friend, required constant vigilance—"keep pounding on the rock," he urged—as did the belief that history was a "mighty current" driven by necessity and divine power.[16]

By spring of 1862 Douglass was convinced, at least for the time being, that "events steadily conspire to make the cause of the slave and the cause of the country identical." That March, Congress abolished slavery in the District of Columbia. "I trust I am not dreaming," Douglass wrote to Charles Sumner, "but the events taking place seem like a dream." At times in his life, Douglass had seriously doubted that he would ever live to see the United States Congress liberate slaves anywhere. Somehow, this war gave reality to dreams that decades of agitation could not accomplish.[17] Abraham Lincoln's preliminary emancipation proclamation of September 22, 1862, elicited from Douglass a grudging but sincere faith in the president's resolve. But even if Lincoln's character turned out to be untrustworthy, reasoned Douglass, "events greater than the President, events which have slowly wrung this proclamation from him may be relied on to carry him forward in the same direction." Douglass waited for emancipation day with great anxiety. But to him, it was not Lincoln's moment, not the work of "individual design." Lincoln, imagined Douglass, was "but the hands of the clock." On January 1, Douglass claimed, the "national ship" would swing around and be wafted off by the "trade winds of the Almighty."[18] Douglass's view of emancipation (in its various stages and meanings) was seldom without this spiritual, millennial component.

The Civil War provided the central event in Douglass's life that reinforced his providential view of history. The war justified and actualized his faith in both reason and revelation. It forged reality and meaning out of strained hope. In a speech on John Brown, first delivered in1860 but repeated numerous times throughout his life, Douglass summed up this providential outlook:

> There is in the moral world a force, a principle, a law, call it by what name you will, retributive justice, logic of events, revenge of time, or

judgments of God, which has asserted itself all along the sweep of history, and the instruments employed in its enforcement, whether dying on the gallows, on the cross or at the stake, have compelled the world to recognize them as its heroes, martyrs, and saviors.[19]

Douglass was not always doctrinaire in determining the source of this control over history. He was certain, though, that the Civil War, as he wrote in December 1861, was "too momentous an affair to be accidental."[20]

While rooted in religion, the apocalyptic tradition also flourished through language.[21] Douglass had discovered his sense of self, and indeed, a portion of his personal freedom through language Through the discovery of literacy while a slave and the exercise of autobiography while free, Douglass had found ways to liberate himself while still living within the racist constrictions of American society. By the same mode, he searched for the meaning of the Civil War. Apocalyptic language runs throughout Douglass's Civil War era rhetoric. Sometimes it took the form of biblical themes and imagery. In the summer of 1857, at a time when black optimism was sparse, Douglass spoke at a commemoration of the twenty-third anniversary of West Indian emancipation. British emancipation, declared the orator, served "as a city upon a hill" for black Americans. It had been a "bolt from the moral sky . . . something God-like . . . commanding the devil of slavery to go out of the British West Indies." Douglass announced on that occasion that he had seen the "apocalyptic vision," and only wished that more Americans could see it with him.[22] Apocalyptic imagery simplified historical complexity and served the nineteenth-century orator well. In times of crisis or despair (such as the aftermath of the Dred Scott decision in 1857), these appeals fell on welcome ears in abolitionist audiences. The cause was not dead while it was still God's cause. An apocalyptic God could change history abruptly in the British Empire (even bloodlessly), so why not in America too?

When the war came in 1861, Douglass used apocalyptic language with more aplomb. In April Douglass refused to deny the charge that James Redpath's Haitian emigration scheme was really a cover for the recruitment of a black army to invade the South (though it was certainly untrue). Instead, he preferred to goad the slaveholders' fears. "Wrapped up" in this claim, he contended, was "the prophecy of the final reign of justice and liberty among men. It is the flaming sword of heaven, bidding the oppressor beware!"[23] At one of his Sunday lectures at Zion church in Rochester, June 16, 1861, Douglass's apocalypticism was in perfect form. "Only mighty forces, resting deep down among the foundations of nature and life," he proclaimed, "can lash the deep and tran-

quil sea of humanity into a storm, like that which the world is now witnessing." Douglass was calling his flock to witness the special historical
moment that seemed to be dawning. Cosmic dualism—the eternal conflict between good and evil—an essential element in the apocalyptic tradition, had never appeared so relevant:

> Men have their choice in this world. They can be angels, or they may
> be demons. In the apocalyptic vision, John describes a war in heaven.
> You have only to strip that vision of its gorgeous Oriental drapery,
> divest it of its shining and celestial ornaments, clothe it in the simple
> and familiar language of common sense, and you will have before you
> the eternal conflict between right and wrong, good and evil, liberty
> and slavery, truth and falsehood. . . .[24]

It is difficult to measure how literally Douglass took his own apocalypticism, especially in its purely religious form. But the frequency with which
he appealed to apocalyptic imagery, the seriousness with which he
preached it, and the general millennial tone of his wartime rhetoric suggests that Douglass's interpretation of the Civil War rested squarely on this
Christian tradition.

Douglass put apocalyptic imagery to many uses during the war. In May
1862 he urged abolitionists to take heart. Abolition was slowly becoming
the policy of the government; Southerners would see to it, for they had
sown the seeds of their own doom. "Pride goeth before a fall," wrote
Douglass, "whom the gods would destroy they first make mad." When the
war was over, Douglass joined his countrymen in trying to understand the
assassination of Abraham Lincoln in apocalyptic terms: "It was as if some
grand convulsion in nature had occurred," Douglass declared in a speech in
December 1865, "for had the solid earth opened and swallowed up one of
our chief towns or cities, had the tombs burst beneath our feet . . . the sen-
sation of horror could not have been more profound." Lincoln's untimely
death, like the cruel war before it, had caused deep spiritual contemplation.
When Lincoln was murdered, "a hush fell upon the land," said Douglass,
"as though each man in it heard a voice from heaven . . . and paused to
learn its meaning."[25] To a millennialist, God seemed to have one final agonizing judgment to cast over the guilty land.

Douglass's apocalyptic interpretation of the Civil War must also be
understood in the context of his growing sense of American nationalism, a
central belief shared with his generation of Northern intellectuals. America's millennial nationalism—the belief in the American republic as a chosen
nation—was pervasive by the mid-nineteenth century and rendered even

more so by the Civil War.[26] The United States was seen as God's redemptive instrument in history. With providential appointments went burdens of world significance. With the notion of an elected nation came both promise and threat. How could the model republic, called to nationality by the founding fathers, endure its own tragic flaws? The Civil War became the crucible in which the nature and existence of that nationalism would be either preserved or redefined, or lost forever.

Douglass embraced virtually every aspect of America's mythology of mission. He believed the very idea of a republic was being tested in the Civil War. He believed the world was watching and he staked his own future on its outcome. Nothing else in Douglass's life stimulated such an outpouring of his own brand of American nationalism as the crisis of the Union. To the oft-repeated assertion by American millennialists that the Civil War was "a crisis in the world's history," as the *New York Independent* put it in 1861, Douglass added his own claims of world significance. As consolation for all the suffering caused by the war, Douglass advocated looking to the "vastness and grandeur of its mission." In a speech he gave all over the North in the fall and winter of 1863–64, Douglass maintained that "the world has not seen a nobler and grander war than that which the loyal people of this country are now waging." The war was prosecuted "not merely to free a country or a continent—but the whole world from slavery." Douglass urged his auditors to mourn the dead but not to mourn their "mission." "We should . . . stand in our appointed place," he challenged, "and do this great service for mankind."[27]

It is true that Douglass did not make such statements quite so zealously before emancipation. But his vision of the chosen republic under divine judgment was prevalent in his rhetoric throughout the war. In January 1862, in language which was both nationalistic and apocalyptic, Douglass described the Armageddon of the model republic:

> The fate of the greatest of all Modern Republics trembles in the balance. . . . The lesson of the hour is written down in characters of blood and fire. We are taught as with the emphasis of an earthquake, that nations, not less than individuals, are subjects of the moral government of the universe, and that . . . persistent transgressions of the laws of this Divine government will certainly bring national sorrow, shame, suffering and death. Of all the nations of the world, we seem most in need of this solemn lesson.[28]

Only in the survival of an American nation, reborn and redefined, could Douglass's nationalism find a true home. Though his confidence needed bolstering in early 1862, there was the assurance that an "earthquake" could radically alter the landscape.

Americans had long invested the Union with sacred qualities. But as disunion in 1861 demonstrated, this sacred trust had always been at best inchoate; the United States was a nation full of promise, but also paradox. Douglass preached a message similar to that of the theologian Horace Bushnell, who believed governments were conceived by God and put into the world through human agents. Nations, like individual sinners, had to experience suffering in order to fulfill their destiny.[29] Douglass returned again and again to the analogy of nations to individuals. In an appeal to the British not to intervene on behalf of the Confederacy, written in November 1862 and published in the *Independent*, Douglass was explicit: "There is no more exemption for nations than for individuals," he argued, "from the just retribution due to flagrant and persistent transgression. For the time being, America is the blazing illustration of this solemn truth."[30] Douglass frequently gave the nation personal qualities in his effort to describe the peril of the war. In January 1862 he described the American republic as but a "young nation" still standing "within the inner circle of childhood." But the youthful nation had lost its way, its "character" had been corrupted, its loyal citizens "sicklied over with a pale cast of thought." A national time of troubles would naturally evoke such lamentations. But Douglass would not let up. "It would seem, in the language of Isaiah," he exclaimed, "that the whole head is sick, and the whole heart is faint." The nation, Douglass seemed to be saying, had a sick soul.[31]

The above remarks came in a speech delivered in January 1862, entitled "The Reasons for Our Troubles." This was well before emancipation became the official policy of the Union war effort, and during a period of some of Douglass's bitterest harangues against the Lincoln administration. But the theme of a national soul persisted in his rhetoric well after emancipation. In April 1863, in the midst of his campaign to recruit black soldiers, Douglass stated that his faith did not ultimately rest in armies and munitions, but the "reform of the national heart." What was at stake in the contest, he contended, was "the soul of the nation."[32] Douglass sought the meaning of the nation's suffering, at least in part, in the doctrine of atonement. If a Christian nation, like an individual, could realize its worst sins and face the consequences of divine retribution, then perhaps a new nation could be born. To Douglass, the prospect of black freedom gathered hope from the nation's woes. But along with his fellow blacks, he would discover that even if the nation experienced a change of heart toward emancipation, it did not necessarily foster the same toward black people.

The religious historian Clebsch has identified the notion of a "cleansing tragedy" as one of the central themes in the Christian interpretation of the Civil War. The tragic sense ran deep in the mid-nineteenth-century American mind. A sentimental age demanded meaning out of death, especially when experienced by the thousands in a catastrophic civil war. Many humanitarian abolitionists could consent to the horrors of the war only when they convinced themselves that it represented divine and regenerative chastisements on the American people. Once persuaded, many millennial nationalists unabashedly called for the righteous shedding of blood.[33]

Though he could not match theologians like Bushnell or Henry Ward Beecher in purely religious nationalism, Douglass certainly contributed to the theme of a cleansing tragedy. In September 1862, just before Antietam and the preliminary emancipation proclamation, Douglass urged his readers not to despair about abolition. "A few weeks more of sufferings, disasters, defeats, and . . . the slaughter of our country's first born," he argued, would force the nation to free the slaves. Douglass's language was strikingly similar to that in Bushnell's famous "Reverses Needed" sermon preached more than a year earlier. "We are saved as by fire," Douglass asserted in words more fitting the pulpit than the editorial page. "We grieve with the sorrow-stricken families all over the North, but their terrible afflictions and heavy sorrows are their educators." This classic Christian notion that people must suffer and repent in order to reform seemed to run deep in Douglass's consciousness. His writings reflect a sense of authentic tragedy. A holy cause could justify almost any level of suffering; indeed, it seemed to necessitate it. "The tears and blood we are now pouring out may at last bring us to our senses," Douglass claimed with some certainty.[34] If through suffering and tragedy individuals found rebirth, then why not nations as well? To Douglass the Civil War was just such an authentic and collective tragedy. He wanted all Northerners to see the conflict as he did: a moral crusade for black freedom in which the American republic would experience a reformation through the fiery trial of war.

Douglass's own mixture of nationalism and apocalypticism was never so bold as when describing the regenerative nature of the Civil War. The Emancipation Proclamation had invested the war with "sanctity," he told a British audience in November 1862. "It will make justice, liberty, and humanity permanently possible in this country." In a flourish of idealism, Douglass claimed that the war's regenerative power applied to everyone, black and white. "We are all liberated by this proclamation," he asserted in February 1863. "It is a mighty event for the bondman, but it is a still mightier event for the nation at large." Douglass thus merged his American nationalism with his own brand of black nationalism. As the historian Wilson Moses has demonstrated, Douglass had always been aware of the peculiar place of black people as a nation within a nation. He had long been an active proponent of black self-help programs and assimilationism, while denouncing virtually all schemes of emigration. But this did not make him any less of a black nationalist, a leader with a sense of the separate cultural identity of his people.[35] The Civil War thrust these two forms of nationalism into vivid juxtaposition, and allowed Douglass to dream that there might one day be only one. If the Union's survival and black freedom could become one cause, then perhaps a truly new nation would emerge.

Like many other millennialists, Douglass believed that the antebellum American republic had been inchoate and temporary. The nation needed to experience a "new birth," as Lincoln put it in the Gettysburg Address. For the nation to survive it had to be recreated. Or, as William Clebsch has put it, the Civil War provided the "anvil of suffering" out of which the nation could finally be "actualized." Douglass delivered this message in December 1863 at the thirtieth anniversary celebration of the founding of the American Anti-Slavery Society. The "old Union" was "dead," he pronounced, its "bones quietly inurned under the shattered walls of Sumter." Northerners were fighting for a new Union, Douglass contended, one in which there would be no North, no South . . . no black, no white, but a solidarity of nation, making every slave free, and every free man a voter."[36] This concluding flourish to a speech which contained numerous allusions to the honesty and wisdom of Abraham Lincoln, was in many ways similar to the brief remarks the president had delivered just two weeks earlier at a cemetery in Gettysburg.

Douglass's analysis of the Civil War as a national regeneration thus illustrates the two central tenets of apocalypticism: the cosmic conflict between good and evil, and the historical, divinely rendered break between two distinct ages. The old Union had represented the dismal, irredeemable first age, and the war had ushered in the beginning of the new one. Douglass may have expressed this best in a recruiting speech to potential black soldiers in Philadelphia on July 6, 1863. He urged his listeners not to be discouraged by the legacy of slavery and discrimination under which all blacks labored. He asked them to try to forget their history down to the dawn of emancipation. "These were all dark and terrible days of the republic," Douglass admitted. "I do not ask you about the dead past, I bring you a living present. Events more mighty than men, eternal Providence, all-wise and all-controlling, have placed us in new relations to the Government and the Government to us."[37] The Battle of Gettysburg had ended just three days prior to this speech, but the news of its horrible casualties must have reached Douglass's audience before he spoke. How could he assuage the fears of these black recruits? How else but by an appeal to their sense of manhood, to their hopes for dignity and citizenship, and by a spiritual invitation to participate in America's millennial future.

In Douglass's millennial nationalism during the Civil War era, we find his frequent use of the jeremiad. Wilson Moses is the first historian to extensively analyze the *black* jeremiad. His working definition is very useful: the "constant warnings" issued to white audiences by black intellectuals, "concerning the judgment that was to come for this sin of slavery."[38] Since his earliest days as an abolitionist, Douglass had lent his voice to this ritual. Indeed, by the late 1850s and especially during the Civil War, he was the principal black Jeremiah. Douglass reached larger white audiences and preached the message of interracial nationalism more than any other black spokesman. This does not necessarily mean that his influence on white America was profound. But on its own terms, the black jeremiad had no more eloquent nor constant voice than Douglass.

Douglass's jeremiads took many forms. He directed his warnings at the nation as a whole, at white abolitionists, and at his fellow blacks. The immediate prewar years stimulated an almost constant wail from Douglass, whether attacking presidents, slaveholders, or abolitionists. In a January 1859 editorial he lamented the "heartlessness . . . and stone-dead indifference" toward the slavery issue of some of the antislavery press and the nation generally. The same month he bitterly attacked President Buchanan's handling of the Kansas question, but true to the jeremiadic tradition, turned his lament into a cry for hope: "Go on, sir; let the nation go on sir. The end is at hand. The haughty Assyrians will yet be brought low—the ire of offended justice will yet flash upon your soul, and burn up your heart strings with unquenchable fire."[39] Warnings of impending doom went hand in hand with attacks on religious hypocrisy, as well as nation declension. In July 1859 Douglass complained that too much of American Christianity had become "emasculated, corrupt, torpid, lifeless, a minister of moral death." The decay of what he like to call the "national heart" was a constant theme in Douglass's prewar rhetoric.[40]

When the war came, millennialists like Douglass responded in their familiar way. The war was both tragedy and prophetic opportunity. In May 1861 Douglass gave his readers a classic jeremiad wrapped in apocalyptic language. "We have sown the wind, only to reap the whirlwind," he charged. "The Republic has put one end of the chain upon the ankle of the bondman, and the other end about its own neck." A chosen but sinful people were about to reap the harvest of their own iniquity: "The land is now to weep and howl, amid ten thousand desolations brought upon it by the sins of two centuries. . . . Could we write as with lightning, and speak as with the voice of thunder, we should . . . cry to the nation, Repent, Break Every Yoke, let the Oppressed Go Free for Herein alone is deliverance and safety!" But it was not too late, Douglass claimed, if the slaves' "cry of vengeance" could be merged with the cry to save the Union.[41] The moment of truth in the nation's life had been reached.

The familiar mode of the jeremiad served Douglass well in responding to national days of fasting. Early in the conflict, President Lincoln declared September 26, 1861, a national day of fasting and prayer. Douglass answered the call with an appeal for prayer and reflection, but also with an attack on the lack of abolitionism in the Lincoln administration. "Our Government no where confesses that slavery is our national sin, nor exhorts to repentance of it," he charged. In a deeply religious editorial, Douglass quoted at length from the first chapter of Isaiah. In the passage, the prophet warns the nation of Israel of God's displeasure with their sac-rifices and burnt offerings, and of his impending judgment. God was not impressed by the entreaties of his sinful people: "I will hide mine eyes from you: yea, when ye make many prayers, I will not hear: your hands are full of blood." Isaiah's Old Testament rebuke of the nation of Israel formed the perfect model for Douglass's warnings to the new Israel. Isaiah calls God's people a "sinful nation . . . gone away backward." Their "whole head is sick, and the whole heart faint." Their country is "desolate" and their cities "burned with fire."[42] The imagery and the message were per-fectly suited to Douglass's purposes. Again and again, the black orator invoked the same language and the same themes to explain the calamity of the Civil War. A chosen but guilty people had to repent, suffer, and reform or lose their destiny altogether. In this crisis, perhaps the most available option to a black editor-orator was to stand with Isaiah and Jeremiah, and issue the warnings. God's people might be listening as never before.

Douglass used the jeremiad as yet another means to express his understanding of the Civil War. The war was the long-awaited calamity in which America's great paradox might be resolved. It was the wedge through which blacks might enter the family of the American nation. It was a moment when Afro-Americans might wrest a new definition out of the terrible duality of their lives. It was a time when America's first princi-ples could be appealed to, not only to free the slaves, but to save the nation. Both causes possessed a sacred quality, and they might be min-gled in one holy war. The war represented, therefore, the act of creation as well as preservation. These were the best hopes of a black abolitionist. The nation, however, had to be awakened to its mission.

The jeremiad provided a means for a black intellectual like Douglass to vent his frustration and rage while still preserving his hope. He could attack the United States government, while at the same time demand a place in its future. Black Jeremiahs, like their white counterparts in historian Sacvan Bercovitch's analysis, lamented declension, while "simultaneously . . . celebrating a national dream."[43] They could express their assimilationist desire while also advocating the distinct purposes of blacks. It was a way to be both black and American, to demonstrate loyalty to the Union and to the slave. This combination had been much more difficult before Fort Sumter. Black spokesmen like Douglass seemed to be saying that blacks were not only a nation within a nation, but a chosen people within a chosen people. If America did not have a special destiny that is must be called back to—or forced to fulfill through a cruel war—then what was to be made of its enslaved race? A powerful sense of mission thrived in nineteenth-century America, fed by republican ideology, boundless land, and evangelical Christianity. If blacks were to stay in America and not resort to wholesale insurrection, Douglass believed they had to share in that mission. Without the mythology of mission, it is difficult to imagine how Douglass could have sustained his hopes for black freedom in America.

Millennial hopes had always been difficult to sustain, though impossible to suppress. For Douglass, moreover, the struggle to keep faith in jubilee by temporal means alone had been too overwhelming. Though always dissatisfied with organized religion, he could not understand his own life nor express the aspirations of his people apart from spiritual considerations. "When all our earthly helps and hopes break down . . . ," he wrote in autumn 1861, "the soul goes up to the eternal and invisible for help."[44]

Undoubtedly, Douglass used apocalypticism and jeremiads as effective rhetorical devices. Appealing to white Christian, nationalistic audiences, Douglass knew the power of his apocalyptic imagery. But we must not mistake belief for expediency in this instance. Douglass believed what he preached. He believed in American mission, in a providential God who shaped history, in history that could reshape nations in a few calamitous years. Douglass's millennialism was genuine.

Thus it was through the idea of national regeneration that Douglass envisioned the purpose of the Civil War. After ceasing publication of his newspaper in August 1863, Douglass wrote a speech entitled "The Mission of the War" which he delivered in city after city across the North well into 1864. It is impossible to determine how many people heard this address, but the total would number in the thousands. The speech was, in part, a series of warnings against backsliding on emancipation, against the racism of the Democratic party and its political threat in 1864, and against the weariness caused by the horrible human costs of the war. But the speech was also a clear and eloquent statement of Douglass's inter- pretation of his American Apocalypse. "You and I know that the mission of this war is National regeneration," Douglass bluntly declared. He invoked the mythology of mission in some of its most widely understood language: "I do believe that it is the manifest destiny of this war to unify and reorganize the institutions of the country—and that herein is the secret of the strength, the fortitude, the persistent energy, in a word the sacred significance of this war."[45] Douglass never expressed the notion of holy war in clearer terms. We might best know the significance of the Civil War in Douglass's life by understanding his own conception of the "sacred significance" of the conflict. Throughout the war, like the apoca- lyptic trumpet in Julia Ward Howe's vision, Douglass spoke with a voice that could never call retreat.

CHAPTER 2

African Americans, the British Working Class and the American Civil War

R. J. M. Blackett

O dear! if yond Yankees could only just see
Heaw they're clammin' and starvin' poor weavers like me,
Aw think they'd soon settle their bother, an' strive
To sent us some cotton to keep us alive.[1]

I N SPITE OF THIS cotton weaver's lament little cotton arrived in England from the United States between the summer of 1861 and the spring of 1865. As a result, by April 1862 only 8,144 of 66,527 cotton operatives in Ashton (31 percent of whose population worked in the cotton mills) were working full time. Not surprisingly, there were passionate debates about the causes of the war and frequent recommendations to the government on the best ways to ensure a resumption of the supply of cotton. Some argued for the immediate recognition of the Confederacy, others for a continuation of British neutrality and still others for open support for the Union's effort to crush the rebellion.

The employment situation in cotton towns like Ashton grew progressively worse as summer moved into fall. As a result, many groups, including the unemployed, attempted through frequent public demonstrations, to pressure local and national authorities to improve conditions. Early in August a town crier called Ashton to a public meeting at Market Place to hear Jacob Green, a fugitive slave from Kentucky, discuss the causes of the war. Only minutes into his speech to a largely working class crowd, the police intervened to stop the meeting on the grounds that it was impeding "public traffic." The crowd's response was to move the meeting to the Plantation Ground, a large open space in the middle of town. There Green leveled a broadside against local working-class supporters of the Confederacy, one of whom, John Matthews, was in the audience. For Matthews, who insisted on the right to reply to Green's charges, the issues turned on the historical fact that England had introduced slavery to the United States and had long benefited from it. Further, he argued, until the firing on Fort Sumter, the Union had done little to emancipate the slaves. During his speech, some of Matthews' opponents climbed on the cart from which he was speaking in an effort to intimidate him. When Matthews made a reference to Green that many thought insulting, a handful of men threatened to throw him into a nearby canal. Only the intervention of friends saved Matthews from a sorry end. In the midst of the turmoil Green retreated to the safety of a supporter's home. But the retreat of the two principals did not defuse the situation entirely. As one reporter recorded, "The neighborhood of the Plantation Ground was in a continued state of excitement throughout the remainder of the night, numerous groups of persons being engaged in talking about the evening's proceedings." Green returned to his lecture the following night when an estimated 4,000 turned out to hear him. England, he insisted, should not recognize a slave power all of whose evils he had personally experienced. As on the previous night, "groups of persons remained on the ground a considerable time discussing the views" of the speaker.[2]

As the dispute between Green and Matthews demonstrates, towns like Ashton, and even those that were not directly affected by the Cotton Famine, were important battlegrounds, contested ground, in the struggles to influence public opinion. In this, visiting African Americans like Green played pivotal roles in the effort to rally public opinion to the cause of the Union. In fact, they were, with very few exceptions, the only American voices in the debate over Britain's policy toward the combatants. Other than Rev. George B. Cheever's brief tour of Britain in the early months of the war and Rev. Henry Ward Beecher's in late 1863, only Moncure D. Conway provided a sustained white American presence in Britain in these years. Gone were the frequent exchange of visits between American and British abolitionists that had kept the transatlantic movement alive during the antebellum period. In these years, the dominant voice in the public debate over the war and British policy was African American.

The dispute in Ashton also speaks to the levels of working-class interest in the effects and outcome of the American Civil War. This interest was longstanding, not just a consequence of the dislocations caused by the shortage of cotton. In fact, the British working class had been active participants in the struggle for abolition in the British West Indies and had taken a keen interest in the cause in the United States in the years after 1834. Samuel Fielden, one of the Haymarket Martyrs, who grew up in Todmorden in the 1850s, remembered the frequent visits of "colored lecturers who spoke on the slavery question in America." These lecturers, he wrote later, "had a very great effect on my mind, and I could hardly divest myself of their impressions, and I used to frequently find myself among my playmates dilating much upon the horrors of slavery." The disruption in the supply of cotton brought into sharp relief all the issues involved in the debate over slavery. As Fielden recalled, "during the summer months every night in the week there would be seen groups of men collected in the streets, and at the prominent corners, discussing the latest news and forecasting the next, and in these groups there were always to be heard the advocates and champions of both sides."[3]

Histories of British reactions to the war have fallen generally into two broad categories. Those written prior to the Second World War tended, in large part, to see the issues in class terms: the British aristocracy and some sectors of the middle class, particularly those involved in manufacturing, were supporters of the Confederacy, while the working class, even those devastated by the Cotton Famine, actively supported the Union and the republican principles for which it stood. Others have since questioned this interpretation, insisting, as Mary Ellison does in her analysis of Lancashire and Cheshire cotton workers' reactions, that those most affected by the shortages were more inclined to support the Confederacy in the belief that independence and the separation of the states would lead to a resumption in the supply of cotton. Self-interest, she argues, not a support for slavery, drove this reaction. While Ellison has provided an important corrective to the rather simplistic picture painted by earlier historians, she never quite comes to grips with Fielden's contention that, politically, the cotton towns were contested ground.[4]

Whatever the interpretation, however, none of these studies has recognized the contributions of black Americans to the debate in Britain. Donaldson Jordon and Edwin J. Pratt, in their comprehensive and still valuable analysis of European reactions to the war, for example, limited themselves to just one observation of black involvement: "A number of escaped slaves, especially the former coachman of Jefferson Davis, were produced as lions at Unionist meetings; and the Reverend Sella Martin, a negro who received a parish in London, was one of the most effective of all workers among the Dissenting bodies." Benjamin Quarles has suggested, but never explored, the existence of a link between the efforts and successes of black Americans to win British support for emancipation in the antebellum period, and British support for the Union during the war. That support, "nurtured by visiting blacks from across the Atlantic, influenced international diplomacy and the outcome of the Civil War."[5]

While the broader issues of diplomacy are outside the purview of this paper, Quarles has pointed to an issue that still needs to be explored. If, as he has shown, African Americans were among the principal actors in the transatlantic abolitionist movement, is it not to be expected that they would have remained actively engaged during the war when the issues surrounding slavery were so starkly drawn? Yet no one has undertaken a systematic evaluation of the role of African Americans in the debate which was so much a part of British economic and political life during the war. Histories of the period have focused either on the tense relationships between governments and the attempts by leading parliamentarians to influence policy or on the efforts of organized societies and prominent individuals to do so. Neither approach is comprehensive enough for each ignores the critical role played by the British working class in the public debate over government policy and the degree to which black Americans attempted to influence public perceptions of the issues involved in the war.

This paper takes up Quarles' challenge by exploring the contributions of African Americans to the public debate over the war. On the eve of the war the textile industry of Lancashire and Cheshire relied almost exclusively on the United States for its supply of cotton. There were, in 1860, almost 2,000 textile factories employing one half million in Lancashire and neighboring counties. (It is estimated that fully four million of a national working population of twenty-one million were employed in cotton.) In Blackburn 34 percent of the workforce was employed in the manufacture of textiles, 30 percent in Preston, 39 percent in Oldham, 31 percent in Ashton and 41 percent in Stalybridge.[6] No wonder Green's lecture attracted such large and keen audiences.

No one in the transatlantic abolitionist movement was surprised when war broke out in April 1861. In fact many had been predicting such an eventuality since the 1830s. But the firing on Fort Sumter created new tensions in the movement that no one could have foreseen. The transatlantic movement was, in all its facets, predicated on the belief that an appeal to shared Anglo-American Protestant and Enlightenment values would lead ultimately to the peaceful emancipation of the slaves. The outbreak of hostilities fundamentally altered the way abolitionists saw the future course of emancipation. Traditional appeals to British public opinion, long considered vital to the success of peaceful emancipation in the United States, had now to be reconsidered. What was once seen as a united transatlantic call by philanthropists for the resolution of differences through peaceful emancipation was now considered, even among some abolitionists, as foreign interference in the internal affairs of the United States. This new development may help explain why white Americans remained aloof from the public debate over the war in Britain.

The outbreak of hostilities also highlighted old tensions and weaknesses in the transatlantic movement, which in Britain had been weakened by prosaic ideological and organizational differences that had their origin in splits in the American movement twenty years earlier. As a result, the British and Foreign Anti Slavery Society, the only truly national organization, lost much of its vibrancy, many of its regional affiliates going to seed in the 1850s. There was a brief revival in the middle years of the decade, following a lecture tour by Julia Griffiths who managed to form a number of active ladies' associations pledged to support Frederick Douglass in Rochester. Even here, however, Griffiths' successes echoed divisions within the movement. British abolitionism was also weakened by the passing of the generation of early abolitionists who had shifted their focus to the United States following emancipation in the West Indies. In 1861 only a handful who could recall the struggles of the 1830s were still alive, and only a few of their descendants seemed willing to carry on the struggle. Henry Highland Garnet touched on this problem during his visit in 1861. He was deeply troubled by his inability to get any support for a meeting in Liverpool and pleaded with friends in Newcastle to ensure that "the anti slavery people of this generation should transmit to their children their hatred of oppression." Finally, Americans with fond memories of British opposition to slavery watched in some despair the rising tide of British racism. Douglass was struck by its appearance in the late 1850s. Unable to fathom the domestic causes for its emergence, Douglass blamed it on the large number of American visitors to Britain who spread the "'leprous distilment' of their pro-slavery poison into the ears and hearts of the British people."[7]

Even if Douglass was slow to understand the nature and extent of British racism in 1860, once war broke out black Americans had a vested interest in ensuring that it did not work to the advantage of the Confederacy. Much of their effort was centered on attempts to influence the British public to reject all pleas for recognition of the Confederacy. In an era when it was generally assumed that "pressure from without" did influence government policy, African Americans believed that they had a responsibility to play an active role in the effort to win public support for emancipation and the Union. Unfortunately, their efforts were partially subverted by the Union's refusal to make slavery an issue in the war, by the economic and social devastation of the cotton shortage, and, at least in the early years of the war, by their own ambivalence toward the Union.

It is impossible to determine with any precision exactly how many African Americans were in Britain between 1861 and 1865. The evidence suggests that the numbers increased during the war as they had done ten years earlier when many black Americans fled to Britain in the wake of the passage of the Fugitive Slave Law. Periodically, there were letters to London newspapers calling for help to support destitute African Americans or to assist them to emigrate to Liberia. There is also evidence that some black Americans found jobs in the north of England and Scotland.[8] There were about forty African Americans involved, at different levels and stages, in the effort to influence British public opinion on the war. Some like Henry Box Brown, James Watkins, William G. Allen, William Howard Day, and William and Ellen Craft were already in England when war broke out. Others, like J. Sella Martin, T. Morris Chester and William Andrew Jackson, went to Britain specifically to campaign against the Confederacy. Still others, such as the Rev. W. Mitchell, were on missions to raise money for fugitive slaves in Canada and used the opportunity to work against the Confederacy. There were also a few students, including William Watson who attended Kings College, London, and R. M. Johnson and C. J. Russell, who read medicine at Scottish universities.

They lectured throughout Britain not just in areas affected by the cotton shortage. Day, William Craft and Martin canvassed the west of England; the Rev. Isaac W. Davison, Jacob Green, Jackson, and Day, Yorkshire; Mitchell, Benjamin Benson, J. W. C. Pennington, Wales; Craft, Garnet, north-east England; and Watson, Mitchell, and Jackson the Midlands. Some were affiliated with organized societies, while others were employed as agents. Day and Garnet, for example, lectured on behalf of the African Aid Society, formed in 1860 following the visit of Martin Delany to promote black American emigration to west Africa. William Craft and Martin worked closely with the London Emancipation Society. Sarah Parker Remond and Ellen Craft were prominent in the Society's ladies' auxiliary. Jackson was employed for a few months as an agent of the Manchester Union and Emancipation Society. Others had no identifiable organizational affiliation. Henry Box Brown's panoramas on slavery, Africa and the Indian Mutiny generated considerable interest. Those like Brown, who operated without any organizational affiliation, did cause dismay in some quarters. Louis Chamerovzow, Secretary of the British and Foreign Anti Slavery Society, expressed concern that there were "itinerant lectures" who were milking the "antislavery community" in "the remoter provinces." Day, he wrote to colleagues in the United States, had "obtained contributions which must in the aggregate have amounted to a considerable sum, but at length in consequence of doubts being raised as to their appropriation, he left the country." It is difficult to determine if Day had defrauded supporters, but there is ample evidence that others did fall foul of the law. Mitchell was brought up before the mayor of Cardiff for trying to slip away without paying his hotel bill. He had evidently done the same in Newport, Penmark and Llancarven.[9]

All of the lecturers used their experiences of American slavery and discrimination as mechanisms for addressing issues involved in the war. The Rev. Nelson Countee, a fugitive from Virginia, but at the time of his visit a resident of Ingersol, Canada, lectured on "The African Race and the American War" at Rochdale, and Jacob Green frequently lectured on the subject "The American War and Slavery." Jackson's lectures mixed traditional anti-slavery themes recounting his experiences in slavery and his escape from it with an attack on Confederate supporters. His was a story of family separation and frequent sales, of a passionate determination to learn to read and write, culminating in a dramatic escape from slavery. The fact that Jackson was Jefferson Davis's coachman at the time of his escape from Richmond in April 1862 lent added poignancy to his narrative. Others gave the sort of anti-slavery lectures that British audiences had come to expect from African-American visitors. The Rev. Isaac W. Davison, for example, lectured on "The Horrors of American Slavery." Then there were those like C. J. Russell who covered a broad range of topics in his lectures including slavery, the war, teetotalism, the dignity of labor and individual responsibility.[10]

Some speakers employed entertainment as a device to attract audiences and to get the message across. Gone were the earlier theatrics of Brown who Fielden recalled marched "through the streets in front of a brass band, clad in a highly-colored and fantastic garb, with an immense drawn sword in his hand." But singing remained a mainstay of many lectures. Brown sang at the end of his exhibit, and Russell sang and played the banjo. Singing what is described as sacred Negro songs, however, was not just meant to entertain; the songs were an integral part of the abolitionist arsenal used to demonstrate the barbarity of slavery and, equally important, to point to the ennobling spirituality of the oppressed. Jacob

Green's singing, for example, was usually preceded by a display of the heavy slave collars used by slaveholders to deter escapes and the paddles used to punish recalcitrant slaves.[11]

Many of these events were organized by individual lecturers who were responsible for advertising, securing support from prominent local figures, and getting the use of local buildings. Others were more structured, the topics determined by the particular needs of the local organizing committee. Martin, for example, was called to Gloucester to counter the activities of M. J. Smith, a pro-Confederate lecturer. Smith, an Englishman who had lived in the South for some time, made his first appearance in Leicester in late 1863 where he gave a series of lectures on behalf of the local branch of the Southern Independence Association, a national pro-Confederate organization formed the previous summer. Union supporters in Gloucester commissioned several lectures from Martin in an effort to counter any positive impressions Smith might have made. Bradford Union supporters brought in Jackson for ten days, and the Hull chapter of the Union and Emancipation Society invited Martin to give three lectures. On many occasions the African-American speakers were paired with a prominent British supporter of the Union: Chester with Frederick Tomkins; Martin with Washington Wilkes; Jackson with George Thompson.[12]

As always, these African Americans, whether free black or fugitive, symbolized America's failure to live up to its democratic promise. When they spoke on slavery and the causes of the war, they spoke, therefore, as representatives of the oppressed yearning to be free. It was a theme that resonated with many in the largely working-class audiences they addressed. Green put it bluntly: African Americans were the best judges of the horrors of slavery and knew best what were the principal causes of the war. When Henry Brougham, one of the leading figures in British anti-slavery since the 1820s, condemned Union policies, D. J. Mac-Gowan of Liverpool reminded him that the "colored people, although well aware that the primary and only avowed object of the loyal States is the preservation of the Union, are fully convinced that Divine Providence has identified the liberty of white and black alike in that momentous conflict."[13]

MacGowan's observation suggests that African Americans in Britain spoke with one voice on the causes and issues involved in the war. Nothing was further from the truth. In the first year of the war, their differing opinions provided ample evidence to support the views of those like Brougham, who believed that the Union was the aggressor and who condemned Lincoln for refusing to pledge himself to free the slaves. Day told a large meeting of the African Aid Society in Birmingham in December 1861 that the war was a direct result of the arrogance of what he called the "Anglo-Saxon races," who refused to recognize the rights of black Americans. Countee insisted that both the Union and the Confederacy were cut from the same cloth, "twin brothers in the unholy transaction . . . an avaricious set of people [who] did not care who sank so long as they swam." As far as Mitchell was concerned the Lincoln government was fighting to preserve the Union for free white labor and had no interest in granting black Americans their freedom. As word of the attack on Fort Sumter arrived in Britain, some, like Craft, who were still wedded to the Garrisonian view of the Constitution as a pro-slavery document, argued that war could have been prevented if the country had lived up to the principles of the Declaration of Independence. Nonetheless, he insisted that the Confederacy could not sustain itself for any length of time with four million slaves in its midst. Green saw things differently. He insisted that the constitution was "perfectly anti slavery" and that the Confederacy was attempting by this war to transform slavery from a local into a national institution.[14]

MacGowan may have underestimated the range of reactions to the war among African Americans, but he was correct when he insisted that they all believed the war would lead ultimately to emancipation. In December 1861 Day predicted that the slaves would be free in two to three years either when the Union heeds the word of God and does what is right, or when the slaves united to take their freedom. Experience taught Craft that the slaves were not docile and that they were likely to exploit the situation to gain their freedom. Without providing much in the way of justification for his position, Mitchell insisted that slavery was doomed regardless of who won the war. Countee was more apocalyptic: the war would end and slavery would come to an end when God was satisfied that both sides were punished enough for their involvement in slavery. Edward Irving, a fugitive from New Orleans who escaped to Britain in 1856, recommended gradual abolition, insisting that sudden emancipation would create unspecified problems for both the freedmen and society; but whatever the timing of emancipation, Chester insisted that the war afforded African Americans an opportunity to come up to the full height of their manhood, to become agents of their own improvement. "He whom the South had endeavored to rob of his rights and manhood had at once come up from the crouching position to the full stature of nature's nobleman, stepped into the ranks of the government at the call of the president, and now, to the astonishment of his former master, kept step to liberty and the music of the Union."[15]

Such disagreements over the origins and objectives of the war quickly evaporated as the Emancipation Proclamation took effect in January 1863. The Union, African Americans now insisted, was entitled to the full support of the British public, but their call for support ran into opposition from many quarters, including those most affected by the cotton shortage. Those who were thrown out of work and forced onto the relief rolls understandably were not always partial to calls for support of the Union. It seemed axiomatic to them that the speedy recognition of the Confederacy by the British government would lead to a rapid resumption of the supply of cotton and a return to work. But recognition of the Confederacy, the opposition argued with some success, ran the risk of pushing Britain into an unnecessary war with the Union without guaranteeing that the supply of cotton would be resumed. Furthermore, recognition would be an endorsement of southern slavery, an unacceptable violation of British abolitionist traditions.

These were just some of the issues involved in the public debate over the war as supporters of both sides endeavored to organized public opinion to pressure the British government to change its declared policy of neutrality. Unable to predict with any certainty that the policy was immutable, each side in the dispute made every effort to rally public opinion to its cause, convinced that "pressure from without" would influence the government's future course of action. Giving the "government a bit of a push," as the pro-Confederate advocate Joseph Barker put it rather quaintly, was the ultimate objective of the public agitation. Similarly, one of Barker's opponents, Peter Sinclair, told a counter demonstration that while the working class had no voice in Parliament they "had a voice outside, and there was something more powerful than guns and of greater strength than ironclads—let them heat once more one roar of that British public opinion that had shaken the thrones of despots in times past."[16]

The efforts to harness that roar gained momentum as it became apparent there would be no quick resolution of the conflict and as the fears of a disruption in the supply of cotton were realized. A Preston mother with two sons in the cotton mills captured the sense of dismay, uncertainty, and frustration felt by many who took the brunt of the economic dislocation caused by the war. The working class (the "backbone" of England and France, she called it) ran the risk of cracking under the strain caused by the high levels of unemployment. The governments of both countries should take a leading role in the effort to stop the war, and if they did not, the working class should compel them to act.[17] As if on cue a group of working-class supporters of the Confederacy, including John Matthews, arranged a series of public meetings in early July 1862 in Bolton, Stockport, Bollington, Blackburn, and other towns in Lancashire and Cheshire. The group had made contact with James Spence, the leading proponent of the Confederacy, who promised to finance and help organize a series of public meetings. Henry Hotze, the Confederate emissary in London, wrote his superiors of plans to allocate a substantial sum of money to finance this public agitation.[18]

What were the principal features of this public debate? The advantage of the early start gained by the pro-Confederate forces was offset to some degree by Lincoln's preliminary Emancipation Proclamation in September 1862. Anticipating its final implementation in January 1863, pro-Union forces began making plans for a series of public meetings throughout the country. A study of how contenders attempted to influence opinion in and around Bury provides some useful pointers as to the nature and outcome of the debate. While the lives of Bury's workers were affected by the shortage of cotton, the town's relatively diverse economy provided something of a cushion against the famine's worse ravages. Although its woolen trade, which manufactured blankets, flannels and quilts, was important to the local economy, almost two thirds of the work force was employed in the cotton mills. The shortage of cotton thus led to sharp increases in unemployment. In April 1862, 133 of 196 mills were closed or operating on short time. The number of those receiving outdoor relief rose by 200 percent between 1861 and August 1862.[19]

Much of the work of organizing meetings in the town and surrounding area fell to David Thomas, the principal reporter on the *Bury Times,* and John Rowlinson, the town's only member of the London-based Emancipation Society. The first meeting in February 1863 adopted a number of resolutions praising the Union and condemning the Confederacy. But some in the audience, like John Dearden who had lived for some time both in the North and South, wondered if the right to secede was not the ultimate expression of democracy. Such a right, William Bell, the old Chartist from Haywood wrote soon after the meeting, would be legitimate if it could be demonstrated that the people of the South were oppressed. More significantly, Bell concluded, if secession was to be raised to the level of a right and principle, then it could conceivably be argued that Lancashire, Cheshire or Yorkshire had a similar right to secede from Britain.[20]

Every effort was made by the opposing forces in Bury to rally support to their cause. Two weeks after the formation of the Bury Emancipation Society, Jackson was the principal speaker at a meeting that condemned slavery and called for support of the Union. As in so many of his other appearances, Jackson told of his experiences and escape from slavery. He called for support for Lincoln's emancipation policy, insisting that it was the only constitutional and logical thing to do; constitutional, because the president acted within the powers granted to the office; logical, because to have done otherwise ran the risk of losing the Border States. Opponents at the meeting forced the issue by insisting that Jackson address continued discrimination in the northern states. Jackson admitted seeing segregated omnibuses in New York City, but these, he insisted somewhat disingenuously, were owned by those who supported the Democratic party and slavery. Only in New York, he observed incorrectly, were there restrictions on the right to vote. There were persons in the North, he argued, using all the traditional stereotypes, who "did not like colored men, but he had only been insulted twice there, and it was by Irishmen who were afraid that if the slaves obtained their freedom they would do the work which the Irish had been accustomed to do."[21]

These pro-Union meetings coincided with the arrival of the *George Griswold*, a ship carrying thousands of barrels of flour, pork, bread, bacon and corn, a gift from major commercial figures in New York City and Philadelphia to the operatives hit hardest by the Cotton Famine. It was in the view of one of the leading working-class newspapers, a "republican gift to the starving and aristocratic-ridden people [which] has no equal in anything recorded of the generosity of princes."[22] Union supporters moved quickly to exploit this act of generosity for all it was worth. Enthusiastic meetings were held in Bury and throughout Lancashire and Cheshire in February and March. The meetings of G. W. Dennison, the *Griswold*'s chaplain, were coordinated with a visit to the area by George Thompson, the leading British advocate of the Union. These were followed days later by another meeting at which Dennison and Peter Sinclair spoke. A Scot, Sinclair had lived for some time in the United States and had only recently returned to Britain as an unofficial emissary of the Washington government. Two weeks earlier Sinclair had teamed up with Jackson at a meeting in Tottington, north-west of Bury, which adopted resolutions thanking Americans for the support sent by the *Griswold* and expressing sympathy with the Union. Running through all of the speeches was the message that there existed an alliance of interests between the British worker and the slave. The working man "ought to have the same protection as the lord," Thomas insisted, "but that could never be while slavery existed." Like the factory operative, whose life was devastated by the Cotton Famine, the slave had shown remarkable political sophistication, eschewing all forms of violence and peacefully awaiting the dawn of his redemption, Sinclair pointed out. "There had been no outbreak by the slave. He had toiled and kept his master and family rolling in wealth. He was waiting the day of his deliverance; so was the factory operative."[23]

Following a meeting in Ramsbottom near Bury, George Rushton, a working-class Union supporter, condemned local mill owners who pressured their employees to adopt resolutions supporting the Confederacy, thus "vindicating a cause so nearly akin to their own way of managing their affairs, for do they not claim us as their own after they have got us in their employ?" Rushton had nothing but contempt for those workers who were willing to do the bidding of their masters in the hope that their sons would find a "living with their coats on." It is clear from Rushton's reactions that Confederate supporters attended pro-Union meetings in such numbers as to cause the organizers some embarrassment. Although Rushton may have exaggerated the influence of factory owners, there is enough evidence to show that the opposition did all it could to limit the impact of the Bury Society's efforts either, by disrupting its proceedings or organizing counter meetings. Similarly and not surprisingly, Union supporters reciprocated by denying organizers of pro-Confederate meetings the stamp of unanimous approval.

In spite of his general popularity, Jackson found himself in some awkward situations once Confederate sympathizers realized that his experiences in slavery and the force of his appeal lent the Union's cause a certain incontestable cachet. At one meeting in Ramsbottom, opponents interrupted his speech with questions that challenged his veracity. He and Thomas were also accused of being paid agents of the federal government. Politically, it mattered little if the accusations were true; once they were made, they were impossible to disprove. Thomas had been serving for some time as the local agent for United States emigration, and Jackson had only recently been enlisted as a paid agent of the Manchester Union and Emancipation Society. To pro-Confederate opponents, both appointments proved the point: to accept pay in the service of the Union was to destroy one's credibility as a disinterested advocate.

Thomas had to indulge in some subterfuge in an effort to outmaneuver his opponents. Prior to a meeting in Bury, placards appeared throughout the town, posted many suspected by the Manchester Southern Independence Association, announcing that the organizers were planning to stifle debate and, what was even more reprehensible, to foist pro-Union resolutions on an unsuspecting audience. Worried that the opposition planned to pack the meeting with their supporters, Thomas called the gathering to order before the advertised time, insisting that its sole purpose was to listen to a lecture by Jackson. The move worked, and at the end of the lecture there were three rousing cheers for Lincoln.[24]

One week later the tables were turned at a meeting organized to hear Jackson and Thomas. It appears that the pro-Confederate manufacturers who earlier had caused Rushton so much concern were better prepared this time and occupied most of the seats on the platform. Thomas and Jackson must have despaired when they found Joseph Barker, one of the major public figures in the pro-Confederate movement, so prominently seated. Before Jackson could begin his speech, someone in the audience insisted that this time he and Thomas not renege on the promise to permit questions. How else, the protester asked, was there to be a full airing of the issues if no questions were permitted. Jackson found the frequent interruptions disconcerting. Those who had hissed at him, he maintained, were generally not working men who were "sound on the question of negro slavery" but those who were only interested in getting a supply of cotton and had no interest in emancipation. Jackson struggled through the early portions of his speech dealing as best he could with the constant heckling, but when someone on the stage was insensitive enough to shout that, as a piece of property, he had no legal right to run away from his master. Jackson could barely contain his anger. Although he countered with an apt rhetorical rejoinder—how would the hecklers react if their wives and daughters were "put on the auction block, and sold, and sent to another part of the country"—Jackson had lost command of his audience. When the heckling and insults continued, he stormed out of the meeting. With one opponent in retreat, Barker moved to gain command of the meeting by asking Thomas a series of ten drawn-out questions that no one could have answered in one sitting. Once he had control of the floor, Barker refused to relinquish it long enough for Thomas to respond to any one of his questions. When it appeared that the meeting would degenerate into a free-for-all, the chairman promptly called the proceedings to a close.[25]

There was no secret about the opposition's intent: disruption would offer a serious challenge to the claim that Bury and Ramsbottom were solidly pro-Union. The pro-Confederate *Bury Guardian*'s report of the meeting concluded approvingly: "and thus ended the second meeting to create sympathy in favour of the Northern States in Ramsbottom." One local observer insisted, but offered no support for his claim, that pro-Confederate organizations had employed groups of agitators to go around the country disrupting Union meetings. In spite of these disruptions, however, it is clear, at least from the testimony of one local pro-Confederate supporter who signed himself "An Operative," that Union sentiment was very strong in the area. After praising the bravery of southern leaders such as Stonewall Jackson, he ridiculed pro-Union supporters whom, he said, were drawn largely from the great unwashed: "This lot, I should think, was the lazy part of the audience, whom one meets running to work unwashed, and their clogs untied, half an hour behind time, and they expect their employers to run their gearing whilst they are skulking in bed."[26]

However satisfying it might be, simply disrupting meetings did little to undermine public support for a cause. As the chairman at Ramsbottom twitted the opposition, Confederate advocates could only determine the true level of the public's endorsement when they persuaded meetings to adopt resolutions supporting secession. Until then, their disruptions of pro-Union meetings were politically meaningless. Local Confederate supporters took up the challenge and arranged a series of three meetings for Barker in Bury. Concerned that pro-Unionists might deploy similar tactics, the chairman of the first meeting pleaded that Barker be given a peaceful hearing, insisting, rather sheepishly, that the Union point of view had been presented "peacefully and without interruption." The chairman's concerns were misplaced. Union supporters opted for a surprisingly different approach: they simply boycotted the meetings. In such an uncontested setting resolutions favoring the Confederacy rang hollow. As a possible result of this boycott, the chairman of the third meeting took the unusual step of reading a telegram which made the startling announcement that the Union army had abandoned its siege of Vicksburg and General Grant had been taken prisoner. It is not possible to locate the exact source of this piece of news from America, but the timing does suggest that Confederate supporters in Bury and elsewhere were willing to use any device to gain an advantage.[27]

If Barker had a relatively easy run in Bury, things were different in Ramsbottom. To a resolution calling on the government to recognize the Confederacy, Jackson proposed an amendment which praised the Union for acting to keep the nation together and called on all those who advocated representative government through electoral reform to support the efforts of the Lincoln administration. Although the amendment was defeated, Jackson, according to one observer, was given "quite an ovation in the village as well as in the Athenaeum, and when the meeting was over he was accompanied by hundreds of people towards the Rev. Maden's house—young men and maidens, old men and matrons—all zealous to show him that bad as things are, and suffering as they never before suffered, they are willing to suffer even more to get for him and his down-trodden brethren the same liberty that they enjoy."[28]

It is clear from the evidence that neither group gave much ground in and around Bury and that what occurred there was duplicated in countless other cities and small towns throughout Britain. Lecturers were challenged by opponents either from the floor or platform to answer a range of questions each aimed at exposing the weaknesses of the other's position. They were also challenged to public debates at which the issues could be freely discussed. When these challenges were unsuccessful, counter meetings were organized within days. At a lecture in Bury in November 1863, T. B. Kershaw, an advocate of Confederate independence, was questioned from the floor and challenged to a debate. When he refused the offer, his opponents held a meeting to refute his arguments publicly. One week after the Rev. E. A. Verity, a Confederate supporter from Havergam Eaves near Burnley, lectured in Bury, 1,100 turned out to hear him debate Thomas. Within days Thomas lectured on the topic "The North for Freedom the South for Slavery" in an effort to consolidate and reiterate the town's pro-Union position. Thomas' lecture was followed soon after by a public meeting at which Mason Jones, the old Chartist and pro-Union supporter, spoke and at which resolutions were adopted condemning the slave-holding Confederacy and praising the British government's policy of neutrality.[29]

As in so many other towns in England, Scotland, and Wales, neither side in Bury gave much quarter in its effort to rally working-class support for its cause. All believed that the outcome of the public debate, as reflected in the resolutions adopted, would have a profound effect on debates in Parliament and on government policy. In a beginning-of-the-year retrospective in 1864, the editor of the *Bee Hive,* a major working-class newspaper, argued that the pro-Union meeting organized jointly by London Trade Unionists and the London Emancipation Society in March 1863 had "considerable influence in shaping the after-policy of the English Cabinet on the American question."[30] The editor may have been correct, but in the long run, the attempt to determine with any accuracy the extent to which public debate and public pressure did influence government policy leads down a blind alley. In a situation where no one could be absolutely certain that the British government was unalterably committed to its policy of neutrality, it was advisable to remain vigilant, to make every effort to marshal public support for one's cause. In such a climate of uncertainty neither side was willing to give ground in places like Bury.

The participation of black Americans in this public debate gave Union supporters a distinct advantage. As MacGowan insisted, black Americans showed a willingness to support the Union in spite of all its shortcomings; for they recognized that, slowly but perceptibly, the country was moving toward emancipation. Their experiences with slavery and discrimination lent legitimacy to this argument especially as their opponents could provide no evidence of the Confederacy's intention to dismantle the "peculiar institution." In fact those who supported the Confederacy were shackled by the insistence of its leaders that slavery was the cornerstone of the nation. Challenged on this issue, its proponents took refuge in the speculation that secession and independence would lead inevitably to emancipation, but the argument carried little weight. African Americans, particularly fugitives like Jackson, were the embodiment of everything the Confederacy rejected. Even Jackson's opponents conceded rather reluctantly that he had been a boon to the Union's cause. Following his return to the United States at the end of 1863, a Confederate sympathizer, clearly relieved that Jackson had left, exaggerated only slightly when he wrote that the Union forces had lost their most potent weapon. They have "ceased to command an audience in Lancashire now that President Davis's mythical ex-coachman (who was really worth seeing and listening to) is no longer available for diversifying the humdrum of an anti-slavery speech with a racy natural joke worth all the money."[31]

While there is no doubt that Jackson was the most influential African American involved in the effort to influence public opinion in 1863, there were others, like Green, who carried on the struggle in the last year of the war. Collectively they represented an important element in the effort to rally public support for the Union. The issue as to whether their activities influenced government policy appears largely irrelevant. At a time when it was generally accepted that "pressure from without" was a vital part of political decision making, African Americans contributed to a public debate with significant implications for international and domestic politics. The fact remains that the transatlantic abolitionist connection, which to a significant degree was consolidated following the visit of the African American Rev. Nathaniel Paul and William Lloyd Garrison in 1832, was sustained during the trying years of the war largely by African Americans.

Part 2

Recruitment and Enlistment of Black Troops

CHAPTER 3

⚊⚌⚊

The Hard Fight Was Getting into the Fight at All

Jack Fincher

IT WAS A CHARGE to remember, that doomed three-quarter-mile rush down a naked beach and up the bristling earthworks of Fort Wagner. When it was over nearly half the 54th Massachusetts, a black regiment of 600 volunteers, had been killed, wounded or captured. Col. Robert Gould Shaw, 25, the pride of his Yankee abolitionist family, fell at the head of his men and was buried in a common sandy grave "with his niggers," as Confederates who buried him would put it.

For some five million Americans who have lately seen the film *Glory*, as well as the recent monumental public television history of the Civil War, the 54th's brave action has stirred interest in what was, for decades, too often ignored—the role of black men in the war that ended slavery. Some 130 years ago, too, Americans were stirred by that demonstration of black courage. "If this Massachusetts Fifty-Fourth had faltered when its trial came," the New York *Tribune* would write, 200,000 black troops "for whom it was a pioneer would never have been put into the field."

But crucial as that moment in mid-July 1863 was, the men of the 54th were not the only pioneers. Black courage in battle had been proved in the American Revolution and in the War of 1812, though white Americans kept refusing to credit it. During the Civil War, the hardest problem for black men was not in being brave; it was in getting a chance to fight at all. At every step, they were confronted with racial scorn and fear, created by the long existence of slavery itself.

Few events offer a better way into the agonies and ambiguities involved than a scene that *Glory* didn't show. Only a few days before the black troops of the 54th stormed Rebel ramparts outside Charleston, South Carolina, other blacks—one related to a member of the 54th—had been killed in the streets of New York City by white rioters.

Most of this was the work of immigrants protesting President Lincoln's latest call for a new federal draft. Union armies had just won their two greatest victories of the war. On July 3, 1863, Lee was defeated at Gettysburg, ending Northern fears that England and France might recognize the South as an independent nation. The next day Vicksburg fell, after 47 days of siege, all but cutting the South in two and threatening to make the Mississippi a Union canal. As usual, casualties had been appalling, and volunteers had long since proved insufficient. But the draft had certain loopholes. Anyone could be exempted from service till the next draft call by paying the government $300, or exempted till war's end by hiring a substitute to fight in his place.

Economics and racism thus combined to make scapegoats of free blacks. Predictably, it had been rumored they were just waiting to step into the jobs left behind when white New York conscripts marched away. The nation was already two years into a war that would claim as many lives as all other U.S. wars including Vietnam. Yet as everyone knew, only a handful of blacks had done any fighting.

"This Is a White Man's War!"

How this came to be so is a tortuous chronicle of politics and racism. When the war started, most men in the North, including military officers, thought that blacks couldn't fight. Early in the war blacks who tried to form a defensive home guard in Cincinnati were threatened by a mob and dispersed by police. Whites shouted at them, "We want you damned niggers to keep out of this, this is a white man's war!" But in political terms, the successful effort to keep blacks from fighting for the Union and their freedom was to a large extent the work of Abraham Lincoln, the man now rightly known to history as the Great Emancipator.

Well into the fighting, Lincoln hoped to save the country from the appalling destruction of a long war, somehow bringing the Southern states back, through a negotiated cease-fire and some informal plan for the gradual and recompensed emancipation of slaves. Yankee abolitionists were still seen as zealots and troublemakers. Political support for the war was shaky in the North, and most of it came from people who wanted to save the Union, not get killed to free the slaves. Preserving the Union was Lincoln's rally cry. Well into 1862, he made his priorities clear: "If I could save the Union without freeing any slave, I would do it; and if I could save it by freeing all the slaves I would do it; and if I could save it by freeing some and leaving others alone, I would also do that." Meanwhile it was all-important to keep the slave-owning Border States, Kentucky, Missouri, Delaware, and Maryland, from joining the South. (In Maryland's case, he would demonstrate his deadly seriousness on this subject by sending federal troops to shut down a session of the State Legislature meeting in Frederick when representatives seemed about to vote for secession.)

Blacks petitioned the President early on for a chance to fight and flocked to enlist. Everywhere they were rejected. Even after Congress had authorized black troops, when Indiana offered to contribute two black regiments, Lincoln replied, "To arm the negroes would turn 50,000 bayonets from the loyal Border States against us that were for us."

The great antislavery leader Frederick Douglass called upon Lincoln to use blacks in the war. "Once let the black man get upon his person the brass letters, U.S., let him get an eagle on his button, and a musket on his shoulder," Douglass declared, "and there is no power on earth which can deny that he has earned the right to citizenship in the United States." As new calls for volunteers were made, he struck pungently at what he saw as the illogic and unfairness of Lincoln's position. The government keeps screaming "Men, men! Send us men!" he wrote. The edifice of state was burning, but the government would let only "Indo-Caucasion hands" help put out the fire.

Pressure from blacks eager to fight, from abolitionists and from a few Army officers who needed men, as well as changing circumstances, eventually altered Lincoln's policy. Along the way, convoluted legal questions involving the Constitution and slaves as property had to be got around. According to the Supreme Court's 1857 Dred Scott decision and the Fugitive Slave Act, slaves were beings without the rights of citizens, property that had to be returned to owners, no matter what.

After secession but before the war had started at Fort Sumter, Lincoln tried to limit the rift between the states by pledging in his First Inaugural Address that the government would not interfere with slavery where it already existed. Constitutional law naturally applied in more dramatic and perplexing terms to the thousands of slaves who soon began fleeing their white masters and taking refuge behind Union lines.

War had hardly begun, in May 1861, when Benjamin Butler, a worldly political general from Massachusetts, adopted the dodge of treating escaped slaves not as returnable property but as captured "contraband of war." On August 30, Gen. John C. Frémont, a hero for his role in claiming California, and the defeated Republican candidate for President on an antislavery platform in 1856, tried to expand the franchise.

Caught in a mini civil war in Missouri, he put the whole state under martial law and declared that slaves of anyone who took up arms against the Union were forfeit—and forever free. Lincoln sacked him. In December, Secretary of War Simon Cameron publicly declared that a time would come when the government would not only have the right but the duty to use freed slaves in the war to suppress rebellion. Cameron had been a loose cannon in other ways, too. Now, Lincoln banished him as U.S. Minister to Russia.

In the new year Lincoln's new Secretary of War, Edwin Stanton, reiterated the Administration's position; blacks, slave or free, were not to fight. But in May 1862, in the Sea Islands and along the coasts of South Carolina, Georgia and Florida, which Union forces had occupied with little resistance, Maj. Gen. David Hunter proclaimed martial law, telling all slaves in his jurisdiction that they were free. In South Carolina he began recruiting them, sometimes at gunpoint. Without approval from Washington, however, the experiment was abandoned.

Throughout the year, casualties kept mounting. So did the political drumbeat from black newspapers and abolitionists, and from officers tantalized by a source of soldiery nearby, yet unable to make use of it. Though George B. McClellan had mostly managed to avoid fighting, other generals had engaged the enemy, with bloody results. In the spring of 1862 at the Battle of Shiloh on the Tennessee River, nearly 100,000 men fought for two days, with 23,000 casualties. It was a draw, with a slight edge to a chunky, unshaven, cigar-smoking general named Ulysses S. Grant. After Shiloh, General Grant gave up all hope of saving the Union with just a few victories and some kind of political compromise. It would take total war and "complete conquest" of the South. And that meant many more men to kill or be killed.

Down in New Orleans, where the North established a large bridgehead at the mouth of the Mississippi, astute and well-connected General Butler had lately become military governor. For weeks he had dickered with Washington about how to deal with the problem of using blacks in war. Now he took action, knowing that at last he might receive official approval. On August 22, Butler shrewdly recruited as part of the federal forces in the area the 1,400-man Louisiana State Guard, an elite force of free black volunteers. They had formed the guard themselves, but the South never called them to combat (*Smithsonian*, March 1979). When Union forces took New Orleans the guard refused to follow the retreating Confederate Army.

Feeling such pressures, Lincoln came to the same conclusion as Grant and was at last sure that the war could not be won without the abolition of slavery. In the summer of 1862 he secretly told his Cabinet about the Emancipation Proclamation. It would be announced after the next successful battle, to take effect in January 1863. Even so, freedom would be limited to slaves in areas in open rebellion against the Union. Slavery was still firmly in place in the Border States and Tennessee, and in Union-occupied portions of Virginia and Louisiana.

The dam was broken, however. Congress passed a new Militia Act, permitting the President to use "as many persons of African descent" as he needed "for suppression of the Rebellion." It also repealed a 1792 ordinance barring "persons of color" from serving in the militia. Free blacks and ex-slaves would be recruited, but they were regarded as laborers and their pay was not to be as much as that of white soldiers—$10 a month less clothing expenses, rather than $13 plus clothing expenses. They were not to have black officers, either.

When Frederick Douglass confronted Lincoln personally about these discrepancies, he was told that the whole idea of blacks as soldiers would be hard for the country to digest. Once that had happened, matters such as pay would be reconciled. About 100 blacks did eventually get commissions in the Union Army; 2,000 became noncommissioned officers.

In September, at Antietam Creek in Maryland, the Union Army under General McClellan finally gave Lincoln something like the victory he needed. Five days after the battle, the President made public his preliminary Emancipation Proclamation. In response, the South declared that captured slaves in Yankee uniforms, as well as their white officers taken in battle, would be executed. Hundreds of Northern soldiers deserted rather than serve with blacks; two Illinois regiments had to be disbanded as a result.

Nevertheless, the recruiting of blacks in Northern states went on apace. Wherever the Union armies were operating, teams of recruiters were authorized to offer $100 to $300 enlistment bounties. This was the period in which Gov. John Andrew of Massachusetts created the celebrated 54th Regiment, mostly composed of literate freemen, recruiting young Col. Robert Gould Shaw as its commanding officer.

Frederick Douglass proved right about the effect of weapons and uniforms on ex-slaves. Especially to men who risked terrible punishment, perhaps death, to escape—who stumbled on foot through the dark toward distant guns in the hope the guns were in friendly hands—the soldierly ritual that followed enlistment had considerable power. Each man was stripped and bathed, his old clothes burned, his Army blues put on. One white soldier described the process: "Put a United States uniform on his back and the *chattel* is a *man*." Black recruit Elijah Marrs, who escaped slavery in Kentucky to join the Union Army, remembered the moment more simply: "I felt freedom in my bones."

Many were treated well and trained well. But many were brutalized, even by Army standards—until some said they were no better off than slaves. Many got inferior equipment and medical care. They died of diseases in the field at nearly twice the rate of whites. Of some 180,000 black men to serve in the Army, only 2,800 died in combat; 34,000 were taken by disease.

The matter of inferior pay was somehow harder to bear, perhaps because it involved both hardship and principle. One of *Glory's* most dramatic scenes, in which the young Colonel Shaw joins his men in tearing up their pay chits rather than accept less money than whites, did not actually take place. But Shaw did write Governor Andrew that his regiment would refuse pay until the matter was corrected. In this Shaw was an exception. All over the country while officers backed their troops in the struggle for equal pay, but ultimately urged them to take what they could and get on with the war. So did many black leaders. But some soldiers remained adamant. "Do we not fill the same ranks?" a private wrote. "Do we not take up the same length of ground in the grave yard?"

The government continued to welch on pay (it did not make amends until 1864 and then only partially). The situation was ripe for some kind of martyr. In 1863, after rumors of the New York draft riots and the Fort Wagner charge had spread throughout the Army, William Walker, a black sergeant in the 3rd South Carolina Volunteers, became one. He ordered his men to stack arms because they would "not do duty any longer for $7 per month." It was clear that he had no idea of the gravity of his act in an army in wartime. Tried and convicted, Walker was executed for mutiny.

The 180,000 black soldiers in uniform by war's end represented nearly 10 percent of all Union forces. This at a time when blacks accounted for only 1 percent of the North's population, as opposed to 13 percent of the whole country, the same percentage as today. Despite their own zeal to volunteer, and objections from their own officers and abolitionist leaders, relatively few were ever allowed to see action. Black soldiers drew excessive fatigue duty, backbreaking work behind the lines that took time away from the training on which their lives might depend in battle. One private from Louisiana actually wrote a letter of complaint to the President: "Instead of the musket It is the Spad[e] and the Wheelbarrow and the Axe."

The first real clash between black troops officially recruited into the Union Army and Confederate soldiers did not take place until the war was almost half over. The time was January 1863. The outfit was the 1st South

Carolina Infantry. The commander, by no coincidence, was Thomas Higginson, a Boston abolitionist already renowned for supporting the idea of blacks as potential combat soldiers. The missions: to free slaves and confiscate lumber at the head of the St. Mary's River on the border between Georgia and Florida.

Shortly after midnight, at the head of a hundred handpicked infantry, Higginson marched through thick forest toward a Confederate camp—and a skirmish that, partly because of his eloquence, has become known to history as the Battle of the Hundred Pines.

"Nobody knows anything about these men who has not seen them in battle," Higginson wrote in his remarkable memoir, *Army Life in a Black Regiment*. "I find that I myself knew nothing." In the dark his troops met some Rebels. "They were as cool and wary," Higginson reported, "as if wild turkeys were the only game," and they fought with a "fiery energy" he had seen matched only by French Zouaves. A brief firefight followed, in which one soldier was killed and seven wounded, as against ten of the enemy killed, including their lieutenant. The rest were routed. Glowingly, Higginson reported, "No officer in this regiment now doubts that the key to the successful prosecution of this war lies in the unlimited employment of black troops."

These views were intended for Northern newspapers, but other observers confirmed them. The enthusiasm, loyalty and humor of black troops were all noted. White commanders, accustomed to having their authority resented, were pleased by the touching allegiance many enlistees showed them. Black volunteers in South Carolina were on their own home ground and new to war. When the bugle sounded for battle, they didn't go on sick call in droves to avoid fighting, as now often happened in battle-weary white outfits.

On the other side of the war, on the lower Mississippi, where Adj. Gen. Lorenzo Thomas had been raising black regiments from escaped slaves, officers also had a high regard for the new troops. Col. Robert Cowden, later the commanding officer of the 59th U.S. Colored Infantry, noted that the Army had to get rid of "plantation manners," including "awkward bowing and scraping, with hat under arm, and with averted look." Once uniformed and trained the men were good soldiers, he reported, except that, because their only free time as slaves had been during the hours of darkness, they were used to leaving camp at night. Strict discipline was needed, said Cowden, so that they would retire at 9 P.M. and "*stay retired till reveille.*"

Stereotyping was common. When given a chance to fight, black troops seemed to excel at quick, all-out, headlong assault—which was encouraged because of the psychological effect it was supposed to have on Confederate fears of uncontrollable slave "savagery." As a result, the notion grew that black soldiers were of little use in tough, rearguard action but charged with a "terrible fierceness." This general impression persisted, despite a brave showing in two bitter fights that occurred far away on the Mississippi.

Complete control of the great river, required the capture of Port Hudson in Louisiana, another Rebel bastion on the river, 250 miles south of Vicksburg. A short march north from Baton Rouge, Port Hudson was defended by 6,000 Confederate troops in heavily fortified positions and had been under siege for weeks that spring. On May 27, 1863, among those forces ordered to make the almost impossible assault were elements of the 1st and 3rd Louisiana Regiments, both black. But the 1st had been the Louisiana State Guard, the only regiment with black officers most notably Capt. André Callioux, a Paris-educated Louisiana landowner who proudly called himself the blackest man in New Orleans.

Six times, a thousand black soldiers of the 1st and 3rd charged across an open field against high battlements Six times, they were driven back by rifle and mortar fire, grapeshot and canister. After each charge Callioux led them forward again, the last time with his arm smashed at the elbow by a rifle ball. There were 212 casualties, with nearly 40 killed, including André Callioux. Except for undeniably demonstrating courage and discipline, these men fell in vain.

Less than two weeks later, on June 7 at Milliken's Bend, 1,400 Union soldiers—the remains of two white companies and three black regiments—took the brunt of a charge by 1,500 Texans. In close combat marked by terrible bloodshed, the men beat back the Rebels. Word went out: the novice black soldiers had held their ground defensively against a second assault.

After the battle, Capt. M. M. Miller, of the 9th Regiment of Louisiana Volunteers of African Descent, wrote his aunt back in Galena, Illinois, "I never more wish to hear the expression the 'the niggers won't fight.'" "The bravery of the Blacks in the battle at Milliken's Bend," Assistant Secretary of War Charles Dana optimistically concluded, "completely revolutionized the sentiments of the Army." The stage was now set for the doomed 54th Massachusetts and Robert Gould Shaw to demonstrate black courage on a national scale.

By the time Shaw's regiment arrived, Northern forces in South Carolina were at last able to turn their attention to the necklace of heavily fortified islands that adorned Charleston harbor, and to Fort Sumter, where the war had started. The key to the Confederate defense was Fort

Wagner. When the attack was planned no black troops appeared on the order of battle. "Our whole experience, so far, has been in loading and discharging vessels," Shaw wrote two weeks before the battle. "I feel very much disappointed." He complained to Brig. Gen. George C. Strong, arguing that "the colored soldiers should be associated as much as possible with the white troops, in order that they may have other witnesses besides their own officers to what they are capable of doing."

Shaw's connections, as well as his logic, were not lost on his superiors. Orders arrived on July 8: be ready to move at an hour's notice. Ten days later, the 54th Massachusetts was poised before Fort Wagner. Three brigades would mount the attack, and Shaw had offered the 54th as its spearhead.

"We May As Well Get Rid of Them"

SEASONED BRIGADE commanders thought a charge up an open beach against defenses as forbidding as Fort Wagner's was foolhardy, but the assault commander, Maj. Gen. Truman Seymour—"a devil of a fellow for dash"—overruled them. The fort, he thought, would be softened by a massive daylong artillery bombardment. Beyond that, according to later testimony before the American Freedmen's Inquiry Commission, Seymour told the operating commander, Maj. Gen. Quincy Gillmore: "Well, I guess we will . . . put those damned niggers from Massachusetts in the advance; we may as well get rid of them one time as another."

All during the day of July 18, Union artillery banged away at the fort. Shortly after 6:30 P.M., 600 men of the 54th formed two wings and moved slowly up Morris Island beach. Just beyond reach of Confederate artillery, they lay down. Shaw dismounted and sent his horse cantering to the rear.

At 7:45, the bombardment stopped and the attack signal came. Shaw spoke to his soldiers: "Move in quick time until within a hundred yards of the fort, then, double-quick and charge!" Off they rushed into history, as 1,700 Confederate riflemen—almost six times as many as Union military intelligence had said were in Fort Wagner—clambered from their shell-battered bombproofs and raced to the ramparts (only eight of them died from the Union bombardment). Confederate batteries, mostly silent during the day to save ammunition, now opened up from the harbor's other islands.

Just before battle, Sgt. Robert Simmons, one of Shaw's men, sent a prophetic note to the members of his family, who only three days before had been under violent racist assault back in New York City: "God bless you all! Good-bye!"

Despite a moat, some wire and a rifle pit, Shaw and a few of his men actually reached the parapets of the fort before being cut down by fire. The rest, less than half of the assault force, were driven back. For having carried the regimental colors despite multiple wounds, Sgt. William Carney became the first black to win the Medal of Honor. "The old flag never touched the ground, boys!" he shouted.

As so often happens with military disasters, the most elementary things had been left undone. "There was no provision for cutting away obstructions, filling the ditch, or spiking the guns," Regimental Historian Luis F. Emilio wrote afterward. "No engineers or guides accompanied the column; no artillery-men to serve captured guns; no plan of the work was shown company officers. . . ."

The attack once again indisputably showed black courage in battle. It also had other effects. One involved the treatment of prisoners. When the Confederate Army refused to exchange prisoners captured during the siege, word spread that those taken alive had been put to hard labor and might be sentenced to death.

If Northern admiration for the gallant 54th was enormous, Northern outrage at mistreatment of prisoners matched it. Within a fortnight Lincoln announced the Union would answer atrocity man for man. Sporadic eye-for-an-eye retribution set in, reaching some sort of apogee on April 12, 1864, at Fort Pillow, Tennessee. There, Gen. Nathan Bedford Forrest and 1,500 Confederate cavalrymen overwhelmed a 570-man, racially mixed garrison, driving survivors into the Mississippi, which was soon, in Forrest's words, "dyed with the blood of the slaughtered for 200 yards." After their surrender, scores of the black soldiers and some of the white soldiers were murdered. For black soldiers, "Remember Fort Pillow!" became a rallying cry, giving them a reason both to fight to the death and to offer no quarter. As another fallout from Fort Wagner, Fort Pillow deeply impressed on white enlisted men the danger of fighting alongside blacks in battle.

Retaliations escalated well into 1864, as the Union realized that victory would require the destruction of the South. Union general William T. Sherman laid waste to Georgia. Grant, at last promoted to commander of all Union armies, smashed away at Lee in Virginia with overwhelming numbers. The appalling series of battles of attrition that resulted became known as the Wilderness to Petersburg Campaign. In six weeks of fighting, Northern casualties amounted to 65,000; Southern, 35,000.

In the North, meanwhile, the 1864 Presidential campaign was being waged, with the Democrats running George McClellan against Lincoln on a "stop the war" platform. Though the war, begun as a fight to save a political union, had become a crusade to free blacks from slavery, the continued carnage with no signs of victory made the Democrats' cause popular, especially in the Midwest, where Yankee abolitionists were still far from loved and dying to free slaves was not exactly popular.

All through the late summer Lincoln was sure he would be defeated, especially without some dramatic military victory to show for the years of killing. But Grant's attempt to wear out Lee and take Richmond ended in the siege not of the Southern capital but of Lee's prime remaining supply depot, Petersburg, Virginia, 20 miles away. During the resulting stalemate, another legacy of the fatal charge of the 54th Massachusetts—government sensitivity to the political implications of consigning black soldiers to slaughter—contributed to one of the more bloody and bizarre blunders of the war.

After five days of Union failure to take Petersburg, Lt. Col. Henry Pleasants, a former mining engineer from the Pennsylvania coal country, offered a daring plan: to tunnel under the Rebel lines and set off a huge blast of dynamite—enough to blow an opening so big that the superior numbers of the North could sweep past dazed and demoralized defenders and wheel toward Richmond.

A 510-foot tunnel, one of the longest of its kind ever dug, was created by troops of the 48th Pennsylvania Infantry, many of them coal miners by trade. On July 27, its two 40-foot lateral galleries beneath Rebel lines were packed with four tons of fused and tamped gunpowder.

Maj. Gen. Ambrose Burnside's four divisions had been chosen to provide "shock troops" to exploit the general chaos that would follow the blast. He selected for special training Gen. Edward Ferrero's black 4th Division. They were new men, untested in battle; his white soldiers were by then exhausted from the Wilderness fighting. Two days before the detonation and long after the 4th had mastered its plan for an attack on both side of the area that was to be exploded, Burnside's superior, Maj. Gen. George Meade, the victor at Gettysburg, abruptly vetoed the plan. Grant backed Meade. "It would then be said," he later testified before Congress, "that we were shoving those people ahead to get killed because we did not care anything about them."

Burnside allowed the white division that would lead the attack to be chosen by lot. Tragically, the short straw fell to Brig. Gen. James Ledlie's 1st Division. Ledlie was a drunk, an incompetent and a coward whom Grant once described as "the poorest division commander that General Burnside had." The 1st Division was a collection of former artillerymen for whom Burnside had little regard, labeling them "worthless."

When the explosion went off, the resulting havoc was beyond anyone's expectations. Most of a Confederate regiment and several artillery pieces disappeared entirely. The fort was blown apart. Confederates on both sides of the crater ran in horror. "Stones, timbers, arms, legs, guns unlimbered and bodies unlimbed" rained back down into the dust-filled, sulfurous crater, 170 feet long, 80 feet wide and 30 feet deep. Ledlie was back in a medical tent, drinking, as his 1st Division stumbled blindly forward through a narrow opening in the Union trenches and into the reeking crater. Caught there, they did not fan out to either side as the plan had intended them to, but having lost critical momentum and nerve, sought cover in the crater and huddled clinging to the shattered, blood-wet earth. Brigades from the 2nd and 3rd Divisions followed, to be lost in the smoke and confusion. By the time the black 4th Division was sent forward, the Confederates had recovered and were mounting a counterattack. The 4th was caught in a withering fire. Buckling at last, the black soldiers also retreated, many falling into the crater.

When the smoke had cleared, the Union had lost 3,798 men killed, wounded or missing.

Reports of the fiasco provided one of the sorriest footnotes of the war. Some Confederate soldiers had followed the 4th down into the crater and killed wounded blacks who were trying to surrender. They, too, remembered Fort Pillow. That was predictable. But there was worse news from the Union side. It was asserted that white Union soldiers bayoneted Union blacks to preserve themselves from Confederate vengeance. According to George Kilmer, a white artillery-man from New York, "Men boasted in my presence that blacks had thus been disposed of."

A lengthy court of inquiry also confirmed that the black division had lost far more men than any of the white divisions. As to white soldiers killing black soldiers, that was never looked into. No one was ever court-martialed.

Grant later said, "General Burnside wanted to put his colored division in front and I believe if he had done so it would have been a success." Nevertheless, in military myth the Battle of the Crater was such a disaster that it cast a general pall over the reputation for bravery that blacks had thus far earned. It was left for General Butler, the first to make use of the "contraband" label, and a man who had once belittled black soldiers for alleged awkwardness in gun handling to fashion a long-overdue tribute. Fittingly, it came after another battle—at New Market Heights, Virginia. There, after having been ordered to remove the caps from the nipples of their guns so they could not fire them (officers believed that stopping to shoot might slow the momentum of the charge), nine black regiments victoriously stormed a Confederate redoubt at bayonet point, suffering 1,000 casualties.

"In a space not wider than the clerk's desk and three hundred yards long, lay the dead bodies of five hundred and forty-three of my colored comrades," Butler wrote, "and as I looked on their bronzed faces up-turned in the shining sun, as if in mute appeal against the wrongs of the country for which they had given their lives, whose flag had only been to them a flag of stripes, on which no star of glory had ever shone for them—feeling I had wronged them in the past, I swore to myself a solemn oath . . . 'to defend the rights of those men who have given their blood for me and my country that day and for their race forever.'"

Before 1864 was out, the all-black XXV Army Corps was formed. The largest black unit ever in American military history, it was commanded by Gen. Godfrey Weitzel who, as a lieutenant, had asked to be relieved of an expedition with black troops because he thought leading them into the South would stir bloody slave insurrections. In the black corps hopes ran high of playing a major role in the spring campaign of 1865 that would end by vanquishing Lee. But then the XXV Corps was dismantled. Divisions were split off, brigades scattered, regiments ordered to temporary duty with white units, the corps' command fragmented and removed to secondary rear echelons. Grant already had 110,000 men in the field to Lee's 50,000. But with some justice, a member of the corps lamented bitterly, "It was clearly not intended that the colored troops should win any glory. . . ."

On the great day when Union troops finally marched into the Confederate capital at war's end, they were led by black detachments from the XXV Corps. A Chicago *Tribune* editorialist reflected on the encouraging fact that representatives of a formerly enslaved race "bore the banner of freedom" into the birthplace of the rebellion. But he also rhapsodized about "sable warriors . . . rolling up the whites of their visual orbs, and exhibiting an untarnished display of nature's dentistry" as they entered Richmond. Immediately thereafter, wonder of wonders, the XXV Corps was reconstituted—and shipped to the Texas border with Mexico. Grant's order left little doubt what fate awaited them there: "You should take a fair quantity of intrenching tools . . ."

CHAPTER 4

―――

Abraham Lincoln and the
Recruitment of Black Soldiers

John T. Hubbell

FOR ALL THE VOLUMES written about Abraham Lincoln, for all the eloquent words spoken by Lincoln himself—for all the polls that mark him
a great man, a national, even international, hero—the Civil War President
remains something of an enigma.[1] Our continuation today of the "Lincoln
and" tradition suggests our preoccupation with his views on great issues.
Given a corollary interest in the topic of race in American history, it is not
surprising that Lincoln's place in that central theme remains a subject of
debate. The revolutionary developments of the post-World War II period in
the area of what is broadly termed "civil rights" have led to a reevaluation of
Lincoln—from the great emancipator to the reluctant emancipator to the
white supremacist, or, in more vulgar terms, Lincoln as just another honkie.

Historians, ordinarily a judicious lot, are as much involved in the
reevaluation as those with more obvious ideological interests. But historians should have a greater appreciation of context. Hence, to wrench
Lincoln from context, from the backdrop of his times, from the exigen-
cies of policy, from the fortunes of war, and from the historical record, is
not a path calculated for arrival at something approximating historical
truth. In our relativistic age, perhaps it is too much to expect fidelity to
the record; perhaps Lincoln should remain more symbol than historical
reality. Perhaps the record is discomfiting; it often is.

Abraham Lincoln was born into a political culture that was profoundly
racist (to use a somewhat anachronistic term). For centuries, Europeans,

whether living on the continent, in the United States, or elsewhere, had deemed the Africans a race apart, one that was in no guise the equal of the European. It was a combination of that racism with economic considerations that made the enslavement of the African fundamentally different from the slavery of other places and other times. Practically speaking, there was nothing in Lincoln's formative years that would lead us to expect him to be other than a man of his culture. The laws of Kentucky, Indiana, Illinois—in common with those of other political jurisdictions within the United States—held the African to be less than a citizen, less than a person.

Yet Lincoln imbibed other influences—the idea of political democracy (however limited); the idea of social mobility (however restricted); the ideas of economic improvement (however problematical). Lincoln believed the words of the Declaration of Independence; he believed that a person should not be constrained by circumstances of birth; and he embraced the Whig notions of economic growth. As an individual he was, from all reports, singularly free from bigotry—against individuals and groups.[2]

As much as any public man of his day, he advocated the widest sharing in the American dream. His reentry into national politics in the wake of the exacerbated sectional conflict of the 1850s was predicated upon the ideas that slavery was an evil and that, in certain instances, racial bigotry was unworthy of a great nation. That his political fortunes, and those of his party, were tied to the geographical restriction of slavery, set him, and his party, apart from his political opponents. In the context of 1858 and 1860 (and 1948 or 1960), he could have been seen as something of a radical.

The threat to slavery perceived by Lincoln's election in 1860 precipitated a train of events that culminated in a civil war. That war, whatever else it may have been, or whatever else we may wish it had been, was a titanic military struggle, fraught with profound political and social consequences. Lincoln, as he remarked in his Second Inaugural Address, did not anticipate, nor did other Americans anticipate, those consequences any more than they anticipated the full horrors of that wretched conflict. Lincoln expected a relatively short war once the apparently overwhelming resources of the Union could be brought to bear against the Confederacy. Thus, the ancient prejudices of his country might have survived the war intact had the war indeed ended with Union victory in the first year or so. But that was not the case. Lincoln necessarily had to accept, and then defend, policies that arose from circumstances—circumstances that forced a reconsideration of the place of the African (more accurately, the Afro-American) in the United States.

The American political and military establishment decreed in 1861 that the war would be fought by white men. Lincoln concurred. The

Congress decreed in July, 1861, that the war would be fought for the Union—not for conquest or the abolition of slavery. Lincoln concurred. When his generals and Cabinet officials moved beyond the President's plan, Lincoln overruled them. When black leaders asked that regiments of black soldiers be enrolled under the flag of freedom, Lincoln and his advisors refused.[3] Many northerners, in stations high and low, seemed to fear a rebellion of slaves more than they feared a rebellion of slaveowners.[4] Had northern arms prevailed in 1861 or even in early 1862, slavery might have remained *status quo ante bellum.*

The political attack on slavery was embodied in a series of laws, termed the Confiscation Acts. Under the provisions of those laws, Lincoln could have enrolled black men as laborers and support elements for the armies in the field. Lincoln chose rather not to invoke those aspects of the Acts. A primary reason was his concern for the border states, especially Kentucky. Lincoln believed that wholesale emancipation or the enlistment of black soldiers would cause Kentucky, and probably Missouri and Maryland, to become even greater obstacles to the Union cause—to say nothing of antagonism elsewhere in the North. In the case of Kentucky he was correct. Holding that state in the Union necessitated either overwhelming military force or some deference to the wishes of its white population. Lincoln's policy reflected a combination of both. Eventually, more black men entered the Army from Kentucky than from any other state except Louisiana. And the reaction of the white population in Kentucky was as negative as had been predicted. But by 1863, negative reaction in Kentucky was considerably less consequential than in 1861 or 1862.[5]

For practical political reasons, Lincoln did not openly lead the movement toward the enlistment of blacks. Prior to 1863, long before he expressed enthusiasm for the idea, he allowed others to take the first steps; he remained silent, overruled them, or caused them to be overruled. He was always sensitive to political considerations and to the perquisites and powers of his office. Timing, the right moment, was critical—and Lincoln always deemed himself a better judge of the moment than those who advised him, formally or informally.

On September 25, 1861, Secretary of the Navy Gideon Welles allowed the recruitment of blacks into the Navy, but only with the rank of "boy" and at a compensation of no more than $10.00 per month. The step caused little comment, perhaps because "boys" on ships were not expected to shoot Rebels or to function as part of the military establishment.[6]

Simon Cameron, Secretary of War, was less subtle. On October 14, 1861, he authorized Brigadier General Thomas W. Sherman to hire black fugitives for service in South Carolina, although he disclaimed any intent to arm them as soldiers. Lincoln seemed amenable to the idea of blacks as "auxiliaries," but the plan failed because General Sherman apparently neither wished to use blacks nor wished to offend unduly the sensibilities of white South Carolinians. In December, Cameron took a more direct step. In his annual report he openly advocated employment of slaves as soldiers. More important, he allowed the report to be copied and distributed before giving it to Lincoln. The President disavowed the offensive portions of the report and ordered them deleted from his own annual message to Congress. Because of that misstep but also because he was a general embarrassment to the administration, Cameron was removed from the Cabinet and named minister to Russia.[7]

During the first half of 1862, Congress moved towards bringing blacks into the Army—March, rendition of slaves by military forbidden; April, abolition of slavery in D.C.; July, Second Confiscation Act and Militia Act. In April and May, the new Secretary of War, Edwin Stanton, encouraged (at least implicitly) the arming of blacks in South Carolina. The situation there caused a great stir, because the general in command, David Hunter, proved to be politically inept and hence a political liability. He managed to offend many officers and men in the white regiments as well as two congressmen of a border state, Kentucky. When those congressmen demanded explanations of what was transpiring in South Carolina, Stanton retreated into his bureaucratic defenses but did ask General Hunter for a report, which he forwarded to Congress. Hunter's report was entertaining to some Republicans (referring to "fugitive rebels"), and to the border state congressmen—insulting.[8]

During the summer of 1862, Lincoln evinced no inclination to support Hunter, to implement the provisions of the Second Confiscation Act liberating the slaves of Rebels, or to employ blacks other than as laborers. He stated his views to the Cabinet in late July, and on August 6 he told a delegation of "Western gentlemen" that he would not arm blacks "unless some new and more pressing emergency arises." Such, he said, would turn "50,000 bayonets" in the border states against the Union. Steps short of actually arming blacks would be continued—upon this he and his critics did not differ. And in the same context, on August 22 he wrote his famous reply to Horace Greeley's "Prayer of Twenty Millions": as President, he would save the Union; all else would be subordinate to that goal.[9]

On August 10, the disheartened (if not chastened) General Hunter reported to Stanton that he was disbanding his regiment of South Carolina volunteers. But, as the curtain fell on Hunter, Stanton on August 25 authorized Brigadier General Rufus Saxton at Beaufort, South Carolina, to "arm, uniform, equip, and receive into the service of the United States such number of volunteers of African descent as you may deem expedient, not exceeding 5,000." Why the reversal? Why had Stanton authorized Saxton to do what had been denied Hunter? A comment by Lieutenant Charles Francis Adams Jr. may be pertinent. Regarding Hunter, "Why could not fanatics be silent and let Providence work for awhile?"[10] (And if not Providence, at least the President.) In short, had Hunter managed to be more politic with respect to his fellow officers and the Congress, had he been able to restrain his rhetorical flourishes, he may not have run afoul of the critics of his policy, to say nothing of the President. The fact was, blacks were now to be brought into the service, not by a general assembly, but by order of the War Department—and the President.

In other corners of the conflict, namely Louisiana and Kansas, other generals proceeded to enlist blacks. In New Orleans, for example, Benjamin F. Butler had negated earlier enlisting efforts but now, encouraged by Secretary of the Treasury Chase (and by Mrs. Butler), called for free blacks to enter the service. By mid-fall three such regiments were formed in Louisiana. On August 5, 1862, the redoubtable abolitionist James H. Lane in Kansas wired Stanton that he was raising black as well as white regiments, and was there any objection? Stanton wrote Lane on August 22 and again on September 23 that such action was without the authority of the President. Lane never received authorization, but he continued enrolling black soldiers for the Union. Benjamin Quarles has termed such enrollment "trial balloons," which when no one of consequence tried to pop, Lincoln allowed to float.[11]

Of course, Lincoln was discussing another matter with his Cabinet in the summer of 1862—namely, emancipation. In his "preliminary" proclamation of September 22, 1862, Lincoln did not mention black soldiers. In October, however, he presumably talked to one Daniel Ullmann of New York, who urged that very course. After hearing Ullmann's argument, Lincoln asked: "Would you be willing to command black soldiers?" Although stunned by the question, Ullmann replied in the affirmative.[12] Given the events of the late summer and early fall in South Carolina, Louisiana, and Kansas, Lincoln seemed to be evolving a plan—perhaps Ullmann would pilot another of those trial balloons.

The Emancipation Proclamation, issued on January 1, 1863, called for the enrollment of blacks in the Union Army and Navy. It was contained in an almost offhand passage—fully in keeping with Lincoln's tendency to hint, approach indirectly, and finally, defend the stated policy. Yet the proclamation was fundamental. It was a war message, a political document. The government of the United States, through the Office of

President, was now unequivocally on the side of emancipation and of bringing black men into the army of the Republic.

Over the next several months the new policy was put into effect. Ullmann, appointed a brigadier general of volunteers, was specifically charged with raising four regiments of volunteers in Louisiana (where he found public opinion far from supportive). Colonel James Montgomery of Kansas was authorized to raise a black regiment in South Carolina, and the governors of Massachusetts and Rhode Island were given similar authorization.[13] Massachusetts Governor John A. Andrew, in fact, raised most of his black troops from the Southern states.[14]

The major organizing effort was placed in the hands of Lorenzo Thomas, adjutant general of the Army. His order of March 25 from Secretary Stanton was to proceed to the Mississippi Valley, in order to enlist black troops and find white officers and enlisted men who would take commissions in black regiments. Thomas was an effective recruiter, stressing that he spoke with the full authority of the President, the Secretary of War, and the General-in-Chief. Henry W. Halleck (who was notorious for his General Order No. 3 in 1861) had fallen in line with administration policy and now was telling other officers in the Mississippi Valley to do the same. Of particular interest was the reaction of Ulysses S. Grant, who early in the war had no more sympathy for emancipation than did many other regulars. Yet Grant was certainly a man to follow orders from Washington. Indeed, he had already made provisions for organizing "contrabands" into a work force. According to John Eaton Jr., in charge of the contrabands, Grant believed that if the occasion arose, the fugitives could carry rifles instead of hoes, rakes, and shovels.

Halleck's advice to Grant, in a friendly if somewhat patronizing letter, was an effective statement of administration policy. "From my position here, where I can survey the whole field, perhaps I may be better able to understand the tone of public opinion and the intentions of the Government." Grant then assured Halleck (and later the President) that he would support the policy even to the extent of ordering subordinate officers to be active in "removing prejudice" against blacks. Thomas's mission, after all, went beyond recruiting black men into the ranks. As Dudley Cornish has stated: "Rather was his task that of initiating Union policy on a grand scale, of breaking down white opposition to the use of Negro soldiers, of educating Union troops in the valley on this one subject, of starting the work of organization," and then leaving others to finish the work of recruiting and training. Lincoln approved of Thomas's work, telling Stanton that Thomas was "one of the best (if not the best) instruments for this service."[15] Perhaps Lincoln had been right after all. It was best to bring the general public along, then put the task in the hands of the professional soldiers who, while not without ideological biases, placed great stock in order, system, and hierarchy. The road to favor with the administration was not in embarrassing the President, but in efficiently following his policy, once that policy was clearly enunciated.

On Independence Day, 1863, Vicksburg surrendered; the "Father of Waters" again flowed "unvexed to the sea." Thanks were given to not only the Great Northwest, but also New England, and the "Sunny South, too, in more colors than one."[16]

In early August, Lincoln wrote to Grant, congratulating him upon his magnificent military achievement, but also noting: "Gen. Thomas has gone again to the Mississippi Valley, with the view of raising colored troops. I have not reason to doubt that you are doing what you reasonably can upon the same subject. I believe it is a resource which, if vigorously applied now, will soon close the contest. It works doubly, weakening the enemy and strengthening us. We were not fully ripe for it until the river was opened."[17] On August 26, Lincoln wrote to a political friend in Illinois that some of his field commanders "who have given us our most important successes, believe the emancipation policy, and the use of colored troops, constitute the heaviest blow yet dealt to the rebellion; and that, at least one of those important successes, could not have been achieved when it was, but for the aid of black soldiers." He could have recited the practical, some might say cynical, reasons given for bringing blacks to the Army—saving the lives of white soldiers. Yet, said Lincoln, "Negroes, like other people, act upon motives. Why should they do anything for us, if we will do nothing for them? If they stake their lives for us, they must be prompted by the strongest motive—even the promise of freedom. And the promise being made, must be kept." One day peace would come. "And then, there will be some black men who can remember that, with silent tongue, and clenched teeth, and steady eye, and well-poised bayonet, they have helped mankind on to this great consummation; while, I fear, there will be some white ones, unable to forget that, with malignant heart, and deceitful speech, they have strove to hinder it."[18]

The force of the effort for recruiting blacks lay in the deep South and in the Northeast. Lincoln still had no wish to press the issue in the border states. And his caution was well founded, although he did authorize (through Stanton) recruiting in Maryland, Kentucky, and Missouri.

Kentuckians were particularly resentful. When Ambrose Burnside suggested in June, 1863, that the administration disavow any intention to conscript free blacks in Kentucky, Lincoln concurred that the effort would cost more than it would gain. In January, 1864, however, the War

Department established a recruiting post in Paducah. Kentucky Governor Thomas E. Bramlette traveled to Washington and protested directly to Lincoln. The President explained that he had come to his policy of emancipation and arming blacks after prudent delay—early in the war it was not an "indispensable necessity." He changed his mind when he knew that he had to choose between "surrendering the Union, and with it, the Constitution, or of laying strong hand upon the colored element." He had not been certain at that time that he had made the right decision, but after a year's experience, he was convinced of it. "We have the men [130,000]; and we could not have had them without the measure. And now let any Union man who complains of the measure, test himself by writing down in one line that he is for subduing the rebellion by force of arms; and in the next, that he is for taking these hundred and thirty thousand men from the Union side, and placing them where they would be but for the measure he condemns. If he can not face his case so stated, it is only because he can not face the truth." That letter contained Lincoln's memorable line, "I claim not to have controlled events, but confess plainly that events have controlled me."[19] Lincoln meant for the letter to be circulated among the white population of Kentucky. Although his correspondents expressed satisfaction with it, Kentuckians in general resented recruitment of blacks more intensely than did people of any other state. But Lincoln knew, and he made the point repeatedly from mid-1863 to the end of the war; without the black soldiers, there would be no Union.

Frederick Douglass said so well in 1876:

> His great mission was to accomplish two things: first, to save his country from dismemberment and ruin; and second, to free his country from the great crime of slavery. To do one or the other, or both, he needed the earnest sympathy and the powerful cooperation of his loyal fellow countrymen. Without those primary and essential conditions to success his efforts would have been utterly fruitless. Had he put the abolition of slavery before the salvation of the Union, he would have inevitably driven from him a powerful class of the American people and rendered resistance to rebellion impossible. From the genuine abolition view, Mr. Lincoln seemed tardy, cold, dull, and indifferent, but measuring him by the sentiment of his country—a sentiment he was bound as a statesman to consult—he was swift, zealous, radical, and determined.[20]

The enlistment of blacks into the Union Army was part of Lincoln's evolving policy on slavery and race, a policy charged with political, social, and psychological overtones. The black man as soldier—with rifle and bayonet—was a different figure from the slave. His presence, while a military necessity, was also a potent blow to the idea of the innate inferiority of the African, an idea not peculiar to the South. Those who urged the enlistment of blacks realized it implications. Some political figures saw it as a necessity calculated to outrage the South. Black leaders saw it from a different perspective. Not only would the enlistment of blacks serve a military purpose, but most assuredly it would also enhance the sense of manhood among black men, a sense deliberately blunted by public policy throughout the nation. Thus, while Douglass remarked on the "tardiness" of the President who "loved Rome more than he did Caesar," he insisted that emancipation and manhood, in the most profound sense, were indispensable steps toward participation in American society.

Lincoln acted as he did from necessity. His almost mystical devotion to the Union and his personal compassion for the dispossessed of the world combined into policy. Events moved him in the sense that events determined the time for action. During the Civil War a basic truth emerged: Black people understood the meaning of the war and contributed to the great goal of freedom. Yet blacks were also objects; in order to defeat the white South, the white North needed black men. Lincoln was their emancipator, their savior, when he spoke as the cautious, prudent political leader and when he eloquently spoke of the magnificent contribution that black soldiers made to the Union. The war brought the time, and Lincoln—"preeminently the white man's President"—became the black man's hero.

CHAPTER 5

Massachusetts and the Recruitment of Southern Negroes, 1863–1865

Richard H. Abbott

ARLY IN 1863, FREDERICK DOUGLASS, militant Negro abolitionist, embarked upon a tour throughout the North seeking volunteers to fill the ranks of the 54th Massachusetts, the first Negro regiment organized in the North to fight for the Union. Douglass told Negroes who came to hear him that they owed a special debt to Massachusetts: "She was the first . . . to break the chains of her slaves; first to make the back man equal before the law; first to admit colored children in her common schools." And now, he declared, Massachusetts "welcomes you as her soldiers."[1] Douglass, bent on exhorting his audience to enlist in the battle for Union and freedom, did not choose to examine carefully the motives of Massachusetts leaders in organizing Negro troops. Had he done so, he would have discovered that while Bay State spokesmen agreed with him that Negroes serving in the army would win the approval of northern white men, as well as win a large measure of self-respect, they were perhaps even more interested in obtaining recruits to fill the state's quotas and keep its white working men out of the draft.

At the opening of the Civil War Massachusetts was the most highly industrialized state in the Union. Twenty-five percent of its entire male population worked in manufacturing establishments in 1860, compared to 13 percent in Pennsylvania and 9 percent in New York. Although the state's cotton industry suffered during the war, its woolen and shoe manufacturers prospered.[2] When the War Department began calling on

Massachusetts for volunteers, the state's businessmen faced the prospect of losing their labor force to the Union Army. Governor John A. Andrew, hoping to ease the distress of the Massachusetts business community while still meeting the state's military quotas, called upon John Murray Forbes to assist him in organizing his recruiting efforts on a more effective and productive basis. Forbes, one of Boston's leading entrepreneurs, had demonstrated his business talents by accumulating a fortune in the China trade at the age of twenty-four. By the time of the Civil War he had accumulated a number of investments on land and sea, and was busy building railroads into the Mississippi Valley. He was quite sensitive to the economic needs of the Bay State, and willingly turned his efforts to finding recruits for Massachusetts regiments.[3]

Forbes and his agents eventually managed to entice approximately one thousand Europeans to migrate to Massachusetts and enlist in the war effort there. Forbes quickly decided, however, that the largest and most accessible source of recruits for Massachusetts could be found among the Negro population, both slave and free, in the United States. Governor Andrew and a number of other abolitionists in the state had been urging the Federal government to permit them to raise a Negro regiment, and in January, 1863, the War Department provided the necessary authorization. Discovering that only 1,973 Negro men of military age lived in the state, Andrew decided he would have to look elsewhere for large numbers of volunteers. Acting quickly, he sent agents into Canada and as far west as the Mississippi River, seeking Negroes to fill the Massachusetts regiments. The chief agent in charge of this recruitment later reported that he had obtained some 1,300 Negroes from Pennsylvania and the West.[4]

This small harvest of northern Negroes was not enough to suit Andrew's needs, especially after March, 1863, when Congress passed a conscription act creating a national draft. Renewed demands upon Massachusetts for troops under new draft quotas produced great anxiety among the state's businessmen. Edward Atkinson, one of the state's leading industrialists, was alarmed at the fact that "our resources are being crippled by the withdrawal of so many working men." Textile manufacturer Amos Lawrence complained that due to the draft, "we have lost not less than 100,000 men, and some kinds of labor are at a stand." According to Forbes, "all our mechanics here are made crazy by the high wages and the draft." The editor of the Boston *Commonwealth* produced a "great law of political economy" which he said "forbids a country to drain out its best industry into the wasteful channels of war."[5]

Responding to the crisis, in the summer of 1863 John Murray Forbes organized a Boston businessmen's committee, formed from the state's leading industrialists, to raise funds to provide bounty money for Negro volunteers. He also helped organize the New England Loyal Publication Society to publish broadsides and pamphlets in behalf of the Union, emancipation, and the use of Negro troops. Forbes and his committee urged President Abraham Lincoln and Secretary of War Edwin Stanton to step up to the Federal government's attempts to enlist Negroes. Forbes reminded Stanton that using Negro troops would not only benefit the Union; it would greatly aid the Negro by treating him "in all respects *as a man*." Yet he also noted that "acclimated Blacks" would be more valuable in the South than white soldiers, and could be more cheaply and easily procured. In one of the Loyal Publication Society's pamphlets, Forbes maintained that using Negroes in the army would "economize our home resources rather than draw on Northern skilled labor."[6]

The inability of Massachusetts agents to find large numbers of Negro volunteers in the North prompted her leaders to seek broader powers to recruit Negroes anywhere in southern territory held by Union arms. The idea of such a measure had been broached by Forbes as early as January, 1863, when he asked Senators James W. Grimes of Iowa and Zachariah Chandler of Michigan to support recruiting in Confederate states "under the stimulus of state competition and state bounties." Forbes, recognizing that many race-conscious people in the North disapproved of Massachusetts' efforts to elevate the Negro, hoped the western senators would uphold the proposal. If enough pressure for the plan could be marshalled, said Forbes, Secretary of War Stanton would implement it without waiting for Congress to act on the matter.[7]

Forbes was doomed to disappointment. Later in the winter, when Massachusetts Senator Henry Wilson, chairman of the Senate Military Affairs Committee, proposed legislation empowering loyal states to recruit Negroes in occupied portions of the South, he encountered stiff resistance from Stanton. Privately the Secretary told Wilson that his bill would not augment the army but instead would merely let northern whites stay home, and he warned the senator that he would resign the day after such a bill passed. Consequently, for several months nothing more was said about state enlistment of Negro troops. Instead, the Federal government developed its own program of recruiting former slaves in the South.[8] At first the government's efforts were halting and confused. Not until May 22, 1863, did Stanton regularize the method of raising Negro soldiers, centralizing full control in the Bureau of Colored Troops. Federal officers recruiting Negroes in the South encountered hostility from white soldiers, and found the former slaves reluctant to step forward to assume duties and responsibilities that were not clearly explained to them.⁹ The fumbling efforts of Federal recruiters gave agitators in Massachusetts a powerful reason for urging once more that states be allowed to seek volunteers among southern Negroes. In August, Amos Lawrence, noting that "whatever opposition existed here to the employment of colored troops had been dispelled by the draft," asked Wilson to persuade Stanton to turn over recruitment of Negroes in the South to "a corps of Yankee-doodle," so that the job would be done. Forbes' committee of businessmen announced that the Federal government's enlistment program would fail unless assisted by the states. In October, Henry Wilson angrily asked Abraham Lincoln to explain why no more Negro troops had been raised, and insisted that if "an eminent businessman of Boston" like John Murray Forbes were permitted to recruit in the South, Union armies would quickly be filled.¹⁰

While Wilson complained to Federal authorities about the slow accretion of Negroes in Union ranks, Forbes, convinced that "it is the only way in which [Massachusetts] quotas *can be filled* within three months," went to Washington to renew his campaign to get Congress to empower northern states to recruit freedmen in the South. Once again he asked Zachariah Chandler to encourage western congressmen to vote for such a measure. He was able to convince Secretary of the Treasury Salmon P. Chase to support the idea. Encountering a delegation of New York businessmen interested in the same proposal, he eagerly encouraged them to press Congress on the matter. As he told Governor Andrew, it would be better if the Bay State did not take the lead in urging the desired legislation, since Massachusetts "is looked upon as entirely monomaniac upon the 'everlasting Nigger.'" According to Forbes, if the bill did pass, Governor Horatio Seymour of New York would oppose enlisting Negro troops, and consequently "Massachusetts with her energy, her bounty and her foresight will get the first pickings." Once again, the Massachusetts businessman and lobbyist ran into resistance from Stanton, who now claimed that in the competition between states for recruits in the South, "the states would give them an advantage over the West," and thus "might create more mischief than the good it would do." In reply, Forbes assured the Secretary that Massachusetts would support the provision even if excluded from its benefits.¹¹

On November 27, Forbes learned to his great pleasure that "the New York *heavy* merchants have signed a letter to the President asking him to let the loyal states recruit in the Rebel states."¹² On December 22, Henry Wilson notified the Senate of his intention to introduce a bill to that effect.¹³ Forbes, telling a fellow member of the Loyal Publication

Society that "if we can get Black [soldiers] . . . from the slave states it is better than draining our artisans and free laborers," encouraged the Society to redouble its propaganda efforts in favor of congressional legislation. He noted that since Stanton still opposed the ides, "we must *make* public opinion."[14] Public opinion was promptly "made." Forbes and the Boston businessmen's committee deluged Stanton and Massachusetts congressmen with pleas to secure admission of state agents into rebel territory. Forbes wrote to clergyman Henry Ward Beecher in New York, asking the dynamic and popular minister to use his influence in behalf of the measure. He also petitioned Reverend William G. Eliot of St. Louis to "get up some western enthusiasm for the plan," assuring him that the whole country would benefit from it.[15] In the meantime, Boston businessmen, noting that Massachusetts industry was already "greatly embarrassed" by the draft, assured Stanton that the "producing states" could afford to pay bounties to southern Negroes and thus relieve their citizens from part of the latest draft call. William P. Robinson, correspondent for the Springfield *Republican,* reflected this reasoning when he wrote that recruiting in slave states had to be approved. "The skilled labor of New England and New York is wanting in factories and shops, and will remain there by a law superior to drafts—must remain there if the national taxes are to be paid and the national credit sustained. There are men enough elsewhere."[16]

Despite the pressures organized by Massachusetts and New York interests, Wilson failed in his attempt to enact a measure permitting state recruitment in the South. Western senators, led by James Grimes, refused to support the idea, claiming that it would permit Massachusetts and other states "delinquent under the draft" to enter the South and use their wealth to purchase "mercenaries" to fill their quotas. In such a competition for recruits, western states like Iowa, which Grimes represented, would be unable to compete. If Negroes were to be enlisted, he maintained, let them be registered as troops belonging to the United States, rather than to any particular state. Wilson denied that Massachusetts was behind in its quotas, insisting that his state had furnished its "full share" to the war effort. The Bay State senator claimed that the draft quotas bore unfairly upon states like Massachusetts that had lost large numbers of young men to the western states. Despite his efforts, Wilson was voted down 27 to 11; nine of the eleven votes in support of his bill came from New England states and New York. Forbes, who had anticipated that if the bill passed it would result in "such a competition for the African as has never been seen outside the Gulf of Guinea," bitterly assigned its defeat to "petty feelings of sectional jealousy existing at the West."[17]

Despite Wilson's failure in the Senate, all was not lost with the Massachusetts scheme. On February 24, Forbes' search for western support bore fruit when Francis P. Blair of Missouri asked Wilson for a copy of his bill, and then introduced it as a resolution in the House of Representatives. Despite determined opposition from men like William H. Wadsworth of Kentucky, who asked why eastern states, "which are growing rich by this war," should be allowed to "purchase their soldiers," the resolution passed the house without much debate by a vote of 82–44.[18] In the Senate, however, the bill languished as members turned to other questions, chief among which was the advisability of repealing commutation provisions in the national conscription act. Commutation, which permitted drafted citizens to pay the government three hundred dollars and avoid military service, played a significant role in the eventual resolution of the argument over recruitment in southern states.

Although some men of influence in Massachusetts, like abolitionist Frank Bird, were skeptical of the House bill, in light of the fact that "we are sending wretched mercenaries [to fight] rather than stop our industries," once again the wheels of Forbes' organization were set in motion. Once more the Boston entrepreneur departed for Washington to lobby for the proposal; he asked Amos Lawrence to accompany him, but Lawrence refused, stating that "we are given to meddling with everybody's business too much." Forbes, hoping to "stir up the dry bones of some of those confounded politicians," visited a number of senators in Washington, and learned that Stanton was still opposed to the recruiting proposal. According to Forbes, the Secretary insisted that passage of the bill "will make civil war at the North, and other such bosh." Senator Wilson, charged with guiding the House resolution through the Senate, complained that many of his colleagues, pointing to Massachusetts' deficit in draft quotas, were reluctant to permit the state to attempt to fulfill her obligations by dragooning southern Negroes into her regiments.[19]

On April 4, when Wilson finally found an opportunity to bring the resolution before the Senate, lobbyists had prepared the way by placing circulars in its behalf on the desks of all the senators. Grimes, expressing irritation at "the great pressures" applied to get them to pass the resolution, demanded that Massachusetts fill its draft quotas as other states had done. John Sherman of Ohio agreed, stating his opposition to permitting northern agents to engage in "ruinous competition" for Negroes in the South. Lyman Trumbull of Illinois demanded that Wilson explain why recruitment of Negro troops should not be left with the Federal government. In reply, the Massachusetts senator complained that "the federal government does not know much about enlisting men" and had been slow to amass colored troops. He claimed that the states, which could pay more bounty than the Federal government, could thereby enlist more Negroes. Despite his efforts, the Senate refused to vote on the House resolution.[20]

Throughout April and May Forbes and the New England Loyal Publication Society continued to campaign for the desired legislation. The New York *Evening Post* and New York *Tribune* published several editorials in its behalf. On May 2, Henry Wilson made a desperate plea before his colleagues, urging them to grant the requisite authority to "raise men by the use of our State and local bounties in the rebel States." The senator reminded his listeners that "the price of labor has risen everywhere; the needs of labor are everywhere upon us both in the workshops and in the fields." In the face of such pressing necessities, he asked the Senate to pass the Blair resolution, and thus "favor our own loyal sections of the country, take care of our own labor and material interests, and put the burdens of the war as much as we can upon those States that have raised the banners of treason." The Senate turned a deaf ear to Wilson's supplications. Nine days later, when he attempted to bring up the resolution "to settle it one way or the other," he was met by dismayed cries of "oh, no," and his motion was defeated.[21]

May gave way to June, and still the Massachusetts senator was unable to gain approval of the Blair resolution. Consequently the bill's proponents turned back to the House, where on June 25 Robert Schenck, Chairman of the House Military Affairs Committee, had just introduced a new conscription measure. Schenck, noting that the Blair resolution, which the House had passed by a large majority, was "permitted to sleep upon the table of the Senate," added the proposal to his new bill. Another provision in the measure provided for the repeal of commutation, and New England congressmen refused to vote for this section unless the Congress approved of state enlistments in the South. Consequently, after a somewhat bitter debate, in which Massachusetts again was charged with dodging her quotas, the House by a vote of 82 to 77 passed a bill uniting commutation repeal with the Blair resolution, and on June 29 sent the package to the Senate.[22]

Forbes and his business associates were now confident of victory in the Upper House. Driven to desperation by draft calls in February and April, the Boston capitalists had been busily "forcing and bringing the New York and Philadelphia Union League to bear" in support of state enlistment in the South. Wilson, upon having the House measure reported to his committee, hurriedly called his committee members together, briefly considered the bill, and reported it out to the Senate the same day.[23]

On the Senate floor, B. Gratz Brown, a member of Wilson's committee, led the attack on the bill, charging that its real purpose was to change
the army into a mass of freedmen enlisted as substitutes for whites. The
Missouri senator had many objections to the proposal. Raising Negroes
in the South by state competition would be more expensive if the states
rather than the Federal government handled the system. Replacing literate, often skilled whites with illiterate, recently-freed slaves would drastically reduce the quality of the Federal armies. Permitting governors to
"run a race" and send thousands of agents into the South for "kidnapping and crimping and bribing to get these substitutes" would destroy
volunteering in the North. Finally, stated Brown, the measure would
"interrupt and destroy the harmony and confidence which during the
progress of this war has existed between the eastern and western states."
The West, he said, would not stand for passage of the bill.[24]

In defense of the proposed legislation, Wilson said it would benefit
the nation and not any particular section. Again he emphasized that the
Federal government was not raising Negro troops, and that the state
governments should take over in this matter. He reminded his colleagues
that the proposal "will relieve [from the draft] . . . a class of men in the
country necessary to its productive industry." Grimes then took the floor
and roundly denounced the bill as a "wild, suicidal, and I would say
ridiculous scheme." William Sprague of Rhode Island, another member
of Wilson's committee, rose to complain that he had not been advised of
the committee's meeting and that the bill had not been properly considered in committee. Wilson, admitting that because he "was pressed up
from all quarters" he had acted hastily, pointed out that even if Sprague
had attended, the bill would have passed the committee by a three to
two vote. He then pleaded for passage of the bill, but the Senate, before
approving the measure, amended it to provide that any soldiers enlisted
in the South be recruited and organized by the Federal government,
rather than the states.[25]

On June 30 the House took up the measure as amended by the
Senate. Henry L. Dawes of Massachusetts led the defense of the original
proposal to permit states to recruit in the South, stating that eastern states
like his own had lost vast numbers of men of military age to the West,
and that they should thus be permitted to make up their state quotas
beyond their own borders. Aaron Harding of Kentucky, after listening to
Dawes, snorted that the congressmen from Massachusetts "might as well
come up and face the music at once," and admit that "their whole effort
is to throw the burden of their share of fighting in this war upon the
negroes they may procure from other states." Francis Le Blonde, Ohio

Democrat, noting that Massachusetts had enlisted hundreds of Negroes in his own state, condemned the whole bill, calling it a "bargain and a sale . . . to suit the wishes of Massachusetts." Despite such bitter criticism of the original House bill, the representatives voted 69 to 53 to stand by it and call for a conference committee to work out the differences between them over the question of state recruitment in the South.[26]

On July 2 the conference committee reported the bill to both houses in much the form that the House had originally proposed. It included the section permitting state recruitment within Federal lines in the South. Once again some of Wilson's colleagues in the Senate protested violently. Garrett Davis of Kentucky claimed that the recruiting proposal would reopen the trading of slaves that Massachusetts had so long opposed. When LaFayette Foster of Connecticut objected to the frequent charge that New England states desired the law to shield their white population, Davis replied that "I did not intend to make an intimation of that kind in relation to any other State than Massachusetts. I think that that State by their representatives on this floor have evinced beyond all question that that is their purpose." In rebuttal, Wilson, after repeating that the proposed legislation would benefit the whole North, admitted that "I do not say we are unselfish about it, but I say the great motive is to get men to break down the rebellion." To this, Thomas Hendricks of Indiana warned that General Ulysses S. Grant, struggling against Robert E. Lee in Virginia, would gain little from receiving Negroes instead of whites to serve under him. "I look for fun," observed Hendricks, "when Massachusetts agents get up from South Carolina with their field hands and bring them to General Grant in new regiments . . . and tell him to take Richmond." Overcoming such irate dissent, Wilson managed to get a vote on the conference committee report, which the Senate approved by one vote, 18 to 17. New England senators in attendance voted unanimously for the report. The resulting bill was signed into law by President Lincoln on July 4.[27] It did not result in Secretary Stanton's threatened resignation.

John Murray Forbes wasted little time rejoicing in his victory. He warned Andrew not to "let the *sharks* go down into the rebel states—such men would discredit our whole plan." Instead, he urged Andrew to appoint a respected figure to superintend agents sent into the South on recruiting missions. Acting immediately after passage of the bill, the Massachusetts governor sent agents to Washington, Fortress Monroe, New Berne, Hilton Head, Vicksburg, and Nashville.[28] In December, when Savannah fell to General William T. Sherman, Andrew immediately dispatched agents to the Georgia city to enlist Negroes at that point. Sherman was not pleased to see the Massachusetts emissaries descend upon him. At Savannah, he was outraged to find them enticing away Negroes who had been serving his own army. Angrily he informed the Army Chief of Staff that the law was "the height of folly," and asked that the agents be banned from his lines. When eager agents at Nashville bombarded Sherman with letters asking where they might enlist Negroes, the irritated general gave them a list of eight cities deep in Confederate territory. President Lincoln finally had to ask Sherman to cooperate in implementing the law.[29]

General Sherman was not the only Union officer disgusted with the July legislation. Ulysses S. Grant, General in Chief of the Union Armies, "was down on the Massachusetts idea of buying out of the draft by filling their quota with recruits at $300, from among the contrabands in Sherman's Army." When Forbes defended the law, Grant answered that "Sherman's head is level on that question. He knows he can get all these negroes that are worth having anyhow and he prefers to get them that way rather than fill up the quota of a distant state and thus diminish the fruits of the draft." General Lorenzo Thomas, charged by the Federal government with raising Negro troops in the Mississippi Valley, complained that state agents were inducing soldiers of several Negro regiments stationed at Vicksburg to desert and enlist with the states. General Napoleon J. T. Dana, commander of the military district of Vicksburg, complained that the agents were taking "diseased men, entirely unfit for the service."[30]

John C. Gray, a young officer from the Bay State, expressed horror at the way in which agents from Massachusetts implemented the law, and asserted that such a system of recruitment brought the state "contempt and sneers." According to Gray, "this traffic of New England towns in the bodies of wretched negroes, bidding against each other for these miserable beings, who are deluded, and if some of my affidavits that I have in my office are true, tortured into military service, forms too good a justification against the Yankees." Albert Gallatin Browne, a former aide of Governor Andrew and in October, 1864, a Treasury agent at Hilton Head, South Carolina, questioned the benefit that his home state received from enlisting freedmen. According to Browne, "the whole system is damnable. I can conceive nothing worse on the coast of Africa. These men have been hunted like wild beasts and ruthlessly dragged from their families." He informed Andrew that the men enlisted by Massachusetts agents got only a fraction of the money promised them, the agents pocketing the remainder.[31]

Such lurid tales of abuse surrounding the implementation of the 1864 legislation led to its repeal in February, 1865. Wilson and his colleague Charles Sumner protested the move, insisting that they knew of no such abuses. Wilson added that the measure had succeeded in pro-

ducing thousands of men for the service. In answer to renewed complaints that Massachusetts had resorted to the law to fill its draft quotas,
Wilson announced that his state was ahead on its draft calls. John Sherman, seeking to shift the debate away from Massachusetts, said the fault
in the bill was not with any particular state, but with the system of
recruitment that it permitted. He observed that in the six months since
passage of the law, he had spoken to many officers, and they were unanimous that "wherever these [state] agents came they created embarrassment, struggle, strife and contention." The Ohio senator also noted that
since the Federal government was now rapidly recruiting Negroes,
Wilson's original motive for the law was removed. The Senate then
voted 28 to 12 to repeal the state recruitment provision. Eleven of the
twelve votes against repeal came from New England and New York. The
House then voted, without debate, 83 to 46 to repeal the law.[32]

In the six months during which the July, 1864 law operated, it had
accomplished little. Long delay in its passage had led its supporters to
assign it undue importance as a means of filling state draft quotas. From
the date of its enactment to its repeal, northern governors sent 1,405
agents into the South, where they were able to recruit only 5,052
Negroes, less than four per agent. Massachusetts obtained 1,257 recruits,
or 25 percent of the total.[33] Despite the meagerness of the results
obtained, the great effort exerted by the Massachusetts businessmen and
politicians to gain the passage and implementation of the law provides an
ironic illustration of how right Frederick Douglass was, back in the early
months of 1863, when he told Negroes that "Massachusetts welcomes
you as her soldiers."

The contention of Massachusetts congressmen that their state was
justified in resorting to Negro troops because the quotas assigned to it
were inequitable is not upheld by the evidence. Senator Wilson and Representative Dawes complained that the quotas were based on total population, thus penalizing Massachusetts for the flow of draft-age men out
of the state to the West. The 1863 conscription act, however, based
quotas for all states upon the number of men enrolled, not total population.[34] Similarly, Wilson's complaint that "the federal government does
not know much about enlisting men," is repudiated by the fact that in
the last two years of the war, Federal recruiters raised almost 100,000
Negroes while all the Northern states together recruited only 55,000.[35]
More to the point was the insistence of Wilson and the Boston businessmen that drafting men from the factories would be harmful to the Union
war effort. The conscription law of 1863, which Wilson himself helped
to draft, provided no exemption by occupation, and made no attempt to

balance the demands of the military forces with the needs of the industry supplying those forces. The solution that Massachusetts industrialists urged to the dilemma was to draft or recruit Negroes, permitting white workers to remain at their jobs. Although abolitionists and idealists like Governor Andrew recognized that service in the Union army would assist Negroes in their quest for freedom and equality, most businessmen regarded the plan from a purely economic viewpoint. To them Negro troops were only a means to an end of maintaining production—nothing more, nothing less. It is small wonder that their efforts, and the efforts of their political representatives, to recruit southern Negroes into Massachusetts regiments, led western congressmen and Union generals to question the real purpose of such activity.

CHAPTER 6

Raising the African Brigade

Early Black Recruitment in Civil War North Carolina

Richard Reid

ECRUITING FOR THE AFRICAN BRIGADE is progressing lively and enthusiastically," wrote Corporal Z. T. Haines, of the Forty-fourth Regiment Massachusetts Volunteer Militia, in late May 1863. "Quite a recruiting fever has seized the freedmen of Newbern. . . . Four thousand colored soldiers are counted upon in this department."[1] At almost the same time another soldier, William P. Derby of the Twenty-seventh Massachusetts Volunteers, recorded the excitement within the city's black population. "One can hardly forget the enthusiasm amongst the Negroes of this place, placards being posted around the city, calling for four thousand men for 'Wild's colored Brigade.' Street processions of the most motley character were the order of the day.[2]

What the two soldiers were describing, the plan to raise four infantry regiments from among North Carolina's African-American population, was one of the first authorized attempts by the Federal government to enlist ex-slaves in the defense of the Union. By the end of the war black recruitment would become widely accepted and North Carolina would provide just over 5,000 of the 179,000 black troops raised.[3] In the spring of 1863, however, the policy was new and controversial. Not surprisingly, it would be implemented in different regions with varying degrees of success. The differences in the ways in which African Americans were recruited and their responses to the Union policy depended greatly upon local conditions, the interplay of widely divergent personalities, and the recent and regional experiences of the black population. In North Carolina the initial attempt to recruit blacks would be strongly influenced by Massachusetts abolitionist zeal and paternalistic altruism, combined with a careful selection of those white officers who would lead the black units. The architects of the project were among the nation's most sympathetic supporters of black service and were drawn from the state with the strongest abolition credentials. Of course, the success of the brigade and any further enlistment would depend most of all upon the willingness of North Carolina blacks to risk all in an uncertain conflict where a blue uniform did not always signify a friend. Nevertheless, the white organizers hoped to establish a model with the brigade in North Carolina that could demonstrate elsewhere how best to serve both Union and black interests. As a result, the recruitment of the African Brigade, and its first months of service, can be used as an effective case study to delineate the upper limits of white altruism and the Federal government's willingness to treat ex-slaves in a fashion similar to white soldiers. The abbreviated career of the brigade also reflects the constantly altering conditions, goals, and priorities facing the organizers and soldiers in the black units. Such a study offers a corrective to current scholarly portrayals of black recruitment.

The most recent study of black troops has described the recruitment of blacks as "one of the most difficult and disagreeable duties of the white officers assigned to the black regiments." All sorts of obstacles were placed in the recruiters' way, and little in the way of assistance or incentives was offered to ease their job. Overall, "too many officers cared too little how they raised black recruits."[4] As a result, the first contact that many African Americans had with recruiters was one of intimidation and constraint. While that was not true in North Carolina, it had been true elsewhere. When General David Hunter began to raise black regiments in South Carolina in May 1862, his conscription of all able-bodied black men ages eighteen to forty-five and other heavy-handed actions terrified the ex-slaves and convinced them that such efforts preceded a return to bondage.[5] Although conditions improved under General Rufus Saxton Jr., later drafts and impressments were almost as draconian as the first. The trial and execution of Sergeant William Walker for mutiny in early 1864 highlighted not only the Third South Carolina Colored Infantry's sense of betrayal over the unequal-pay issue and its onerous fatigue duties but also the number of incompetent regimental officers in it who faced dismissal or military charges.[6] In Louisiana, conflicting groups of "planters, Northern lessees, contrabands, and free blacks, all claiming to be loyal to the Union, as well as officials of both War and Treasury departments" prevented the formulation of any orderly and rational policy of black enlistment.[7] Moreover, they ensured that the interests of the black slaves would receive a very low priority. General Benjamin Butler's refusal in July 1862 to let Brigadier General John Phelps openly encourage slaves to join Union forces and to enroll them in black regiments was largely a result of Butler's initial reluctance to disrupt the social status quo. Butler's subsequent enlistment of New Orleans's free black militia was rooted in that group's perceived social status as well as the rapidity of changing attitudes and events.[8] Conditions in North Carolina, a few people hoped, offered a chance of black recruitment by carefully chosen men who would bypass those problems.

The decision to raise a brigade of black troops in North Carolina was a by-product of several factors. The Federal occupation of coastal areas of the state, which occurred in 1862, was necessary before significant numbers of potential black recruits became available. Even then, however, until white attitudes concerning the appropriateness of black service changed and until African Americans had convinced the North of their willingness and ability to support the Union, few people championed black enlistment. One group that did so ardently and whose support for the African Brigade was crucial to its success was led by the governor of Massachusetts, John A. Andrew. Andrew, an abolitionist, had long been an advocate of black recruitment at all ranks including commissioned officers, initially among Northern free blacks. Encouraging him and supporting his goals were abolitionists such as Wendell Phillips, Francis W. Bird, George L. Stearns, and Edward W. Kinsley. As the war progressed, the governor expanded his arguments to include Southern slaves.[9] By the end of January 1863, he had succeeded in getting authorization to raise a black regiment in Massachusetts, the Fifty-fourth Massachusetts Volunteers, and Stearns began to develop a network of black recruiting officers throughout the North.[10] The response to the call for black volunteers was so good that a second black regiment, the Fifty-fifth, was soon added.

Andrew's achievement led him to propose to Secretary of War Edwin M. Stanton, on April 1, 1863, that "some able, brave, tried, and believing man" be sent to North Carolina to raise black troops.[11] Andrew had cause to believe that conditions and the time were favorable. Not only did he have information that there were between twenty-five hundred and five thousand potential recruits within Union lines, but he was also aware, from published and unpublished accounts by soldiers in the thirteen Massachusetts regiments making up part of the occupying forces, of the enthusiasm and aid for the Union cause exhibited by the ex-slaves.[12] Colonel Frank Lee of the Forty-fourth Massachusetts Regiment had informed Robert Gould Shaw, commander of the Fifty-fourth Massachusetts Volunteers, and others that "a brigade of coloured men could be easily raised in North

Carolina."[13] His opinion carried greater weight because one of his men, Private Henry A. Clapp, was compiling a census of the freed black population in Federal-occupied North Carolina for the Union commander.[14] The census was completed for New Bern by March and indicated that there were at least eighty-five hundred black refugees in the town and in three outlying camps.[15]

Moreover, by the early months of 1863 the idea of using former slaves as soldiers was slowly becoming more acceptable throughout much of the North. Equally important, Andrew believed that one of his state's black regiments could serve a vital role in North Carolina. Attracting escaped slaves to join a whites-only Northern army, he argued, would be very difficult. On the other hand, "it would be comparatively easy to gain large numbers to join an army in part already composed of black troops. I suggest that if you sent some colored troops down there the result would shortly be a general attraction of the blacks to our Army unless the business of dealing with those people should be badly managed."[16] He reminded Stanton that his act of raising "a colored regiment in Massachusetts was begun upon talking with you about North Carolina and the difficulty of attracting negroes to join white troops." He proposed that Stanton send the Fifty-fifth to North Carolina to form "the nest egg of a brigade."[17] The governor had originally planned on sending the Fifty-fourth to New Bern, and as late as April 8 Robert Shaw was preparing his regiment to go to North Carolina.[18] Ultimately, however, Shaw's regiment was sent to South Carolina, where there was greater opportunity for it to demonstrate its military value. Shaw had told Andrew that there was more hope for action there under Hunter than in North Carolina under Major General John G. Foster. "The latter," wrote Shaw, "as likely as not, would make us do all the digging in the department."[19]

Shaw's concerns underlined the fact that Andrew's enthusiasm was absolutely critical because Union officials in the state were far less sanguine about the prospect of raising black soldiers there. Edward Stanly, who had been appointed provisional governor in May 1862, was very hostile to any attempt to alter the status quo. He believed that the conflict was "a war of restoration and not of abolition and destruction."[20] The governor was convinced that many slaveholders were sincere unionists and that their property should be safeguarded. In January 1863, when former slaves who were employed as stewards in the navy or as servants for Union officers returned to Edenton to release their families, Stanly and the slave owners were outraged. He demanded that the blacks and the soldiers who accompanied them be punished for their "insolent" conduct.[21] Until his resignation in protest of Lincoln's Emancipation Proclamation, Stanly would oppose the use of black troops. Even Major General John G. Foster, who had replaced General Ambrose E. Burnside as Union commander in eastern North Carolina in July 1862, was more interested in raising white troops in the state than enlisting African Americans. Despite the number of contrabands around New Bern, he believed that "not more than one Regiment, if even that could be raised in this Department by voluntary enlistment, and forced enlistment would of course alienate the negroes, the very object the Governor of Massachusetts wishes to avoid." He not only distrusted their "lack of discipline" but also believed that they would not enlist while they could work as civilians for the government.[22]

Foster's concern resulted partly from the shortage of Federal troops left in his department following General Burnside's departure for Virginia with two full divisions.[23] The shortage of troops did, however, open the door to limited black military service, which in turn began the slow transformation of white attitudes toward the black male. Some Northern soldiers serving in the South were struck by the enthusiasm and emotional outpouring of Southern slaves to the Union occupation.[24] The general Northern response, on the other hand, was at the very best ambivalent. While some men such as Corporal Haines might refer to "our friends, the contrabands," one officer in Plymouth responded to calls for "protection" from blacks by giving them "a dozen stripes" with a rope.[25] William F. Draper wrote from New Bern to his father, who he believed would be celebrating the emancipation of the slaves in the West Indies. Draper then voiced his own views on abolition. "I hope ere many years to be able to celebrate the emancipation of the slaves in the U.S. I wish they would be colonized though."[26] Another Massachusetts soldier, Thomas J. Jennings, scoffed at such abolitionist attitudes. "You who are at home," he wrote a friend, "are as ignorant of the position and qualification of the Negroes, as they are of education."[27] In July 1862, when a New York soldier freed a slave who had sought freedom in Plymouth only to be recaptured by his owner, five other Northern soldiers seized the slave and arrested the would-be liberator.[28]

Despite discriminatory attitudes and overt violence, blacks continued to aid Northern efforts in the state, frequently providing information on Confederate troop movement. Perhaps as many as fifty of the freedmen worked continuously as "spies, scouts, and guides" for the Union forces.[29] During the summer of 1862 Confederate forces captured two blacks who had been "sent out as emissaries to induce others . . . to run away and enlist." According to the Confederates, the two captives "had U.S. money and enlistment papers with them." The two men were hanged.[30] In New Bern, Burnside had formed the numerous black refugees into a pioneer corps despite the complaints of some soldiers in this command that they were "sick, tired, and disgusted with the sight" of the many slaves.[31] Rumors quickly spread among Confederates that "the yankees wir raising negro volunteers at Newbern," and there were exaggerated accounts "that eleven hundred up to Saturday evening had volunteered."[32] Months later the supervisor of black refugees at Elizabeth City, a former cavalry sergeant, claimed that "he could easily raise a company of [black] cavalry there and that he knew they would make splendid soldiers." He supported that claim by the fact that about fifty freedmen were already being used "as a sort of night-picket in half-defiance of the directions from head-quarters." Those men proved to be very effective at guarding the lines. Indeed, they were "models of courage, vigilance and trustworthiness, and the bands of rebel guerrillas who infest the out skirts and who caused almost constant alarms at night, before these men were put on, stand in the greatest dread of them." Their knowledge of local roads and paths, plus their capabilities as night fighters, made them formidable. In addition, they had exhibited "great eagerness to fight." The men had been formed into a unit and had developed some proficiency at drill before the "company was broken up by Gen. Foster's orders."[33]

The general was soon forced to reconsider his actions. The number of Union troops under his command was reduced in the early spring of 1863, just as the Federal-occupied area was threatened by Confederate activities. Ten thousand of Foster's soldiers were transferred from North Carolina to the anticipated attack on Charleston. At almost the same time, Confederate General James Longstreet sent General D. H. Hill with reinforcements to move against New Bern and Washington.[34] The possibility of using black soldiers to defend against those attacks led at least some Union soldiers to have second thoughts about fighting. In mid-March Confederate planters claimed that some of the Federal soldiers at Plymouth, upon hearing rumors that black troops were to be sent there from Massachusetts, had threatened to "throw down their arms" if that happened.[35] During the next month, however, the Confederate offensive highlighted the military capacities of blacks and convinced many white United States soldiers of their value. On March 16 two companies of the First North Carolina Union Volunteers, a white regiment, were attacked just outside the river town of Washington and driven back under fire to their boats. During the retreat a number of soldiers were saved from capture or death "by the self-sacrifice of a gallant negro, who, seeing [a] boat was aground, . . . jumped overboard and pushed the flat into the water. In the course of his heroic actions the brave man was hit by gunfire and fell lifeless into the water, but the launch floated away to a place of safety."[36] Two weeks later, when the Confederates laid siege to the town, the number of Union troops, only 1,139, was too small to defend the entire perimeter. As a result, the able-bodied black males were organized, armed, and put into the line. "This was the first experience with armed negroes," wrote William Derby, "and it was wonderful how quietly it was submitted to by many who had loudly declared 'they would never fight side of a nigger!' Whitworth shots, exploding shells and bullet tz-z-zps are wonderfully persuasive arguments on such a question, and settled it once and for all with the garrison of Washington."[37]

Another Union soldier described the seriousness with which the ex-slaves took on their new roles. Led by blacks already employed as laborers in the white units, the new recruits began drilling and studying the field manual. He recorded the change in white opinion: "[O]ur colored recruits are already winning golden opinions for their soldierly qualities. Our most bitter negrophobists admit that they will *fight,* and one of their sincere haters has been detailed to officer them. Some of the poor fellows lie behind their breastwork with a spelling book in one hand and a musket in the other."[38] When D. H. Hill withdrew his attack on Washington, the hastily recruited freedmen gave back their guns, but their willingness to fight had convinced many that they could make useful soldiers. The demonstration of black military ardor coupled with the withdrawal of white Union troops was an effective catalyst for black recruitment in the state.

Even before Hill had abandoned his siege of Washington, Secretary of War Stanton had decided to accept Andrew's plan to raise black troops in North Carolina. In less than two weeks, Edward A. Wild, colonel of the Thirty-fifth Massachusetts Volunteers, was authorized to form a brigade of four regiments from North Carolina's African-American population.[39] Wild had not been Andrew's first choice. The governor had initially proposed Brigadier General Francis C. Barlow of New York.[40] Nevertheless, Wild had much to recommend him. Born in Brookline, Massachusetts, in 1825, he had graduated from Harvard before going on to practice medicine. At the outbreak of the Crimean War, he had sailed for Constantinople and offered his services to the Turkish government. He was commissioned as surgeon of artillery with the rank of lieutenant colonel and attached to the army corps of Omar Pasha, commander in chief of the Turkish forces. For several years he supervised Turkish hospitals before returning to Brookline. An active member of the Independent Corps of Cadets in Boston, Wild immediately helped to raise a company of volunteers in Brookline and Jamaica Plain when the Civil War began. In May 1861 he was mustered in as captain of Company A in the First Massachusetts Volunteers. During the next eighteen months he fought in six major engagements and gained a reputation as an effective and courageous officer. His right hand was badly maimed at the Battle of White Oak Swamp. "A warm personal friend" of

Governor Andrew, Wild was promoted colonel of the Thirty-fifth Massachusetts Volunteers in August 1862, but only three weeks later, at the
Battle of South Mountain, "an exploding bullet" struck him in the left arm
After several operations, surgeons removed the arm at the shoulder joint
"under his own direction."[41]

While Wild recuperated in Boston from the last wound, Andrew asked
him to help in the effort to raise the Fifty-fourth and Fifty-fifth black regiments. His tasks were to "receive applications for commissions, to read
and judge of their recommendations, to see and examine candidates, and
to advise with Col. Robert G. Shaw and Lt. Col. N. P. Hallowell, commanders of the Fifty-Fourth and Fifty-fifth regiments respectively, in the
selection of their officers."[42] Those activities not only familiarized him with
a number of qualified officer candidates whom he would later appoint to
his own regiments but also confirmed Andrew's faith in his ability to raise
and lead black troops. In a number of ways Wild was well prepared for his
new assignment. He was sympathetic to the problems facing black Americans, and he held a firm belief in the value of black troops. He could draw
upon his abolitionist connections throughout the Northeast. Above all, he
had demonstrated, through two years of arduous campaigning, his
courage and capability as a military leader. He could not be accused by
officers contemptuous of black troops that he was just a political appointment who knew nothing of war. On the other hand, Wild's abolitionist
background and his wartime experiences embittered him toward a Southern slaveholding class. The loss of his left arm and part of right hand,
wounds that ended his career as a physician, may partly explain the deep
hatred that he displayed at times against "rebels."[43] Nevertheless, he made
a positive impression on many people. Robert Shaw told his mother that
Wild "is an excellent man," although Shaw expressed concerns that
because of his wounds, the commander "may not be able to remain in
active service, though he is determined to try it."[44]

The work that Wild had done in screening commission applicants for
Andrew was put to immediate use as he began to organize his prototype
regiment, the First North Carolina Colored Volunteers (NCCV). His first
objective was to staff the regiment with the proper type of officers. For
both him and Andrew that meant men with previous military experience
who were ardently committed to both abolition and temperance.[45] For
both men it also meant including some African Americans as officers.[46]
Their hopes were mostly thwarted, and the fact that officers, with only a
few exceptions, remained white throughout all the United States black
regiments reflected the enormous difficulties that they faced. It also high-
lights what they were able to accomplish. Wild was hampered in his search

for white noncommissioned officers with military experience to serve as officers because he could not draw any of them from the Army of the Potomac and, therefore, had to select them from units stationed elsewhere or from soldiers who had in some way become disabled. Not surprisingly, Wild looked first to Massachusetts regiments stationed in New England or just completing service in North Carolina. The limitation on where he could draw officers, however, was more than balanced by the unusual freedom granted him by the War Department in assigning commissions. Officers in the African Brigade, unlike officers seeking positions in other black regiments, did not have to face a board of examiners or be assigned a rank considered appropriate by the Bureau of Colored Troops. Instead, Wild had been given authority to select men who he felt were qualified and to establish their relative seniority in his regimental structure. That allowed him to staff the First NCCV quickly and effectively. Three days after he formally accepted his appointment to raise the brigade and become a brigadier general, he had selected most of the regiments officers, including virtually all of the junior officers.[47]

The ability to select whom he wished, he later wrote, was "by far the most valuable privilege attached to my mission." It allowed him "to get the very best men for my particular work and to secure a unanimity of feeling and a harmony of action unparalleled, and unattainable otherwise."[48] Wild wanted men of practical experience. Even the civilians he commissioned were all old soldiers. "Not one man have I taken," Wild later wrote, "who has not seen service (chaplain excepted). Most are real veterans. Not a few were discharged from the ranks crippled by wounds, but not disabled from using the sword or pistol, and again facing the enemy in his bitter mood."[49] He was particularly pleased to be able to combine many of those qualities in soldiers who had already served part of their military terms in North Carolina and who were therefore somewhat familiar with the state and the nature of black refugees in towns such as New Bern, Washington, and Plymouth. Seven officers were drawn from the Seventeenth, Twenty-third, and Twenty-fifth Massachusetts Volunteers, all regiments that had been stationed in Eastern North Carolina, while most of the remaining officers had served in other regiments from Massachusetts.[50] The case of one individual, Leonard Lorenzo Billings, revealed the political connections and the personal convictions that influenced Wild in his selection of officers. Billings had served as a corporal in the Twenty-ninth Massachusetts Volunteers and had seen combat. He was recommended to Wild by Edward W. Kinsley, a close friend of Governor Andrew who, in a letter that included the governor's warm greeting, summarized the corporal's qualifications. "He is," wrote Kinsley, "Anti-Slavery. Temperance *ultra*—and a good soldier."

Billings received a commission as a second lieutenant.[51] At the same time another candidate, W. H. R. Brown, who was apparently well qualified and had letters of recommendation, was unsuccessful. He had served in the Thirty-ninth Illinois Volunteers and claimed that he wanted to lead "African troops." A notation on his application indicated that his wife objected "to seeing niggers with stripes on."[52]

Although the vast majority of the officers of the First NCCV had served in Massachusetts regiments, the two senior officers had not. Wild's first choice to lead the regiment, Colonel Edwin Upton of the Twenty-seventh Massachusetts Volunteers, was unavailable. Instead, Wild selected James Chaplin Beecher, son of the prominent minister Lyman Beecher and half brother of Harriet Beecher Stowe. Beecher had most recently held the rank of lieutenant colonel in the 141st New York Regiment. Unlike Wild, however, he may have joined the service in part to escape domestic troubles, and he had a history of nervous breakdowns.[53] The lieutenant colonel of the regiment, William N. Reed, was also a resident of New York and had been selected because of his abolitionist sentiments and his military background. Reed had graduated from the military school at Keil, Germany, and had reached the rank of etat major in the imperial army. He was very competent and interested in the welfare of his men. Some sources describe Reed as a mulatto, in which case he may have been the highest-ranking African American in the Union army, although he was not recognized as such.[54]

Two other appointments reflect the racially progressive attitudes of the organizers. John V. De Grasse, an assistant surgeon with the rank of major, was one of the very few blacks throughout the Union army to receive a commission prior to the last months of the war. He had already proved himself an exceptional man. After receiving his medical degree in 1849, he had become the first black man to be admitted to a medical association when he became a member of the Massachusetts Medical Society in 1854.[55] Although discharged supposedly for drunkenness in 1864, De Grasse was, in fact, cashiered for reasons that had as much to do with pigmentation as with intoxication.[56] Wild also commissioned the Reverend John N. Mars as the regiment's black chaplain, a policy he would continue with the other regiments.[57] Unfortunately Mars, at age fifty-eight, could not withstand the rigors of army life. He remained in a North Carolina hospital when his regiment left the state, and he ultimately resigned his commission in early 1864 for reasons of "chronic rheumatism in the ankle joint, and old age."[58] The careers of De Grasse and Mars (and possibly Reed) illustrate that, as initially conceived, the brigade espoused advanced racial attitudes. Unfortunately, the pressures of the war and widespread white hostility served to erode that policy, especially after the regiment left Wild's command. After Reed's death at the Battle of Olustee, both the doctor and the minister would be replaced with white officers. Those reversals, however, lay in the future.

On May 18 the general and fourteen of his officers reached New Bern and immediately began to recruit soldiers from among the freedmen gathered there. A soldier in the Forty-fifth Massachusetts, Thomas Hale, wrote home discussing Wild's arrival and the response of many white officers to his black surgeon, "who wears the uniform of a major and is of course to be 'obeyed and respected accordingly.' I wonder," suggested Hale, "how the nice young men of Boston, the ladies' pets, the 'gallant' 44th, will like the idea of presenting arms, the most respectful salute they can make, to a negro?" Hale predicted that "it will come rather hard for some of them but they will have to submit to it."[59]

Of much greater concern to Wild and his officers was the danger that both they and any black recruit faced from bitter Confederate hostility. Those risks were made very clear the next week. The *Wilmington Journal* carried a report of the law passed at the start of the month by the Confederate Congress to deal with black soldiers and their white officers. "All commissioned officers," the paper reported, "who shall be captured in command of negroes, shall suffer the penalty of death." The black prisoners of war would be subject to the laws of the state in which they were captured—in other words, treated as slaves engaged in insurrection. The newspaper justified the summary process as extreme but necessary. Since the Union officers had "organized and armed half civilized beings and urged them . . . even to the annihilation of the white population of the South," the only recourse was to treat them as outlaws and murderers.[60] It was right and proper, the editor continued, "that the Yankee officers who would put themselves at the head of a negro brigade . . . should fight with halters around their necks."[61] The war in North Carolina did not descend to that level of barbarism, in part because at the end of July 1863 President Lincoln had issued a policy of retaliation if prisoners of war were executed.[62] Nevertheless, the early recruitment of the African Brigade proceeded with all officers and men facing that very real threat. Moreover, aside from the official Confederate policy toward black troops, there was always the danger from individual Southern soldiers offended and outraged by blacks in the army. A soldier in the Forty-sixth Massachusetts wrote in his journal at the end of May that "the enemy's pickets at the ferry had considerable to say about the niggers being around in this department. They swore they would shoot every b——d nigger taken up arms against them."[63] When a squad from the Forty-sixth Massachusetts was captured a few days later, the Confederate interrogator's primary interest was the state of black recruitment and the time when the nine-month regiments would go home.[64]

The process of filling the First NCCV and the type of soldier enrolled established a pattern for the next two regiments in the brigade. On May 20 Luke Measel, age thirty, became the first man to enlist in Company A.[65] Of all of the companies in the regiment, for some reason this one filled slowest. The Fifty-fifth Massachusetts Volunteers would not arrive for several more months, and the North Carolina freedmen, who probably hoped for civilian jobs around New Bern, may have been cautious about what they would face in a white Union army. The day after Measel joined, enrolling officer Captain Josiah White, operating in Beaufort County, signed on Taft Godfrey, who at age forty-three was the company's oldest recruit. In New Bern another eight men joined. By May 26 company strength had reached fifty-one and included men recruited at New Bern, Beaufort, and Newport. Another ten men were added by June 1, including the first man to volunteer from Morehead City. A week later eighty-one men were in uniform, but it was not until June 18 that Company A reached a complement of one hundred men. By that time most of the other companies had been manned. Captain James Croft had signed eighty-seven men into Company D by May 22. Company E had eighty-nine men from New Bern by May 28, and Company G numbered ninety-two soldiers as of June 1. The other companies, organized in June, filled even more quickly when their books were opened. On June 9 Croft enlisted ninety-seven men at Washington into Company C. Only two other men would be added to that company before the end of the war. Six days later, when Captain Charles A. Jones began forming Company B, eighty-seven men, all at New Bern, enlisted and only one other man, Frank Harrison, who joined on July 13, was added to the unit until May 1865.

The increased pace of enlistment within the First NCCV suggests that Wild was able to encourage enlistment in a number of ways to capitalize on the willingness of the freedmen to join the Union army. He began by going over the census returns compiled by Clapp.[66] He then spent several weeks visiting the various parts of the department to encourage recruitment personally. In mid-June, on one of his trips, the general and his effectiveness were described by an officer stationed on Hatteras. Wild, "a tall slim man with a reddish beard" and an empty sleeve dangling at his side, appealed to the freedmen on the island, with impressive results. He "succeeded in getting about 150 men from the colored people on the bar, leaving only the old and decrepit."[67] There and elsewhere, in filling out his regiments the general used his own funds to cover some of the costs of recruiting.[68]

Wild relied on more than just his own presence to attract African Americans to his regiments. When he came to North Carolina, he was accompanied by several civilians who were to help him raise black troops. Edward W.

Kinsley is reputed to have been a major force in attracting recruits. One account, written by Albert W. Mann long after the war, claimed that recruiting had been slow until Kinsley held a secret, late-night meeting with influential New Bern blacks, headed by Abraham Galloway. At that meeting Kinsley gave an unauthorized promise to accept certain demands. The freedmen's requests included pay equal to that of the black Massachusetts troops, rations for the soldiers families, education for their children, and a government commitment that captured colored troops must be treated as prisoners of war by the Confederates.[69] The meeting that took place, however, must have been very different in substance from Mann's account. Abraham H. Galloway was certainly influential in New Bern, but he was described by Wild as "my special and confidential recruiting agent, a mulatto, originally sent to me by George L. Stearns." The general praised Galloway, writing that he "has served his country well, since the commencement of the war—formerly as a spy—now as recruiting emissary."[70] As a recruiter, Galloway was probably a much more persuasive spokesman for the general than was Kinsley. A black abolitionist from Pennsylvania who had come with Wild, Joseph E. Williams, was less useful in raising troops.[71] Although Williams had been very active initially when volunteering was popular, he became less interested and effective as the pool of ready recruits dried up. He became involved in some unspecified swindle in New Bern and was forced by Wild to leave the state. Several months later, he had been employed by George Stearns to recruit and was headed for Vicksburg.[72]

The late-night meeting attended by Kinsley may have been organized by Galloway to reassure other freedmen in New Bern. It certainly underlined what the freedmen saw as the crucial contractual nature of any agreement into which they might enter with the government. If they offered their services, then the government was morally obligated to protect them and their families. The meeting also accorded with a protest of black laborers who had refused to work after their wages were long overdue. Wild seems to have understood their concerns. Certainly, in addition to his military duties, the general initiated a number of programs to aid the refugees, including a policy to place the families of soldiers volunteering for his regiments upon vacant land. General Order No. 103 authorized him to take possession of all unoccupied and unowned land on Roanoke Island "for the purpose of distributing the same to the families of Negro soldiers and other contrabands in the service of the United States."[73] Wild was convinced that he should give "much time and labor to the care ad provision of negro families."[74] He understood that a guarantee to provide support for the families of his new recruits was both fair and a strong encouragement for further recruitment. One of the Northern teachers at New Bern, Oscar

Doolittle, reported that Wild "tires out his staff daily," although he seemed "as fresh as ever" despite his many responsibilities, long hours, and the oppressive heat. In addition to recruiting, organizing and training his brigade, and supervising plans for Roanoke, the general found time for the black civilians. Doolittle wrote that he was "in consultation with [Wild] a number of times a day in regard to the establishment of Schools and other matters pertaining to them."[75] Although the general believed himself to be overextended, not until July 1863 did an officer specifically appointed as superintendent of Negro affairs assume some of Wild's duties concerning the black refugees.[76] The assistance offered to the families of black soldiers had a special significance. It marked a new role for many of those men as a direct provider for their families.[77] At the same time, the recruits were often encouraged to join by family members. William Derby was struck by the enthusiasm shown by black women in encouraging their men to enlist in the African Brigade. He claimed that "they seized every able-bodied man of their race, shouting '. . . you's look a heap better in de crowd dar!' at the same time shoving him by force into the ranks."[78]

The regimental descriptive books of the First NCCV allow a cautious assessment of the background of the enlisted men. In addition to indicating where, when, and under which officer the men enlisted, the books also give the ages, heights, and complexions of the recruits. Their places of birth are recorded and there are spaces, not always filled, for their occupations. General remarks concerning mortality, discharge, and desertion were added for some soldiers, although other records indicate that the descriptive books were often incomplete and must be used carefully. If the place of birth can be used as a crude measure of residency for the prewar slaves, however, certain patterns are clear. The regiment drew heavily from those areas opened up by the Union occupation. Beaufort, Martin, and Pitt counties produced the largest block of the first recruits, while considerable numbers of men came from the region of Pasquotank and Camden counties. Washington and Hyde counties also yielded many recruits. Nevertheless, one of the striking features of the evidence is that the soldiers in the first regiment had come originally from at least thirty counties in North Carolina. By September, Wild's brigade had in it men drawn from forty counties (see appendix A). Each company in the first regiment would also recruit men in South Carolina at the end of the war.[79]

The pattern of many counties' providing the men for each company suggests one way in which the experience of the black soldier differed significantly from that of the white troops raised in either the North or the South. Each company of a white regiment was usually raised from a specific region, often a single county or large town. That practice allowed family and friends to enlist together, bringing into the army a sense of a particular community, which was then reinforced by letters and visits to home and by replacements drawn from the original locale to fill depleted ranks. For the African-American soldiers, usually ex-slaves who had managed to free themselves of the planter's control, a different picture emerges. Most had become refugees and had sought protection within Union lines prior to May 1863. In many cases, their local black communities had already begun to fragment as eastern planters tried to move large numbers of their slaves into the interior of the state. Union military excursions allowed some but not all of the slaves left behind the opportunity of flight. Some, singly or as families, grasped the chance. The result was that, among the freedmen who congregated at towns such as New Bern, ties of family and old friendships had been badly disrupted although not completely destroyed. Companies raised at these towns, as a result, were often conglomerates of strangers. One of the exceptions, in the First NCCV, may have been Company H. Slightly over 60 percent of all the men who joined the company in 1863 came from Hatteras Island in the wake of Wild's visit there. It is likely that, for this unit, the prewar community ties carried over into military life in ways not possible in the other companies.[80]

The lives of many of the men in the African Brigade had been significantly and permanently altered even before they volunteered. Unlike most white troops, the men filling the ranks around them were less likely to be kin or old friends. Extended family ties had been broken by the war, and little in the way of contact with absent family members could be hoped for until the conflict was over. Of course, some of the soldiers' families were already behind Union lines. For those men service in the army was one of the best ways to ensure that family members were provided with at least some care, as the men of Wild's regiments had been promised, upon their enlistments, that their family members would receive adequate rations while they were in the service.[81]

The descriptive books of the first regiment provide some limited insight into the prewar occupations of the soldiers. Most, of course, had worked as agriculturalists, and some company clerks, such as in Companies B and K, simply listed all men as "laborers." Three companies listed no occupations. In those cases where a number of occupations were given, a consistent pattern emerged. About 90 percent of the men apparently indicated that they were farmers or laborers, and only a handful claimed other occupations. The most common of the latter were servants and carpenters, followed by drivers and sailors. A scattering of men reportedly worked as caulkers, masons, blacksmiths, and teamsters (see appendix B). The information recorded by the company clerks also allows a minimum assessment of the mulattoes in the regiment. The clerks described 7.5 percent of the men as having "light" complexion.[82] The soldiers recorded as light complexioned made up about 40 percent of the men in nonfarm occupations. The same body of men made up a disproportionate share of the first noncommissioned officers. Three of Company A's sergeants were typical of this group. All were light and engaged in a skilled prewar occupation. Their ages ranged from eighteen to twenty-seven, probably below the company average, while their heights were slightly greater than the norm. It is not clear whether the selection of these men was a result of a white bias in favor of mulattoes, an indication that most may have been free before the war, or a reflection of their position among their fellow African-American soldiers. In the case of at least one sergeant, John Monroe of Company A, rank was very likely a result of literacy; by 1864 Monroe was handling a portion of the company's paper work.[83] Alternatively, previous occupation rather than skin color may have been the crucial determinant.

Almost as soon as recruiting officers began enlisting men, the site for the camp of the First NCCV was selected—on the south bank of the Neuse River just outside New Bern. The site was quickly laid out, the brush cut down, hundreds of stumps removed, and a parade ground set up. By June 7 seven companies were in camp, two were uniformed, and all had started to drill. Regimental commander Colonel James C. Beecher reflected the attitude of most, if not all, of the officers of the African Brigade on the necessary and crucial role of religion. Camp grubbing and drill were important, but so too, he believed, was religious instruction. Initially Beecher served in the role of regimental chaplain as well as commanding officer, and he was very much moved by his own preaching. When the nearly seven hundred newly uniformed men of the First NCCV knelt down and bowed their heads without instruction, "[I]t affected me beyond measure," Beecher wrote, "and I prayed for them in faith. . . . I know not that I ever felt the reality of prayer more deeply."[84] Whatever doubts Beecher initially had about the quality of his soldiers, by the time the troops had been in camp for a few weeks he confided to a friend in the North that he wished that "doubtful people at home could see my three week regiment. They would talk less nonsense about negro inferiority. Our discipline is to-day better than that of any regiment I know of, and I believe, by the blessings of God, our efficiency will be second to none."[85]

By mid-July, just before the Fifty-fifth Massachusetts Volunteers arrived at New Bern, Beecher contended that his regiment could make a fair fight if necessary. He knew that the New England regiment would be better clothed and equipped and was more fully officered, but as far as the "soldierly efficiency" of his regiment was concerned, he had no apprehension.[86] Military effectiveness is always difficult to assess, but the quarter-master returns for Company A of the First NCCV, the only records remaining, suggest that at least that company received adequate arms and training through 1863. The company received ninety-six "Enfield rifled muskets, calibre .577," including accoutrements and cartridges, on June 11, 1863. Not until July 1864 did they receive another sixty-four Enfields.[87] The last quarter returns of 1863 for the company of about one hundred men indicate that they fired four thousand practice rounds, or about forty rounds per man. That was twice what they used in action over the same period and suggests that they entered combat with much better marksmanship training than many of the other new regiments, black or white. Yet, like many other black regiments, the First NCCV found that it had received much substandard equipment. Senior regimental officers condemned large parts of the regiment's equipment. "The Arms (Spring-fields, Enfields, & Swivel Bore)," Major Archibald Bogle wrote, "being mostly second hand and many of them more or less imperfect are hardly suitable for Field Service." Most of the equipment was used previously, he believed, and in very poor condition.[88] His concerns were justified. In the midst of the regiment's first battle, a number of soldiers found their muskets unserviceable, "[m]any bursting in action."[89]

Despite the range of difficulties confronting black enlistment in North Carolina, by June 25 General Wild was able to announce that the first regiment had been completed and that he had begun to raise a second one.[90] In fact, the first soldiers in the new regiment had been enlisted on June 13 at New Bern. The Second NCCV was in many ways very similar to the first regiment. Wild appointed all of the regimental officers on July 3, with two exceptions, but not until August did most begin to muster in. As with the First NCCV, Wild drew heavily from his home state to staff the Second NCCV. Sixty percent of the captains whom Wild commissioned in the new regiment, and all of the lieutenants, had been promoted from the ranks, including nine privates and eight corporals.[91] Excluding Lieutenant Joseph Hatlinger, all those men had soldiered in Massachusetts regiments, and fourteen of the officers had been previously stationed in North Carolina.[92] Wild explained that he selected them for what they had "done in camp and field" rather than for any performance before an examining board. He claimed that "there are no two regiments in the service, more uniformly well-officered than my first and second."[93] One of the few captains selected with a previous commission was Wild's son, Walter, who had been a lieu-tenant and who would become the general's aide-de-camp. Not surpris-ingly, given the entire family's sentiments, Walter had held his commission in the Fifty-fourth Massachusetts Volunteers. He was, however, the only officer in the African Brigade to transfer from either of Massachusetts's black regiments. The young colonel of the second regiment, Alonzo G. Draper, had been a journalist and a city official in Lynn, Massachusetts. When Wild selected Draper, he was serving as a major in the Fourteenth Massachusetts Volunteers. The only black commissioned officer in the Second NCCV was the chaplain, David Stevens, a Methodist minister from Harrisburg, Pennsylvania, whose muster was later suspended.[94]

The soldiers who made up the rank and file of the second regiment were in most ways identical to those in the First NCCV. The average age of the recruits was the mid-twenties, with the extremes ranging from sixteen to fifty-one years.[95] As with the First NCCV, the largest group by age were the nineteen- and twenty-year-olds (see appendix C). Most of the soldiers were originally from the coastal counties, but a number came from inland counties such as Bertie, Duplin, Edgecombe, and Halifax. One man had been born as far west as Raleigh. Most of the soldiers were ex-slaves who had worked the land, but abut 10 percent indicated that they had previous trades. Among them were a few carpenters, coopers, teamsters, fishermen, and lumberers, plus the occasional steward, barber, or brakeman. The one man listed as an engineer, Ansom Farrier, remained a private from his enlistment in July 1863 until his final discharge in March 1865.

One difference between the first two regiments of the brigade arose from their varying rates of enlistment. Black enthusiasm for enlistment remained evident when the Second NCCV began recruiting, and Wild played on it. He personally visited the town of Washington to encourage recruitment. "He remained only two days," the local newspaper, the *New Era,* reported, "but such was the willingness manifested by the negroes to become soldiers that he carried back with him to Newberne some two hundred sable volunteers."[96] Despite that case, the companies in the Second NCCV filled much more slowly than the first. Many companies had only one-half to three-quarters of their establishment by the end of August. The regiment would continue to fill its ranks after it left the state in 1863. The result was that a few companies had up to 45 percent of their soldiers drawn from Virginia, although the average was much lower. The Second NCCV was significantly less a North Carolina regiment than was the First NCCV.

Long before the second regiment had been filled, soldiers from the first regiment had seen their initial service in the field. Twenty men had taken part in a raid on the Wilmington and Weldon Railroad in early July. The expedition, led by Lieutenant Colonel George Lewis of the Third New York Cavalry, left New Bern on July 3, occupied Trenton, and two days later cut the railroad line at Warsaw. It then retreated to New Bern. In that raid, the African-American soldiers were used as pioneers to build bridges and to destroy the railroad tracks. The tasks assigned them, as laborers and not combat soldiers, reflected the current attitude among many of the white Union troops. Nevertheless, the engineer in charge of the black unit, Captain H. W. Wilson, praised his soldiers. They were, he wrote, "more efficient than any colored men I have taken out on former expeditions."[97] That contrasted sharply with Wilson's description of the usefulness of Lewis and his white cavalry gangs, who performed poorly. Recruiting agent Joseph Williams accompanied the raiders to encourage slaves in the area to flee to New Bern and enlist in the African Brigade.[98]

Although events occurring in Pennsylvania overshadowed this raid and others like it, the expedition generated considerable concern in North Carolina, in large part because it involved the black population. Although the first rumors in state newspapers that half of the raiders were black were quickly corrected, the reports made clear that hundreds of slaves were taking advantage of the raid to try to escape to Union-occupied areas.[99] The *Wilmington Journal* estimated that about 200 slaves left with the raiders. In another raid a few weeks later aimed at destroying the railroad bridge at Rocky Mount, even more African Americans were involved. Conflicting newspaper accounts indicate that 500 slaves had left with the Union cavalry, that 150 had been intercepted at Burney Place, twenty-two miles northeast of Kinston, and that elsewhere Confederate troops "succeeded in capturing and killing four hundred negroes."[100] The paper tried to play down the obvious disaffection of so many slaves by relating an anecdote concerning a free black named Jackson, "an enlisted Bugler in Cummings' Battery" who was detailed and acting in the Confederate commissary department. The enraged Union soldiers, the paper claimed, placed a bounty of five hundred dollars on his head and destroyed much of his property in his absence.[101]

The Confederate propaganda notwithstanding, Wild was well aware of the real situation and the opportunity that it offered for his partially raised brigade. Filling the first two regiments, he later reported, had absorbed much of the available pool of black recruits in the Union-occupied areas. Civilian jobs had attracted many of the remaining candidates. Wild had not resorted to any form of impressment of blacks, although it was being ordered in Virginia at the time. Instructions had been sent from Washington to Fortress Monroe "to impress all able-bodied colored men for Service in the Qr Masters Dept at Washington." The result, George Stearns argued, was that the "ablest of them run for the woods imparting their fear to the Slaves thus keeping them out of our lines, and we get only those who are too ignorant or indolent to take care of themselves. I feel sure we can get more men by fair enlistment."[102] Wild's refusal to compel recruitment may have resulted in more soldiers' signing up, or it may simply have allowed more black men to take civilian jobs with the various Union departments. For some refugees, the civilian jobs must have been more attractive than a soldier's pay of $10 a month and a chance of death offered by the army. Upon the occupation of New Bern, General Burnside had established civilian pay scales that in many cases exceeded the soldiers' wages. Stevedores received $15 and teamsters $20 per month, while the day rates for carpenters, blacksmiths, masons, and mechanics ranged from $1.25 to $3.00. Even laborers were paid $10 a month, the same wages as soldiers but without the danger. In New Bern alone more than fifteen hundred black civilians were employed by November 1863.[103] The pay rates gave the quartermaster's, commissaries', engineer's, and other departments an advantage over what Wild could offer.

While black civilian occupation did not represent an absolute loss to the Union war effort but rather a redistribution of resources, it did force Wild to consider new ways to find further recruits in order to raise all four regiments envisioned. As a result, he planned in the summer of 1863 to conduct expeditions with his troops into Confederate counties, "each one of which would have brought us hundreds of recruits."[104] To do that he needed the Fifty-fifth Massachusetts, and its delay in arriving set back his plans.[105] As soon as the regiment arrived, the general gave instructions for a planned new raid. Before the expedition could be launched, however, Wild was ordered to leave immediately with all available troops for Charleston, South Carolina. On July 30, less than six days after the arrival of the Massachusetts regiment, Wild and more than two thousand soldiers of the African Brigade embarked for South Carolina. General Foster predicted that "they will do well and fight well under their fighting general."[106]

The brigade, in response to the unexpected orders, left in such haste that they took their arms and not much else. Knapsacks, camp equipage, officers' horses, baggage, and even the company books were all left at New Bern, and not until well into September could the regiments regain what had not been lost or stolen.[107] Wild had ordered things left at New Bern because he believed the transfer of his brigade to the new department to be merely temporary.[108] With that in mind, he integrated elements of the Second NCCV accompanying the brigade into the First NCCV. Those men would fill the vacancies created in the First NCCV because of sickness. The extra troops brought the brigade up to 2,150 men and forced the general to crowd more soldiers onto the transport vessels than had been expected. Although much was left behind, all guns and stretchers, plus hospital tents, were taken.[109]

In many ways the move to South Carolina, which had been seen as a temporary response to a crisis, marked the end of the original experiment in raising and training a brigade of black North Carolinians under abolitionist guidance. After Wild left New Bern, recruitment of the Second NCCV slowed and delayed a start to the Third NCCV. Colonel Alonzo Draper, who had been left in charge of recruitment for the brigade, tried unsuccessfully to get authorization for "an expedition to bring in Colored recruits," and without that stimulus his efforts showed few results.[110] Enlistment picked up again in October and November only after Wild returned to New Bern, following his repeated protests that he was needed there to carry on recruitment of the third regiment. Within a month, however, he would be transferred to Fortress Monroe.[111] While Wild did conduct subsequent military operations within North Carolina in later 1863 from his base in Virginia, his ambitious plans for recruiting raids into interior counties were largely unfulfilled. Although the Third NCCV was ultimately formed, the fourth regiment of black infantry never materialized. Instead, a heavy artillery regiment was gradually mustered in from the freedmen in occupied North Carolina throughout 1864.[112]

Wild did not stay in North Carolina in the fall because, well before his return from Charleston, all black troops had been ordered out of the state. On August 12, 1863, Major General John J. Peck, a West Point graduate and a New York Democrat, was given command of the District of North Carolina.[113] Within two weeks of Peck's arrival in the state, the remaining components of the African Brigade, Colonel Draper's Second NCCV plus a detached unit from the First NCCV, were informed that they were "destined (with all the other colored troops in NC) to Fortress Monroe."[114] Unlike the transfer of the First NCCV, this relocation was to be permanent. All of the property and the sick of Draper's command that could be moved must go. The move, in part, reflected Foster's fears that his base in Virginia was about to be attacked before his fortifications there were complete.[115] Since he was reluctant to ask for troops from either the Army of the Potomac or from Charleston, and since he wanted, first of all, a labor force, Draper's men served his purpose. At the same time, Peck appeared pleased to let them go. In his assessment of the defenses of North Carolina, Peck never regarded the African-American units highly. At the first intimation that black troops in his command would be relieved or replaced by white soldiers from Virginia, he sent them off even though it meant leaving some posts unguarded.[116] By the end of the year only white units were stationed in North Carolina. Additional black infantrymen would be mustered in by recruiting officers scattered in places such as New Bern, Roanoke Island, Plymouth, and Morehead City and then forwarded to the regiments in Virginia.

Although Wild continued to command an "African Brigade" until April 1864, it was not what Governor Andrew had first proposed, a North Carolina black brigade. At Folly Island, South Carolina, in August 1863, the brigade consisted of the Fifty-fifth Massachusetts, the First NCCV, and the small detached part of the Second NCCV.[117] Four months later Wild's brigade, still called the African Brigade but now based in Norfolk, Virginia, contained the Second NCCV, the Third NCCV (only partly formed), the First Regiment United States Colored Troops (USCT), the Fifth USCT, and the Tenth USCT, plus two small and temporary detachments of the First NCCV and the Fifty-fifth Massachusetts.[118] By April the general's brigade had been stripped of all North Carolinians. It then consisted of the First USCT, the Tenth USCT, and the Twenty-second USCT; the North Carolina regiments had been transferred to separate commands. The First NCCV had been sent to Florida in mid-February and would never serve with the other North Carolina regiments. Indeed, on February 8, 1864, the three regiments had lost their official designations as North Carolina soldiers and been renamed the Thirty-fifth United States Colored Troops, the Thirty-sixth United States Colored Troops, and the Thirty-seventh United States Colored Troops, respectively.[119] In official eyes, what made the African Brigade distinct and gave it cohesion was not the fact that all the soldiers were North Carolinians but rather that they were black and largely ex-slaves. Apparently there was no belief that the three Tar Heel regiments formed a natural entity, and even Wild indicated that he would fill his ranks "by picking up recruits by the wayside" wherever he might be located.[120] That attitude helps explain why, in an army in which white regiments retained their state designations and felt strongly about their state identifications, all black troops raised in the South became, in early 1864, merely numbered regiments of the United States Colored Troops.[121]

There were other, more important signs that the original progressive ideas behind the African Brigade were eroding or, with the departure of Wild, ceasing to be major concerns. The First NCCV received its first taste of military discrimination shortly after it arrived in South Carolina. Detachments of the regiment were ordered to lay out and police the camps of white New York soldiers on Folly Island. After heated protests from both Colonel Beecher and General Wild, such practices were officially prohibited, although evidence suggests that similar abuse continued well into November.[122] Moreover, in late October, while Beecher was absent, Lieutenant Colonel Reed was placed under arrest after he stopped the misuse of one of his soldiers. The soldier, Private Lafayette Spencer, had been detailed for duty in the quartermaster's department on Folly Island but was being required to serve as cook for some white soldiers. When Reed removed him from the quartermaster's department without authorization, the officer was arrested for going outside the proper line of command. Two days later, however, Reed was released from arrest and resumed his temporary command of the regiment.[123]

More alarming than those events were the signs of internal discrimination or racial unease within the brigade. The appointment of De Grasse as assistant surgeon had created tensions among the white medical officers, the one group of officers whom Wild could not entirely handpick. De Grasse's authority proved particularly galling for Daniel Mann, the other assistant surgeon. After Wild returned to New Bern, leaving the First NCCV on Folly Island, Mann complained in writing to Surgeon Horace R. Wirtz that De Grasse had been disputing Mann's seniority, and he implied that De Grasse wanted to get control of the medical liquor supplies. Wirtz felt compelled to support the white doctor and claimed that "the Lieut. Col. of the Regt. (which is commanded by Col. Beecher) is a mulatto and while he has been temporarily in command of the Regt. he has used every endeavor in his power to elevate the negro doctor over the white one."[124] Wirtz also claimed that De Grasse "had committed misdemeanors in the way of appropriating Hospital Rations," which would compel Wirtz to prefer charges, although no such charges were ever made.[125] The following year Henry O. Marcy, the white surgeon of the regiment, orchestrated charges that led to De Grasse's being cashiered.[126] In a less dramatic event, when the black chaplain of the First NCCV resigned his commission because of disability, a white chaplain, Thomas A. Hall of Otis, Massachusetts, replaced him. The shift from a black chaplain for the soldiers to a white minister for the officers reflected "the expressed desire of the officers of [Beecher's] command."[127]

Not only were the few blacks holding commissions not replaced with other African Americans, but there were also signs that faith in black leadership at all levels was slipping. When the first two regiments were formed a certain number of white noncommissioned officers were selected, but they appeared to be attached exclusively to the field and staff.[128] Regulations posted in early June 1863 established how noncommissioned officers were to be chosen for the First NCCV. "Two sergeants and Eight Corporals should be selected from the most promising and be under the special instructions of the Company Officers." Three more sergeants would eventually be selected from the eight corporals, and those vacancies would be filled from the ranks.[129] The same was done for the Second NCCV, but by the time the Third NCCV was being established a new policy seems to have been adopted. The first sergeant in each company was now to be white. The commander of the Third NCCV, Lieutenant Colonel A. G. Chamberlain, recruited a detachment of twelve men in Boston before his first companies were mustered in. Most of them were reenlisting veterans who, prior to the war, had been artisans, clerks, or students in Massachusetts. Their ages, with one exception, ranged from nineteen to twenty-seven. They became the first sergeants and the regimental noncommissioned staff when the regiment was formed. Their appointments expressed a belief that the new companies each needed at least one white noncommissioned officer to function properly. The men who signed on in Boston may have been motivated by abolitionist sentiment, or by the three-hundred-dollar bounty, and most believed that they could expect a commission in the future if they performed well.[130]

Even the families of North Carolina's black soldiers were not untouched by changing events. On September 10, 1863, after Wild and his soldiers had been reassigned to Folly Island in South Carolina, the authority that the general had received to colonize Roanoke Island with the families of his soldiers was transferred to Horace James, a former chaplain of the Twenty-fifth Massachusetts Volunteers. Although James sympathized with North Carolina's freedmen and worked long hours on their behalf, he admitted that he was "not personally a believer in negro equality."[131] It is not clear that James supported the interests and equal treatment of the soldiers' families to the degree that Wild had, and certainly the transfer of the regiments out of North Carolina created real difficulties for the dependents. In late 1864, men of the old Second NCCV, then at Chaffin's Bluff, Virginia, complained that they could not get word to or from their families at Roanoke. They requested that a member of the regiment be allowed to go to the island to check on their relatives.[132] By the end of the war, men of that regiment believed that James was closing his eyes to mistreatment of their families on Roanoke Island. Although they placed the greatest blame on assistant supervisor Holland Streeter, who, they charged, sold rations and abused the soldiers' dependents, they claimed that "Captn James the Suptn in Charge has been told of these facts and has taken no notice of them." Indeed, the soldiers of the Thirty-seventh USCT, another of the North Carolina regiments, believed "the cause of much suffering is that Captn James has not paid the Colored people for their work for nearly a year and at the same time cuts the ration's off to one half so that people have neither provisions nor money to buy it with."[133]

Given the rapid change of events and attitudes in 1863, the demise of the African Brigade was perhaps inevitable. Its existence depended, to a large extent, on the concerns and actions of a few men whose powers were limited and circumscribed. The fact that the brigade's regiments had to be raised sequentially meant that at some point Wild would have to split his attention between raising and training black soldiers and leading his first regiments into active theaters. The escalating demands, in 1863, for combat soldiers, and the pace of his recruitment, would ensure that the general could not complete his brigade. More importantly, however, the two major issues that Governor Andrew had hoped to address—whether Southern ex-slaves would serve voluntarily in a white Union army, and whether white Americans would accept those men, even grudgingly and with conditions, as an integral part of the Union forces—had been largely answered in the affirmative by the end of 1863. Black troops were being raised successfully throughout the South. As a result, the model for enlistment offered by Andrew and Wild, in which North Carolina served merely as a crucible to test the recruiting of ex-slaves, proved largely unnecessary by 1864. For all but a few individuals, the soldiers themselves were just pawns in a larger game. As they served their purpose and the game moved on, the pawns became intermingled with the other pieces. As a result, what began as a distinct state brigade was ultimately integrated into the larger pool of United States Colored Troops.

Yet, even though the three North Carolina regiments ceased to exist as a combined unit by the start of 1864 and were amalgamated into larger units of African-American troops, the nature of their recruitment and staffing left an imprint on the regiments that would influence their military records. The officers had been as carefully selected as conditions would allow, to bring to the regiments not only military experience but also a set of abolitionist values initially sympathetic to black North Carolinians. Thus it was that, twenty-five years after the war ended, one of the black veterans, John Hadley, still described the regiment in which he had served as the Thirty-seventh Massachusetts.[134]

Appendix A

Numbers of Black Recruits from North Carolina by County of Origin

Northeastern counties

Beaufort	44
Bettie	60
Camden	39
Carteret	75
Chowan	22
Craven	81
Currituck	58
Dare	8
Cates	5
Greene	19
Hertford	37
Hyde	46
Jones	31
Lenoir	26
Martin	91
Pamlico	6
Pasquotank	102
Perquimans	21
Pitt	89
Tyrrell	26
Washington	126
Total	**1,012**

Central counties

Chatham	0
Durham	0
Edgecombe	25
Franklin	1
Halifax	9
Johnston	0
Nash	0
Northampton	3
Vance	0
Wake	1
Warren	1
Wayne	5
Wilson	1
Total	**46**

Southeastern counties

Bladen	1
Brunswick	0
Columbus	0
Cumberland	2
Duplin	21
Harnett	0
Moore	1
New Hanover	15
Onslow	17
Pender	1
Richmond	0
Robeson	0
Sampson	2
Total	**60**

Western counties

Guilford	2
Iredell	3
Macon	1
Total	**6**

Total	**1,124**

SOURCE: Descriptive Books, Thirty-fifth, Thirty-sixth, and Thirty-seventh Regiments United States Colored Troops (USCT), Records of the Adjutant General's Office, Record Group 94, National Archives, Washington, D.C. (1,124 records).

Appendix B

Ages and Occupations of Early Black Recruits

Occupation	Age								Total
	15–19	20–24	25–29	30–34	35–39	40–44	45–49	50+	
Barber	1	2							3
Blacksmith			2						2
Brickmaker		1							1
Caulker				1	1				2
Carpenter	1	6	5	1	5	1			19
Cook		3							3
Distiller		1							1
Driver	4		2						6
Engineer			1						1
Engraver		1							1
Farmer	114	195	83	40	27	17	9	1	486
Fisherman	1	1			1				3
Fishmonger			1						1
Government employee	1								1
Laborer	103	193	78	24	24	11	5		438
Lumberman			1						1
Mason	1	1							2
Painter	1	1							2
Porter		3							3
Sailor	1	3	1	1	1				7
Servant	8	6	4	2	1	1			22
Shoemaker					1				1
Steward				1					1
Teamster	1		1			1			3
Waiter	9	3	1		1				14
Total	246	420	180	70	62	31	14	1	

SOURCE: Descriptive Books, Thirty-fifth, Thirty-sixth, and Thirty-seventh Regiments USCT, RG 94 (1,024 records).

Appendix C

Ages of Black Soldiers Recruited before September 1863

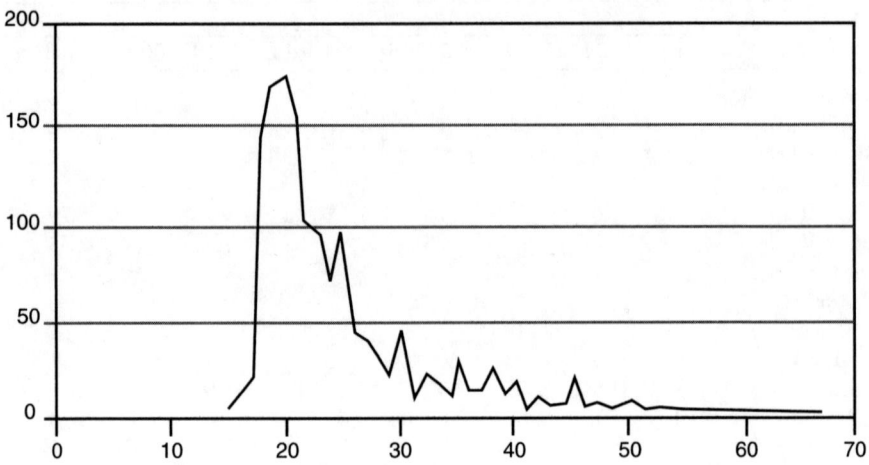

SOURCE: Descriptive Books, Thirty-fifth, Thirty-sixth, and Thirty-seventh Regiments USCT, RG 94 (1,427 records). Graph supplied by the author.

CHAPTER 7

Terrible Dilemmas

Black Enlistment in the Union Army During the American Civil War

Gary Kynoch

DURING THE AMERICAN CIVIL WAR, approximately 180,000 black soldiers served in the Union Army—twenty-one percent of the black male population aged eighteen to forty-five.[1] In many areas of the North, free blacks served in a higher proportion than whites; however, an overwhelming majority (more than 140,000) of black Union soldiers were slaves when the war began.[2] There are important distinctions to be made between white and black enlistment in the Union army. All men, regardless of color, had to weigh the consequences of personal safety along with family and financial welfare when considering enlistment. A Union officer observed that, "The negroes reindicate their claim to humanity by shirking the draft in every possible way; acting exactly like *white men* under similar circumstances."[3] Nevertheless, black men joined the army despite a great many disincentives particular to their race. They were motivated to enlist for some of the same reasons as whites (adventure, patriotism and so on), but also for reasons that would never have occurred to the majority of white soldiers. Additionally, thousands of black recruits were pressed into service. Although they shared much common ground, the black population of the Union and Confederate states was by no means a homogeneous group. Slaves in Confederate territory, border state slaves and free blacks in the North often enlisted for reasons that were peculiar to their status. The same, of course, holds true for obstacles to enlistment.

Some historians have stressed the considerable enthusiasm displayed by black men (especially in the North) to take up arms for the Union.[4] Implicit in this depiction of black enlistment as a massive lemming-like migration to Union army depots is the assumption that blacks rushed to the army to hasten the end of slavery and to gain equal rights for a "down-trodden and oppressed race." Certainly a sense of racial solidarity was an important motivator for black soldiers and the Civil War had a distinct importance for African Americans. As Corporal James Henry Gooding of the 54th Massachusetts wrote shortly before his death in battle, "Supposing we became involved in war with some foreign power, the incentive to the black man to fight would not be the same as in this war."[5] However, the desires to free the slaves and to obtain equal rights were not the only factors which determined the patterns of black enlistment. Indeed, such an approach ignores the agonizing complexity of the black man's position in America during this period and obscures the fact that tens of thousands of potential recruits chose not to serve. A more nuanced exploration of the varied ways in which African Americans reacted to the prospect of fighting on the side of the Union is important precisely because it illustrates this complexity. By examining the reasons men enlisted, and avoided enlistment, much can be learned about the nature of American society and the range of strategies different segments of the black population employed to improve their situations during this tumultuous period.

For free men in the North, enlistment involved surrendering oneself to white authority and military discipline with no chance of advancement to officer's rank; yet many were convinced that fighting on behalf of the Union provided their best opportunity to secure equal rights. Liberated slaves who acquired lucrative positions as military laborers had to judge whether this new-found employment was worth forsaking enlistment and the chance to gain revenge against their former masters. For those still in bondage, the benefits of enlisting to gain freedom and fight against slavery had to be weighed against the dangers of escape and the prospect of abandoning friends and family to the abuses of enraged masters.

For some, the decision to enlist may have been relatively simple, while for others, a number of variables would have come into play. One man may have been enthusiastic to join the fight but could not support his family on a soldier's meager wages and so stayed out of the war—until he was offered a substitution fee or bounty of several hundred dollars. Another may have enlisted primarily to gain freedom, but also for the hope of personal revenge. A third man who may otherwise have joined, could have been deterred by the discriminatory terms of enlistment. Thousands of black men were denied the luxury of choice as they were drafted, "collected" by

Union army patrols, or pressed into service at bayonet point. Thus, this article is devoted to articulating the larger issues which most likely impacted enlistment from the black man's point of view, and to discussing the relative importance of these issues to free blacks in the North and to slaves/newly liberated slaves.

When attempting to assess the information available to potential recruits, it must be remembered that the black community in the North was well informed of every aspect of black military life through letters, newspapers, word of mouth and recruiting meetings, in other words by all the various means that white people acquired news. For slaves from the border states and the Confederacy, access to information was more restricted, but by no means unobtainable. No doubt the vast informal network of communication, known as the "grapevine telegraph" which caused a Louisiana planter to exclaim, "Damn the niggers, they know more about politics than most of the white men. They know everything that happens,"[6] kept many well informed of the progress of the war and the status of black soldiers. After its editors interviewed a number of fugitive slaves in 1861, the *Anglo-African,* probably the most widely read black newspaper, concluded that, "One cheering fact in reference to this war is that the slaves are in possession of all the necessary information in regard to it."[7] Therefore, it is reasonable to assume that African Americans, enslaved and free alike, were reasonably well informed of both the potential benefits and the drawbacks of enlistment.

The Early Days

When the war began in 1861 there is ample evidence that blacks (or at least their literate representatives) in the North were eager to join the fray. The declaration of the "colored citizens of Cleveland" who announced during an assembly at the National Hall in October 1861 that, "We will pray for the Union, will give our money for the Union, and will fight for the Union," was typical of the sentiment expressed at such gatherings.[8] However, the Union was not prepared to entertain the idea of black men in uniform other than as servants. The prospect of black soldiers was alarming to the vast majority of the white populace, who were not yet convinced of the need for such a desperate measure—it was expected to be a short war. Thus all black offers of military assistance were initially refused or ignored.[9]

By the end of 1862, for a variety of reasons public (white) opinion regarding the use of black soldiers began to change. Popular enthusiasm for the war, along with voluntary enlistment, had dropped drastically. As casualties continued to rise and with no end to the war in sight, military service, instead of being viewed as a privilege of race, was increasingly seen in a negative light. Gradually, as a result of the incessant demand for troops, resistance to black enlistment began to wane. A passage from a letter written by the Governor of Iowa to the General-in-Chief of the Army in August 1862 provides an insight into the shift in white attitude. "When this war is over & we have summed up the entire loss of life it has imposed on this country I shall not have any regrets if it is found that a part of the dead are *niggers* and that *all* are not white men."[10] White soldiers often expressed similar sentiments: "I would a little rather see a nigers head blowed of then a white mans [*sic*]."[11]

Faced with a critical manpower shortage, Lincoln issued the Conscription Act in March 1863. Widespread resentment, even resistance, was expected. Although this Act did not apply to black men, it provided further impetus for the government to approve voluntary enlistment. In the words of Mary Frances Berry, "If the administration expected the public to accept compulsory service as necessary, all obvious manpower resources had to be utilized."[12] For some, need dictated policy and prior to receiving official authorization, Generals David Hunter in South Carolina, Benjamin Butler in Louisiana, and Senator James Lane of Kansas recruited black soldiers on their own authority. The actions of these men provide an early look at some of the issues that became critical to large-scale black enlistment.

Union occupation of Hilton Head South Carolina in November 1861 resulted in the flight of Confederate slave masters and brought thousands of slaves under Union control. The Treasury Department initiated a project known as the Port Royal experiment, designed to transform the plantations into a productive free labor system. General Hunter saw things differently and in April 1862 he (unlawfully) ordered the conscription of all able-bodied black men aged eighteen to forty-five. In this manner, the first numerically significant impressment of black men by Union officials began in South Carolina. The regiment never saw active service and Hunter was forced to disband it in August because the War Department was as yet unwilling to recognize or supply black regiments.[13]

As a result of Hunter's draconian recruiting methods, many of these former slaves remained deeply distrustful of the Union army. Colonel Thomas Wentworth Higginson, commanding officer of the First South Carolina Volunteers, complained that Hunter's actions were detrimental to later recruiting efforts.

> The trouble is in the legacy of bitter distrust bequeathed by the abortive regiment of General Hunter—into which they were driven like cattle, kept for several months in camp and then turned off without a

shilling, by order of the War Department. The formation of that regiment, was on the whole, a great injury to this one . . . those who now refuse to enlist have a great influence in deterring others.[14]

In New Orleans (captured by Federal forces in April 1862) General Butler was successful in organizing the first black regiment in the Union army. Desperate for troops, Butler recruited the Louisiana Native Guards, a regiment of free New Orleans blacks, whose services the Confederacy had previously refused. These men remained in New Orleans during the Federal occupation and were quickly mustered into Union service. Within a short time they made up two regiments.[15]

Senator Lane of Kansas began recruiting blacks in July 1862. He adopted a very successful policy of appointing black recruiting agents with the promise that they would serve as officers with the men they enlisted. Lane also guaranteed that black soldiers would be treated well and paid the same as whites. Spurred by these promises his agents did their jobs well (Lane filled in the gaps by impressment) and the 1st Kansas Colored Volunteers was formed by October 1862. However, since Lane had acted without federal authority his volunteers went without wages until January 1864. Additionally, his officers did not received commissions.[16]

In early 1863 the Lincoln government began to extend permission to the states to recruit regiments of black troops.[17] Once the conscription bill was signed on 3 March, Lincoln ordered the War Department to develop a general policy for the enrollment of blacks and in May, the Bureau of Colored Troops was created to standardize recruitment and administer the organization of newly enlisted black soldiers.[18] This policy finalized the Union government's commitment to utilizing black troops.

The "Dual" Factors

The Black Elite

THE LEADERS of the black community in the North—men such as Frederick Douglass, J. Sella Martin, J. W. C. Pennington, William Wells Brown, Martin Delany, Henry Highland Garnet and John Mercer Langston—backed by white abolitionist and black publications, served a dual role in the great drama of black enlistment. The *Christian Recorder*'s stance on enlistment was widely representative of the position taken by the majority of influential blacks.

The *Recorder* will take a bold stand for our soldiers, and will advocate all the rights that they now have, and all that belongs to them which they do not now enjoy. Any information that any old or young man desires, that will enable him to enlist, we will cheerfully give to the best of our ability—for we are well aware that we have a large and extended influence among all the classes and denominations of our people throughout pretty much all the States of the Union, both inside and outside the Church. Already a number have enlisted through our influence, which we shall continue on with unremitting zeal.[19]

The *Anglo-African* took a very practical view: "The South must be subjugated, or we shall be enslaved. In aiding the Federal government in whatever way we can, we are aiding to secure our own liberty; for this war can only end in the subjugation of the North or the South."[20] On this one hand, the elite of black society engaged in extensive recruiting, travelling the country to urge young men to join the Union army.[21] On the other hand, in the campaign to achieve equal status for black soldiers, they publicized the mistreatment and discrimination to which these men were subjected. Newspaper editorials excoriated the government for denying blacks equal pay and the right to be commissioned as officers, and letters from soldiers disillusioned with the conditions of service featured prominently in such black publications as the *Anglo-African* (New York) and the *Christian Recorder* (Philadelphia), as well as sympathetic white newspapers like William Lloyd Garrison's *Liberator* (Boston). The black elite implored the government to afford blacks equal treatment, but almost without exception they worked as recruiting agents in the hope that large-scale enlistment would, in the end, benefit their people.[22]

Not all well-to-do blacks supported the idea of enlistment, especially their own. Having attained a certain station in life, military service in an army that refused to accept blacks as officers held little appeal for these men. As a result, a number of wealthy blacks furnished substitutes when they were drafted.[23]

Remuneration

THE DEBATE over whether remuneration served as a stimulus or a barrier to enlistment illustrates the differing circumstances and attitudes of potential recruits. The evidence suggests that money was an important incentive for some enlistees and the principal deterrent for other men. The earliest regiments formed (up to June 1863) had been promised equal pay with white troops, which was important from both a financial standpoint and as a matter of principle.[24] White privates received $13 per month plus a $3.50 monthly clothing allowance. This rate of pay likely appeared quite attractive to Northern freemen, many of whom had probably never earned as much as $13 per month.[25] Furthermore, some states offered attractive bounties. As a result, thousands of men, free and contrabands alike, enlisted on these terms. However, after much bureaucratic wrangling, the legal advisor to the War Department decided that the only legislation dealing specifically with black soldiers was the Militia Act of July 1862 which stated that blacks were to paid $10 per month with $3 deducted for clothing. Beginning in June 1863 all black soldiers had their pay reduced to this rate.[26]

Entire regiments refused to accept the lesser amount. Corporal Gooding protested in a letter to his local newspaper, "Too many of our comrades' bones lie bleaching near the walls of Fort Wagner to subtract even one *cent* from our hard earned pay."[27] Another member of Gooding's regiment made a similar complaint: "Now it seems strange to me that we do not receive the same pay and rations as white soldiers. Do we not fill the same ranks? Do we not take up the same length of ground in the graveyard that others do?"[28] Some troops did not limit themselves to written protest and instead deserted or mutinied over pay, an offense for which more than one black soldier was executed.[29]

The ruling on pay had an immediate impact on recruiting. The Governor of Ohio complained to the Secretary of War in July 1863 that, "The item of pay is a most serious obstacle in my way," while the Commissioner for the Organization of Black Troops in Middle and East Tennessee informed his superior that "the tardiness of the Government to accord equal pay to all its Soldiers, acts disadvantageously for Recruiting Colored Troops."[30] The Brooklyn Correspondent for the *Christian Recorder* was adamant that "Men in the North will not leave their homes and families, their avocations, at wages of $25 and $30 per month, to be sent to South Carolina, or Georgia, to fight rebel white men, with a prospect of a dog's death by the minions of Jeff Davis, should they be captured, all for $10 a month."[31] Letters to the editor from soldiers who told of families suffering great hardship as a result of the wage reduction must have been particularly damaging to the recruiters' cause. A Private in the Sixth United States Colored Regiment (Pennsylvania) registered the following demand in May 1864:

> We were conscripted and enlisted under the stipulation of thirteen dollars per month and $102 bounty. Our families—hundreds, nay thousands, of helpless women and children—are this day suffering for the natural means of subsistence, whose husbands and fathers responded to the call. . . . There should be but one of two things to do—pay us full wages and bounty, or else send us home.[32]

Those who urged enlistment were forced to address the pay inequity. At a Philadelphia rally in July 1863, Douglass beseeched his audience: "Do you get as good wages now as white men get by staying out of service? Don't you work for less everyday than white men get? You know you do. . . . Young men of Philadelphia, you are without excuse. The hour has arrived and your place is in the Union army."[33] Appealing to its readers in a similar vein, the *Christian Recorder* implored: "We hope that our men will not stand on dollars and cents, but will consider that their country has called for their services, and if it has not heretofore been considered their country, it will be hereafter."[34]

Some historians claim that a booming war economy worked against black enlistment as it provided black men with increased employment opportunities and access to higher wages.[35] Others argue that while the war economy opened doors for some black men, many found their options decreasing in this period due to mounting competition from recent (particularly Irish) immigrants and increasing racial hostility evident in many Northern cities. Lorenzo Green and Carter Woodson state unequivocally that "no improvement took place in the economic status of northern Negroes during this period."[36] The chapter dealing with the Civil War period in Foner and Lewis' documentary history on black labor is entitled "The Worsening Status of Free Black Workers in the North During the Civil War" and consists primarily of newspaper articles highlighting white fear of black competition in the workplace and the corresponding backlash of violence to exclude blacks from certain sectors of employment. Reporting in the aftermath of the 1863 New York City Draft Riots, a New York *Tribune* editorial provides an indication of how deeply threatened some whites felt by black labor: "The mob exults in the belief that if it failed in its other objects, it has at least secured possession of the labor of the city, and has driven the blacks to seek work elsewhere."[37]

In border states and liberated territory, army wages were often the only remuneration other than plantation labor available to unskilled former slaves. When provided with a choice between army service and other forms of waged labor, black men were quite discriminating. Military labor often paid substantially more than a soldier's wages and men were not eager to forsake the extra money to join the army. In North Carolina, black men working for the Quartermaster's Department made $20 a month as teamsters and $15 a month as stevedores in November 1863. These wages prompted an army commander to complain that "while such prices are being paid in North Carolina, it will be impossible to make much headway with recruiting." In Tennessee the Commissioner for the Organization of Black Troops reported that the poverty of recruiting was due to "the higher price commanded by the laborers in this town as compared to soldiers. The Quartermasters Schedule of prices for colored laborers in this town is $25 a month and a Ration."[38] Additionally, the demand for military laborers was so high in some areas that local authorities refused to allow workers to leave their positions to join the army.[39]

The cumulative effect of the employment situation on black enlistment is difficult to judge. It seems logical to conclude that it worked both for and against enlistment. For men driven out of, or otherwise excluded from employment, the army was a paying option. For others the war may have provided opportunities which made them loathe to sign up for the lower wages and uncertainties of a soldier's life. Denied the opportunity to serve as officers, educated blacks of means had absolutely no financial incentive to enlist. One of the few exceptions was the commissioning of black chaplains, a handful of whom served in the Union army, usually as a reward for recruiting services.[40]

Enlistment did offer further monetary inducements to black men in select circumstances in the form of state bounties and, until it was outlawed, as paid substitutes for white (or wealthy black) conscripts. Enthusiasm for enlistment was closely tied to bounties and states which offered substantial amounts were guaranteed a positive response. To attract black recruits to its newly formed heavy artillery company, Rhode Island began offering a $300 bounty in June 1863. Volunteers from across the free states poured in until a total of 1700 filled a regiment by the end of the year.[41] The Rhode Island recruiting campaign was so successful in New York City that the native Frémont Legion, unable to compete, closed down its recruiting office. Likewise, when Connecticut offered the same $300 bounty late in 1863, it was noted that, "The colored men are enlisting very fast."[42] In most instances blacks were not eligible for bounties over $10, consequently substitution bonuses attracted large numbers of men determined to maximize the financial benefits of enlistment. A Commissioner for recruitment reported to the Secretary of War in August 1863 that "of late the draft has interfered with recruiting, but when it is filled and colored men have no chance to be paid as substitutes I think recruiting here will be resumed here with spirit."[43] A number of black men already in uniform were determined that their patriotism would pay dividends. Northern recruiters were offering large bounties to obtain men to fill their state quotas by the middle of 1864 and some black soldiers (like their white counterparts) took advantage of this opportunity to desert their regiments, re-enlist and pocket the money.[44]

Bounties and substitution fees did serve as an incentive to some men; however, substantial numbers of soldiers were cheated out of this money by recruiting officers and military officials. The *Christian Recorder* warned its readers of this practice: "There are those who are engaged in the matter of enlistments who are fit representatives of the race; F. Douglass, Wm. W. Brown and a few others; but there are as many pretenders as there are sharks in the wake of vessels in the gulf stream."[45] Indeed, Martin Delany was implicated in a recruiting scandal in early 1864. "He has persuaded young men who have been taught to hold his name sacred, to go into the army by promising them bounties which they were not to get. Yea, he has even managed to filch from them that which they should and would have received but for him."[46] Certainly, some men who considered enlistment would have been dissuaded by the actions of unscrupulous recruiters.

All things considered, a military career was not a lucrative one for the majority of black soldiers. Many regiments did not receive pay for extended periods of time, either because of their refusal to accept reduced wages or as a result of bureaucratic bungling.[47] When black recruits did enlist for money it was most likely because of a paucity of other opportunities. A verse sung by the men of Colonel Higginson's regiment, which began "De Buckra [poor white] 'list for money," indicates that at least some black soldiers considered their white counterparts more mercenary than themselves.[48]

Family

FOR BLACK men in the South and the border states, enlistment decisions often revolved around one primary consideration—family. Concern for family was a major impediment to recruiting in the South. Potential recruits worried that loved ones left behind would suffer at the hands of vengeful masters, yet families who fled with their men often had no means of survival once these men enlisted. Some of the ugliest stories of the period concern the abuse inflicted upon soldiers' families by slaveholders. Clarissa Burdett testified that when her husband Elijah enlisted ". . . my master beat me over the head with an axe handle saying as he did so that he beat me for letting Ely go off."[49] If a man managed to spirit his family away, the army rarely provided sanctuary, especially in the border states, where in the view of many military officials, the enlistee's family remained the property of their masters.[50] Mistreatment of dependents reached it peak with the eviction of hundreds of woman and children from Camp Nelson, Kentucky in November 1864. These relations of black soldiers were expelled from camp on a freezing day, most of them with nowhere to go and nothing to eat. Joseph Miller of the 124 U.S.C.T. Infantry testified:

> My little boy about seven years of age had been very sick and was slowly recovering. . . . A mounted guard came to my tent and ordered my wife and children out of Camp. The morning was bitter cold. . . . At

night I went in search of my family. . . . I found my wife and children shivering with cold and famished with hunger. They had not received a morsel of food all day. My boy was dead.[51]

In light of such events it is hardly surprising that black men began to demand support and protection for their families as a condition of enlistment. In November 1864, a Colonel of the 72nd U.S. Colored Infantry stationed at Covington, Kentucky reported that a large number of slaves had offered to enlist provided that "they had assurances that the Government would free their families or the Army would protect their families from the cruelty of their masters."[52] Army recruiters soon discovered that a willingness to enlist rested on the army's commitment to the dependents of recruits. General Butler, recognizing this, pledged family protection and support to his recruits in December 1863. Other military officials, including Adjutant General Thomas in the Mississippi Valley, soon followed suit with very positive results.[53]

Manhood and Racial Pride

GERALD LINDERMAN has masterfully demonstrated the centrality that the concepts of "courage" and "manhood" assumed in the consciousness of white soldiers in the Civil War. In his words, "Many soldiers called combat the test of manhood."[54] All the evidence indicates that the notion of "manhood" was even more critical to black men for it was inextricably intertwined with demonstrating not only their individual worth, but that of their race. At an enlistment meeting in Nashville in 1863, one man exhorted his comrades to join with the plea, "Let us make a name for ourselves and our race, bright as the noonday sun."[55] The enlistment of black soldiers also "designated black men as the liberators and defenders of black women and children."[56] Emasculated in the South by slavery and in the North by their status as pariahs, the prospect of combat was seized by many black men as an opportunity to reclaim their manhood.

The whole question of the manhood of "a long enslaved and despised race" was a potent weapon in the hands of those who advocated enlistment. Black recruiters like Frederick Douglass advised that "Liberty won by white men would lose half its luster. Who would be free, themselves must strike the blow."[57] After listing the rights enjoyed by free blacks in the North, the *Anglo-African* stated that, "It is illogical, unpatriotic, nay mean and unmanly of us to shrink from the defense of these great rights and privileges."[58] The black New Orleans newspaper, *L'Union* queried, "In what land has man made himself respected in wartime for cowardice?" while the *Christian Recorder* challenged its readers, "We have been denounced as cowards. Arise and cast off the foul stigma. Shame on him who would hang back at the call of his country."[59] The number of men influenced by such appeals cannot be calculated, but such blandishments were a staple of recruiting campaigns.

The transformation from slave to soldier could be a powerful and uplifting experience. "This was the biggest thing that ever happened to me in my life. I felt like a man with a uniform on and a gun in my hand," observed a newly enlisted former slave.[60] Taking a larger view, Daniel Walker of the 54th Massachusetts assured the readers of the *Christian Recorder* that "wherever we are, whatever may be our fate, we shall always try and be an honor to the race we represent."[61] One of the great ironies of the Civil War was observed by W. E. B. Du Bois: "The slave pleaded; he was humble; he protected the women of the South, and the world ignored him. The slave killed white men; and behold, he was a man."[62]

There was of course another side to the issue of manhood being tied to enlistment. Some black men refused to join an army that denied them equal rights. A chaplain in the 54th Massachusetts resigned as a result of the disparity in pay between black and white soldiers, declaring that while keen to suppress the rebellion, "I cannot enter the field till I enter as a man."[63]

Collection and Impressment

NONVOLUNTARY ENLISTMENT resulted in the addition of thousands of black soldiers to the Union ranks, although it is impossible to calculate exact numbers. Likewise, it is impossible to accurately estimate how many recruits were scared off or so angered by these policies that they refused to enlist. There were several ways in which a man could end up in the army without having exercised free choice. The practice that probably affected more men than any other was "collecting." In certain circumstances the men who were collected enlisted voluntarily, but in many cases collection differed little from impressment. Collection involved squads of Union soldiers being sent into Confederate territory (and the border states) to round up as many blacks as possible. The following, issued by the Commander of the Department of Virginia and North Carolina in December 1863, was typical of collection orders, ". . . all officers commanding expeditions and raids shall bring in with them all negroes possible . . . so that they may be cared for and protected, enlisted, or set to work."[64] Addressing the officer commanding an expedition into Arkansas in the summer of 1863, Adjutant General Thomas ordered him to "collect as many blacks—men, women and children as possible," and to organize the men into regiments.[65] Rushed to the alien environment of Union army camps, newly liberated slaves were clearly expected to enlist. As a soldier in the 54th Massachusetts stationed in Florida reported, "As soon as the male contrabands reach here they are put into the army."[66] The majority of these contrabands had no immediate means of support, many had families and at least the army offered a wage. Consequently, most able-bodied slaves who were collected ended up enlisting. Sometimes the line between collection and impressment was very fine indeed. A Federal official wrote from South Carolina, "You wish to know whether the refugees are kept in the guard house until they are willing to volunteer. I do not know whether they are kept confined till they volunteer, but I do know that they always let them out when they do volunteer."[67]

Impressment involved the use or threat of force to persuade men to enlist and while it brought thousands into the ranks of the Union army, it was also detrimental to recruiting efforts. Northern agents casting about the South to fill their state quotas (and their pockets with commission money) had a particular reputation for brutality. A Treasury Agent in Hilton Head wrote of the practices of Northern recruiters, "I can conceive nothing worse on the coast of Africa. These men have been hunted like wild beasts and ruthlessly dragged from their families."[68] Impressment in New Orleans reached epidemic proportions as recruiting agents colluded with the local police and many blacks were marched to recruitment depots at gunpoint.[69] In Norfolk and Portsmouth, Virginia, troops reportedly arrested black men, abducting them from their homes and workplaces as well as off the street. They were taken to the Craney Island Camp where it was common for them to be forced to carry fifty pound iron balls until they agreed to enlist.[70] Black troops were not above impressing fellow blacks and were frequently sent on expeditions to round up recruits. Soldiers quartered at Mason's Island just outside Washington, D.C. raided the city from time to time to kidnap black men to fill up their regiments.[71] As the lyrics of a popular song, "One more valiant soldier here, To help us bear de Cross," illustrate, black troops were appreciative of all the help they could get.[72] All of these activities served to make a wary black populace more distrustful and less likely to enlist voluntarily.[73]

Black men also ended up in the army as a result of being conscripted, sold and tricked. On 24 February 1864 the Federal draft was amended so that black men between the ages of twenty and sixty-four were subject to conscription.[74] Some border state slave owners saw the writing on the wall and salvaged some of their investment by enlisting their slaves, thereby collecting the state or Federal bounty and up to $300 compensation from the Federal government.[75] In some Northern cities, unscrupulous police officers threatened to arrest black men for fictitious crimes if they did not enlist. When this ruse worked, the men were sold as substitutes.[76]

The Disincentives

THERE WERE a few factors which definitely retarded black enlistment. The three most prominent were: discrimination in American society and within the military; the dangers involved for some slaves in attempting to enlist; and the fate of captured black soldiers.

Discrimination

NOTWITHSTANDING THE recruiting efforts of the black elite, many blacks in the North believed it was folly to enlist in the service of a government (and society) which persistently discriminated against them on the basis of race. At a large New York recruiting meeting in April 1863 the combined efforts of Frederick Douglass, Henry Highland Garnet and J. W. C. Pennington produced only a single volunteer. When they appealed for more men to come forward, a member of the audience responded that "if the government wanted their services, let it guarantee them all the rights of citizens and soldiers, and, instead of one man, he would ensure them 5,000 men in twenty days." The crowd applauded this speech resoundingly.[77] In an 1861 letter to the *Anglo-African* one dissenter advised "that the raising of black regiments would be highly impolitic and uncalled for under the present state of affairs, knowing as we do the policy of the Government in relation to colored men." Another indignant writer reminded the editors "that this government has played so ignoble a part in the execution of the fugitive slave law," and urged readers to resist joining an army that forcibly returned slaves to their masters.[78] The *Christian Recorder*'s Brooklyn correspondent summed up the feelings of many reluctant enlistees when he declared, "War is a reality, and the glory of riding in the *Jim Crow car* in 6th Avenue . . . is not considered by some gentlemen as sufficient compensation."[79]

The Union army reflected the views of the society from which its members were drawn and although they risked their lives in the service of their country, black soldiers enjoyed no special protection from racism. With very few exceptions the commissioned officers in black regiments were white.[80] Some of them were abolitionists or simply decent men, who (by the standards of the time) treated their troops well; others served with black regiments only because it offered a quicker route to promotion and were openly disdainful of the soldiers under their command. In the words of one Illinois soldier. "I would drill a company of alligators for a hundred and twenty a month."[81] Military discipline was harsh regardless of color, but racial contempt meant that many black soldiers were excessively punished. Traditional slave punishments were justified by one officer on the grounds that blacks "have been used to very severe treatment, any light punishment is of no account whatsoever."[82] A soldier in the 32 Regiment (Pennsylvania) reported that once the troops refused to accept their reduced pay, the officers "began to treat the men like dogs. The least thing the men would do, they were bucked and gagged, and put on the knapsack drill, and made to stand for four hours in the hot broiling sun at a stretch."[83] Resistance of any kind by black soldiers was met with the harshest severity. Although African Americans made up less than ten percent of the Union army, nearly twenty-five percent of the 272 troops executed by the end of 1865 were black. The vast majority of troops executed for mutiny (72.2 percent) were members of the United States Colored Troops, as were nearly half of those executed for rape.[84] The prejudice of white officers and military courts was not lost on black troops. In an April 1864 letter, a soldier from the 54th Massachusetts wrote: "There have been four inflictions of the death penalty on colored soldiers since the landing of the expedition [in Florida] February 7, 1864. Is this not strange?" This penchant for executing blacks was one reason soldiers begged for black officers. A sergeant explained, "We want to be represented in court martials, where so many of us are liable to be tried and sentenced."[85] Black soldiers were also subject to attack from white Union troops and civilians; the sight of a black man in uniform being sufficient to incite murderous assaults on a number of occasions.[86]

The fact that a black soldier's chances of becoming an officer were virtually nonexistent worked against black enlistment. It was yet another obstacle that men like Frederick Douglass had to deal with at recruitment meetings. "Do I hear you say you want black officers? Very well. . . . But it is not ridiculous in us all at once refusing to be commanded by white men in time of war, when we are everywhere commanded by white men in time of peace?" The *Anglo-African* used a different approach to persuade black men to ignore this prejudice: "Can you ask any more than a chance to drive bayonets or bullets into the slaveholders' hearts? Are you more anxious to be Captains and Colonels, or to extirpate these vipers from the face of the earth?"[87]

Despite pleas from recruiters (both black and white) that the commissioning of black officers would stimulate enlistment, the War Department steadfastly refused to appoint black men to ranks where they might one day be in a position to give orders to whites.[88] In one case where whites did find themselves serving under a black officer, they protested indignantly. Dr. A. T. Augusta had been commissioned into a black regiment as the senior surgeon with the rank of major. The other surgeons, who were all white, petitioned the President. "When we made applications for positions in the Colored Service, the understanding was universal that *all*

Commissioned Officers were to be white men. Judge of our surprise and disappointment, when upon joining our respective regiments we found that the Senior Surgeon was a Negro."[89] Dr. Augusta was subsequently transferred because the government pandered to the fear that black officers, even if exclusive to black regiments, would cause great discontent among the majority white portion of the army.

Another worry of potential recruits was that enlistment in no way guaranteed an opportunity to distinguish oneself in combat. A number of black regiments performed exceptionally well in battle, yet many white officers preferred their black troops to perform labor rather than combat duties, prompting one black soldier to write, "Instead of the Musket it is the Spad and the Whelbarrow and the Axe."[90] A Union Colonel described the benefits of putting black soldiers to work in an 1863 letter: "They relieve us of our fatigue duty entirely, and have built some fine breastworks besides. When soldiers see them hard at work in the hot sun, doing what they would otherwise have to do, the 'opposition' and 'prejudice' to the plan of organizing and enlisting them soon disappear."[91] This practice became so pervasive that in June 1864 Adjutant General Thomas ordered commanding officers to work their black troops less and drill them more, otherwise they would be useless for combat.[92] The prospect of constant labor duties no doubt deterred black men who for various reasons were eager to fight.

In select circumstances it appears that instead of being restrained from fighting, black soldiers were used as cannon fodder. A *New York Times* reporter testified immediately before an attack that he heard a Union General comment, "Well, I guess we will . . . put those damned niggers from Massachusetts in the advance; we may as well get rid of them one time as another."[93] Additionally, black soldiers who had been taken captive testified that they had been used as "breastworks for white troops."[94] The *Christian Recorder* was incensed by reports of such abuses:

> It is reported that the 2nd Louisiana native guard, a regiment of blacks which lost six hundred in the gloriously bloody charge at Port Hudson, were placed in front, while veteran white troops brought up the rear. Great God, why is this? We care not so much for the loss of men, however bravely they may die, but we damn to everlasting infamy, those who will thus, pass by *veteran troops of any color,* and place a regiment of raw recruits in the front of a terrible battle.[95]

Perils of Enlistment

MALE SLAVES contemplating escape and enlistment placed both themselves and their families in jeopardy. Abandoned families often bore the brunt of the master's wrath; however, escapes involving entire families had a reduced chance of success and exposed all to great danger. When runaways were captured, punishments were severe. One slave reported, "We'en de Union soldiers wur near us, some o' de youn han's run off to git to de Union folks, an' massa ketch dem an' hang dem to a tree, an' shoot dem."[96] Captured runaways were often sold, chained at night, put to work for the Confederate army or moved to areas further from the Union lines. The orders of a Confederate officer in Louisiana illustrates that being captured was not the only danger. "The passing of negroes, slaves or free, towards or into enemy lines is positively prohibited. . . . Every negro who shall violate this order, will be shot, unless he or she shall immediately submit to arrest."[97]

Slaves in border states faced similar problems when they attempted to enlist. They were frequently encouraged to join by Union officials, but only sporadically offered protection *en route* to recruiting stations. Prior to June 1864 border state slaves required their master's consent to enlist and were turned away if they sought to join without it. A Kentucky Provost Marshall's report describes the predictable result of this policy: "Of course as it was foreseen, slave-holders refused to give their slaves permission to enlist in the army. These slaves, however, flocked to my Hd. Qrs. begged to recruited and returned to their masters to be met with torrents of abuse and the merciless lash."[98]

Even after June 1864, when an order was issued giving slaves the right to enlist without consent, they had to get past hired patrols, hostile white civilians and Confederate guerrillas. Harsh penalties were meted out to those who failed to negotiate this gauntlet.

> In Kentucky two white inhabitants cut the left ears off two men who sought to join the Union ranks. Some locals in Missouri caught a party of black men trying to enlist, whipped each of them, and returned them to their owners. One of the slaveholders was so furious with her bondsman for running off that she offered five dollars to anyone in the group who would shoot the slave on the spot; a partisan promptly obliged her.[99]

Slaves who were collected were spared this danger, but for thousands of potential recruits getting to Union lines involved great personal risk.

The South's Revenge

THE CONDITIONS in prisoner of war camps during the Civil War were appalling, and the suffering of prisoners at such notorious institutions as Andersonville received wide publicity. Thus it is telling that black soldiers counted themselves lucky if they were imprisoned when captured or forced to surrender. The murder of black troops following the conclusion of battle reached its apogee with the Fort Pillow massacre, but there were numerous such episodes on a lesser scale.[100] A Confederate soldier recorded that carnage of one such slaughter: "The battlefield was sickening to behold. No orders, threats, or commands could restrain the men from vengeance on the negroes, and they were piled in great heaps about the wagon, in the tangled brushwood, and upon the muddy and trampled road."[101] If troops did survive capture there was still no guarantee they would make it to a prisoner of war camp. President Davis' 1862 Christmas Eve Proclamation stated that "all negro slaves captured in arms be at once delivered over to the executive authorities of the respective States to which they belong to be dealt with according to the laws of the said States."[102] Considered guilty of insurrection these slaves were subject to the death penalty. This law applied only to slaves, free blacks who were captured could not officially be executed but were sometimes sold into slavery.[103]

Lincoln's General Order No. 233, passed on 31 July 1863, which pledged that for every Union soldier executed, regardless of race, a Confederate soldier would suffer the same fate, greatly reduced the likelihood that black prisoners would fall victim to official executions. A much more common practice was to return slaves to their masters, sell them or put them to work on Confederate fortifications.[104] The Confederate Department of War decided on 8 April 1863 that blacks, whether slave or free, did not qualify as prisoners of war, and the Confederate Agent of Exchange, Robert Ould refused to hear propositions regarding black prisoners, declaring that the South "would die in the ditch" before it would give up the right to return captured slaves to their masters.[105] Black troops were, of course, aware of the dangers of falling into Confederate hands. Corporal Gooding wrote that "There is not a man in the regiment who does not appreciate the difficulties, the dangers and maybe the ignoble death that awaits him, if captured by the foe." Colonel Higginson recorded that he and his men felt that they fought with ropes around their necks and his troops frequently commented, "Dere's no flags ob truce for us."[106]

Those involved with recruiting recognized these disincentives and did their best to overcome them. Recruiting posters stressed equal rights, equal pay and the protection that General Order No. 233 proffered. Glowing tributes to black valor were coupled with appeals to "liberate your brethren in bondage." States offering bounties to black troops emphasized that other states offered less or nothing at all. The recruiters exhibited a shrewd awareness of the key issues and worked to assuage the fears of their clientele while at the same time providing incentives for enlistment.[107]

The Incentives

Personal Freedom and the End of Slavery

ENLISTMENT EQUALLED freedom; the choice was that simple for tens of thousands of black troops—a Union soldier could not be a slave. When slaves in border states were emancipated and freedom was no longer contingent on joining the army, there was a precipitous drop in enlistment.[108] Conversely, when enlistment resulted not only in personal freedom, but freedom for the recruit's family, the response was tremendous. In March 1865 Congress passed an act that guaranteed the freedom of the wives and children of black soldiers and of those of future enlistees. Consequently, thousands of men volunteered in the last few weeks of the war.[109]

Other than gaining personal freedom the most universal reason for slaves to join the army was the destruction of the institution of slavery. A slave from Tennessee declared that, "I fought to free my Mammy and her children all through Nashville and Franklin and Columbia, Tennessee and all down through Alabama and Georgia."[110] While ending slavery was a more immediate stimulus for men whose families remained in bondage, it was also a powerful motivator for Northern blacks. The *Christian Recorder* emphasized the special nature of the war:

> If the negro goes to fight for his liberty, he goes upon the economy of human life. Slavery has been a war upon the negro race for over two hundred years, and between the horrors of the middle passage and the Southern plantation, were the war to last for one hundred years it could hardly consign more human beings to an untimely grave. If the war should consign nine out of every ten men, women and children of the negro race to the grave before it closes, the purchase will be cheap, if it shall secure the balance their liberty. And with that understanding the negro accepts the war.[111]

Frederick Douglass appealed to Northern blacks, "can you ask for a more inviting, ennobling and soul enlarging work, than that of making one of the glorious Band who shall carry Liberty to your enslaved people? Enlist, therefore, enlist without delay, enlist now, and forever put an end to the human barter and butchery which have stained the whole South with the warm blood of your people, and loaded its air with their groans."[112] The white population of the North may have called it a war to preserve the Union but for the black population of all the states, this war had an entirely different meaning.

Equal Rights

IF FREEDOM was the primary catalyst for the slaves, equal rights and citizenship occupied this position in the free black's hierarchy of motivation.

Edwin Redkey's study of more than four hundred letters that black soldiers (the vast majority from the North) wrote to newspapers during the Civil War led him to conclude that "these men clearly believed that the primary reason they joined the army was to win citizenship and voting privileges for themselves and their people."[113] There was a strong connection between manhood and equal rights. A speaker at an 1863 meeting of blacks in Washington, D.C. assured the audience that "when we show that we are men, we can then demand our liberty."[114] In its campaign for equal rights the *Christian Recorder* urged the government to remember "how manfully many of our brave boys have sacrificed their lives for their country."[115] Frederick Douglass encouraged the idea embraced by so many black soldiers from the North that if they fought for the Union and helped defeat the rebellion, they would no longer be denied equal rights. "Nothing can be more plain, nothing more certain than that the speediest and best possible way open to us to manhood, equal rights and elevation, is that we enter this service." One of Douglass' more celebrated passages spoke directly to the concerns and hopes of many Northern blacks: "Once let the black man get upon his person the brass letters U.S.; let him get an eagle on his button, and a musket on his shoulder, and bullets in his pocket, and there is no power on earth which can deny that he has earned the right of citizenship in the United States."[116] Corporal Gooding believed that the conflict was crucial to blacks in the North and berated those who resisted enlistment: "Our people must know that if they are ever to attain to any position in the eyes of the civilized world . . . they must fight for it."[117]

While this concern with equal rights and citizenship was predominantly an incentive for free blacks, slaves also expected a dramatic elevation in their status as a reward for their participation in the war. Thomas Higginson recorded the following speech by a sergeant in his regiment:

> Now tings can never go back, because we have showed our energy and our courage and our naturally manhood. Anoder ting is, suppose you had kept your freedom without enlisting in dis army; your chilen might have grown up free and been well cultivated so as to be equal to any business, but it would have been flung in their faces—"Your fader never fought for his own freedom"—and what would dey answer? Neber can say that to dis African race any more.[118]

Revenge

REVENGE WAS a powerful motive, especially for slaves who had been free for just a short while. The opportunity to confront on more equal terms "men who had recently sold their parents, put their sisters in the field and scarred them with the lash"[119] was a compelling incentive to enlist. As one soldier observed, "We is gwine to pay our respectable compliments to our old masters." Another commented, "Jess put de guns into our hans, and you'll soon see dat we not only know *how* to shoot, but *who* to shoot."[120] Corporal Gooding, whose regiment was comprised almost entirely of free blacks from the North, made this observation, "They do not, some of them, yet exactly comprehend the future benefits of enlisting, but they have an impulse equally as great, so far as they are capable of understanding it, and it is revenge."[121] The *Anglo-African* took a more historical view: "Should we not with two centuries of cruel wrong stirring our blood, be but too willing to embrace any chance to settle accounts with the slaveholders?"[122]

Conclusion

IRA BERLIN, when discussing the atrocities visited upon captured black soldiers, argues that, "Black soldiers came to realize that while they might have more to gain in the war than whites, they also had more to lose."[123] This statement is also applicable to slaves as compared to Northern blacks. The newly freed slaves who enlisted in the Union army were fighting for a new way of life for themselves and their families. A Confederate victory might well have resulted in generations of continued slavery. The fact that slaves often risked considerable danger just to get into the army reflects this realization. For blacks in the North it was a great moral and humanitarian crusade to participate in the liberation of the slaves, a crusade they hoped would also result in equal rights for all African Americans throughout the United States. However, the extent of black enlistment in the Union army cannot be solely attributed to these overarching issues. While the destruction of slavery and the quest for equal rights provides the larger backdrop to black participation in the Civil War, black enlistment was a complex process which reflected the terrible dilemmas faced by so many African Americans during this period of upheaval.

Part 3

THE BLACK MILITARY EXPERIENCE

Service to a People and a Nation

CHAPTER 8

—⊸ᗐ᎗ᗑ⊷—

In the Service of the United States

Comparative Mortality Among African-American and White Troops in the Union Army

Andrew K. Black

T HE GLORY OF THE Civil War lies firmly in the valor of the soldiers on both sides who fought and died for liberty as they saw it. Partially in response to their record, the literature on the war is extraordinarily voluminous. One group whose story has yet to be fully told is the African Americans who fought for the Union. Men who served in the "United States Colored Corps" regiments did not experience the same conditions as other troops. Among a galaxy of differences, they suffered from disease at a considerably higher rate than white troops who served in the Union Army. There were, however, exceptions in reference to particular disorders and regions. The causes of the disparities between these two groups can be explained by their different environmental experiences, and included the locations where they served, the type of duty to which they were assigned, their medical experiences from the antebellum era, and the type of clinical treatment they received from the Union medical staff.[1]

This disparity has only been discussed at length in two works: Bell Irvin Wiley's *The Life of Billy Yank: The Common Soldier of the Union,* and Ira Berlin's *Freedom: A Documentary History of Emancipation 1861–1867; Series II: The Black Military Experience.* Wiley's work is interesting, but limited; African Americans appear only to provide context for the descriptions of white soldiers, Berlin's work, while much more effective, makes little attempt at specificity in regard to disease and region. All the different ingredients that caused the disparity between whites and

blacks have yet to be addressed in a comprehensive manner. Consequently a full treatment of the most important aspects of this topic from a
comparative viewpoint will be attempted as the subject of this study.[2]

In this most deadly of American war Union fatalities from all causes
exceeded 300,000 men. Of these, the distribution for white troops was
90,638 killed in battle or as a result of wounds, and 171,806 from disease. For black troops 3,331 were killed in battle or as a result of
wounds, and 29,963 from disease respectively. In simple terms, white
troops were twice as likely to die for reasons of ill-health as in battle,
while black troops where almost ten times as likely to do so.[3]

The large amount of illness reported suggests that during the first
two years of the war the average Union soldier (almost all of whom were
white until late 1863) must have been ill much of the year. Indeed Union
troops appear to have served in conditions of perpetual epidemic. Since
the sick rate for black troops did not decrease (until March 1866) to less
than that for white troops, it seems clear that the normal state of health
within the "United States Colored Corps" was marginal at best.[4]

For Union troops as a whole the medical records were organized into
Atlantic, Central, and Pacific regions, and segregated by race. The
Atlantic zone extended from the East coast including Florida to the crest
of the Appalachian mountain range. The Central zone started at the
Appalachians and included all the territory up to the crest of the Rocky
mountains. The Pacific zone included everything from the Rockies to the
West coast, where the black presence was so small that no records were
tabulated for them in that area. Of the three, by far the greatest mortality
for all causes other than battle occurred in the Central region.[5]

The Mississippi river valley experienced an extraordinary number of
epidemics both in the antebellum period and after which caused it to be the
area of the nation with the greatest risk of ill-health from disease. For example, yellow fever alone, beginning with its first large-scale outbreak in New
Orleans in 1796, reappeared consistently until well into the twentieth century. In 1823, Natchez, which was located well up the river from the Crescent City suffered a very severe epidemic. As a result of this and similar
incidents, Natchez would later establish one of the first quarantines on the
river. Throughout the nineteenth century the entire Mississippi Valley continued to experience extraordinarily high rates of disease. It is possible that
one of the reasons for this pattern was the extremely high number of slaves
as a proportion of the population, and their normally poor health.[6]

It was well known in this period that epidemics on the river usually
began in New Orleans. It was even suggested at the time that "after
speedy communication by speedboat navigation became common, and

large numbers of persons and packages were transported fresh from the poisoned atmosphere, and heavy quantities of the poison, the epidemics were engendered." Such movements up and down the Mississippi River had been normal during the antebellum era, but became much more frequent during the war as a result of Union Army traffic, thereby continuing and exacerbating the epidemiological environment.[7]

The disparity in mortality by region affected both blacks and whites. The statistics did not indicate any significant difference between the two groups in relation to the degree of suffering attributable to region. Table I shows the comparative mortality for African-American and white troops in the different areas. These numbers seem even more striking in light of the fact that those black troops who served in the Atlantic region did so in the most unfavorable, disease-ridden areas, where they would have been expected to suffer a much higher rate of mortality than whites who generally found themselves posted in healthier locations. Many were assigned to posts along the coasts of the Carolinas, Georgia, and Florida; all well known since colonial times as epidemiologically deadly. Nonetheless, until the year after the war ended their rate of death because of disease continued to be greater in the central region.[8]

This is especially interesting since the places they served were so dangerous to the black troops' health. For example, much of Charleston, South Carolina's early development came from wealthy planters who, fleeing the pestilence endemic on their marshy estates (in many cases located on islands later occupied by black troops), took up residence in the city. While the Union may have been fighting for the end of secession or the abolition of slavery, equality was not an important part of the rationale for the war. This situation resulted in black troops being routinely stationed in locations considered unhealthy for whites.

The Atlantic region placed after the Central region with respect to mortality, while the Pacific region placed a distant third. In addition, the rate for all diseases (whether fatal or not) illustrates precisely the same tendency. For both groups the numbers of cases for each 1,000 men who served were greater every year of the war in the Central region. In the case of black troops, only the year after the war (ending June 30, 1866) did they show a higher rate in the Atlantic region than in the Central.[9]

How these men died presents as interesting a problem as where their deaths occurred. Among both black and white Union troops the biggest killer was called "camp fever," which included the separate disorders "diarrhea and dysentery." Dysentery in all its forms is an "inflammation of the intestine, especially of the colon, that may be caused by chemical irritants, bacteria, protozoa, or parasites" which in modern times is limited to lesser developed areas of the world, and other locations where as a result of disaster or a breakdown of social organization, clean food and safe water become unavailable. In the nineteenth century such conditions prevailed to a considerably greater extent than in the twentieth. In one such instance President-elect James Buchanan spent much of the time shortly before his inauguration suffering from what was called the "National Hotel Disease," which was almost certainly some form of dysentery. Even in the nation's capital this disease prevailed. In the countryside, on military maneuvers conditions could only have been worse.[10]

The Surgeon General was so impressed by the virulence of this class of disorders that an entire volume devoted to enumerating and explaining the Union Army's experience with them began:

> The various forms of flux which appeared among the troops during the war were recorded on the monthly reports of sick and wounded under four headings—Acute Diarrhoea [sic], Chronic Diarrhoea [sic], Acute Dysentery, and Chronic Dysentery. These disorders occurred with more frequency and produced more sickness and mortality than any other form of disease. They made their appearance at the very beginning of the war, not infrequently prevailing in new regiments before their organization was complete, and as a rule comparatively mild at first, were not long in acquiring a formidable character. Soon no army could move without leaving behind it a host of victims. They crowded the ambulance trains, the railroad cars, the steamboats. In the general hospitals they were often more numerous than the sick from all other diseases, and rivaled the wounded in multitude. They abounded in the convalescent camps, and formed a large proportion of those discharged [from] the service for disability. The majority of our men who were so unfortunate as to fall into the hands of the enemy suffered from these affections. Finally, for many months after the cessation of the war, and after the greater portion of the troops had returned to their homes, deaths from chronic diarrhoea [sic] and dysentery contracted in the service continued to be of frequent occurrence among them.[11]

Considering the state of medical knowledge at the time and the poor diagnostic procedures then in practice, what were listed as acute diarrhea, chronic diarrhea, acute dysentery, and chronic dysentery may all have been caused by different stages of the same illness. Out of black mortality of 29,963, due to disease, those reported in this classification amounted to 6,764 or 22.57 percent of the total. Of these, 1,368 were attributed to acute diarrhea, 3,278 to chronic diarrhea, 1,492 to acute dysentery and 626 to chronic dysentery.[12]

The next two types of diseases in order of severity of the mortality they caused were pneumonia and the disorders classified as either typhoid or malaria. The largest killer of black troops after dysentery, reported both as "inflammation of lungs" and "inflammation of pleura," would now be labeled as pneumonia. Table III shows comparative figures on this group of disorders for both white and black troops. In this classification, including all kinds of respiratory disorders, 6,198 deaths were reported for black troops, or 20.69 percent of total deaths from all causes. White troops suffered 17,896 deaths, or 10.42 percent of total mortality from all causes. Clearly the experience of whites with respect to respiratory disorders was not as severe as that of blacks.[13]

The largest killers of white troops after dysentery were typhoid and the various types of malaria. These disorders are treated as one classification for the purposes of this study as a result of the inability of the medical personnel of the era to distinguish between them. Indeed, in the nineteenth century they were often diagnosed either as the same disease or mistaken for each other. This resulted to a certain extent from their normal temporal congruence. One medical expert of the antebellum period went so far as to say that "malaria and miasmata are also said to be causes of typhus fever." In the Surgeon General's records they were shown in several variations including "typhoid fever," "typhus fever," typho-malarial fever," and five kinds of remittent and intermittent fever that would most likely be diagnosed today as one or another kind of malaria.[14]

Table IV shows the specific distribution between the variations within this category. One understanding available from this data is the difficulty Civil War doctors had separating typhoid and malaria. While it came to be known at a later period that these conditions were more distinct than indicated in these records, in the era before germ theory and bacteriology such differences were not understood. The transition in names in this table from typhoid fever to typhus fever and from typhomalarial fever to the remittent and intermittent fevers, all of which were the terminology in use at the time, graphically demonstrates the lack of understanding. All of the diseases in this category were thought at the time to be miasmatic, which suggested that they were caused by foul or polluted air in specific topographical locations.[15]

Another difficulty leading to imprecise diagnoses was the similar patterns the diseases displayed. An intermittent fever is one in which the symptoms take place, stop, and then start again. On the other hand remittent fevers waxed and waned, but never entirely disappeared before recovery. In the context of the medical knowledge of the period, it seemed logical to group these infections together as related. Indeed, it is not unreasonable to suppose that diagnostic differentiation was less than accurate in the conditions under which the Union Army commonly operated.[16]

The class of illness known as "eruptive fevers," characterized by some form of physical manifestation on the skin, were next in order of importance, accounting for 3,521 deaths or 11.75 percent of all disease mortality for black troops. These consisted of erysipelas, smallpox, and varioloid measles, and scarlet fever. Of these erysipelas accounted for 247 deaths, smallpox and varioloid for 2,341, measles for 931, and scarlet fever for 2.

Erysipelas, a variety of streptococcus, was one of the infections caused as a result of wounds and surgical procedures in this era before the appearance of sanitary operating theaters. This and others of the eruptive fevers are infections of childhood, but those coming from rural areas where previous exposure may not have occurred were susceptible as adults. Indeed farm boys were highly likely to suffer from these and other diseases at higher rates than their urban brethren. At times entire regiments were stricken in precisely this fashion.[17]

The causes leading to blacks and whites suffering from different diseases at disparate rates, and for the special virulence of specific disorders in both groups are extremely important. Table V shows the comparison for the most important causes of mortality. Indeed, during the Civil War germs, parasites and microbes of all types were not part of the knowledge available to practitioners. While there was a certain amount of understanding that cleaner camps meant healthier troops, this insight proved of limited value. Other considerations such as the miasma, or disease-causing properties of the air, in a particular location, received as much attention in the effort to combat infection as sanitation. Incomplete knowledge of this type made preventive efforts unlikely to succeed since much of the effort expended went into unproductive avenues. In an army staffed by a rural people with no true knowledge of biology, sanitation was marginal at best. "Country boys" were as likely to use open slit trenches as latrines (a couple of feet outside the tent door). Dysentery, the class of disease with the highest rate of mortality for both white and black troops, did not originate with the idiosyncrasies of any one group of troops. Instead, it derived from the level of social development and patterns of settlement of all soldiers which were as easily associated with white troops as black, thereby explaining the lack of difference in the rates of suffering.

Black susceptibility to pneumonia at rates much higher than that for white troops may also be traced to environment. In the antebellum South, the concept of "states-rights medicine" developed in the era before the Civil War and had been used as one of the supports for the pro-slavery argument. This school of thought directly attempted to adjust Southern medical practice and thought to the intellectual needs of Southern slave-holders. Medical knowledge could then be used to display a biological justification for slavery.[18] One of the supposed weaknesses proving black inferiority had been their high rate of respiratory infections. What this analysis ignored were the different backgrounds and living conditions of slaves and Southern whites.

The rural white person in the South lived in contact with many fewer people than their Northern counterparts, but slaves experienced different conditions. A planter and his family came into contact with their house slaves, and possibly, but not necessarily, the overseer on a regular basis, and their living quarters were as spacious as income would allow. In contrast slaves lived in overcrowded, poorly maintained quarters which were perfect environments for the transmission of respiratory diseases.[19] In Union Army camps the conditions were just as conducive for the transmission of airborne disease as they were in the slave quarters. Overloaded accommodations in tents, and on the ground, in the midst of large camps of men carrying a variety of diseases, provided an open invitation to infection. After 1845 pneumonia and the other disorders in this classification caused increasing mortality among bondservants in the South. Because of exposure to the weather and the possibility of being required to work in the fields during rain and even snow their daily lives presented a perfect environment for the propagation of disease. The fact that black troops came into the army with medical backgrounds that made pneumonia a likely part of their history made them more susceptible to reinfection than the whites who did not share that history. Clearly, a combination of experiential rather than genetic factors led to their high rate of suffering from this cause.[20]

Regional differences in the rate of disease were another reason for the greater mortality of black troops. Since the Central region was the most lethal, troops most likely to serve in that area could be expected to suffer in higher numbers. Since the vast majority of black Union regiments either saw some or most of their service in the Mississippi Valley, they suffered most from that area's propensity to cause disease. Table VI shows the number of black regiments that served in the Atlantic and Central regions, as well as those who saw service in both places.

Fully 68.15 percent of all regiments in the "United States Colored Corps" served in the Central region, and were, therefore, exposed to the greatest concentration of disease experienced by Union troops. Another 13.38 percent saw at least some of their duty in the Central region, while only 18.47 percent served entirely outside the area. One consideration which should be remembered in relation to disease differentials between the races is the fact that black troops were stationed in locations considered unhealthy for whites. According to the records compiled by the Surgeon General, because of ". . . the then generally accepted belief in their partial immunity . . . they were often stationed in localities that would have proved specially dangerous to white men"[21]

Adjutant General Lorenzo Thomas made frequent trips into the area by order of President Lincoln to raise troops from the large populations of contrabands that followed the Union Army wherever it went. On one such trip he reported to Secretary of War Stanton that he had succeeded to the extent of being able to recruit 56,320 men. In the same communication he mentioned having difficulty finding sufficient recruits because of another one of the factors causing greater disease among black troops:[22]

> . . . More troops would have been put into the army but for the pressing demands of the several departments on the Mississippi, and for laborers with the troops operating in the field. The number of blacks used in this way, excluding cooks and servants must be very large. Most of the labor is done by this class of men, and the forts on the Mississippi river have been mainly thrown up by them.[23]

In many instances throughout the war black troops were assigned to what was known as fatigue duty. This consisted of construction and maintenance and other duties considered too demeaning for whites in locations with available black labor. In a later part of the above letter to Stanton, Thomas says:

> Where white and black troops come together in the same command the later [*sic*] have to do the work. At first this was always the case, and in vain did I endeavor to correct it, contending that if they were to be made soldiers, time would have to be afforded for drill and discipline, and that they should have only their fair share of fatigue duty. The prejudice in the army against their employment as troops was very great; but now, since the blacks have fully shown their fighting qualities and manliness it has greatly changed.[24]

The fact that blacks experienced an increasingly improved state of health may be partly explained by the fact that they began to be assigned less fatigue duty. Since this kind of service was understood even at that time to produce a higher rate of illness, the reduction in disease which followed a lessening of such duty is not a surprise.

Other considerations, however, contributed to this improvement. The most important among these was the greater availability of medical personnel for black units later in the war. Thomas Wentworth Higginson, a prominent abolitionist and minister before the war, commanded a regiment in the "United States Colored Corps" during the conflict. In his memoirs he prominently mentioned a number of reasons for the poor health suffered by his men, conspicuous among them, fatigue duty and the lack of medical personnel:

> In what respect were the colored troops a source of disappointment? To me in one respect only,—that of health. Their health improved, indeed, as they grew more familiar with military life; but I think that neither their physical nor moral temperament gave them that toughness, that obstinate purpose of living, which sustains the more materialistic Anglo-Saxon. They had not, to be sure, the same predominant diseases, suffering in the pulmonary, not in the digestive organs; but they suffered a good deal. They felt malaria less, but they were more easily choked by dust and made ill by dampness. On the other hand they submitted more readily to sanitary measures than whites, and with efficient officers, were more easily kept clean. They were injured throughout the army by an undue share of fatigue duty, which is not only exhausting but demoralizing to a soldier; by the unsuitableness of the rations, which gave them salt meat instead of rice and hominy; and by the lack of good medical attendance. Their childlike constitutions needed prompt and efficient surgical care; but almost all the colored troops were enlisted late in the war, when it was hard to get good surgeons for any regiments, and especially for these.[25]

Nor was Higginson the only person to note the difficulty in obtaining doctors for black units. Lorenzo Thomas, when writing to Secretary Stanton to report on his recruiting trip to the Mississippi, said:

> . . . Great difficulty was experienced in the early part of the work in getting medical officers, but this has been remedied by sending a medical officer through the New England States, who induced a number of physicians to appear for examination and receive appointments.[26]

Other problems experienced because of the shortage of doctors for black units included the use of surgical assistants in their place when no physicians were available. In conditions of primitive medical knowledge such personnel were of dubious value at best. In one instance when a qualified black doctor was found for one of these regiments the surgical assistants that he worked with chose to write a letter to President Lincoln. In it they said:

> When we made application for position on the Colored Service, the understanding was universal that all commissioned officers were to be white men. Judge of our surprise when, upon joining our respective regiments, we found that the Senior Surgeon of the Command was a negro.
>
> We claim to be behind no one, in a desire for the elevation and improvement of the colored race in this country, and we are willing to sacrifice much in so grand a cause, willingly compromise what we consider a proper self-respect; nor do we deem that the interests of either the country or of the colored race, can demand this of us. Such degradation, we believed to be involved in our voluntarily continuing in the service, as subordinate to a colored officer. We therefore most respectfully, yet earnestly, request that this unexpected, unusual, and most unpleasant relationship in which we have been placed, may in some way be terminated.[27]

It boggles the imagination to assume that such attitudes as cited above, both in the surgical assistants' protest and by Higginson, did not affect the medical treatment received by black troops. While Higginson may have held advanced notions on race relations for his time, the equality of the races clearly was not part of his ideology. Nor should he be considered unusual. The medical data upon which much of this study is based comes from the Surgeon General of the United States who saw fit to present them in segregated format. In one volume of the series, as a justification for segregating the records by race, the statement is made that:

> The propriety of endeavoring to present separately such facts as it has been possible to collect, with regard to the sickness and mortality of Colored Soldiers, would appear too obvious to require extended remark in this place. Aside from all considerations of a scientific or historical nature, motives of humanity would seem to dictate that the statistics should be presented in the form most likely to render them serviceable as a contribution to our knowledge of *race-peculiarities on disease* [emphasis added].[28]

As black troops were treated differently by Union doctors on account of race in the records, it stretches belief to assume that their treatment by those same men, on the battlefield and off, was equal to that afforded to whites.

One so-called racial peculiarity in disease was the different experiences of white and black troops with respect to malaria. Peter Wood has suggested that this difference, which he also found in colonial South Carolina, resulted from genetic factors. This theory seems ripe for reexamination. The sickle-cell carrier trait that Wood credits for this difference does indeed provide greater protection for a carrier than for a noncarrier. However, only a portion of the black population was actually carriers, while one hundred percent had been exposed to malaria in their environment.[29]

Traditionally, malaria had been endemic throughout North America from the time of the European conquest. By 1850, however, it had been eradicated in New England. Since mosquitoes, who were the mechanisms for transmission for malaria, died out in the frost each year, only a new source of infection in the spring made possible a continuance of the endemic presence. The northern Mississippi valley retained an endemic presence as a result of its trade with the areas bordering the southern part of the river. In contrast, as trade with the Caribbean began to be centered in New Orleans rather than New York, Philadelphia, or Boston, and the sources of renewed spring time infection left with the changing patterns of trade, malaria disappeared from all but isolated pockets in New England. At the same time no annual frost killed mosquitoes in the South and the infection remained as an endemic presence throughout the region.

Consequently, blacks generally came from the part of the country where they had an almost one hundred percent likelihood to have been exposed to malaria and acquired some resistance. Since white troops mostly came from regions where it was either unusual, or where the type of malaria was different from that in the South, they faced the Southern disease environment with little or no resistance. Since the greatest resistance to malaria for an entire population comes from acquired immunity, Wood's theory that a genetic factor only present in a portion of the black population was responsible for their greater resistance entirely ignores epidemiologically important geographical and environmental factors. White troops suffered more than blacks from this infection for reasons directly traceable to environment and geography, with genetics only a minor consideration.

African Americans who served in the Union Army did so in conditions of considerably greater distress than their white compatriots. They were assigned more onerous duties which exposed them to a greater likelihood of disease. When they became ill they received substandard care. They suffered more from disease because of their background in slavery, but also found themselves with greater resistance to one of the biggest killers for the same reason. In the face of these obstacles they became more and more likely as the war lasted to be assigned to battle, which for them turned out to be healthier duty.

Table 1

Black Regional Mortality for the Years Ending June 30
(Per 1,000 Men)

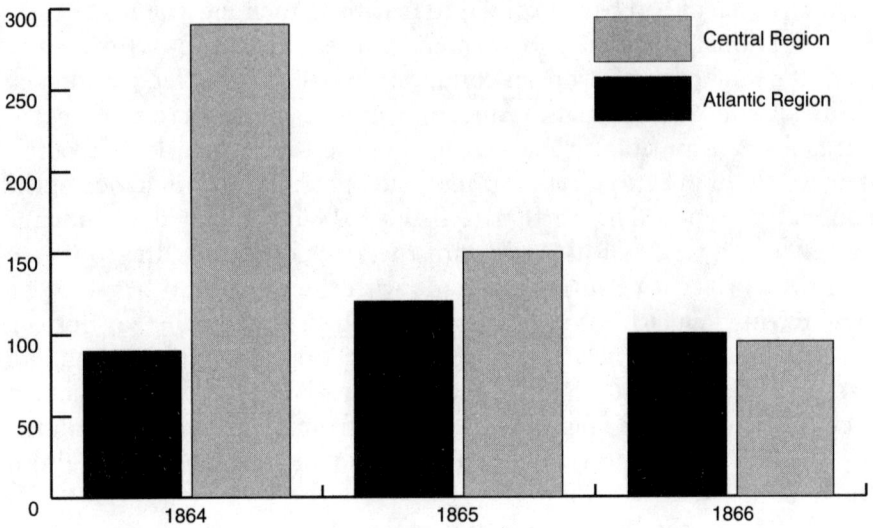

White Regional Mortality for the Years Ending June 30
(Per 1,000 Men)

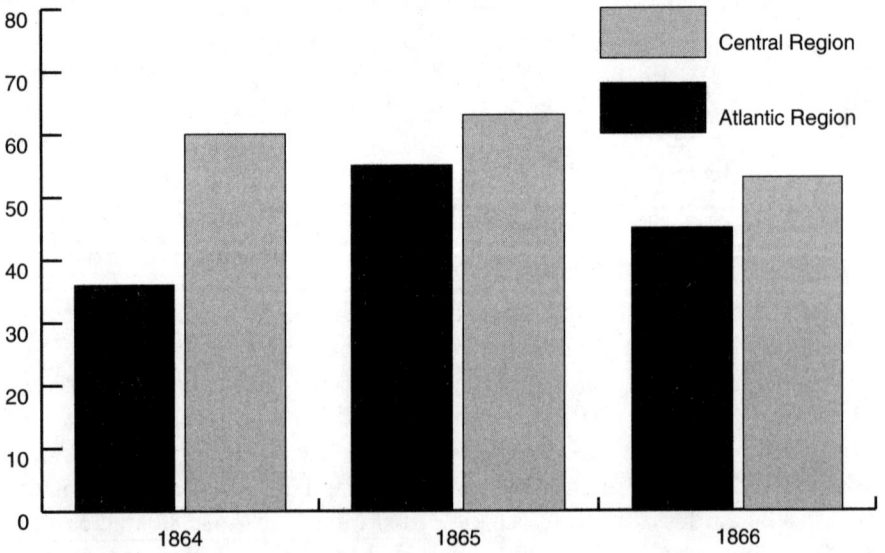

SOURCE: *Medical and Surgical History*, 3:1, 8

Table 2

	White Troops		Black Troops	
	May 1, 1861 to June 30, 1866		July 1, 1863 to June 30, 1866	
	Cases	Deaths	Cases	Deaths
Acute Diarrhea	1,155,226	2,923	113,801	1,368
Chronic Diarrhea	170,488	27,558	12,098	3,278
Acute Dysentery	233,812	4,084	25,259	1,492
Chronic Dysentery	25,670	3,229	2,781	626
Total	1,585,196	37,794	153,939	6,764

SOURCE: Surgeon General of the United States, *The Medical and Surgical History of the War of the Rebellion* (Washington, D.C.: United States Government Printing Office, 1879), vol. 1, pt. 2, p. 2.

Table 3

	White Troops		Black Troops	
	May 1, 1861 to June 30, 1866		July 1, 1863 to June 30, 1866	
	Cases	Deaths	Cases	Deaths
Asthma	9,365	75	762	18
Acute Bronchitis	168,715	650	22,648	255
Chronic Bronchitis	26,912	529	2,733	149
Dropsy of Chest	508	82	129	49
Hemorrhage from Nose	2,722	19	257	6
Inflammation of Larynx	17,318	234	2,738	40
Inflammation of Lungs	61,202	14,738	16,133	5,233
Inflammation of Pleura	31,852	590	7,175	304
Hemorrhage from Lungs	5,745	209	405	60
Other Disease of this Order	38,907	770	2,209	84
Total Respiratory Disorders	363,246	17,896	55,189	6,198

SOURCE: Surgeon General of the United States, *The Medical and Surgical History of the War of the Rebellion* (Washington, D.C.: United States Government Printing Office, 1879), vol. 1, pt. 1, pp. 639, 711.

Table 4

	White Troops		Black Troops	
	May 1, 1861 to June 30, 1866		July 1, 1863 to June 30, 1866	
	Cases	Deaths	Cases	Deaths
Typhoid Fever	75,368	27,056	4,094	2,280
Typhus Fever	2,501	850	123	108
Typho-Malarial Fever	49,871	4,059	7,529	1,301
Remittent Fever	286,490	3,853	30,645	1,002
Quotidian Intermittent Fever	447,258	452	63,992	58
Tertian Intermittent Fever	375,170	381	51,045	54
Quartan Intermittent Fever	41,223	84	3,923	15
Congestive Intermittent Fever	13,673	3,370	2,536	794
Total Typhoid and Malaria	1,291,554	40,105	163,887	5,612

SOURCE: Surgeon General of the United States, *The Medical and Surgical History of the War of the Rebellion* (Washington, D.C.: United States Government Printing Office, 1879), vol. 1, pt. 1, p. 637.

Table 5

	White Troops		Black Troops	
		Percentage of Total		Percentage of Total
	Deaths	Disease Fatalities	Deaths	Disease Fatalities
Diarrhea and Dysentery	37,794	21.98	6,764	22.57
Respiratory Disorders	17,896	10.42	6,198	20.69
Typhoid and Malaria	40,105	23.34	5,612	18.72

This table is a compilation of the four others which precede it.

Table 6

Regional Distribution of Black Regiments

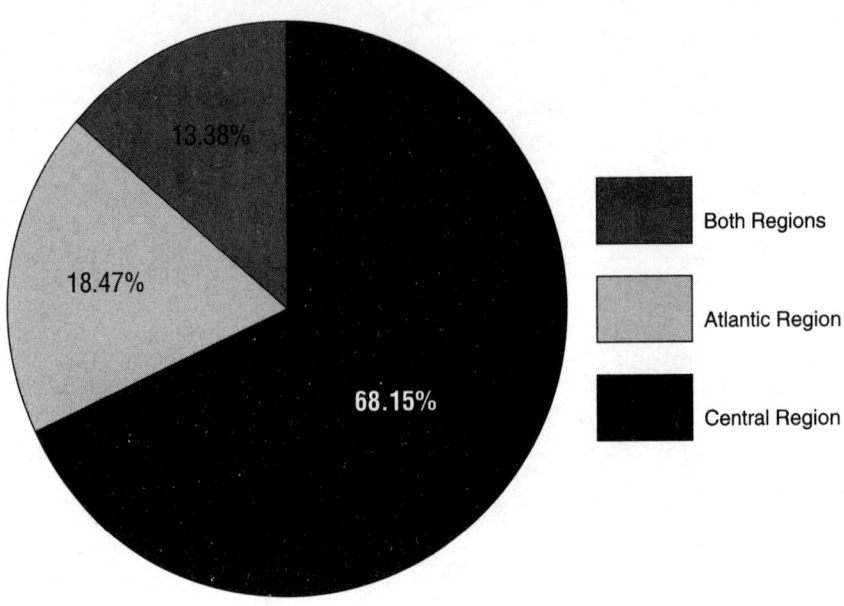

SOURCE: Frederick Dyer, *A Compendium of the War of the Rebellion* (New York: T. Yoseloff, 1959, 1879), vol. 1, p. 245–53.

〜⊶⊷⊶〜

CHAPTER 9

"To Come Forward and Aid in Putting Down This Unholy Rebellion"

The Officers of Louisiana's Free Black Native Guard During the Civil War Era

Manoj K. Joshi and Joseph P. Reidy

HE SOCIAL TRANSFORMATION SURROUNDING slave emancipation profoundly affected Southern free blacks, but none more so than
Louisiana's free people of color. The Civil War and Reconstruction at once
threatened their privileged position and promised to enlarge their liberty
along with that of all blacks. By so doing, wartime and postwar events
magnified the forces that had historically pulled free blacks in contradictory directions: toward the world of the white planters and toward the
world of the black slaves. Struggling to maintain their balance and, if possible, to enhance their own position as the old order crumbled, the free
people wavered between the two worlds. Despite nearly universal white
opposition to black equality, the free people developed only a shaky
alliance with the former slaves, seemingly natural allies in the battle against
prejudice. Differences rooted in the eighteenth century continued to
haunt relations between those free before the war and those freed by the
war. The free blacks' response to civil war and reconstruction illuminates
both their unique past and the new postwar order they helped shape.

From the time of Spanish and French rule in Louisiana, New Orleans
free people of color enjoyed privileges far beyond those of black slaves.
Openly claiming European as well as African ancestry, many freemen
flaunted their cosmopolitan backgrounds and culture. On the eve of the
Civil War, New Orleans freemen owned two million dollars' worth of

property, and fully 85 percent worked as artisans, professionals, and pro-
prietors. The most prosperous owned large plantations and hundreds of
slaves. Unlike free blacks elsewhere in the South, they could travel without restriction; they could testify against whites; and they did not have to
register with the state or acknowledge dependence upon a white
guardian. Though they lacked the vote, on several occasions they successfully mobilized white patrons and allies to defeat attempts to limit their
liberty. In short, the Louisiana free black community enjoyed economic,
social, and cultural privileges scarcely matched by any free black caste in
the Western Hemisphere.[1]

Free blacks in New Orleans had long used military service, first on
behalf of the French and Spanish and later on behalf of the United
States, to protect their privileged position. For their efforts in the War of
1812 and particularly during the fighting at New Orleans in 1814 and
1815, they earned the praise of General Andrew Jackson.[2] Although
Louisiana authorities eventually stripped them of their arms, the state
paid free colored soldiers pensions and the federal government granted
them bounties. Denied the chance to maintain their military organization, the soldiers refused to let die their proud tradition. They formed a
benevolent association, the "Association of Colored Veterans of 1814
and 1815," which provided mutual support in the event of death or
incapacity to work and celebrated their martial past.[3]

With the outbreak of the Civil War, Confederates viewed the free
black community suspiciously, fearing a potentially explosive union
between freemen and slaves. Rebel partisans threatened severe reprisals
to any free person of color suspected of disloyalty and watched closely
for suspicious signs. In the circumstances, many free people of color
viewed military service as the surest guarantee of their security.[4] Confederate authorities concurred, and, beginning in November 1861, sponsored mass meetings in New Orleans to promote enlistments in a free
black regiment. Under the plan, leading freemen would recruit companies (of one hundred men each), then serve as officers (one captain and
two lieutenants) for the companies they raised. Ten companies would
form the regiment, which trusted whites would command. In March
1862 Confederate Governor Thomas O. Moore inducted the regiment
into the state militia, denominating it the "Native Guard." The regiment received neither clothing nor arms from the state. It did not drill
with the white units and never fought for the Confederacy. Expressing
little enthusiasm for Confederate service, the men attended regimental
musters only irregularly,[5] apparently exerting the least effort necessary to
allay Confederate suspicions.

Within weeks of their formal muster into the state militia, the Native Guards resolved the dilemma created by their mobilization on behalf of the rebel cause. In April 1862 Union military and naval forces attacked New Orleans, and the Confederates fled. Unlike their white counterparts, the colored militiamen remained, not to resist but to welcome the federals. Discreetly disbanding, they skipped quickly back into the comparative anonymity of the French Quarter, but soon they desired to serve the Union, hoping thereby to protect and perhaps enhance their privileges.

Filled with a sense of duty "to come forward and aid in putting down this unholy rebellion and save our country from her awful threatened doom," as one later expressed it, the Native Guard officers tendered their services to General Benjamin F. Butler, commander of the newly created Department of the Gulf.[6] Butler admitted being struck by the intelligence and sincerity of the officers, "the darkest of whom was about the color of the late Mr. Wester." Nonetheless, he declined their offer on the grounds that the War Department did not then permit black soldiers, let alone black officers.[7] The officers received a more sympathetic hearing from General John W. Phelps, commander at Camp Parapet, several miles above New Orleans on the Mississippi River. Phelps, a Vermont abolitionist, was anxious to organize an army of slaves to destroy the Confederacy. Service of privileged free blacks in such a force would compromise his vision, to be sure, but Phelps had no objection in principle to such service and recommended the former Native Guard officers to General Butler. While Butler stalled, Phelps pushed. The ensuing struggle between the two over Phelps's proposal to arm slaves provided cover for the free blacks to enter federal service.

Through the summer of 1862 Phelps repeatedly requested authority to enlist slaves. Butler rejected each such request but dutifully submitted it to Secretary of War Edwin M. Stanton asking that President Abraham Lincoln rule on the question. Rather than allow Phelps to arm the slaves who had taken refuge in his camp, in July Butler ordered the abolitionist to employ them as wood choppers. Phelps resigned rather than serve as a "slave-driver."[8] When Confederates reversed the momentum of federal advances, recapturing Baton Rouge later in the summer and threatening to attack New Orleans, Butler had to act. Desperate to enlarge his fighting force, he invited the Native Guard officers to his headquarters. When they assured the general that their men would welcome the chance to serve the Union, Butler authorized their muster. The Confederate Native Guard became the 1st Louisiana Native Guard.

Try as he might, Butler could not recruit enough white Louisianans to fill his growing military needs. Hence, through the fall of 1862 he continued to "call upon Africa," authorizing formation of two more regiments of freemen. As he had done with the first regiment, he permitted free blacks to command the companies they raised. While he also followed the Confederate precedent of placing white colonels in command of the regiments, he appointed Francis E. Dumas, a freeman serving as a captain in the first regiment, major in the second. Dumas, a wealthy slave-owning sugar planter and distant relative of French poet Alexandre Dumas, thus became the first nonwhite to hold a field office in the United States army.[9] In mid-December 1862, when Butler relinquished command of the Gulf Department of General Nathaniel P. Banks, the 1st Louisiana Native Guard was at full strength and the two additional regiments were well on their way toward completion.

The change of commanders boded ill for the free black officers. Banks had a history of opposition to black soldiers. In 1859, in his capacity as governor of Massachusetts, he vetoed legislation that would have admitted blacks to the state militia on the grounds that it violated the whites-only provision of the 1791 federal Militia Act.[10] Upon assuming command in New Orleans, Banks again resorted to formalities. Considering the freemen unqualified to hold commissions, he intended to remove them from the service, by persuasion if possible, by force if necessary.

He moved first against the officers of the third regiment, summoning them for an interview early in February 1863. Inquiring whether they had any complaints, Banks suggested that those who voiced grievances resign.[11] Within weeks, the eighteen free black officers of the regiment submitted a joint letter of resignation. Their statement affirmed that they "did most certainly expect the Privileges, and respect due to a Soldier who had offered his services and his life to his government, ever ready and willing to Share the common dangers of the Battle Field," though they denied any expectation of full social equality. Denouncing the "Scorn and contempt" that whites of all ranks had heaped upon them, they claimed that "This treatment has sunk deep into our hearts. We did not expect It therefore It is intolerable. We cannot serve a country in which we have no more rights and Privileges given us."[12] Without so much as an investigation of the charges, Banks accepted their resignation.

In the eyes of General Banks and the white commanders of the Native Guard regiments, the free colored officers lacked the qualifications required of Union officers. In the words of Banks's adjutant, the officers' presence "led to much ill-feeling among the officers and men of some of the white regiments, resulting often in controversy and on several occasions in violence. By their arrogance and intolerant self-assertion, the officers . . . had conclusively shown that they were not the men to pioneer this experiment, even before they proceeded to demonstrate their hostile and uncompromising spirit by seeking occasions to force their complaints upon the Dept. Commander." Although the freemen admitted to a "limited Knoledge of military Disciplin" in their resignation letter, they fully understood that officers in white regiments often had no greater formal military training than they. They considered their ouster a flagrant violation of military etiquette. Having entered federal service with General Butler's full assurance of equal treatment, they refused to have that promised equality abridged.[13]

In the spring of 1863, sensing that Banks would soon oust them, officers in the 2nd Louisiana Native Guard also began to leave federal service. In early March, after consulting among themselves, five officers stationed at Fort Pike, Louisiana, resigned, submitting nearly identical letters of resignation. "When I Joined the united States army," declared Lieutenant Robert H. Isabelle, "I did so with the sole object of laboring for the good of the union supposing that all past prejudice would be suspended for the good of our Country and that all native born americans would unite together to sacrifice their blood for the cause as our fathers did in 1812 & 15 to save our native soil from her threatened doom."[14] Although they expressed disappointment that their performance had not demolished long-standing prejudices, all affirmed that military success required harmony, and they consented to resign in the face of undiminished hostility among whites. When several officers in the second regiment refused to take their cue, Banks delivered a clearer message. He convened a special board to examine their qualifications. The freemen pointedly observed, "the officers detailed to compose said Board are in the Majority of inferior rank (1st Lieutenants of the same Regiment) whose promotion would be Effected by our dismissal." When the composition of the board remained unchanged despite the clear violation of protocol, still other black officers resigned in protest.[15] Undaunted by Banks's threats, several black officers appeared before the board and passed examination, but by the fall of 1863 the last holdouts, Major Dumas and Captain P. B. S. Pinchback, had had enough. They, too, resigned.

The officers of the 1st Native Guard Regiment escaped the frontal attack their counterparts in the second and third regiments endured, but, early in 1864, resenting the constant sniping at their qualifications, they too began to resign. "I respectfully tender my immediate and unconditional resignation," wrote Captain Joseph Follin, "because daily events demonstrate that prejudices are so strong against Colored Officers, that no matter what would be their patriotism and their anxiety to fight for the flag of their native Land, they cannot do it with honor to themselves."[16] The officers of the first regiment, admitted earliest into service, appropriately remained in service the longest, the last until the summer of 1864. Despite their pride in being first and their reluctance to depart, they abandoned the military rather than submit to the disrespect of white comrades.

While General Banks considered black officers an incumbrance, he desperately required black troops to protect the ever-expanding Union-occupied domain. When rebels threatened attack, as they did repeatedly during the spring and summer of 1863, his need increased in proportion to the credibility of the threats. Sensing Banks's vulnerability, a group of resigned officers, for the most part from the 3rd Native Guard, requested permission to recruit a black regiment "to assist in putting down this wicked rebellion, And in restoring peace to our once peaceful country." Once again citing the precedent of their forefathers who fought with Jackson, they reasoned: "The commanding Gent may think that we will have the same difficulties to surmount that we had before resigning. But sir give us A commander who will appreciate us as men and soldiers, And we will be willing to surmount all other difficulties."[17] In the same vein, the secretary of the association of resigned officers expressed to General Daniel Ullmann, commander of black troops in the Gulf Department, his desire to raise a "Company of Cavalry of picked men of full stature who are free Born intelligent men who have been used to the saddle from infancy never having done any thing Else since they were old enough But Catch wild attakapas Cattle and hunt." The officer confidently boasted, "They are men who understand the use of the Lassoe so well that they will wager to Catch a beef at full speed by any one of his feet."[18] Ullmann responded, as he did routinely in such cases, that he lacked the authority to commission blacks as officers though he would gladly issue warrants for noncommissioned offices to those deemed qualified.[19] The freemen declined Ullmann's offer, and Banks held fast to his course.

Flouting Banks's determination to keep the officer corps white, the resigned officers repeatedly sought permission to raise new companies of black soldiers. Robert H. Isabelle, a former Lieutenant in the 2nd Native Guard who had passed the board of examination before resigning, offered the services of more than 1,000 free blacks in New Orleans whose only request "is the privilege of selecting their own line officers or for you to select from our own race such persons as you might find qualified."[20] In midsummer 1863, as rebel threats on New Orleans intensified, Banks capitulated. He authorized the resigned officers to raise and serve as company officers of two regiments, the 6th and 7th Louisiana Infantry, whose term of service would be sixty days. One officer, Charles W. Gibbons, later reported having reassembled his company in two hours.[21] Jordan W. Noble recruited with similar ease, drawing upon his illustrious military background as a drummer during the War of 1812, the Seminole War, and the Mexican War.[22] Although the Confederates did not attack, the incident demonstrated Banks's continuing dependence upon the resigned officers. While he considered them unqualified to command, he knew that no one could enlist black recruits as quickly as they.

Banks's successor, General Stephen A. Hurlbut, proceeded from scratch in learning the same lesson. In the fall of 1864 declining black enlistments plagued Hurlbut, desperately short of soldiers to guard the ever-extending lines and to protect the freedmen working on government plantations. To complicate Hurlbut's plight, his superior, General Edward R. S. Canby, weary of the constant complaints about recruiters' "excesses," had banned forcible impressment of blacks into the army. To solve his problem, Hurlbut somewhat sheepishly followed Butler's and Banks's precedents and turned to the freemen. Late in October he began organizing new black regiments, authorizing the former Native Guard officers to recruit companies and promising them commissions provided they passed the qualifying examination. On the brink of implementing his plan, Hurlbut changed his mind. Black recruitment languished as a result, but more important, the free blacks lost another chance to serve as commissioned officers. It proved their last.[23]

From beginning to end, the purge of the black officers of the three Native Guard regiments lasted nearly eighteen months. The earliest fatalities, the officers of the third regiment, for the most part left the service together in February 1863. The last holdouts, officers of the first and second regiments, did not succumb to the pressure until the summer of 1864. Those who remained in service with the odds stacked increasingly against them at times found room in which to preserve their dignity and retain some semblance of respect. Even they eventually gave up in desperation.

Through it all, Banks demonstrated a curious combination of vindictiveness and benevolence. Despite his numerous violations of established protocol in forcing the officers to resign, Banks scrupulously adhered to other guidelines of military decorum in apparent contradiction of his larger strategic aims. For example, in the midst of his purge, he did nothing to block the promotion of two lieutenants, James H. Ingraham and Alfred Bourgeau, found qualified for the rank of captain.[24] Pending the final success of his campaign to oust the officers, Banks supported their demand for equal pay. When General Butler first enlisted the Native Guard regiments, he promised pay, bounties, and other emoluments equal to those received by whites, and it appears that the freemen drew at least one pay on those terms.[25] In a celebrated decision of July 1863, the War

Department ruled that all blacks, regardless of rank, should receive a mere $10 per month.[26] The Native Guard officers protested the new policy to Secretary of War Stanton, describing it as an affront both to their dignity and to Butler's promise of equal pay, and Banks endorsed their petition affirmatively.[27] Even while Banks maneuvered to eliminate the freemen from the officer corps, he apparently considered them entitled to the full benefits of Union officers.

As Banks quietly purged the free black officers, they and their men won unexpected national attention. In May 1863 volunteers from the first and third regiments took part in the ill-conceived assault on Port Hudson, Louisiana, which resulted in the virtual massacre of the Native Guards who spearheaded the attack. One of the colored officers, Captain André Callioux, died in the fighting, and commanders up to General Banks himself praised the gallantry of both officers and men. In the same month, at East Pascagoula, Florida, and Ship Island, Mississippi, officers and men of the second regiment also won the praise of their superiors, with Major Francis E. Dumas achieving special distinction.[28] Black officers hoped that battlefield heroics would demolish all opposition to their service and assure full acceptance into the officer corps. Resigned officers of the third regiment, seeking readmission to the service, posited precisely such a connection when they requested to "be allowed to share the dangers of the battle field and not be Kept for men who will not fight. If the world doubts our fighting give us A chance and we will show them what we can do."[29] Nonetheless, as black soldiers later recruited from among former slaves would find out, valor provided no guarantee of honorable treatment, either within military ranks or among whites in general.

While their struggle for equality in the Union army ground slowly to a halt, the resigned officers broadened their campaign, at first aiming to capture for themselves the privileges of full citizenship previously denied them, and ultimately incorporating the freedmen into the struggle for equal rights. Segregated public transportation facilities offered a clear target. While still in federal uniform, the black officers were repeatedly denied first-class railroad accommodations. The officers resisted such discriminatory treatment and on occasion used their pistols to back their arguments.[30] When expulsion from the army removed the cloak of authority represented by their uniforms and shoulder straps, they helped organize a public campaign against the long-despised, segregated "star cars" and petitioned military authorities to put an end to that hallmark of inferiority. After the war, the agitation spread and eventually succeeded in integrating the New Orleans streetcars for the rest of the nineteenth century.[31] The campaign to integrate the cars represented one prong on the all-out assault on the vestiges of slavery.

Perhaps the most important prong of that attack centered upon the extension of voting privileges to blacks. From antebellum times, free people of color had desired the suffrage, but the particular turn of wartime events gave them an unprecedented opportunity to press their case. In light of the Emancipation Proclamation and the service of blacks in the Union army, the political reorganization of Louisiana in 1863 and 1864 set the stage for broadened political participation. Freemen pressed for the suffrage in mass meetings and in the columns of their newspapers, *L'Union* and the *Tribune,* and persuaded sympathetic white Unionists to support suffrage extension. During months of agitation, they refused to be rebuffed by the cool indifference of General Banks, Lincoln's point man in Louisiana. On the eve of the 1864 state constitutional convention, they circulated a petition demanding that intelligent, free-born blacks have the right to vote. They dispatched two emissaries, John B. Roudanez, brother of the *Tribune*'s owner, and Arnold Bertonneau, a former Native Guard Captain, to Washington. After consulting with Congressional Radicals, the two men included in the petition the demand for universal black suffrage, a clear signal that freemen had begun to view their own political future as inseparable from that of the soon-to-be-liberated slaves. When the delegation returned to New Orleans, the implications of that realization grew.[32]

In January 1865, in the aftermath of the National Convention of Colored Men held in Syracuse the previous October, New Orleans freemen sponsored a state equal rights convention. True to form, the resigned Native Guard officers played a prominent role. Of the eight former officers—all captains—among the hundred-odd delegates, three particularly distinguished themselves: James H. Ingraham, Jordan B. Noble, and Ernest C. Morphy constituted the organizing committee, and each subsequently served as a convention officer. The three-part program for economic, political, and social change called for the removal of all federal restrictions upon the labor contracting process, unrestricted manhood suffrage regardless of color, and an end to all civil distinctions based upon color. The convention marked the first organized bid by blacks who had long enjoyed freedom to join hands in struggle with blacks who had just gained freedom, but the subsequent implementation of the program exposed differences which threatened to keep them apart.[33]

Significant divisions, rooted in different relationships to productive property, provided the most serious obstacle to unity between freemen and freedmen. Whereas, freemen had for years owned land, buildings, tools, merchandise, animals, and even slaves, freedmen had until recently been property and now owned little of productive worth. Property ownership in turn conferred upon the freemen a measure of economic independence denied to many whites as well as to former slaves. In abolishing slavery and nationalizing the free market in labor, the Civil War enabled the freemen to exercise their entrepreneurial talents without the restraints put upon them by the bondage of blacks. At the same time, while the war liberated the slaves, it consigned them to continuing economic dependence as wage laborers or share croppers. These material differences between the free and the freed blacks gave rise to profound social and cultural distinctions that the mere sharing of African ancestry could not bridge.

In some ways the forces unleased by the Civil War helped to narrow the gap between free and freed blacks. For instance, service of several companies of Native Guards in the plantation districts supervising the transition from slavery to freedom forced free colored officers and enlisted men to scrutinize their own biases. Socially, the free black officers frequently had more in common with the loyal planters and plantation lessees than with the freed people working on the plantations. The officers dined at the big houses and, in turn, entertained the leading figures of plantation society. They listened sympathetically as employers described insolence and insubordination on the part of plantation hands and exhorted the freedmen to labor faithfully and industriously. That notwithstanding, black officers saw disturbing signs that the old order had not completely died, and they waged all-out war on whipping and all similar vestiges of slavery. In turn, employers charged the officers with prompting unrest among their hands and demanded removal of the Native Guard from the countryside.[34] The officers strove to supervise the new plantation system with strict impartiality, protecting the rights of both employers and employees, but with the balance of experience and force on the side of the former, the officers often had to take sides openly with the latter. They and the larger free black community faced similar choices in the years that followed, as their African ancestry and their social position drew them in apparently opposite directions.

Just as material circumstances differentiated free and freed blacks, the two groups had different ideological perceptions of federal policies toward the liberated slaves. Most free people viewed the economic problems of the freed people through lenses tinted by their own privileged position before the war. Whereas most freed blacks welcomed federal supervision of plantation labor, the free blacks opposed government interference. To an extent matched by few of their contemporaries in the North or the South, Louisiana's free people of color adhered to the tenets of economic laissez faire. They felt that unrestrained market forces would mediate the transition from slavery to freedom more efficiently than the contrived plans of civil or military officials possibly could. Hence, they sternly criticized the tightly circumscribed and closely supervised labor system devised by General Banks. At a mass meeting held in New Orleans in March 1865, co-chaired by former Captain James H. Ingraham, the freemen stated their case. The key resolution argued "That the right of the employee to freely agree and contract according to his best judgment, with his employer, for the term of labor is the unquestionable attribute of every freeman." Other resolutions called for the removal of all restrictions upon mobility and for the abolition of the army's Bureau of Free Labor, established to safeguard the interests of the former slaves. In response to the resolutions, General Stephen A. Hurlbut stressed the "bitterness of feeling" between those born free and those freed by the war: "You are striving for social equality, they for personal freedom." Hurlbut vigorously defended the army's plan; without it, he argued, freed people would be entirely at the mercy of their former owners.[35]

Hurlbut's characterization served to demonstrate how the economic and social differences dividing the free and the freed black communities had given rise to strong prejudices on both sides. Inasmuch as the free people did not shy away from making their feelings known publicly, even Hurlbut's unsophisticated eye could quickly comprehend the situation. More than once, free blacks attempted to magnify the social distance separating them from slaves in an apparent attempt to close the gap between themselves and whites. Late in 1864, for instance, freemen in Baton Rouge, led by former Native Guard Captain Samuel W. Ringgold, vehemently protested being rounded up and "placed on an equality with contrabands" during a military impressment of laborers to work on the levee. Claiming a respected position on the "social scale" by virtue of their education, their property ownership and their payment of taxes, they demanded to be "treated as freemen."[36] Throughout the war and after, certain freemen preferred to use freedmen as mudsills upon which to erect their own rights rather than as allies in a common struggle for mutual rights.

Countering the forces pulling the two groups apart, a few stalwart free blacks worked to strengthen the alliance between the freeborn and the slaveborn that had tentatively emerged during the closing months of the war. The Bureau of Industry, established by the 1865 Louisiana Equal Rights Convention, investigated conditions on the plantations in an effort to increase freedom of contract and mobility, but it apparently accomplished little. Louis C. Roudanez, influential owner of the *Tribune*, continued to advocate the unity of economic and political interests between free people and freed people throughout Reconstruction, but he fought an uphill battle with steadily decreasing numbers of free black allies.[37] Profoundly different economic interests and circumstances daunted the alliance: the two found common ground in struggling first for the extension of and then for the protection of political and civil rights.

Black manhood suffrage became a reality under the Reconstruction Acts of March 1867, and in the following months Louisiana blacks registered and voted for the first time. As earlier, the former Native Guard officers stepped to the fore, moving quickly into leadership of the fledgling Republican party. In the state's first gubernatorial contest after passage of the Reconstruction Acts, former Major Francis E. Dumas ran for the Republican nomination against Henry Clay Warmoth but lost. In 1872 Dumas ran for secretary of state on the Liberal Republican ticket and again lost. Undaunted by Dumas's setbacks, approximately twenty former Native Guard officers won public office in Louisiana during Reconstruction. The most prominent, P. B. S. Pinchback, served as lieutenant governor and for a short time as acting governor.[38]

In the hothouse atmosphere that characterized Radical Reconstruction, social differences within the free black community eventually assumed political form. The main fault line there fell between free people of Gallic-American and those of Anglo-American ancestry. For the most part, the latter remained faithful to the regular Republican party, where they sought first public office and later party patronage in their quest for economic security. The freemen of French descent, however, displayed less fealty to the regulars and had to live without the crumbs of patronage as a result. Instead, they pursued economic and social security within the French Quarter and cultivated a fierce pride in their Gallic past.[39] In the postwar era, differences in social background crippled the efforts of black Louisianans to establish a unified political movement, dividing free people from former slaves and fragmenting the free community within itself.

As successive Republican administrations, beginning with that of Rutherford B. Hayes, abrogated responsibility for protecting the rights of Southern black voters, the long struggle of New Orleans freemen for equality took on renewed significance. In 1871, for instance, P. B. S. Pinchback threatened to sue the Pullman porter company for denying sleeping berths to blacks who held first-class passenger tickets. In practice, such rights meant little to plantation freedmen who could not afford first-class fares in any event; but in principle, the fight for equal accommodations kept alive the larger struggle for equality. Throughout the rest of Reconstruction, the former free people fought for educational privileges and equal public accommodations and challenged all efforts to curtail the advances they had won.[40] In the post-Reconstruction years, when Democrats assaulted the advances in civil and political rights, Louisiana blacks tried to resist the onslaught, but in the face of new political realities, most of the earlier fire was gone.

In 1890 Louisiana legislators enacted bills to deprive blacks of equal accommodations on railroads and other public conveyances, and the fateful final episode in the freemen's struggle for equal rights began. Sparked by the new laws, the handful of surviving former officers organized immediate opposition. Pinchback and James Lewis, joined by blacks from around the country and a handful of whites like the renowned carpetbagger Albion W. Tourgée, organized the American Citizens' Equal Rights Association. In conjunction with the ad hoc Citizens' Committee to Test the Constitutionality of the Separate Car Law, the association sponsored a series of lawsuits against the railroads, which eventually led to the landmark 1896 Supreme Court case of *Plessy v. Ferguson.*[41] The court's adverse decision marked the end of the Civil War era and the beginning of the era of segregation. And it paralyzed the free black community. In 1906 the star cars reappeared.

The free blacks of New Orleans attempted to use military service to gain full admission into free society. When that effort failed, they shifted tactics, pressing for full citizenship rights in society at large and joining forces with the newly emancipated slaves in a common struggle for economic, political, and civil rights. The alliance of groups with such vastly different social backgrounds and historical experiences proved fragile, and the partners quickly drifted apart. While freed people fought for the economic and political fruits of freedom, free people concentrated on civil equality. During the early postwar years, when both groups enjoyed some success, the partnership held hope of lasting. When Reconstruction ended, and many of freedom's achievements fell victim to Democratic assault, the allies separated again. Freed people on the plantations struggled to free themselves from share cropping's close confines, and the former free people struggled to maintain equal public services and accommodations. By the end of the nineteenth century, neither struggle held much promise of success.

Most of the Native Guard officers did not live to see Reconstruction's dénouement in the Plessy case. Perhaps it is just as well. Some of the veterans may well have contemplated a return to arms rather than wait indefinitely for Congress to complete the unfinished business of the Civil War era.

CHAPTER 10

<del>━━⊶⊷⊶━━</del>

A Brothers' Fight for Freedom

Harold T. Pinkett

THE CIVIL WAR IN the Upper South sometimes has been characterized as a "brothers' war."[1] In this region kinsmen frequently
enlisted and fought in opposing military units for the Union and the
Confederacy. The conflict also has been called a brothers' war in another
sense. It brought about the creation of military organizations, north and
south, in which brothers and other relatives served side by side.[2] In this
sense the characterization of the conflict as a brothers' fight had special
meaning for thousands of African-American kinsmen who fought for
Union and freedom.

This article sketches the story of how four brothers—Sandy, Stephen,
Adam, and Wilson Pinkett—of an African-American family in Somerset
County, Maryland, won freedom from slavery by joining and serving in
the Union army. Their objectives and experiences were probably typical of
many African-American brothers in the Civil War. Their own regiments
included many men who had the same family names and were recruited in
the same locality at the same or nearly same dates and thus were probably
brothers or other kinsmen.

The Pinkett brothers were born between the years 1833 and 1843,
apparently on the farm of William Records Byrd in an area of Somerset
County then know as the Upper District and later as the Salisbury District.
The area was a few miles west of the town of Salisbury. Byrd was a descendant of colonial settlers who had lived in the same community when it was

known as Rewastico. His great-grandfather, grandfather, and father—William, Jesse, and Thomas Byrd—were owners of land and slaves that were partly inherited by him.

The father of the Pinkett brothers was Denard Pinkett, son of Jacob and Anne Pinkett, free African Americans, lived in the Upper District of Somerset County as early as 1820 and probably had obtained free status during or shortly after the American Revolution. During the 1830s Denard was employed as a free laborer on the Byrd farm. There he became a member of the household and the husband of Byrd's slave named Mary. From this union were born twelve children, including four brothers who enlisted in the Union army. As children of a slave mother they were slaves under Maryland law.

Sandy, Stephen, Adam, and Wilson Pinkett doubtless worked with their father, Denard, in various tasks on Byrd's property. These tasks included the cultivating of corn, wheat, and potatoes, and the care of livestock. They also entailed wood chopping and probably work in Byrd's grist- and sawmills located on Rockawalking Creek, a tributary of the Wicomico River. The family remained together until Byrd's death in 1855, after which Denard's wife and children became the property of their late owners' two sons, William J. Byrd and George Byrd, and daughter, Elizabeth A. Byrd. Sandy and Wilson became slaves of George. Stephen and Adam were bequeathed to William. Denard eventually became a laborer on the farm of Josephus Humphries in the Quantico District of Somerset County.

The division of the Pinkett family served as a reminder of how harsh slavery could be to family relations, and it doubtless strengthened the slaves' desire for freedom. William J. Byrd, a lawyer, lived in the Princess Anne District of Somerset County and had extensive legal practice in partnership with John W. Crisfield, a former Eastern Shore congressman. He apparently did not have a great need for the labor of his slaves and, accordingly, hired them to other persons. George Byrd inherited his father's mills near Salisbury and seems to have had surplus slave labor that he made available for hire. Slaves of Elizabeth A. Byrd may also have been offered for hire. Whatever limited independence from their owners this hiring practice might have given the Pinkett brothers, it probably was overshadowed by the disruption of family ties. "Only the caprice of owners and hirers determined how often family members could see one another—unless they ventured to do so without permission," Barbara Jeanne Fields has observed convincingly. "A limited term of hire provided no automatic guarantee that the following term would place an individual any closer to family and friends."[3] The division of the Pinkett family continued after 1860, when William J. Byrd died and his widow, Adeline H. Byrd, inherited the slaves.

Mrs. Byrd soon had reason to worry about the security of this peculiar property, for the war to preserve the Union evolved into a crusade against slavery. Owners of the Pinkett family, like other slaveholders in the state, dreaded the Union government's demand for increased manpower. As early as June 1863 the War Department authorized Col. William Birney, son of the abolitionist politician James G. Birney, to recruit free blacks in Maryland. Activities began in Baltimore and soon extended to the entire state. Some of Birney's agents in their zeal began to sign slaves, without specific authority, as well as free blacks. By the beginning of October 1863 news of this development had reached slaves on the Eastern Shore, and many of them did not hesitate to flee from their owners to enlist in the army. On 21 October Stephen Pinkett (aged 24) enlisted for three years and was enrolled in Company G, 7th Regiment Infantry, U.S. Colored Troops.

Meanwhile, in deference to the concerns of Unionist slaveholders in Maryland, President Lincoln for a few weeks ordered suspension of all black enlistments in the state, pending negotiations with Governor Augustus W. Bradford. At the end of October 1863, Lincoln approved implementation of War Department General Order No. 329, which authorized the Bureau of Colored Troops to establish recruiting stations in Maryland, Missouri, and Tennessee, where free blacks and slaves, with their masters' consent, could be enlisted. If county quotas were not filled in thirty days, slaves could be enlisted without their masters' consent. Loyal masters whose slaves were recruited or who consented to their recruitment could receive as much as $300 in compensation upon filing a deed of manumission. The order declared that "all persons enlisted into the military service shall forever thereafter be free."

General Order 329 led to the establishment of an army recruiting station near Salisbury. The station's existence and purpose soon became known to Sandy, Adam, and Wilson Pinkett, because within a month of its establishment, on 22 November, they fled from their owners and joined the Union army. They apparently acted without the consent of their pro-Southern owners; Adam's enlistment record referred to his owner's being a "strong rebel." The brothers' determination to enlist doubtless was increased by Stephen's flight and enlistment one month earlier. Sandy, Adam, and Wilson were enrolled in companies of the 9th Regiment Infantry, U.S. Colored Troops. Other African-American family members, recruited largely on the Eastern Shore, were also to be found in these ranks. The fact that many of these persons possessed the same family names and enlisted at the same time and in the same locality strongly suggests that they were brothers or other close kinsmen (see table 1).[4]

All four of the Pinkett brothers began their army service at Camp Stanton in Charles County, near the village of Benedict and the Patuxent River.[5] There they received instruction in military regulations and discipline and engaged in rigorous drilling in preparation for field duty. They also received some rudimentary training in reading and writing.[6] Unhealthy conditions at the camp caused the brothers much physical suffering. They slept in cold shelters built of timber plastered with mud that had to be replaced after each rain. During the latter part of November they suffered an epidemic of measles and later a siege of congestive chills. For several days in December 1863 and January 1864 Adam received treatment in the camp hospital and Sandy was "sick in quarters." During December eight members of Adam's company died from congestive chills and twenty-three (approximately one-fourth of the company) received hospitalization. Many men of Stephen's regiment perished from sickness during their winter encampment at Benedict.

The 7th and 9th regiments departed from Camp Stanton in early March 1864. Both units traveled by steamship to Hilton Head Island, South Carolina, which Union troops then held as a base for attacks on Confederate coastal areas. The 9th Regiment remained in South Carolina until August 1864, during which time it performed guard duty at Union staff headquarters at Beaufort and engaged in skirmishes with Confederate troops on John's Island.

En route to South Carolina the 7th Regiment was diverted briefly to Portsmouth, Virginia, to assist in protecting Union lines against menacing Confederate forces, who then occupied nearby Suffolk. Maj. Gen. Benjamin F. Butler, commander of Union troops in eastern Virginia, in a letter read to the regiment at dress parade on 31 March 1864, commended this assistance. Soon thereafter the early military conduct of both the 7th and 9th regiments won praise from Gen. William Birney, who had supervised their recruitment and had become their field commander. Birney declared: "My Seventh and Ninth Regiments are very much admired in this department [of the South]. I am proud of having raised two such fine bodies of men."[7]

Meanwhile, on 13 March, the 7th Regiment had received orders to proceed by ship to Jacksonville, Florida, where it was to join several Union regiments engaged in efforts to weaken Confederate positions in Florida. Less than a month earlier Confederate forces had won an engagement at the village of Olustee near Jacksonville. Stephen's first major combat experience probably came in the Jacksonville area on 6 May 1864, when Confederate cavalry attacked outposts of his regiment and were speedily repulsed. Later in May his regiment had an important

Table 1

Brothers and Other Kinsmen in the 9th Regiment Infantry U.S. Colored Troops 1863

Company G:

Franklin Chew	Charles H. Hargus	Dennard Northern
William H. Chew	Henry Hargus	Raymond Northern
	Peter Hargus	
Henry Dennis	Shepard Hargus	John J. Purnell
Littleton O. Dennis		Levin Purnell
	Spencer Laws	Lewis Purnell
Daniel Fossett	Stephen Laws	Saco Purnell
Frederick Fossett		Sevron Purnell
Handy Fossett	Benjamin Massey	
	Joseph Massey	
	William Massey	

Company H:

Arthur Bailey	James Jacobs	Henry Wood
James Bailey	Peter Jacobs	John J. Wood
Charles Davis	Richard Morris	Daniel Wright
John W. Davis	Samuel J. Morris	James H. Wright
	George Somerville	
	John Somerville	

Company I:

Nathan Cottman	Alfred Dashiell	Elsey Pullett
Robert Cottman	James W. Dashiell	John Pullet
Samuel Cottman	John Dashiell	Joseph Pullet
	Joseph Dashiell	
John Steward		
Noah H. Steward		
Sandy Steward		

role in skirmishes with the enemy at Cedar Creek. The disciplined men and energy of the regiment impressed the Union's Florida military commander, Gen. George H. Gordon, who called the 7th "the best colored regiment in the service of the United States."[8]

On 27 June 1864 the 7th Regiment sailed to Hilton Head, South Carolina, to participate in a Union army expedition to the North Edisto River, John's Island, and James Island. The 9th Regiment, which had been in South Carolina several months, joined the expedition. This development placed the four Pinkett brothers in the same theater of action for several

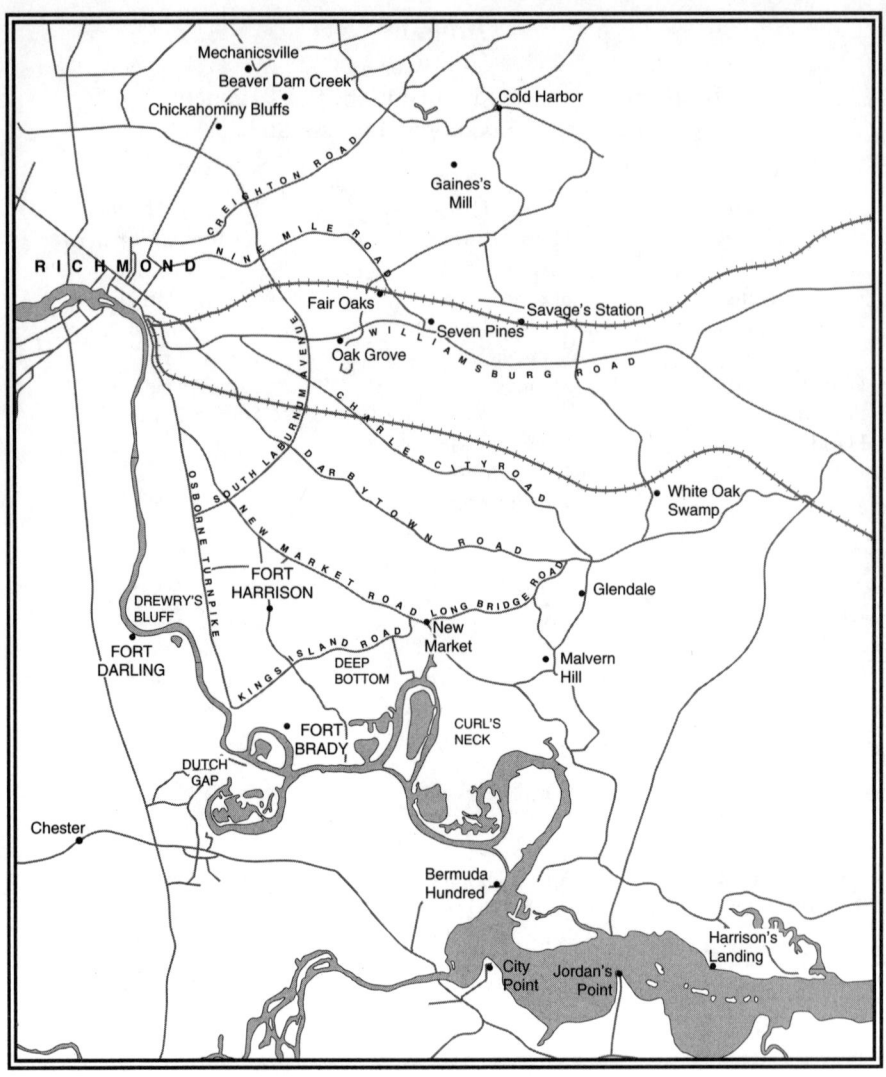

The military-operation sites of the Pinkett brothers' regiments during the Union
campaign against Richmond, Virginia, 1864–1865.

days. Union troops sought to capture a Confederate fortification in the
Charleston area near White Point. Men of the 7th, 9th, and other Union
regiments fought valiantly but were held off by superior enemy artillery
fire. In an attack on 3 July 1864 Stephen received a gunshot wound in his
abdomen, for which he was hospitalized at Beaufort for one month. The
attack continued for several days. On 9 July the 7th Regiment rescued the

veteran 104th Pennsylvania Infantry, a white regiment, which had run out of ammunition. As the black men advanced, the Pennsylvanians broke before a strong Confederate assault and fled through the 7th's line. Lt. Joseph M. Califf reported the bravery and discipline of the black soldiers of his regiment: "It was a position to have tried veterans, but our men, for the first time under fire of a line of battle, moved steadily forward . . . in perfect order and without firing a shot until the order was given."[9]

Stephen returned to duty in South Carolina shortly before his regiment transferred to Virginia. There his wound required further treatment in army hospitals at Fort Monroe and City Point. His transfer to Virginia in August 1864 coincided with that of his brothers in the 9th Regiment. By that time the Pinketts, like thousands of other black soldiers, were assembling in Virginia for the Union's final struggle against Confederate forces. The 7th and the 9th Regiments were transferred to Bermuda Hundred on the James River, a base for Gen. Ulysses S. Grant's campaign against Richmond. There they became a part of the Colored Brigade, 3rd Division, 10th Army Corps, and immediately began to take an active part in the Union operations of the Richmond-Petersburg area.

In a strategy designed to test a part of the defense of Richmond, the 7th and the 9th Regiments with other army units crossed the James River at Deep Bottom on 13 August 1864. The next day they charged through a cornfield under heavy fire and captured a line of Confederate rifle pits. Two days later the regiments advanced under continued heavy fire in an attack on breastworks, a stronger line of enemy defense. In this encounter they were forced to withdraw after a strong rally by enemy reinforcements. Thomas Morris Chester, black Civil War correspondent of the Philadelphia *Press,* described the gallantry of their withdrawal: "The colored troops were last to retire, which they did with unwavering firmness and in obedience to orders, not, however, before they gave three cheers, which evinced their dauntless spirit."[10]

In this encounter at Deep Bottom, Sandy, Adam, and Wilson probably engaged in the most severe fighting of their war experience. Union casualties were thirteen men killed, ninety-one wounded, and forty-four missing. Wilson was among the men wounded in action. He received a gunshot wound to his left ankle which disabled him for the remainder of the war.

After Deep Bottom the next major military experience of the Pinkett brothers came on 29 September 1864, in the Union Army's ill-fated attack on Fort Gilmer a few miles south of Richmond. At that time battle injuries precluded participation of Stephen and Wilson, although the former's 7th Regiment engaged strongly in the attack. Sandy and Adam, however, were present for duty and apparently participated in their 9th Regiment's costly storming of a strongly defended Confederate fortification. Lieutenant Califf of the 7th, calling 29 September "the most unfortunate day in the history of the regiment," stated critically:

> First, the Ninth was sent unsupported to charge a work . . . across an open field where its line was enfiladed by the enemy's fire, and was repulsed; then four companies of the Eighth, as skirmishers, were sent against the same work, with no better success, and after this bitter experience, four companies of the Seventh were sent to their destruction on an errand equally hopeless. Had the [Colored] brigade been sent in together, instead of its three regiments in detail, the rebel line would have been carried and the road to Richmond opened to us.[11]

During most of the autumn of 1864 the Pinkett brothers engaged in several military operations north of the James River that General Grant planned in his long siege of Richmond. Among these operations were encounters with Confederate forces at New Market Heights, 28–30 September; Darbytown Road, 13 October; and Fair Oaks, 27–28 October. They also spent much time laboring in trench construction, helping to hold Union lines in rifle pits, and performing picket duty and reconnaissance. In November Stephen returned to duty from the hospital and Sandy was promoted from private to corporal, a significant accomplishment for a soldier who had been a slave one year earlier. The brothers probably had their most exciting and memorable experience of the year when, on 1 November, General Birney informed them of Maryland's adoption of the constitutional amendment abolishing slavery. Their mother, sisters, and brothers were no longer slaves.

The brothers' fight for freedom continued to be linked on 1 December 1865, when their regiments and other black military units were consolidated to form the 25th Army Corps, representing the largest concentration of black troops during the war. Soon after this reorganization a lull developed in Grant's siege of Richmond and the 7th and 9th Regiments went into winter quarters at Fort Harrison (then called Burnham), the Union Army's strongest position in the Richmond vicinity. Lieutenant Califf vividly described the experience of the regiments at Fort Harrison:

> When the weather permitted, we had battalion or brigade, and occasionally, division drill. Snow fell frequently and we had much cold weather. We turned out each morning an hour before daylight and stood to our arms until it was so light that an attack from the enemy was improbable, and then went to our quarters.[12]

Philadelphia Press correspondent Thomas Morris Chester reported the severe wintry experience of the regiments:

> Soldiers gathered around their fires, in their quarters, communing with the absent loved ones, while the ever watchful and faithful sentries upon their beats covered over with ice, were the only persons stirring about the camp. The pickets, standing at their post, looked like men who had been glaciated.[13]

The spirits of the Union regiments in Virginia, however, were lifted as the weather became warmer during March 1865 and reinforcements arrived for the coming fight for Richmond. On 19 March 1865 General Grant and Secretary of War Edwin M. Stanton reviewed the 25th Corps. A week later President Lincoln did the same. Chester made this observation of the presidential review: "Both white and colored troops looked well, and, if possible, marched better than on former occasions. It was a grand sight, and must have been a source of considerable satisfaction to his Excellency."[14]

A few hours after the president's visit black troops received orders to move as Grant began his attack on Lee's lines at Petersburg. Stephen's 7th Regiment marched south to cross the James and Appomattox rivers and the Weldon Railroad and reach a position west of Petersburg near Hatcher's Run. After a terrific cannonade against all Confederate lines from Richmond to the south of Petersburg, the 7th Regiment on 2 April received an order to advance on Petersburg. It pressed forward eagerly but eventually found that the city's principal fortifications had been abandoned. Lieutenant Califf described this effort and one of the war's greatest triumphs:

> Pushing ahead the regiment was the first to reach the centre of the city, where it was joined a few moments later by troops that had entered from the other side. The stronghold that had baffled us so long, for whose capture so much blood had been poured out, was ours at last. Petersburg had fallen![15]

Meantime, under the command of Gen. Godfrey Weitzel, Sandy and Adam on 3 April advanced beyond Fort Harrison toward Richmond, which the Confederate government had already begun to evacuate after the loss of Petersburg. Weitzel's troops advanced along the Osborne Turnpike, entered Main Street, and proceeded to Capitol Square to take formal possession of the city. The Pinkett brothers participated in one of the ironies of American history: the first forces to enter the Confederate capital following its evacuation were black. Although other Union troops jostled for the distinction, it went to the black 5th Massachusetts Cavalry, followed by elements of the all-black 25th Corps. Men earlier denied an opportunity to serve their country found themselves in the vanguard of forces that had helped to save it and expand its freedom.[16]

While Sandy and Adam were participating in the military occupation of Richmond and later Petersburg, Stephen was pursuing remnants of the Confederate Army of Northern Virginia. The route taken by the 7th Regiment led through Burkeville and Farmville and across the Appomattox River. The troops covered nearly one hundred miles in three and one-half days, reportedly "without a single straggler" and were praised by Gen. Edward O. C. Ord, commander of the Department of Virginia. Arriving within four miles of Appomattox Court House on 9 April 1865, the regiment heard reports of General Lee's surrender and shortly thereafter joined the victorious Army of the Potomac at Appomattox. Reporting from Petersburg on 19 April 1865, the day after the 7th Regiment returned there from Appomattox Court House, Chester of Philadelphia *Press* praised the regiment and other units of the 25th Corps for participating in what he called the "vigorous campaign which has crowned the Army of the Potomac with immortal glory."[17]

The euphoria experienced by the Pinkett brothers and other black soldiers over the surrender of Lee's army and the end of the war was quickly diminished by the news of Lincoln's assassination. The news reached Stephen's regiment in Petersburg on 16 April and was reported to have fallen on the regiment "like a thunderbolt from a clear sky." The men felt that it was "a personal as well as a national misfortune."[18] Hence it doubtless seemed fitting to them that the first camp they helped build after the assassination was named Camp Lincoln. Situated at City Point (now a part of Hopewell, Virginia) at the confluence of the Appomattox and James rivers, this camp became the installation to which the Pinkett brothers' regiments were assigned during their final military service in Virginia. Here on 21 May 1865 Stephen received a promotion to the rank of corporal.

The Union triumph in 1865 ensured the freedom for which the Pinkett brothers had been fighting, but it did not immediately relieve them of the obligation they had assumed when they enlisted for three years of military service. Accordingly, less than two months after the fall of the Confederacy, they along with the rest of the 25th Corps were sent to the Texas border as a show of force against the French-supported regime of the Emperor Maximillian in Mexico. The U.S. Army's commanding officer in the Richmond-Petersburg area, Gen. Henry W. Halleck, supported this assignment because he and other army officers wished to eliminate white protests against the use of black troops in the occupation of former strongholds of the defeated Confederacy.[19]

Stephen's 7th Regiment sailed on 24 May 1865 and, after a long, tedious voyage with stops at Mobile Bay and the mouth of the Mississippi River, arrived at Indianola, Texas, on 23 June. Sandy's and Wilson's 9th Regiment embarked at City Point on 7 June 1865 and reached Brazos Santiago, Texas, on 1 July. Fortunately, the French threat in Mexico subsided, leaving U.S. Troops in Texas with the duties of military occupation. The Pinkett brothers' regiments stood provost-guard, built and maintained military installations, and handled sequestered Confederate property. The 7th Regiment saw service at Indianola, Matagorda, Lavoca, and Victoria; the 9th served at Brownsville and Brazos Santiago. There was time for some elementary education, from which the Pinketts benefited. Adam's promotion to corporal on 22 September 1866 was probably aided by this instruction, for he and Stephen learned to read and write during their enlistments.

Service in Texas, however, was not free from trouble. In the summer of 1865, a shortage of fruits and vegetables in army rations led to a massive outbreak of scurvy among the troops, estimated by a medical officer to have affected 60 percent of the 25th Corps. Adam was hospitalized with the disease in September 1865 and again in March of 1866. An epidemic of cholera spread to Stephen's regiment at Indianola during the summer of 1866. Lieutenant Califf reported: "It was hard to see men who had safely passed through the dangers of three years of service, and were on the eve of returning to their homes and friends, stricken down without a moment's warning, and dying in a few hours."[20]

In late 1866 the end of the Pinkett brothers' enlistments was in sight. By the middle of October they had left Texas with their regiments en route to Baltimore. At Fort Federal Hill on 15 November Stephen was mustered out. Eleven days later, Sandy and Adam followed. As they journeyed home to rejoin their relatives on the Eastern Shore, they doubtless remembered their regiments' casualties: 130 men had been killed in action or died from wounds, and 570 more had perished from disease. But, in addition to their survival, the Pinketts had much to be thankful for. They had begun the Civil War as slaves and emerged as freedmen, noncommissioned officers in the army of their country. More importantly, their contributions to the preservation of the Union helped to establish a firm basis for the claims of their race to the benefits of American citizenship.

CHAPTER 11

Negro Troop Activity in Indian Territory, 1863–1865

Lary C. Rampp

A
T NOON, JULY 1, 1863, THE long column of black infantry was
halted. Their white commander, Union Colonel James M.
Williams, broke away from the main body of resting troops and moved
his horse ahead to meet his two returning scouts. He was informed that
the opposite bank of the nearby Cabin Creek was held by Confederate
troops of an undetermined, but large number. The Confederate enemy
soldiers were so positioned as to command the ford and the fortified
encampment located there. Colonel Williams wheeled his mount around
and returned to his command where he ordered the regiment to fall in
back on the Texas Road.[1]

Major John A. Foreman, commanding officer of the Third Indian
Home Guard Regiment, had already moved forward through the parallel
woods and pastures to make contact with the entrenched Confederates at
Cabin Creek. When he came within sight of the banks of Cabin Creek,
Confederate pickets began to harass his line with scattered musket fire.
One company of the Third Indian Home Guard Regiment surged forward into a forward protective line of skirmishers and engaged the enemy
pickets, killing three and capturing three more. Being overrun by the
pressing Union skirmish line, the remaining Confederate pickets retired
across the creek and merged with the main Confederate troops.[2]

Union horse artillery was ordered to deliver a covering fire while a
depth sounding was taken of the rain-swollen creek. Finding it too high

for fording by his colored infantry, Colonel Williams posted a heavy line of pickets along the creek banks and moved back out of range to organize the attack for the morrow. The wagon train was posted two miles back from the ford and secured in a temporary park on an open prairie. Holding conference with this staff, Colonel Williams laid out his plan of attack: The Union flanks would be secured by detached portions of the attached Indian Battalion. The ten companies of the First Kansas Colored Volunteers Infantry Regiment were to make up the main attack force, along with parts of the Third Indian Home Guard Regiment and a battalion of Second Colorado Infantry Regiment.[3]

At dawn the troops were roused from a fitful sleep and moved anxiously into their assigned combat positions. By eight o'clock that morning the troop placements had been made ready. Colonel Williams, locating himself at a vantage point in the center of the line behind his black regiment, ordered the artillery on the wings to commence firing. For forty minutes the Second Kansas Artillery Battery poured solid shot and shell upon the entrenched Confederates across Cabin Creek. Believing that the cannonade had driven the enemy from their placements, Williams ordered Major Foreman forward with one company of the Third Indian Home Guard Regiment. Major Foreman rose to his feet, saber in hand, and yelled for his men to charge. As one unit, the entire company quickly moved to the banks of Cabin Creek. Meeting no serious defensive fire from the opposite shore, the Indian company negotiated the steep bank and moved into the deep water. By holding their weapons and ammunition above their heads, these articles were kept operative and dry. As the attack force from the Third Indian Home Guard Regiment neared the enemy shore, concealed Confederates began to pour a merciless fire upon them. On a horse, Major Foreman was a prime target. He was one of the first to be hit. After five musket balls had hit his mount, two balls found Major Foreman, pitching him violently into the water. Seeing their gallant major taken from the fighting, the Indian troop quickly lost all heart for combat and began a confused withdrawal back across Cabin Creek.

Colonel Williams immediately ordered forward reinforcements. The First Kansas Colored Volunteers Infantry Regiment, waiting a short distance back from the creek, rushed to the edge of the bank and began a covering fire, trying to mask the fire of the Confederate musketry. Three companies of the colored troops were maneuvered to the right of the Union center and there began to lay down a permanent blanket of covering fire for the second attack column. The Federal artillery also began tearing away at suspected Southern positions in an effort to dislodge them from the far bank. Colonel Williams ordered the artillery to cease firing and instructed the company officers to take their commands across the creek.

Before the din of the artillery pieces had completely stilled, the black troops began moving down the banks of Cabin Creek and into the murky waters. All of these black companies were plunging on across the creek trying to be the first unit to get ashore on the far side. Confederate musket fire began to tear small holes in the immersed double blue line when the three reserve black units returned the enemy fire and completely masked it. Climbing up the slippery banks the colored units quickly realigned and began moving forward in regimental front.

Cavalry rushed across the creek and took up a position on the right flank of the long Union line. Another mounted unit, commanded by Lieutenant Philbrick, moved through the advancing colored infantry, assembled into a heavy skirmish line and with a yell of command and encouragement charged the Confederate secondary entrenchment across the prairie, pistols blazing, sabers held high. The weight of the cavalry attack, along with the heavy infantry musket fire of the black soldiers was too much for the Confederate line to bear. It fell apart and Southern troops ran for their lives, oblivious to their officers' entreaties to stand and fight.

Seeing the Confederate line put to flight, Colonel Williams stopped the infantry pursuit and ordered forward his reserves of cavalry to continue the chase. Despite the heavy firing on both sides only fifty-one soldiers were killed and seventy wounded. Of these figures, one killed and twenty wounded belonged to the Union casualty list. Putting his column into line and returning to his parked wagon train, Colonel Williams pushed on to Fort Gibson, his mission being accomplished.[4]

Ever since the first gun sounded the beginning of the Civil War, interested people north and south of the Mason-Dixon Line continually asked about the role the Negro was to play in the war. The Negro, in general, was individually quick to catch the war fervor. Upon learning of the massacre of Sixth Massachusetts Volunteers in the streets of Baltimore, Maryland, April 19, 1861, a large group of Negroes rented a public hall in which they practiced drill and manual of arms hoping to thereafter enlist.

President Abraham Lincoln in 1861 was very reluctant to use Negroes as troops. His hesitance was due to the fear of alienating the border states. Lincoln's Secretary of War, Simon Cameron, actively advocated the use of Negro troops but, because of his ineffectiveness as a cabinet member, was removed before he could lay any groundwork on enrolling Negro regiments.[5] Major General David Hunter, Commander of the Department of the South, was the first military man to take any direct action in the recruitment of Negroes. On May 9, 1862, General Hunter called together his staff and issued orders that all able-bodied Negro males capable of bearing arms were to be sent, under guard, to departmental headquarters. Hunter formed these men into the First South Carolina Colored Volunteers Regiment; but, due to political pressure and lack of Federal recognition for the black regiment by the government, it was disbanded in August, 1862. Though not sanctioned officially, the First South Carolina Volunteers Regiment was the first actual recruitment and arming of Negro men.[6]

Activity for Negro recruitment was present in the trans-Mississippi area as well as in the Department of the South. The pro-Union state of Kansas did not lag behind in the recruiting of Negroes for military purposes. A discussion of the military uses of the Negro would not be complete without a mention of James Henry Lane. Lane, a United States Senatorial candidate representing Kansas, was elected in 1861. Speaking in Fort Leavenworth, Kansas, early in 1862, Lane said, "I do say that it would not pain me to see a Negro handling a gun and I believe the Negro may just as well become food for powder as my son."[7]

Actual recruitment of colored men in Kansas began on July 22, 1862. It was on this date that Lane was designated recruiting agent in the Union Department of Kansas. Because his commission did not mention the particular race to be recruited in the enrollment of enlistees for United States infantry regiments, Senator Lane signed up colored as well as white recruits. The actual enrollment of Negroes into the army brought forth many objections: Sympathizers for the rebellion feared the addition of the Negro manpower to the reserves of the United States. Some just disliked the race as a whole. Making the Negro a soldier gave him undeserved social stature and a few believed that enrollment in the army would not be in the best interest of the Negro. Still others were present who believed that the Negro did not have the necessary qualifications to make a courageous and efficient soldier.[8]

Colonel Williams was placed in charge of raising the first regiment of colored troops. He was hampered at every opportunity by resentful civilians. His recruits were arrested and jailed on fraudulent charges by county officials, and the white officers of the proposed regiment were harassed with trumped-up charges, such as unlawfully depriving a person of his freedom.[9]

By January 13, 1863, the Kansas First Colored Volunteers Infantry Regiment, as the colored unit was called, was ready to be mustered in, comprising six of the ten companies necessary to make up an infantry regiment. By May 2, 1863, the remaining four companies were filled and mustered in, filling the regiment completely.[10] Before the new companies had time to pitch tents alongside their sister companies, the commanding general of the Kansas department, Major General James G. Blunt, ordered the entire colored command to report to Baxter Springs located in southeastern Kansas. Baxter Springs was less than a day's ride from Indian Territory.

Colonel Williams was to open up a permanent line of communication with the outermost Federal post in Indian Territory, Fort Gibson. Being so close to Indian Territory, it is doubtless that many Negro scouting patrols weaved back and forth across the Kansas and Indian Territory border. The regiment of colored soldiers occupied the Baxter Springs fortification and vicinity until June 26, 1863. On this date instructions were received from departmental headquarters stating that the Kansas First Colored Volunteers Infantry Regiment would form part of an escort to a very important supply and provisions wagon train. Because of the rough topographical features in eastern Indian Territory the only dependable route of supply to Fort Gibson and the Union garrison stationed there was the Texas Road.[11] The post and troops stationed at Baxter Springs testified to the value of the dusty artery. On June 26, 1863, the Kansas First Colored Volunteers Infantry Regiment was joined by Major Foreman and his reinforced Union Indian Brigade. Forming his column into line and throwing out flankers Colonel Williams, the commander of the train by seniority of rank, ordered the train and cavalry escort southward. The wagon train and escort was spread over a two-mile stretch of the Texas Road. Sometimes on rough portions of the Texas Road, the length of the train extended up to three miles. The infantry would stretch along both sides of the road and keep a watch for Confederate snipers. The cavalry scoured the point, both flanks and rear for signs of enemy troop movements. The train entered Indian Territory on the night of June 30 or early morning of July 1. All was quiet for the Union train until midday July 2. Major Foreman, commander of the point and reinforced vanguard, sent back a message to Colonel Williams who was riding with the main body that a Confederate force of an undetermined number had been encountered on the south bank of Cabin Creek. The skirmishing of Foreman's point resulted in three Confederates dead and a like number captured; no Union soldiers were killed or wounded.[12]

Receiving word of the encounter, Colonel Williams moved forward with a twelve-pound field howitzer. This gun joined the lighter artillery of Foreman's Brigade and together they began to prove the opposite bank of Cabin Creek for Confederate emplacements and trenches. Solid

shot and salvos of canister forced the Confederates to call in their skirmishers and consolidate their fortifications leaving the Federal colored
troops in command of the north bank of Cabin Creek and the surrounding woods. After making reconnaissance of the creek and discovering it
to be too deep for his infantry force to ford, Colonel Williams decided to
hold off on an immediate attack and ordered his colored regiment into
camp a safe distance from the Confederate fire. The attack was scheduled
to begin at dawn. The black regiment posted a strong security on the
banks of Cabin Creek and then retired back from the bank and set up
camp. While his colored troops were preparing for the next morning's
fight, Colonel Williams ordered the bugler to sound an officer's call as he
planned that evening a war council.

Colonel Williams outlined his plan to his staff and line officers as thus:
Lieutenant Colonel L. H. Dodd, commander of the original wagon train
escort, would remain in that position and remove his wagons to a point
two miles to the rear of the Cabin Creek ford. The prairie located there
would offer enough space to corral the entire train; a minimum guard
escort would accompany Lieutenant Colonel Dodd. The artillery sections
would be positioned on both flanks of the enemy not more than two hundred yards from their entrenchments. Two six-pounder cannons would be
located on the left flank, one twelve-pound howitzer and one mountain
howitzer would hold down the right flank. These artillery pieces would lay
down a cover of fire while the Kansas First Colored Volunteers Infantry
Regiment, supported by Foreman's Union Indian Brigade troops, made
an attempt to force a crossing, having the intention of routing the Confederate soldiers located there. Following this general operation order,
Colonel Williams issued his attack order: Major Foreman and one company of his Indian Home Guards Regiment would lead the attack; Lieutenant Colonel John Bowles would lead the ten companies of the Kansas
First Colored Volunteers Infantry Regiment; behind Lieutenant Colonel
Bowles would be one battalion of the Second Colorado Infantry Regiment, commanded by Major J. Nelson Smith. In reserve and guarding the
Union flanks would be the three companies of Wisconsin and Kansas cav-
alry; included in this reserve was the remainder of Major Foreman's Indian
Brigade, having the secondary mission of being infantry flank guards.[13]

On July 2, 1863, the Negro and Indian soldiers broke camp and by
daylight, the long swaying columns were marching to their assigned positions. The Confederate troops across the creek were greeted at dawn with
an alarming sight. Cannons, caissons, and outriders were surging back and
forth along the rear of the forming Union battle line with reckless abandon. From the dense woods near the creek emerged a long column of col-

ored soldiers. On reaching the designated position for the infantry line to begin the attack, Lieutenant Colonel Bowles stood up in his saddle, saber aloft, shouting orders and giving instructions. Like the ribs of a mammoth fan, the columns of infantry separated from the main body, stopping with the completion of the double rank formation, of linear tactics used by Civil War infantry units. Mounted officers rode up and down the lines, filling gaps, offering encouragement, and straightening the battle formation where necessary. By eight o'clock that morning all was ready. With a deafening roar the Union artillery on the flanks began to lay down heavy covering fire. For forty minutes the artillery barrage barked at the Confederate ditches; both solid shot and infantry-killing canister hurtled toward the Confederate positions. Colonel Williams ordered soundings taken of the creek; upon satisfactory reports that the creek had fallen sufficiently to allow fording, he prepared to attack. After a last-minute conference with his staff, he ordered these officers to post. The attack was about to begin. The colored soldiers knelt in position waiting for the word to move forward, involuntarily flinching with each artillery report. There was neither fear nor demoralization in these black troops since they had been bloodied in Kansas and they were prepared to die for the Union.[14]

Colonel Williams ordered the artillery to cease-firing and instructed Major Foreman to move on the Confederate positions. Company officers carried these orders to the men in the ranks. As one entity the Indian units rose to their feet and rushed forward, yelling and screaming. Jumping into the chest-high waters, these soldiers fighting the sharp current crossed the creek. Holding guns and ammunition above their heads, the Indian troops kept these invaluable supplies dry and usable. As the Northern Indian forces neared the opposite shore, concealed Confederate Indian troops opened up on the vulnerable Union Indian Brigade. Major Foreman was shot twice by musketry, and his horse receiving five wounds was shot out from under him. The fall of their commander was too much for the Indian company to bear; they began a perfidious retreat back across the creek to their former positions.[15]

Colonel Williams immediately issued instructions, which would send his own regiment across the creek. The awaiting colored soldiers, upon receiving the order to advance, leaped to their feet with a yell and dashed to the creek bank. Once in the creek the black unit pursued the opposite shore and the Confederates hidden there. To prevent a similar surprise volley on the black regiment Colonel Williams pulled three companies of the Kansas First Colored Volunteers Infantry Regiment out of the main attack column and stationed them along the Union bank of Cabin Creek to the right of the Union column. These troops began firing at the far

bank in an effort to force the Confederates down behind their entrenchments until the rest of the regiment could overrun the position. The
artillery fired salvos again and the vicinity of Cabin Creek echoed and re-
echoed with the din of cannon reports. The Kansas First Colored Volunteers Infantry Regiment quickly and without serious casualties cracked
the Southern earthworks and secured the far bank. The black regiment
displayed superb discipline in the manner they responded to the orders of
their officers. New lines were formed on the enemy's side of the creek
and the colored Union regiment moved out on the nearby prairie to offer
battle to the Confederates drawn up on the far side.

Lieutenant R. C. Philbrick, commander of Company C, Ninth Kansas
Cavalry Regiment, moved segments of his mounted unit across the creek
to the support of the vulnerable flanks of the long Union line. With less
than 400 yards separating them, the two lines of infantry faced each other.
The Negro troops knew that only complete vanquishment of the enemy
would do; it was a well-known fact that no prisoners or quarter was given
when colored troops were involved in an engagement. The deathly quiet-
ness hanging over the Confederate and Union lines was broken with the
renewed fire of the Union artillery and the three companies of black
infantry renewing their covering fire. The aligned Federal infantry did not
attack as expected; instead the center portions of the colored line fell back,
allowing two companies of Captain John E. Stuart's cavalry through. One
company moved to the left; the other column dashed to the right forming
a single line of horsemen. Halting long enough to align, the Kansas horsemen drew sabers and giving a piercing yell, lunged toward the Confederate line. Opening fire, the Confederates tried to unsaddle the charging
Union Cavalry. The colored troops began to give a supporting fire, which
had an immediate and revealing effect. Charging cavalry on the Southern
Indian was too much to bear. The Confederate line fell apart under the
weight of the mounted assault and the men in the ranks made for the rear
and safety. Colonel Williams ordered fresh cavalry to pursue the defeated
Southerners and moved up his black regiment to secure the abandoned
Confederate positions and care for the wounded enemy.[16]

The Federal pursuit was called back after a five-mile chase. Union
losses included only one colored soldier killed and twenty Indian and
colored troops wounded. The Confederate loss was estimated at fifty
killed, a comparative number wounded, and nine prisoners. From the
captured Confederate soldiers, information was learned that the leader
of the enemy attacking force had been Colonel Stand Watie, the most
able Confederate Indian in Indian Territory. With a force of only 900
men Colonel Williams had beaten off a serious attack of a Confederate

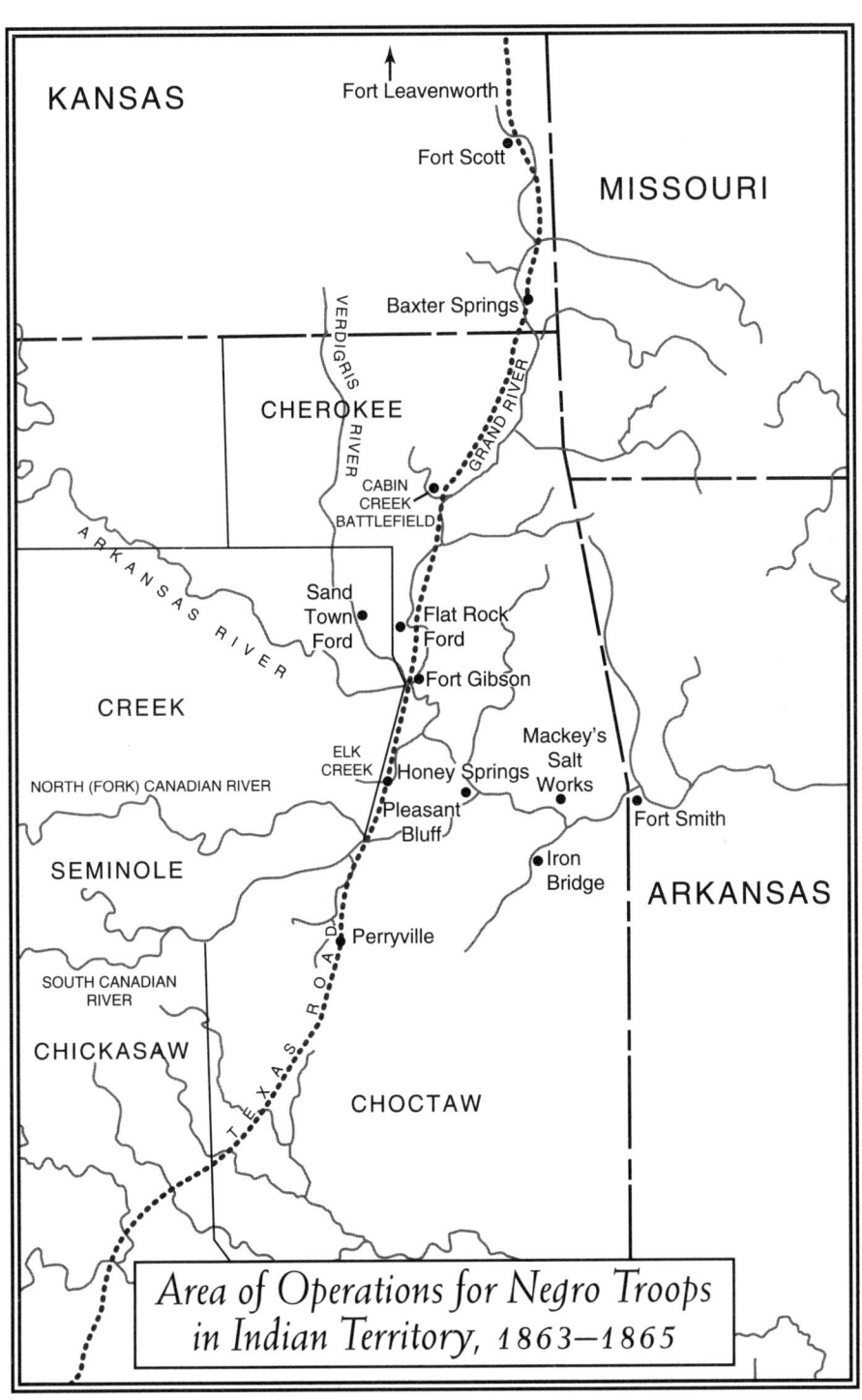

KANSAS

Fort Leavenworth

Fort Scott

MISSOURI

Baxter Springs

CHEROKEE

VERDIGRIS RIVER

GRAND RIVER

ARKANSAS RIVER

CABIN CREEK BATTLEFIELD

Sand Town Ford

Flat Rock Ford

Fort Gibson

CREEK

Mackey's Salt Works

NORTH (FORK) CANADIAN RIVER

ELK CREEK

Honey Springs

Pleasant Bluff

Fort Smith

SEMINOLE

Iron Bridge

ARKANSAS

TEXAS ROAD

Perryville

SOUTH CANADIAN RIVER

CHICKASAW

CHOCTAW

Area of Operations for Negro Troops in Indian Territory, 1863–1865 force numbering close to 2,200 men. The Kansas First Colored Volunteers Infantry Regiment and attached units had definitely proven their mettle in battle. Sending for the parked supply train, Colonel Williams put his victorious column on the Texas Road and continued south toward Fort Gibson. The victory at Cabin Creek had a noticeable effect on all the Union forces concerned; the morale was high, the step lively and the spirit of soldierly unity grew.[17]

The action at Cabin Creek proved without a doubt that the Negro troops were good fighters. They had fought and defeated a superior foe who did not give quarter. Colonel Williams had a regiment he could be proud of and depend on in tough situations. Action and combat is what these colored troops hungered for and within a few days all appetites would be satisfied.

The addition of the Kansas First Colored Volunteers Infantry Regiment to the Indian and white units already stationed at Fort Gibson now made it possible for the Union forces to assume an offensive attitude. Word was filtering back across the Arkansas that the Confederates were massing for a big offensive campaign. This push would have to be stopped whatever the cost or everything that the Union present represented in Indian Territory would be obliterated. On July 11, 1863, Fort Gibson was surprised by an unannounced visit of their Commanding General, Major General Blunt. Accompanying him were six hundred cavalry troopers, representing various Kansas and Wisconsin cavalry units.

Major General Blunt went into immediate conference with all of the company and staff officers about the impending campaign he planned to launch below the Arkansas River. Blunt organized his mounted troops and infantry companies into two brigades. The First Brigade, commanded by Colonel William R. Judson, held the colored regiment; the Second Indian Regiment dismounted as infantry and various sections of artillery. The Second Brigade made up of mostly white soldiers was commanded by the Fort Gibson commander, Colonel William A. Phillips.[18]

Because of the July rains the Grand River was quite swollen and impassable. Major General Blunt began constructing rafts, which were to be used to transport his units at the earliest opportunity. On the evening of July 15, 1863, scouts reported that the Grand River was fordable a short distance above the juncture point with the Verdigris River. At midnight on July 15, Major General Blunt led 250 cavalry and supporting artillery, taken from the First Brigade, out of Fort Gibson to force a passage across the Grand River. The remainder of the Union offensive force could then cross safely, opening the campaign. The remainder of the First Brigade under Colonel Judson, including the First

Kansas Colored Volunteers Infantry Regiment, and the Second Brigade under Phillips, also moved out of Fort Gibson taking a more direct route to the ford selected as the point of crossing. Arriving at the ford, near the mouth of the Grand River, the Negro troops settled down to await the outcome of vanguard on the enemy side of the river. Scattered shots and infrequent volleys could be heard all the rest of the night.

By early morning Union soldiers appeared opposite the waiting Federal columns and waved for them to cross. The barges were brought forward, the infantry units were ferried across, and the opposite shore and vicinity was tightly secured, allowing the rest of the column to be poled across. This ferrying maneuver was not completed until well after dark. By 10 o'clock the night of July 16, all of the Federal troops and their equipage were on the hostile side of the Grand River. Choosing not to encamp for the night the Negro and Indian companies formed up in the stealth of the darkness in their marching order and immediately began to trek southward. The entire Union force numbered only slightly less than 3,000 men. The Confederate force was estimated by the reports of spies to surpass 6,000 men, all heavily armed and deeply entrenched on the banks of Elk Creek. Marching throughout the night, the long Federal column lumbered toward its objective on Elk Creek. By daylight the point squad brushed with the forward element of the Confederate outpost. Quickly reinforced, the Federals drove the Southern soldiers back on their own column and entrenchment which were formed in attack order on the south side of Elk Creek. The Confederate emplacements extended their lines for one and a half miles on either side of the Texas Road. Leaving orders to close up the column which had become strung out in the darkness, Major General Blunt took a small escort and moved to the front to examine the defenses of the waiting Confederate force. Blunt was close enough to the concealed Confederates' trenches that he could tell they were ready for an attack. He could not locate the Southern artillery and, in an effort to move closer and pinpoint it, the small mounted party was spotted and drew musket fire from Confederate outposts. Withdrawing to a place of safety one of Blunt's escorts, shot dead, was toppled from his horse.[19]

Returning to his fast-approaching column, Blunt found his men and horses exhausted from their all-night forced march. He directed them to take cover behind a nearby ridge to rest and eat some food from their haversacks before going into battle. Men of the Kansas First Colored Volunteers Infantry Regiment ate a quick lunch and then readied their weapons for the coming fight. Major General Blunt issued an officers' call and when all the company commanders were assembled, he outlined his plan to them. The column would be divided into two parts: The First Brigade under Colonel

Judson would form up on the west or right side of the Texas Road and the Second Brigade under Colonel Phillips would position itself on the east or left side of the Texas Road. Both columns would have their infantry formed by company, the cavalry in platoons, and artillery stationed by sections. All units would keep a tight and closed formation so as to deceive the Confederate forward observers of the Federal strength.

Having issued these instructions and cleared away any questions, Blunt ordered his officers to post and prepare to march. As if on parade the one large column broke into two smaller ones, one on either side of the road. The columns moved out rapidly and closed the distance from the enemy to less than one-quarter mile. As soon as Blunt began receiving musket fire from Confederate outposts, he ordered his columns into a battle line of two ranks. Without halting, the battle formation was formed. Similar to spokes of a wheel emanating from a central point, the ranks broke from the main body and moved forward in double ranks. Skirmishes were thrown out in front of the main line in order to probe the enemy defenses for a weak point. The secreted Confederate artillery revealed its location when it opened fire on the Union skirmish line.[20]

Colonel Williams, previous to forming a line of battle, spoke to his colored troops encouraging them to fight for honor, duty and country. Williams told his troops, "I want you all to keep cool, and not fire until you receive the command; in all cases aim deliberately and below the waist. I want every man to do his whole duty, and obey strictly the orders of his officers."[21] Receiving orders to be in the right column on the west side of the road, Colonel Williams moved his regiment into line with precision and accuracy. The Kansas First Colored Volunteers Infantry Regiment, 500 men strong in this engagement, was to support Captain E. A. Smith's artillery located also on the right flank; as a secondary mission the colored troops were to seek out a weak point in the Southern line and exploit the enemy weakness, if located. The men in the ranks were nervous, but anxious to meet the enemy across the prairie and finish the task of liquidation they had begun at Cabin Creek. Once in position these black troops fixed bayonets and knelt in the dew-laden grass to await the word of attack. The colored regiment held the most important point of the Federal line, the center portion of the line astride a section of Smith's artillery.

The battle opened with a deafening roar as the Union cannon blazed into life, pouring shot and canister into the Confederate positions. After a period of bombardment, Lieutenant Colonel Bowles, commanding this section of the Federal line, rode his horse out in front of the black regiment and ordered them forward. The entire regiment stepped out and marched with perfect alignment toward the concealed enemy. The

300-yard gap between the two positions began rapidly closing. The Confederate artillery began pounding the black phalanx, tearing huge gaps in the oncoming Union line. Seeing this courageous example of daring, several of the other Federal units marched out to offer battle. The Second Colorado Cavalry Regiment (dismounted) joined with the Kansas First Colored Volunteers Infantry Regiment's right. The Second Indian Home Guards Regiment, commanded by Colonel W. F. Schaurt, moved up on the black regiment's left. Pushing through the tall prairie grass and isolated islands of trees and brush, the colored unit moved up to within forty yards of the enemy line. Lieutenant Colonel Bowles halted the unit and ordered it to, "ready, aim, fire."[22]

Instantly, two long rows of smoke and flame blazed forth as the double rank of the Union line erupted with a volley of musketry. At the same moment the Confederate line returned the Union volley with one of their own. Both lines loosed their fire at the same instant making it appear that the Confederates thought the command to fire given by Union Lieutenant Colonel Bowles was given by their own commander. It was at this point that Colonel Williams, now located on the extreme right of the Federal line, was felled, severely wounded on the face, breast and hand. Lieutenant Colonel Bowles, upon receiving word of the wounding of Colonel Williams, assumed command and pushed the attack of the Kansas First Colored Volunteers Infantry Regiment along all the line. Due to over enthusiasm, the Federal Second Indian Home Guard Regiment mistakenly placed itself between the Union and Confederate fields of fire. Lieutenant Colonel Bowles immediately ordered a cease fire of his units and yelled at the Union Indian command to fall back out of the line of fire.

The Confederates thought the withdrawal command was meant for all of the Northern forces to their front and immediately moved to take advantage of the black regiment. Colonel Charles DeMorse, commanding the Confederate's Twenty-Ninth Texas Infantry Regiment, ordered his companies forward to press the supposed retreat. Meantime the Indian troops had removed themselves from the line of fire and the colored troops steadied themselves for the onrushing Confederate Twenty-Ninth Texas. On command the double line of the black soldiers delivered two calm volleys into the charging Southern troops. Having reached a distance of only twenty-five paces from the Union line, the fire of the Federals was disastrous. The first rank of the Twenty-Ninth Texas simply disappeared, and the second Federal volley tore huge holes in the next rank and the Southern attack slowed. The line stalled and with the firing of another volley, it stopped completely and began a disorganized retreat. Momentarily the screams of the wounded and triumphant yells of the black troops rose above the din of gunfire signifying all up and down the line that a Federal victory was within their grasp. The entire Union front seemed to gather courage and strength from the colored soldiers' coup and surged forward. The pressure of the combined Union attack was too much; the Confederate troops broke ranks and made for the rear and safety. All along the mile and a half front, the Southerners began breaking contact; the battle of Elk Creek was a decisive Union victory.[23]

Major General Blunt ordered in cavalry to push the Confederate rout to the utmost. The retreating Confederates made several counterattacks, but all proved too feeble to stall their vigorous pursuers. Regaining their unit integrity, the Kansas First Colored Volunteers Infantry Regiment secured the battlefield and pushed onto the supply depot located two miles further south at Honey Springs. The Confederates, seeing the tide of battle change against them, set fire to their commissary building destroying practically all edible supplies. Moving post the smoldering buildings and dropping off a detachment of Union troops to secure the Southern supply depot, Blunt continued the chase for three more miles before he ordered recall. The terrain prevented further pursuit with artillery; the cavalry horses were in a jaded state and the black infantry was short of ammunition and exhausted. Blunt moved up his orderlies and staff stationing field headquarters at the Honey Springs compound. Colonel Williams' soldiers found many sets of shackles amid the ruins of the Confederate depot. Captured Confederate prisoners reported that the shackles were to be used to secure any black soldiers captured during the fight and subsequent return to his Southern master.[24]

Union losses at Honey Springs amounted to seventeen killed in the fighting and sixty wounded, most of which were superficial. The Southern casualties were much greater, having 150 killed and buried on the field, 400 wounded and seventy-seven captured. Also taken from the Confederate force were one artillery piece, one stand of Confederate colors, 200 stand of arms and fifteen wagons found at the Honey Springs depot, which were later burned on Blunt's orders. Major General Blunt praised his entire command for its actions at Elk Creek and the Confederate supply depot at Honey Springs. He singled out the Kansas First Colored Volunteers Infantry Regiment for singular courage and valor saying they "particularly distinguished . . ." themselves. "They fought like veterans, and preserved their line unbroken throughout the engagement. Their coolness and bravery I have never seen surpassed . . ."[25]

The defeat of the Confederate forces at Honey Springs, June, 1863, marked the twilight of the Southern dominance in Indian Territory. The valor and fighting ability of the Negro troops greatly helped in pushing and containing the Confederate forces below the Arkansas River. For the remainder of the war in Indian Territory these black units would again meet Southern Indians on the field of battle and prove to all doubters their victory at Honey Springs was not chance. The Kansas First Colored Volunteers Infantry Regiment moved to Fort Gibson and was temporarily attached to the permanent garrison there. The Kansas First Colored Volunteers Infantry Regiment remained at Fort Gibson the entire month of August, 1863, performing routine patrol and garrison duties.[26]

On September 14, 1863, the Kansas First Colored Volunteers Infantry Regiment joined its sister regiment, the newly formed Kansas Second Colored Volunteers Infantry Regiment at Fort Smith, Arkansas.[27] Both Negro regiments were then attached to the Second Division, Army of the Frontier. For the next two and one-half months these two units conducted various operations deep in Confederate Indian Territory. Several of their combat raids ventured as far south as Perryville, deep in the Choctaw Nation. On December 1, 1863, the Kansas First Colored Volunteers Infantry Regiment and the Kansas Second Colored Volunteers Infantry Regiment were transferred to Arkansas to operate against Confederate Major General William Steele, who was launching a counterattack against Federal Major General Frederick Steele. The Kansas First Colored Volunteers Infantry Regiment remained in Arkansas after the Confederate thrust had been thwarted and was involved in heavy fighting until May, 1864, when it was transferred back to temporary garrison duty and fatigue detail at Fort Smith, Arkansas.[28]

On June 15, 1864, the Kansas Second Colored Volunteers Infantry Regiment became involved in a brisk skirmish with Brigadier General Watie at Iron Bridge, Choctaw Nation. The Federal general headquarters at Fort Smith had decided to experiment with supplying the Union outpost of Fort Gibson by water. Usually summer rains raised the Arkansas River enough to allow shallow draft craft through to the upper parts of this important tributary. In early June the craft, *J. R. Williams,* was selected and loaded with basic condiments and other important necessities. In planning the re-supply of Fort Gibson by water the escort assigned to guard the valuable supplies was much too small. Upon arrival at the steamer, only twenty-six men comprised the entire guard mount. The cargo had an assessed value of over $120,000 and seemingly deserved more security than twenty-six men could supply if difficulty arose.

Arriving at a point five miles below the mouth of the Canadian River, the *J. R. Williams* was brought under Confederate artillery fire. Lieutenant Horace A. B. Cook, Company K, Twelfth Kansas Volunteers Infantry Regiment was taken by complete surprise and his men managed to return only a scattered, ineffective volley of musket fire before the Southern cannon had completely disabled the Union ferry craft. The captain of the *J. R. Williams* managed to maneuver and ground the disabled craft on the far shore of the Arkansas River, opposite the Confederate artillery and infantry entrenchments.[29]

Believing the situation aboard the *J. R. Williams* hopeless, Lieutenant Cook moved his men off the steamer to a nearby sandbar. Outnumbered, and having no known relief in the vicinity, Cook soon decided to break contact with the entrenched Confederates. He would try to reach Fort Smith and come back with reinforcements to retake the ferry boat. A party of Cook's command, which had become separated from the main body made its way about ten miles distant from the disabled steamer to Mackey's Salt Works, where Colonel John Ritchie had a command of 800 men from the Second Union Indian Regiment. Ritchie moved a part of his force to the crippled *J. R. Williams* and quickly brought the looting Confederate Indian troops under fire. During the interval of Cook's retreat and the arrival of Ritchie, Colonel Watie had towed the Union steamer across the river.[30] By evening of June 16, Watie was informed that a large force of Union Negro troops, with several pieces of horse artillery, was coming up from the direction of Fort Smith. This unit was the Kansas Second Colored Volunteers Infantry Regiment, an infantry regiment of about 700 men under the command of Colonel S. J. Crawford. Colonel Crawford had thrown to his front an extended line of skirmishers and it soon brushed with elements of Watie's security net. Receiving reports of contacts with Confederate personnel, Crawford ordered a harder push along the front in order to ascertain their numbers. The colored skirmish line attacked the task with vigor and peppered the encountered Confederate patrols with musket balls.

The Kansas Second Colored Volunteers Infantry Regiment easily pushed the Confederate scouts aside, and when they came within sight of the Iron Bridge, Crawford ordered a halt. Colonel Crawford put his troops into a battle formation of double lines of infantry with the artillery and cavalry in support, positioned to the rear of the massed infantry. So aligned, the colored troops moved forward keeping precision combat alignment. When well within musket range, the Confederates opened a heavy fire in an effort to break the black Union line. Crawford ordered the fire returned and sent for the Federal artillery section, stationed in the Union rear. The center of the Union line broke open momentarily as the artillery caissons raced forward to their position in front of the Union formation. After a few well-placed rounds of solid shot and canister, the Confederate cavalrymen broke ranks and fled to the rear for their horses. The exhausted condition of the Kansas Second Colored Volunteers Infantry

Regiment prevented any prolonged pursuit of the retreating Southern raiders. Colonel Crawford ceased the forward movement of his troops, put them into column formation and moved them to the Arkansas River where he allowed them to rest. Infantry cannot effectively follow cavalry; thus, there was no need to exert his tired men unnecessarily. That same evening, after their much needed rest, the colored troops moved back to the Federal post at Fort Smith, elated over their victory.[31]

In September 1864, the Southern high command launched the largest raid-invasion into Federally held Indian Territory since July 1863. Vied against this Confederate thrust was the Kansas First Colored Volunteers Infantry Regiment. On September 16, the Confederate columns filed out onto the Texas Road at Sand Town Ford and began their trek northward. In command of this raiding force were two of the most distinguished officers in the Confederate army stationed in the Trans-Mississippi West, Brigadier General Watie and Brigadier General Richard Gano from the Texas Confederate sub-district and commanding officer, by date of rank, of the combined units being used on the raid. The force was made up of an 800-man brigade commanded by Watie and 1,200 men, cavalry and infantry, from various Texas units under Brigadier General Gano; 2,000 men totaled the count. Marching in single column formation on the Texas Road, the Confederate force stretched out for over two miles. Proceeding northeast, the raiders made their way to their first objective; the haying station reported to be on the prairie located near Flat Rock. A patrol of scouts had been sent ahead, and it was soon confirmed that a party of Federals lay to the Confederate immediate right front. Gano and Watie proceeded to the top of a nearby ridge for a better vantage point. Using spy glasses, they watched the Federals making hay.[32]

The Union haying operation at Flat Rock was commanded by Captain Edgar A. Barker. Captain Barker had only two reinforced companies of his regiment with him at the haying station, the Second Kansas Cavalry Regiment and four companies of the Kansas First Colored Volunteers Infantry Regiment, a total force of only 125 men. Barker's Union colored scouts returned to camp and reported that a large force of Confederates had crossed the Verdigris River and was advancing on his camp from the southwest. The first intelligence reports from the colored scouts set the Confederate party as numbering approximately 200 men. With his command only slightly smaller, Captain Barker elected to fight the advancing enemy force. When recall was sounded by the bugler, the black soldiers out on the prairie hurried to camp to erect a defense.

With his men assembled together, Barker formed them in a half-circle formation in a ravine to the rear of his camp. Taking a small mounted detachment of men, the Federal captain moved forward to reconnoiter the exact number and designs of the Confederates advancing on his front. Captain Barker and his Negro escort detachment met Gano's command two miles southwest of his camp. Here he correctly estimated the Confederate host at being near 2,000, vastly outnumbering the previously reported 200. The flat prairie also disclosed the six pieces of field artillery the Confederates had with them. Barker made his intended reconnaissance on the enemy flanks and immediately fell back when approached by a Confederate advance party. He skirmished with this advance patrol all the way back to the Federal haying camp. Arriving at the ravine, to the rear of the Union camp, Barker dismounted the patrol detachment and prepared to meet the Confederate attack.[33] For the Negro troops with Captain Barker, it would be a fight to the death, and the Negro soldiers intended to make the Confederates pay dearly for their lives. A well-known fact to the Federals, white and black, was that the Confederate forces did not take prisoners.[34]

General Gano could see from his vantage point that the Confederate party sent to cut off the escape of the Federal haying detail were in position. Captain S. M. Stayhorn of the Thirtieth Texas Regiment, sent with the advance element to aid in cutting off the Union party was beginning to advance his skirmishers; the engagement at Flat Rock Ford had begun. Watie and his entire brigade, minus the First Cherokee Regiment, which was with Lieutenant Colonel C. N. Vann at the rear of the Union camp, advanced to the left of the field. Gano dispatched Lieutenant Colonel William G. Welch with a cavalry column to the right. It was composed of Colonel DeMorse and the Twenty-Ninth Texas Cavalry Regiment and Lieutenant Colonel Peter Hardeman of the Thirty-First Texas Cavalry Regiment. Welch advanced to a position about 200 yards to the right of Gano and halted. Gano and the remainder of the Confederate cavalry force, including the artillery, made up the center. Increasing musketry fire to the Federal rear indicated that Lieutenant Colonel Vann was advancing in force. Gano gave the order, and the V-shaped formation of the Southern units began to move in on the haying camp. The infantry accompanied by Gano, advanced to within 200 yards of Captain Barker and his besieged Negroes and white soldiers and opened fire. Watie and Welch with their cavalry forces charged the flanks of the Federally-held ravine repeatedly, but on each assault the Negro troops effectively repulsed them.[35]

The Negro troops under Captain Barker held their ground well for a half-hour, but the Federal position grew more untenable as the Confederates began gaining ground and moving in closer. With the Confederate Indian troops positioned as they were, the Federal haying party was assailed from five directions at once. Barker knew by the disproportioned odds it would be only a short time before his command would be over-whelmed and wiped out to the last man. With Negroes in the Federal party, the Confederate force around him would not be inclined to show much mercy to any person in the unit, white or black. Barker spotted a weak point on the Confederate left in Watie's section of the line and decided to mount all those of his party who had horses, break through if he could and attempt to save at least a portion of the doomed command. Mounting sixty-five men, he charged the Confederate left. Watie in com-mand of that portion of the line ordered reinforcements in, and all but fifteen of the Federal cavalry were captured or killed. The colored soldiers and some white infantry left in the ravine rallied under Lieutenant Thomas B. Sutherland, a company commander of the Kansas First Col-ored Volunteers Infantry Regiment.

For two more hours the repeated Confederate charges were success-fully repulsed. On their knees and bellies the black soldiers volleyed the Confederate advances into oblivion. When the ammunition supply became exhausted, Sutherland told his colored troops they would have to save themselves as best they could. Thirty-seven colored troops had been at the hay camp when the engagement started at noon and by that evening only four remained alive. These four colored soldiers had secreted themselves in the prairie grass or in the nearby pools of water which were runoff areas of the Grand River, When darkness came, these four survivors crawled between the Confederate sentries and mounted patrols and wormed their way to Fort Gibson to relate their story.

The Confederates moved about the camp looting and observing their captured prize. The hay—exceeding 3,000 tons—was burned in its ricks. Destroying all they could not use, the Confederate commands of Watie and Gano spent the night at Flat Rock. The next morning, Sep-tember 17, 1864, the Southern cavalry and infantry units with the artillery sections stationed to the rear formed into columns and began their trek anew in a northerly direction.[36]

The Federal forces stationed in Indian Territory knew that the large Confederate Force reported in the area was out to break the all-impor-tant supply line between Fort Scott, Kansas, and Fort Gibson. Should the Texas Road be effectively blocked for any length of time, Fort Gibson, without a doubt, would fall. Since the experiment with *J. R. Williams* had failed miserably, the only alternative was to keep the Texas Road functioning as a Federal supply line. On September 14, 1864, the entire command of Colonel Williams, the Kansas First Colored Volunteers Infantry Regiment, was sent to Fort Gibson to ensure that Confederate raiders making sorties through the Cherokee Nation would not break the vital supply artery.[37]

By September 14, Major Henry Hopkins, Second Kansas Cavalry Regiment, commander of the supply train then making its way to Fort Gibson, was putting forth every effort to prevent a surprise attack on his little command. On September 17, Major Hopkins was located approximately fifteen miles north of Cabin Creek. He had received an additional one hundred men from Baxter Springs to add to his 260, totaling 360 men, white and Indian. The Federal train, consisting of 300 wagons, 205 of which were government wagons, four ambulances, and ninety sutler wagons, was immense for a military supply convoy. Hopkins received word from Colonel Stephen Wattles, the new commander of Fort Gibson, that a hostile force of more than 1,500 Confederates was headed in his direction and accordingly ordered Hopkins to move his train with all possible dispatch to the safety of the Federal stockade at Cabin Creek.[38]

Major Hopkins acted immediately and began moving toward the Union fortification and safety. To increase the speed of the train, the wagons were put into double column formation. Traveling throughout the pre-dawn and early morning, the train covered the fifteen miles to the Cabin Creek stockade in six hours. The train arrived at Cabin Creek at 9:00 A.M. on the morning of September 18, 1864. Reinforcements were waiting there and with these additional units, the entire escort numbered 150 cavalry and 460 men acting as infantry. Patrolling that same afternoon, the Confederate advance party was sighted in a gully three miles south of the stockade. Instead of waiting for a new day to dawn, the Gano and Watie commands began their attack shortly past midnight. Forming their battle line in the dark, the attack was started with great enthusiasm on the part of the Confederate Indians. General Gano held the Confederate center and right wing of the line, and General Watie fastened down the left section of the battle formation. Furious fire fighting ensued for the duration of the night and extended well into the next morning without a letup. By 9:00 A.M. September 19, the engagement at Cabin Creek was over.

The Federal forces had been, after a tenacious defense, pushed back out of the stockade and finally routed and scattered throughout the woods surrounding the fortification. The retrograde movement, started by the Federal commander, quickly evolved into a race for safety when the wagon teams, composed of both horses and mules, usually six to eight animals per team, began to go berserk and charge aimlessly around as a result of the din created by the fighting and discharging of muskets.

When the musketry had died down to scattered shots and volleys, the booty left on the field and in the possession of the Confederate forces was enormous. The Confederates had salvaged 130 Federal supply wagons and herded together 740 Union mules and horses suitable for service. Although over one hundred wagons had been burned, the remaining wagons and their cargos were valued exceeding $1,500,000. The casualties had been unusually slight for the number of engaged men and the viciousness of the fighting between the rival units. The Confederate loss was no more than forty-five men, killed, wounded, and displaced. The total Federal casualties was not in excess of fifty-four men.[39]

By 10:00 A.M. General Gano had all of the captured wagons in line, his men positioned in columns on either side of the wagons and was ready to return to Confederate Indian Territory below the Arkansas River. After moving for an hour, scouts returned to the Confederate column and reported that a Federal force, a large one, was in front of the Confederate raiders and was at that moment pressing the Confederate advance party. Gano reacted immediately. He ordered his entire command forward, except the security party left with the wagons and remuda. Placing his men in double ranks, Gano massed onto the prairie in such a position that he intercepted the path of the pursuing Federals. Gano, by his show of force and aggressiveness, held the Union relief brigade at a respectable distance.[40]

The advancing Union brigade was commanded by Colonel Williams and his Kansas First Colored Volunteers Infantry Regiment, recently changed to the Seventy-Ninth U.S. Colored Troops (new). Williams had crossed Pryor's Creek and his point element had brushed with Confederate General Gano's advance party; the Confederates quickly fell back to warn the recently captured Union supply train. Colonel Williams ordered his command in battle formation of double ranks, with his artillery moved to the rear and flanks. The discipline of the colored regiment and skill in moving from the column formation to the battle line was a sight to behold. Functioning as a well-oiled cog the colored infantry companies smoothly took their respective slots on the combat line. With their Federal colors and standards flashing and flopping in the wind, the line began to advance. Skirmishers moved out ahead of the first line to test the enemy defenses as the main body marched at a slightly slower pace. When in range of the Confederate musketry, the quarter-mile-long blue line was halted and given parade rest. Because of the exhausted condition of his men and a total lack of cavalry, Colonel Williams elected to permit the enemy to approach him. Putting his colored troops at rest, Williams reinforced his skirmishers to the front, moved skirmish elements to secure the flanks and rested his men for the Confederate attack.

The Confederate and Union skirmishing continued until 4:30 P.M. that afternoon when the noise of increased firing and activity from the Southern line told the colored veterans an attack was in the making. Ordering his rear sections of artillery forward, Williams directed them, as well as the artillery sections posted on the flanks, to open fire with shot, shell and canister at the enemy infantry came within range. The combined fire of the Federal guns drove back the massed ranks of Confederate troops, showering them with huge clumps of prairie. The Confederates made no further efforts to advance and the skirmishing resumed as the Federal colored scouts began anew their probing of the Southern position, continuing actions until dusk. Colonel Williams bivouacked on the prairie in line of battle to prevent any surprise attack by the Southern units. The next morning, September 20, the Confederate units and all of the captured Federal wagons and valuable supplies were gone, slipping across the Verdigris to the west. During the night the wily Gano and Watie had tricked Williams and his colored regiment. The exhausted condition of Williams' infantry prevented any pursuit of the retreating Confederates.[41]

The engagement at Cabin Creek was the last serious employment of the Negro as a fighting man within the confines of Indian Territory. The Kansas First Colored Volunteers Infantry Regiment did not stop serving the trans-Mississippi district as a capable fighting unit, nor did the black enlisted man stop functioning as a Federal combat soldier. Immediately after the Cabin Creek action of September 18, 1864, most of the colored units were transferred out of Indian Territory to adjacent states. The Kansas First Colored Volunteers Infantry Regiment was transferred into the Second Brigade, Frontier Division. Colonel Williams, commanding the brigade, remained in that position for a short time before being transferred again. Colonel Williams was rotated back to direct command of his colored regiment and then the entire unit was sent briefly to Little Rock, Arkansas, and later was sent to a permanent duty station at Fort Smith. The black regiment remained at Fort Smith engaged in heavy escort duty and fatigue calls until it was mustered out by the Federal government on October 30, 1865. It received its final muster pay and was discharged at Fort Leavenworth, Kansas.[42]

The sister regiment to the Kansas First Colored Volunteers Infantry Regiment, the Kansas Second Colored Volunteers Infantry Regiment, officially the Eighty-third U.S. Colored Troops (new), served most of her remaining active military life as a fighting unit outside the borders of

Indian Territory. During the early months of 1865, the Kansas Second Colored Volunteers Infantry Regiment did garrison duty in Little Rock, Arkansas. In August the regiment was moved to Camden, Arkansas where it was mustered out, October 9, 1865. Because of the location of the Federal paymaster the unit was again moved, this time to Fort Leavenworth, Kansas, where it received its severance pay and discharge, October 27, 1865.[43]

An accurate and definitive evaluation of the Negro as a soldier in the Civil War is virtually impossible in a project of this size. But a few observations can be made without stepping out of the realm of pure objectivity. The reason for the difficulty in evaluation is because the Negro was not used uniformly by the Union army. Negro units were used in labor battalions, garrison duty, pioneer units, construction gangs and as combat soldiers. Usually the employment of these black soldiers depended on the desires of their commanding general. For the most part, the colored soldier was an integral part of the Union fighting team in the trans-Mississippi West, particularly the Kansas-Arkansas-Indian Territory area. The Kansas First Colored Volunteers Infantry Regiment was employed as a separate and independent fighting entity, and on occasion was fused with a larger component for combat missions, such as the Army of the Frontier, in 1863. In both instances this black regiment, and her sister regiment, the Kansas Second Colored Volunteers Infantry Regiment, served with valor and distinction, being specifically praised by their field commanders on several occasions.

While the Negro soldier was helping the Union suppress the rebellion of the Southern states they were also doing great benefit for themselves. It was while the black ex-slaves were in the blue uniform that they learned how to accept the reins of authority and how to properly serve in positions of responsibility and leadership within their regiments, usually as noncommissioned officers. Many Negroes had their first opportunity to learn to read and write while in the Federal armed services. It was not unusual for a white company commander to drill his black recruits in the manual of arms during the work day and drill these same men in their letters at night while off duty.

The fighting ability of the Negro soldier can be demonstrated in one respect by their long casualty list. The losses among black units were very high. It is reported from figures available that out of all the black troops enrolled in the ranks, over one third of these were reported killed in battle. This figure would be higher when applied to the trans-Mississippi West because all the black soldiers in that department were used as combat troops, while most of the colored units east of the Mississippi

River were utilized proportionally less as fighting commands. The desertion in the Negro units was also much less that in the white companies. Taken as a whole, the colored units had a seven percent desertion rate while the overall white desertion figure was nineteen percent.[44]

One of the most important results of the using of the Negro fighting man was in changing the white man's attitude toward the black man. Doubtless if the Negro had sat on the sidelines of the Civil War the Fourteenth and Fifteenth Amendments would have been a very long time in coming. As it was, the Negro did not sit idly by, letting someone else fight his battles for him. He formed drill units on his own, flocked to the recruiting stations to enlist, and hung on the fringes of the Union armies helping the war effort in every way possible; menial or otherwise. After the Civil War the citizens of the trans-Mississippi West no longer considered the Negro an animate piece of chattel property, but began to think and trust the black Union veteran as a man. The Civil War for the Negro was the stepping stone from slave to citizen, in less than five years. For a decade or two he would be granted wide political, economic, and social opportunities and responsibilities. Though political motives would remove the privileges that attend citizenship, no selfish move could remove the pride the Negro had gained in himself and his race for his part in the Civil War.

CHAPTER 12

—⁓⚭⚭⏖⏖⁓—

Black Chaplains in the
Union Army

Edwin S. Redkey

UNTIL RECONSTRUCTION, NO AFRO-AMERICAN achieved higher official public status than the black army chaplain. During the Civil
War, the federal government waited long to use black soldiers; it waited
even longer to authorize black officers. Racial prejudice among white
soldiers and officers made the War Department reluctant to commission
black officers, who even though serving in all-black units, might some
day give orders to whites and who, in any event, would have to be
saluted by whites. Yet blacks and their white allies insisted that some
were well qualified to serve despite their color. One way of solving the
dilemma was to appoint blacks as chaplains. Although officers, they did
not command soldiers; although black, they were less threatening to
white superiority.[1]

Their military experiences provide insights into the lives and
thoughts of several black clergymen at a time when the fortunes of all
Afro-Americans were changing rapidly. Most were from the northern
states and now encountered masses of southern slaves for the first time.
Some served as "race men" on behalf of their troops. Some wrote extensively about army life. All shared with the black soldiers the burdens of
racism and all shared with their white counterparts the poorly defined
tasks of the army chaplain.

By war's end, over one hundred eighty thousand blacks served in the
Union army, but most never saw a black chaplain. In May 1863, the War
Department established the "Bureau for Colored Troops," and soon all

but one Connecticut and three Massachusetts regiments were absorbed into the category of "United States Colored Troops" (USCT). For these black regiments, the appointment of officers, including chaplains, was controlled by the federal government. Line officers were appointed for their military skill, not their abolitionist sympathies or their views on racial equality. Chaplains, in turn, were selected by the white officers of each regiment, most of whom did not want to share the officers' mess with a black man. Of the 133 men who served as chaplains to black units, only 14 were black.[2]

Gov. John A. Andrew of Massachusetts was the man most responsible for getting the first black chaplains into the army. Most of the white soldiers who fought for the Union served in "volunteer regiments" raised by the individual states. When the Emancipation Proclamation, on 1 January 1863, stated the intent of the government to use black troops, it was natural for the states to recruit black regiments to help meet their quotas. Andrew, an eager abolitionist, in January 1863 sought and received permission from the War Department to raise the first black volunteer regiment in the North. He immediately requested authority to appoint a few black officers: "Give me leave to commission Colored Chaplains, assistant surgeons, and a few second Lieutenants. My discretion may be trusted. The mere power will be useful." Secretary of War Edwin M. Stanton refused, leaving the matter to the discretion of President Abraham Lincoln, who was unwilling then to act. Andrew raised three black regiments, the 54th and 55th Massachusetts Volunteer Infantry and the 5th Massachusetts Cavalry, each with an all-white corps of officers. He continued to press his case for black officers, but not until the end of the war was he able to commission a few battle-tested blacks as lieutenants.[3]

Chaplains, however, were a different matter. As the black recruits gathered for training at Camp Meigs, near Boston, Governor Andrew decided that, even if the federal government would not yet permit black chaplains, Massachusetts, at least, could have black clergymen in the state-operated camp to minister to the needs of the men. On 23 March 1863 he appointed two black "post chaplains," William Jackson, a Baptist, and William Grimes, a Methodist, both from New Bradford. Under pressure from highly placed abolitionists such as Secretary of the Treasury Salmon P. Chase, the government finally permitted Andrew to make Jackson the first official black chaplain in the Union army when he appointed him chaplain of the 55th Massachusetts.[4]

Jackson's new role was poorly defined, as was the case with *all* army chaplains until late in the war. Before 1861 chaplains had conducted common schools at army posts—no regulation required them even to hold worship services. In the hectic days of 1861, "General Order No. 15," which organized the volunteer forces to fight the Confederacy, had allotted to each regiment (about one thousand men) one chaplain, but it did not prescribe his duties.[5] Until 1863 there were no "how-to-do-it manuals." Not until April 1864 would Congress give more shape to the pay, rank, status, and work of the chaplain. Even then he, his regimental officers, and their men had to formulate his role in that particular regiment.

That role depended on the commanders and the chaplains. Some commanders welcomed the presence of spiritual leaders in their regiments and did all they could to make the chaplain's work effective. Many more seem to have viewed the chaplain as a nuisance, an officer whom they did not understand or appreciate. Some actively opposed religious work among the troops because they thought it hurt their fighting abilities. A few commanders filled the chaplain's vacancy with more "useful" men; the story is told of one regiment that used the chaplain's slot to hire a French chef to cook for the officers.[6]

Chaplains varied in quality. Initially they needed only be Christian ministers for state governors to appoint them. Once in the regiments, many proved lazy or stupid; some were corrupt. Others could not adjust to army life, especially to the rigors of campaigning; they soon resigned and went home, having done their bit for the war. Most found difficulty adapting their peacetime messages to wartime soldiers. Even the energetic, able, and adaptable had to carve out their own places in their regiments. This lack of direction combined with indifference or hostility from regimental officers made the role of all army chaplains marginal. "Relatively few became honored and indispensible pastors to their regiments."[7]

Into this ill-defined, marginal office black ministers eagerly climbed. Getting to be a chaplain was not easy for these black men. Army regulations required that the chaplain must be elected by the other officers, all white, of the regiment. Each candidate had to be a regularly ordained clergyman and have the endorsement of at least five other clergymen of his denomination. There were no denominational quotas, and the ages of the black chaplains ranged from twenty-one to sixty-one years. For the state regiments, the governor had some authority in this process, and other politicians might have had some influence. For the federal units, it was mostly an internal matter for the regiments, although the politicians also brought pressure from time to time, especially early in 1863 when the government was first deciding on its policy on black chaplains.

Each of the fourteen gained his commission in a different way, but most seem first to have won favor with the army by recruiting soldiers for the black regiments. Henry M. Turner served as pastor of Israel

African Methodist Episcopal (AME) Church on Capitol Hill in Washington, D.C. There he attracted public attention of both blacks and whites for his ardent sermons advocating the use of black soldiers. When it became known that the government would begin recruiting early in 1863, Turner offered his centrally located church as a rallying point: speeches were made there, and in its churchyard the first volunteers signed up for the local regiment, soon to become the 1st USCT. As soon as the unit started training on a nearby island in the Potomac, Turner began regular visits, preaching and encouraging the men to prove their manhood and protect their rights.[8]

Recommended by the colonel of the regiment and by five ministers of his AME denomination, Turner applied for the post of chaplain in July 1863, about the time Jackson was appointed in Massachusetts. The War Department delayed, but Turner persisted, writing impatiently to Secretary Stanton, "Your honor would greatly relieve me, by informing me ONCE FOR ALL whether it is the intention of the government to have colored chaplains or not." Still no reply came from the War Department. Early in September, Tuner solicited a recommendation from his fellow abolitionists, Secretary of the Treasury Chase and Congressman Owen Lovejoy, who jointly wrote of Turner, "He has been very useful in raising the first colored regiment raised here." This must have persuaded President Lincoln, for on 10 September, the appointment was approved—but no one notified Turner until November. Finally, he was mustered in and joined his regiment in North Carolina.[9] Once the War Department appointed Turner, others soon followed.

Samuel Harrison, a Congregationalist minister from Pittsfield, Massachusetts, also encouraged young black men to enlist. Early in 1863 he applied to Governor Andrew for the post of chaplain in one of the colored regiments, but the War Department had not yet authorized black chaplains.[10] On 18 July 1863, just after William Jackson was commissioned in the 55th Massachusetts, its sister regiment, the 54th Massachusetts, fought a bloody battle at Fort Wagner near Charleston, South Carolina. The black troops fought well and won national acclaim, but they suffered heavy losses, including the death of their commander, Colonel Robert Gould Shaw. Governor Andrew, wanting to express the sympathy of the people of Massachusetts, asked Harrison to be his emissary to the 54th. Harrison, having persuaded other men to leave their families to join the army, could hardly refuse. In South Carolina, where he could meet the men of the 54th in person, he soon learned that the officers of the regiment had elected him chaplain. He went home, put his affairs in order, and then returned south as a commissioned chaplain.[11]

Other black clergymen, after helping recruit soldiers, joined the army as enlisted men in hopes of later being commissioned chaplain. This was a risky choice. William J. Hodges went south in early 1864 to be chaplain but became a sergeant major of the 36th USCT when David Stevens was commissioned instead. Francis A. Boyd had better luck—for a while. A young minister of the Christian Church in Louisville, Kentucky, Boyd was told by a recruiting colonel that in order to become a chaplain he must first enlist. But it was the regimental officers, not the recruiter, who must elect the chaplain, and the officers of the 109th USCT refused to elect Boyd; they elected a white man instead. As a sergeant, Boyd performed many of the duties of a chaplain, and when the white chaplain resigned, Boyd wrote a confidential letter to Gen. Benjamin F. Butler, commander of the Army of the James. Boyd laid out the history of his claim, and the impetuous Butler replied by unilaterally appointing him chaplain of the regiment on 23 November 1864. This process, of course, ran counter to army policy, and the colonel of the regiment protested that the appointment was "made against the expressed wish of the field officers and Co. commanders." Boyd complained that as chaplain he was coolly and contemptuously treated by the Officers of this regiment with some exceptions. Prejudices are Dark and Bitter, and I feel that my life is in peril." On 22 February, the army revoked Boyd's commission, and he returned to the ranks as a private, his pride much damaged: "I have been offered the position of Hospital steward and orderly sergeant by the colonel of my regiment, but I refused to accept it for the sake of the service, because it would look bad to see a man who had been a commissioned officer on his staff and whose only dishonor was the color of his skin, holding the place of a noncommissioned officer."[12]

Recruiter Garland H. White succeeded in getting his commission but only with help from influential people. Before the war White had been the slave of Robert A. Toombs, United States Senator from Georgia, ardent secessionist, and later Confederate secretary of state and general. As Toombs's personal servant, White claimed to have been in the Senate chamber in 1856 when Congressman Preston Brooks beat Senator Charles Sumner senseless. Furthermore, he had met a variety of statesmen, especially William H. Seward, senator from New York who would become Lincoln's secretary of state. White ran away from Toombs sometime in 1859 or 1860 and went to London, Ontario, where he became pastor of an AME Church. When the war erupted, he wrote to Secretary Stanton offering his services and those of other refugee blacks in Canada. But it was too early for black soldiers, and there is no record that Stanton replied. A year later, when Stanton had decided to use black troops, White wrote directly to Secretary Seward, this time from Toledo, Ohio, where he was busily recruiting soldiers for the Massachusetts regiments and hoping to become chaplain. Disappointed again, he continued recruiting, and by the end of the year had helped enlist many of the men for an Indiana regiment. Gov. Oliver P. Morton apparently promised him the chaplaincy, but when the regiment went under federal control and became the 28th USCT, he would have to be elected by the white officers. He enlisted "as a private to be with my boys. . . . My officers have me acting as a chaplain," he wrote to Seward, "but no man seeks my commission. I pray you will see me justified after having done as much as I have in raising such troops." Slowly the process began to work: the regiment's colonel on 1 September certified that the officers had indeed elected White as chaplain, and on 27 October the War Department approved. On 1 November 1864, after almost a year as "acting chaplain," White received his commission.[13]

The life and work of the black chaplains is revealed in several sources. Starting in April 1864 all chaplains were required to send monthly reports to the adjutant general of the army, since there was no central office of chaplains. The reports were to tell of "the moral condition and general history of the regiments, hospitals, or posts to which they may be attached."[14] These reports were actually filed sporadically, but they provide a general picture of the chaplains' work and occasional useful details. Sometimes the commanding officers would mention the chaplains in their official or personal correspondence, and there are some examples of the enlisted men writing about them. But the primary body of evidence is the letters of the chaplains themselves. Several of them wrote to the two black weekly newspapers of the Civil War era, the *Weekly Anglo-African,* of New York, and the *Christian Recorder,* the journal of the Philadelphia-based AME church. The most prolific writer was H. M. Turner, whose full and frequent letters to the *Christian Recorder* provided a window not only on the black troops but also the chaplain himself.

Army life for the chaplains brought both satisfactions and frustrations. Being part of the great national crusade gave them a sense of belonging, of being "full-fledged men." Like other men who served in the Civil War, the army brought black chaplains out of their provincial activities into the public arena. As black men, army service gave the opportunity to prove that they were as brave, as loyal, as any other American, and that they deserved full citizenship rights. But the chaplains had to deal with racial insults and slights from fellow officers, from white soldiers, and from white civilians. They also considered themselves the defenders of their black troops against attacks by the white press.

The chaplains shared with their men the general hardships and joys of army life in wartime. Separated from their families and communities, they suffered the personal concerns of family men. "Since leaving home my wife has become an invalid and had two small children to whom she is unable to give the care and attention required. Consequently they need to be provided for. My private affairs are also in such a condition as to demand my personal attention," wrote George W. LeVere, applying for thirty days leave from the 20th USCT. Much of the soldiers' time was spent in preparing for battle, preparation that was exhausting, hard work. Jeremiah Asher, of the 6th USCT, wrote in a monthly report, "The last month has been one of constant excitement and fatigue. The men have been working on the fortifications day and night, not excepting the Sabbath." The routine of hard labor was punctuated, however, with combat action against the rebels. In a war in which personal valor and courage still counted for much, the chaplains shared the dangers and triumphs with their men. Their letters stressed the bravery of the gallant black soldiers in battle and their worthiness for equal rights. War also had its grim side, and sickness and death were frequent visitors. "I have seen just as many men killed as I wish to see. . . . I am case-hardened to death, as men generally get to be; for when I am tired I had much rather sleep at night in a house with dead people than living, because the dead don't bother me," wrote Turner, "and a man can rest quietly, yet feel that he has company."[15]

Sickness and disease were constant threats during the Civil War, and the chaplains shared that hazard. Samuel Harrison, of the 54th Massachusetts, contracted malaria soon after arriving in the Sea Islands and was discharged after only four months in the service. David Stevens, of the 36th USCT, who was over sixty years old, and who claimed to have been a drummer boy in the War of 1812, tried to resign his commission for prostate and intestinal problems. His resignation was denied by Gen. B. F. Butler: "He is certainly but six months older than when he took his commission. . . . If ever he were fit for his position, he is as fit now as ever." Stevens stayed at his post for another year. H. M. Turner spent two months in a hospital, and another month convalescing from smallpox. He later fell from his horse while fleeing Confederate soldiers. Although several of the chaplains were with the troops during battle conditions, none of them was wounded in combat. Jeremiah Asher, 6th USCT, was the only black chaplain to die while in the army; he died of disease on 27 July 1865.[16]

Sources reveal little about the theological assumptions and beliefs of the black chaplains. They seem to have fitted into the mainstream of American Protestant religion of the time, with its focus on evangelism and morality. Only Turner recorded specific study of theology: "Having had a little more leisure time than usual, I have been devoting it to reading James McCosh's great work on Divine Government, physical and moral, &c., which work cannot be too highly esteemed." Later, when he observed the black churches in North Carolina, he noted,

> Most of the Baptists here have those old worn-out ideas still, that you must go under the waters before you are right; while a more liberal-thinking portion regard true Christian fidelity as the standard of moral rectitude only. . . . The Methodist Church . . . appeared to worship under a lower class of ideas, or to entertain a much cruder conception of God and the plan of salvation, than the Baptists—Hell fire, brimstone, damnation, black smoke, hot lead, &c., appeared to be presented by the speaker as man's highest incentive to serve God, while the milder and yet more powerful message of Jesus was thoughtlessly passed by.[17]

No transcripts have survived to reveal what the sermons and prayers of the black chaplains contained of theology and devotion. They probably paralleled those of white chaplains, who preached on the religious duty of patriotism, the necessity for moral living, the familiar evangelistic call for personal salvation, and the comfort of God's promises to the suffering faithful.[18] To these topics the black chaplains undoubtedly added a theme that often appeared in their letters, that the future of the race in America depended on the faithful bravery of the black soldiers.

Although no sermons remain, other evidence clearly shows that the black chaplains actively cast the gospel net of evangelism among their men. Methodist White reported that "we now have some 20 or more converts to be baptized before admitting them in the church as full members. We have a glorious revival of religion now going among us. I have already baptized forty persons in my regt. since reaching here." Baptist Leonard reported, "Agreeable to request, I have administered the ordinance of Baptism to one young man, who has given good evidence of conversion." Presbyterian Randolph reported eighteen conversions since his last monthly report. Methodist Turner, who preferred baptism by sprinkling, wrote, "Some of my brave soldiers wish baptism by immersion. Their wish shall be granted, God being my helper. I wish I could baptize the whole regiment, Colonel and all."[19]

On special occasions the chaplains would be called upon to speak to the entire regiment. When the president set aside special days for prayer and fasting or for thanksgiving, the men would be ordered to a parade formation to hear the chaplain's message. On Thanksgiving Day of 1863, the year of the Emancipation Proclamation, Chaplain Hunter preached on the text, "Thou crownest the year with thy goodness, and thy paths drop fatness" (Psalm 65:11).[20]

Preaching, of course, for the center of Protestant worship, and part of the chaplain's reputation rested on his speaking ability. One civilian visited the camp of the 1st USCT near the front at Petersburg, Virginia, and inquired about Chaplain Turner. A soldier told him that "sometimes his discourses were very eloquent and rose to sublimity, and at other times he was equally as dull and very poor. But none questioned his being a Christian, a scholar, and a gentleman."[21]

The core of faithful believers was usually organized into some kind of church within the regiment. Garland White reported, "I have organized a thorough church system in my regiment, and large numbers are coming in every day." He added that "the law governing the Protestant Church of the U.S. is in full force among us as we are all Protestants when at home." Benjamin Randolph reported that, of the 1018 men in his regiment, 76 were members of the "regimental church." By setting up such nondenominational "churches," the chaplains were following the broad patterns of American Protestantism thy had learned in civilian life—the gathered church called out from the world.[22]

The chaplain's responsibilities, however, extended beyond his "church" of believers; he was thus to become the priest of his regimental "parish." In the chaplains' required reports on the moral condition of the troops, the most common complaint was profanity. White complained that "profane swearing is too prevalent both with officers and men, yet I hope the influence of our protracted meetings may [have] checked it to a great extent." Randolph asserted that

> the greatest ostensible evil in this regiment is, profanity. Some of the white Com. Officers *persist* in this evil habit, which makes it very difficult for the Chaplain to check it on the part of the men. The poor oppressed negro of this land needs the most wholesome example set before him to elevate him, but this is one sad example, set by those whom he looks up to for example, and one which confirms him in his degredation. Would that for humanity's sake it could be stoped!

Randolph noted that of the twenty-eight white officers in the 26th USCT, ten were "habitually profane."[23]

There is no direct evidence about the soldiers' relations with the local women, but the records show that the chaplains performed a great number of marriages for the men, especially after the fighting ended in April 1865. There were even special orders issued in some areas regulating such marriages and requiring that certificates be issued when soldiers married ex-slaves. Serious moral incidents occurred in some regiments, but Garland White could proudly report that "no one in our regiment has been executed or punished with capital punishment. No mutinous act can be found upon the record of the 28th USCT."[24] The chaplains undoubtedly had some influence on the behavior of some of their men, reminding them of their duty to God, nation, family, and race.

Conducting worship services was the most public of the chaplain's official duties. Worship and prayer meetings were open to all, both enlisted men and their white officers. Most chaplains apparently tried to hold regular services each Sunday, even though army regulations did not call for such until the spring of 1864. But wartime conditions frequently made such services impossible, and the regulations added that phrase, "when practicable." In winter, when the troops were in camp, regular services were "practicable." But when spring made the roads passable, the fighting began again and routine vanished.

May of 1864 saw the start of the great campaign against Richmond, the Confederate capital. Black troops were fully involved in the main action of the war for the first time. In particular, they led the offense against Petersburg, the rail center south of Richmond. Chaplain Asher reported that "our opportunities for holding service while in the field are usually much fewer than when in winter quarters, but we have managed to hold service with but two exceptions each Sabbath since we have been in our present location. The exceptions were when the regiment were in the trenches."[25]

Turner, returning from sick leave to join his regiment in time for heavy fighting along the James River, told his superiors, "Since my return to duty my regiment has been so continually moving or otherwise actively engaged in front of the enemy that it has not been my privilege to have those religious exercises which are necessary to counter balance the demoralizing influences incident to army life." A year later, however, he could write:

> After we left the front of Richmond and started on the Fort Fisher [North Carolina] expedition, our campaign was so constant and uncertain . . . [it] subjected our religious exercises to so many disappointments. . . . During the intermedium, however, we have had preaching, prayer meetings, and other moral or religious exercises as much as circumstance would permit. So much so, that no one could frame an excuse that his identity with sin was founded upon the ground that he was not taught better. But for the last six weeks our regimental church has been systematically carried on.[26]

With the end of the war, the occupying soldiers had more leisure for worship. Chaplain White could report that "we preach every Sunday unless on a march or prevented by bad weather. We have prayer meeting twice a week when in camp, but here of late we have prayer meetings every night & things as regard religion progress finely." Those prayer meetings, of course, gave the chaplain encouragement—they were the evidence of the efficacy of his work. "I have to admire the soldiers' prayer meeting in my regiment," Turner wrote. "I have repeatedly stood and looked at my soldiers, when holding their prayer meeting, until I cried like a child, standing out under heaven's broad canopy singing and praying, in the most inclement weather."[27]

Worship and prayer meetings were the most visible parts and most pleasant of the chaplain's duties. The less attractive formal duties included burying the dead and attending condemned men at their executions. According to modern estimates, over 180,000 blacks served in the Union army; 2,751 were killed in action, and perhaps 60,000 more died of wounds or disease. Funerals, of course, were not something the chaplains liked to write about. White mentioned in 1865 that his troops were falling to disease: "No men in any country suffered more severely than we in Texas. Death has made festful [*sic*] gaps in every regiment. Going to the grave with the dead is as common to me as going to bed, for I also attend on such occasions in other regiments, rather than see men buried indecently. Chaplains are very scarce out here." Turner concludes a long soliloquy to Death with these words:

> At the end of time, O Death! thy dagger, bloody with the gore of billions of hearts, shall be snatched from thy ruthless hands, and those heroes who have fallen on many battle-fields, died in many hospitals for want of proper care, and have sacrificed their lives for all that is dear to man on earth, will rise before your face to recount the fruits of their labors and join in the chorus of the anthem, for ever to sing, "The world is redeemed, the slaves are free."[28]

There was more melodrama in executions, and the details were relished by the tellers. Congregationalist George LeVere, chaplain of the 20th USCT, told readers of the *Christian Recorder* the step-by-step details of his visit with a condemned murderer to inform him of his death sentence: three hours of tearful contrition and prayer, the hand-cuffed trip to the scene of execution, the firing squad, and the body falling into its coffin. Chaplain White provided similar detail for another execution. "The order was now given: Ready! Aim! Fire! About as long as it would take me to speak a word was the interval. I approached the corpse, and found that all life was gone. Five or six bullets had pierced his heart. It was the saddest spectacle I ever witnessed."[29]

The official duties of the chaplains—to bury the dead, conduct worship services, and to report regularly on the moral condition of the regiment—occupied much of the attention of the black chaplains. But since each of these men had to carve out much of his own role in his regiment, his nonofficial work as a leader, as an officer concerned with the well-being of his men, frequently took more of his time and energy than the official tasks.

Foremost among those other duties was service in the army hospitals set aside for black soldiers. Before the Civil War there had been no army hospitals as such. After the First Battle of Bull Run, in July 1861, emergency hospitals had to be established in Washington, D.C., to received the sick and wounded. At the urging of pious citizens, President Lincoln first appointed volunteer civilian clergymen to minister to the patients. In May of 1862, Congress authorized the appointment of military chaplains specifically to serve in army hospitals. As "contraband" runaway slaves entered Union lines, and as black soldiers began serving in the army, the government established hospitals to care for the sick and wounded blacks.[30]

Chauncey M. Leonard, a prominent black Baptist pastor from Washington, D.C., served as chaplain at the L'Ouverture Hospital for Freedmen in Alexandria, Virginia. An ardent abolitionist and missionary, Leonard had returned from West Africa early in 1864, his health too damaged to go back to Liberia. In August President Lincoln appointed him an army hospital chaplain. His work there included conducting regular worship services and a school, distributing religious tracts and papers, organizing a literacy society, publishing "Day Star," a newspaper written by the patients, and, of course, burying the dead. Presumably he spent time counseling and comforting the men.[31]

Washington was a major hospital center for the Union armies fighting in northern Virginia. But closer to the front lines other hospitals also treated black soldiers. Portsmouth, Virginia, received the sick and wounded blacks during the bloody battles around Petersburg and Richmond in the summer of 1864. "There are in the hospitals here about five hundred sick and wounded colored soldiers. . . . Some few are without arms and legs, but the greater part of them are slightly wounded, and will be ready for duty in a few weeks," wrote an observer. Such hospitals sprang up in the wake of battle, and no chaplains were available to serve the patients. The temporary solution was to assign regimental chaplains to visit their own men. "Look In" reported to the *Christian Recorder* on 16

July that "Henry M. Turner, Chaplain of the 1st USCT . . . is here looking after wounded soldiers, giving them good cheer, and pointing them to Christ." Chaplain Jeremiah Asher reported that, after the fighting of the early summer, he had sought and received permission to visit the hospitals at Hampton and Portsmouth. "The number of sick and wounded collected in the hospitals from the different regiments is quite large. I had supposed that they had been favored with the preaching of the word," he wrote, "but I was informed by one who had been there from the beginning: he told me they never had a sermon preached to them since they had been there. . . . Query: While the regiments are situated as these here, and some in front of Petersburg, would it not be well for one of our chaplains to spend some time with them?"[32]

When the chaplains were away from the regiments, they faced a peculiar problem: military identification. The uniform for chaplains was so plain and nonmilitary that they could easily be mistaken for civilians. They were clothed in "a plain black frock coat with standing collar and one row of black buttons, plain black pantaloons, and a black felt hat or army forage cap." For black chaplains that plain dress created special difficulties. Turner, on behalf of several chaplains, black and white, complained to the War Department: "We not having any badge or mark by which we are known, subjects us to a thousand inconveniencies, especially at Hospitals where we are the most needed, unless the guards know us personally, we are often treated below a private, not allowed to enter where we have important business, and some times driven away." He requested that the army provide a more distinguishing uniform for the chaplains. The appeal, probably in concert with others, was heard, and in August 1864, the chaplain's uniform was spruced up to include "herringbone braid around the button holes of their coats and . . . on their hats the letters 'U.S.', in silver, Old English design, encompassed by a wreath." This not only facilitated the hospital visits but helped distinguish the black chaplains from the ordinary run of black civilians.[33]

Recruiting new black soldiers was another special duty assigned to some of the black chaplains. As the war progressed and as the regiments with black chaplains moved into the South, the government needed increasing numbers of newly freed slaves to bear arms. The methods used to recruit those men varied from patriotic speeches to payment of bounties to trickery to outright kidnapping. Black chaplains were assigned to recruiting duty, presumably, because of their oratorical skills and their example of black achievement. Turner reported from North Carolina that "hundreds of these men stand ready to enlist at a moment's notice, while a few sermons or speeches would only be necessary to induce the rest."[34]

Recruiting had, for white men, frequently been the path to high rank and command. Indeed, many of the black chaplains had gained their commissions because they had recruited successfully in the North. In February 1865 President Lincoln had opened new doors by commissioning Martin R. Delany, a leading black physician, abolitionist, and journalist, as an army major with responsibility to raise black regiments in South Carolina and Georgia. William Waring (or Warring) of the 102nd USCT, resigned his chaplaincy in May 1865 to received a commission as second lieutenant in Delany's 104th USCT. With the new possibility of gaining high rank by enlisting freedmen as soldiers, Chaplain Turner decided in April 1865 that he could be of greater service to the Union as a recruiter, since he had little opportunity to preach to his own regiment, which was then continually on the move through North Carolina. Writing to Secretary of War Stanton, he claimed, "I have no motive in this other than to serve my country, and to be so situated that I can be able to inspire my race with those manly principles, which they are in many respects devoid of, owing to their former condition. . . . I can provide thousands [of recommendations] for that, or any other position you might give me, if it were to be a *Colonel*."[35] Turner did not get his promotion to colonel.

Before the war the main duty of army chaplains had been education, and the black chaplains considered teaching one of their most important responsibilities. Prewar chaplains on army posts had taught the children of the soldiers; the wartime black chaplains taught their own men. The prewar crusade for public education had valued learning as a way to break down class barriers and promote responsibility in a democratic society. Those same ideas were shared by abolitionists and blacks; one of the sins of the slaveowners had been their deliberate attempt to keep their slaves ignorant and illiterate. Free blacks believed that education would be a necessary priority for bringing the freedmen into full citizenship. Thus, black churchmen urged their people to get literacy as a way of gaining white respect, and some black ministers had augmented their low salaries by teaching school. When those men became army chaplains, they brought with them not only a respect for learning but also a strong belief that education would be the means of elevating the race. Turner spoke for all of them when he wrote that he hoped "to leave my regiment with every man in reading and writing. If I can accomplish that I shall say to myself, Well done!"[36]

The soldiers themselves eagerly embraced the opportunity to learn to read and write. For some it was an avenue to promotion, because the sergeants had to read orders and keep assorted records. Chaplain Boyd told of "our color corporal, Preston Johnson, who was entirely ignorant in books on the first of last August. In that month I commenced teaching him and learned him to write his name in two days. He is now able to write his company sick list [and] read his Bible." But most of the men went to school because they sensed that education somehow made them better men. Chaplain Turner told of receiving newspapers, *The Christian Recorder* and *The Weekly Anglo-African,* in camp:

> One very ordinary fellow takes up the paper, and begins to lay open its columns, and to throw a glare of interest where, to the uneducated, all seems to be darkness and gloom, and a more stalwart and finer-looking fellow listens a while, and becoming jealous at the idea, starts off in search of a spelling-book, saying to himself (as he fancies his superior abilities,) 'I won't listen to him. I am going to do my own reading,' and away he wends himself from tent to tent, and from one place to another, until a spelling-book is procured, regardless of price. All that is then necessary, is to watch him a few months, and you will see him blundering through a newspaper like a child learning to walk. You had as well loose him, and let him go then, for you may be sure he is gone.[37]

Chaplain Leonard, conducting school in his hospital, reported that "the day school keeps up with much interest and is increasing in numbers. The scholars are becoming quite interested with the historical part of their lessons." "The men are actually clamoring for books and readers," Boyd told his superiors. "Enter their quarters at what time you may, and you will find them engaged in trying to decipher lessons in their spellers." As the white chaplain of a Louisiana black regiment wrote, "A majority of the men seem to regard their books as an indespensable [*sic*] portion of their equipments, and the cartridge box and spelling book are attached to the same belt."[38] Not every soldier took advantage of this schooling, but the response of these men foreshadowed the eager reception of missionary teachers by freedmen of all ages across the South.

Much of the time, especially when the regiments were on the move or near the battlefront, the actual instruction was done by the chaplains. Some were aided by the literate noncommissioned officers, and some of the white officers or their wives taught the men. But whenever possible, the chaplains tried to get civilians from the North to teach. Especially after the fighting ended in a particular area, civilians taught the men, who now had more time free from military duties. Turner wrote from Roanoke Island, N.C., that "several young ladies, white and colored, are coming from the North to teach in my regiment besides two young men from New York, who will soon be here also: [we will pay] them $50 a month." "The soldiers themselves pay all the expenses incurred by the employment of teachers."[39]

Despite the eagerness of the men and the intentions of the chaplains, education in the army was not a simple matter. Military duties interrupted school, and when the regiments manned the trenches or marched against the rebels, there was no time for classes. There were never enough teachers, and it was often difficult to find a place to sit down for school. The biggest problem was the lack of textbooks. Some chaplains, especially white chaplains, could appeal to their denominations for books. But the black denominations were too poor to give much help, so black chaplains had to find other sources. Turner went on leave to Washington, D.C., to buy books for his men with money from his own pocket. But the hazards of war defeated his effort: "Hundreds for whom I had gotten books had them destroyed in their knapsacks by the sinking of a boat in the Cape Fear River." So he appealed to the army for help: "I renew my application, asking that you have my Regiment furnished with five hundred advanced spelling books. . . . As there are no promotions made in colored regiments for gallantry or merit, it would be a very small manifestation of regard to supply those at least who are trying to improve their minds with the necessary books." There is no evidence that the army bought any books, but from a variety of churches, missionary boards, freedmen's relief associations, and private donors came enough Webster's spellers and McGuffey's readers to make the chaplains' lessons successful for many black soldiers.[40]

There is, of course, no accurate way to measure this success. Chaplain White reported at the end of the war that his regiment, theoretically a thousand men but probably much smaller by then, contained three hundred men who could "read & write & cipher," and 474 who could "spell & read." Turner, reporting on the success of his schools, wrote, "I have never seen the fruits of my labor so visibly as I do now." James M. Trotter, of the 55th Massachusetts, was one of the handful of black soldiers who gained commissions as line officers. Twenty years later he recalled the army as a school for the black soldiers: "Not a few of the best workers were colored chaplains, who wisely divided their time between preaching, administering to the sick by reason of wounds or otherwise, and to teaching."[41]

One side benefit of the chaplains' education programs was that literate soldiers could write their own letters to the folks back home. Chaplains wrote for the nonliterate men frequently and in a variety of circumstances. Some letters were more or less routine. For example, Chaplain Bowles wrote for Private John H. Jenkins, of the 55th Massachusetts, informing Mrs. Jenkins in Boston of the situation near Savannah, Georgia, in January 1865:

Dear wife: I take these few minutes to write you a few lines to let you know how my health is wich is verry good at present and hope wen you receive this you will be injoying the same blessing. I have got the box at last the pies was all spoilt and as hard as a stone. The cake was a littel moldy but we eat it. . . . We have been 2 months in the field with but one sute of cloaths on our backs and [most] of the time nothing to eat. . . . Dear Amanda, do send me some tobacco and paper envelopes and post stamps in a small box as soon as you recive this letter. Give my love to Brother and Titus, Maria, Mary Ann, Mrs. Dawson and children and all of my friends. I must close by bidding you good day and may god ever bless you in the prayer of your true and affectionate husban[42]

More dramatic were the letters from wounded men in the hospital and the letters home announcing the deaths of soldiers. Chaplain White wrote that, just before the infamous Battle of the Crater at Petersburg, the men asked him to write home if they were killed: "'I want you, brother White, to write to my father and mother,' in New York, Philadelphia, Chicago, Boston, Cincinnati, Cleveland, and other places, 'that George (Thomas, John, or Peter, as we call each other out here) died like a man; and when pay-day comes, if it ever does come, send what money is due to my wife, and tell her to raise Sally and Mary in the fear of the Lord.'" From a hospital in North Carolina, Chaplain Turner told of one man's last request, "Well, Death's got me at last. I will soon be gone. Please write to my dear wife. Tell her Williams lives no more. Give my five little children their father's dying kiss. Tell her also, to raise them in the best way she can with her scanty means, and to teach them to fear their God, and love their country."[43]

This part of their work not only strained the emotional and spiritual resources of the chaplains but took much of their time and energy. Because of their involvement with the mails, some found themselves placed in charge of the regimental post office. Furthermore, as the most articulate, and probably the most literate of the black men in the regiments, some of the chaplains considered it their special duty to correspond with the newspapers to keep the home folks informed about the doings of the regiments—their activities, battles, casualty lists, and religious progress.

When the war ended in 1865, most of the fourteen returned to civilian lives and to the familiar tasks of ministering to black congregations. Samuel Harrison, for example, returned to western Massachusetts to resume his Congregational pastorate, respected by black and white alike. George LeVere, on the other hand, answered the call to be a missionary among the freed men of East Tennessee, founding several Presbyterian churches around Knoxville. William Waring became an attorney and trustee of

Howard University. Some of the chaplains went south to share in the heady excitement of Reconstruction politics. Benjamin Randolph became a newspaper editor and politician in South Carolina; as chairman of the state central Republican Committee, he was assassinated by an angry white man. Henry M. Turner went to Georgia to work for the Freedmen's Bureau and stayed there to win black Methodists to his AME Church. After serving in the state constitutional convention and legislature, he later became a bishop and ardent black nationalist.[44]

The black chaplains could look back at a period of rapid change both for their race and for themselves. The slaves had been freed, and black men had fought in the victorious Union cause—two events that had seemed impossible five years earlier. These fourteen clergymen had played active roles in the army while it held center stage. As officers, they had held highly visible and prestigious positions. They shared a sense of accomplishment that few Afro-Americans could have hoped for. But they had also experienced new forms of discrimination, and even as they returned home several northern states were refusing to reward black soldiers with the right to vote. Their army service had been but one battle in a much longer war.

Appendix

Black Chaplains in the Union Army

ASHER, Jeremiah. Baptist. Born free, Hartford, Conn., 1812. 6th USCT. Residence: Philadelphia, Pa.

BOWLES, John H. Baptist. Born free, Lynchburg, Va., 1827. 55th Mass. Infantry. Residence: Chillicothe, Ohio.

BOYD, Francis A. Christian. Born free, Lexington, Ky., 1843. 109th USCT. Residence: Louisville, Ky.

HARRISON, Samuel. Congregational. Born slave, Philadelphia, Pa., 1818, 54th Mass. Infantry. Residence: Pittsfield, Mass.

HUNTER, William H. AME. Born slave, Raleigh, N.C., 1831. 4th USCT. Residence: Washington, D.C.

JACKSON, William. Baptist. Born free, Norfolk, Va., 1824. 55th Mass. Infantry. Residence: New Bedford, Mass.

LEVERE, George W. Congregational. Born free, place unknown, 1821. 20th USCT. Residence: Brooklyn, N.Y.

LEONARD, Chauncey. Baptist. Origins unknown. L'Ouverture Hospital, Alexandria, Va. Residence: Washington, D.C.

RANDOLPH, Benjamin F. Presbyterian. Born free, Kentucky, 1837. 26th USCT. Residence: Buffalo, N.Y.

STEVENS, David. AME. Born: 1803, place and status unknown. 36th USCT. Residence: Harrisburg, Pa.

TURNER, Henry M. AME. Born free, Abbeville, S.C., 1834. 1st USCT. Residence: Washington, D.C.

UNDERDUE, James. Baptist. Born: 1828, place and status unknown. 39th USCT. Residence; Philadelphia, Pa.

WARING [WAHRING], William. Baptist. Born free, Fredericksburg, Va., 1833. 102d USCT. Residence: Oberlin, Ohio.

WHITE, Garland H. AME. Born slave, Richmond, Va., c. 1830. 28th USCT. Residence: Toledo, Ohio.

CHAPTER 13

Occupying the Middle Ground

African Creeks in the First Indian Home Guard,
1862–1865

Gary Zellar

MANY PEOPLE ARE FAMILIAR with the part African American soldiers of the First and Second Kansas Colored Regiments played in the Indian Territory and the trans-Mississippi theater during the Civil War. The role other African American soldiers performed in the First Indian Home Guard regiment is less well known. The former slaves and free blacks from the Creek and Seminole nations were the first African American soldiers officially mustered into the federal army and to participate in combat during the Civil War. Though their numbers were few, the blacks in the First Indian were an essential element in the tri-racial unit. The Africans served as interpreters and soldiers and provided a cultural bridge between the full blood Upper Creek soldiers and the unit's white officers. Their duties, however, went beyond merely translating orders, They served as negotiators, clerks, orderlies, medicine men, soldiers, and scouts. Occupying the middle ground had both advantages and hazards for the blacks as they struggled to define their role in the red, white, and black cultural equation.[1]

Relations between the African Creeks and the Creek Indians in the Indian Territory prior to the Civil War were marked by a fluidity that could not be equaled in most areas of the slave-holding South, particularly in the neighboring slave states of Arkansas, Missouri, and Texas. The pro-Southern Creek Council had adopted black codes during the years leading up to the Civil War that restricted the African Creeks' emancipation, property, and citizenship rights. However, as historian Daniel Littlefield has pointed out, they were not as severe as those found in neighboring slave states. In any case, the evidence indicates the laws were seldom enforced, except on the plantations of a few wealthy Creek aristocrats of mixed white and Creek ancestry who represented the Lower Creek faction of the tribe and who identified more closely with the cultural and racial attitudes of Southern whites.[2]

Most African Creek slaves were accustomed to scant supervision from their Indian "masters" who allowed them considerable freedom of movement. They were allowed to come and go as they pleased, decide their own work schedules, choose what crops to plant, and select where to live. According to Nellie Johnson, one of chief Roley McIntosh's slaves, "Old chief just treat all the Negroes like they was just hired hands." Jacob Perryman, a slave on the neighboring Mose Perryman plantation, lived under similar conditions and was allowed enough range land to accumulate livestock that included cattle, mules, and hogs as well as "ten fine American horses." Under those conditions many African Creek slaves accumulated personal property contrary to the provisions of the slave codes.[3]

Some African Creek slaves even kept firearms among their personal possessions. Although the black codes barred African Creeks from owning guns, the untamed character of the Creek country and the way the slaves settled in outlying areas apart from their masters made such strictures either impractical or unenforceable. Many slaves regularly supplemented their food supply with the abundant wild game in the area. The need to protect livestock from predators that roamed the countryside was an immediate concern that motivated some slave owners to supply their slaves with guns. Whatever the reason, many African Creeks owned or at least had ready access to firearms and knew how to use them.[4]

Creek slaves also were active in creating their own economic niche. Besides providing the field labor that generated the wealth enjoyed by the Creek aristocrats, African Creek slaves played a key role in the trading and mercantile activities in the Indian Territory. Many Creeks, particularly those who spoke little or no English, depended on their slaves to carry out their trading and commissary transactions with Euroamerican traders. African Creeks not only bridged the language barrier for their owners, but also had the ability to understand the Euroamerican culture and thus arrange a more advantageous trade. Consequently, many white traders in the Creek country reversed the cultural equation and began to employ African Creek interpreters at their stores.[5]

The slaves' freedom of movement also was indicated in how they arranged family life. Married slaves who had different masters frequently lived together with their families with little concern from their masters over where they located, as long as they rendered their masters' due. Under those conditions African Creek slaves formed wide-ranging community and kinship ties that enabled them to communicate with each other freely and if necessary quickly.[6]

African Creek slaves also were active in the cultural and social life of the Creek Nation. Black slaves were instrumental in bringing Christianity into the Creek Nation in the pre-removal days. They helped establish the first churches in the Indian Territory and provided the first preachers. Indeed, church membership in the Creek country remained predominantly African Creek until the mid-1840's. Even after Creek Indians began to embrace Christianity in larger numbers, many congregations depended on African Creeks to provide translations of sermons and scriptures. African Creek freedom of movement and independence of action was further indicated in how black devotees and preachers traveled some distance from their homes or their owners' plantations to attend church services, camp meetings, and revivals.[7] The African Creek slaves also participated in a wide variety of more worldly pursuits. They joined the traditional Creek inter-town ball games as valued players and attended horse races that were a popular pastime in the Creek Nation. Jacob Perryman no doubt entered his "American horses" in the races. Dances, called "bangas," also were popular. Indians and blacks of both sexes intermingled freely on such occasions, dancing to fiddle music provided by African Creeks while imbibing illicit whiskey smuggled into the Indian Territory.[8]

Free blacks also experienced a wider latitude of freedom in the Creek Nation than those in the surrounding slave states. While the Creek codes imposed taxes on all free blacks living in the nation, forbade them to marry Creek Indians, and in some cases denied them adopted citizenship, the laws posed no great barrier to living an unrestrained life in the Creek Nation. A majority of the free blacks were either small farmers or laborers, but many took advantage of the unfettered atmosphere and established stores, trading posts, hotels, and wagon train stations. Other free blacks held some of the largest stock herds in the Creek Nation. They also were employed as merchants' interpreters, teamsters, blacksmiths, stonemasons, and carpenters.[9]

According to the 1860 census, there were 1,651 black slaves and 277 free blacks living in the Creek Nation. As civil war approached, pro-Southern Creeks took steps to place the African Creeks under tighter control. Consequently, the Creek Council enacted a harsher set of laws. New laws that took effect in March, 1861, confined slaves to their masters' lands, instituted a pass and patrol system, and forbade slaves ownership of livestock or property or to hire out their labor. African Creek preachers were forbidden to preach before mixed congregations, and slaves could only attend churches within the immediate area of their masters' holdings. The new code also instructed all free African Creeks to select a master by March 10, 1861, or face being sold to the highest bidder. Free blacks also had to dispose of all property before their return to slavery. Violations of the codes carried severe penalties for blacks or anyone aiding them in circumventing the laws. The new laws struck at practices the African Creeks had come to regard as their rights. The African Creeks were unnerved by those developments, but in the early months of 1861 there appeared to be little they could do to reverse the course of events. The blacks were equally alarmed when leaders of the Lower Creek faction signed a treaty with the Confederacy in July, 1861, and then mustered two Creek Confederate regiments, giving the pro-Southern Creeks the ability to enforce the new laws.[10]

The African Creeks were not the only ones in the Creek Nation unsettled by the alliance with the Confederacy. Upper Creek leaders, who had counseled neutrality in the "white man's war," were driven into opposition after the Lower Creeks signed the Confederate treaty. Opothleyohola, the aging spiritual leader of the Tuckabatchee Creeks, organized the Loyal Creeks and along with other Upper Creek leaders repudiated the terms of the new treaty. The split between the Lower and Upper Creeks over the alliance with the South had more to do with longstanding intratribal antagonisms than with the issues of slavery or secession. Nonetheless, Opothleyohola and the Loyal Creeks found the African Creeks willing allies. In that new situation, and given their experience with freedom of action, most African Creeks chose to arm themselves and leave the Creek country rather than give up the relative freedom they had come to expect.[11]

The first blacks to join the First Indian Home Guard came from the estimated 200–300 African Creeks and African Seminoles who joined Opothleyohola's exodus from the Indian Territory to Kansas during the fall and winter of 1861.[12] Opothleyohola took active steps in forging an alliance with the blacks in the Creek and Seminole nations. The Creek leader sent agents into the slave settlements and free black enclaves throughout the two nations bearing promises of freedom to all blacks who joined the Loyal Creek cause. The blacks needed little convincing. They left their stores, farms, and the plantations of their masters to join Opothleyohola at his camp in the western Creek country.[13]

How did changing conditions move some African Creeks into active resistance and alliance with Opothleyohola and later to enlist in the First Indian Home Guard? One example involved Simon Brown. Brown was a trusted slave of Hannah Brown, who lived near Tullahassee Mission.

In accord with the relaxed Creek attitude toward slavery, Brown lived and worked at Tullahassee for the Robertson missionary family earning wages in the pre-Civil War years. "Uncle Simon" regularly made trips to Fort Gibson Station or Park Hill in the Cherokee Nation on errands for the Robertsons, frequently traveling alone.[14]

In July, 1861, Brown drove the wagon that carried the Robertsons into forced exile out of the Creek Nation for the duration of the war. On that trip, however, he scrupulously followed the provisions of the new slave code and only carried the Robertsons as far as the boundary of the Creek Nation on the Verdigris River. From there the dutiful Brown bade his patrons goodbye and returned to Hannah Brown's plantation on foot.[15] History has not recorded what went through Brown's mind as he made his way back, but by November the "trusted slave" fled the increasingly restrictive and oppressive atmosphere and took his family to Opothleyohola's camp because of "atrocities committed against Negroes by rebel troops."[16] Brown later enlisted in Company H of the First Indian.[17]

There were a number of blacks who fought in the battles of Round Mountain, Bird Creek, and Caving Banks during the flight to Kansas. A Confederate Cherokee scouting party reported confronting a group of armed African and Creek allies prior to the battle at Bird Creek. When the Cherokee scouts identified themselves as "soldiers of the South," one of the blacks "reprimed his gun" then "spoke back impudently," before continuing on. The Confederates, outnumbered and outgunned, decided to withdraw rather than confront the African and Creek allies.[18]

When the Loyal refugees finally reached Kansas, officials from the Indian Office observed that the Indians not only shared their camps with blacks but also "treat them as their equals." G. C. Snow, the Seminole agent, counted sixty African Seminoles among the refugees when they arrived in Kansas. United States Army surgeon A. B. Campbell found fifty-three African Creeks slaves and thirty-eight free African Creeks in the Creek camps.[19]

Although Creek contact with whites was on the increase in the years immediately before the outbreak of the Civil War, communication was still limited, especially among full-blood members of the tribes. Moreover, the contact was usually confined to occasional trading and financial transactions. After the Native Americans and African American s became refugees in the white man's country and their very survival was at stake, the need to communicate with whites on a daily basis took on a new urgency. Accordingly, the blacks' responsibilities as "linksters" expanded enormously as they became the key liaison between the white officials who provided subsistence and medical care and the Indians who spoke little or no English and were desperately in need of such care.[20] The blacks' role as middlemen in the cultural equation took on another dimension after the African and Indian allies enlisted in the First Indian Home Guard.

The War Department granted authority to raise the Indian troops in April, 1862, and the African Creeks and African Seminoles among the refugees eagerly enlisted. A Kansas newspaper reported that one black said he wanted "to return to shoot his master, who is secesh."[21] When the First Indian Home Guard was officially mustered into the federal army in May, 1862, there were between twenty-five and thirty African Creeks in the regiment.[22]

Creek and Seminole Indians served as company officers in the ten companies of the First Indian. Among them were Tuckabatchee Harjo and Tulsey-Fixico, two leading voices in the more traditional Upper Creek faction. They commanded two of the eight Creek companies. Halleck Tustenuggee and Billy Bowlegs, war leaders in the Second and Third Seminole Wars, captained the unit's two Seminole companies. White regimental officers commanded the regiment and oversaw its operations. Colonel Robert W. Furnas, a free-soiler from Nebraska, had command of the regiment. With him he brought his aide-de-camp, Stephen H. Wattles, and his friend, Andrew Holladay. Wattles was commissioned as a lieutenant colonel and Holladay the regimental surgeon.[23] A. C. Ellithorpe, who left Chicago to answer the Union's call and received a lieutenant's commission, served as one of the most active junior officers. William A. Phillips, one of John Brown's chief supporters in Kansas, also served as a lieutenant.[24]

The first action seen by the blacks in the First Indian as well as the first combat experienced by regularly mustered blacks in the federal army during the Civil War came on the ill-fated Indian Expedition in the summer of 1862. The ostensible purpose of the expedition was to clear the area north of the Arkansas River in the Indian Territory of rebel troops so the Loyal Indian and African refugees in Kansas could return to their homes. Six thousand white troops were detailed to the expedition to aid the First and Second Indian Home Guard regiments.[25]

On July 2, 1862, the Indian and African allies routed the Confederates at Locust Grove. Other victories followed later that month at Sand Town Ford, and Bayou Menard as the African and Indian forces succeeded in pushing the demoralized rebels south of the Arkansas River. Meanwhile, the thousands of white troops contributed to the demise of the expedition by staying in camp, consuming the dwindling rations, and swilling whiskey in the 100-degree heat before staging a mutiny and returning to Kansas on July 18. Reportedly, the only shot fired in anger by the white federal troops at the Battle of Locust Grove succeeded in killing Surgeon Holladay.[26] The Indian troops were left behind to guard the retreat of the white troops and hold the area if possible. Both Ellithorpe and Phillips reported their men were eager to stay and defend the area in spite of meager rations and unrelenting heat. By the end of July Colonel Furnas, disgusted with the whole enterprise, and believing the Indian troops were on the verge of their own mutiny, also ordered a retreat to Kansas. Furnas later tendered his resignation to Secretary of War Edwin Stanton and stated his reasons:

> I have always doubted the propriety and the policy of arming and plac-
> ing in the field Indians. . . . All communication has been through inter-
> preters, all of whom are ignorant and uneducated Negroes, who have
> been raised among the Indians and possess to a great degree their pecu-
> liar characteristics. The commander has but little assurance that orders
> are correctly given . . . or understood.[27]

For Colonel Furnas, who stayed in camp most of the time issuing orders, using African Creeks as middlemen was a problem because they often identified with the needs of the Indians. However, Ellithorpe and Phillips, the white field officers, saw the Indian-African alliance in action against the enemy and judged it successful.[28]

After their return to Kansas in August many of the blacks and Indi-ans in the First Indian made their way back to the refugee camps around LeRoy, rather than report to the regimental camp near Fort Scott.[29] Approximately 300 of the 900 effective members in the First Indian refused to march when General James G. Blunt ordered them into Mis-souri at the end of September. The soldiers and their leaders felt betrayed by the white troops while on the Indian Expedition, and they also believed ordering them into action in the white man's country violated the agreement to serve only as "home guards" in the Indian Territory.[30]

Those who obeyed Blunt's marching orders found additional white offi-cers attached to their companies. Blunt believed the additions were neces-sary to improve discipline and to aid in keeping the company books and accounts.[31] The reorganization also included assigning African Creek sol-diers specific duties. Hessiah-hupt-keh received an appointment as first sergeant in Company A, which later became one of the most active and effective companies in the regiment during the fall campaigns. Joe Barnett and Jim Barnett of Company C had assigned duties at the regimental hospi-tal and as interpreters. Other interpreters included John Adams for Com-pany E, Cully Adams for Company G, and Ya-fa-la-mart-la for Company I.[32]

The truncated version of the First Indian participated in the Battle of Maysville on October 22. According to E. C. Manning, one of the recently appointed white officers assigned to Company C, the First Indian soldiers were among the first on the field and then actively pursued and harassed the Confederates after their retreat.[33] The victory at Maysville revealed that the African-Indian alliance could provide effective service in the white man's country when called upon and helped bolster the morale of the troops. Their defeat affected the morale of the Creek Confederate troops as well, some of whom began to reconsider their Confederate alliance.[34]

When the defeated Creek rebels came thundering back to the Creek country, they brought with them alarming stories of the imminent arrival of federal Indian Home Guard troops bent on revenge. The wealthy planters and slave owners in the Arkansas-Verdigris river valley panicked and hurriedly planned to move their slaves and stock to safety farther south.[35] Meanwhile, the African Creek slaves in the area began to make arrangements of their own.

William McIntosh, Jacob Perryman, and Hector Perryman, three brothers who lived in the Choska bottoms area on the north bank of the Arkansas River, huddled together over several nights secretly making plans for a dash to freedom after learning of their owners' intentions.[36] African Creeks from the surrounding McIntosh, Perryman, Marshall, Lewis, and Hawkins plantations also joined the exodus that included several hundred blacks.[37] In Cherokee country on their way to the Union lines, the party fought several skirmishes with rebel bushwhackers and encountered Stand Watie's Confederate troops. Lieutenant Colonel R. C. Parks, Watie's adjutant, reported "four wagons and a good battalion of Negroes" passing through the area in early November.[38] When they finally reached the Union lines at Camp Babcock on the Arkansas-Cherokee Nation line after the second week in November, it was reported that "a good many [of the] Creek contrabands . . . had arms" and lost seven men in their skirmishes with the rebels.[39] Among those enlisted "in the field" were Peter Johnson, who immediately became a sergeant in Company C, and Charles Hawkins, enrolled as a private in Company D. Simon Brown also enlisted at Camp Babcock and joined Company H, although he had been attached to the First Indian since its inception, as a civilian interpreter.[40] Major Ellithorpe described others in the party as "in a suffering condition" and "many almost naked." Consequently, those not enlisted at Camp Babcock were sent to Fort Scott and eventually were recruited at the refugee camps near LeRoy and Burlington, Kansas, in the last week of November. Among them were

Book, Tally Lewis, Dennis Marshall, and Jacob Perryman detailed to Company C, and Daniel Miller, Isaac Perryman, and Pompey Perryman assigned to Company I. The new recruits made up for the loss of seven African Creeks who deserted during the same period.[41]

In the weeks leading up to the battles of Cane Hill and Prairie Grove, Colonel Wattles took a leave of absence and Major Ellithorpe took command of the First Indian. Ellithorpe was not one to stand idly by and took steps "to reinvigorate" the unit. The earnest major, aided in his negotiations by black interpreters, made some headway in convincing the soldiers who refused to march in September to return to their units. In the process he uncovered a series of frauds in the regiment involving white officers cheating soldiers and interpreters of their pay. Ellithorpe brought charges against Wattles and Lieutenant George Dobler of Company G. The black interpreters were instrumental in bringing the scheme to light and with Ellithorpe's help they eventually recovered their money as well as that of the Indian soldiers.[42] One interpreter, Cully Adams of Company G, used his position as middleman to aid Dobler in defrauding the soldiers.[43] The whole affair shows the key role blacks played in negotiating the cultural terrain in the tri-racial unit as well as the growing importance of the white men in the equation.

At the Battle of Cane Hill on November 28, a running fight that stretched some four miles through wooded hills and rocky ravines, communicating orders was of critical importance. Lieutenant E. C. Manning commanding Company C later commented that his service with the First Indian was "very irksome" because "With each company were three or four Negroes who were enlisted men. The Indians either could or would not speak English, so the Negroes were used as translators. If I had no Negro at hand, I could give no orders."[44]

The black interpreters/soldiers, including the newly enlisted Sergeant Peter Johnson in Company C, apparently translated the orders effectively because they kept the men moving and aided in pushing back the Confederate attempt to establish themselves north of the Boston Mountains.[45]

African Creeks in the First Indian also saw service in the skirmish at Reed's Mountain on December 6. The entire regiment, except Company B, which was on detached service guarding Blunt's train at Rhea's Mill, and those holdouts still in Kansas, participated in the Battle of Prairie Grove on December 7. At least twenty African Creeks were under arms at Prairie Grove, making them the first regularly mustered blacks in the federal army to participate in a major battle.[46] Various reports in Southern newspapers spoke alarmingly of seeing "Negroes in federal uniforms" at the battle, some even "wearing officers' swords."[47]

The close association of the soldiers in the First Indian with white troops during the fall campaigns of 1862 necessitated clear communication between the Indians, blacks, and whites. Often enough it was a matter of life or death. The black soldiers and interpreters were in the unenviable position of having to bear part of the responsibility if orders were misunderstood or ignored by their Indian allies. In that situation the African Creek alliance with the Indians, while still important, became a secondary consideration as the contingencies of "the white man's war" guided the movements and the role of the First Indian.

Following the Battle of Prairie Grove, the regiment joined in a foray into the Indian Territory at the end of December. The soldiers who had remained in LeRoy since September rejoined the command after hearing that the First Indian would be dispatched to the Indian country. William A. Phillips, who had gained a promotion to colonel and was given command of the "Indian Brigade" consisting of the three Indian regiments, led the expedition. Although the Indian Brigade failed to occupy permanently the Indian country north of the Arkansas at this juncture, they did succeed in destroying Fort Davis, the rebel stronghold across the river from Fort Gibson, and provoked another panic among the Confederate sympathizers in the area.[48]

The expedition also brought another wave of African Creek recruits into the First Indian's ranks. Major Ellithorpe wrote at the time that "nearly 400 contrabands" from the Indian country had come into the Union lines and many of them "found ready employment in our army."[49] Ellithorpe went on to say the blacks "have somehow been impressed with the idea that the war is being waged on their account and the present is the long looked for time when their shackles shall fall and their race shall be free."[50]

Pickett Rentie believed the time had come. Their master took Rentie and his family south after the war started to resettle on the Red River, "where slavery was more like that among the white people."[51] Rentie escaped and at the beginning of the hazardous journey through the rebel-occupied Indian Territory he and his party had a skirmish with rebel bushwhackers. Rentie was separated from his companions, who gave him up for dead. Unscathed, Rentie continued on alone, eventually enlisting in Company B at the First Indian's camp near Bentonville, Arkansas, on January 14, 1863. Other African Creek recruits at that time included Jerry, John Steadham, and Warrior Rentie [Pickett's cousin] in Company C, William Marshall in Company D, Hardy Steadham and John Thomas in Company G, and Peter Collins in Company I.[52]

In April, 1863, Colonel Phillips and the Indian Brigade reoccupied Fort Gibson for the duration of the war. The men in the First Indian—

blacks, Indians, and whites—worked shoulder to shoulder with "shovel in one hand and gun in the other" building fortifications and throwing up earthworks. Phillips also ordered drill and training exercises in an effort to improve the "military appearance" of his soldiers. Phillips forwarded the orders to the new commander of the First Indian, Lieutenant Colonel George Dole, who had replaced Wattles. The new regimen required the African Creeks to be on the training field every step of the way. Apparently the efforts were successful; Phillips later reported, "[T]he progress of the First gives me great pleasure, for I had despaired."[53]

As the regiment settled into the routine of garrison life at Fort Gibson the white officers further defined and enlarged the duties of the blacks. That included orderly detail, assignment at the regimental quartermaster's, and duty as teamsters.[54] Many of those assignments were in keeping with the white racial stereotypes of blacks as a servile class. Additionally, the Indians viewed such assignments as beneath the dignity of a warrior. However, acute white observers noted that the African Creeks carried themselves with a self-assurance that was anything but servile.[55] Hospital duty was another assignment that regularly fell to the blacks. From the time when the refugees fled to Kansas, the white doctors found black interpreters "indispensable" in bridging the wide cultural gap between the Indian and white ideas of healing and medicine.[56] Sentry, guard, and picket duties at the fort required the African Creeks' bilingual abilities to identify friend or foe. Scouting assignments necessitated the clear transfer of intelligence gathered and that was particularly important in the wilds of the Indian Territory. The blacks' knowledge of the terrain and its inhabitants, coupled with their language abilities, made them valuable scouts. Black scouts reportedly furnished vital information to General Blunt on the disposition of Confederate troops under Generals Douglas Cooper and William Cabell that led to the victory at Honey Springs.[57] The important role the African Creeks played in the unit was further underscored in an August, 1863, order Lieutenant Colonel Dole issued. Dole posted a list of the soldiers, most of them African Creeks, who had to "hold themselves in readiness to answer to any detail when called for."[58] Thus, the African Creek soldiers did double duty and shouldered double the responsibility. While they had to be "in readiness," they were still accountable for their regular company duties.

One of the most important duties the blacks were called to perform was escort service for the subsistence trains that traveled between Fort Scott, Kansas, and Fort Gibson. Because of their communication skills and their familiarity in handling supply and financial transactions for their

Indian owners in prewar days, the African Creek soldiers were regularly detailed to escort and/or drive the trains on the long and hazardous trip. While the escort and supply details carried the stigma of unwarrior-like grunt work for the Indians, being directly connected to the workings of the supply system had its advantages in a country stripped of subsistence.[59]

The "regular" company duties of the African Creek soldiers included participation in the extensive combat that erupted in the Indian Territory during 1863. In addition to involvement in the constant skirmishing around Fort Gibson during the spring and early summer, the black soldiers also participated in the battles at Greenleaf Prairie, First Cabin Creek, and Honey Springs. Pickett Rentie said he could predict two days in advance when a battle was going to happen, because his body would begin to shake nervously, only to calm before the enemy arrived.[60] Jacob Perryman, promoted to sergeant in Company C in May, 1863, following Peter Johnson's death, prepared for combat in a different way. Reportedly his captain would get the soldiers "steamed up" on corn whiskey before a battle to make them "mean enough to whip their grannie[s]."[61] However they prepared for battle, the African Creeks' duties as translators and transmitters of orders put them in the front lines in every fight. They played an essential role in the 1863 summer campaign in the Indian Territory, as they had in previous campaigns.

The combat duties of the blacks carried an extra danger. If captured, they could expect no mercy. Following the Battle of Honey Springs in July, 1863, the First Indian took part in the effort to establish a federal presence in their native Creek country. The federal push into the area in August and September was initially successful in driving out the rebels and securing a large amount of corn and forage in the seemingly abandoned countryside.[62] In October rebel forces under William C. Quantrill entered the area and massacred eleven First Indian soldiers on a scouting detail near the Creek Agency. Several African Creeks, including John Steadham of Company C, were among those murdered. There also were other examples of atrocities committed against blacks in the First Indian. George, an African Creek in Company D, was captured and then murdered while on picket duty in early 1863. Bob Grayson, also from Company D, similarly was murdered after being captured while on scouting duty in October, 1864.[63]

The Union troops abandoned the Creek country soon after Quantrill's appearance, but not before enlisting two dozen African Creek and African Seminole recruits, many from settlements along the North Fork of the Canadian River. Among those enlisted was Sugar T. George, mustered into Company H, who became one of the most visible and active African Creeks in the regiment.[64]

In February, 1864, Colonel Phillips commanded another expedition into the western and southern regions of the Indian Territory. His effort had both military and diplomatic purposes. He intended to clear the area of remaining rebel forces and distribute copies of President Abraham Lincoln's Emancipation and Amnesty proclamations. The expedition met little rebel resistance, but Phillips had less success in getting rebel soldiers to surrender and accept amnesty.[65] However, the blacks taken into the far country by fleeing Indian masters earlier in the war flocked to Phillips' party. Thirty blacks enlisted in the First Indian during that period, among them former slaves from the Choctaw and Chickasaw nations. The regiment then included at least seventy-five blacks from the various Indian nations in its ranks. Nearly one-third of the men in companies D, E, and I were black.[66]

While there were a greater number of African Indian soldiers in the unit, few blacks were promoted. Except for Sugar George, who was promoted to sergeant in May, 1864, only a handful of blacks even attained the rank of corporal. George's promotion followed the dismissal of the company commander and the desertion of the second-in-command. Thus, George was the ostensible commander of the unit until September, 1864, when he was reported as sick in quarters. Rather than have command of the unit devolve to a corporal, Second Lieutenant Co-so-gee from Company G was attached to George's company as commander. The fact that George continued as de-facto commander of his company for five months spoke well for his leadership abilities, but he was not compensated or promoted for his increased responsibilities, which was typical of the army's inability to recognize the contributions of individual African Creeks.[67]

However, the important role blacks as a whole played in the unit was recognized in an unofficial way. Orders from the War Department in March, 1864, called for the blacks to be mustered out of the Indian regiments and enlisted in United States Colored Troops units. However, the local commanders realized the blacks were "indispensable" to the "good service and discipline" of the unit and wisely ignored the directive.[68] Not only did the blacks remain in the First Indian, but their enlistments increased throughout the summer of 1864.[69]

That summer more than 5,000 refugees returned to the Indian Territory from the camps in Kansas. They joined the 10,000 Indians and blacks who had already congregated around Fort Gibson for protection. The living conditions at Gibson, already frightful, took on truly alarming proportions as disease and hunger grew rampant.[70]

Under those conditions it was not surprising that a rash of violence spread through the regiment. There were six murders in the regiment between August and December, 1864, and two more in January, 1865.

Four of them, those of Sam Nero, Caesar Smith, Moosey, and Harry Jamison, involved Indians killing blacks. In another case, Jerry Stead-ham, an African Creek from Company C, killed John Wannack, a recent black recruit in Company I.[71] Two Indian soldiers from Company D, Su-lik-koh-hih and Tas-he-hia-e-ha, were charged with murder in Smith's death. The court sentenced Tas-he-hia-e-ha to ten years' hard labor, and Sul-lik-koh-hih to death by hanging. The testimony revealed that Smith's killing was at least in part racially motivated, but whether or not the killers' views typified the feelings held by a majority of Indians in the regiment is hard to say.[72]

Blacks in the First Indian also participated in the last major engage-ment of the Civil War in the Indian Territory at Second Cabin Creek in October, 1864. However, most of the soldiering done by the First Indian during the final ten months of the war involved herding cattle to subsist the soldiers and refugees clustered around Fort Gibson or chasing the cattle rustlers that plagued the Indian Territory.[73] It was estimated that as many as 300,000 cattle, much of the stock belonging to Loyal Indians, were run out of the Indian country to beef contractors in Kansas during the war.[74] Because many African Creeks, such as Jacob Perryman and Daniel Childress, were experienced stockmen, they were frequently detailed to round up cattle for subsistence, which brought them into fre-quent conflict with the rustlers, as well as the Loyal Creeks who claimed the cattle. Their operations often resembled combat missions. The bands of rustlers were like small armies themselves, allegedly supplied with weapons and ammunition from the Fort Gibson sutler's shop.[75] The line between official army operations, which were intended to subsist the sol-diers and civilians, and cattle rustling, was blurred by the conflicting claims to the cattle and the involvement of army officers and Indian Office offi-cials in the illegal trade.[76] Once again the blacks found themselves in the middle ground where their own interests were difficult to define in the clash between white army officers and Creek Indians.

In early 1865 the First Indian returned to the Creek country and established permanent camps near the Creek Agency and Tullahassee Mission on the eastern edge of the nation. The soldiers gave some mea-sure of protection for the Creek and African Creek refugees who wanted to return to the area. Many of the African Creeks, among them Simon Brown and Pickett Rentie, resettled in the rich bottom lands in the Arkansas-Verdigris river valley formerly occupied by their rebel masters. While the First Indian detachments had no specific orders to protect the blacks in reclaiming the lands, their presence pacified the area and held rebel bushwhackers at bay while the refugees returned.[77]

As the war neared its end Phillips asked the War Department to keep the soldiers in service long enough to assist in planting spring crops, mending fences, and repairing buildings in the devastated countryside. The African and Indian soldiers worked together beating their swords into plowshares for several weeks before they were mustered out in May, 1865. It was a fitting end to a long and brutal conflict.[78]

The African Creek and other black soldiers in the First Indian Home Guard played a vital role in the regiment, though their contribution was seldom recognized or rewarded. Nevertheless, they served. Many of the future leaders of the postwar Creek freedmen community, including Sugar T. George, Pickett Rentie, Simon Brown, Tally Lewis, and Jacob Perryman, served in the First Indian.[79] The rigors of war tested the African-Indian alliance, but it survived to play an important part in the Creek Nation's politics in the postwar era. The blacks sacrificed much for their service in the First Indian, but in the process they won their freedom. A testament to that sacrifice and how it was linked to that of the Native Americans in the Creek Nation can be seen at the Fort Gibson National Cemetery where the graves of African Creeks and Creek Indian soldiers lie side by side.[80]

Part 4

THE BLACK MILITARY EXPERIENCE

Atrocities, Injustices, and Black Response

CHAPTER 14

"We Cannot Treat Negroes . . . As Prisoners of War"

Racial Atrocities and Reprisals in Civil War Arkansas

Gregory J. W. Urwin

THE BATTLE OF POISON SPRING, April 18, 1864, was one of the most complete victories ever won by Confederate forces in Arkansas. Fewer than four thousand cavalrymen sprang a cleverly laid ambush within the hearing of thirteen thousand Union soldiers in nearby Camden, capturing a large wagon train carrying food for their foes. As the exulting Rebels scattered the train's escort, they refused to take prisoners from its largest unit, the 1st Kansas Colored Volunteer Infantry Regiment. Thus a glorious Confederate triumph was transformed into Arkansas's most notorious war crime.[1] The atrocities at Poison Spring, along with the retaliatory measures adopted by other African American troops serving in Arkansas, reveal the essence of a savage conflict whose central issue was race.

Though more than 130 years have passed since that terrible day, the memory of Poison Spring still troubles many of those who prefer to view the Civil War in romantic terms. The Arkansas Department of Parks and Tourism, which maintains a historic park at Poison Spring, has tended to ignore the dark deeds that stained that particular patch of hallowed ground. Despite such indifference, the murder of captured black soldiers at Poison Spring deserves a prominent place in any history of the Civil War west of the Mississippi River.[2]

The clash at Poison Spring marked the beginning of the end for the Camden Expedition, the last major Federal offensive in Arkansas. In late March 1864, Maj. Gen. Frederick Steele, the commander of the Union

Department of Arkansas and Seventh Army Corps, marched south with roughly fourteen thousand troops drawn from his garrisons at Little Rock and Fort Smith. The five thousand soldiers from the latter post belonged to Brig. Gen. John M. Thayer's Frontier Division and were veterans of successful operations in Indian Territory. Among Thayer's regiments were the 1st and 2nd Kansas Colored Infantry, composed of runaway slaves from Missouri and Arkansas and led by white officers. Steele's column penetrated further into southern Arkansas than the Federals had ever gone before. The expedition also represented the first time that black units in the state were employed as anything more than garrison or labor battalions. Both of these facts struck terror into the hearts of the region's white inhabitants.[3]

Steele carried orders to rendezvous at Shreveport, Louisiana, with a larger Union army and a gunboat flotilla under Maj. Gen. Nathaniel P. Banks. Once Steele joined him, Banks planned to invade Texas, seizing vast supplies of cotton in the process to enrich Northern speculators. But the two armies were destined never to meet.[4]

Hampered by muddy roads and constantly harassed by more than six thousand Confederate cavalry, Steele pushed southward by starts and stops. A feint toward Washington, the capital of Confederate Arkansas since Little Rock's capture the previous year, threw the Rebels so off balance that Steele was able to march into the fortified town of Camden without fight on April 15.[5]

The country through which Steele's army passed had been picked over by Confederate foragers since the autumn of 1863. By the time the Federals reached Camden, they had been on half rations for three weeks, and their rations were soon halved again. But relief lay close at hand. Capt. Charles A. Henry, Steele's chief quartermaster, learned of the existence of five thousand bushels of corn stored at a point sixteen miles west of Camden. Henry assembled a forage train of 198 wagons to secure the corn.[6]

Steele turned to the Frontier Division for an escort to guard the train, and General Thayer detailed a total of 1,170 troops for that purpose. There were 438 officers and men from the 1st Kansas Colored Infantry, 383 from the 18th Iowa Infantry, 291 troopers from the 2nd, 6th, and 14th Kansas Cavalry and 58 artillerymen manning four guns. Command of the escort went to James M. Williams, the 1st Kansas's colonel and an officer known for his zeal, competence, and courage. A lawyer in civilian life, Williams had distinguished himself at several battles in Indian Territory in 1863 and would end the war a brevet brigadier general of volunteers.[7]

The Confederates destroyed 2,500 bushels of corn before Williams could reach the scene on April 17, but the Federals saved the remainder and loaded it aboard their wagons by midnight. At sunrise the next day, Williams started his column back toward Camden, detaching small parties to gather additional corn from the farms lying near his route. After marching some four miles, Williams encountered Confederate brigadier general John S. Marmaduke with twelve cannon and over 3,600 cavalry deployed for battle at Poison Spring.[8]

Marmaduke's hastily assembled force represented a cross-section of Confederate mounted strength in the Trans-Mississippi theater; a brigade and an independent battalion containing 786 of Marmaduke's fellow Missourians; 1,500 Arkansans in brigades led by Brig. Gen. William L. Cabell and Col. William A. Crawford; and 655 Texans and 680 Choctaw Indians in a division brought from Indian Territory by Brig. Gen. Samuel B. Maxey. Most of these horsemen carried infantry rifles, weapons with greater range and stopping power than the Rebel cavalry's traditional carbines and shotguns.[9]

Colonel Williams deployed the 1st Kansas in an L-shaped line to shield the head and southern side of the forage train from the enemy's main thrust. The black soldiers had only gotten fifteen hours of rest during the past seventy-eight and were now caught in a three-way artillery crossfire. Nevertheless, they held their ground in the face of superior numbers, repulsing two Confederate attacks with rapidly delivered volleys. Many Rebels present, impressed by such tenacity but unwilling to concede that former slaves could match them as soldiers, later stated that the Federals had 1,500 black troops at Poison Spring instead of 438.[10]

By the time Marmaduke was ready to mount a third attack, the 1st Kansas's ranks had been badly thinned by death and wounds, and ammunition was running low. Advancing with cheers and war whoops, the Rebels turned the battered regiment's flanks and drove the crumbling blue line back through the parked wagons. Colonel Williams rallied as many men as he could and conducted a fighting withdrawal to the comparative safety of a swamp north of the battlefield. From there, he guided what was left of his escort on a circuitous retreat to Camden. The first of these weary fugitives began entering Steele's lines around 8:00 P.M.[11]

A gloating Camden resident watched as Colonel Williams's men "held groups of soldiers in the streets in solemn silence, to hear the story of the fight at Poison Spa." The tales spread by the battle's survivors contained elements more horrifying than the experience of military defeat. As Williams himself reported: "Many wounded men of the First

Kansas Colored Volunteers fell into the hands of the enemy, and I have the most positive assurances from eyewitnesses that they were murdered on the spot." The 1st Kansas's major and adjutant confirmed the colonel's accusations, as did other members of the escort.[12]

Williams's casualty figures told Steele's veterans at Camden that they could not dismiss these atrocity stories. Of the 301 men listed as killed, wounded, or missing from Williams's escort, 182 belonged to the 1st Kansas. That by itself proved nothing, as the blacks had borne the brunt of the battle. What aroused suspicion was the disclosure that the 1st Kansas had suffered 117 slain but only 65 wounded. "It will be seen," reasoned a trooper in Steele's 3rd Missouri Cavalry, "that the number of our killed exceeds the number of our wounded in this engagement, an unusual occurrence in warfare of the present day, as it is generally found from the reports of the many battles being daily fought in our land, to be just the contrary. This can be accounted for when it is known as we were informed by one of the 2nd Kansas Cavalry who made his escape a few minutes prior to the completion of the struggle, that the inhuman and blood thirsty enemy . . . was engaged in killing the wounded wherever found."[13]

In letters, diaries, reminiscences, and oral testimony handed down from generation to generation, the victors at Poison Spring described the fate that befell those black soldiers who failed to escape. Lt. William M. Stafford, a Texas artilleryman in Maxey's division, confided to his journal: "The surprise of the enemy was complete—at least 400 darkies were killed. [N]o black prisoners were captured." Three different Arkansas cavalrymen expressed pride in the fact that the Union dead were "mostly Negroes." A trooper in the 1st Arkansas Cavalry boasted that "we almost exterminated the troops that had the train in their charge." Ordered to remove the captured wagons to a place of greater safety, Cabell's Arkansans drove over the dead and dying blacks, competing to see who could crush the most "nigger heads." When Gen. Edmund Kirby Smith, the commander of the Confederacy's Trans-Mississippi Department, reached the Camden vicinity two days later, his jubilant subordinates informed him that they had left six hundred Federal dead rotting at Poison Spring, "primarily Negroes who neither gave or rec'[eived] quarter." Local civilians were soon referring to the fight as the "Poison Spring Massacre."[14]

Of all those who succumbed to the homicidal frenzy at Poison Spring, none surpassed Col. Tandy Walker's Choctaws for sheer ferocity. As Lieutenant Stafford scribbled in his journal, "The havoc among the negroes had been tremendous—over a small portion of the field we saw at least 40 dead bodies lying in all conceivable attitude, some scalped & nearly all stripped by the bloodthirsty Chactaws." "You ought to see Indians fight Negroes—

kill and scalp them," marveled Pvt. Charles T. Anderson of the 2nd Arkansas Cavalry. "Let me tell you, I never expected to see as many dead Negroes again. They were so thick you could walk on them." The Choctaws' behavior was still a topic of conversation when Brig. Gen. Thomas J. Churchill's Arkansas infantry division arrived in the Camden area a few days after Poison Spring. "The Chocktaw was at Camden when we came up," James McCall Dawson of the 34th Arkansas wrote his family. "They caught out one Regt of Steels negros and killed all of them. They take no prisoners. They would shoot a negro as long as he could breathe." Mrs. Elizabeth Godbold Watts, whose home was close enough to Poison Spring to be pressed into service as a field hospital, complained that her slave, Henry, did nothing to protect her hogs from Choctaw foragers "for fear that someone will kill him since the negroes were killed so in that fight."[15]

The Choctaws harbored so much animosity for their black victims that killing them was not enough. In addition to scalping and stripping, the Indians devised other ways to desecrate the 1st Kansas Colored's dead. The *Washington (Ark.) Telegraph* treated its readers to this example of "CHOCTAW HUMOR": "After the battle of Poison Springs, the Choctaws buried a Yankee in an ordinary grave. For a headstone they put up a stiff negro buried to the waist. For a foot-stone another negro reversed, out from the waist to the heels." Three days after the battle, a Union burial detail discovered that three dead white officers from the 1st Kansas had been scalped, stripped, and turned on their faces as a sign of dishonor, while the corpses of their black soldiers were laid in a circle around them.[16]

News of these atrocities traveled quickly throughout southern Arkansas. For years afterward, Mrs. Martha Holcomb thrilled her children and grandchildren in the little village of Moscow with this version of the battle:

> By noon Marmaduke's men had routed the Federals who had put into the front line of the battle the untrained negro slaves. It was easy enough for these Southern planters when faced to face with their own slaves, to attack with a rage which put to flight the unskilled . . . negroes. They fled in terror to hiding places and were pursued by their masters like infuriated demons.
>
> A few miles below the battle field was an old mill with its beautiful pond fed by an abundant spring; here was refuge for the fleeing negroes. These Southern soldiers' revenge was not appeased by flight. The negroes were hunted and either shot or bayonetted in their hiding places.[17]

General Marmaduke and his senior officers never openly admitted that their men had butchered black prisoners, but they strongly hinted that such had been the case in their official reports. "The number of killed of the enemy was very great, especially among the negroes," noted General Cabell. "You could track our troops by the dead bodies lying on the ground." Colonel Walker asserted that during the engagement his "hungry, half-clothed Choctaws" had been animated solely by the desire to shed "the blood of their despised enemy." Col. Charles DeMorse, who led the Texas brigade in Maxey's division, offered this sinister revelation: "But few prisoners were brought in by my command."[18]

While acknowledging no complicity in any war crimes, some of Marmaduke's officers felt the need to justify the carnage committed by their troops. Colonel DeMorse implied that his Texans were outraged to find the Federal forage train "laden with corn, bacon, stolen bed quilts, women's clothing, hogs, geese, and all the *et ceteras* of unscrupulous plunder." Lt. Col. John M. Harrell of Cabell's brigade recalled that "little children's and women's clothing" were "piled upon the wagons," including "little baby frocks, shoes, stockings, women's bonnets, shawls, and cloaks."[19]

It was only natural for Confederates to be infuriated by such discoveries. Brutalized by hunger and the frustrations of campaigning in rough and hostile territory, Steele's bluecoats blazed a path of destruction across southern Arkansas. But that does not explain why the winning side at Poison Spring made the 1st Kansas Colored the sole object of its vengeance. After all, the 1st Kansas composed less than half of Colonel William's escort, and the African Americans were so drained by a lack of food and rest that they were in poor shape to go ranging about the countryside collecting forage and plunder. By sunup on April 18, one hundred black infantrymen were so worn out that Williams classified them as "unfit for duty."[20]

The escort's 291 white Kansas cavalrymen were far better equipped to loot the farms along their route, and they apparently made the most of their opportunities. "Many of the cavalry, in violation of orders, straggled from their commands," Williams fumed. Shortly before the battle broke out, some of these wayward troopers showed up at the home of Mrs. Sara Elizabeth Gillespie, about three miles from Poison Spring. "The soldiers," wrote Gillespie's great-granddaughter, "took what meal, hams and sides of meat, dried beans, peas and fruit that Sarah had not sent deep into the woods and buried."[21] According to the same source, the Kansans were even more ruthless in ransacking the farm next door: "A neighbor of Sarahs climbed up into her meal barrel when the soldiers started to take it, but the man just picked her up and set her out on the floor and took the barrel of meal away. They also took all of her silver. . . . She had one fork left that they did not find. The Federals took feather pillows and mattresses, ripped them open and emptied the feathers out, then used them as sacks to carry their "loot" in. They could sling them across the backs of their horses if there was no room in the wagons."[22]

From the existing testimony of Confederate civilians who lived in and around Camden during Steele's occupation, it is incontestable that the Union troops to be most feared were white Kansans—especially cavalrymen. "The real yankee's I was not afraid of," insisted Mrs. Clara Dunlap, "they treated me gentlemanly enough, but the Kansas jay hawkers, that were most always sent with the wagon trains I was afraid off, they looked mean enough for any thing, & the officers, as bad as the men!" Dunlap testified that the Kansans "took all of our mules, *corn, sugar, molasses, flour, everything* in the world we had to eat . . . , they even took all my *soap, candles, coffee* & every *hen, chicken,* turkey, *eggs* &c on the place except two or three setting hens, that ran off in the woods; all my *cooking vessels,* pan, *blankets* &c then searched the house over, broke the lock on every trunk (but one) & took a good many little things all my good *shoes, stockings, soda,* spirits, even . . . took my *wedding slippers.*" The invaders ravaged the nearby farms of Dunlap's relatives with the same merciless thoroughness. Many of these "Jayhawkers" bore grudges against Southerners that dated back nearly a decade to "Bleeding Kansas" days, and they rarely missed a chance to settle old scores.[23]

In contrast to their white comrades, Steele's black troops were reasonably well behaved, and the guilt for relatively few depredations can be laid at their door. On the night of April 6–7, 1864, some of the 2nd Kansas Colored may have burned a cotton barn south of Hot Springs after word got out that the white men from that plantation "were all in the Southern army." A week later, two black soldiers forced their way into a house at Moscow, but all they demanded was food.[24]

For the most part, however, enlisted personnel from the 1st and 2nd Kansas Colored gave Confederate civilians few legitimate grounds for complaint. "I did not find the negro soldiers impudent to a firm white man," an anonymous Camden resident informed the *Washington Telegraph.* During the Federal evacuation of the town on April 26, this same observer spotted a black regiment protecting a doctor's home from marauding white stragglers.[25]

Where Steele's black troops deliberately disregarded Southern white sensibilities was in their enforcement of the Emancipation Proclamation. Once at Camden, they wasted no time in notifying local slaves that they were now free to leave their masters and mistresses. Black soldiers also encouraged male slaves to enlist in the Union army, sometimes resorting to press gang tactics to snare recruits. Yet in all these activities, the men of the 1st and 2nd Kansas avoided direct confrontation with whites, and alert slaveowners managed to hold onto most slaves who were too timid to go willingly with the Federals. When an armed black squad tried to spirit off the household servants of businessman Henry Merrell, he succeeded in talking the soldiers out of it: "I interposed a long-winded argument to the colored patriots & they listened respectfully enough, until suddenly the drums beat for 'Roll Call,' & my audience vanished in obedience to discipline." Merrell also obtained a speedy release for his body servant, Munroe, who was bullied into enlisting after other black soldiers threatened him with hanging.[26]

If Federal looting really was the primary cause of the Poison Spring Massacre, then the Confederates had as much reason to murder the 120 white prisoners who fell into their hands—and not just the African Americans. The fact that the victims of this massacre belonged exclusively to the 1st Kansas leads to the conclusion that the perpetrators' motives were racial. The *Washington Telegraph*, the voice of Confederate Arkansas, admitted as much seven weeks after the battle.[27]

With the onset of civil war, John R. Eakin, the *Telegraph*'s editor, dedicated his newspaper to ensuring unwavering public support for the Confederacy across southern Arkansas. His importance as an opinion-maker received an enormous boost for Washington became the state's Confederate capital. In a June 8, 1864, editorial titled "THE SLAVE SOLDIERS," Eakin turned his persuasive talents to justifying Confederate excesses at Poison Spring:

> How shall we treat our slaves arrayed under the banners of the invader, and marching to desolate our homes and firesides? . . . It is a case in which it well becomes our rulers to pray most earnestly for Divine guidance. May they have it soon! Meanwhile the problem has met our soldiers in the heat of battle, where, there has been no time for discussion. They have cut the Gordian knot with the sword. They did right. It was not theirs to untangle its knotty folds. It is far better for the deluded victims, as for us, that the fate which may perhaps be considered inevitable, should come upon them in hot blood, and the excitement of the battle field.[28]

African Americans are such a conspicuous and valued part of today's American military that it is difficult to appreciate the revolutionary nature of Abraham Lincoln's decision to let slaves become soldiers. Yet when John Eakin proclaimed that "the crime of Lincoln in seducing our slaves into the ranks of his army" should be ranked "amongst those stupendous wrongs against humanity, shocking to the moral sense of the world, like Herod's massacre of the Innocents, or the eve of St. Bartholomew," multitudes of

Confederates on both sides of the Mississippi would have agreed. "All minor and local massacres," Eakin added defensively, "pale before it."[29]

To Eakin and other guardians of Southern slavery, the African American was two persons rolled into one. On the one hand, he was a simple and childlike soul, needing white care and guidance to lead a happy and productive life. On the other hand, he remained a savage at heart, purportedly like his ancestors in Africa, and had to be restrained by slavery. If ever those bonds should slip, he would revert to his animal nature and attempt to kill every white person he came across.[30]

White Arkansans schooled in such prejudice viewed any Northern action against slavery as more than just a threat to their economic and social status, but as a deliberate attempt to stir up servile insurrections. If slavery were abolished, whites would either have to exterminate blacks or suffer extermination themselves. The question was literally a matter of life and death, or so whites believed.[31]

When the Lincoln administration followed the Emancipation Proclamation with authorization to accept blacks into the Union army, Confederates in Arkansas fretted that the South's worst nightmare was about to come true. Little Rock's *True Democrat* accused the Federals of escalating the conflict into "a war for extermination, not only of men, but of women and children." The competing *Arkansas Gazette* anticipated this shift in enemy policy months before it took place, and its reaction was similar to the *Democrat*'s: "Our course is plain. A savage war has been forced upon us. We will have to meet, and deal with it as we find it." In particular, the *Gazette* urged the Confederate government to adopt the following course of action: "Arming negroes, as soldiers or otherwise, or doing any thing to incite them to insurrection is a worse crime than the murder of any one individual: Therefore, all officers and soldiers . . . guilty of such practices . . . should be punished as murders."[32]

Arkansas journalists charged the North with violating the rules of civilized warfare by fielding black regiments. Only the most drastic action could save the Confederacy and what she represented. "It follows irresistibly that we *cannot* treat negroes taken in arms as prisoners of war," proclaimed John Eakin, "without a destruction of the social system for which we contend. In this we must be firm, uncompromising, and unfaltering. We *must* claim the full control of all negroes who may fall into our hands, to punish with death, or any other penalty, or remand to their owners. If the enemy retaliate, we must do likewise; and if the *black flag* follows, the blood be upon their heads."[33]

Eakin's readers shared his indignation, especially after the 1st and 2nd Kansas Colored appeared in the midst. Reflecting in 1911 on the depredations committed by white Federals during Steele's stay in Camden, Virginia Stinson revealed: "Only one thing stirred my Southern blood to heat, was when a negro regiment passed my home going to fight our own dear men at Poison Springs. How fierce they did look, it was then that I gave vent to my feelings." When three wounded white prisoners from Poison Springs were delivered to the house of Elizabeth Watts, she taunted them by asking "if they felt as though they were fighting their equals."[34]

These feelings prevailed at the highest command levels in the Trans-Mississippi Department. Ten months prior to Poison Spring, Gen. Kirby Smith chided one of his senior officers in Louisiana: "I have been unofficially informed that some of your troops have captured negroes in arms. I hope this may not be so, and that your subordinates who may have been in command of capturing parties may have recognized the propriety of giving no quarter to armed negroes and their officers." Fear of Federal retaliation prevented the Confederate government from openly endorsing this draconian policy, but Kirby Smith's subordinates needed little prodding from above to put it into practice. In raids on Pine Bluff and Clarksville, Arkansas, between the fall of 1863 and the spring of 1864, Rebel irregulars shot or hanged captured black soldiers. Confederate guerrillas in Missouri habitually executed any male slaves caught trying to sneak off to Union recruiting stations. In a skirmish south of Lake Providence, Louisiana, on June 29, 1863, a Texas colonel directed his cavalry brigade to charge a fort held by two companies of black infantrymen and to "take none with uniforms on."[35]

As the first black combat unit in the Union army, the 1st Kansas was the paramount symbol of Yankee malice to every Confederate soldier and guerrilla in "Kirby Smithdom." In a clash that presaged Poison Spring, more than 150 Confederate bushwhackers surprised a foraging party of twenty-five men from the 1st Kansas at Sherwood, Missouri, on May 18, 1863. The black soldiers had stacked their rifles to load some corn into wagons, and most could not recover their arms before the Rebels were upon them. The guerrillas showed the defenseless Federals no mercy—shooting, stabbing, or beating thirteen of them to death. The others saved themselves by fleeing into the brush.[36]

Despite this setback, the 1st Kansas Colored developed into a first-rate regiment, which maddened its enemies all the more. At the Battle of Honey Springs in Indian Territory on July 17, 1863, the 1st Kansas squared off in a head-to-head musketry duel with the dismounted 29th Texas Cavalry. The blacks outshot the 29th Texas, downing its colors twice and finally putting it to rout. The Texans never got over the humiliation of being bested by former slaves. When the 1st Kansas and 29th Texas next met at

Poison Spring, the Texans recognized their opponents and shouted with vindictive glee: "You First Kansas Niggers now buck to the Twenty-ninth Texas!" After the fight, a black soldier feigning death heard the Texans chanting a macabre litany as they searched the battlefield for wounded men to kill. "Where is the First Kansas Nigger now?" one would crow. "All cut to pieces and gone to hell by bad management," another would answer.[37]

An African American did not have to bear arms for the Union to become the object of Confederate wrath. Simply running away to the Federals was considered enough of a threat to Southern society to warrant the severest penalty, as was seen at the Battle of Marks' Mills, Arkansas, April 25, 1864.

Like Poison Spring, the clash at Marks' Mills was a consequence of General Steele's logistical problems at Camden. On April 23, he dispatched 240 wagons to Pine Bluff to pick up a load of supplies. Mindful now of the sting of the Confederate cavalry, Steele detailed an entire infantry brigade of three regiments (1,200 men), 240 cavalry, and two artillery sections under Lt. Col. Francis M. Drake as the train's escort. Drake noted that his column was accompanied by "a large number of cotton speculators, Arkansas refugees, sutlers, and many other army followers, and 300 negroes." Two days out from Camden, Drake linked up with a relief party of 150 Union cavalry from Pine Bluff.[38]

That same day, four thousand Confederate horsemen directed by Brig. Gen. James F. Fagan and Joseph O. Shelby converged on Drake's force at Marks' Mills. Hitting the Federals from two directions at once, the Rebels annihilated the escort in short order, taking 1,300 prisoners and the entire supply train. But according to General Fagan, only 150 of the 300 runaway slaves with Drake were taken into custody by the victors. What happened to the others?[39]

The diary of Lt. Benjamin Pearson of the 36th Iowa Infantry, captured with most of his regiment at Marks' Mills, provides a partial answer: "There was not an armed negro with us & they shot down our Colored servents & teamsters & others what ware following to get from bondage as they would shoot sheep dogs." A wounded Colonel Drake fell into enemy hands midway through the engagement, and he subsequently learned that "a large number [of] negroes . . . were inhumanly butchered by the enemy, and among them my own negro servant." A graphic account of this massacre comes from Confederate major John N. Edwards, the adjutant of Shelby's brigade. "The battle-field was sickening to behold," Edwards wrote in 1867. "No orders, threats, or commands could restrain the men from vengeance on the negroes, and they were piled in great heaps about the wagons, in the tangled brushwood, and upon the muddy and trampled road." An Arkansas soldier saw General Shelby himself bring a clubbed rifle crashing down on the head of a frightened slave. Then Shelby drew his revolver and casually shot the prostrate black man to death.[40]

The exact number of fugitive slaves killed at Marks' Mills will probably never be known, but it undoubtedly topped one hundred. The day after the fight, Lieutenant Pearson's captors allowed him to walk the battlefield to search for his son, who was listed as missing. "The number of Negroes I could not get," Pearson complained. "I saw perhaps near 30, & the Rebs pointed out to me a point of woods where they told me they had killed eighty odd negroes men women & children this is their report to me & . . . I fully believe they are hartless enough to do any act that wicked men or devils could conceive." Those few runaways who survived the carnage were apparently hunted down by local whites and carried off to Texas for resale into slavery—much to the chagrin of their original owners.[41]

The war crimes at Poison Spring and Marks' Mills were not isolated outbursts of senseless racial violence but part of an ongoing program of racial intimidation that took its cues from the basic values of antebellum Southern society. As far as the men who did the killing were concerned, they had simply made examples of some disloyal slaves to deter other blacks from betraying their masters or giving further aid and comfort to the enemy.[42]

Despite the additional peril, there was no restraining the emancipation movement. When Steele's desperate Federals finally evacuated Camden on the evening of April 26, hundreds of slaves followed in their wake. Likewise, most black men already wearing Union uniforms were not demoralized by the Confederates' no-prisoners policy. A few weeks after Lt. William Blain of the 40th Iowa Infantry returned from Camden, he encountered a former servant named Alfred who had joined a black regiment at Little Rock. "I asked him," Blain wrote the next day, "if he intended to give the 'rebs' any quarter when he fought with them?" "No Sah," Alfred replied, "dey don't gib us any, and we don't intend to gib dem any. Why sah, dey just kill us like brutes and we's gwine to use dem de same way."[43]

Those were not empty words. Black troops had redeemed Alfred's harsh pledge a full month before Lieutenant Blain first heard it. Within a day of the bloodbath at Poison Spring, Col. Samuel J. Crawford called the officers of the 2nd Kansas Colored Infantry into council at Camden to discuss the enemy's treatment of their sister regiment. Before they adjourned, Crawford and his officers solemnly swore "that in future the regiment would take no prisoners so long as the Rebels continued to murder our men."[44]

The 2nd Kansas fulfilled that dreadful oath on April 30, 1864, when Kirby Smith and three Confederate infantry divisions overtook Steele's retreating army amid the flooded bottoms on the south side of the Saline

River at Jenkins' Ferry. At one point in the battle, the Rebels unlimbered two cannon opposite Crawford and his black troops. Crawford accepted the challenge and ordered a charge, which was closely supported by the white 29th Iowa Infantry. With one volley, the blacks immobilized the enemy artillery by killing most of its horses, and with a second volley they dispersed a supporting line of infantry. Then the 2nd Kansas dashed forward with leveled bayonets, the men shouting "Poison Springs" and "Here comes your 'Iron Clads.'" The blacks easily overran the battery position, impaling every Confederate within reach, including three gunners who raised their hands in surrender. Only the timely arrival and forceful intervention of the 29th Iowa saved the lives of Lt. John O. Lockhart, the commander of the captured cannon, and his five remaining men.[45]

In his 1911 memoirs, Colonel Crawford admitted that the 2nd Kansas used Jenkins' Ferry to repay the enemy for Poison Spring, but he insisted that his troops behaved in a humane fashion. "After the Poison Springs massacre," Crawford recalled, "we were resolved to take no prisoners. And yet, there lay scores of Rebel wounded all around us; but we left them as they were, to be cared for by their comrades." But Pvt. Milton P. Chambers of the 29th Iowa told a very different tale in a letter home seven days after the fight. "The negroes want to kill every wounded reb they come to," he wrote, "and will do it if we did not watch them."[46]

In the fury of their charge, Crawford's vengeful blacks drew no distinction between able-bodied or wounded foes. As Private Chambers related, "One of our boys seen a little negro pounding a wounded reb in the head with the but of his gun and asked him what he was doing. [T]he negro replied he is not dead yet! I tel you they won't give them up as long as they can kick if they can just have their way about it."[47]

Yet even after the heat of combat cooled, the 2nd Kansas continued to exact revenge for Poison Spring. Having fought Kirby Smith to a standstill, Steele's white regiments started to disengage and slip across the Saline River, leaving behind the 2nd Kansas for approximately two hours to cover their retreat. Crawford claimed that he utilized that interval to send "men all along where our lines had stood to pick up such of our wounded as might have been overlooked." His soldiers, however, combined this mission of mercy with acts of merciless cruelty.[48]

Earlier in the day, Pvt. John H. Lewis of the 18th Texas Infantry took a bullet in the leg and crawled behind a tree stump for shelter. "After a while," Lewis explained, "the firing ceased and our army was gone. Soon I looked around and saw some black negroes cutting our wounded boys' throats, and I thought my time would come next." Forcing himself to walk on his wounded leg, Lewis hobbled away to a place of safety.[49]

Other Confederates, following the Federals at a prudent distance, eventually stumbled across the horrors described by Private Lewis. Surgeon Edward W. Cade of Col. Horace Randal's Texas brigade revealed: "Our command fell back, and when they again advanced they found several of our wounded who had their throats cut from ear to ear by the Negroes." James Dawson of the 34th Arkansas Infantry wrote his family that "the negros killed some of our Wounded." Assistant Surgeon Junius N. Bragg of the 33rd Arkansas Infantry informed his wife that A. J. Williams, the regiment's acting sergeant major, "had his throat cut by a negro" and lived long enough to tell about it. David S. Williams, the 33rd's senior surgeon and A. J.'s brother, added more details in his own harrowing revelations: "We found that many of our wounded had been mutilated in many ways. Some with ears cut off, throats cut, knife stabs, etc. My brother . . . was shot through the body, had his throat cut through the windpipe and lived several days. I saw several who were treated in the same way. One officer . . . wrote on a bit of paper that his lower jaw and tongue were shot off after the battle was over or during the falling back as referred to above."[50]

News of these reprisals quickly became common knowledge throughout Steele's army, but no one censured the 2nd Kansas Colored. "It looks hard," Private Chambers conceded, " but the rebs cannot blame the negroes when they are guilty of the same trick." Lieutenant Blain resigned himself to the increasing dehumanization of the conflict as symbolized by Poison Spring and Jenkins' Ferry: "The 'rebs' appear to be determined to show no quarter to Black troops or officers commanding them. It would not surprise me in the least if this war would ultimately be one of extermination. Its tendencies are in that direction now."[51]

Colonel Crawford liked to pretend that the retaliatory measures he sanctioned at Jenkins' Ferry taught the Rebels to stop killing black prisoners. He was mistaken. Of the 150 badly wounded men that the retreating Federals abandoned at a field hospital on that battlefield, nine belonged to Crawford's 2nd Kansas. Before sunset, some Confederate cavalry rode up to the hospital and began robbing the patients. "One," reported indignant Surgeon William L. Nicholson of the 29th Iowa, "dressed like an officer, drew his revolver and shot three wounded 'niggers' who lay in the yard." Two weeks later, the Confederates moved Nicholson and the six surviving 2nd Kansas men to more permanent accommodations at Princeton, Arkansas, where the blacks were lodged in a small storehouse. Shortly after their arrival, Nicholson hard gunshots and someone shouting, "The niggers are catching it." Next he saw a Rebel gripping a revolver in each hand emerge from the storehouse. "I went over at once," Nicholson related, "and found all the poor negroes shot through the head."[52]

The unfortunate 1st Kansas Colored had several more of its member murdered at a hay-cutting camp fifteen miles from Fort Gibson, Indian Territory, before 1864 came to a close. On September 16, Brig. Gen. Richard Gano and a brigade of 1,200 Texas cavalrymen fell on Company H of the 1st Kansas at Flat Rock. The company's thirty-seven men took shelter in a ravine and kept the Rebels at bay for two hours until their ammunition ran out. At that, the blacks' white lieutenant told them to save themselves, but only four succeeded in getting away. Those few escapees relayed what happened next to Capt. John R. Graton, their acting regimental commander: "The men were all killed except a few who concealed themselves in a ravine until dark and then crawled away."[53]

Graton's words jibed well with Confederate accounts. "The negroes were nearly all killed in a little creek into which they had jumped," remembered Pvt. Jefferson P. Boze of the 30th Texas Cavalry. "The water was red with the blood of the dead negroes." Pvt. W. T. Sheppard of the 5th Texas Partisan Rangers rejoiced: "The Federals were short a company of negro troops and after the battle they were all 'good' negroes." To their credit, some of Gano's Texans abstained from the general bloodletting and spared six blacks as prisoners, but up to twenty-seven other Company H men were massacre victims.[54]

The racially motivated killings at Poison Spring, Marks' Mills, Jenkins' Ferry, Princeton, and Flat Rock sprang from deep-seated fears that had permeated white Southern society during two centuries of slavery. Such atrocities were not peculiar to the Trans-Mississippi, even though that theater had earned a reputation for brutality well before black troops entered the Union army. In 1864, incidents like the Poison Spring Massacre occurred from one end of Dixie to the other. To cite only the more conspicuous examples, Confederate soldiers refused to take black prisoners at Fort Pillow in Tennessee and in battles around Petersburg, Virginia.[55]

Confederates regarded the employment of African American soldiers as such a crime against humanity that they felt absolved from any obligation to treat black troops and their white officers as honorable opponents. Rebellious slaves and white abolitionist agitators had to be exterminated to keep other blacks in their place and save a social system based on racial subordination. These convictions added a unique element of savagery to the Civil War, and they persisted for a century after Appomattox. During Reconstruction, many Confederate veterans joined terrorist organizations that frequently assassinated assertive blacks who dared to press for political equality. As heirs to this heritage of racial oppression, the descendants of those veterans would preserve much of the old Southern order down to the 1960s. Thanks to the civil rights movement and the aggressive actions of the national government, expression of much of America's ingrained racial hatred has been driven underground, but students of the dark side of the Civil War should not be surprised to see it still surface from time to time.[56]

CHAPTER 15

Black Experience in the
Union Army

The Other Civil War

Richard M. Reid

VIEWED FROM AN INTERNATIONAL perspective, one of the distinctive
features of the American Civil War, especially given the widespread
material destruction and the bloody loss of life, was the restraint and control exercised by the armed participants on both sides. It stood in sharp
contrast to many of the wars, civil and international, in Europe, Asia, and
Africa, where the line between combatants and noncombatants blurred
and where atrocities became all to frequent. A major factor contributing
to his restraint had been the Union decision at the war's start, "to treat the
Confederate forces *as if* they were the army of a legitimate belligerent"
even though the Union denied legitimacy of the Confederate government.[1] As long as the rebel army and the Southern population observed
the laws and usages of war they were effectively treated as a foreign power.
Moreover, courage, combat, and a common background, as Gerald Lindeman and James Robertson have recently shown, helped create a bond
between Johnny Reb and Billy Yank which acted "to contain violence
within the limits of formal battle."[2]

For one group of Americans, however, the conflict was a very different civil war, one which included a strikingly brutal and savage side.
Black Americans, primarily Southerners, became increasingly caught up
in the conflict as Union armies first occupied significant parts of the
Confederacy and then began to use the blacks as a military resource. For

249

them the formalized rules of war did not always apply and for them the distinction between combatants and noncombatants was frequently ignored. Moreover, for black soldiers and their families it was not always possible to identify their enemies by the color of the uniforms.[3]

In the first year of the war both sides agreed that it was a "white man's war," and the Union War Department refused to accept even Northern black volunteers.[4] This kept black involvement in the early stages of the war to a minimum. The first attempts by Union officers, acting independently, to enroll blacks as soldiers led to failure and reprimands. In April 1862 General David Hunter had sought permission, unsuccessfully, to arm 50,000 blacks in South Carolina.[5] Three months later General John W. Phelps began to raise black troops in Louisiana despite the hostility, at that time, of General Benjamin Butler.[6] Both men were checked by their superiors and their black enlistees were never officially recognized. Rapidly moving events, however, soon achieved what Hunter and Phelps could not. Manpower demands, Union occupation of larger parts of the South, and a changing war goal forced the Northern government to alter its policy on black enlistment. The militia act of July, 1862, authorized the enrollment of blacks, envisioning their use in labor battalions which would free white soldiers for combat. The Emancipation Proclamation of January 1, 1863, went further, and provided for the enlistment of black soldiers and sailors. Two months later, the nation's first draft act accelerated white demands throughout the North that blacks be recruited, a demand which had produced a popular war song, "Sambo's Right to be Kilt." Several New England states, led by Massachusetts Governor John A. Andrew, took steps early in 1863 to raise regiments of black soldiers, initially made up of free Northern blacks, but later including Southern ex-slaves credited to the Northern states. Soon after, the Union army began to raise its own regiments of black soldiers.[7] Major recruiting efforts were conducted in the spring of 1863 in Louisiana by General Daniel Ullmann, in the upper Mississippi Valley by Adjutant-General Lorenzo Thomas, and by General Edward A. Wild, who was ordered to raise a brigade in North Carolina "from the freedmen of that state."[8]

These soldiers, their families and blacks elsewhere in both the North and South began to experience, in a series of ways, a very different civil war from their white comrades. One immediate difference faced by some lay in the way by which they were enlisted. For a minority, neither choice nor due process played a part. Instead they were virtually kidnapped. In April 1863, Captain Alfred Sears complained that Colonel Thomas W. Higginson had forcibly impressed black laborers whom he had been employing. "My men, Colonel," he wrote *have not been drafted. They have been kidnapped in the night.* And that by men who profess to be their peculiar friends. A panic has seized the negroes remaining here and many of them, unless closely watched will escape to the enemy.[9]

Late in the war, fifty-three black soldiers enrolled in Kansas complained that they had been

pressed into Service by force of numbers without any Law civil or military to sanction it many of us were knocked down and beaten like dogs others were dragged from our homes in the dead hour of [night] and forced into a Prison without Law or Justice others were tied and thrown into the river and held there until forced to subscribe to the Oath. Some of us were tied up by the thumbs all night we were starved beaten kept out all night until we were nearly frozen and but one alternative to join the service or nearly suffer death.[10]

Of course, these were the experiences of only a small minority of the 186,000 black soldiers.[11] However, once enlisted, they all faced a form of discrimination unknown to white soldiers. Despite earlier promises, the secretary of war decided in June 1863 to pay black soldiers not the $13 a month plus a $3.50 clothing allowance granted to white soldiers, but rather $10 a month with $3.00 deducted for clothing provided. Blacks who had enlisted with the promise of equal pay, and who were after employed extensively on work details, were outraged.[12] When the soldiers of Company A, Third South Carolina Colored Infantry, stacked their arms and refused to return to duty because of the pay question, one of their sergeants, William Walker, was charged with mutiny and subsequently executed.[13]

In addition, blacks could not realistically hope to become commissioned officers. Because of the possibility that a black officer might be placed in the position of ordering white soldiers, the war department refused throughout most of the war to consider allowing blacks line commissions.[14] Ultimately the animosity which these discriminatory policies caused among potential black recruits, and the ever-increasing manpower demands of the war, forced the government, in several stages, to alter its policy. By March 1865 all black soldiers were eligible for equal pay. In addition, the government had been persuaded, by wartime necessity and by men such as Andrew, Vice-President Hannibal Hamlin, James A. Garfield and Henry Wilson, to begin granting commissions to certain black combat officers, although the numbers remained few.[15]

As bitter as these issues became for some black soldiers, they did not deter freedmen from volunteering in large numbers. Blacks enlisted heavily in areas where that enlistment provided a basic claim to freedom for a man and perhaps his family, and where there was no competing demand for free black labor. Perhaps most importantly, blacks volunteered in large numbers when there was a general faith in the individual recruiting and commanding of the black troops.

General Wild's activities in North Carolina provide an example. Despite the discriminatory recruitment policy, blacks in eastern North Carolina flocked to join Wild's first regiment. By late June 1863 the 1st North Carolina Colored Volunteers Regiment (NCCV) had been raised and Wild was recruiting for the second regiment.[16] Just before he and his brigade were temporarily assigned to Folly Island, South Carolina, he had filled a third regiment. His soldiers were overwhelmingly ex-slaves drawn from the coastal counties of North Carolina, although often from countries held by Confederate forces. Less than five percent were mulattos, while only a slightly larger percentage was made up of out-of-state blacks.[17] Getting officers for his regiments was much more difficult, for he was not allowed to draw soldiers or officers from the Army of the Potomac, while the secretary of war, Stanton, refused in this case, as in others, to grant commissions to black line officers. Only with great difficulty did General Wild succeed in getting commissions for two blacks—Assistant Surgeon John V. De Grasse and Chaplain William A. Green.[18]

Wild's recruiting successes, and the numbers of blacks enlisting elsewhere, were remarkable given the sinister threat facing black, but not white, Union soldiers. What would be their status if captured? As early as the summer of 1862, Major General David Hunter, acting on his own authority, had armed black troops. Four of his soldiers had been captured in November, 1862. The Confederate secretary of war, James A. Seddon, had ruled that "they cannot be recognized in any way as soldiers subject to the rules of war and to trial by military courts. . . . Summary execution must therefore be inflicted on those taken."[19] In addition, Hunter or any other commissioned officer organizing blacks as soldiers was not to be regarded as a prisoner of war but rather was to be "held in close confinement for execution as a felon at such time and place as the President shall order."[20] This latter order was never carried out, but Hunter's unfortunate men were never considered part of the Union army and were thus not under its protection. It was a clear indication of what might occur when large numbers of black soldiers began serving in the Union army. By 1863 the issue of what to do with captured black soldiers was being unsuccessfully tackled by the Confederate government through a series of savage, but confusing and conflicting, directives.[21] Sometimes captured blacks were ordered executed and in one recorded instance they were sold.[22] In response, the Union War Department issued, then modified, General Order 100 stipulating that if a black soldier were killed in violation of the laws of war, a Confederate prisoner would be executed in retaliation. It was a policy which some officers were prepared to enforce. When Lieutenant Oscar Orillion and twenty of his Louisiana Native Guard were captured, hanged and cut to pieces by Confederate soldiers, retribution followed. General George Andrew at Port Hudson selected ten of his Confederate prisoners and executed them.[23.]

General Kirby Smith, operating in Louisiana, handled the question by advising his subordinates "who may have been in command of Capturing parties" to recognize "the propriety of giving no quarter to armed negroes and their officers, in this way we may be relieved from a disagreeable dilemma."[24] Sometimes the murder of captured black soldiers was a covert action. In September 1863 Colonel Frank Powers, a Confederate cavalry officer at Jackson, Louisiana, reported on the fate of a squad of black soldiers captured by his cavalry. "The morning after the affair," he wrote:

> Col. Griffith and myself ordered the Negroes Several hours in advance of the comd. . . . On the route . . . four of the Negroes attempted to escape. I ordered the Guard to shoot them down. in the confusion the other Negroes attempted to escape likewise-I then ordered every one shot, and with my Six Shooter I assisted in the execution of the order. . . . There was not any Federal prisoners [*sic*] with the Negroes.[25]

The cavalry commander for that department assumed "that the negroes were summarily disposed of," but took no action.[26] A citizen of Jackson subsequently testified that

> he saw Lieutenant Shattuck, of Scott's Confederate Cavalry, dismount from his horse and deliberately shoot dead a wounded U.S. colored soldier then lying wounded on the ground; also that he heard said Lieutenant Shattuck say that he had shot thirteen negro soldiers that day, and that they took no prisoners. There was no fighting on the day referred to; also that he saw Confederate soldiers taking other negro soldiers outside of town, as they said, to shoot them, and he saw their bodies afterwards on the ground.[27]

The cumulative effect of such acts was to threaten the control of law on both sides. In December 1863 General Edward Wild led two of his regiments into the northeastern part of the state, an area outside effective Union or Confederate control. After several of his black soldiers had been captured by irregular Confederate forces and after Samuel Jordan of the

5th U.S. Colored Regiment was hanged, Wild retaliated.[28] He seized the wives of two Confederate soldiers, Mrs. Phoebe Munden and Mrs. Elizabeth Weekes, burnt the former's house, and brought them both to Elizabeth City where they were held under guard by his black soldiers.[29] Wild warned that as his captured soldiers were treated "so shall they be; even to hanging." This act, and the holding of seventy-three-year-old Major Gregory of Camden County, infuriated Southerners and resulted in an investigation of the matter by a special committee of the Confederate Congress.[30] Despite the cries of outrage, actions such as this effectively controlled widespread mistreatment of black prisoners of war in North Carolina and elsewhere.

They could not ensure, however, that black soldiers would be taken prisoner; a constant specter facing black troops was that they would be given no quarter. At Milliken's Bend, where two regiments of badly-equipped black soldiers were able to beat off a superior force, Confederate soldiers reportedly shouted "no quarter" and cut down the few black soldiers who tried to surrender.[31] At Wilson's Wharf, General Wild's black regiments faced superior Confederate numbers and he was informed that unless his force surrendered immediately, General Fitz Lee, the Confederate commander, could not be responsible for the consequences.[32] Although Wild's soldiers drove off the Confederates after six hours of fighting, they and fellow black soldiers faced a level of warfare different from that encountered by white soldiers: they entered every battle with the possibility that no prisoners would be taken.

This possibility became a reality only a month before the fight at Wilson's Wharf. In April 1864 Confederate cavalry led by Major General Nathan B. Forrest overran Fort Pillow. The federal garrison there consisted of 580 men, over half of whom were black, men of the 6th United States Colored Heavy Artillery and the 2nd United States Colored Light Artillery.[33] One Confederate soldier described what happened after the fort was captured:

> The slaughter was awful. Words cannot describe the scene. The poor deluded negroes would run up to our men, fall upon their knees and with uplifted hands scream for mercy but they were ordered to their feet and then shot down. The white men fared but little better. Their fort turned out to be a great slaughter pen.[34]

The death toll for the white soldiers was under thirty-six percent, while sixty-six percent of the black soldiers were killed.[35] The white officers fared particularly badly. The commanding Union officer, Major William F. Bradford, was captured and subsequently shot "while attempting to escape."[36]

It might be argued, of course, that incidents such as that at Fort Pillow, or cases of black prisoners-of-war being executed or sold into slavery were the exceptions, and that statistically they were few. It would have been small comfort to the men involved. More importantly, while such a fate may have been increasingly unlikely as the war progressed, it was still a possibility which was faced by all black Union soldiers, but only those white Unionists who chose to lead these troops.

In other ways, moreover, the blacks' Civil War was a very different experience. The line between combatant and noncombatant blurred when it involved Southern blacks who were or had been slaves, especially if they were seen as helping the Union forces, relating to a black soldier or trying to escape to Union lines. One case in Virginia graphically revealed Confederate attitudes toward black refugees. In September 1864 some black government employees at the hospitals at Fort Monroe and Hampton had requested help from Union forces to get their families out of Confederate territory. An officer and fifteen black soldiers, with strict orders not to plunder, were sent out at night up the Smithfield Creek to get the women and children and to return immediately. The expedition became delayed when more and more women and children sought to join them, and more boats had to be obtained. When the expedition finally set out, it was early morning, the boats faced a head tide, and a warning had gone out to the surrounding farms. Three miles down the creek, the refugees were attacked "by a force of irregular appearance, numbering about 100, having horses and dogs with them, armed variously with shotguns, rifles, etc., and posted behind old breast-works." The opening fire was directed not at the uniformed soldiers in the rear boats, but rather at the leading boats, packed with women and children. Several were killed and more wounded before the remainder managed to get to the far bank and "scattered over the marshes. How many more have been slaughtered we know not," reported the officer in command.[37]

This pattern was repeated elsewhere in various forms. One of the most notable incidents occurred late in 1864 at Ebenezer Creek during Sherman's march from Augusta to Savannah. Here the Fourteenth Corps, commanded by Major General Jefferson C. Davis, crossed on a pontoon bridge which was ordered taken up before the black refugees following the army could use it. Hundreds were abandoned either to Wheeler's cavalry or to the river. Many blacks preferred the river. Unknown numbers drowned trying to cross while others, northern soldiers reported, were cut down by the Southerners.[38] The action, which shocked many of the Northern soldiers, caused one to wonder: "Where can you find in all the annals of plantation cruelty anything more completely inhuman and fiendish than this."[39] It is hard to imagine that white Union refugees would have been treated in a similar fashion.

One result was that some white commanders themselves began to ignore the rules of war and indulge in emotional revenge. Just before the battle at Wilson's Wharf, General Wild had been rebuked by his divisional commander, Brigadier-General Edward Hinks. Hinks wanted a report on "all the circumstances attending the killing of a citizen by an armed party of your Brigade, and the whipping of a Citizen Prisoner of War within your camp."[40] Wild was incensed at the rebuke.

The citizen, a district enrolling officer and a member of a Rebel signal party, was killed in a skirmish before the Confederates surrendered to Wild's soldiers. The whipped prisoner, William H. Clopton, had been arrested by Wild for disloyal activities. He apparently had gained notoriety as the cruelest slave owner in the region, and Wild allowed several women whose backs were scarred from the lash to return the very same treatment. Clopton was stripped naked and whipped by the women. In closing his letter, Wild revealed one of the key issues which exacerbated the relations between officers of white and black troops. Hinks, Wild wrote, had once again evoked the rules of civilized warfare, calling for the "exercise of magnanimity and forbearance," But, Wild continued,

> I would respectfully inquire for my own information and guidance whether it has been definitely arranged that black troops shall exchange courtesies with Rebel soldiers? And if so, on which side such courtesies are expected to commence? And whether any guaranties have been offered on the part of the Rebels calculated to prove satisfactory and reassuring to the African mind.[41]

Not all Union officers shared Wild's concern for the welfare of black troops. Indeed, blacks may have wondered for a variety of reasons whether all their enemies wore grey uniforms. A concern of many black soldiers was the welfare of their families, some of whom were still held as slaves, while others had been forced to relocate to avoid retaliation. All too frequently, even the latter families were treated callously by the federal government and given little support. Frequently, families who had set up crude squatters' camps were driven out of what little shelter there was. At Camp Nelson, Kentucky, some four hundred women and children were forced off the base; their shacks were destroyed and "many died" of exposure.[42] A similar act took place at Memphis, Tennessee, even in the face of some black soldiers who attempted to interfere.[43] Other Union officers had attempted to forestall such problems by preventing black refugees from entering their lines.[44]

Even the families of blacks who had enlisted in states still within the Union faced persecution. In Maryland, William Birney described the white terrorism that was used to dissuade black volunteers:

> Encouraged by their success, the enemies of the enlistment of U.S. Colored Troops have within the past week resorted to the most inhuman outrages against the families of free men of color who have enlisted: the cornfields of these poor people have been thrown open, their cows have been driven away and some of the families have been mercilessly turned out of their homes.[45]

Reports from Missouri indicated that a number of the wives and children of black enlisted men were being smuggled into Kentucky and sold.[46] The local provost marshal pleaded that,

> for the sake of down trodden humanity, use your influence to have the Negro recruiting Stopped—or else protect the families of the poor Soldiers who are enlisting to defend the Government. If the Government calls on the negro to fight her battles—in Gods name protect their wives and children while they are in the army.[47]

Sometimes the wife of a black soldier paid a heavy price. A Missouri provost marshal complained that the "wife of a colored recruit . . . says that she has been severely beaten and driven from home by master and owner." The letter had a note added to it that "this is but one of dozens of similar applications of like character."[48] The families of white Union soldiers killed in service were aided by cities and states, but little was done for blacks until July, 1864, when the federal government began providing survivors' benefits to black families.[49]

Even when black soldiers were free from concerns for their family's safety, they might fact discriminatory treatment from fellow Union soldiers, including their own officers. While some officers were sympathetic to black goals, even a man such as Robert Gould Shaw, a prominent Bostonian whose death at Fort Wagner provided the abolitionist press with a martyr, had misgivings about leading black soldiers.[50] Others had volunteered to lead black soldiers for reasons very different from those of Gould. It provided a rapid path for promotion. One such officer, Brigadier-General August Kautz, revealed his prejudice. "I shall feel less regret," he wrote, "over the slain than if my troops were white. . . . If I must fall myself I should prefer to die with my own [kind]."[51] When the Confederate capital fell, the senior Union officer, Major General Ord, warned the general leading a black division: "Now you must get these damned niggers of yours out of Richmond as fast as you can."[52]

In extreme cases, the prejudice of some Union officers created bizarre situations. In December 1863 Wild had used his newly-recruited black regiment in a major raid in eastern North Carolina, partly in an attempt to free black families and to raise new recruits. The raid was undermined by cavalry outriders who had been sent in advance of Wild's soldier to warn the inhabitants that his "nigger-stealers were coming to plunder them of everything."[53] The Confederate planters may have been grateful for the warning, but they must have been perplexed by the fact that the warning had been sent by a Union officer, Colonel John Ward of the 8th Connecticut Regiment.[54]

The black experience in the Civil War reveals two opposite forces in a precarious equilibrium. On one hand were emotions, fears, prejudices and hatred with roots deep in antebellum prejudice and slavery. Here was the potential for a bloody race war, with few, if any, civilizing restraints. Here lay the desire to treat captured blacks as insurrectionists, not prisoners of war. On the other hand was the fundamental need by both sides to observe formalized rules of war, which could alone prevent a descent to barbarism, a need deeply entrenced in American values. The realization that the rules of war could not be applied arbitrarily or selectively without being completely undermined ultimately won out. The precariousness of the balance of those forces had been made all too clear to black soldiers and their families by the time the scales had tipped the other way. That helped explain why, for them, it was a very different civil war.

CHAPTER 16

❦

Captive Black Union Soldiers in Charleston—What to Do?

Howard C. Westwood

"THIRTEEN PRISONERS FIFTY-FOURTH MASSACHUSETTS, black. What shall I do with them?" That message, hastily penned by Confederate General Johnson Hagood on the night of July 16, 1863, near the beginning of the Union attack on Fort Wagner, also noted that two of the blacks were "refugee" slaves, the rest free.[1]

The general's question posed a conundrum. The Confederacy had been struggling with it for months and would continue to struggle with it until the war was dwindling to an end. By mid-1863, the Union, after long hesitation, was taking blacks into its army by the thousands. Inevitably some had become Confederate captives. In time there were many more. Some had been slaves in the state where captured. Some had been slaves in a Union slave state. Some had been free, residents of a Union state or even of the Confederacy (notably Louisiana). Many blacks had donned the Union uniform voluntarily; but not a few, especially among slaves of Confederate states, had been forced into the army, either by formal conscription or by irregular means. Nearly all would be in the ranks, and eventually some would be commissioned. Captive, too, would be some of their white officers. Finally, among captives there would be officers and men of white units operating in conjunction with black units. The law of every Confederate state made slave insurrection or aiding such insurrection a crime; and, as viewed by the Confederates, slaves in arms as Union soldiers were engaged in insurrection. The conundrum: were all these captives regular prisoners of war or were they all common criminals; or were some the former and some the latter? Or were some captives in between, in some new, unprecedented status? Or were some simply to be slain, without ceremony? Confederate statesmen, politicians, military commanders, judges, lawyers, and ordinary soldiers and civilians were to face this puzzle. Nowhere in the Confederacy was it posed more starkly than in Charleston. For, from late 1862 until almost the end of the war, in Charleston and its near regions there was repeated conflict with Union forces that included slaves of the local citizenry and, by 1863, slaves from elsewhere as well as free blacks.

General Hagood's query, after receipt at district headquarters, was forwarded at once to General Beauregard, commander of the Department of South Carolina, Georgia, and Florida, headquartered in Charleston. With it went word that the captive blacks had been ordered to the city under a strong guard and "without their uniforms."[2] On the next day, July 17, the department sent a copy of Hagood's note to South Carolina Governor M. L. Bonham. At the same time, Beauregard informed Richmond that he had black prisoners from the Union forces, several of whom "claim to be free, from Massachusetts." He asked, "Shall they be turned over to State authorities with the other negroes?"[3]

It reflected the confusion in the Confederacy at that time—the time of Chancellorsville, Gettysburg, Vicksburg, and Port Hudson—that neither General Beauregard nor Governor Bonham yet knew that on May 1, 1863, President Davis had approved a joint resolution of the Confederate Congress that, as we shall see, answered Beauregard's question. The general and governor both thought that President Davis's proclamation of December 23, 1862, promulgated on Christmas Eve, was still applicable: that "all negro slaves captured in arms be at once delivered over to the executive authorities of the respective States to which they belong to be dealt with according to the laws of said States" and that "like orders be executed in all cases with respect to all commissioned officers of the United States when found serving in company with armed slaves."[4]

Doubtless Beauregard thought that the proclamation had been carefully formulated, for it had followed by less than a month quite different instructions that he had received from Secretary of War Seddon. In mid-November 1862, one of Beauregard's district commanders had captured four slaves, armed and in Union uniform, and Beauregard immediately had sought Seddon's guidance. After checking with the president, Seddon on November 30 had instructed Beauregard to avoid a dilemma. On the one hand, delay and "military inconvenience" would be caused by turning the slaves over to civil tribunals, and, on the other hand, they could not be recognized as "soldiers subject to the rules of war and to trial by military courts." The way between the dilemma's horns, Seddon instructed, was to have the "general commanding the special locality of the capture" inflict on the slaves "summary execution."[5] Obviously, Davis's proclamation, coming so soon after Seddon's harsh instruction, must have been thought through. And notably, it said nothing about free blacks. So Beauregard wanted further guidance. Indeed, as it turned out, most of the black captives claimed that they had not been slaves.

A very recent episode had shown Beauregard that he was in a delicate area. It had been only a month since General Hagood had forwarded a report that several young Confederate soldiers had been captured by Union forces at an observation outpost along one of the coastal waters. They were "sons of wealthy planters or themselves owners of slaves" and were lodged in the Beaufort jail instead of being treated as prisoners of war subject to exchange. It was said that the young men were kept hostage for black Union troops or their officers who might be captured by the Confederates.[6]

It was well for Beauregard to take warning from that report, for the facts behind it were sobering. It seems that the young Confederates were a sergeant and eight privates captured by the Union navy and that the navy had acceded to a demand of Union General Hunter, then army commander in the Sea Islands region, that they be turned over to him. Hunter knew that regiments of former slaves in his command had been one of the causes for the institution of a Confederate policy denying prisoner-of-war treatment to blacks and their officers. When he had found that among the navy's prisoners were "young darlings" of southern families, "rich, powerful and malignant," "pets of the aristocracy," he wanted them as hostages.[7] Moreover, on the very day of the report that Hagood had forwarded, Hunter had instructed the commander of one of his black regiments, a one-time Jayhawker, Colonel James Montgomery, that "every rebel man you may capture, citizen or soldier, you will send in irons to this place to be kept as hostages for the proper treatment of any of your men who may accidentally fall into the hands of the enemy."[8] While Beauregard would not have known of Hunter's instruction to Montgomery, he did know of a letter that Hunter had written to President Davis as recently as April 23, 1863, that revealed his attitude. Back in August 1862, when Hunter had been first trying to take slaves into his army, Davis had had his War Department issue an order declaring Hunter an outlaw and providing for his execution as a felon, on presidential order, if captured, and the execution of any other captured Union officer engaged in "instructing slaves, with a view to their armed service in this

war." In his April letter, Hunter had announced to Davis that if the
August order were not revoked, "I will at once cause the execution of
every rebel officer and every rebel slaveholder in my possession."[9]

While, by the time of the Union expedition against Fort Wagner,
Hunter had been superseded by General Gillmore as the Union army
commander,[10] it was obvious enough to Beauregard that measure and
countermeasure, retaliation met by retaliation, might soon make war
uncivilized, and that he should exercise caution in his treatment of captive blacks. Indeed, there already had been a breakdown of the Union-
Confederate prisoner exchange cartel so that any exchange was limited to
"special agreements." The Confederate treatment of blacks had been one
of the principal causes of the breakdown and would persist as an obstacle
to repair.[11]

While Beauregard was writing Richmond, Governor Bonham was
asking his state attorney general what evidence was required to render
blacks captured in arms "amenable" for delivery to the state's executive
under the presidential proclamation. On the next day, July 18, the attorney general opined that, since 1740, "by the laws of South Carolina a
negro is presumed to be a slave until the contrary appears." Moreover,
he advised, authoritative commentary had declared that "color is prima
facie evidence that the party bearing the color of a negro, mulatto or
mestizo is a slave." Hence, he concluded, General Beauregard must
deliver to the governor all Negroes captured in arms in South Carolina
"unless by evidence before him he is satisfied that the prima facie pre-
sumption of slavery arising from color had been rebutted."[12]

The governor sent Beauregard a copy of his attorney general's opinion, and they conducted "some informal proceedings."[13] though more
blacks than those first reported by General Hagood were being captured,
of the few who did not claim to be free none was a South Carolinian. The
presidential proclamation had ordered that slaves should be turned over
to the executive of the state "to which they belong." Also, among the
captives, there were white officers of black units, and the proclamation
had ordered that "like orders be executed" for such men. Beauregard
apparently thought that the proclamation meant what it said, that his
slave captives and their officers were not to be turned over to South Carolina authorities, but, presumably, were to be sent to the "belonging"
state. The governor—who was a lawyer and formerly had been both a
United States and a Confederate congressman[14]—read words not for
what they said but for what they intended; in his view, however strained,
the state "to which they belong" was intended to be the state where the
"offense" of slave rebellion and the capture had occurred—South Caro-

lina. But on the question of the free blacks, Beauregard and the governor did agree that further word from the president was needed.

As a result, on July 21, Beauregard followed up his recent inquiry to Richmond with a wire: "What shall be done with the negro prisoners who say they are free? Please answer."[15] And on the next day the governor wrote Beauregard formally demanding custody of the captured slaves and white officers and asking that the free blacks be retained—not exchanged or paroled—pending word from Richmond. As to the slaves, said the governor, if Beauregard disagreed with his interpretation of "to which [state] they belong," they also should be retained until the president could resolve the question. On the following day, July 23, the governor wrote Secretary of War Seddon, enclosing a copy of his letter to Beauregard, requesting not only the slaves and white officers but also the free blacks; the latter, he said, had violated a South Carolina statute of 1805 prescribing death for any person "concerned or connected with any slave or slaves in a state of actual insurrection within this State."[16]

On the day the governor had written Beauregard, Seddon had wired the general that, pursuant to a resolution of the Confederate Congress, "all negroes taken in arms" were "to be handed over to the authorities of the State where captured to be dealt with according to the laws thereof." And on the day the governor wrote Seddon, Beauregard wired the secretary of war that he did not know of the resolution, that, indeed, a congressman had informed him that "it failed to pass."[17] But finally the governor located a copy of the resolution and, on July 27, sent it to the general.[18]

This was the resolution of May 1. It provided, as Seddon's wire had indicated, that all "negroes and mulattoes" (slave or free) who are "engaged in war . . . against the Confederate States" or who "give aid or comfort to the enemies of the Confederate States" shall, on capture, "be delivered to the authorities of the State or States in which they shall be captured to be dealt with according to the present or future law of such State or States."[19] Hence, on July 29, the governor was advised by Beauregard that the blacks, slave and free, were at his disposal. The governor, however, was not yet ready to take custody, and at his request they were kept in Castle Pinckney, the military prison, until August 19, when they were transferred to the Charleston jail.[20]

For a time, however, the governor was confused about the white officers. Perhaps he had not read closely the congressional resolution before sending it to the general. For, on August 8, he wrote Seddon requesting that the officers also be delivered to him.[21] Two days later, though, he had found that the resolution explicitly provided that captured officers from black units would not be turned over to state authorities but would be tried by a Confederate military court and "be put to death or be otherwise punished at the discretion of the court," subject to the president's power to commute sentence.[22] Thus, on August 10, the governor wrote Seddon again, withdrawing his request for the officers. But in this further letter, Bonham raised a question: would it be quite right for a free black to be given one sentence—South Carolina law, as we have seen, prescribed death, subject only to the governor's general power of commutation—but his officer to be given a less severe punishment, as was possible under the congressional resolution? His letter suggested some arrangement between the state and Confederate authorities for uniformity of treatment. Bonham also advised Seddon that he would proceed with the trial of slaves and any free blacks from Confederate states but would delay action on free blacks from the North, hoping to hear word on the question he had raised.[23] The governor was beginning to glimpse something of the conundrum.

In the meantime, there was mounting public outrage that the defenders of Charleston were confronting armed blacks. The press reported that the Confederate troops were indignant at the thought that a white man might one day be exchanged for a Negro. The northern blacks were described as "a mongrel set of trash." Incidents were reported of blacks, seeking to surrender, being summarily shot. To lend grim humor to the issue, there was quoted the story of a Frenchman who begged for quarter from a Scot: "'I canna stop to quarter ye,' he remarked, 'but I'll cut ye in twa.' And suiting his actions to his words he passed on." Indeed, the account of the opening engagement in the Fort Wagner attack told that the blacks "received no tender treatment during the skirmish, and the marsh in one place was thick with their dead bodies."[24]

One of the local papers, virulently anti-Davis, knowing that the governor had demanded that free black captives be turned over to him, assumed that their continued residence in Castle Pinckney was due to "that serbonian bog of indecision—Richmond."[25] The authorities were quick to correct the paper's misunderstanding; already the governor was preparing for criminal proceedings. On August 10, he had instructed his attorney general to convene a court for the trial of such of the captives as appeared to be slaves or to be free blacks of the Confederate states, and on the next day Bonham ordered a three-man commission—two of his staff and another "prominent citizen"—to examine all the black prisoners.[26]

On August 14, the commission reported to the governor. There were, by then, twenty-four black captives other than hospitalized wounded. Each of the twenty-four was questioned separately. One prisoner seemed defiant; all the others were respectful. Only four appeared to be slaves. Of the twenty free men, none was from a Confederate state (though one seemed to be from Maryland). All were from the Fifty-fourth Massachusetts Regiment (Colored). Questioning disclosed, however, that the entire unit contained not more than fifty or sixty blacks from Massachusetts and but a few more from other New England states; in fact, about a third of the regiment had come from Ohio.

The commissioners had, for the most part, believed the stories they heard, for they were convincingly similar. All but the one defiant captive were utterly disillusioned by their treatment in the Union army and were eager to return to civilian life. In substance their complaints were three: (1) their enlistment had been solicited by the promise that their service would not be for combat but merely for garrison and fatigue duty; (2) promises of bounty and rates of pay had been grossly violated; and (3) in battle they had been put in the forefront, "as breastworks for the White Troops," told by their officers that they would be shot from behind if they did not advance. Some said that their officers deserted them. Two prisoners were unarmed officers' servants, carrying into the attack only canteens for their officers.[27]

On August 14, the day the commission filed its report with the governor, Seddon was writing Bonham in reply to the letter of August 8, which had requested custody of the blacks' officers. Seddon pointed out that the congressional resolution superseded the presidential proclamation and that the officers were thus to be handled by the military. He assured Bonham that "appropriate proceedings will be instituted and severe punishment inflicted upon the officers taken in the unworthy and criminal service of commanding negroes, thereby inciting to servile insurrection and all its attendant horrors within your State."[28]

Though Seddon's letter was not in fact a reply to the governor's letter of August 10, in which he had withdrawn his earlier request but had raised the question of uniformity of punishment for free blacks and their officers, it seemed to say that the military would deal harshly with the officers. So, on August 19, with Seddon's letter received, the governor transmitted a copy to his attorney general, telling him to "defer no longer the trial of the free negroes of the Federal States found in arms with slaves."[29] By August 21, the governor had assigned as counsel to the blacks a very able Charleston lawyer, Mr. Nelson Mitchell; on that day Bonham sent instructions to the Charleston sheriff to allow Mitchell and "lawyers associated with him," to have access to the prisoners "for the purpose of preparing for their defence."[30]

Soon—perhaps at Mitchell's request—the governor appointed as his co-counsel Mr. Edward McCrady, also a very able Charleston lawyer.

The governor ordered the attorney general personally to prosecute the case, designating as his co-counsel one of the members of the commission that had examined the prisoners.[31] The matter was now coming to a head. On August 25, the court met and organized for the trial.[32] It was the police court for the Charleston District, sometimes called the provost marshal's court, with criminal jurisdiction over slaves and free blacks, and its decisions were not subject to appeal. The proceedings began on September 8; but only the four alleged slaves were brought to trial, despite the governor's instruction of August 19 that the free black captives were to be tried also.[33]

It is not known whether the trial was confined to the four slaves as a result of the lawyers' tactics or as a result of the receipt by the governor of a further letter from Seddon, written on September 1, replying to Bonham's letter of August 10.[34] When the governor read this further letter, he was to find new confusion injected into Confederate policy. In Richmond, the complexity of the conundrum was becoming apparent. In early June, Seddon had written an old school friend, who had suggested that captured officers and men of black regiments be put to work "in the Chesterfield coal-pits," that the law required that slaves be turned over to the states and that blacks "without free papers when not claimed by the owners" would "be liable to be sold as slaves."[35] But that easy dictate hardly met the problem. The problem was soon to be posed to Richmond more insistently by General Kirby Smith, commanding the Department of the Trans-Mississippi.

In mid-June, Smith sent to Richmond copies of letters written to General Richard Taylor, one of his district commanders who had custody of some blacks "captured in arms." Smith did not know of the congressional resolution; like Beauregard, he had understood that the legislation had not been adopted, leaving in force the presidential proclamation. One of the letters to Taylor had been sent by Smith's assistant adjutant general; it told Taylor that "no quarter" should be given to slaves in arms, but, if quarter were given, they should be turned over to the executive authorities of the state where captured. (Apparently Smith, like Governor Bonham, interpreted "to which they belong" in the proclamation not to mean what the words said.) The letter went on to say that if such were executed by the military, Union retaliation would be provoked; but the author naively added that if they were turned over to the civil authorities to be tried under state law, "no exception can be taken." The other letter to Taylor was from Smith himself, who hoped that Taylor's subordinates "recognized the propriety of giving no quarter to armed negroes and their officers. In this way we may be relieved from a disagreeable dilemma." But if blacks were taken captive, Smith added, they should be turned over to state authorities for trial. In sending copies of the two letters to Richmond, Smith wrote, "Unfortunately such captures were made by some of Major-General Taylor's subordinates."[36]

With Smith's communication in hand by mid-July, Seddon had a reply sent which suggested a different policy. The reply did not mention officers, only the blacks. They, "as deluded victims," ought to be "treated with mercy and returned to their owners." However, "a few examples might perhaps be made," though "to refuse them quarter" would make them, "against their tendencies, fight desperately."[37] If, by the time Smith received this word, he had been informed of the congressional resolution, he must have wondered if his secretary of war intended to follow it; for the resolution was perfectly clear—all blacks, slave or free, were to be turned over to state authorities to be dealt with under state law; it made no provision either for refusing quarter or for the military's return of a slave to his owner.

In any event, Governor Bonham's letters, especially that of August 10 suggesting uniform treatment of free blacks and their officers, forced Seddon to seek instruction from his president. Perhaps he wanted such guidance because of a recent action by the president of the United States. On July 31, the Union's War Department had promulgated a proclamation by President Lincoln announcing that the Union would protect all its citizens, "of whatsoever class, color, or condition," and that "for every soldier of the United States killed in violation of the laws of war a rebel soldier shall be executed, and for every one enslaved by the enemy or sold into slavery a rebel soldier shall be placed at hard labor on the public works. . . ."[38] When Seddon received Bonham's August 10 letter, he sent it to President Davis for instruction. The president returned it, inviting Seddon to state his own views. On August 23, Seddon resubmitted the letter with his endorsement, saying that "the free negroes should be either promptly executed or the determination arrived at and announced not to execute them during the war." They should not be treated as prisoners of war, said Seddon, but dealt with so as "to mark our stern reprobation of the barbarous employment of such inciters to insurrection." Seddon suggested that the way to do this "effectually" would be "by holding them to hard labor during the war." Seddon did not suggest how this course might be squared away with the May 1863 congressional resolution.

On August 25, President Davis returned Bonham's letter to Seddon with his own endorsement added. He noted that the congressional resolution "gives no discretion to the Executive so far as the captured negroes are concerned." But, said Davis, the statute did provide, in the case of "white men serving with negroes" (Davis did not say "officers"), that he had the power "to commute penalty" that might be imposed by a military court. This, Davis noted, indicated "a purpose to make discriminations" between individual cases. So, Davis concluded, Bonham's suggestion that there be "the same line of action" by the state and by the Confederate governments (in their respective treatment of free blacks and officers) could not be given a definite answer "as each case must depend upon its circumstances"—unless (and here the conundrum surely was confessed), "as you intimate," it be decided "not to bring any case to trial." As to that possibility Davis said that he did "not know how far the power of the Governor extends."[39]

It was with the problem thus back in his lap that Seddon wrote to Bonham on September 1. His letter quoted his own endorsement to the president and the president's return endorsement. To the governor he recommended that "the captured negroes be not brought to trial, or if condemned, that your power of executive clemency be exercised" to allow for the possibility of an "arrangement on this question, so fraught with present difficulty and future danger." The difficulty and danger referred to, of course, was Union retaliation.[40]

Whether or not it was this word from Seddon that prompted the decision not to go forward with the trial of the free blacks when the four alleged slaves were tried, that decision at least was consistent with a position then being taken by the Confederate agent of exchange in a conference with his Union counterpart on the breakdown of the prisoner exchange cartel. At the conference, as the Union agent reported to his superior on August 25, the Confederate agent said that his people would "die in the last ditch" before giving up their right to send captured slaves back to slavery but that they were willing to make "exceptions" for free blacks.[41] Obviously, the seeming neat simplicity of the Confederate Congress's resolution was becoming befogged.

The trial of the four slaves, however, did proceed. It lasted for three days, from September 8 to 10. The court was a five-man tribunal. There were two charges: that, being slaves, the defendants had been in insurrection against the state; and that they had been "concerned and connected with slaves" in insurrection. Allegedly, two of the defendants had been slaves in Missouri and two in Virginia. The second of the two charges presumably was designed to cover the case were it decided that only its own slaves could be deemed to be in insurrection against South Carolina; the evidence was to show that in any case the defendants had been encamped with two Union regiments of South Carolina slaves.

At the trial, the only evidentiary conflict was whether or not one of the defendants in fact had been a slave. Time was largely devoted to lawyers' arguments, chiefly on the question of "the jurisdiction of the court, as a Civil Tribunal, to try offenses committed by persons engaged as soldiers in the act of war, and in the ranks of the enemy." The unanimous decision of the judges, announced without elaboration, was that the court had no jurisdiction. Thereupon the court ordered that the prisoners be recommitted to jail and that the governor be notified of its decision.[42] The captives were subsequently held in the Charleston jail, month after dreary month, along with other captured blacks. Already in the jail when they had arrived were four black Union sailors, at least three of whom were free-born New Yorkers.

Despite the fact that from the Republic's early days the Union to which the Confederate states had been parties had enlisted blacks in its navy (though not in its army),[43] the Confederates treated these black sailors harshly. As crew members of the Union gunboat *Isaac Smith,* they, with the boat's officers and rest of the crew, had been captured in Charleston's waters in late January 1863. In time, the officers and white crewmen were exchanged. The Confederate exchange agent had included the names of the blacks in the exchange list furnished to the Union agent, but that had been a deception. Not until August did Union authorities hear that the blacks in fact were incarcerated in the Charleston jail. The three black New Yorkers had managed to have smuggled out a note to the United States consul in Nassau telling of their fate: "in close confinement," "almost dead," fed "but a little corn bread and water." Their note was forwarded to Washington, where, on August 3, Secretary of Navy Welles sent it on to Secretary of War Stanton for his "special attention." General Hitchcock, the Union commissioner for exchange, advised Stanton that there had been "other cases like this" and that, in his view, "they can only be effectually reached by a successful prosecution of the war." Stanton then ordered Hitchcock to have three South Carolina prisoners held "in close custody as hostages for the three colored men" and to communicate that action to Richmond.[44] Three captive privates of a South Carolina Confederate cavalry unit were put to "hard labor on the public work" in Washington.[45] But in Charleston jail the three New Yorkers and a fourth black crewmen remained confined.[46]

For Governor Bonham, by mid-September, the conundrum had become most sharply posed. The Confederate Congress had decreed that all captured blacks were to be turned over to state authorities "to be dealt with according to" state law. But the governor's own state court had ruled that a South Carolina crime had not been committed by "persons engaged as soldiers in the act of war," even though they had been slaves. While Bonham later was to write Seddon that "the correctness" of that decision "may be questioned," he could hardly defy it. Aside from its finality under state law, the standing of the counsel involved gave it force. Prosecuted by the attorney general and defended by two of the state's leading lawyers—characterized by Bonham himself as "eminent"—the outcome of the case could not be shrugged off.[47] Carolina as well as other states, the governor in time did have at least some South Carolinian slaves tried before other state courts, and they were executed. But beyond that he did not go; with his president fuzzily suggesting that blacks not be brought to trial and with the secretary of war, obviously troubled by the problem of Union retaliation, recommending that the governor postpone a decision, Bonham simply "suspended further action," leaving the blacks in the Charleston jail at the expense of the state and local civil governments.[48] His bafflement must have increased when he found, as surely he soon did, that white officers of black units were not given the severe treatment by the military that Seddon had so confidently predicted. With only a few exceptions, nowhere in the Confederacy was the pertinent provision of the congressional resolution actually carried out; the officers were treated rather as prisoners of war.[49]

Nearly a year after the Charleston trial, the governor picked up word from Richmond press that further complicated the problem. It was reported that recently captured Union soldiers who had been slaves were being delivered to their former owners. Puzzled, on June 24, 1864, the governor wrote Seddon asking for pertinent regulations.[50] There is no record of a reply. Two months later, on August 23, he wrote Seddon again, saying that, in line with Seddon's letter of September 1, 1863, he had suspended action as to all captive blacks except those who had been South Carolina slaves, but he wanted to bring the question "again to your attention, in order that something definite may be done if practicable." He explained that his term of office would end in December and that he would "be glad" to dispose of the matter before then.[51]

That the governor was in a mood to place the whole business behind him is suggested by the fact that his office had just requested the state auditor to recommend "a suitable and proper fee" to be paid to the lawyers who had conducted the prosecution and the defense in the trial of the previous September. In early September 1864, the auditor, after consulting "eminent members of the bar," recommended that a proper fee would be one thousand dollars "to each of the Council on the part of the State and on the part of the prisoners respectively"[52] This recommendation reached the governor just after he had received a reply from Seddon to his August 23 letter. Seddon's reply, dated August 31, must have made Bonham wonder whether all the trouble and expanse undertaken by the state had been worth the candle.

Seddon said, in effect, that the Confederate executive and military were ignoring the congressional resolution of May 1, 1863, because of "embarrassments" from its "rigid enforcement." ("Embarrassments," of course, referred to Union retaliation.) Moreover, some state authorities had objected to having blacks turned over to them and often complained about the "inability . . . to obtain criminal trials." So, said Seddon, captives who had been slaves were being returned to their owners under a statute of October 1862. But "free negroes of the North are held in strict confinement, not as yet formally recognized in any official dealing with the enemy as prisoners-of-war, but, except in some trivial particulars indicative of inferior consideration, are treated very much in the same manner as our other captives." Seddon concluded with advice that the governor deliver slaves to their owners and free blacks "to the Confederate authorities."[53]

The October 1862 statute referred to by Seddon had been adopted at the closing of the second session of the First Confederate Congress as a reaction to President Lincoln's preliminary Emancipation Proclamation. It had provided that the secretary of war should establish depots in each state to hold slaves captured by the Confederate military. Each slave would be returned to is owner on due proof of the owner's claim; newspaper advertisements of the slave would be published, and until proof of claim was forthcoming the slave would be employed by the military on public works. The bill whence came the statute had provided also that captured free blacks should be delivered to the governor of the state where captured "to be dealt with according to the laws of such State," but the House committee handling the bill had eliminated that provision.[54] Thus, the measure was very different from the severe congressional resolution of May 1, 1863. Indeed it may be that the 1862 statute had been intended initially to apply only to noncombatant slaves, fugitive or seized by Union forces, captured by the Confederate military; and it certainly had not been designed to cover the case of slaves of a non-Confederate state (Delaware and Maryland).[55] In any case, whatever the intended scope of that statute, and even though the 1863 resolution had not amended it in express terms, the latter most certainly had superseded the former with respect to slaves captured in arms. But now the Confederate executive, by sheer fiat, had superseded the 1863 measure in its entirety with the much narrower and milder 1862 statute.

If, on Governor Bonham's reading of Seddon's August 31 letter, he questioned what the military would do with free blacks "not as yet formally recognized . . . as prisoners-of-war," that uncertainty was removed in a letter sent a few weeks later, at Seddon's instruction, by General Lee to General Grant. This letter, sent on October 19, defended the propriety of the Confederates' returning to their owners captured Union soldiers or sailors who had been slaves of "citizens or residents of the Confederate States," but stated, unambiguously, that all other blacks in the Union armed services "are regarded as prisoners of war, being held to be proper subjects of exchange, as I recently had the honor to inform you. No labor is exacted from such prisoners by the Confederate authorities."[56]

When, if ever, that authoritative word reached Bonham it must have heightened his confusion. Obviously, in his Charleston jail there were many free blacks, and they certainly were not being treated as prisoners of war. Further, he felt that some among his prisoners had been slaves, and Seddon's August 31 letter had advised that they be delivered to their owners, not kept in jail. But from the evidence available to him, Bonham could not identify either the slaves or their owners. Even as to the four who had been tried the year before, there was a problem. As to one, an alleged Virginia slave, evidence of his slavery was not clear; he may have been a free-born Ohioan. Two of the others were from Hannibal, Missouri, and the third from Norfolk, Virginia.[57] Identifying their owners and returning them would be, to put it mildly, impractical at that stage of the war. Finally, as the end of his term loomed near, the governor gave up. On December 8, he wrote Seddon that on that day he had ordered the Charleston sheriff to deliver all the prisoners to the Confederate military. "A few of them, it is supposed, may be slaves," he wrote, "but the State has no means of identifying them or their masters." He told Seddon that he had given the military "the evidence from which it is supposed that some of them may be slaves."[58]

In the meantime, for nearly a year and a half, the blacks had been suffering a jail confinement with scantest fare and most miserable conditions.[59] Neither the Confederacy nor the state ever notified the Union authorities of their identity; they had been nonpersons. While rumors reached the North that there were black prisoners in South Carolina, there was no way for the Union authorities to know who of the missing were dead and who were imprisoned. But finally there came in August 1864 another smuggled note brought by an exchanged white officer. The note pleaded that something be done to release the prisoners from their "destitute condition." The note was signed, "Mass," but appended a list of forty-six blacks in the Charleston jail as of June 13, 1864, most from the

Fifty-fourth Massachusetts, including the four who had been defendants in the trial of the preceding September. In a few days the list was published in the New York press.[60] But, as we have seen, the blacks remained in jail until turned over to the Confederate military in December.

From that time, their circumstances, miserable as they had been, worsened. For their destination was the military prison stockade at Florence, South Carolina, which rivaled Andersonville. Disease was rife, and some died, including two of those who had been defendants at the September trial, victims of fever.[61] The Confederacy was disintegrating. By late January 1865, General Winder, in charge of prisons in the area, wanted to move his Florence prisoners; but he was "at a loss to know where," for "in one direction the enemy are in the way. In the other the question of supplies presents an insuperable barrier." He urged "paroling the prisoners and sending them home." Bonham's successor as governor and General Chesnut, a leading South Carolinian, agreed with him.[62] But Winder's proposal was not accepted. Instead the prisoners were moved from place to place in North Carolina.[63] In the meantime, by the end of January the Confederate Congress had drastically amended the May 1, 1863, resolution so that it became nothing more than a condemnation of the employment of Confederate slaves as Union soldiers and a mere authorization to the president to retaliate as he thought proper. President Davis approved the amendment on February 8.[64] Finally, in early March, as General Sherman drove northward, most if not all of the black captives who had survived were released near Goldsboro, North Carolina. It is uncertain from records whether they were paroled, exchanged, or simply released.[65] No matter. The nonpersons had become persons again. And in Charleston, the struggle with the conundrum was no more. On February 18, Charleston had been occupied by the Union army.

CHAPTER 17

The Execution of White Officers
from Black Units by Confederate
Forces During the Civil War

James G. Hollandsworth Jr.

O N MAY 1, 1863, BOTH CHAMBERS of the Confederate Congress
passed a resolution in response to the Emancipation Proclamation declaring that "every white person being a commissioned officer"
who commanded, armed, trained, organized, or prepared black men for
military service was guilty of "inciting servile insurrection, and shall, if
captured, be put to death or be otherwise punished." Dudley Cornish
drew attention to the resolution in his important book, *The Sable Arm,*
when he quoted Charles W. Eliot's comments during the dedication of
the Shaw Monument on the Boston Common.

> The white officers, taking life and honor in their hands, cast in their lot
> with men of a despised race unproved in war and risked death as inciters
> of servile insurrections if taken prisoners, beside encountering all the
> common perils of camp, march, and battle.[1]

References such as these sparked this writer's curiosity. The fact that the
Confederate Congress had adopted the controversial resolution is
beyond dispute. Yet, to what extent was the threat implemented?

Federal military records provided the answer. At the end of the war the
federal government published the *Official Army Register of the Volunteer
Forces of the U.S. Army, 1861–1865,* containing a roster of all officers who
served in the infantry, cavalry, and artillery regiments constituting the

United States Colored Troops. If the Confederate government's policy was carried out in the field, the names of its victims would be found here.

The *Official Army Register* lists 7,773 Civil War officers from black units. One of the author's graduate students went through these names and identified every officer who died of noncombat causes. She also compiled a list of officers who were recorded as "missing" and presumably dead.[2] Her research determined that nine officers were "murdered," "executed," or "killed" under circumstances not involving combat, while ten others are listed as "missing." To put these figures into perspective, one must consider that eighteen officers died during the war of accidental causes and 160 men were killed in action. Another ninety-four died of disease.

Armed with the names of those killed or missing, this writer visited the National Archives in Washington and reviewed the compiled military service and pension records for each man. I also consulted the *Official Records* for references to these individuals.

My findings regarding individuals killed under noncombat conditions are presented in Table 1. Three of the nine (Sanborn, Schwartz, and White) were killed by civilians behind the front lines. Although their affiliation with black units may have contributed to these murders, violent acts by civilians in Union-controlled territory tells us little about the enforcement of official Confederate policy. I consequently focused my attention on the remaining six officers who were apparently killed by Confederate troops.[3]

The compiled military service and pension records of the ten missing officers generated a less consistent picture, as can be seen in Table 2. Three of the ten (Alman Bassett, John Cochran, and James Wilson) were dismissed from active duty. The search did not produce any records regarding a fourth man (F. Comstock), who was also presumably rejected by the army. Of the remaining six missing officers, Elisha Dewitt was reported to have been paroled after his capture at Milliken's Bend. Five others were captured, four in battle and one while on recruiting duty near Washington, La. One of the latter five, Capt. Corydon Heath, was reportedly murdered near Monroe, La. The other four—William B. Hamblen, Oscar Orillion, David W. Parmenter, and James C. Spry—were never heard from again. These five names plus the six men noted earlier thus constitute my list of candidates for the dubious honor of having been victims of the Confederate government's policy regarding white officers serving in black units (see Table 3).

Out of the eleven cases, I was able to locate reports regarding six, one of the earliest of which involved Lieut. Oscar Orillion.[4] On August 3, 1863, Confederate cavalry swept down on a detachment of Union infantry near Jackson, Louisiana. Twenty-two black enlisted men and Orillion were among the Federal prisoners. The next morning, Gen. John L. Logan, who commanded the raiders, ordered a guard from the 17th Arkansas Mounted Infantry to march the prisoners toward Confederate lines with Orillion at the head of his men. The guard set out several hours before the main body broke camp, took the wrong road, and eventually rejoined the main column later minus the prisoners. Col. John Griffith, who commanded the 17th Arkansas, reported that four of the black soldiers had attempted to escape and were fired upon, which "created some excitement and a general stampede among them, all attempting to effect their escape." Col. Frank Powers, commander of Logan's cavalry, was more explicit. "I ordered the guard to shoot them [the four escapees] down. In the confusion the other negroes attempted to escape likewise. I then ordered every one shot, and with my six shooter assisted in the execution of the order." Lieut. James W. Shattuck of Scott's Cavalry later boasted of having killed thirteen of the prisoners himself. Although neither Griffith or Powers mention Orillion by name, he was probably killed along with his men.[5]

Another account of an officer being shot "while trying to escape" involved Lieut. Hamblen, who was captured while on recruiting duty near Washington. In January 1868 Hamblen's mother placed an advertisement in the *New Orleans Times* for information regarding her son. The notice attracted the attention of one Crouch, formerly of 173rd New York Infantry, who claimed to have been a prisoner in Opelousas when young Hamblen was captured. Crouch reported to Mrs. Hamblen that her son was ordered to Texas, presumably to the Confederate prison at Camp Ford, but "was shot dead by the guard" about five miles from the town. Crouch stated that Opelousas residents were aware of the incident, talked about it among themselves, and justified the guard's actions because Hamblen had been recruiting and running off negroes from the Plantations."[6]

Actually, this was the second account the family had received regarding Hamblen's death. In May the year before, Robert M. McClermont, formerly of the 11th New York Cavalry, had written Hamblen's brother-in-law from Baton Rouge to give the following report.

> I was captured on the 14th of Nov. 1864, by Confederate forces of this state [Louisiana]. While a prisoner at one time there were three (3) sergeants appointed to guard me also to conduct me to a place of safety in the interior—Jackson, Miss. At one time the three sergeants held a sort of a council as to the propriety of shooting me, and accounting for it on the plea that I had made an attempt to escape, as the Vice President's son had been served. I immediately spoke up and denied their ever having the Vice President's son in their custody. They positively affirmed it and stated when and where he had been captured—which I have now

forgotten . . . I understood them to say that Young Hamblen was recruiting in this state for some Negro Regiment, and that they thought he was the Vice President's son, on account of his name and his being a New England Yankee. He was placed under the charge of a young Texan Cavalry man who shot Willie in the back of the head killing him dead, for attempting to escape. The sergeant who told me about it saw the young man's dead body, and heard the shot.[7]

McClermont made it safely to Jackson and was exchanged six weeks later. His report seems plausible, although it should be noted that McClermont was captured east of the Mississippi River, while Hamblen's murder occurred in the Trans-Mississippi Department. Nevertheless, the pension office accepted his account and awarded a pension to Hamblen's mother in 1890.[8]

Two months prior to Lieut. Orillion's demise, Second Lieut. George Conn and Capt. Corydon Heath respectively of the 9th and 11th Louisiana Infantry, African Descent, were captured at Milliken's Bend on the west bank of the Mississippi River near Vicksburg. Shortly thereafter, Thomas Cormal claimed that a white captain and all of the black soldiers taken in that battle had been hung in Richmond, La., in the presence of district commander Richard Taylor and his staff. Ulysses S. Grant wrote directly to Taylor to inquire about the charge. Taylor responded with a strong denial, adding that he had "remained at Richmond and its vicinity for several days after the skirmish to which you allude, and had any officer or negro been hung the fact must have to come to my knowledge, and the act would most assuredly have met with the punishment it deserved." Grant accepted Taylor's denial, and there is no evidence to suggest that Taylor was lying. In fact, the black troops captured at Milliken's Bend were not killed but sent to Texas, where they survived the war to return to their regiments after the Trans-Mississippi Department surrendered. Yet, Lieut. Conn and Capt. Heath were never heard from again.[9]

As Grant and Taylor exchanged messages over Cormal's allegations, several citizens living in the vicinity of Monroe came forward with another report of a violent end for two white officers from black units captured about the same time. They told Capt. W. H. Welman of the 59th Indiana Infantry that two white officers captured by Confederate troops near Lake Providence, La., had been taken into the woods one night and shot. They identified the gunmen as Maj. M. W. Sims and Lieut. Sparks, both members of Gen. Paul O. Hébert's staff. (Hébert was commander of the sub-district of northeast Louisiana.) In fact, three white officers from the 1st Arkansas Infantry, African Descent (later the 46th Infantry, USCT) had been captured along with 113 of their men by

Parsons' Texas Cavalry near Lake Providence on June 29, 1863. The Federals occupied a stout fortification on top of a large Indian mound. The white officers had offered to trade their strong defensive position for a promise of proper treatment but agreed to surrender the black soldiers unconditionally. Gen. Parsons accepted the terms, but apparently something went wrong. One of the white soldiers, Lieut. John East, did make it safely to Camp Ford, where he remained until his release at the end of the war. The other two officers disappeared.[10]

The fate of the two officers captured with East is clouded further by the absence of any reference to them in the *Official Army Register.* Of the five fatalities among officers in the 1st Arkansas during the course of the war, the *Official Army Register* indicates that four died of disease and one drowned in the Gulf of Mexico. No one is listed as missing or killed. I hoped to resolve this discrepancy when I learned that Maj. Sims had been captured by Federal troops in July 1863 as he attempted to cross the Mississippi River with dispatches for Joseph E. Johnston. After a brief stay in Northern prison camps, Sims returned to Vicksburg, where he was jailed until he could be court-martialed for the murder of the still unidentified officers. Unfortunately, this writer could find no evidence in the National Archives that Sims's court-martial ever took place. What I did find was a pardon for Sims after the war, ordered by President Andrew Johnson and signed April 23, 1866. Thus, the question of whether Sims and Sparks murdered two men and, if so, who they were remains.[11]

The most credible of the execution reports concerns another pair of fatalities. This time the accuser, First Lieut. George W. Fitch of the 12th Infantry, USCT, was an eyewitness to the event, and his statement is riveting.

> I was captured on the 20th of December fourteen miles in a southeasternly direction from Murfreesborough, [Tennessee,] in company with two other officers, Lieut. D. G. Cooke, Twelfth U.S. Colored Infantry, and Capt. Charles G. Penfield, Forty-fourth U.S. Colored Infantry, by a company of scouts belonging to Forrest's command, numbering thirty-six men, commanded by Captain [Addison] Harvey. As soon as captured we were robbed of everything of any value, even clothing. We were kept under guard for three days with some other prisoners . . . until we reached a small town called Lewisburg, some eighteen miles south of Duck River. There[,] the officers were sent under a guard of four men to report, as I supposed, to General Forrest's headquarters. The guard told [me] that was their destination. They took us along the pike road leading from Lewisburg to Moorsville, about four miles, and then left the road and turned to the right for the purpose, as they said, of stopping at a neighboring house for the night.

After leaving the road about half a mile, as we were walking along through a wooded ravine, the man in advance halted us, partially turned his horse, and as I came up, drew his revolver and fired on me without a word. The ball entered my right ear just above the center, passed through and lodged in the bone back of the ear. It knocked me senseless for a few moments. I soon recovered, however, but lay perfectly quiet, knowing that my only hope lay in leading them to believe they had killed me. Presently I heard two carbine shots, and then all was still. After about fourteen minutes I staggered to my feet and attempted to get away, but found I could not walk. About that time a colored boy came along and helped me to a house nearby. He told me that the other two officers were dead, having been shot through the head. That evening their bodies were brought to the house where I lay. Next morning they were decently buried on the premises of Col. John C. Hill, nearby.[12]

Fitch eventually made his way back to Union lines and reported the incident to George H. Thomas, who wrote to John Bell Hood on January 13, 1865, to express his outrage. Hood did not reply, possibly because he was forced to relinquish command of the Army of Tennessee a few days later.[13]

Did any white officers from black units who were captured live to tell about it? Thirty such instances are known to have occurred. As noted earlier, Capt. Elisha Dewitt was evidently paroled after his capture at Milliken's Bend, although corroborative evidence of his release has not been found. Records also indicate that Capt. Penfield, who met his fate at the hands of Forrest's scouts in December 1864, had been captured and paroled at Dalton, Ga., only two months earlier. Second Lieut. Joseph K. Nelson of the 11th Infantry, USCT, was captured near Sulphur Branch Trestle, Ala., on September 25, 1864, only to be paroled less than two months later. First Lieut. George B. Coleman, of the 10th Infantry, Corps d'Afrique (later the 82d Infantry, USCT) was taken prisoner in August 1863 near Jackson, La., and survived to return to duty at the very end of the war, as did Lieut. John East.

A particularly interesting incident involved Capt. Albert Allen and Second Lieut. Charles E. Page of the 6th and 9th Infantry, Corps d'Afrique (later the 78th and 81st Infantry, USCT), respectively. Nathaniel P. Banks wrote Dick Taylor in August 1863 to protest the detention of the two officers "in close confinement and in irons" at Shreveport because they served as officers in black regiments. Taylor made an inquiry and reported to Banks a few weeks later that the allegation was "incorrect and without foundation," although he admitted that the two men were no longer under his control. When Allen and Page were exchanged a year later, both reported that they had been "kept in close confinement in *irons* forty days, on account of being *suspected* of belonging to a colored regiment." (The second italics were added.) Their denial may have worked, for both men were exchanged and eventually given a discharge from the Union army.[14]

Certainly the single largest capture of white officers from black units occurred during the Battle of the Crater outside of Petersburg, Va., during which a group of eleven fell into rebel hands. "What disposition was made of these officers?" Lee's assistant adjutant-general asked. In spite of the Confederate resolution, they were sent to Columbia, S.C., as prisoners of war. By Christmas, at least three of them had been exchanged, with the remaining eight reaching the Federal exchange point at Annapolis, Md., by early March 1865. Furthermore, my examination of a list of Union officers held prisoner at Columbia turned up the names of eleven additional officers from black regiments who were held there. Seven of these had been captured before Petersburg, while three others had caught up with Forrest at Brice's Crossroads. The eleventh prisoner had been captured at Olustee, Fla. These officers also survived the war and were duly discharged or mustered out of the Union army at the end of the conflict. This evidence suggests that by mid-1864 white officers from black units were being treated in the same manner as officers from white regiments, particularly if they were fortunate enough to fall into the hands of front-line troops.[15]

It is probable that Lincoln's well-publicized threat to retaliate in equal measure was a major reason why the Confederate government failed to carry through with the terms of the congressional resolution. The correspondence between the commissioners of exchange is full of references regarding the proper treatment of these officers. In fact, the threat of retaliation was so effective that Confederate authorities and commanders in the field consistently denied that the policy was being carried out.[16] For example, Joseph E. Johnston directed Gen. Stephen D. Lee "to inquire into the truth of the report that after the recent action [August 3, 1863,] near Jackson, La., twenty-three prisoners (one white officer and twenty-two colored and negro privates) were put to death in cold blood and without form of law, and if it is true, to bring the culprits to trial." This was the skirmish in which Lieut. Orillion was captured. However, this writer could find no evidence that Griffith, Powers, Shattuck, or any of the guard from the 17th Arkansas were punished. The "shot wile trying to escape" excuse apparently worked.[17]

Although the Confederate threat to execute white officers from black units was not carried out officially, there was another way in which the spirit of the decree could be followed without fear of retaliation. Confederate troops could avoid taking prisoners in the first place. This was precisely the position Kirby Smith took when he learned that a number of black soldiers and their officers had been inadvertently captured at Milliken's Bend. Writing to Dick Taylor on June 13, 1863, Kirby Smith put the matter bluntly.

> I have been unofficially informed that some of your troops have captured negroes in arms. I hope this may not be so, and that your subordinates who may have been in command of capturing parties may have recognized the propriety of giving no quarter to armed negroes and their officers. In this way we may be relieved from a disagreeable dilemma.[18]

It should not be surprising, therefore, that when Confederate troops overran positions held by black soldiers, the number of prisoners they took was usually far less than when the defenders were white. This can be documented by incidents at Milliken's Bend, Poison Springs, the Crater, and Fort Pillow. In these instances, the white officers were less likely to survive than the black troops they commanded. As the reader may recall, the rebel battle cry at Milliken's Bend was "No quarter for white officers, kill the damned abolitionists, but spare the niggers."[19]

In summary, the evidence suggests that the Confederate government did not officially carry out its threat to execute white officers who volunteered to command black troops in the Union army. On the other hand, there were a number of instances in which individuals serving the Confederate army carried out the spirit if not the letter of the law by shooting prisoners who, they claimed, were trying to escape. As far as can be determined, none of these persons were ever brought to trial for their misbehavior, in spite of official condemnation of their acts by superior officers.

Although the number of white officers from black units executed by Confederate forces during the war was not great (none died of accidents), the death of each man was still tragic. This point was brought home to this writer when he encountered the following letter while reviewing Oscar Orillion's compiled military service record.

New Orleans, September 20, 1864

General:

My brother Oscar Orillon [*sic*] duly commissioned by Maj. Gen. Banks First Lieut. of the 1st Regt. of the Louisiana Native Guards have [has] been made a prisoner since the month of August last in a place nearby Port-Hudson[.] I have been for all that whole time deprived of any news concerning his situation or whereabouts[.] After much inquiry, they tell me that you, only you Sir, could give to an affectionate sister some consolation, and calm the anxiety that I suffer on account of my beloved brother, being my support, and enlist for the purpose of aiding me in my living, being a widow with two little children. I am sure Sir that you will understand uneasiness about him and that you will excuse a poor Sister who comes to trouble you in your camp duty to have some news of dear brother who was for the present all my hopes in this world.

If you can let me have any information, Sir, I shall be in the future very grateful to you, and will learn to my young ones to pray for you, and to respect your name, and I shall be for ever one of your most faithful Servant[s]

[signed] Rosella Debergue Orillon [*sic*]

There ends the record of Lieut. Orillion's military service in the United States Army.[20.]

Table 1

Officers "Killed" in Situations Other than Combat*

Name	Unit[21]	Disposition
2d Lt. Ellis Bentley	3rd HA[22] (1st Tenn. HA)	"Killed by guerillas Sept. 22, 1864, near Wacomah Creek south of Memphis."
2d Lt. George L. Conn	49th Inf. (11th La.)	Captured at Milliken's Bend, June 7, 1863. "Reported to have been hung by the enemy; Murdered by the rebels at Monroe, La., during Aug., 1863."
2d Lt. David G. Cooke	12th Inf.	Killed near Columbia, Tenn., Dec. 22, 1864.
Asst. Surg. Eli M. Hewitt	15th Inf.	"Killed by guerillas near Springfield, Tenn. July 24, 1864."
2d Lt. John A. Moulton	67th Inf. (3rd Mo.)	Captured at Mount Pleasant Landing. La. on May 16, 1864. "Information has been received of his being killed 12 hours after capture."
Capt. Charles G. Penfield	44th Inf.	"Murdered by Capt. Harvey Scouts. Forrest's Cavalry, near Columbia, Tenn., Dec. 22, 1864." (Ironically, Penfield had also been captured at Dalton, Ga. on October 13, 1864, and paroled two days later.)
2d Lt. Anson L. Sanborn	1st Inf.	"Killed by Dr. Wright at Norfolk, Va., July 11, 1863, while on recruiting service."
2d Lt. Jacob Schwartz	59th Inf. (1st Tenn.)	"Killed by 3 men names unknown at Memphis, Tenn., Sept. 13, 1864." Also "Assassinated in South Memphis on the evening of the 11th Sept., 1864."
2d Lt. Eben White	7th Inf.	"Murdered by John H. Southoron & son, Oct. 20, 1863, at Benedict, Md., while on recruiting duty."

*SOURCE: Individual compiled military service and pension records in the National Archives, Washington, D.C.

Table 2

Officers Listed as Missing and Presumed Dead*

Name	Unit[23]	Disposition
2d Lt. Alman Bassett	54th Mass. Inf.	Commission dated Feb. 14, 1863. "Not accepted."
1st Lt. John Cochran	93rd Inf. (25th Cd'A)[24]	"Failed boards, Nov. 25, 1863, dismissed for incompetency, July 10, 1865."
1st Lt. F. Comstock	3rd HA (1st Tenn. HA)	No complied military service or pension record.
Capt. Elisha Dewitt	5th HA (9th La. Inf.)	Captured at Milliken's Bend, La., June 7, 1863. "Absent on parole of honor," July, 10, 186 3.
2d Lt. William R. Hamblen	4th Cav. (1st Cav. Cd'A)	On recruiting service, "captured March 22, 1864, near Washington, La." Still no record as of Feb. 28, 1866.
Capt. Corydon Heath	5th HA (9th La. Inf.)	"Was taken prisoner and murdered by the enemy at or near Monroe, La., June, 1863."
2d Lt. Oscar Orillion	73rd Inf. (1st NG)	"Missing at Jackson, La., Aug. 6, 1863." No information as of Sept. 1864.
2d Lt. David W. Parmenter	10th Inf.	Captured at Plymouth, N.C., April 20, 1864. "Not been heard from since and dropped from the Rolls."
2d Lt. James C. Spry	26th Inf.	"Wounded and taken prisoner at the Battle of Bloody Bridge," Johns Island, S.C., July 7, 1864.
Capt. James Wilson	57th Inf. (4th Ark.)	Commission revoked and dismissed from the service, Feb. 29, 1864.

*SOURCE: Individual compiled military service and pension records in the National Archives, Washington, D.C.

Table 3

Officers Most Likely Executed After Being Captured by Confederate Forces

Bentley, Second Lieut. Ellis. Date: Sept. 22, 1864; Place: Memphis, Tenn.; Report: Yes; Confederate operation: Forrest raids north Alabama and middle Tennessee.

Conn, Second Lieut. George L. Date: June 7, 1863; Place: Milliken's Bend, La. Report: Yes; Confederate operation: Taylor attempts to relieve Vicksburg.

Cooke, Second Lieut. David G. Date: Dec. 22, 1864; Place: Columbia, Tenn.; Report: Yes; Confederate operation: Forrest retreats from Nashville with Hood.

Hamblen, Second Lieut. William B. Date: March 22, 1864; Place: Washington, La.; Report: Yes; Confederate operation: Taylor moves against Banks on Red River.

Heath, Capt. Corydon. Date: June 7, 1863; Place: Milliken's Bend, La. Report: Yes; Confederate operation: Taylor attempts to relieve Vicksburg.

Hewitt, Asst. Surg. Eli M. Date: July 24, 1864; Place: Springfield, Tenn.; Report: No; Confederate operation: Forrest chases A. J. Smith in north Mississippi.

Moulton, Second Lieut. John A. Date: May 15, 1864; Place: Mount Pleasant Lending; Report: No; Confederate operation: Wirt Adams disrupts leased plantations.

Orillion, Second Lieut. Oscar. Date: Aug. 6, 1863; Place: Jackson, La.; Report: Yes; Confederate operation: Lyon orders harassment of federal troops.

Parmenter, Second Lieut. David W. Date: April 20, 1864; Place: Plymouth, N.C.; Report: No; Confederate operation: Pickett undertakes 1864 offensive in North Carolina.

Penfield, Capt. Charles G. Date: Dec. 22, 1864; Place: Columbia, Tenn.; Report: Yes; Confederate operation: Forrest retreats from Nashville with Hood.

Spry, Second Lieut. James C. Date: July 7. 1864; Place: Johns Island, S.C.; Report: No; Confederate operation: Jones directs operations around Charleston.

CHAPTER 18

⸺◈⸺

Betwixt Wind and Water

A Short Account of Confederate Major General Nathan Bedford Forrest's Attack on Fort Pillow

William R. Brooksher

FIFTY OR SO HIGHWAY miles above Memphis, on top of a high bluff pushing out to help form the S the Mississippi River makes between Plum and Pecan Points, sits Fort Pillow, Tennessee. In April 1864 it was a nondescript post staffed by 557 black and white Union troops, men who were neither worried about nor prepared for an enemy attack. By the end of the month nearly half those same men were dead, wounded or prisoners, their fort a shambles and the cataclysm that had brought them all down was the subject of a controversy that dragged in Americans both north and south of the Civil War's battle fronts.

Much of the controversy swirled around one soldier, former land speculator, railroad investor and slave trader Nathan Bedford Forrest. Then a Confederate major general responsible for what he termed the "Cavalry Department of West Tennessee and North Mississippi," in Spring 1864 he and his troops were raiding in Tennessee and Kentucky looking for supplies and recruits. On April 12, it would be his force that assaulted Fort Pillow.

Poorly educated but wealthy, at the war's outset a virtual novice at all things military, possessed of fearsome temper and absolute fearlessness, Forrest confounded all his superiors' expectations, employing his troops in combat like a seasoned professional. Military historians would one day claim he was among the best cavalry commanders America ever produced. During the war some of his countrymen would brag he was

nearly invincible and call him the "Wizard of the Saddle." His opponents would grumble that he constantly did the unexpected.

Forrest's steadily blossoming reputation made it easy to recruit men to
ride with him: a certain amount of prestige was attached to his command
and the rumor was that his soldiers ate well. His unexpected assaults on
Union army positions supplied his force with abundant material resources.
But Southern enthusiasm for the Rebel leader was not universal. Some,
who professed gentility—while not necessarily opposing slavery—held a
low opinion of this one-time practitioner of "the trade." A Mississippian
new to his command once commented: "The dog's dead. Finally we are
under N. Bedford Forrest. . . . I must express my distaste at being commanded by a man having no pretension at gentility—a negro trader, gam-
bler—an ambitious man, careless of the lives of his men so long as
preferment be *in prospectu*. Forrest may be, and no doubt is, the best cavalry officer in the West, but I object to a tyrannical, hot-headed vulgarian's
commanding me."

Then and later, this trooper probably found himself a member of a
distinct minority: most of Forrest's troops and veterans demonstrated a
remarkable degree of loyalty and commitment to him. It was loyalty that
would be tested off the battlefield, after their attack on Fort Pillow, when
word spread that they had not merely overrun the Federals there, but had
murdered many of them.

Winding up a successful foray through the region, Forrest noted in
his April 4, 1864, report to Confederate Lieutenant General Leonidas
Polk, commanding the Department of Alabama, Mississippi, and East
Louisiana, "There is a Federal force of five or six hundred at Fort Pillow,
which I shall attend to in a day or two, as they have horses and supplies
which we need."

On Sunday, April 10, from his temporary base near Jackson, Tennessee, about 75 miles northeast of Memphis, Forrest issued instructions placing Confederate Brigadier General James R. Chalmers in
command of the brigades of Colonels Robert "Black Bob" McCulloch
and Tyree H. Bell, outfits camped all along a long stretch of Forked
Deer Creek many miles farther north, ordering them to take Fort Pillow.
Chalmers immediately sent Colonels J. J. Neely and John McGuirk
south toward Memphis to create a diversion and hold Federal forces
there in position. Union Major General Stephen A. Hurlbut, commanding the XVI Corps in the Army of the Tennessee and serving in the
Memphis region, acted as Forrest expected when Neely and McGuirk
moved his way. He acknowledged he was tied in position, reporting: "I
have ordered up the four regiments of the third division of the Seven-

teenth Corps, now in Vicksburg, as soon as practicable, that I may have some movable troops."

At the same time, Chalmers ordered the remaining portions of McCulloch's and Bell's brigades, which would form his division, toward Fort Pillow. Bell, who had 70 miles to travel, moved at midnight Sunday, while McCullough, 50 miles from the target, waited until Monday morning to march. Once underway, both units plunged doggedly forward, moving without rest through drizzling rain and clinging mud and arriving at Fort Pillow at about 5:30 A.M. Tuesday, April 12.

The object of their military interest had actually once been a Rebel post. Their department commander Leonidas Polk had designed it and started its construction early in the war. It was named for Tennessee military personality Gideon Pillow and was originally made up of three lines of defensive works. The Mississippi River flowed directly beneath the bluff on which it stood. A stream named Cold Creek flowed southwest and entered the river directly below the fort; the opening of Cold Creek Ravine, a steep cut running down from the bluff to the creek, sat less than 100 yards outside Pillow's southeasternmost wall. After Confederate defeat in the Battle of Shiloh and the June 1862 fall of Memphis to the Union navy, Southern troops abandoned it. Union gunboats showed up immediately afterward claiming the site for the Federals. From then on Union troops garrisoned it and from there watched over their army's supply and communication lines. One of their few additions to the site were strings of huts or shanties that sat not 100 yards outside the walls to the southwest. Called "barracks" in old records, these shelters would one day contribute to the fall of Fort Pillow.

The fort's two outer defense lines were networks of breastworks and trenches long out of use. By Spring 1864, the Federals used only the thick-walled inner fortification. These horseshoe-shaped works measured about 70 yards from end to end behind a parapet about 120 yards long. The walls were 6 feet high, 6 feet thick, flat on top and cut to accommodate six gun emplacements. On the outside, they rose from the lip of a ditch 8 feet deep and 12 feet wide that surrounded all but the river side of the fort. The terrain outside the walls was marked by ravines and depressions, much of the land littered with brush, logs, and stumps left from the original clearing of the land. On the riverbank beneath the fort, rifle pits had been dug to protect sharpshooters firing on river traffic. An unused water battery site was positioned there as well and a couple of empty barges tied up to the bank. Back inside the walled fort itself, there were only four field cannon covering the overland approaches, two 6-pounders and two Parrot guns.

When McCulloch's and Bell's troopers first rode up they unceremoniously drove the Federal pickets in. Daylight found the Confederates firmly ensconced inside the two lines of dilapidated outer works battering disorganized Union skirmish lines.

The force on the skirmish lines and inside the fort, commanded by Major Lionel F. Booth, was made up of the 11th U.S. Colored Troops (6th U.S. Colored Heavy Artillery and 1st Alabama), Battery F, U.S. Colored Light Artillery, and Bradford's Battalion, 13th Tennessee Cavalry. Looking for protection inside the fort were about 20 white noncombatants—all men—and, it was said, a few women of color. The ethnic make-up of the garrison itself could be said to be divided this way: about half were former slaves who had only recently joined the Union army; the rest were local whites who had maintained their loyalty to the North. Forrest's men looked on the blacks inside Pillow as property in revolt against their masters and hated them. Their opinion of the troops of the 13th Tennessee, if it can be believed, was even lower. Looked on as traitors, they were called "Tennessee Tories" or "Homemade Yankees."

These black and white Federals had little or no combat experience. But they were supported by Union navy Captain James Marshall's lightly-armored "tin-clad" gunboat *New Era,* anchored not far from the banks below their fort, and felt secure behind the overly-wide walls of their fort. Many of them also held Forrest's troops in moral contempt; this disdain may have contributed to making some of them overly confident.

Forrest had sent his men off to Pillow with orders to "invest" the Federal position. Once in front of the fort, Chalmers followed through and kept up a steady forward movement. With McCulloch's Brigade on the left, Colonel A. N. Wilson's 16th Tennessee covering the center and the remainder of Bell's Brigade on the right, and with Colonel C. R. Barteau's 2d Tennessee taking the extreme right, the Confederates, making the most of the cover offered by the stumps, logs and brush cluttering the approaches, gradually pushed their opponents toward the heavily walled fortification. Though the garrison's skirmishers tried to hold together firing lines and put up a fight in front of their barracks and the southeast face of the fort and the *New Era* lobbed in shells to support them, well-concealed Rebel sharpshooters made their struggle miserable.

Describing this action, post adjutant Lieutenant Mack J. Leaming of the Union's 13th Tennessee reported, "The firing continued without cessation, principally from behind logs, stumps and under cover of thick underbrush, and from high knolls. We suffered pretty severely in the loss of commissioned officers by the unerring aim of the rebel sharp-shooters, and among this loss I have to record our post commander, Major L. F.

Booth, who was killed almost instantly by a musket-ball through the breast." With Booth's death command passed to Major William F. Bradford, later described by XVI Corps commander Hurlbut as "a very young officer, completely inexperienced in these matters." The change in command would have major consequences as the battle unfolded.

In spite of heavy fire from both the fort and the gunboat, by late morning the Confederates had succeeded in almost completely ringing the fortification. Barteau's and Bell's troops had gained the shelter of Cold Creek Ravine northeast of the fort; Wilson occupied the second set of redoubts—the dilapidated breastworks and trenches that ringed the walled fort—and was sheltered from fire from embrasures along Pillow's east face; McCulloch was situated behind the line of shanties or barracks to the southwest. At this point Chalmers stopped his troops from moving forward and had his sharpshooters keep up a steady fire, taking out any enemy solder unwise enough to present a target.

Confident his subordinates had the operation well underway, Forrest did not arrive on the site until sometime near 10 A.M. As was his habit, he started reconnoitering the area. Then a Union bullet struck his horse. The mortally wounded animal reared and fell backward, painfully bruising the general. Undeterred, he gathered himself up, mounted another horse and continued his survey. In a few minutes the second animal dropped from under him, the victim of another deadly round. Again, the general remounted, dismissing the pleas of his adjutant, Captain Charles W. Anderson, to continue the reconnaissance on foot with the comment that he was "just as apt to be hit one way as another and that he could see better where he was."

Though his third mount was also severely wounded, Forrest eventually finished his reconnaissance and concluded he had learned two important things from his adventure. The ravines in the area would allow his troops to move up against the walls of the inner redoubt in relative safety and, by taking advantage of the high knolls, his sharpshooters could sweep much of the inside of the fort and the top of its walls. He ordered the number of sharpshooters greatly increased and asked McCulloch what he thought about taking the barracks. McCulloch recalled later: "I replied that if I could get possession of the houses I could silence the enemy's artillery. He then said, 'Go ahead and take them.' I made the charge in short order, and very soon had my men in and behind the houses, from which the artillery on that side was silenced by sharp-shooters."

Forrest ordered the remainder of the force forward. They carefully worked their way toward the fort until all were positioned for a charge if it was called for. At that point, the defenders discovered their protective walls were working against them. Forrest's adjutant Captain Anderson summed the situation up: "The width or thickness of the works across the top pre-vented the garrison from firing down on us, as it could only be done by mounting and exposing themselves to the unerring fire of our sharp-shooters, posted behind stumps and logs on all the neighboring hills. They were also unable to depress their artillery so as to rake these slopes with grape and canister, and so far as safety was concerned, we were all as well fortified as they were. . . . it was perfectly apparent to any man endowed with the smallest amount of common sense that for all intents and pur-poses the fort was ours."

The firing died down as Forrest waited for runners to bring up rifle ammunition to refill the nearly empty cartridge boxes of his troops. The fresh rounds arrived at about 3:00 P.M.

Ready to assault the fort at that point, but eager to keep his losses as small as possible, Forrest called a truce and sent a note forward demand-ing the unconditional surrender of the garrison. Should his demand be obeyed, he assured the occupants, they would be treated as prisoners of war. Then he concluded, "Should my demand be refused, I cannot be responsible for the fate of your command."

Young Major Bradford, unaware Forrest had used similar—usually empty—threats before, and obviously completely unsure of himself, penned a reply to Forrest and signed dead Major Booth's name to it. In his note, he asked for ". . . one hour for consultation and consideration with my officers and the officers of the gunboat."

It was about 3:30. Forrest was alerted the Union navy steamboats *Liberty* and *Olive Branch* were approaching, both apparently loaded with troops. Believing "Booth" was attempting to gain time to reinforce the fort, he gave him twenty minutes to make up his mind. While he waited, watching the boats press ahead in apparent violation of the truce, For-rest ordered Anderson and Barteau to secure the landing sites on the river; he had four small mountain howitzers to train on the fort's naval support. He told Anderson to "hold his position on the bluff, prevent any escape of the garrison, to pour rifle-balls into the open ports of the *New Era* when she went into action, and to fight everything blue betwixt wind and water" until the fort's flag came down.

Union critics later looked on Forrest's repositioning of his troops as a truce violation and evidence of "misconduct" or an infraction of the rules of war. It would be the published opinion of U.S. Government officials that Forrest used the truce to gain a favorable position for an assault. Post adjutant Leaming, who hand-carried Bradford's notes outside the walls, recalled it this way: "During the cessation of firing on both sides in con-sequences of the flag of truce offered by the enemy, and while the attention of both officers and men were naturally attracted to the south end of the fort, where the communications were being received and answered, Forrest had resorted to means the most foul and infamous ever adopted in the most barbarous ages of the world for the accomplishment of his design. Here he took occasion to move his troops partially under cover of a ravine and thick underbrush into the very position he had been fighting to obtain throughout the entire engagement up to 3:30 P.M."

Forrest's view of the situation was different: he stated he felt justified in taking this action since Fort Pillow's defenders did not signal the approaching naval vessels that a truce was in force. Forrest's opinion regarding the lack of a signal is supported by Union Brigadier General George F. Shepley who was aboard the *Olive Branch*. In response to a message from the *Liberty*, which had just sailed past the fort, "All right up there; you can go by. The gunboat is lying off the fort," the *Olive Branch* pushed on upstream. As the boat arrived opposite the fort, Shepley reported, "There was no firing at the fort at this time. The Union flag was flying, and after we had passed the fort we could see a flag of truce outside the fortifications. No signal of any kind was made to the boat from the fort or from shore. No intimation was given us from the gunboat, which had the right to order a steamer of this description, other than . . . [an] order to proceed to Cairo and send down . . . ammunition."

While all this was taking place, the defenders passed around buckets of whiskey taken from the commissary, called out to the enemy they did not believe Forrest was with them, and took the opportunity to insult the Confederates in language recalled as colorful, profane, and obscene; they seemed intent on raising the ire of the Rebels to the highest possible level. Barteau noted, "During the truce they openly defied us from the breastworks to come and take the fort."

Bradford, still signing Booth's name, finally responded to Forrest's surrender demand with a rather cloudy communication saying, "Negotiations will not attain the desired object."

Forrest, who had ridden forward to demonstrate to the doubting Yankees that he was indeed present, had no patience for such messages. He handed the note back to the couriers saying, "I am General Forrest; go back and say to Major Booth that I demand an answer in plain, unmistakable English. Will he fight or surrender?"

Forrest did not have long to wait. The couriers quickly returned and handed him a note, again signed in Booth's name, that read, "I will not surrender."

Forrest saluted, returned to his position some 400 yards from the fort and ordered the assault. He later wrote: "I dispatched staff officers to Colonels Bell and McCulloch . . . to say to them that I should watch with interest the conduct of the troops; that Missourians, Mississippians, and Tennesseans surrounded the works, and I desired to see who would first scale the fort."

Forrest's men already despised the soldiers inside the fort. They believed they were traitors and racial inferiors. The dirty taunts had blackened their moods. Before their general issued the attack order, they wanted to make these blue-uniformed antagonists regret this day. Then Forrest asked them to compete to see who would breach the walls first. Fueled by contempt, anger, and competition, the Confederate attack that followed was almost guaranteed to be intense.

It was not characteristic; Forrest elected to wait out the fight in a spot well behind his attacking troops. It's been speculated he may have still been shaken up from the fall from his dying horse. He turned to his bugler, Corporal Jacob Gaus, and said, "Blow the charge, Gaus."

Gaus' horn sported two bullet holes. He raised the battered instrument to his lips and sounded the command. As soon as the first few notes rang out, a Rebel Yell drowned out the bugle and the Rebels rushed forward.

The attack was no disorganized affair. Moving forward in well-drilled order, the troops were told to hold their fire until inside the fort. The first Rebel wave jumped into the muddy ditch and placed their backs to the bank, serving as ladders to boost those who followed to the top of the fort's wall. Sharpshooters swept the parapet with heavy fire, forcing the defenders, who crouched behind it, to keep their heads down.

The attackers, who had yet to fire a round, scrambled across the parapet virtually ignoring a largely ineffective Union fusillade and emptied their weapons point-blank into the defenders. A second wave followed immediately, pouring a second devastating sheet of lead into the hapless Federals before they could reload. Leaming reported Rebels were everywhere "as if rising out from the very earth." The result was chaos. Cacophony engulfed the combatants as men fired through the swirling smoke of battle. Yells, screams of pain, and curses mingled with the roar of weapons as the Rebels drove the attack home. The defenders fought briefly then gave into panic and turned to dash toward the river with the attackers in hot pursuit.

By the river, several open cases of ammunition waited for the Federals. The *New Era*, bristling with heavy cannon, sat strangely silent nearby.

The *New Era*'s Captain Marshall later reported, "Major Bradford signaled to me that we were whipped. We had agreed on a signal that, if they had to leave the fort, they would drop down under the bank, and I was to give the Rebels canister." But he fired no canister: Marshall had expended most of his ammunition earlier firing on the attackers as they approached the fort. Low on all ammunition and unable to fire without hitting Bradford's men, Marshall kept his vessel's ports shut tight, applied steam and moved away upriver. He later justified his action by saying he was afraid Confederates would commandeer a steamer and attack him with 400 or 500 men.

For the hapless Yankee troops on shore their retreat became a debacle. Running down the hill under a hail of Rebel fire, they saw the gunboat move away and broke to the right where they ran headlong into a scathing fire from Anderson's troops. They quickly reversed course only to meet the same treatment from Barteau's men. Many dashed into the river only to drown or be shot by sharpshooters on the bluff. Others turned in terror to surrender. Some became prisoners, some were shot down. Through most of this activity, the Union colors continued to fly above the fort. Finally, Confederate Private John Doak Carr cut the halyard and let it fall.

As soon as Forrest saw his men pour into the fort, he and his staff dashed forward. Ignoring that the Union flag was still flying and the Federal troops were trying to escape, they were able to bring the fighting to a halt.

Though Rebel officers quickly showed up on the scene, for a time they did lose control of their forces. During those minutes, the hatred and animosity smoldering inside their men burst into full flame. With passions let loose, the "rules of conflict" were thoroughly disregarded.

The fight lasted about 20 minutes. In that time, the Federals absorbed an outrageous number of losses. According to figures complied by the state of Tennessee, only 226 Union men survived unscathed. Approximately 110 black and white troops were wounded. About 42 percent of the black troops—110 men—were killed. About 21 percent of the white soldiers—62 officers and enlisted men—perished. Forrest reported, "The victory was complete, and the loss of the enemy will never be known from the fact that large numbers ran into the river and were shot and drowned. . . . The river was dyed with the blood of the slaughtered for 200 yards." He did not repeat stories that circulated in the North later, of wounded or surrendered men begging for their lives before being shot or knifed to death by incensed Rebel troops. For their part, Northerners were unaware of Rebel casualties. The Confederates lost 14 killed and 86 wounded.

Forrest immediately put Union survivors to work burying the dead. At nightfall, he moved out, taking the 226 unwounded prisoners with him. The next day he sent Captain Anderson back under a flag of truce to contact a gunboat that was shelling the area unaware the fort had fallen. Anderson managed to contact its captain and to arrange for the seriously wounded to be take off and moved to Memphis. The Battle of Fort Pillow was over, and the recriminations and charges were just starting.

Northern newspapers, politicians, and civilians yelled, "Massacre!" Confederate civil and military authorities denied the fort's garrison had been murdered or abused. Mounds of testimony were available from both sides to bolster anyone's claim of anything. Members of the U.S. Congress' Joint Committee on the Conduct of the war, a considerably less than objective body, was dispatched from Washington to look into the matter. They reported "an indiscriminate slaughter, sparing neither age nor sex, white or black, soldier or civilian. No cruelty which the most fiendish malignity could devise was omitted by these murderers."

Southern authorities denounced the testimony collected by the Northern Congress, calling it lies. Union garrison surgeon Doctor C. Fritch later said: ". . . early in the morning all of the women and all of the noncombatants were ordered onto some barges and . . . towed upriver to an island . . . before anyone was hurt." Minnesota soldier, Charles Robinson, wrote, "As soon as the rebels got to the top of the bank there commenced the most horrible slaughter that could possibly be conceived. Our boys when they saw they were overpowered threw down their arms and held up . . . their hands in token of surrender, but no sooner were they seen than they were shot down, & if one shot failed to kill them the bayonet or revolver did not."

Barteau denied it, saying, "They, [the Federals] were in a frenzy of excitement or drunken delirium. Some even, who had thrown down their arms, took them up again and continued firing. Some of my own men had to take down the flag. The Federals did not do it nor at any time make a surrender." He further contended: "All was done that could be done by General Forrest and his subordinates to save unnecessary loss of life and protect all who surrendered as soldiers in good faith."

The issue of excesses has never been settled. And after almost 130 years, it appears nothing but new, conclusive, and startling testimony could quiet one group of partisan historians or another. It is clear, however, many Southerners were excessive in the use of force. It cannot be denied black soldiers bore the brunt of their hatred and some extraordinary malice; they and their white comrades were clearly defeated and, whether or not their flag was still flying or senior Confederate officers ordered a halt to the battle, their attackers were personally responsible for most of their actions. It is equally clear most of Forrest's troops were not motivated by a calculated, cold-blooded desire to commit murder.

But the battle provided a setting where old antagonisms between master and slave, Secessionist and Union man, could be vented freely and where the only device governing the mechanism of destruction was carried in the heart of each soldier.

This is not to say all blame for excesses or muddy thinking rests with individual soldiers, that Forrest, his senior commanders, or the Union's immature Major Bradford bore no responsibility. They clearly lost control of their respective forces for a short time. Had that not happened, the story of Fort Pillow would have undoubtedly been vastly different. It did, however, and those charged with leading the Southern force must bear the bulk of the responsibility for the results. The body of available evidence will not, however, conclusively support the charge of intentional atrocity.

Immediately after the battle, U.S. President Abraham Lincoln asked Secretary of War Edwin Stanton to have the matter investigated. He, in turn, handed that duty over to Lieutenant General U. S. Grant who made things plain to his ranking subordinate in the region, Major General William T. Sherman. He told Sherman, one of Forrest's most implacable military foes, "If our men have been murdered after capture, retaliation must be resorted to promptly." Sherman, known for his belief in making war hard on civilians and soldiers alike, conducted his own investigation and, in the end, exacted no retribution. That, as much as anything, indicates no intentional massacre or atrocity. Had there been one, just as sure as day follows night, Sherman would have take a full measure of revenge—and then some.

CHAPTER 19

The Jacksonville Mutiny

B. Kevin Bennett

AT 1200 HOURS ON DECEMBER 1, 1865, six soldiers from the 3d United States Colored Troops (USCT) were led from the guardhouse at Fort Clinch, Fernandina, Florida, and executed by a firing squad drawn from white troops at the garrison. The six soldiers, Privates David Craig, Joseph Green, James Allen, Jacob Plowden, Joseph Nathaniel, and Thomas Howard, were executed for mutiny, the last servicemen in the American armed forces to be executed for this offense.[1] Inasmuch as the Civil War period marked the first time in American history that blacks served in the military in appreciable numbers, the Jacksonville Mutiny is a tragic but instructive beginning milestone from which the progress of the black soldier within the military justice system can be measured.

As a result of large-scale operations and resultant massive casualties, the Civil War created a manpower crisis, which in turn led to the enlistment of large numbers of blacks into the Federal military and naval services. Free blacks served in a limited capacity in the Revolution and War of 1812, their participation limited by the relatively small number of free blacks (and by the prejudices of society). The Civil War, however, was the first real opportunity for blacks to join organized military units and to strike a blow for the freedom and status of their race. Recruitment for the military was spurred on by the exhortations for black leaders like Frederick Douglass, who declared, "Let the black man get upon his person the brass letters U.S., an eagle on his button, and a musket on his shoulder and bullets in his pocket, and there is no power on earth which can deny that he had earned the right of citizenship." In response, blacks turned out in large numbers. By the end of the war, over two hundred thousand had joined the Union army and navy.[2]

One of the earliest units formed was the 3d USCT, which was organized at Camp William Penn near Philadelphia in July 1863. Comprised of escaped slaves and freedmen from the various northern states, it was, like all black units, officered by whites.[3] After a brief period of basic training, the regiment embarked in August 1863 for Morris Island, South Carolina, where it served in the trenches before Fort Wagner (a campaign recently made famous by the movie *Glory*). Having suffered substantial casualties during this campaign, the regiment was transferred in February 1864 to Jacksonville, Florida, which was occupied by Union forces. From then until the end of the war the men served on outpost duty, continually fighting skirmishes and mounting raids and expeditions into the Confederate-held interior of the state. After the cessation of hostilities, the regiment continued to be stationed in Florida on occupation duty. Assigned the unenviable chore of trying to reestablish and uphold federal authority in a hostile environment, the soldiers of the 3d USCT found the duty marked with endless hours of boredom and frustration. In the absence of the excitement and challenge of combat, many of the soldiers turned to alcohol and chafed under the continuing restrictions of military discipline.

Commanding the regiment was twenty-three-year-old Lt. Col. John L. Brower, a native of New York City. Unlike most white officers assigned to black regiments, Brower had no previous enlisted military experience when he obtained a direct commission as a captain in August 1863. Rather, it appears that he obtained his commission through political connections. Brower had only recently been promoted, assuming command on September 12, 1865, when the former regimental commander, Colonel Bardwell, was promoted to the position of military district commander.[4] Unfortunately for the enlisted rank and file, it appears that in addition to his inexperience, Brower was something of a martinet. Despite the fact that the 3d USCT had served honorably as a combat regiment and was shortly due to muster out, Brower was determined not to slacken military discipline. While strictness and control were necessary to keep troops in line during battle, this inflexible discipline only served to exacerbate an already strained relationship between most of the officers and the enlisted men of the 3d USCT. Indications of this discontent was evidenced in a "letter to the editor" from a back soldier to a black religious publication. Decrying the contemptuous and callous treatment of black laundresses and camp followers by white officers of the 3d USCT, he noted, "We have a set of officers here who apparently think that their commissions are licenses to debauch ad mingle with deluded freewomen under cover of darkness. The conduct of these officers is such that their presence among us is loathsome in the extreme."[5]

For their part, the officers were concerned about the growing insubordination and drunkenness of troops. While willing to serve in black regiments despite the negative connotations attached to such an assignment, the officers were by and large a cross section of the society from which they were drawn. While they may have desired the abolition of slavery and respected the fighting qualities of their black troops, rare indeed was the individual officer untainted by some form of racism. From letters and journals it seems that most white officers considered blacks just one step removed from barbarism. As recent descendants of primitive peoples, black soldiers, so their officers felt, lacked self-control and discipline. "The Negro is very fanciful and instable in disposition," stated one officer. White officers greatly feared that their troops could go wild and riot at any time.[6] Just as the fear of brutal violence in slave revolts terrified Southerners, so too it made the Northern white officers uneasy with the possibility of armed mutiny. One officer in a black regiment wrote his wife, "I do not believe we can keep the Negroes from murdering everything they come to once they have been exposed to battle."[7] Additionally, it seems that some officers were at a loss on how to teach and administer discipline to their troops. As one enlightened regimental commander pointed out, "Inexperienced officers often assumed that because these men had been slaves before enlistment, they would bear to be treated as such afterwards. Experience proved to the contrary. Any punishment resembling that meted out by overseers caused irreparable damage."[8] Given the volatile environment that existed within the regiment, it did not require much for the long-simmering discontent to explode into confrontation. The incident providing the spark occurred on Sunday, October 29, 1865, two days before the regiment was to be mustered out.

From the testimony recorded in various court-martial transcripts, it appears that during the midmorning hours of Sunday, October 29, an unnamed black soldier was apprehended while attempting to pilfer molasses from the unit kitchen. The arresting officer was Lieutenant Greybill, who was acting as Officer of the Day. Greybill then undertook to punish the soldier by having him tied up by his thumbs in the open regimental parade ground.[9] When the prisoner resisted the efforts of Greybill and Lieutenant Brown (the regimental adjutant) to tie him up, Brower arrived on the scene and the prisoner was bound "after some difficulty."[10]

During the time that the prisoner was being strung up, a crowd of enlisted men gathered and threatened to free him. Pvt. Jacob Plowden, a forty-four-year-old former slave from Tennessee, began "talking loudly" and disputed the authority of the officers to punish a man by tying him up by the thumbs. Plowden, who was alleged to "have been considerably in his liquor," stated, "it was a damn shame for a man to be tied up like that, white soldiers were not tied up that way nor other colored soldiers, only in our regiment." He further announced that "there was not going to be any more of it, that he would die on the spot but he would be damned if he wasn't the man to cut him down."[11] Plowden was not alone in his attempts to incite the crowd. Pvt. Jonathan Miller began moving among the crowd, shouting, "Let's take him down, we are not going to have any more of tying men up by the thumbs."[12]

According to an eyewitness account by another officer, a group of about 35 unarmed enlisted men started advancing toward the three officers and the prisoner. Pvt. Richard Lee was in the lead, telling the crowd to "Come on, the man has been hanging there long enough." Brower, standing by the side of the prisoner, waited until the group was within 15 feet. Drawing his revolver, he fired into the crowd. Two of the shots struck Pvt. Joseph Green in the elbow and side, and he fell wounded in the parade ground. Pandemonium broke loose, and the crowd retreated with a number of soldiers yelling, "Go get your guns, let's shoot the Son of a Bitch."[13]

While a number of the soldiers dispersed after the firing—some 15 to 20 did, in fact, get their weapons and return to the parade area where they opened fire on Brower and other officers—Greybill departed the camp to obtain assistance from the town, several shots whistling close behind him.[14] The adjutant, Lieutenant Brown, mounted his horse and proceeded to the section of camp where Company K was located. There he attempted to have the company fall in so as to quell the mutiny. As the company was forming, several of the armed mutineers, Privates Harley, Howard, and Nathaniel, also arrived in the area. Several shots were fired at Brown whereon several soldiers forcibly subdued Nathaniel and Howard and took their muskets away. The company by this time was gathering about Brown, querying him as to what was going on. During this confusion Harley took Brown's service revolver from its holster and attempted to take him prisoner. In a matter of minutes, however, the noncommissioned officers of Company K had restored order in that area.[15]

At the time this was occurring, Lieutenant Fenno came out from his quarters to investigate the firing. He was quickly surrounded by several enlisted men whom he attempted to question. He met with curses and "improper language" from Pvt. Calvin Dowrey. Fenno responded by drawing his saber and slashing Dowrey on the left arm, slightly wounding him. While Fenno's attention was distracted by several other soldiers, Dowrey returned with a fence rail and walloped Fenno on the right side of the head. While Fenno was attempting to pick himself off the ground, another unknown soldier forced him down again into the dirt with a buttstroke of his musket. The soldier with the musket then disappeared into the crowd, and several soldiers took the fence rail away from Dowery.[16]

Meanwhile, a fairly brisk firefight took place at the regimental parade ground between Brower and several of the mutineers. The gunfire abruptly ended after an estimated 30–40 shots when Brower's finger was shot off. Pvt. Richard Lee, one of the original instigators, yet one who had not take up arms, rushed over to Brower and, with the help of several others, escorted him to the relative safety of the cookhouse. Several of the mutineers followed close behind, notably Pvt. James Allen, who yelled, "Let me at him, let me shoot the son of a bitch."[17] Lee tried to ward the pursuers off, warning them to "stop their damn foolishness."[18] As Brower was seeking refuge in the cookhouse, Captain Walrath arrived with a number of troops, who disarmed the mutineers and quelled the disturbance. Brower then left the cookhouse and started for town, aided by several enlisted soldiers. A number of mutineers who had not been apprehended followed a short distance behind, shouting threats and insults. The mutiny had pretty much spent its force at this point, although Allen did take Captain Parker prisoner, tying him up in the officer's tent. Colonel Bardwell, the former regimental commander, arrived as the mutiny was winding down. Inasmuch as Bardwell was well respected by the troops, he was able to settle the situation, obtain aid for the wounded, and effect the immediate release of Parker.[19] With respect to the immediate cause of the mutiny, it appears that Pvt. James Thomas took advantage of the confusion and worked furiously to release the prisoner; however, just when he had succeeded in cutting the post down he was apprehended at gunpoint by Captain Barker.[20]

As was to be expected, fifteen of the suspected mutineers were confined, and charges drafted and preferred against them With a speed that would please many a modern-day prosecutor, a convening order was issued on October 30, 1865, with the court-martial scheduled to convene on October 31, 1865. The proceedings were a general court-martial, composed of seven officers headed by the provost marshal of the 3d USCT, Maj. Sherman Conant.[21] The accused were all offered but declined the assistance of counsel and proceeded to trial representing themselves. The separate trials began on October 31, 1865, and ran until November 3.

By the time of the Civil War, three kinds of court-martial had evolved in the army: general, regimental, and garrison. Of those, only a general court-martial could try officers and capital cases, impose sentences of death, dishonorable discharge from the service, forfeiture of more than three months pay, or any lengthy period of imprisonment.[22] A general court-martial could be convened only by the president, the secretary of war (acting under the order of the president), a general officer commanding an army, or a colonel commanding a separate department. Exceptions made during the Civil War allowed the commander of a division or separate brigade (as was true in this case) to appoint such a court.[23]

Of the fifteen soldiers who were to stand trial, fourteen were charged with mutiny, a violation of Article 22, Articles of War. Mutiny was defined as the unlawful resistance or opposition to superior military authority, with a deliberate purpose to subvert the same or to eject that authority from office.[24] The remaining accused, Pvt. Archibald Roberts, was charged with a violation of Article 99, conduct prejudicial to the good order and military discipline. Roberts did not take part in the actual mutiny but afterwards was overheard to say, "Lt. Colonel Brower, the God-Damned Son of a Bitch, he shot my cousin. Where is he, let me see him."[25]

The maximum punishment for mutiny in time of war, rebellion, or insurrection was death by shooting. Unfortunately for the accused, Florida was still considered to be in a state of rebellion, notwithstanding that the last organized Confederate forces had surrendered in May 1865. Since a state of rebellion was considered to exist, the court-martial that was convened had the authority to assess the death penalty, and this "state of rebellion" status also limited the amount of appellate review that would be afforded to any soldier sentenced to death. In times of peace any death sentence was required to be transmitted to the secretary of war, who would review it and present it to the president for his consideration along with his recommendation.[26] If a state of war or rebellion existed, the division or department commander had the power to confirm and execute sentences of death. He could, if he so desired, suspend the execution of a death sentence so as to allow review by the president and the condemned an opportunity to petition for clemency. This suspension and review process was not required while a "state of rebellion" existed.[27]

In regard to the composition of the court-martial, black troops were afforded one advantage in that they were usually tried by officers assigned to black regiments. Although not specifically required by regulations, the practice was first instituted by Maj. Gen. Benjamin F. Butler to shield the black troops from abuse and prejudice.[28] While this was obviously a prudent safeguard for the black troops in general, it was of dubious value in a mutiny case such as this where the prosecution witnesses were for the most part officers from the same regiment.

The trial procedure for general court-martials and utilized in the Jacksonville cases was as follows: first, the judge advocate read the order assembling the court and asked the accused if he had any objections to being tried by any member of the court. Following the negative response received in each case, the judge advocate administered the oath to each member of the court, and the president administered the oath to the judge advocate. The judge advocate then read the charges, the general nature of the offense, and the specifications. The accused would then enter his plea of guilty or not guilty. The witnesses for the prosecution were then sworn in and questioned by the judge advocate, the court, and the accused. After all its witnesses had testified and were cross-examined, the prosecution rested its case. Then the defense witnesses and the accused were sworn in, questioned, and cross-examined. Before the court was closed, the accused had the opportunity to make a statement, either oral or in writing. This statement, though not considered evidence, could be considered by the court in its deliberations. After "having maturely deliberated upon the evidence adduced," the court announced its findings, and, if the accused was found guilty, the sentence. Decisions on guilt required only a simple majority; a sentence of death, however, needed a two-thirds majority. The summarized transcript was authenticated by the judge advocate who would then forward the court record to the officer having authority to confirm the sentence.[29]

Once commenced, the Jacksonville trials were carried out with great dispatch. The longest appears to have been four hours in length, the shortest, one hour. Starting with four court-martials on October 31, three were held on November 1, three on November 2, and five on November 3. Twenty-two witnesses provided testimony in the various court-martials, the most appearances being logged by Lieutenant Brown, the prosecution's star witness. Indeed, Brown seems to have possessed an uncanny ability to remember the faces and mutinous acts of quite a number of individuals. From the testimony offered it appeared that he was most eager to provide damning evidence against the various accused. Particularly in the case of Pvt. Joseph Nathaniel, his questionable testimony that Nathaniel fired upon him cost Allen any chance of escaping the death penalty. The defense strategy, to the extent that there was one, was first to show that a soldier had not taken up arms. If that fact was beyond controverting, then it was crucial to show that he had not fired at the white officers during the mutiny. This act clearly was the dividing line between a death sentence and a lengthy prison term. In his testimony, Brown swore that a shot that had whistled over his head came from Nathaniel's weapon. The two black noncommissioned officers who had apprehended Nathaniel and taken his weapon testified that they had not witnessed Nathaniel discharging his musket. Further, they checked his musket for signs of firing and found it capped and loaded.[30] Despite the obviously exculpatory nature of this evidence, the court-martial panel either discounted or disregarded it and found Nathaniel guilty of firing at Brown.

Another troubling feature of Brown's and several other officers' testimony was the issue of Lt. Colonel Brower firing into the unarmed group of soldiers. During the first few court-martials, all the officers including Brown testified that Brower had fired into the crowd and that the soldiers were unarmed at the time. On the second day of the proceedings, however, Brown asserted that Brower had fired warning shots into the air. Perhaps realizing the inconsistency of this testimony with the wounds suffered by Private Green, both Brown and Greybill later claimed that the crowd was armed at the time Brower opened fire.[31]

Curious also was the part played by Brower in the court-martials. He testified in only one, that of Pvt. Joseph Green. Brower did not testify about the events leading up to the mutiny, nor did he discuss the specifics of his actions or the mutiny. He testified that Green advanced upon him with a musket and that he had fired to disable Green. Green disputed that account, claiming that he had not taken up arms until after he was shot.[32] Shortly after testifying, Brower was mustered out and quickly shipped back home to New York City. In light of this, one cannot help but wonder what transpired between Brower and his superiors in the two days between the mutiny and his mustering out. Considering his incredible overreaction by opening fire combined with his allowing punishments that, while not specifically prohibited, were looked upon with great disfavor, one had to suspect that the command was anxious to be rid of an embarrassment.

Given the expedited nature of the proceedings and the sentences handed down, one might readily conclude that the trials were nothing more than "kangaroo courts." Notwithstanding the brevity of the trials and the fact that the accused were not represented by counsel, it appears that the president, Major Conant, endeavored to ensure each accused a full and fair hearing. Conant, a former noncommissioned officer with the 39th Massachusetts Volunteers, consistently asked questions of the various witnesses in an effort to ascertain facts and resolve inconsistencies. Unfortunately, the same balanced approach was lacking from the judge advocate, Lieutenant Knight. Procedurally, he was required to assist the accused in eliciting favorable testimony when they were not represented by counsel, but his questions were leading and seemed designed to elicit only incriminating evidence.[33]

When the last court-martial had adjourned on November 3, thirteen of the accused had been found guilty of mutiny. Another, Private Roberts, was convicted of conduct prejudicial to good order. Only one accused, Pvt. Theodore Waters, was acquitted of the charge of mutiny. Privates Plowden, Craig, Allen, Howard, Green, and Nathaniel were sentenced to execution by shooting. Private Dowrey received a sentence of fifteen years at hard labor with Privates Morie and Harley receiving ten years. A sentence of two years at hard labor was adjudged against Privates Lee (both Richard and Alexander), Miller, and Thomas. Roberts received a relatively light sentence of two months' confinement. All received dishonorable discharges and total forfeiture of pay.[34]

Upon the conclusion of the trials, the mission of mustering out the remainder of the regiment was completed. The court record was authenticated and forwarded for review on November 10 to the department commander, Maj. Gen. John Foster.[35] In reviewing the records, Foster declined to exercise any leniency, approving each finding of guilty and adjudging sentence. Interestingly, Foster disapproved the findings of not guilty with respect to Private Waters, noting on the record that there was insufficient evidence![36] Foster set the execution date for December 1, 1865, between the hours of noon and 2 P.M. and further designated the place of imprisonment as Fort Jefferson, located on Dry Tortugas Island in the Florida Keys.[37]

The court records of the proceedings were apparently forwarded to the Bureau of Military Justice in Washington, D.C. on November 13, 1865, but no actual legal review of the cases appears to have taken place until after the executions. This was evidenced by the troubling case of Pvt. David Craig, one of the soldiers sentenced to death. Contained within Craig's service file is a letter from his foster father H. C. Marehand, dated December 10, 1865, to U.S. Sen. Edgar Cowan (Pa.) requesting that the sentence of execution be suspended pending a review and investigation of the case. Craig, a twenty-one-year-old laborer from Pennsylvania, had been raised by Marehand. The letter indicated that Marehand had received correspondence the previous day from Craig indicating his dilemma and proclaiming his innocence in that "he [Craig] had been excused to take the guns from some of the mutineers and then was arrested."[38] In response to the congressional inquiry, a telegraph was sent to General Foster to suspend the sentence and to transmit the record for review. Unfortunately the telegraph and suspension were too late as the executions had been carried out nine days earlier. Foster replied by telegraph on December 16 informing the War Department of the execution and the fact that the court records had been forwarded on November 13. There is an additional handwritten notation on the telegraph: "Senator Cowan informed, Dec. 20."[39] Apart from the questions of the late delivery of Craig's letter and the belted legal review is the mystery of what happened to the record of Craig's court-martial. Among all the records arising from the Jacksonville Mutiny, his record alone has either been lost or destroyed.

Fortunately for the imprisoned soldiers the legal process did not end with the deaths of their six comrades. In December 1865, a review of the court-martial records was accomplished by the judge advocate general of the army, Joseph Holt. Although his review was limited to strictly procedural matters, a further review on the merits was conducted by the Bureau of Military Justice in late 1866, which resulted in the prison sentences of the surviving mutineers being commuted. Pvt. Jonathan Miller was released in November 1866, and the others, Privates Calvin Dowrey, Morie, Harley, Thomas, and Alexander Lee, were discharged in January 1867. Pvt. Richard Lee had previously died from typhoid fever.[40]

From that point the lives of the participants in the mutiny slip into obscurity. Of the officers, there remains no further record of Lt. Col. Brower as he failed to file for a pension. Lieutenant Brown returned to Indiana, married, and died in 1912.[41] Major Conant left active duty immediately after the trials. Interested in promoting the welfare of newly freed blacks, he accepted a position with the Freedmen's Bureau in Florida. He later returned to New England and died in Connecticut in 1924.[42] Of the black mutineers who survived prison, even less is known. Having been dishonorably discharged they were ineligible to apply for a military pension, thus no recorded information is available. About the only postscript is a letter contained within the file of Pvt. Jacob Plowden. Dated in 1878, it was written by his brother on behalf of Plowden's minor son Jesse, attempting to collect any arrears in pay due Plowden.

In light of the severe sentences handed down, it appears that the court-martial failed to consider as mitigating the egregious actions of the commanding officer. By his condoning the use of a disreputable and inflammatory punishment and in imprudently firing into a group of unarmed soldiers, he essentially provoked an armed mutiny from what appeared to be insubordination. While it is perhaps too easy to criticize the commander's actions, less drastic methods could have been used to quell the initial disturbance. Nor were the harsh sentences meted out that unusual in the context of the black soldier in the Civil War. While blacks comprised 9 percent of the total manpower in the Union Army, they accounted for just under 80 percent of the soldiers executed for the offense of mutiny during the Civil War.[43] Based upon this statistical data, the appearance of disproportionate punishment and racial bias in mutiny cases is clearly suggested. Additionally, one has to question the fairness of these court-martials given their composition, the absence of defense counsel, and the rapid fashion in which they were tried and the sentences carried out. While the concept of due process was not well defined, even by the minimal standards of the time, an element of fairness was lacking.

In reviewing the transcripts and the testimony offered, however, there seems to be little doubt that Privates Plowden, Green, Howard, and Allen were among the group of soldiers that took up arms and fired upon their officers. Additionally there was no dispute that Privates Nathaniel, Morie, and Alexander Lee took up arms; however, there was considerable evidence that they did not fire their weapons. In the case of Lee, which was the shortest court-martial, the accused merely proffered that he had been drunk during the mutiny and did not remember a thing. With respect to the cases of Privates Harley, Dowrey, Richard Lee, Miller, and Thomas, the court was probably justified in finding them guilty of mutiny for their various acts in inciting, assisting, and attempting to free the prisoner. Likewise there was no dispute that Roberts had uttered the disrespectful language about Brower in public hearing and was guilty of conduct prejudicial to good order. Therefore, with the exception of the unusual case of Craig, it seems likely that the findings of guilty on the charges of mutiny were supported by the evidence.

The Jacksonville Mutiny, was a tragedy. Black soldiers had achieved remarkable gains through their noteworthy participation in the Civil War, not the least of which was the end of slavery. Their gains in the administration of military justice were evident.

CHAPTER 20

"Remember Poison Spring"

Mike Fisher

I N THE LATE SPRING of 1864, Colonel Samuel J. Crawford's regiment of the 2nd Kansas Volunteers moved south from Fort Smith, Arkansas, with the Union Army of the Frontier toward the Confederate supply depot at Shreveport, Louisiana. Rendezvousing 110 miles to the south with General Frederick Steele's VII Corps, Crawford's men found themselves confronted by both difficult terrain and aggressive Confederates under Major General Sterling Price. On April 18, rebels mauled a Union forage train at Poison Spring, fourteen miles east of Camden in southern Arkansas, murdering many of the soldiers in the 1st Kansas Colored Volunteers. A week later, Confederate cavalry, under Brigadier General James F. Fagan savaged another Union forage train at Marks' Mills, northeast of Camden. On the night of April 27, Steele's force, reduced to 8,000 men, slipped out of Camden, retreating northeast toward the safety of Little Rock, the Confederates pursuing. At dawn, April 30, Confederates, now under the command of Lieutenant General Edmund Kirby Smith, looked down into the river bottom at Jenkins' Ferry, seeing the VII Corps desperately fording the rising Saline River. Bugle calls gave way to the rolling thunder of musketry as the story of Crawford's 2nd Kansas Colored Volunteers began.[1]

Throughout the afternoon of April 29, 1864, skirmishing flared periodically between Major General John S. Marmaduke's Confederate cavalry and Union Colonel Adolph Englemann's 3rd Brigade. Fighting between the exhausted Union and Confederate troops ceased during the night. Before daylight the following morning, however, Marmaduke again felt for the VII Corps, striking elements astride the ridgeline just south of the Saline bottoms and driving them five hundred yards east into the valley.[2]

Colonel Colton Greene followed Marmaduke's cavalry up the ridgeline and there, looking east, saw woods and marshes to the east of the road, leading down to the Saline crossing. Directly to his front lay two ploughed fields, separated by a skirt of heavy brush and timber. To the north, an impassable bayou of cane and underbrush extended beyond Toxie Creek which flowed into the river from the west, closely paralleling the ferry road. Across the open portions of the fields, large trees had been felled, providing rude breastworks for the Federal troops. In both fields stood dead trees, providing better cover for Union sharpshooters. As the ferry road approached the river it sank into defilade, high ground on the south giving way to the dense underbrush on the north, rising abruptly to a steep hill. This funnel-like terrain, which began a mile and a half below the base of the hill from which Greene looked down, extended the final mile to the ferry crossing. There the Federals again had begun crossing their pontoon bridge.[3] Within that funnel trashed the remainder of the VII Corps wagon train, extending some two miles back from the river to the east. Only five hundred yards from the base of the ridgeline, Greene watched with his growing Confederate force, now being reinforced by additional infantry.[4]

General Frederick Salomon, commanding Union troops on the west side of the Saline, sought to consolidate his force of some 4,000 men. As Federal wagon trains slowly moved forward, Marmaduke broke off skirmishing. He had encountered elements of the 50th Indiana and the 33rd Iowa, falling back in the face of their musket fire. Salomon ordered General Samuel Rice to move the exposed western elements of the Federal rear guard east one-half mile, to the tail of the Union train, snarled in the morass of mud leading to the pontoon bridge. Salomon directed Rice to use the cover and concealment on the west side of the westernmost open field. The site immediately fronted the van of Greene's dismounted Confederate cavalry, moving down the bluff into position.[5]

General Rice had moved the veteran 33rd Iowa west to reinforce elements of Englemann's 2nd Brigade on the afternoon of April 29. Trotting forward on horseback the following morning, Rice found the Iowa unit exposed to the enemy attack he believed imminent. He called in the regiment's skirmishers and sent a messenger back to 3rd Division headquarters, asking Salomon's permission to move the unit farther to the rear. Simultaneous with the movement of the 33rd Iowa's skirmishers to the rear, the Confederates struck the command near the base of the ridgeline to the west of the Saline bottom. Colonel Greene led his Missourians forward. Rice quickly threw forward the 50th Indiana, reinforcing the Iowans to the west as the musket fire grew.[6]

Colton Greene discovered the Federals now in force as he developed the Union position. The commander of the Missouri Brigade found himself faced by two Union regiments, the 50th Indiana and 33rd Iowa, extending the Union from across the narrow gateway down the Jenkins' Ferry road. The roar of small arms fire increased as the engagement became general along the entire front. Slowly, the Confederates pressed the Federals back from the base of the ridgeline. After moving forward under heavy fire, they encountered intense musketry striking their position from the north and east of the battlefield.[7]

The Second Kansas Colored Volunteers about-faced and double-timed west from their position near the western end of the pontoon bridge when Greene's Missourians struck the 33rd Iowa in force at 8 A.M. Increasing their firepower, the black volunteers stopped Greene's advance. Colonel Samuel Johnson Crawford, commanding the Second Kansas, led his men in four ranks down through the mud of the ferry road, double-timing them where the footing permitted toward the musket fire. Halting his black troops to allow them to throw off their haversacks and overcoats, Crawford left his regiment momentarily. They resumed the march toward the fire light, and he galloped over to General Rice's headquarters, three hundred yards to the rear of the battle.[8]

"What regiment have you?" General Rice calmly asked of Crawford.

"Second Kansas Colored Volunteers," Crawford replied as his regiment continued streaming up the ferry road, moving toward the fight.

"Do you think you can take them in?" Rice asked.

"Yes, General, I can take that regiment where any live regiment will go," Crawford answered confidently.[9]

With a smile, Rice then ordered Crawford to relieve the 29th Iowa which was short of ammunition. Crawford, without halting his black troops, formed them into a column of companies, passing them to the front of the 29th Iowa.[10] There, he tied his northern flank into Toxie Creek while his left flank stood astride the road leading down to the ferry. Tangled thickets of scrub trees and heavy underbrush provided cover for the Second Kansas.[11]

Crawford knew his men would fight. He had trained the regiment since the previous November, culling out the rejects, both officer and enlisted, and providing the strict discipline and training essential to the élan he knew the men would need.[12] Additionally, the colonel knew that his troops understood the meaning of Confederate policy toward black soldiers. They realized that surrender or capture meant virtually certain death.[13] After the Poison Spring massacre, the officers of the Second Kansas had agreed to take no Confederate prisoners until the enemy stopped murdering captured and wounded black soldiers.[14]

Brigadier General James C. Tappan's Arkansas brigade of infantry had marched fifty-one miles through heavy rain and ankle-deep mud since the previous Thursday; now, between intermittent rain showers, they built fires a mile south of the ridgeline where Colton Greene had first looked down on the Federal command in the Saline River bottom.[15]

No sooner had the Arkansas troops built their fires than they were ordered forward by their division commander, General Thomas Churchill. Marmaduke's cavalry had bent and broken before the 50th Indiana Infantry and the veteran 33rd Iowa. Tappan's command reached the brow of the ridgeline. After conflicting orders, they moved down the ridge to reinforce Colton Greene, with two regiments in skirmish line. The third followed in trace as reserve. The Confederate infantry passed through the first of the open fields which immediately fronted the ridge to the east and then worked through a skirt of woods approximately 300 yards wide. Here Tappan's men came on the Federals. Union skirmishers waited in the middle of the second ploughed field, four hundred yards from east to west. The main Federal defensive perimeter lay along the western edge of the timber skirting the second field, two hundred yards beyond the Federal skirmishers.[16]

Tappan's command advanced quickly, reinforcing Greene's battered Missourians and driving in the Federal skirmishers. Moving to within close range of the main Federal defensive line, the Arkansas troops opened with rifle and musket fire. As the engagement grew, Tappan ordered forward his reserve, the 33rd Arkansas. As the regiment came on the line, they faced increased Federal fire which tore their ranks and killed instantly the regimental commander, Colonel H. L. Grinsted.[17] By ten o'clock, Tappan called for additional reserves. Confederate General Alexander T. Hawthorn responded, leading forward his brigade under the direct command of Colonel Lucien C. Gause.[18]

Gause's Arkansas troops had marched since midnight, and when the battle began at daybreak they had been ordered forward. They took position on the brow of the hills surrounding the western edge of the bottoms as Tappan's men quick-stepped forward. No sooner had Gause's troops formed in skirmish line than they were ordered to advance and support Tappan's troops. They found Tappan in position a half mile down the ferry road on the south side of the muddy lane and fronted by Federal infantry firing from the timber. As Gause positioned his men, he saw the infantry of General Parsons move up adjacent to Tappan's hard-pressed command on the northern edge of the battle-field.[19] Across the muddy fields, centered on the ferry road the musketry rolled in continuos thunder. As the violence grew, rain squalls continued to fall intermittently throughout the morning on the Saline bottoms.[20]

General Mosby M. Parsons had led his Missouri division of Confederate infantry to within three miles of Jenkins' Ferry during the night of April 30. He had halted his men west of the Saline crossing to rest in an open field. His men lit fires to dry their clothes when the first volleys of musketry to the north warned that the battle had begun. Shortly after eight o'clock, Parsons arrived at the brow of the ridgeline and looked down in the valley below. He saw the Confederate infantry heavily engaged in the second of two ploughed fields to his immediate front. At 10 A.M., Tappan's calls for reinforcement sent Parsons's Missourians sliding down from the high ground to form a skirmish line centered on the ferry road. Arriving at the strip of woods which separated the two cleared fields in the valley. Parsons met his commander, Sterling Price. Price ordered him to move to the south of the engaged Arkansas troops and then advance to the front.[21]

As Parsons advanced through the woods he next encountered General Thomas Churchill, who requested immediate support for his Arkansas troops north of the road. Countermanding Price's orders, Parsons sent his 2nd Brigade, under Colonel Simon B. Burns, to reinforce the Arkansas infantry on the north side of the ferry road, under heavy fire from the timber and felled trees on the far side of the second ploughed field.[22] Now reinforced, the Arkansas troops vigorously moved forward, steadily pushing back the Federals on the north side of the road a quarter of a mile amidst constant small arms fire. Suddenly, Union reinforcements smashed into the Confederate lines, hurling them back on both flanks and the center. The Confederates retreated from the ground they had so dearly bought across the second field to the west.[23]

Tappan's first attack of the morning had concentrated on the northern flank of the Union perimeter. Tappan had attempted to outflank the Federals by moving infantry across Toxie Creek and through the swamps, enfilading the Federal position stretched north to south across the ferry road. Elements of the 2nd Brigade and the 29th Iowa moved across the creek and successfully resisted this Confederate envelopment. Tappan then concentrated his Arkansas troops on the Federal southern flank, driving vigorously forward on the 50th Indiana.[24]

The Confederates came down hard on the southern flank of the Union line, anchored on the bog fringing the southern edge of the battlefield. Sensing the Confederate tactic of striking each portion of the Union line successively to find a weak point, General Rice double-timed the veteran 33rd Iowa forward to the left flank. There they reinforced the 50th Indiana under heavy attack. Despite the added support, the Federal line fell back some 250 yards on the southern flank as Parsons's Missourians joined the Arkansas troops in attacking the entire Federal front in the narrow valley.[25] Rice now ordered forward the 12th Kansas Infantry to support the rapidly deteriorating situation on his left flank. The Kansans, under Colonel Josiah E. Hayes, went in with a cheer and drove the Missouri and Arkansas enemies before them. Rice advanced his command some three hundred yards, driving the Confederates back through the more westerly of the two ploughed fields.[26]

On the northern edge of the rain-soaked fields, the Union position now improved. Confederate efforts to flank the Federal northern flank by crossing Toxie Creek brought instant Federal response. Two companies of the Second Kansas Colored waded the narrow but swollen creek and reinforced the 43rd Illinois. The swift flowing creek varied from three to four feet in depth and filled many of the Federals' cartridge boxes.[27]

Colonel Sam Crawford conferred briefly with General Rice just south of the ferry road early on the morning of the battle. He moved his black soldiers up the ferry road, relieving the 29th Iowa and 9th Wisconsin. The latter had withstood attacks first by Marmaduke's skirmishers, then Colton Greene's Missourians, and finally, Tappan's Arkansas troops reinforced by additional Missouri Confederate units under Mosby Parsons. With the 43rd Illinois moving across Toxie Creek, the combined Missouri and Arkansas troops, under Sterling Price, struck desperately at the Federal northern flank, securely tied to the bayou fringing on the Union right.[28] A section of Confederate artillery unlimbered on the Federals in the middle of the most westerly ploughed field, as the Confederates began a renewed effort to storm the Federal right.[29]

Crawford placed his 600 men in a skirmish line facing the veteran Confederate infantry under Tappan, Parsons and Hawthorn. As Tappan's Arkansas troops, with the other Confederate units in reserve, advanced on his position, the commander of the Second Kansas gave his men the command to fire at will. The first Federal volley staggered the enemy, and then both Federal and Confederates blazed away at each other at close range. As the two skirmish lines exchanged fire, Crawford galloped up and down behind his black troops, urging them to "aim low and give them hell."[30]

For over an hour, the Kansas regiment exchanged small arms fire with the Arkansas troops. The Confederates finally broke, and Hawthorn's men with Parsons' reinforcements moved up to take their place. After forty minutes the second Confederate line broke before the accurate and steady fire of the Second Kansas. During the time when the Second Kansas outdueled the Arkansas and Missouri troops at close range, the Union right had held, but the left and center had been driven back by the superior numbers and firepower of the Confederates. Seeing that the Confederates had come up almost on line with his southern flank, Crawford quickly changed front with five companies of the Second Kansas. His well-drilled troops immediately poured a murderous fire into the long axis of the enemy skirmish line to his south. The Confederates retreated across the open field from the wood line they had fought valiantly to take only moments earlier.[31]

Having driven the Confederates to his front and flank, Crawford saw a section of Confederate artillery unlimber in the center of the ploughed field over which much of the morning fighting had raged. Three Confederate guns stood to the immediate front of the Second Kansas Colored while three additional guns lay to the south and rear of the first battery. All six guns, supported by Confederate infantry, opened on Crawford's position with canister, causing heavy casualties among the Federals. Crawford notified General Rice by courier that he must either take the battery to his front by bayonet charge or fall back. Rice replied instantly:

"You can charge the battery as soon as you hear cheering on the left."[32]

Crawford ordered his regiment to fix bayonets and moved them out into the open field as cheering began.[33] After advancing a hundred yards, Crawford halted the Second Kansas Colored. His regiment levelled a volley into the battery of artillery immediately to the front, killing many horses and holding the three guns in place. The other three pieces limbered as the Confederates retreated from the field. Crawford ordered a second volley poured into the enemy infantry to his front and then moved his black soldiers forward.[34] With the same calmness they had exhibited during the two-hour exchange of small arms fire, the black troops advanced, surging across the muddy field with hearty and continuous cheering.[35]

Crawford's men, still at the quickstep, passed the Confederate battery where over thirty enemy horses lay dead. With the bayonets "freely used," the Second Kansas Colored continued past the battery, following the retreating Confederate Infantry.[36] Crawford continued 150 yards past the battery and halted his regiment. Here, he sent a sufficient force back to secure the rebel guns. This done, Crawford's regiment retired to the rear to resupply their nearly exhausted ammunition.[37] Although the

Second Kansas Colored had taken no prisoners during the charge, Crawford proudly noted that his men killed none of the wounded Confederates they had passed in the ploughed field.[38]

As a momentary lull fell over the battlefield, a lieutenant of the captured Missouri battery, John O. Lockhart, was brought before Crawford. Knowing of the massacre of wounded and captured black soldiers two weeks earlier at the engagement at Poison Spring, Lockhart appeared markedly nervous.[39]

Regaining his self-control, Lockhart told Crawford, "We have been unfortunate to-day and here I am a prisoner of war."

"You are not a prisoner of war," Crawford answered.

> Your President [Davis] has placed his army under the 'Black Flag' insofar as our colored troops and their officers are concerned, and General Price's troops carried out that order to the letter at Poison Spring . . . But we are not going to kill you . . . I am going to send you back to your lines as a messenger . . . tell [your commanders] that I accept their new flag [the black flag implying no quarter in battle] . . . and . . . so long as they bear it aloft . . . I shall simply tell the men to remember Poison Spring.[40]

Following the Lockhart interview, Crawford resupplied his men with ammunition and double-timed them into position at the center of the Federal line. The battle again intensified. Once again the rolling thunder of small arms fire crackled through the valley.[41]

For over six hours the battle had raged, most of it fought over an area only 150 yards wide. Dense smoke from the continuous musket fire hung over the battlefield; black rain clouds also pressed down on the site. Over the field, now covered with the bodies of both Confederate and Union dead and wounded, lay a sheet of water, varying from ankle to knee-deep.[42]

While desperately continuing to move wagons and artillery across the pontoon bridge over the Saline River, the Federals had beaten back successive attacks by Marmaduke's cavalry and Price's Arkansas and Missouri divisions under Generals Churchill and Parsons.[43] General Kirby Smith now directed Walker's Texas division to the front in one last desperate effort to destroy the Union men. The Federals still resisted along the eastern edge of the ploughed field in which the Second Kansas had captured Parsons's cannon.

Walker's division had trudged up the muddy road leading to the bluff overlooking the battlefield just as the Second Kansas regiment captured the guns in their bayonet charge. Two miles back they had filed by their commander, Brigadier General John G. Walker, who, astride his iron gray horse, urged his men forward. As the intermittent rain began anew, the

Texas division stumbled down the steep hill leading to the ferry crossing. They shook out their ranks in a double skirmish line and moved toward the now ebbing roar of musketry. On the field so dark from cloud and smoke, friend and foe could be identified only by the flash of almost constant small arms fire.[44]

Having covered twenty-two miles on muddy roads since 2:30 A.M. Brigadier General Thomas N. Waul led his brigade of Walker's Texas division toward the fight. By 10:30 A.M. Waul had his men in place, behind the other two Texas brigades led by Brigadier William R. Scurry and Colonel Horace Randal.[45] With Kirby Smith exercising direct command of the division, Waul set his troops in motion as reserves, following the other two brigades. As the Texans moved forward in skirmish line, they met General Price, leading remnants of his Arkansas and Missouri divisions from the field following the bayonet charge of the Second Kansas Volunteers.[46] The Texans threw forward a battalion of skirmishers as they pressed through the skirt of timber separating the two open fields. They moved into the gateway to the pontoon bridge where most of the morning's action had taken place. Here, General Waul found Federal skirmishers pursuing the retreating Confederate Arkansas and Missouri troops. After a brisk fight between the skirmishers, the Federals retired to the Union defensive line in the eastern skirts of timber, where they used logs, rails, and fallen trees as cover.[47]

In addition to the main body of the 4,000 Federal troops frontlining the center of the Texas division, elements of the VII Corps now held a position along the banks of Toxie Creek on the western edge of the narrow battlefield. This element extended at right angles south of the main Federal line and enfiladed the advancing Confederates. Additionally, the Union commanders had extended their lines to the south and the west, to create a cone of fire into which the attacking Texans moved.[48]

Waul's brigade moved forward, guided on the center of the Federal line while Scurry and Randal led their brigades toward the northern flank of the Union position. Quick stepping through continuous small arms fire as they left the cover of the western skirt of timber, the Texans came under heavy fire as they neared the Federal lines. Sheets of flame smashed the advancing Confederate line in a killing crossfire. Waul's Confederates on the northern edge of the field pressed back a Union charge, and the two skirmish lines fought at close quarters, neither line wavering.[49] So thick hung the battle smoke over the field that troops crouched down to see their targets below the black curtain.[50]

Waul prepared his Confederates for a charge against the Union right. Aligning his troops in the timber, he advanced against the center of the

Federal line. Simultaneously, he received word that brigade commanders Scurry and Randal had fallen mortally wounded.[51] In the confusion, elements of the Confederate divisions began retreating. Moments later, the Confederates' advance wavered and then disintegrated.[52]

Edmund Kirby Smith rode in the vanguard of the fight, moving among the Texans and remnants of the torn Missouri and Arkansas divisions, cheering the men forward. As elements of those Arkansas troops began to give way before the Federal crossfire, Kirby Smith dismounted. Taking up a musket, he personally led the men forward.[53] General Churchill followed his commander's example, also dismounted and joined the ranks of his Arkansas troops, musket in hand.[54]

With only a remnant of his small army still effective, Kirby Smith ordered a withdrawal. Walker's men retired to the western edge of the field where they set up a defensive line to command the field and, in the words of General Waul,

> protect any wounded that might have accidentally been left, and prevent their mutilation and murder, which the barbarity of the enemy had inflicted on some who had been left on the field in the conflict before our [Walker's Texas Division] arrival.[55]

Waul, although badly wounded himself, remained on the field, working with Kirby Smith to maintain a Confederate defensive line on the western edge of the ploughed field.[56]

As Marmaduke struck the Federals on the west ridgeline about noon, the almost constant musket and rifle fire abated.[57] Proudly, the battered Federals displayed three sets of captured Confederate colors. Two had been seized by the 50th Indiana, while the 9th Wisconsin had taken the other. As the firing diminished, General Salomon feared that the Confederates were receiving reinforcements. He determined to shorten his lines and called back the 43rd Illinois. From their northern position flanking Toxie Creek, the Illinois troops had pursued Confederate elements nearly to the base of the western ridgeline.[58]

Salomon intended to shorten his lines by moving his command closer to the pontoon bridge to the rear. General Frederick Steele arrived on the field for the first time. He agreed with Salomon's decision, and immediately the 3rd Division commander began an orderly withdrawal. As the Federals drew back, Salomon's directed the collection of wounded and dead. Others, to be left behind, were collected and left at a small house on the battlefield that had been used as a field hospital. Surgeons and attendants remained with the Federal casualties.[59]

Across the rain soaked battlefield, the moans of the wounded and dying now replaced the roars of musketry and shouts of triumph. Slowly the black clouds of smoke lifted, revealing the field littered with wounded and dead.[60] As the Federals gathered their casualties, the Confederates retreated to the ridgeline, covered by Marmaduke's cavalry. The same troopers had begun the engagement nearly seven hours before at dawn.[61]

Crawford's tough Second Kansas Colored Volunteers rested gratefully on their arms as the battle ceased. During the fight they had suffered over eighty killed and wounded. An additional forty casualties remained on the field.[62] Ordered to retire with the rest of the command, Crawford's men spent over two hours caring for the Federal wounded and dead. At four o'clock the Second Kansas left the field, covering the rear of the Union column. Subsequently they were ordered by General Thayer to destroy the pontoon bridge that had been crossed by virtually the entire VII Corps. In the late afternoon, Crawford's regiment passed over the bridge and commenced its destruction. The black soldiers used bayonets to puncture the India rubber pontoons on which the spans rested.[63]

At nightfall, Confederates held the battlefield, the main body of Kirby Smith's force camping on the high ground of the ridgeline to the south of Jenkins' Ferry. Safe across the Saline with the pontoon bridge sunk, the VII Corps bivouacked in the muddy bottom on the east side of the river.[64] Brigadier General James F. Fagan finally arrived with 2,500 cavalry. He threw Brigadier General Joseph O. Shelby forward in pursuit of Steele only to find the bridge gone. Fagan had hesitated following the victory at Marks' Mills on April 25. Unaware of the Federal retreat from Camden, he had galloped thirty-four miles during the night and morning of the battle only to arrive too late.[65]

Although returns were incomplete, Salomon's 3rd Division listed 63 dead and 458 missing and wounded.[66] Thayer did not file a report, but his casualties must have been at least as large as the 3rd Division's. The Second Kansas Colored alone suffered over 100 casualties.[67] Estimates of 1,000 would approximate the number of Union soldiers killed, wounded, and missing in the engagement.

Confederate returns proved equally incomplete. Price reported 86 men killed and 358 wounded in the Missouri and Arkansas divisions and Marmaduke's cavalry. Walker's division, which bore the burden of the final Federal crossfire and lost General Scurry and Colonel Randal, made no report. Estimates of Texas casualties reached 500 dead, wounded, and missing.[68] Thus, Confederates lost 1,000 in the fight, a total of 2,000 casualties in seven hours.

As both Confederate and Union forces regrouped, General Steele ordered the worst of his wagons destroyed and the teams doubled on the remaining wagons and ambulances. On the western bank of the Saline one federal surgeon, two assistant surgeons, and a team of attendants cared for the grisly litter of the battlefield. Steele wrote, "I regret exceedingly the necessities which have caused me to lose so many brave men in detail. . . . The conduct of the colored troops of my command proves that the African can be made as formidable in battle as a soldier of any other color."[69]

Then, the night shrouded it all. Only the wind in the Arkansas pines, the occasional moaning of the wounded, and the rushing of the rising Saline, broke the silence of the spring night. As the survivors of the battle of Jenkins' Ferry slept, rain fell on the two armies.[70]

Part 5

AFRICAN-AMERICAN WOMEN AND THE WAR EFFORT

CHAPTER 21

—~~◁◁◁╲╱▷▷▷~~—

The Southern Side of "Glory"

Mississippi African-American Women
During the Civil War

Noralee Frankel

On the Clark plantation in Hinds, Co., until the battle of Vicksburg
ended in [July] 1863, which was the first time we knew we were
free, all the slaves in the surrounding country was gathered into a
camp on a plantation about five miles from Vicksburg. We
remained in this camp until October 1863. My husband with
others were sent up to Vicksburg to enlist. I went with him; he was
examined, pronounced sound and was accepted and went
immediately into camps with the troops, he was made a cook for
the company. I followed and for several week I assisted him in
cooking. . . . [from Maria Clark's widow's pension testimony. Maria
Clark was a slave and the wife of Henry Clark, also a former slave,
who served in the Third Cavalry, United States Colored Troops][1]

T HE MOVIE *GLORY* DEPICTS the Civil War experiences of the Fifty-
fourth Massachusetts Regiment of African-American soldiers. For
most Americans, the movie represents their first exposure to the fact that
thousands of Black troops fought and died in the Civil War. Unlike the
Fifty-fourth, most of these soldiers were not born in the North, but lived
as slaves in the South. Initially resistant, the federal government finally
allowed African-American men to become soldiers in 1862, and slave
men throughout the South enlisted. In Mississippi, for example, they
formed the core of six regiments exceeding seventeen thousand men.

African-American women such as Maria Clark joined their men in their quest for freedom. The impact of army life on African-American women in the South has yet to be told.

Each Northern victory in Mississippi, particularly the capture of Vicksburg, Jackson, and Natchez in 1863, encouraged increasing numbers of slave men and women to flee their enslavement. While Black young men went into the army, the women, both single and married, followed the soldiers. John Eaton, a military chaplain in the Mississippi Valley, saw slave women after the fall of Vicksburg, "following the army, carrying all their possessions on their heads, great feather beds tied up in sheets and holding their few belongings."[2] When William Tecumseh Sherman advanced through the state of Mississippi in 1863–64, behind his army were "10 miles of negroes . . . a string of ox wagons, negro women and children behind each brigade that equalled in length the brigade itself."[3]

These former slave women and children migrated to areas, usually cities, where the army stationed the soldiers. As ex-slave Frances Brown recalled, "The soldiers came through there [Hinds Co.] and I came away with them. I did not know one regiment from another; all I knew was that they were Yankee soldiers. I came right here to Vicksburg, Mississippi, with them. I don't know what year that was but I guess it was after Vicksburg surrendered for they were mustering in colored soldiers when I got here."[4]

Upon arrival, the women sometimes lived in army tents.[5] Gradually, though, the majority of women, including family members of Black soldiers, moved into other residences outside of the barracks. They lived as near to the enlisted men as the army officers permitted. Accommodations ranged from boarding houses to shanties, although to a soldier even the poorest housing looked better than army barracks. One soldier recalled that a fellow comrade, when not on duty, stayed with his wife, "who lived but a short distance from the barracks" in a shanty. "This house was covered with boards. . . . I have been in the house. It was a comfortable house. The house was more comfortable than a tent."[6] Still, Northern philanthropists journeying South to help the newly freed slaves were greatly distressed over the women's living conditions. According to one observer, the ex-slaves in Natchez, mainly women and children, "live in a community by themselves in the outskirts of the town, a cabin is built . . . say 12 feet wide with walls, 7 feet in height and divided off into compartments . . . and each one is appropriated to a family."[7] One army officer bluntly stated that "soldiers' wives and children are living in wretchedness and miserable hovels. . . ."[8]

Located near the army, some of the African-American women obtained employment as nurses, cooks, laundresses, as well as personal servants to white officers.[9] For example, the woman living in the shanty "more comfortable than a tent" worked as a washerwoman for thirty men in the Fifth Heavy Artillery, soldiers of which built her that house. The soldiers probably ensured housing for her because she provided a necessary domestic service for them. While both Black soldiers and Black women served as cooks and nurses, the army only hired women as laundresses. Washing and ironing clothes for the same men over a period of months, they kept close contact with the soldiers, especially if they had known them during slavery.

Unmarried women performing domestic work in the army camps found willing mates among the soldiers. Having left her slave master to come to Vicksburg with her sister and brother, Ellen Creevy became a soldier's bride. A laundress for several Black soldiers, she met her future husband while visiting the army camp.[10] As with other slave women, Anna Roberts also followed the Union soldiers to Vicksburg. Once there, she moved in with a woman who baked for the soldiers. Roberts later remembered that "the Fifth Heavy Artillery was camped right up on the hill above where we lived and I would go there every morning and sell the pies about all out." Anna felt quite comfortable in camp since she had known several of the soldiers before the war. One soldier, who had lived on the same plantation with Anna, recalled that during one of her visits, "she met Richard Roberson and she got stuck on him and told me that she and Roberson were going to get married."[11] Similarly, Lucinda Westbrooks, who married Frank Morris during the war, recalled that she "had been washing for Morris and we decided to marry and so we did."[12]

Unlike Anna Roberson and Lucinda Westbrooks who met their mates during the war, many former slave women were actually remarrying their slave husbands while these men served in the army. Even though slave marriages possessed no legal standing, couples took these unions seriously. While enslaved, men and women considered themselves married when they lived together with consent of their master, often following a small wedding ceremony performed by the slave owner or slave preacher. During the war, some of the slave couples legally remarried. While slaves, Eliza Foreman and Nathaniel Foreman wedded in 1858. When Eliza Foreman came to Vicksburg as a domestic servant for a Yankee officer, she remarried her soldier husband. Their marriage certificate stated that:

> This certifies, that I have this day joined in lawful marriage, Nathaniel Forman . . . and Eliza Todd . . . in compliance with the ordinance of God, and by authority of the United States of America, vested in me, in accordance with No. 15, special Order of the Secretary of War . . . signed Joseph Warren, chaplain 25, Inf. assistant in charge of freedmen, . . ."[13]

African Americans kept army chaplains busy performing marriage ceremonies. Former slave Lucinda Westbrooks recalled being "married by a white man preacher Miller—who came there with the first Yankees and went around marrying the soldiers. He married lots of other soldiers the same day."[14] Chaplains also held weddings for several couples simultaneously. One army wife recalled that "there were about a dozen married at the same time and stood right around in a row . . ."[15] Soldiers invited their comrades to these festivities. While in the Fifth Heavy Artillery, John Dollins attended the marriage of his pre-war companion and fellow slave, Louis Caston.[16] Women friends, known since slavery or met during the war, also came to the ceremonies.[17]

While the army gave former slaves the first access to legal marriages, army officials used legalized marriage of African Americans as a means to restrict civilian interaction with soldiers. In order to control the numbers of women entering army camps, Samuel Thomas, an officer in Vicksburg, decided to forbid any nonlegally married couples from living together. After Emily Fulgert joined her slave husband Gordon Fulgert's "regiment, . . . orders [were] enforced that soldiers should remarry under the laws and flag then Gordon Fulgert . . . remarrie[d] [Emily] again this being the second marriage once by the owner and once by Provost Marshal Samuel Thomas at Vicksburg,"[18] The army applied the new orders to women living inside and outside of the barracks. One ex-soldier, when explaining how he knew a couple was married so that the widow could obtain her husband's military pension, emphatically stated that "I have personal knowledge that said parties lived and cohabitated as man and wife in the camp and [as she was] so treated by the officers and all others, and if she had not been recognized by the officers as his lawful wife she would not have been allowed to remain in the camp as such."[19] The army forcefully encouraged couples such as Private Benjamin Lee and Winnie Moore to wed. Having known Benjamin Lee before the war, Moore moved in with Lee when she came to Vicksburg. While living together, "there was a law passed by the officers that no man should live with a woman unless he married her and then Ben and Winnie went up to [Samuel Thomas' headquarters] . . . and were married or they said they married any how. Most all the boys were living with women and went up and were married."[20]

Besides encouraging legal marriages, white officers such as Samuel Thomas used more extreme methods for dealing with the large numbers of former slave women and children in the army lines. They banned women from army quarters and sent them to deserted plantations to raise cotton for the Northern government to sell. Overcrowding of the areas where soldiers were stationed and sexual activity between African-American women and soldiers, both white and Black, became rationales for moving African-American women out of the cities. The army officers considered the women disruptive to military procedure. Samuel Thomas complained that "the Regiments are crowded with women of bad character and soldiers' wives and children are living in wretchedness and miserable hovels, when land can be furnished in safe localities where they can build good houses and support themselves by cultivating it."[21] A few officers even worried about the white soldiers' sexual exploitation of former slave women, but most perceived any African-American women consorting with Union soldiers as corrupting the troops.[22]

In Natchez, General Tuttle at the suggestion of chief health officer A. W. Kelley decided to rid the city of large numbers of civilian African-American residents. They ordered every Black man and woman "to present a paper certifying that he or she was living on the premises of some responsible white person and was *employed* by them." While allowing African-American women who worked for the military such as laundresses to remain, the army forcibly began to remove other former slave women from the city. The military only modified the policy when Black soldiers marched into the office of one of the Union officers and informed him that "they could no longer endure the trial of seeing their wives and children driven in to the streets and if he would not at once interfere and protect them they should *positively* do it themselves."[23]

The military, however, continued to initiate civilian removal plans. A year later, Lieutenant L. W. Brobet grew concerned as more former slaves arrived in Natchez. Brobet, as with military officers elsewhere, believed that ex-slave women should be rounded up and taken to Union-held plantations. Another military commander in Natchez thwarted Brobet by allowing the wives and children of African-American soldiers to stay, even though Brobet considered the soldiers' families the "main cause" of the congestion in Natchez.[24] In spite of the soldiers' protests, the army moved hundreds of African-American women onto land abandoned by Southern planters.

Soldiers acted individually as well as in groups against the army's insistence on relocating the soldiers' families. When Samuel Williams's wife was "taken to a government farm . . . he came after her and she came to Vicksburg to her husband."[25] Similarly, when another soldier found his family on federally controlled land, "he hired a wagon and carried [his wife] and the children . . . here to Vicksburg."[26] One of slavery's worst horrors had been the threat of a family member being sold and sent away to work elsewhere. Since insuring a stable family life motivated slave men to enlist, African-American soldiers were unwilling to tolerate the army's breaking up of Black families.

Northern officers failed to appreciate the emotional ties formed during slave marriages nor did they approve of any relationship other than legalized marriage. Certainly, some of the Black women visiting the army camps of Black soldiers engaged in sexual activity, but few of the women sleeping with these men were paid prostitutes. Occasionally, soldiers lied by falsely indicating that the women with whom they were intimate where their legal wives.[27] These exceptions, however, failed to negate the devotion shown by African-American couples.

African-American soldiers and wives displayed their mutual affection by seeing each other whenever possible. When their wives lived outside the barracks, soldiers obtained passes to see them. Couples enjoyed their conjugal visits. Richard Robert's bunk mate recalled that "whenever [Richard] could get away at night he was with [his wife, Anna]."[28] Benjamin Lee's passion for his new wife caused him to obtain "a pass to come from home whenever he wanted to and often ran in home without a pass."[29] Moses Wilson's wife recalled "I was there near my husband in the camps and he came often to see me of nights."[30] Soldiers, like Allen Alexander, who spouses stayed on the plantation even sent for their wives to join them.[31] When their husbands became unable to visit them, wives, when able, came to camp to visit or nurse their husbands staying in hospitals from war-related injuries and illnesses.[32]

Former slaves maintained their family life as best as they could throughout the war. They remained committed whenever possible to their extended family as well as to their spouses and children. For example, washerwoman Ellen Creevy met her husband while visiting her brothers in the army. The army also gave African Americans the opportunity to meet former slaves from outside their plantation neighborhood, greatly expanding ex-slaves' physical and social geography, although, the ex-slaves continued to value older landmarks such as the slave family and the plantation community. Slave women ran to the Union lines to gain liberation from enslavement. They discovered during the war that freedom and even legal marriage failed to provide family autonomy removed from white interference. As they fought for family stability, during Reconstruction, they continued to learn that their Northern liberators would often play a confusing and contradictory part in their struggle. Due to the movie *Glory*, African-American soldiers' contributions to the Northern victory are finally receiving recognition. Black women's experiences during the Civil War also deserve attention and continued study.

CHAPTER 22

Presence and Precedents

The USS Red Rover During the American
Civil War, 1861–1865

Steven Louis Roca

O N JUNE 10, 1862, A VESSEL left Cairo, Illinois, and entered the
Federal army's Gunboat Service on the Mississippi River. By all
accounts, it was a large and aesthetically pleasing craft. In many respects,
however, it was a singular vessel, distinct from its fleetmates.[1]

The USS *Red Rover* had been extensively refitted, first at St. Louis,
then at Cairo, into the first hospital ship in U.S. naval history. Throughout its career, *Red Rover*'s crew included significant numbers of African
Americans, and, for the first time on board a U.S. warship, women were
employed, Catholic nuns and African Americans among them. Several of
the latter became the first female nurses in the U.S. Navy.

On April 7, 1862, following the three-week battle for Island No. 10
in Missouri, the Federal gunboat *Mound City* discovered *Red Rover*. It
had been a commercial sidewheel steamer, purchased by the Confederacy
in November 1861 for use as an unarmed accommodations ship or float-
ing barracks.[2] During the battle for Island No. 10 it was struck by plunging shot that penetrated all of its decks and caused flooding. To avoid
sinking, it was run aground and then abandoned. *Mound City*'s engineers
made temporary repairs so that the captured vessel could be towed
upriver to St. Louis.[3]

At the time of *Red Rover*'s capture, the Union needed every vessel
which it could procure and convert for service on the sprawling Mississippi and its tributaries. Flag Officers Andrew H. Foote, however, ordered

Fleet Capt. Alexander M. Pennock "to procure a good comfortable steamer to be fitted as a hospital boat with surgeon, steward, etc., complete" to support the Union army's Western Flotilla. *Red Rover* was selected and underwent refitting as proposed by Quartermaster George D. Wise and approved by Comm. Charles Henry Davis. Pennock oversaw the hull and engine overhauls, while Wise procured items needed to equip a hospital boat. On May 25 he reported that "I am in St. Louis preparing the *Red Rover* for a hospital for our sick and wounded. The Sanitary Commission have rendered me valuable advice and aid, and the *Red Rover* will have every requisite for the purpose she is intended."[4]

At the time, facilities for the care of sick and wounded were limited and primitive. Various steamers temporarily housed and transported casualties but lacked the personnel and facilities required for proper medical treatment. *Red Rover* was to ease the burden of the Western Fleet by removing casualties from the fighting vessels. It would also serve as a transport, delivering medical supplies and provisions to fleet vessels wherever needed. To meet these requirements, *Red Rover* was refitted in innovative ways, making it a unique vessel. The refit transformed *Red Rover* into a craft that emphasized both comfort and sanitation. The Western Sanitary Commission provided medical and other supplies worth $3,500 and arranged for two well-respected Boston physicians, Drs. George H. Bixby and George H. Hopkins to become the ship's senior medical officers. Bixby served in that capacity until the ship's final decommissioning in the fall of 1865.[5]

Red Rover featured separate operating and amputating rooms and distinct crew and patient galleys with below-deck kitchen facilities. An aft cabin's walls were opened to provide better air circulation for patients suffering from communicable illnesses, and the windows were covered with "gauze blinds . . . to keep the cinders and smoke from annoying the sick." Several enclosed or canvas-covered barges were assigned to *Red Rover* to accommodate those with infectious diseases and moored along protected banks of the Mississippi. Other additions included a separate steam boiler for laundry, nine bathrooms and water closets, three elevators to move patients and supplies, and a cold-storage locker that held three hundred tons of ice.[6]

Red Rover carried sufficient medical supplies and provisions to support its crew and two hundred patients for up to three months. Everything available and considered essential for the treatment of sick and wounded was carried on board. Wise wrote from the naval depot at Cairo: "I wish you could see our hospital boat, the *Red Rover,* with all her comforts for the sick and disabled seamen. She is designed to be the most complete thing of the kind that ever floated, and is in every way a decided success."[7]

Sisters Mary Adela and Veronica, the first women carried as nurses on board a U.S. vessel, were entered into the books on June 1, 1862. Sister Angela, superior of the Order of the Holy Cross, volunteered the services of the order to the navy, but most of the nuns would serve at shore facilities.[8] Although not a nursing order, these women provided experience and discipline, trained as they were to "procure cleanliness, nourishment, and safety for the sick, the administration of simple medicine, kitchen and laundry work, supervision of the wards, and care of the spiritual welfare of the patients." This made them valued assets to the ship, where their duties, along with those of other nurses, included general cleaning, cleaning and distributing laundry and supplies, preparing special diets, and writing letters and providing spiritual comfort for patients. Adela and Veronica remained on board *Red Rover* throughout the war, while two others, Sisters Calista and St. John, came on board "for a while."[9] These were not the only women on board *Red Rover,* however.

From early on, the greatest presence Union forces exerted in the South was on the Mississippi. For enslaved African American "Contraband" trying to reach Federal lines, especially in the western theater, the Union flotilla offered the best chance of escape and safety. Throughout the war, numerous African Americans made their way onto flotilla vessels, including *Red Rover.* Records show them initially listed as "Contraband," and most of them were employed and "entered on the Ship's books." Men achieved ranks as cabin boys, laborers, carpenters, coal heavers, landsmen, cooks, stewards, seamen, and other rated members of the crew and Medical Department. Most women received the rating of laundress, and several attained the rank of nurse (Appendix).[10]

These nurses and laundresses, however, were not the first women to serve on board *Red Rover.* Ann Graves was hired on April 13, 1862, by Wise as "Chambermaid" for twenty dollars a month. She soon had plenty of company. Mary Warfield joined the chambermaid staff in May at the rate of fifteen dollars. Mary Bryant, Maria Cassidy, and Eliza McLothian came on board as laundresses in June, at fifteen dollars each per month. Mattie Perkins, Betsy Bishop, and Nancy Rogers hired on as laundresses in August for ten dollars a month, while Sarah Watson joined them in the laundry room in September for only seven dollars per month, though one month later she received a raise to fifteen dollars.[11]

Two additional facts should be considered here: throughout the war, men serving as nurses on board *Red Rover* greatly outnumbered their female counterparts, and, by way of comparison with the women's pay, the average Union army infantryman only received thirteen dollars per month.[12] Missing from the records, are the chambermaids' race, ethnicity, and physical descriptions. With the exception of the October 13, 1862, entry for Sarah Watson, these women disappear from *Red Rover*'s records.

One final item regarding *Red Rover*'s women warrants passing note. On June 27, 1862, Davis wrote to Pennock: "It has been reported . . . officially, that there is a woman on board *Red Rover* dressed in men's clothes . . . known to be the mistress of the commander of the vessel [Captain A. McDaniel]. . . . [M]ake a formal investigation into this charge and . . . make a brief report of your conclusion." On July 18, Davis informed Pennock that "Capt. McDaniel . . . informs me that he is desirous of giving up his command."[13] McDaniel resigned on June 21, and on September 16 Acting Master William R. Wells arrived to take command of *Red Rover*.

After a delay caused by additional hull damage, *Red Rover* entered service on June 10, 1862, assigned to the Federal army's gunboat service under Fleet Captain Pennock. *Red Rover* received its first five patients from Ram Fleet vessels on June 11 and fifty-one additional patients from flotilla vessels over the next two days. Davis wrote often of *Red Rover*'s valuable service to the Western Flotilla, describing conditions prior to its arrival:

> I have waited until I had an opportunity to make a personal examination of the Hospital Boat *Red Rover* before expressing . . . my great admiration . . . for your success in this undertaking and the gratitude felt . . . by myself and the officers and men . . . for the judgement and humanity with which you have executed this important work.
>
> No one but those who have witnessed it can comprehend the sufferings to which our sick have been exposed by the absence of proper accommodations on board the gunboats. . . .
>
> When the ship was cleared for action, as often happened when lying near Fort Pillow [Tennessee], it was necessary to take down their cots and hammocks more than quickly into out-of-the-way and uncomfortable places.
>
> This must always have been attended with pain and distress, if not positive injury.
>
> The arrival of the *Red Rover* will put a stop to all this, promote the efficiency of the squadron by procuring comfort and the means of restoration of the sick.
>
> All the conveniences and appliances of a hospital are fully provided, and to these are added the neatness and order essential to so large an establishment.

In fact, by June 14, *Red Rover*'s accommodations and "conveniences" made admittance so desirous that Davis issued a General Order in an attempt to restrict and regulate the "sick persons . . . sent on board the hospital boat indiscriminately."[14]

Nonetheless, numerous men from other vessels received treatment on *Red Rover.* Wells's and the surgeons' log entries noted them as having been admitted "without papers" or "without papers, on orders of Rear Admiral Porter [or] Surgeon Pinkney [or] Surgeon Bixby."[15]

On June 17, infantry-carrying gunboats of the Western Flotilla attempted to open army communications along Arkansas's White River, resulting in the capture of Confederate forts at St. Charles and the securing of Union control over the White. During the fighting, the gunboat *Mound City* was struck. A shell penetrated the port casemate, killing three crewmen before crashing into the steam drum, which exploded. Eight men were scalded to death, eighty-two died in the casemate, and forty-three others drowned or were shot after escaping overboard. Only twenty-three of the 175 *Mound City* crewmen were left unwounded. Injuries like those suffered by the crew of the *Mound City* increased as the war dragged on, due mainly to the vulnerability of the primitive and fragile steam plants. *Red Rover*'s medical department records are filled with cases of "Ambustio," or burns, of varying degrees of severity.

Most of *Mound City*'s injured were taken to the army hospital at Memphis, Tennessee. On June 19, thirty-seven of *Mound City*'s casualties left on *Red Rover* for transport to the Mound City Naval Hospital. Before departing Memphis, Davis ordered McDaniel to take *Red Rover* to Cairo to "suggest . . . the following changes" for his boat: move the galley below deck and open the cabin aft for air circulation; install a steam boiler for the laundry; and add a awning for the "cabin upper side lights."[16]

On June 24, Dr. Bixby received a letter from Davis concerning his treatment of the *Mound City* wounded:

> The hospital boat *Red Rover* will leave this evening for Cairo . . . You will report to commander Pennock . . . as to the best method of disposing of the wounded from the gunboat Mound City.
>
> To transfer them either to the Mound City Hospital or . . . still farther up to St. Louis seems to me . . . the best plan. It is a source of the greatest satisfaction for me to know that those poor wounded men are in the hands of so able, attentive and humane a physician as yourself. I have witnessed your devotion to them with profound gratitude and I am sure you must enjoy the highest of all rewards the consciousness of having done your duty.

Bixby responded to Davis on June 27:

> I cannot resist acknowledging, with the deepest gratitude, your kind approbation of my humble efforts toward the unfortunate victims of

the past week. While your words send a thrill of encouragement through the heart of one anxious to serve his country, yet he feels that in the performance of one's plain and positive duty there lies no merit. The satisfaction of having endeavored to do my duty is mine, which, as you truly remark, is the greatest reward . . . [17]

On June 26, *Red Rover* transported thirty-five of the thirty-seven *Mound City* wounded, along with two prisoners of war and several other patients, to the Mound City hospital. An inspection revealed a broken stern post, so it was moved to the Mound City shipyards for repairs. *Red Rover* got underway again on July 8 and rejoined the flotilla above Vicksburg, Mississippi, four days later. Commander James Alden of the Steam Sloop USS *Richmond* entered in his log that "the steamer *Red Rover* came down the river; she is the hospital steamer of Davis's fleet; is one of the largest and most beautiful steamers on the river, and has splendid accommodations for the sick."[18]

On July 15 CSS *Arkansas* ran through the Western Fleets. *Red Rover* accommodated the injured left in *Arkansas*'s wake, along with numerous casualties around Vicksburg caused by combat and the harsh climate. Six weeks later, near Helena, Arkansas, *Red Rover* suffered a fire that caused little damage but required the assistance of the flagship *Benton* to extinguish the blaze.[19]

As a captured vessel, *Red Rover* came under the jurisdiction of the Federal Prize Court in Illinois. At the end of September 1862, the Prize Court sold *Red Rover* to the navy for $9,314.28. All officers, crew, and vessels of the Western Flotilla were transferred to the Navy Department, and on October 16 David Dixon Porter arrived t take command, placing his flag on USS *Black Hawk*. The Army Ram Fleet became the Mississippi Marine Brigade and was "temporarily attached" to Porter's command, while the Western Gunboat Flotilla now became the Mississippi Squadron.[20]

Shortly before the transfer, Bixby recommended changes to make *Red Rover* fit for winter operations, which were approved by Davis and Pennock. With all naval facilities filled, Pennock arranged to house *Red Rover*'s patients at the army's Mound City hospital during its refit at Cairo, which lasted through December. Among these modifications were the installation of an additional boiler and steam ducts throughout the ship for heating purposes.[21]

On December 26, 1862, *Red Rover* was commissioned into the U.S. Navy under the command of Acting Master Wells. It was not what would today be considered a typical hospital ship in one very important respect: it was an armed vessel. It carried a 32-pounder cannon with grape, canister, and shell projectiles; muskets, bayonets, cutlasses, and revolvers; a full complement of boarding pistols and pikes and all the associated accoutrements and ammunition needed for a combat vessel.[22] No special considerations applied to this new type of craft. *Red Rover,* regardless of its role as hospital ship, was expected to perform the same military duties as any other fleet vessel.

Wells commanded "12 Officers; White Men 25; Contrabands 10; In All, 47 Souls," plus persons "not shipped," most of whom worked in the Medical Department. Sisters Adela, Veronica, and Calista returned to *Red Rover* on December 1 to continue their work as nurses and were joined in February by Sister Mary John/St. John. Contraband women were brought on board during the winter of 1863, greatly enhancing the care provided by the Medical Department. Newly appointed Fleet Surgeon Ninian Pinkney arrived in December and made *Red Rover* his headquarters ship. From the start, he strove to improve the care of the squadron, urged the Bureau of Medicine and Surgery to provide standard training and policies for all squadron surgeons, and recommended that all iron-clad and light-draft vessels be supplied with medical officers and surgeon's stewards, respectively. This allowed vessels operating on detached duty to provide emergency care for their sick and wounded until they could reach *Red Rover.* Bixby's medical staff gained a wide reputation for the unequaled quality of care they provided to their patients, including the extensive use of fresh food for patients' diets, which was unsurpassed in the fleet.[23]

The medical journal kept by Pinkney and Bixby, containing detailed accounts for all of *Red Rover*'s patients, vividly demonstrates the level of care given. A typically moving example is the entry for patient "No. 302," admitted from the *General Price:*

> *April 10* Melvin, Amassa. Boy [rank], 16 [age]. Native of Indiana. Afflicted with Nostalgia. His disease originated in the line of duty from a desire to return home. Complains of great pain in head, which has continued for two weeks, tried cold to head, with effect.
>
> *April 12* Says he feels nicely, no pain in head. Home with his Mother is the best place for him.
>
> *April 18* Returned to duty on board USS Black Hawk.[24]

On December 29 *Red Rover* moved to Memphis to receive five seamen transferred from the gunboat *General Bragg,* and then continued downriver, passing Helena, Arkansas. There it met USS *Longside,* whose officers reported a Confederate blockade at Bolivar, Mississippi. Both vessels traveled back to Helena to gather additional intelligence. They returned on December 31 with the gunboats *Lancaster* and *Tigress,* which were to escort *Red Rover* past the blockade. At midnight, while *Lancaster* took on wood for its boilers, Wells decided to run *Red Rover* through the blockade unescorted. With bales of straw surrounding the boiler area and the entire crew at general quarters, its single 32-pounder loaded with grapeshot, *Red Rover* passed the Confederates undetected.[25]

Arriving on January 1 at the mouth of the Yazoo River, Wells took *Red Rover* and rendezvoused with Porter on *Black Hawk*.[26] The next day, both returned to the Yazoo's mouth and awaited troop transports, which anchored along the Louisiana shore. They then steamed to the White River and on January 7 met with the ordinance ship *Judge Torrence*. *Red Rover* and *Judge Torrence* were to guard the White's mouth and protect the fleet's coal barges while *Black Hawk* joined the main flotilla.

Preparing for action, *Red Rover* transferred its patients to an army hospital transport. A light flotilla including tin- and cottonclads soon approached, led by *Rattler* and followed by Porter's flagship *Black Hawk*, which led the heavy flotilla of ironclads and troop transports. Covering the flotilla's rear was the gunboat *Lexington*. The objective was to bombard Fort Hindeman, Arkansas, to support an infantry assault. In addition to guard duty, *Red Rover* and *Judge Torrence* notified vessels to remain at the river's mouth until further orders from Porter.[27]

After Fort Hindeman fell on January 11, *Signal* and *New Era* headed downriver to deliver wounded to *Red Rover* and take on stores, including ice and fresh beef. "Stormy gales" with rain changing to heavy snow lasted from January 14 through 16, during which time *Red Rover*'s crew "was employed cleaning snow and burying the dead," and eleven crewmen were "reported on the sick list." By January 18 the weather changed to "clear and cold," but *Red Rover* remained "at anchor at the mouth of White River." The tedium of long periods at anchor in support of the fleet was noted in Well's log entries on numerous occasions.[28]

By January 21 the fleet was underway again. *Red Rover* and *Black Hawk* moved from the White to anchor just below Napoleon, Mississippi, where they came under Confederate cannon fire. Two plunging shots penetrated *Red Rover,* one of them smashing through the hospital wards. Astonishingly, no serious damage or injuries were recorded. The crew replied with rifle fire and the ship withdrew four miles for the night.[29]

On January 23 *Red Rover* arrived at the Yazoo's mouth to support the squadron in its attempt to interdict supplies intended for the Confederate defenders of Vicksburg and to gain control of the Yazoo and its tributaries. Occasionally, *Red Rover* left station to conduct burial parties, transfer patients to shore facilities, or "procure" chickens, ducks, and eggs from the "Jefferson Davis plantation." For much of this time, however, it merely lay at anchor "near [the] mouth of Yazoo River."[30]

The siege of Vicksburg exacted a high toll on all combatants involved. *Red Rover*'s wards were filled to capacity, while along river banks more casualties accumulated without access to proper medical attention. In February 1863 Admiral Porter sent Pinkney to secure permission from Maj. Gen. U. S. Grant to occupy buildings suitable for conversion into a naval hospital. Because of its central location and reputation as the healthiest place on the Mississippi, Memphis was the site chosen. The navy occupied an ex-Confederate hotel and adjacent buildings to establish the required hospital. Named in honor of the fleet surgeon responsible for its procurement, Hospital Pinkney was soon caring for over 240 men. Sister John/St. John left *Red Rover* at the end of September 1863 to take charge of the hospital's nursing facilities.[31]

On April 16, 1863, *Red Rover* moved to the Louisiana shore above Vicksburg, arriving just as Union gunboats and transports prepared to break the Confederate blockade. By the time the blockade was broken, some sixteen thousand Union navy shells had rained down upon the Confederate defenders. The price for the fleet's success was high, and the decks and wards of *Red Rover* overflowed with casualties.[32]

The boredom and tedium of lying at anchor for long periods, providing burial parties, and the almost daily loading and unloading of coal, ice and stores took their inevitable toll on *Red Rover*'s officers and crew. By the spring of 1863, this become all too apparent. On April 23 *Red Rover* delivered casualties from Vicksburg to Hospital Pinkney before berthing at the Memphis Navy Yard for repairs, which lasted several weeks. On April 26, the ship's log records "Capt. Wells unwell." Six days later Wells went ashore, accompanied by Pinkney, and did not return until May 15. For the crew, this meant a modicum of freedom—and shore leave (with or without permission), their first in four months of service on the Mississippi. Crewmen took quick advantage of their circumstances. Listed among *Red Rover*'s initial ordinance stores were ten pairs of "Hand Irons" and six of "Leg Irons." By late April these restraints were seeing almost daily use. At least fifteen crew members and convalescing patients were placed in single or double irons for "drunken and riotous conduct," "going ashore without leave," returning late, "disobedience," and "disorderly conduct." The greatest problems stemmed from alcohol, its consumption or desire thereof. On April 29, for example, a carpenter's mate named Blackmun "was arrested . . . passing the Guard Boat, in a dingy with a clothes bag with 10 bottles in. Said he was going for Whiskey. Put him in double irons . . . in the Brig."

During this time *Red Rover* was also the focus of some unexpected attention in the press. The May 9, 1863, issue of *Harper's Weekly* printed a full page of illustrations by renowned artist Theodore R. Davis that depicted various aspects of *Red Rover.* The accompanying text read:

> This institution is . . . an untold comfort to our sick or wounded sailors. The sketch shows the main ward, in which are accommodations for over two hundred patients. The Sister is one of those good women whose angelic services have been sung by poets and breathed by grateful convalescents all the world over. The convalescents are placed in a ward for their sole use, where they smoke, read, and generally enjoy themselves. The boat itself, a clean, roomy craft, is under the command of a gallant old sailor.[33]

With repairs completed *Red Rover* returned to Hospital Pinkney to take on eleven new crewmen and then headed downriver to rejoin the fleet engaged in operations to destroy everything of value around besieged Vicksburg. On May 22 it "arrived at mouth of Yazoo . . . at old anchorage." For several weeks, *Red Rover*'s crew evacuated numerous fleet casualties. On June 7 Wells recorded "heavy firing heard in direction of Millikens Bend . . . Light Draft No. 3 shelling woods near us . . . *Thistle* came alongside with 20 shells, in . . . anticipation of an attack. Gun trained to Louisiana shore." The following afternoon *Red Rover* received several "leading men of Iowa" who came on board to visit and inspect the hospital ship. On June 11 Wells entered into his log: "Held a sale of clothing of deceased patients." This practice was repeated several times during the war, along with entries stating that the ship's paymaster held "sale[s] of new Hammocks, Mattresses & c."[34]

On June 20 *Red Rover*'s crew and lone 32-pounder stood armed and ready above Young's Pass to help deny escape to Vicksburg's defenders. On June 29 it transferred ice and medicines to *Rattler;* then "at 1 P.M. a crazy man named Perkins from USS *Petrel* jumped overboard from upper Hospital room and drowned." Pinkney and Bixby dutifully and with compassion recorded the suicide's sad story. Their entry for patient "No. 510" concludes "James Perkins was not his true name, and [he] gave another name of his own, which was not written down and is now forgotten."[35]

Meanwhile, casualties mounted from the siege of Vicksburg, and *Red Rover* received a steady flow of squadron wounded. In addition, it ranged thirty miles upriver from its station at the Yazoo, where the crew procured meat, poultry, eggs, milk, and produce from the Harrison Plantation. They built livestock pens on shore, provided burial details, and off-loaded medical supplies and fresh provisions to squadron ships. *Red Rover* also "sent 10 Contraband to load shell[s] to Mortars . . . [and] sent 14 Seamen and 2 Contraband to man a gun."[36]

Wells proudly recorded the "Unconditional Surrender of Vicksburg" in his log at ten o'clock on July 4, 1863, adding: "32,000 prisoners taken. Rockets shooting in Evening from Vicksburg." The completion of the Vicksburg campaign signaled the end of major fleet actions in the western theater. For the remainder of the war, *Red Rover*'s crew primarily occupied their time with resupply operations. On July 14 *Red Rover* docked at Memphis to deliver wounded and receive additional medical stores. Continuing the support, the Western Sanitary Commission supplied the ship with hospital clothing, storage chests, books, and other medical supplies.[37]

Two weeks later *Red Rover* proceeded downriver to the Jefferson Davis Plantation, where the crew transferred medicines to *Carondolet* and other gunboats. It continued making stops as far as New Orleans, supplying stores to vessels in exchange for their wounded. At Natchez, Mississippi, Adela "went to see Archbishop [William] Elder . . . exiled by the United States officers, and he confided to my care some official documents which they would not permit him to send without examination." Adela smuggled these documents, the content of which is unknown, on board *Red Rover* and later "mailed them at Cairo."[38]

Red Rover made numerous stops on its way back to Memphis, arriving in mid-August and remaining there for three months. On August 23 Wells "placed James Gray, a nurse in single irons for theft." Gray was released on August 28. The following day, John Jackson and Henry Mitchell were placed in irons "for exhibitions of pugilistic propensities." On September 25 "Engineers Long and Goodlow [were] ordered in [*sic*] arrest for dissolute conduct for improper intimacy with two Colored girls employed in the Hospital Department of this Ship. Georgina and Ellen [Harris and Campbell, both nurses] were put in the Brig for immoral conduct by order of the Commanding Officer." The women gained their release "by order of Surgeon Bixby" the next day, followed by Long and Goodlow, who were "ordered to duty."[39] The unanswered questions that arise from this episode include the scope and nature of official policies concerning fraternization on board *Red Rover* and whether or not additional "contact" occurred between men and women.

Red Rover moved to the Mound City shipyard on November 19 for extensive repairs, where it remained until the following spring. On December 2, Wells was promoted to acting volunteer lieutenant. After loading wounded from *Clara Dolson* and various stores on April 12, 1864, *Red Rover* steamed downriver to aid the survivors of the infamous Fort Pillow massacre. On April 13 "the United States naval hospital boat *Red Rover* landed, and Fleet Surgeon Ninian Pinkney, with his usual Promptness, provided comfortable quarters for them, and with his little army of assistant surgeons soon had their wounds dressed." Acting Ensign Charles King entered into *Red Rover*'s log that "2:20 [P.M.] landed at Fort Pillow found the enemy in possession. . . . At 3:30 started down river, took on at Fort Pillow 10 white and 3 black soldiers, all wounded . . . one of the black soldiers died." All thirteen wounded are listed as suffering from "Vulnus Scloptarium," or gunshot wounds.[40]

Steaming to Memphis, *Red Rover* readied its 32-pounder in anticipation of hostile fire from Fort Randolph, which it passed "without molestation." Arriving on April 14, it delivered wounded soldiers to Overton Army Hospital and squadron sick to Hospital Pinkney. From April 17 through May 12, *Red Rover* supported the disastrous army-navy Red River expedition, delivering medical supplies and provisions to the fleet in exchange for their sick and wounded, who were then transported to shore facilities. On May 24, while the ship traveled from "Baton Rouge to Red River," the following appears in *Red Rover*'s log-book: "Acting Volunteer Lieutenant William R. Wells, Acting Master H. E. Barlett & Acting Master T. A. Oliver detached, Acting Ensign Charles King took command," where he would remain at least through the year's end.[41]

By June 1864 the Mississippi Squadron was operating one hundred vessels with some fifty-five hundred crew. Kentucky, Tennessee, Arkansas, Louisiana, and the upper regions of Mississippi, including the northern banks of the Ohio River, were now firmly under Union control. Patrolling this expanse from Cairo to New Orleans while securing the Ohio, Tennessee, and Cumberland Rivers was a formidable task. To facilitate such vast operations, the areas patrolled by the Western Flotilla were divided into ten naval districts. Squadron vessels were assigned to specific districts, although required to extend mutual support when needed. By contrast, *Red Rover* had no assigned district and ranged over the full western riverine theater serving the entire fleet.[42]

Red Rover headed upriver on May 25, 1864, to deliver medical supplies to Natchez, Vicksburg, the White River, and Helena, and then docked at Memphis on June 3, 1864, as usual delivering patients to Hospital Pinkney and taking on stores. The vessel departed on June 7 for Mound City for repairs, which were completed within a month. On July 6 *Red Rover* headed to Memphis to transfer patients to Hospital Pinkney and replenish supplies; it then steamed as far south as Donaldsonville, Louisiana, on a routine medical and supply voyage, returning to Memphis on August 4.[43]

Memphis was assaulted on August 22 by twenty-five hundred Confederates under the command of Gen. Nathan Bedford Forrest, whose troops seized limited control for a few hours before being driven out by Federal units. During the raid *Red Rover* rendered assistance to the iron-clad *Essex,* which was damaged and without steam. Hospital boat *Red Rover* tied up alongside, to tow Essex out of harm's way, but the measure proved unnecessary.[44]

Red Rover remained near Hospital Pinkney until October 24 before beginning its final medical supply mission. The vessel stopped at Helena, at the White, Red, and Yazoo Rivers, and at New Orleans, returning to Memphis on November 23 to deliver patients retrieved along the way. On December 7 *Red Rover* headed upriver but returned to pick up some forgotten documents. That done, it continued upstream, returning to Mound City on December 11, 1864, where it remained until its final decommission.[45]

The Civil War wound down through the spring of 1864. With the war's impending conclusion, the light-draft ironclads of the Mississippi Squadron were sent to Mobile Bay, where Confederate naval forces formally surrendered on May 10, 1865. Within weeks, the Mississippi Squadron was greatly reduced, with many vessels decommissioned and readied for sale or dismantlement.

The first major reduction occurred on May 3, when navy secretary Gideon Welles ordered a reduction of the squadron "to 25 vessels." *Red Rover* remained in service longer than most of the squadron, but on May 29 its name appeared on the list of "Vessels . . . which it is proposed to dispose with." On June 26 the squadron was reduced "to five vessels only in commission," and on July 6 Welles notified Lee that the "[Navy] Department intends to break up the Mississippi Squadron." On August 12, 1865, Lee notified Welles that "I have . . . issued orders for turning over . . . the remaining vessels . . . *Tempest, Kate, . . . Volunteer,* and the hospital ship *Red Rover.* My flag will be hauled down on the 14th instant." Even with many of its officers and crew transferred or detached, *Red Rover* operated until November 17, 1865, when the eleven patients still on board were transferred to the steamer USS *Grampus.*[46]

According to the "Cruise of U.S.N. Hospital Ship 'Red Rover' . . . General Recapitulation," of the 1,697 patients admitted between June 1862 and March 1865, 1,282 had their "Nativity Ascertained." Of the "Americans," 343 came from Northern states, 231 from Western states, and 332 from Southern states; 376 "Foreigners" are listed, while 415 birthplaces went unrecorded. Of the patients treated 1,365 were discharged and 157 died on board. Unmentioned are the two women admitted as patients from other squadron vessels. Mary Dorcas Robb was treated for "Debilitas" and eventually returned to duty, while Eliza

Jenkins, a twenty-two-year-old laundress from the USS *Black Hawk*, admitted with "Hydrops" on July 5, 1863, succumbed to her illness and died on September 30.[47]

Red Rover's April 1, 1865, muster roll shows Sisters Adela and Veronica, Mary Dalton, and Betsy Young still serving on board, although Sister Veronica left on March 31. Betsy Young remained until August 20, followed by Sister Adela and Mary Dalton eleven days later. From then until the ship's final decommission, no women are listed in any capacity among the remaining crew of eighty-three. In addition to the women, many men worked as nurses and stewards, including contraband and convalescent patients detailed to *Red Rover* from shore hospitals or from its own wards.[48]

The cessation of hostilities and preservation of the Union brought rapid, ignoble ends to many careers. *Red Rover*'s unique contributions to Union victory, shipboard medical treatment, and historical precedents for the reduction of racial and gender barriers in the armed services constitute a remarkable legacy. The vessel itself, however, along with much of the Mississippi Squadron, met a swift and unseemly end at public auction. Stripped of its gun and iron plating, *Red Rover* was auctioned on November 29, 1865, at Mound City by Solomon A. Silver to A. M. Carpenter for the sum of forty-five hundred dollars. Thus ended the days of the USS *Red Rover*, first hospital ship of the United States Navy.[49]

Red Rover's female medical personnel, too, have left a historic legacy. They were the first women in history to serve officially on board a naval vessel. In virtually every account, the Sisters who served on *Red Rover* are credited as the progenitors of the U.S. Navy Nurse Corps and the first U.S. naval nurses. Yet the records reveal that from the close of the Civil War until 1908, when the U.S. Navy Nurse Corps (Female) was created, women were excluded from service in the U.S. Navy.[50]

Who were the first U.S. Navy nurses? Technically, the Catholic order volunteered its services, yet they were compensated by the Medical Department and the U.S. Navy. In the muster rolls and the Medical Department's "Reports—Deaths—Invoices & c.," the nuns are listed simply as Sister[s] of Charity." These same records, however, when referring to the "Contraband," "Mulatto," or "Negro" nurses and laundresses, recognized said categories as rated members of the crew. The records indicate that the contraband women, hired outright after being brought on board, trained, and paid by the Medical Department of the U.S. Navy, actually deserve the distinction of *first* true female personnel in the United States Navy. Representatives of extant records are the "Amounts Paid Persons 'Not Shipped' on Board *USN Hospital Ship*

'*Red Rover,*' Employed in the Medical Department During Quarter Ending Sept. 30th 1863," wherein Sisters St. John, Veronica, and Adela are listed individually as "Sister of Mercy." The African American women Sarah Bohannon, Ellen Campbell, Betsy Young, and Georgina Harris, in turn, are all listed under the "Rank or Rating" heading as "Nurse" and were paid the same rate as the Sisters. Ann Stokes, Mary Dalton, Margaret Jackson, and Nancy Buel appear as "Laundress" and received a lower rate of pay for their work.[51]

The "Complete Descriptive List or Muster Roll of the Crew of the Naval Hospital '*Red Rover,*'" also filed quarterly, supports elevating the African American women to the status of first female naval personnel. At the end of the muster ending October 1, 1863, Paymaster Alex W. Pearson wrote, "In addition to the above there are sundry employees hired by the Medical Department as nurses who cannot strictly be said to belong to the service. Therefore I do not muster these." Sisters Adela and Veronica do not appear on this muster, although they were on board at this time. During the muster ending December 31, the Sisters are not listed with the crew but instead appear in the section reserved for Pearson's "Sundry employees," which list "Three Supernumberie's [*sic*]" followed by the two "*Sisters of Charity.*" Throughout the records from October 1863 through August 1865, Adela and Veronica remain "Sister[s] of Charity," while Ellen Campbell, Sarah Nothing, and Betsy Young are rated as "Nurse"; and Nancy Buel, Sallie Bohannon, Lucinda Jackson, Sabra Miller, and Mary Dalton (who in March and April 1863 worked as a nurse at the Overton Army Hospital in Memphis) are rated as "Laundress." Margaret Jackson and Ann Stokes are simply recorded as "Contraband." Susan Hicks, Josephine Hicks, and, later, "Ann White, Colored," were mustered under the title "Supernumeran."[52] Ann Stokes rose in rank from "Contraband" to "Nurse," while most of the contraband women ended their careers ranked as they began.

"The Records of the General Accounting Office, [for the] Hospital Ship *Red Rover,*" covering the period from October 1862 through August 1865, provide additional evidence. Again, Adela, Veronica, Calista, and St. John appear throughout as "Sisters of Charity," while Ann Stokes, Ellen Campbell, Betsy Young, Georgina Harris, and Sarah Nothing are entered as "Nurse." Filling out the roster for female Medical Department personnel on board *Red Rover* are Alice Kennedy, Sarah Kinno, Mary Dalton, Nancy Buel, Sallie Bohannon, Lucinda Jenkins, Adelia Robertson, Mary Ann Donald, Ann Rogers, Alice McLean, Sabra Miller, and Ann Ragan, all rated as "Laundress," with Eliza Owens and Margaret Jackson being recorded simply as "Contraband."[53]

The records speak clearly. The muster rolls, surgeon's reports, and records of the General Accounting Office were recorded and filed by separate clerks from different departments. In all three sets of documents the "Rank or Rating" sections consistently identify these women as to their designation on board *Red Rover* and within the U.S. Navy. In the sections headed "Remarks" or "Personal Description," the lines are blank for the Sisters yet relatively detailed for the African American women, listing them variously as "Contraband," "Mulatto," or "Negro," often including as well their ages and physical descriptions. With such detailed record keeping, it is clear that while the U.S. Navy welcomed, accepted, and compensated the Sisters for their services in the Medical Department, they were clearly identified and recorded as nonnaval personnel, retaining their titles as members of an organization *outside* of the U.S. Navy. These Sisters worked *for* the navy as nurses, though they were not considered U.S. Navy nurses.

Just as clear is the evidence that *Red Rover*'s officers and medical officers trained contraband, both female and male, after being brought on board. Acting Master Wells, *Red Rover*'s commander, has left compelling evidence of this in his deck log entries. A sampling from these records helps illustrate the process by which contraband women and men were brought into the ranks of the navy. On January 2, 1863, Wells wrote: "Received from *USS Juliet* the following Contraband and entered them on the ships books for duty." By June 5 he was referring to the duty assignments of the "Colored crew." On August 23, 1863, Wells "Rated 4 Contraband as Firemen and 8 as Laundresses."[54]

The Catholic Sisters of the Order of the Holy Cross served unselfishly, even heroically, on board *Red Rover* as well at hospitals ashore. For too long, however, the valuable contributions and sacrifices of the African American women who also served on board *Red Rover*, and who in fact constitute the first true female U.S. Navy personnel and shipboard navy nurses, have been overlooked, or simply ignored.

Post-Civil War events help to explain how the Holy Cross Sisters on board *Red Rover* came to be recognized as the first navy nurses. The federal government bestowed belated recognition to the vast number of women, considered noncombatants, who performed in many capacities during the war. Bills passed in 1890 awarded backpay and pensions to female nurses who had served during the Civil War. These women were divided into seven "classes" by the chief clerk of the Surgeon General's Office, Samuel Ramsey. Two classes pertained to *Red Rover*: "Sisters of Charity [generic name] who received forty cents a day, when paid at all"; and "Colored women hired under General Orders in 1863 and 1864 at $10 a month."[55]

It was necessary for eligible women to apply to the government to receive benefits under this program. Many Catholic Sisters applied for and received their benefits. With one exception, however, the contraband women who served on *Red Rover*, many of whom were probably illiterate, had moved or had no knowledge of this program and cannot be found in the pension records. Only Nurse Ann Stokes, Application #20,335, who served on *Red Rover* and *Black Hawk* and who filed on July 28, 1890 from Illinois, received a pension.[56]

The roles played by African Americans during the Civil War have long been neglected, and it comes as no surprise that their contributions on board *Red Rover* and other vessels of the western fleet have been overlooked. The men initially listed as "Contraband, Negro, Mulatto, Black, Slave, Farmer and Field Hand" and eventually obtained official naval ratings. In his log entries for January 27 and 29, Wells mentions "Negroes drilling in 1st Cutter." His entries indicate that these people were not just brought on board and put to work, but they were trained in the ways of the U.S. Navy before being admitted into the ranks. In January 1863, for example, twenty-two-year-old contraband Goodfer Nothing was brought on board. He was one of several "Nothings" on *Red Rover* who actually became crew members. Initially rated as a cabin boy, Goodfer changed his name to Gasper, and by September 1 had earned the rating of "Coal Heaver' in the engineering department, serving in that capacity until May 31, 1864, when he transferred ashore to Hospital Pinkney. Contraband Sarah Nothing, described in the muster books as "Contraband-Mulatto," served as a nurse in the Medical Department.[57] These were two of many African Americans who provided valuable service on *Red Rover* during the Civil War.

Another striking fact is the sheer number of African Americans who served as crewmen. For most of *Red Rover*'s career a majority of its crew was African American, at time outnumbering other crewmen by more than two to one. Not until 1865 did whites regularly outnumber blacks as crewmen. Evidence suggests that these numbers hold for most of the Mississippi Squadron. The implications of this fact for a revised appraisal of African American contributions to Union victory are as important as failure to consider them is disturbing.[58]

Appendix

The following is a complete listing of the women who served on USS *Red Rover* between April 1862 and November 1865, including ratings and dates of service.

Western Gunboat Flotilla, while in army service

NAME	HIRED AS	FROM	TO
Mary Warfield	Chambermaid	5-22-62	8-31-62
Ann Graves	Chambermaid	4-13-62	8-31-62
Mary Bryant	Laundress	6-8-62	9-30-62
Maria Cassidy	Laundress	6-21-62	8-31-62
Eliza McLothian	Laundress	6-27-62	7-31-62
Sister Adela	Nurse*	6-1-62	9-30-62
Sister Veronica	Nurse*	6-1-62	9-30-62
Mattie Perkins	Laundress	8-1-62	9-30-62
Betsy Bishop	Laundress	8-1-62	9-30-62
Nancy. Rogers	Laundress	8-1-62	9-30-62
Sarah Watson	Laundress	9-17-62	9-30-62

*While Sisters Adela and Veronica are listed as nurses, this records personnel hired to serve in a particular capacity in the Army's Western Gunboat Flotilla and does not necessarily represent an official rank held. Also; this represents the precommission status of *Red Rover* and its crew into the U.S. Navy.

Mississippi Squadron, U.S. Navy Service

NAME	RANK/RATING	FROM	TO
Sister Veronica	Sister of Charity	12-1-62	3-31-65
Sister Adela	Sister of Charity	12-1-62	8-31-65
Sister Calista	Sister of Charity	12-1-62	2-28-63
Alice Kennedy	Laundress	1-1-63	7-16-63
Ann Stokes	Contraband	1-25-63	5-31-64
	Nurse	6-1-64	10-25-64
Eliza Owens	Contraband	1-26-63	4-30-63
Sarah Kinno	Laundress	2-13-63	4-25-63
Mary Dalton	Laundress	2-21-63	8-31-65
Sister St. John	Sister of Charity	2-21-63	9-30-63
Margaret Jackson	Contraband	5-10-63	10-4-63
Nancy Buell	Laundress	9-1-63	10-26-63
Sallie Bohannon	Laundress	9-1-63	11-23-63
Ellen Campbell	Nurse	9-1-63	3-26-64
Betsy Young	Nurse	9-1-63	8-20-65
Georgina Harris	Nurse	7-1-63	9-26-63
Sarah Nothing	Nurse	12-1-63	6-15-64
Lucinda Jenkins	Laundress	1-1-64	6-13-64
Sabra Miller	Laundress	1-1-64	3-26-64
Adelia Robertson	Laundress	7-1-64	10-25-64
Mary Ann Donald	Laundress	10-24-64	11-23-64

| Ann Ragan | Laundress | 10-24-64 | 11-23-64 |
| Alice McLean | Laundress | 1-1-64 | 3-24-64 |

Susan and Josephine Hicks, along with Lucinda Jenkins (who later worked as a laundress), appear in the December 1863 muster as "Supernumeran's." Susan and Josephine Hicks remained in that category through the April, July, and October 1864 musters. The April 1865 muster recorded "1 Supernumerary, Ann White, Colored." Harriet Adams may very well be another of those "sundry employees" that Paymaster Pearson referred to. In "Reports—Deaths—Invoices, &c" she is listed as a Medical Department laundress during the fourth quarter of 1864, having come on board November 15. No other mention of her occurs in any other records.

CHAPTER 23

Sojourner Truth and President Lincoln

Carleton Mabee

THE EX-SLAVE SOJOURNER TRUTH, a compelling advocate of equal rights for blacks and women, gathered intriguing myths around her, including myths about her association with President Lincoln. These myths helped make her into an American heroine. If we peel back the myths about Sojourner and Lincoln, what view of Sojourner emerges?

Sojourner met with Lincoln at least once, on 29 October 1864. What we know about this visit depends primarily on Sojourner's recollection of it soon after the event, briefly in her letter of 3 November, which still exists in its original form, and more fully in her letter of 17 November.

Like many other slaves, Sojourner, when she was growing up in New York State in the early 1800s, did not learn to read or write.[1] So when she "wrote" her letters, someone else wrote down her words for her.

Sojourner addressed her letter of 17 November to a New Jersey Quaker and gave him permission to publish as much of it as he thought suitable. He evidently sent the letter to both the *National Anti-Slavery Standard,* in New York, and the *Liberator,* in Boston, both abolitionist weeklies which had long been printing news of Sojourner. The *Standard* published the letter on 17 December 1864, the *Liberator* on 23 December. The *Standard* version, being fuller, is probably more authentic.

Many claim about Sojourner's association with Lincoln go beyond what she wrote in her letters. Probably the claims that have been most frequently repeated are those that most deeply fulfill the psychological and political desires of the friends of Sojourner and Lincoln, desires that some-times changed over the years and sometimes contradicted each other.

First, there are the claims that seem to reflect a desire to perceive Lincoln as welcoming a poor, illiterate, black grandmother to the White House. For example, we find that in the 1870s, Sojourner's old friend, the Vermont-born anti-slavery editor Oliver Johnson, asserted that Lincoln "treated her with the utmost respect, and even reverence."[2] On the other hand, we also find that in the activist 1960s, when sit-ins were a powerful weapon against segregation, an article in a historical journal claimed that when Sojourner went to see Lincoln, she sat in his office "quietly and resolutely," as if she were unwelcome there, until he was willing to see her, and that thus Sojourner staged "the first Sit-In."[3]

What really happened as far as we can tell, from the most authentic early sources available, is this. Hoping to visit Lincoln, Sojourner, when she was about sixty-seven years old, made a long, round-about journey from Battle Creek, Michigan, which was then her home, to Washington, D.C. After she arrived, she found to her surprise that she was unable on her own to secure an appointment to visit Lincoln. Sojourner then asked Lucy Colman—a white, Massachusetts-born schoolteacher who had become an anti-slavery lecturer—to arrange it for her. After some weeks, Mrs. Colman, using Mrs. Lincoln's black dressmaker as a go-between, succeeded in arranging an appointment. When Mrs. Colman finally took Sojourner to the White House on 29 October, the two women had to wait several hours until it was their turn to see the busy president. Having every expectation of being welcomed, they were not "sitting-in" in protest.

When the president was finally able to see Sojourner and Mrs. Colman, as Colman recalled on 1 November in a letter to the Rochester *Evening Express,* Lincoln received Sojourner with "pleasing cordiality." However, long afterward, Colmon, in her 1891 memoirs, written when she was free of any compulsion to make Lincoln look better, gave a less favorable impression of Lincoln's attitude toward Sojourner. This time Mrs. Colman wrote caustically: "Mr. Lincoln was not himself with this colored woman; he had no funny story for her, he called her aunty, as he would his washerwoman."[4]

Sojourner, despite her cruel experiences of slavery, was more buoy-ant than Yankee teacher Colman. Sojourner reported soon after the interview, in her letter about it published by the *Standard,* that "I never was treated by any one with more kindness and cordiality than were shown to me by that great and good man, Abraham Lincoln." Sojourner added, as if she were proud of it, that Lincoln, in signing his name in her autograph book, called her "Aunty."

In 1940 an article in *Opportunity* magazine made the large claim that Lincoln "always welcomed" Sojourner at the White House.[5] However, while Lincoln was president, blacks were sometimes excluded from the White House on racial grounds, and on at least one occasion Sojourner herself was barred from a public reception there, according to both Colman and Fred Tomkins, a British journalist. Tomkins happened to be present at the reception on 25 February 1865 when he saw Sojourner being refused admission because she was black. Two days later, when he interviewed Lincoln, Tomkins expressed his regret that Sojourner was "the only person I saw who had been refused admission." In reply, according to Tomkins, Lincoln "expressed his sorrow, and said that he had often seen her, [and] that it should not occur again."[6]

Altogether, available evidence indicates that although Sojourner was not welcomed at Lincoln's White House as quickly as she would have liked, nor always welcomed, nor clearly welcomed with "reverence," at least she was welcomed once, and probably more often.

Next, we can see how the desire of blacks, abolitionists, and their friends to perceive Lincoln as the Great Emancipator, who was motivated above all else by personal conviction rather than merely the circumstances of the Civil War, affected reports of Sojourner's interview with him. According to what Sojourner stated soon afterward in her letter in the *Standard,* when she told Lincoln that he was the best president America had had, implying that he was so because he had issued the Emancipation Proclamation, Lincoln replied that any other president, including Washington, would have freed the slaves "if the time had come." If the Southerners "had behaved themselves," Lincoln continued, "I could not have done what I have." Then, according to the *Standard* version of Sojourner's letter, Lincoln concluded, "But they did not, and I was compelled to do these things." However, according to the version of Sojourner's letter published eleven years later, in the 1875 edition of the *Narrative of Sojourner Truth,* Lincoln concluded instead: "But they did not, which gave me the opportunity to do these things."[7] Thus the *Narrative* makes Lincoln look more favorable from the abolitionist point of view, as if he had not been "compelled" to free the slaves but had been looking for an "opportunity" to do so all along. One cannot help but speculate that Frances Titus, a Michigan abolitionist who edited the 1875 version of Sojourner's *Narrative,* deliberately altered Sojourner's letter to make Lincoln look more like a friend to the slaves and less like a political opportunist.

Blacks, abolitionists, and their friends sought to project the image of Sojourner as receiving Lincoln's guidance for her work, thus contributing to her effectiveness and prestige. Neither Sojourner's letter of 17 November as published in the *Standard* nor her letter of 3 November gives us any evidence that she asked Lincoln's advice on what work she should be doing or that Lincoln encouraged her to do any particular kind of work. In 1869 and 1871, however, friends of Sojourner's, apparently after listening to her, reported that Lincoln had led her to work with the freedmen.[8] In the 1875 edition of the *Narrative,* Frances Titus claimed, perhaps on the basis of what Sojourner had said to her, that Lincoln gave Sojourner a "commission" to work among the freedmen in the Washington area. In 1879 Sojourner herself, according to an interview with a Chicago journalist, said that when she met Lincoln, he "wanted me to see to the colored people [freedmen] at Arlington Heights and Mason's Island [near Washington], where they came running in and died like cattle." Many later writers have repeated such claims, but can they be corroborated by persuasive evidence?[9]

In the 1875 *Narrative,* Titus prints what she calls a "commission," dated 1 December 1864, from the National Freedmen's Relief Association of New York appointing Sojourner a counselor to freedmen at their camp in Arlington, Virginia. Titus's presentation of the commission seems designed to encourage readers to assume that Lincoln was responsible for it, and yet she makes no direct claim that he was involved. It seems unlikely that he would have been since the National Freedmen's Relief Association was a private organization. In September 1865, the Freedmen's Bureau, which was a government agency, recommended to its Freedmen's Hospital in Washington that it give Sojourner authority to promote "order, cleanliness, industry and virtue" among its patients, but this recommendation was, of course, issued five months after Lincoln had been assassinated.[10] No direct evidence is available that Lincoln encouraged, much less authorized, Sojourner's work with the freedmen.

Moreover, in early 1864, when she had begun to plan her trip to Washington, in two separate letters Sojourner had already expressed her intention to seek out the freedmen in the Washington area; in fact, as she then explained it, the purpose of her trip was to see not the president but the freedmen.[11] Since Sojourner was in Washington several weeks before her interview with Lincoln, she could easily on her own have become acquainted with the ragged freedmen who were crowding into Washington and have begun work with them. In her letter of 3 November, written only five days after seeing the president, Sojourner stated that already she was staying at the house of an official who was working with the freedmen, had twice spoken publicly in Washington on behalf of the freedmen, had spoken twice to the freedmen themselves, and had decided that the freedmen needed her, all of which seems likely to have taken more than five days to accomplish. Indeed, although she described her visit to Lincoln briefly in this same letter, she did not make any connection between Lincoln and her efforts on behalf of the freedmen. In addition, the *Standard,* on 17 December, published a letter from Captain G. Carse, a U.S. military officer assigned to work with the freedmen, describing what Sojourner was doing with him for the freedmen. He, too, made no mention of Lincoln's having encouraged her to do this work. Nor did Colman or Tomkins, though both described her visiting Lincoln and her work with the freedmen, suggest that Lincoln led her in any way toward this work.[12] Accordingly, it seems reasonable to conclude on the basis of available evidence that despite later claims by Sojourner and her friends, she came to dedicate her labors to the freedmen essentially not by Lincoln's guidance but by her own initiative.

An even more ambitious claim sometimes made about Sojourner is that she significantly advised President Lincoln on national policy. In 1929 an article in a popular magazine asserted that Lincoln "gained much of his knowledge of slavery, its cruelties and atrocities, from her."[13] As it is well known, however, Lincoln was born and spent his earliest years in the slave state of Kentucky. After he moved to the free states of Indiana and Illinois, he still occasionally traveled to slave states, as when he crewed on a boat taking cargo down the Mississippi. While a congressman, he served in Washington, a center for the sale of slaves. Before being elected president, he had taken part as a lawyer in court cases involving slaves; he had often read anti-slavery papers, including the *National Anti-Slavery Standard;* and he had long been required in his political life to consider the nature of slavery. While it may be doubted that anyone who has not been a slave can fully feel its cruelties, by the time he met Sojourner, Lincoln undoubtedly had considerable knowledge of slavery.

Another claim, by Sojourner's friend, anti-slavery editor Oliver Johnson, can be easily dismissed. In 1876 he noted, "When the war broke out she went to Washington, to urge the President to free the slaves," and Lincoln was "deeply moved by her appeals."[14] Of course, the Civil War broke out in 1861, and Sojourner did not meet Lincoln until October 1864, by which time he had not only issued the Emancipation Proclamation, which abolished slavery in the rebel states as a temporary war measure, but also, as part of his presidential reelection campaign, had called for a Constitutional amendment that would abolish slavery permanently in the United States. Sojourner herself had correctly sensed as early as the summer of 1863 that the war had set in motion events that would eventually free all slaves.[15] Moreover, Sojourner's predominant goal in visiting Lincoln, according to both Mrs. Colman in her letter of 1 November and Sojourner herself in her letter of 17 November, was not to push Lincoln to grant further rights to blacks but to thank him for what he had already done, particularly in issuing the Emancipation Proclamation.

Another overstatement about Sojourner's role is more widespread. In an early 1940s textbook for black children we find the assertion that Sojourner urged Lincoln to arm free blacks to fight for the Union. In the late 1940s, Executive Secretary Walter White of the NAACP even insisted extravagantly that Sojourner returned to the White House "time and time again" to urge Lincoln to enlist free blacks and that "her arguments, combined with the manpower needs of the Union Army, eventually won over Lincoln and Congress." Since then many writers, including, alas, the present writer, have made similar, if less extreme, claims.[16]

It is true that early in the Civil War Lincoln opposed enlisting blacks. By at least the summer of 1863, however, he was praising the performance of black soldiers and pushing for more blacks, both the traditionally free and the newly freed, to enlist, and they were enlisting in considerable numbers. By that same summer, Sojourner's grandson James Caldwell had enlisted in a Massachusetts black regiment, with her enthusiastic blessing, and Sojourner was welcoming the enlistment of blacks as "the most hopeful feature of the war."[17] When she first met Lincoln in October 1864, his policy to support the enlistment of blacks was well established, so it seems unlikely that Sojourner would have felt it necessary to urge the cause further.

Altogether, the claims that Sojourner advised Lincoln on the cruelty of slavery, freeing the slaves, or enlisting blacks have not been substantiated and in any case seem inherently improbable.

Finally we consider how an old, uneducated, ex-slave-woman has been portrayed as being cleverly brash to a president, manipulating him, and getting away with it. In particular two often-repeated tales convey this impression. The first one opens when Sojourner tells Lincoln that she had never heard of him until he was proposed as a candidate for president. This episode was not mentioned in the *Standard* or *Liberator* versions of Sojourner's 1864 letter describing her visit to the president, but according to a newspaper report, she recounted it in a speech in Detroit in 1869.[18] When Frances Titus prepared the 1875 edition of Sojourner's *Narrative,* without acknowledging what she was doing, she inserted the story into Sojourner's 1864 letter as if it had been there in the first place. According to this inserted passage, Sojourner said, "I told him [Lincoln] that I had never heard of him before he was talked of for president. He smilingly replied, 'I had heard of you many times before that.'"[19]

This story tends to suggest that Sojourner was well known and could even be said to hint that she had long influenced Lincoln. Its appeal to those who would enjoy seeing a poor, uneducated person being unafraid of, if not impudent to, a person of power is obvious, and the remark attributed to Sojourner is in accord with the pert retorts she was fond of making. Still, if this story is even partially true, we must ask—since it is so striking and such a delightful example of the tall-tales Sojourner relished and could enhance her reputation for daring—why doesn't it appear in her 1864 letter as originally published in the *Standard* or the *Liberator*?

The other apocryphal story portrays Sojourner trying to sell Lincoln her photograph for a "greenback" which bore a picture of Lincoln. This story was published in abbreviated form in 1880.[20] It was published in detail in 1890, twenty-five years after it supposedly occurred, in a version offered by Calvin Fairbank, an anti-slavery hero whose health had been broken by his long imprisonment in Kentucky for helping slaves escape and who, of special interest here, had a reputation for being inaccurate. Fairbank said he had been at a huge public reception at the White House celebrating Lincoln's second inaugural on 4 March 1865, when Sojourner came in and asked to see the president. When she saw him, she handed him a copy of her photograph (which she often sold to help support herself, normally for about 35 to 50 cents). She said, "It's got a black face but a white back; an' I'd like one o' yourn wid a green back." According to Fairbank, the president "laughed heartily" at her request and then drew a ten-dollar greenback out of his pocket for her, saying, "There is my face with a green back."[21]

Since ten-dollar "greenback" bills carrying Lincoln's picture were in circulation at the time and since Sojourner had given President Grant a copy of her photograph in 1870, for which he gave her a five-dollar bill, the story does wear a face of plausibility.[22] However, the Lincoln story seems more improbable than the Grant story. The Lincoln story seems too outrageous, portraying her, as it does, as requesting money for herself from a president, while the Grant story does not so portray her. Moreover, Sojourner told the Grant story soon after it happened, and retold it in her 1875 *Narrative*, while she never told the Lincoln story. It seems probable that some wag picked up the lumpish Grant story, jazzed it up, and gave it panache by attaching it to Lincoln instead of Grant.

Because of her eccentricity and inability to read and write, Sojourner Truth's exploits were prime material for myth-makers. Moreover, when the myths developed in her lifetime, she did not appear inclined to puncture them. As an activist who felt a mission to speak out for God, Sojourner did not think much in terms of the linear truth of details about her own past. She interpreted her own life and the world at large more in terms of images, parables, and prophetic truth.

If Sojourner was not all that mythmakers, past and present, claim, nevertheless she rose magnificently above her circumstances as a slave, an illiterate, a black, a woman. She insisted on applying her childlike evangelical Christianity to help set the world "right side up," as she said;[23] and with her original, whimsical illustrations and her strange blend of the brash and the wise, she was often persuasive. She felt at ease with black and white, rich and poor. She was welcomed into the homes of some of the nation's far-seeing, if embattled, leaders, including Elizabeth Cady Stanton, William Lloyd Garrison, and Lincoln. But she often chose to identify with the poor, as with the freedmen; and she is a more impressive example of such an identification because she did not depend on Lincoln to assign it to her but found it essentially by herself.

Part 6

AFRICAN AMERICANS AND AID TO THE CONFEDERACY

CHAPTER 24

Free Men of Color in Gray

Arthur W. Bergeron Jr.

A NUMBER OF WRITERS HAVE studied the use of blacks as soldiers by the Union and Confederate governments during the American Civil War. Most of these workers have focused on the Union army since it employed large numbers of black soldiers during the conflict. When the authors do cover the Confederate side, they usually limit their coverage to the free blacks of New Orleans who formed a regiment of "Native Guards" for the Louisiana militia and to efforts late in the war to employ slaves as soldiers.[1] Various Southern states enacted legislation accepting free blacks as laborers or in other noncombat roles, but until early 1865, the official policy of the Confederate government prohibited blacks from serving as armed soldiers.[2]

Scholars who have investigated the role of blacks in the Confederate armies usually have described only the body servants who occasionally picked up a weapon during a battle, though several writers have discussed the largely unsubstantiated cases of slaves serving in other combat situations.[3] Two studies which look closely at blacks who aided the Confederate war effort fail to document satisfactorily the enlistment of free blacks as combat soldiers. One of these books exhibits a strong Confederate bias but cannot substantiate its assertion that "many of these [free blacks] were in active war participation."[4] In dealing with "the question as to whether or not any Negroes ever fought in the Confederate ranks," Professor Bell I. Wiley found no firm evidence to say that they did. He concluded, "If persons with Negro blood served in Confederate ranks as full-fledged soldiers, the percent of Negro blood was sufficiently low for them to pass as whites."[5]

Contrary to Professor Wiley's contention, a number of Louisiana free blacks did serve as soldiers, and their white comrades in arms did know them to be "free men of color." Some fifteen hundred or more New Orleans free blacks made up the First Regiment Louisiana Native Guards. Free blacks in several country parishes of the state organized themselves into military companies. Professor John D. Winters has estimated that nearly three thousand free blacks had volunteered for militia duty by early 1862.[6] With this many men in militia service, it seemed reasonable that a few individuals could have seen combat duty. In researching this theory, I documented fifteen free blacks who volunteered for and served in regular Confederate units as privates. Twelve of these men enlisted in Louisiana volunteer regiments, two in a home guard or reserve unit, and one in a Texas cavalry unit. Three of the first twelve fought in several battles, and two of the three received wounds. This manuscript will summarize the military service of these fifteen men and speculate briefly on their reasons for wanting to fight for the Confederacy.

The three most prominent examples of free blacks who volunteered for Confederate military service all came from St. Landry Parish.[7] The three were Charles F. Lutz, Jean Baptiste Pierre-Auguste, and Lufroy Pierre-Auguste. Charles F. Lutz, born in June 1842, was the son of Frederick Guillaume Lutz and Caroline Marx (or Manse), a mulatto woman. Charles Lutz joined Captain James C. Pratt's Opelousas Guards company, which became Company F, Eighth Louisiana Infantry Regiment, on June 23, 1861. This regiment went to Virginia and formed part of a brigade commanded by Brigadier General Richard Taylor. The Eighth Louisiana fought in the battles of Winchester, Cross Keys, Port Republic, the Seven Days, Second Manassas, Sharpsburg, and Fredericksburg. In the battle of Second Fredericksburg, or Marye's Heights, on May 3, 1863, Lutz fell into enemy hands with more than one hundred of his comrades. He remained in Federal prisons for about two weeks before being exchanged to rejoin his unit. At the Battle of Gettysburg, on July 2, 1863, Lutz received a severe wound in his left forearm and again became a prisoner.

After holding him in a prison hospital in New York, Federal authorities exchanged Lutz on September 16, 1863, at City Point, Virginia. He went home on furlough after his release. While at Opelousas, Lutz became involved in some kind of difficulty in May or June 1864. As a result of this mysterious event, Lutz lost his right arm. He claimed in a pension application after the war that he was shot in the arm but did not elaborate on the nature of the affair. Lutz went to Texas to live with his brother in Polk

County. On May 9, 1865, he received a discharge at the General Hospital at Houston on the basis of a surgeon's certificate of disability. Lutz married after the war and later moved to Westlake in Calcasieu Parish. After two attempts, Lutz finally received a Confederate pension from the state of Louisiana in 1900. Of the men discussed here, Lutz was probably the only one who passed for and enlisted as white. The federal censuses of 1880 and 1900 list him as such.[8]

Jean Baptiste Pierre-Auguste was born in St. Landry Parish in May 1842. He was possibly the son of Ursin and Caroline Pierre-Auguste, both free persons of color. Jean Baptiste joined Captain James W. Bryan's company at Lake Charles in early 1862. He may have been living in Calcasieu Parish when the war began. Bryan's unit became Company I, Twenty-ninth Louisiana Infantry Regiment, on April 15, 1862. The regiment went to Vicksburg, Mississippi. There the unit participated in various campaigns in defense of the city, particularly the Battle of Chickasaw Bluffs, December 28–29, 1862. The Twenty-ninth Louisiana was part of the Confederate garrison besieged at Vicksburg between May 19 and July 4, 1863. The men fought back two major Union assaults on their trenches. Jean Baptiste received a slight wound to his thigh during one of these actions. Following the surrender of the Confederate garrison, he went home on parole.

The men of the Twenty-ninth Louisiana returned to duty in the summer of 1864 near Alexandria. From that time until the end of the war, the regiment did little except routine garrison duty. In February and March 1865, Jean Baptiste was detailed as a cook for his company's officers, possibly a duty he received because he was free black. A clothing-issue book kept by Captain Byran shows Jean Baptiste in service as late as May 12, 1865. The Twenty-ninth Louisiana disbanded near Mansfield about May 19, and the men went to their homes without official paroles. Jean Baptiste was married at least twice. The 1900 census for Calcasieu Parish lists him as a single parent, but he stated he had a wife and four children when he applied for a Confederate pension in 1912. The State Board of Pension Commissioners originally rejected his application because he had no official parole. Several of his former comrades sent in affidavits attesting to his service until the end of the war, and he received his pension in 1915.[9]

Lufroy Pierre-Auguste was born in St. Landry Parish about 1830. He was the son of Pierre Pierre-Auguste and Gabriele Tessier, free persons of color. The 1860 census shows that Lufroy worked as a stockherder for Francois P. Pitre Jr. Lufroy left his farm and joined Captain Daniel Gober's Big Cane rifles, which became Company K, Sixteenth Louisiana Infantry Regiment. The first two muster rolls of this company list him as a free man of color—the only such instance found in researching these men. None of the men discussed in this manuscript, except for Lutz and possibly Gabriel Grappe, pretended they were white. The other men in their units undoubtedly knew them as free blacks.

The Sixteenth Louisiana fought in the battles of Shiloh, Farmington, and Perrysville. On December 8, 1862, while in camp at Murfreesboro, Tennessee, Lufroy received a discharge from Confederate service. The reason given for his discharge was that he was a "a colored man." Apparently superior authorities had finally discovered that he was black and ordered his separation from the army. Lufroy went home, but he did become involved in one other incident before war's end. On May 13, 1865, he surprised two Jayhawkers near Opelousas. These men made up part of a band of outlaws, deserters, and draft dodgers who resisted Confederate authority. The two Jayhawkers fired at him, and he returned fire, hitting one of the men. Lufroy married in 1869, but no further information on his life after the war has come to light so far.[10]

Two free men of color—Evariste Guillory Sr. and Evariste Guillory Jr.—saw some service as home guards. Both father and son were free mulattoes living on Bayou Mallet west of Opelousas when the war began. They joined Captain M. McDavitt's Company I, Second Louisiana Reserve Corps. No information exists on when they enlisted in this unit, but the regiment did not form until July 1864. The Reserve Corps consisted primarily of men who were over or under draft age or who were in some manner ineligible for regular service, such as discharged or disabled former soldiers. The men of the Reserve Corps saw practically no fighting with the enemy, but Confederate authorities called them out to chase Jayhawkers and deserters when needed for such service. They sometimes acted as drovers gathering cattle for the army in the field. Both of the Guillorys surrendered to Federal authorities and received their paroles at Washington, Louisiana, on June 17, 1865.[11]

Jacques Esclavon, a forty-year-old free mulatto farmer of Calcasieu Parish, saw service in a Texas military unit late in the war. Jean Esclavon and Adelaide de la Fosse, free mulattoes, possibly were his parents. On September 11, 1864, he enlisted in Company A, Ragsdale's Battalion Texas Cavalry. This unit had moved into southwestern Louisiana to perform guard and picket duty around the Calcasieu and Mermentau rivers and had enlisted several dozen Louisianians. It is possible that the Texans did not know that Esclavon was black, but existing battalion records showing his assignment to menial duties such as teamster and company cook may indicate they knew his status. Official records show Esclavon in service until at least March 1865. He may have remained on duty until his command broke up and dispersed to their homes at the end of the war.[12]

The remaining free men of color who wore gray all came from the area of Campti, and did not, with one exception, join a military unit until relatively late in the war. There appear to have been more men enlisted than the nine mentioned here, but other names have not yet been discovered. An authority on this area of northwestern Louisiana has observed that these free blacks "lived as white, in almost all respects. There was hardly an aspect of Campti life or society (male, that is)" in which they "were not freely accepted. Almost all of the old Campti families (white) were their relatives and freely acknowledged it."[13] Thus, it is not hard to understand why they entered easily a predominantly white military company.

Gabriel Grappe became the first of these north Louisiana free blacks to enlist. On April 6, 1862, at Monroe, Grappe joined Captain Thomas W. Fuller's Bossier Cavalry company. Gabriel, born in 1825, was the son of Jacques Grappe and Marie Rose de la Cerda. Jacques Grappe was "half-Negro, one-eighth Chitimachas Indian and three-eighths French." Rose de la Cerda was of Spanish ancestry and probably had no black ancestors. The 1860 census shows Gabriel Grappe was a wagoner, but when he enlisted he gave his occupation as farmer. From Monroe, Fuller's company went to Tennessee and fought in skirmishes both there and in northern Mississippi. Grappe appears on a muster roll for January and February 1863 as being absent sick at Okalona, Mississippi, and makes no further appearance in official records until October 1, 1864. On that date a Confederate officer in Natchitoches wrote that Grappe had joined Captain R. B. Love's Company H, Sixth Louisiana Cavalry Regiment. It is possible that Grappe received a discharge from Fuller's company and later enlisted in Love's, or he may have transferred from one company to the other shortly after the formation of the Sixth Louisiana Cavalry (the Bossier Cavalry now serving as Company C of the regiment). The regiment saw no combat duty in late 1864 or early 1865 but served on courier and guard duty. Grappe surrendered and received his parole at Natchitoches on June 15, 1865.[14]

The eight remaining free men of color from the Campti area served in Company H, Sixth Louisiana Cavalry, with Gabriel Grappe. One man was Gabriel's brother McGhee (or Margil), born in 1835 and by occupation a carpenter.[15] Two of the men were a father and son—Jesse (or Jessy) and William Gardner. William was the son of Jesse and Jane Laury and was born February 24, 1840.[16] Two others—Joseph G. and Alphonse Perot—were brothers born in 1843 and 1838, respectively. They were sons of Valery Perot and Marie Felonize Condet, and both men operated farms.[17] Sylvester Perez was, as his name indicates, of partial Spanish ancestry. He married his first cousin, also a free person of color, Trinidad Armandine Simon, whose ancestors came to Campti from the Opelousas area.[18]

Ambroise Lebrun was a descendant of Paul Etienne Le Brun *dit* Dagobert, a Frenchman who with Suzette Grappe, a sister of Jacques, fathered a number of mulatto children.[19] Little information has come to light on John Adams, the last of the Campti group. Born in 1842, he made his living as a shoemaker. A descriptive list gives his complexion as quadroon.[20]

The service of these men first came to my attention through a letter written by Lieutenant J. Alphonse Prudhomme, the Confederate enrolling, or conscript, officer in Natchitoches. On October 1, 1864, Prudhomme wrote to his superiors in Shreveport that he had discovered the Perot brothers and McGhee Grappe in possession of passes from one of their lieutenants. The three privates told Prudhomme that the other five men had joined Captain Love's company also. Prudhomme reported that he had enrolled the Perots and Grappe under provisions of an order calling for conscription of free men of color as laborers. He also said he intended to send the men to Alexandria to work on fortifications there. Prudhomme then asked for instructions.[21]

While awaiting a reply, Prudhomme allowed Grappe to go home for clothes. Under this pretext, Grappe sought assistance from a family friend. On October 7, P. A. Morse, an influential citizen of Bossier Parish, wrote to the commander of the Louisiana conscript district and had Grappe take the letter to Shreveport. Morse stated that he knew well the Grappe family and recounted some of their family background. He asked for orders permitting the Grappe brothers to stay in Captain Love's company because they wished to remain in it and because Prudhomme had enrolled them illegally. Morse pointed out that although their father was a free man of color, the Grappes' mother "was a Mexican white woman." Colonel Edmund G. Randolph responded quickly to Morse's letter. The next day, he ordered McGhee Grappe back to Natchitoches and advised Prudhomme to send him back to his regiment. Grappe continued to serve with his unit until he surrendered and received his parole.[22]

The Perot brothers did not fare as well as McGhee Grappe. Prudhomme sent Alphonse on October 7 to Alexandria to serve as a laborer. Joseph received orders to appear before a medical examining board no later than October 16 to determine if his health would permit him to do heavy labor. No further information on him has come to light and his ultimate fate is unknown. Prudhomme finally caught John Adams, enrolled him on December 30, and sent him on the same day to work on the Alexandria fortifications.[23] No other official records exist to show what happened to Jesse and William Gardner, Sylvester Perez, or Ambroise Lebrun. If any of them remained in Captain Love's company after the controversy of October 1864, none received a parole at the end of the war. Prudhomme's record book showing enrollments of free blacks contains no entries after December 1864. He may have eventually enrolled these last four men as laborers or at least forced them out of active service in Love's company.

Unfortunately, none of the men discussed here left any letters, diaries, or memoirs yet discovered either to elaborate on their wartime activities or explain why they chose to enlist as volunteers in Confederate units. This leaves us to speculate on their motivation in risking their lives for a cause many people would not expect them to espouse. They undoubtedly followed a stronger urging of the same impulses which led thousands of their fellow free blacks to form militia units. In assessing the actions of New Orleans free blacks, David C. Rankin and Mary F. Berry emphasize the historical state-patriotism these men felt as well as their long tradition of service in the militia.[24] General studies of the roles played by free blacks elsewhere in the South, whether in labor or militia units, center on their state loyalty. As Benjamin Quarles noted, "these Negro volunteers placed the cause of their respective commonwealth above every other public duty."[25]

Gary Mills's study of the free blacks in the Natchitoches area also speaks of state loyalty but adds, "Most . . . realized that a Union victory would mean the complete destruction of their economy, the basis of their livelihood, and their special status as *gens de couleur libre*." Claude Oubre has written that St. Landry Parish's free blacks "knew where their loyalties lay" when the war started because they stood to lose "the status they enjoyed as a free people." These writings fall in line with the statewide study done by H. E. Sterkx, who observed that "many well-to-do colored freemen prized their distinctive economic positions so strongly that they deplored any prospect that would endanger it. . . . Equally feared by this group of colored planters was the prospect of a general emancipation, which would submerge them in great black mass of Negroes."[26]

Another factor, related to this view of their place in society, comes into play when considering the Campti free blacks (except Gabriel Grappe) and the Guillorys of St. Landry Parish. These men found themselves faced with a choice in the late summer or early fall of 1864—they could enlist in combat units or wait for conscription as laborers. A Natchitoches free black wrote from one labor camp, "We are in a way slaves." He described the squalor of the camp and told his wife, "The negroes [slaves] are treated better than we are. We are obliged to do the hardest kind of work and the negro looks on."[27] To avoid the degrading conditions and work of the labor camps, where they would find the same treatment given the slaves around them, these men chose an action that would emphasize their distinctiveness from other blacks.

Several historians have questioned the sincerity of the free men of color who formed Confederate militia units. They say that those men did so out of fear or under pressure from whites. They also point accurately to the fact that the Native Guards regiment disbanded when New Orleans fell into Union hands and that most of the men later joined the Union army.[28] These historians may indeed be correct in appraising the majority of the free blacks involved. Yet fear or coercion does not seem to have motivated the men discussed in this manuscript to join regular Confederate units. As stated, Confederate law prohibited any blacks from serving in combat units. If coercion forced these me to enlist, why didn't many more free blacks face the same pressure? We should not doubt the sincerity of these fifteen men, especially the ones from St. Landry Parish. A study of that area states, "The Opelousas *Patriot* was the most virulently anti-free Negro journal in the whole of Louisiana." Many residents of the parish advocated the expulsion of mulattoes from the state, and in fact, some eighty-one free persons of color left St. Landry for Haiti in 1860.[29]

The actions of these free blacks seem to argue for what may be to some an unpopular conclusion. By volunteering for combat duty in regular Confederate service, these men took what can be seen as the final step of their acceptance or acculturation into the local white societies where they lived. Their decision reinforces what Gary Mills and others have written about the social and economic interactions of certain segments of Louisiana's antebellum population. In areas of Natchitoches, St. Landry, Calcasieu, and possibly other parishes, many whites and free blacks must have enjoyed a freedom of association that has received relatively little attention by social scientists. The actions of these free men of color in volunteering for—and of their white comrades in accepting them into—military units should lead us to take a closer look at race relations in Louisiana's pre–Civil War period.

In summary, state or local patriotism and the desire to protect their standing which kept them above blacks in slavery would seem to have motivated all of the men discussed here to join the Confederate army. There is no evidence that anyone forced them to take that step. Rather it seems that they followed the dictates of their consciences and made a bold move many whites shunned.

CHAPTER 25

Black Southerners in Gray

Richard Rollins

O NE OF THE LEADING Southern historians of our time, C. Vann Woodward, remarked on the relationship between black and white in the South:

> The ironic thing about these two great hyphenate minorities, Southern-American and Afro-American, confronting each other on their native soil for three and a half centuries, is the degree to which they have shaped each other's destinies, determined each other's isolation, shared and molded a common culture. It is, in fact, impossible to imagine the one without the other and quite futile to try.[1]

Woodward's insight holds true for the Civil War era. We often imagine the armed forces of the Confederate States of America as all-white, but that is far from accurate. The South was a biracial, caste society, and the armies it fielded reflected that peculiar social reality. To imagine the Confederate armies without black Southerners in their ranks is to perpetuate the ahistorical myth of the South as a compartmentalized society. It ignores the real relationship between blacks and whites in the Old South, as well as the role and experiences of a small but significant portion of black Southerners in the Confederacy. The question then, is not *if* black Southerners played a role in Southern armies, but *what* and *how* they contributed to the war effort.

This essay will outline the process through which some black Southerners found their way into combat in Confederate armies. Black participation in Confederate armies can be divided into three categories. They served and bore arms as servants; as private individuals; and as units either predominantly black or made up of all black Southerners.

When the guns of Fort Sumter startled the nation in 1861, they released a great tension that had built up during the long years of controversy between the sections. Both North and South broke out into near-hysterical demonstrations of patriotism. In cities large and small, frenzied demonstrations of patriotism filled the streets with people pledging their lives and fortunes to the war effort. Volunteers signed on to put down the Rebellion or to defend their homeland against Northern aggression.

Black Southerners were also caught up in the emotion of the coming of war. While many awaited anxiously the "year of jubilo," some had a different response. As individuals and in groups, black Southerners across the South took actions that indicated their support for the South. Even before Sumter a group of free blacks in Charleston and Columbia, S.C. had sent messages to public officials, including Governor Pickens. "We are by birth citizens of South Carolina—In our veins flows the blood of the white race, in some half, in others much more than half white blood," said one. All indicated their support for the South. "Our attachments are with you, our hopes of safety & protection from you. Our allegiance is to So. Ca. and in her defense, we are willing to offer up our lives, and all that is dear to us." They offered themselves for "any service where we can be most useful." We are ready, they said, "whenever called upon to assist in preparing the State a defense, against any action which may be brought against her."[2] Another groups of "able bodied free colored men" offered to work without pay on the breastworks being built on the coast.[3]

In Georgia another group published the following letter in the *Savannah Evening News:*

> To Brigadier General Lawton
> Commanding Military District
> The undersigned free men of color, residing in the city of Savannah and county of Chatham, fully impressed with the feeling of duty we owe to the State of Georgia as inhabitants thereof, which has for so long a period extended to ourselves and families is protection, and has been to us the source of many benefits—beg leave, respectfully, in this the hour of danger, to tender to yourself our services, to be employed in the defense of the state, at any place or point, at any time, or any length of time, and in any service for which you may consider us best fitted, and in which we can contribute to the public good.[4]

An observer in Charleston noted a "thousand Negroes who, so far from inclining to insurrections, were grinning from ear to ear at the prospect of shooting Yankees."[5] A group of black musicians in Richmond, calling themselves the "Confederate Ethiopian Serenaders" gave the returns of one of their concerts to help pay for gunboats and munitions.[6] Just after Sumter a company of armed blacks was seen passing through Charleston.[7] In Nashville a company of free blacks offered their services to the Confederate government and in June the state legislature authorized Governor Harris to accept into Tennessee service all male persons of color.[8] In Memphis in September a procession of several hundred free blacks marched through the streets under the command of Confederate officers. "They were brimful of patriotism, shouting for Jeff Davis and singing war songs."[9] One black company was sent to Augusta, Georgia to serve with the 3rd and 4th Georgia Regiments.[10] In Montgomery blacks were seen being drilled and armed for military duty.[11] Two companies of black Confederates were formed in Fort Smith, Arkansas. They had no weapons, but prepared themselves by drilling and declared themselves determined "to fight for their masters and their homes."[12]

Similar occurrences took place in Virginia. In Lynchburg 70 men enlisted to fight for the defense of Virginia soon after it seceded; a local newspaper raised "three cheers for the patriotic Negroes of Lynchburg."[13] A week later a group in Richmond volunteered "the work of defense, or any other capacity required" and were ordered to report "to the Captain of the Woodis Riflemen."[14] In late April, 60 black Southerners carrying a Confederate flag asked to be enlisted. In Hampton 300 blacks volunteered to serve in artillery batteries.[15] In Petersburg a group of blacks who had volunteered to work on defenses held a mass rally at the courthouse square. The former Mayor, John Dodson, presented them with a Confederate flag and promised them "a rich reward of praise, and merit, from a thankful people." Charles Tinsley, a bricklayer and spokesman for the group, accepted the flag and said "we are willing to aid Virginia's cause to the utmost of our ability. We do not feel that it is right for us to remain here idle, when white gentlemen are engaged in the performance of work in Norfolk that is more suitable for our hands and of which it is our duty to relieve them. We promise unhesitating obedience to all orders that may be given us."[16] Off they went, probably dressed in red shirts and black pants, bearing the flag of the Confederacy "of their own free will."[17]

The largest demonstration of all came in New Orleans. A mass meeting attended by black residents was held just after the news had arrived from Fort Sumter. They declared themselves resolved and "ready to take up arms at a moment's notice and fight shoulder to shoulder with other citizens."[18] Later one black man said to a commanding General of the State Militia, "our fathers were brought here as slaves because they were captured in war, and in hand to hand fights, too. Pardon me, General, but the only cowardly blood we have got in our veins is the white blood."[19] They proceeded to organize a regiment of black Confederate troops with black officers, a unit that will be discussed in more detail later in this essay. Thus all over the South there were black men who responded to the news of war by making public demonstrations of their support for the Confederacy.

Free blacks and slaves provided much of the infrastructure of the Southern war effort. In the course of four years of war hundreds of thousands worked on fortifications. Breastworks, trenches, forts, and other defensive works were built in nearly every city and town in the South, largely by black laborers. Indeed, one of the persistent themes in Confederate politics was the labor question. How should black labor be used? What compensation should be given owners of slaves used on national projects? Blacks staffed Southern hospitals and ran the weapons manufacturing plants in Virginia and Georgia. One historian estimates that at least 20% of the workers in the Confederate Ordnance Department were black. Another states that half of the workers at Richmond's Tredegar Iron Works, the largest and most important in the South, were black.[20] Blacks built the enormous Chimborazo Hospital in Richmond; drove wagons for Southern armies; planted and harvested the crops on Southern plantations while whites were in the army, and dug coal and saltpeter out of Southern mines. As James Brewer has shown, blacks played a central and essential role in Virginia's Quartermaster and Commissary Departments, in Confederate Naval and Ordnance works, the Quartermaster Department, hospitals, railroads, and as transportation workers.[21] By February of 1865, 310 out of 400 workers at the Naval works in Selma were black, and by September of 1864 there were 4,301 black and 2,518 white workers in Confederate iron mines.[22]

Southern blacks also supported the rebellion in individual ways. In New Orleans, black lithographer Louis Pessou produced and sold beautiful full-color pictures of Confederate camp scenes and a copy of the Ordinance of Secession in his shop.[23] In Fort Smith, Arkansas, a black-sponsored ball raised money for soldiers.[24] Richard Kinnard of Petersburg gave $100, and Jordan Chase of Vicksburg, a veteran of the War of 1812, gave a horse for Confederate cavalry and pledged an additional $500 to the cause. A New Orleans real estate broker also gave $500 to the war effort. Not all could give money, but even some of the poorest slaves supported the war: an Alabama slave gave a state regiment a bushel of sweet potatoes, possibly all he had to give. The black residents of Helena, S.C., rounded up $90 for soldier relief and in Charleston a little black girl sent "a free offering of 25 cents."[25] The free black women of Savannah made uniforms for Southern soldiers and among the subscribers of a Confederate loan in Columbus, Ga., was a free man who contributed $300.[26] The "Ladies Gunboat Fund" in Savannah, which eventually produced the CSS *Georgia,* had significant black support.[27] Free blacks in Vicksburg held a ball to raise money for soldiers in Virginia. "The colored folks in every town in the South had given balls, parties, and fairs, for our benefit, and sent thousands of dollars, clothes and blankets, etc . . ." wrote one Southerner. Blacks even echoed the white tendency to brag about their fighting prowess. "In truth, our servants feel as much pride in this holy war as we do, and are ever ready, as we have frequently seen to prove in battle 'dat de Soufren colored man can whip a norfern nigger and de Yankee to back him'"[28]

In the town cemetery of Canton, Mississippi, just outside of Jackson, stands a 20' obelisk in memory of the black Mississippians who served in a partisan unit attached to Nathan Bedford Forrest's cavalry in 1864 led by a young Mississippian, Addison Harvey, and known as "Harvey's Scouts." It was built sometime between 1894 and 1900 by William Hill Howcott, a private in the unit. It is dedicated to "the good and loyal servants who followed the fortunes of Harvey's Scouts during the Civil War." It carries a tribute to the "faithful servant and friend Willis Hoscott, a colored boy of rare loyalty and faithfulness whose memory I will cherish with deep gratitude."[29]

The feelings of black Southerners about the war have received scant attention from historians. Perhaps the concept of freedom is so overwhelming in our culture that we assume that all black Southerners believed that victory by the North would bring freedom, whatever might be their interpretation of that idea, and that they naturally sympathized with the North. Certainly this is the framework of perception that Northern soldiers carried south with them.[30] Just as surely we have been misled by the Southern writers before, during and after the war who propagated and endorsed the "myth of the happy slave" to support their view of slavery as a benign institution. We have apparently just begun to comprehend the minds and hearts of black Southerners during the war, and to study and understand how they truly felt about it, and how the war actually affected their lives.

Recent research suggests a very different sensibility. Some sided with the South, some with the North, but the majority were loyal to themselves and their families, and tried to do what was the best for themselves, without regard to abstract political causes.[31] One recalled that he had fought for both North and South, "but I neber fought for the Yankees till dey captured me and put me in a corral and said, 'Nigger, you fought for de South; now you can fight for de North.'"[32] Black Southerners gave support to both sides, and that support was conditional, based on individual assessments of the situation at hand. For the majority, the war brought not elation and joy but anxiety, wariness, and difficult choices. As Clarence Mohr, a historian of slavery, has written recently, there is much to suggest that throughout the war black Southerners "maintained a strong sense of local identity and a bittersweet affinity for the land of their birth." He went on to conclude that during the war "an almost bewildering array of emotions and private considerations" shaped the behavior of individual bondsmen:"

> Concern for friends or relatives in slavery, uncertainty over the war's outcome, personal esteem for white owners, disillusioning contacts with racially prejudiced Northerners, awareness of religiously inspired efforts at ameliorative reform, and the actual expansion of slavery's customary prerogatives all served to bind particular Afro-Americans to the Southern cause.[33]

The primary fact was that the South was home. Some of the 4,000,000 who lived there had roots going back over 200 years. The African "griot" tradition of a village "historian" passing family and tribal history down the generations orally often kept family traditions alive.[34] Despite the oppression of slavery and racism, and sometimes because of it, they had developed intricate networks of relationships to families, friends (both black and white), in local towns and on plantations. Many felt a strong sense of attachment to their home states, towns and rural areas. In New Orleans, Mobile, Richmond and Charleston, black Southerners had long served in local militia units and had played a significant role in the Revolution and War of 1812. Their strongest loyalty and bittersweet affinities lay with their local area and state, not the Federal government, or some far-off ideal world. Like whites, they thought of themselves as Virginians, Carolinians and Louisianians, or members of a local community, *not Americans.* As Bell Wiley has point out, even some of those who followed the Union armies away from their homes returned after short periods of time. Homesickness and a growing awareness that the army could not care for them drove them back to where they started.[35] As Benjamin Quarles, one of the leading black historians of this century has said, "like thousands of white Southerners who personally hated slavery and felt that it was doomed with the coming of the war but who nevertheless defended the Confederacy, these free Negroes had a sense of community responsibility which impelled them to throw their lot with their neighbors."[36]

Many hoped that a victorious South would show its appreciation of its black citizens and loosen the bonds that held them. As one body servant said when he was captured with his master and was questioned about his loyalty by a Northern officer, "I had as much right to fight for my native state as you had to fight for your'n, and a blame sight more right than your furriners, what's got no homes." He was paroled as a member of the Seventh Virginia Cavalry.[37] On the march to Gettysburg one servant talked to a wife of a Pennsylvania farmer who suggested that he slip away from the army and remain in Pennsylvania, a free man. He refused and she asked him "are you treated well?" "I live as I wish," he boldly replied, "and if I did not, I think I couldn't better myself by stopping here. This is a beautiful country, but it doesn't come up to home in my eyes."[38] Another black Confederate underscored the wish to improve life in the South by defending it when he stated they hoped to raise esteem for blacks amongst both blacks and whites by fighting for the South: "no matter where I fight," he said, "I only wish to spend what I have, and fight as long as I can, if only my boy may stand alone in the street equal to a white boy when the war is over."[39]

Many reasons existed for black Southerners not to perceive the North as a land of freedom and opportunity. Stories circulated throughout the South that the Yankee soldiers were monsters who would treat them badly, as indeed they often did.[40] Sherman's troops in Georgia were especially rough on black Southerners.[41] Several Northern states had laws prohibiting black immigration and even residency, and all had discriminatory laws. Lincoln himself, "Father Abraham" to some, repeatedly declared that he was no abolitionist, and did little to make Southern blacks feel they were welcome in the North. Combined with the difficulty of the escape process, these factors probably caused some to seek ways to work within the context of the Civil War South.

In addition to psychological and emotional ties, many free black Southerners had economic and material reasons for siding with the South. Significant divisions existed between free blacks and slaves, and some free blacks aligned themselves with whites against slaves. In their eyes, the degradation of slavery elevated their own status just as the degradation of all blacks elevated the status of all whites.[42] John Chavin, a free Negro preacher and schoolteacher, opposed emancipation and urged his friends to oppose abolitionism.[43] Ethnic and religious differences also caused divisions because slaves, noted a writer in the *New Orleans Picayune*, felt that free blacks, "put on too many airs, and he scoffs at him and hates him accordingly."[44]

The number of affluent free blacks in the South grew dramatically in the 1850's, a decade of unprecedented prosperity and continuous economic expansion in the South. In Charleston, 75 whites rented homes from blacks. By 1860, there were 26 free black residents of Nashville who, with no property in 1850, had managed to accumulate net assets of $1,000. Labor shortages caused increases in wages for skilled craftsmen, and free blacks prospered as bricklayers, barbers, machinists, carpenters, and in many other professions.[45]

Many prosperous free blacks were mulattos who had been given or inherited property from their white parent. While marriage between blacks and whites was outlawed, racially mixed couples were numerous, so much so that in Louisiana a special term, "placage," was coined to designate it. They became successful as plantation owners as well as farmers, artisans and skilled craftsmen. By 1860 in Charleston alone they owned $500,000 in property. They formed small clans of related families and friends and aligned themselves with the planter aristocracy. For example, the two wealthiest black farmers in Virginia were Priscilla Ivey and Frankey Miles, both of whom had been mistresses of white slave-owners. A successful North Carolina barber-planter was the son of a prominent merchant-shipper and an Ibo woman. Former slave Robert Rentfro owned a famous hotel in Nashville. St. Louis had a long Spanish and French Creole tradition and there the four most prosperous free families were all descendants of white settlers and black women. Louis Rutgers, who eventually amassed an estate of $50,000 was the slave son of a Dutch immigrant.[46]

Perhaps the group that had the strongest vested interest in seeing the South victorious were the black slaveowners. In 1830 approximately 1,556 black slaveowners in the deep South owned 7,188 slaves. About 25% of all free blacks owned slaves.[47] A few of these were men who purchased their family members to protect or free them, but most were people who saw slavery as the best way to economic wealth and independence for themselves. The American dream in the antebellum South was just as powerful for free blacks as whites and it included the use of slaves for self-improvement. They bought and sold slaves for profit and exploited their labor just like their white counterparts. In South Carolina, John Stanley owned 163 and William Ellison owned 97. The Metoyer clan of Louisiana owned nearly 400. By 1860, so many black women in Charleston had inherited or been given slaves and other property by white men, and used their property to start successful businesses as caterers, dressmakers, and other small businesses, that they owned 70% of the black-owned slaves in the city.[48] Horace King of Russell County, Alabama, was born a slave but was freed and became a highly skilled and successful bridge-builder, employing slave labor in his business. During the war he was a frequent contributor to the Southern cause and furnished uniforms and money to the sons of his former master.[49] These black slaveowners undoubtably understood that a Northern invasion and victory would bring economic and social ruin to them. And it did.[50]

Even some slaves might believe they had a vested interest in a Southern victory. Skilled labor was in great demand before and during the war, and slaves with training benefited from the economic pressure. They were often rented out by their masters for goodly sums and because of their value were given incentives to do good work and stay with their masters. Some were allowed to live on their own away from their owners and to live nearly as freely as whites. They earned wages that made many whites envious and the war stimulated this trend. One slave blacksmith bragged that his income exceeded that of "any white man in the shop with him." In addition, skilled slaves could keep any money they earned in their spare time. For example, in 1864 one black Southerner made $7.50 per day in basic wages, plus an additional $6.00 for each breech-band he made for Southern cannon. He made $127.50 in one month in overtime wages alone.[51]

Finally, like their white counterparts, some young black Southerners went off to war because it was an exciting thing to do, the great adventure of their generation. A servant from South Carolina wrote a letter to his sister which summed up his feelings in battle as well as his self-identity, as many other black Southerners must have felt, as a soldier:

> I've bin havin' a good time ginerally—see a heap of fine country and a plenty of purty gals . . . I have also bin on the battle fields and hear the bullets whiz. When the Yankees run I . . . got more clothes, blankets, overcoats, and razors than I could tote. I've got an injin rubber cloke with two brass eyes keeps the rain off like a meetin' house. Im a made man since the battle and cockt and primed to try it again. If I kin kill a Yankee and git a gold watch, and pair of boots, my trip will made. How other niggers do to stay at home, while we soldiers are havin' such a good time is more than I can tell.[52]

Black Southerners found their way into combat in Confederate armies in three ways, but perhaps the largest numbers were the ubiquitous "body servants." At Fort Mill, South Carolina, there is an unusual monument, with the following inscription:

Dedicated to
the faithful slaves
who, loyal to a sacred trust
toiled for the support
of the Army with matchless
devotion . . . guarded
"Our Confederate States of America."[53]

These were not the laborers in work-gangs, nor were they the soldiers who volunteered on their own. Body servants were those slaves who before the war had been cooks, butlers, carriage-drivers and other skilled workers who had not worked in the fields but in the "big house" on plantations and on small farms with whites. As Eugene Genovese has pointed out, they often grew up with the children of their masters and had close, though often ambivalent, relationships with them.[54] Sam Newsom of Tennessee remembered the relationship he had with a white boy and linked it to his Confederate service:

> We was sort of brought up together, master Will and I was, and maybe that's why everybody seemed to sort of trust him to me. I used to rock him to sleep. He got to be a fine and reckless sort of gentleman. Then the war came. I went with Master Will. Nothing could stop him and I knew he would need me. He got to be a first lieutenant in the cavalry. I slept in the same tent. When he was fighting I stayed with the ambulances. . . . I got wounded once at the battle of Sullivan's Creek. Master Will was killed at Chickamauga. I brought his body home. I smuggled him by the pickets, hired a wagon and got him to Chattanooga. From there I brought him on home.[55]

When an English observer estimated that there were 30,000 body servants in the Army of Northern Virginia in 1862 he meant the cooks, valets, and personal attendants.

Blacks seemed to be everywhere in the Southern armies, especially early in the war. A Union surgeon, caught behind Confederate lines in 1862, observed the Army of Northern Virginia moving toward Sharpsburg and remarked in his diary on the presence of black Confederates:

> Wednesday, September 10
> At 4 o'clock this morning the Rebel army began to move from our town, Jackson's force taking the advance. The movement continued until 8 o'clock P.M., occupying 16 hours. The most liberal calculation could not give them more than 64,000 men. Over 3,000 Negroes must be included in the number. . . . They had arms, rifles, muskets, sabers,

bowie-knives, dirks, etc. They were supplied, in many instances, with knapsacks, haversacks, canteens, etc., and they were manifestly an integral portion of the Southern Confederacy army. They were seen riding on horses and mules, driving wagons, riding on caissons, in ambulances, with the staff of generals and promiscuously mixed up with all the Rebel horde.[56]

Black Southerners, and especially body servants, became an integral, important part of Southern armies. One soldier sent his servant home to get supplies and wrote a note to his wife about him:

> He is a great darky—worth his weight in gold even in these hard times. . . . He can tell you what things I principally need & more fully than I can write—he knows more about it anyway than I do, knows more about what I have and what I need—he attends to it all.[57]

In 1861 the 3rd Alabama Infantry marched to war with 1,000 white soldiers in the ranks, and almost as many blacks. This was not unusual. Of the 3,000 free blacks in Alabama, nearly all served the Confederacy in one capacity or another.[58] One brigade had a "washing corps" of 150 blacks.[59] Some became superb foragers and made important contributions to food supplies.[60] For their masters, and often for many others, they set up and struck tents, cleaned clothes, cared for the sick and wounded; in the Navy they stoked the fires in steamships and tended the sails on older ships. In short, they performed virtually every act of labor of a personal sort one can imagine.

There were so many black musicians in Southern armies that in April of 1862, the Confederate Congress passed a law authorizing their use and setting their wages as the same as white musicians.[61]

The Confederate government acknowledged their presence in various ways. For example, Samuel Cooper, Adjutant and Inspector General, issued an 1862 order that "the adjutants of the regiments throughout the Army will inquire into and report all cases of slaves serving with their respective regiments without written authority from their masters."[62] In other words, the Confederate government recognized that black Southerners had gone off to join the army: the *Southern* army.

Not all were slaves, owned by whites; many were free blacks with attachments—economic and otherwise—to the people they served. Robert Greene, in *Black Defenders,* lists several who were hired, not owned, and who served for three or four years.[63] Stonewall Jackson's servant, Jim Lewis, was "inconsolable" at Jackson's death. He led Jackson's horse in the funeral procession, then returned to the army and served

Colonel "Sandie" Pendleton until Pendleton died at Fisher's Hill in 1864. Lewis was eventually buried in Lexington, not far from where Jackson and Pendleton rest.[64] Peter Vertress, a Kentucky mulatto, served his white uncle as Assistant Surgeon for three years.[65] Silas Young of Alabama served for three years.[66]

It was not unusual for a servant to work for more than one person over a period of time. Several of the men in Greene's study not only served the entire war, but also with several individuals.[67] Benjamin Singleton of Beaufort, South Carolina entered the army as a servant of Capt. John J. Thompson and stuck with him until he was killed at Second Manassas in 1862. He then worked for Sergeant William Thompson and later Corporal David Thompson until late in the war, when he was with Robert and James Thompson of the Citadel Cadets.[68] It is not recorded whether these were all members of the same family.

Others revealed their dedication to the South's war effort in different ways. One servant who was captured by a Yankee was made to serve a Northern officer, but when sent to a spring to get water, kept on going through the Confederate lines and returned to his former master, taking two Yankee horses with him.[69] Another, Leroy Jones of the 4th Tennessee, joined up with his master and was captured with him. When his master died of typhoid fever, Jones slipped through the lines and went to his master's home, where he remained until given his freedom. Fifty-nine years later he applied for a pension and had several whites support his application.[70] Some of the servants indicated their military feelings by wearing uniforms. The Cahaba Rifles had servants who "with gray blankets, haversacks, and cedar canteens strapped on their shoulders and wearing the Confederate gray uniform, marched behind the company."[71] One slave was even more loyal to the cause than his master. Both were captured and sent to Point Lookout, then exchanged, whereupon they were asked to sign an oath of loyalty to the Union. The master signed, the slave did not. When asked why he refused to sign as his master had, the slave replied: "Massa has no principles."[72]

Servants occasionally captured white or black Northerners. Colonel Arthur Fremantle, a British officer of the Coldstream Guards, visiting the Army of Northern Virginia in 1863 spotted a black Confederate,"dressed in full Yankee uniform, with rifle at full cock, leading along a barefooted white man, with whom he had evidently changes clothes. General Longstreet stopped the pair, and asked the black man what it meant." The black Confederate said that two white Confederates had captured the Yank, then had a bit too much Brandy, whereupon they turned the prisoner over to him. Fremantle was impressed with the slave's earnestness and serious-

ness, as well as the "supreme contempt with which he spoke to his prisoner."[73] At another point about 20 servants, on their own initiative, made a
night raid on a Northern camp and captured a number of black laborers.[74]

One Confederate reported that when his regiment went into battle
their servants went in too, picking off Federal officers. During one
charge they found that a half-dozen blacks had actually preceded them,
and each brought back a black Federal prisoner. The Southerners kicked
and abused the Federals, saying:

> you black rascal you!—does you mean to fight agin white folks, you
> ugly niggers, you? Suppose you tinks yourselves no 'small taters' wid
> dat blue jacket on and dem striped pants. You'll oblige dis Missippi
> darkey by pulling dem off right smart, if yer doesn't want dat head o'y-
> ourn broke" said one of our cooks to his captive; "comin' down Souf
> To whip the whites! You couldn't stay 't home and let us fight de
> Yanks, but you must Come along too, eh! You took putty good care o'
> yourself, you did, behind dat ole oak! I was a lookin' at yer; and if you
> hadn't dodged so much, you was a gone chicken long ago, you ugley
> ole Abe Lincolnite, you![75]

And of course they were occasionally captured in battle by Union
troops. Hiram Conaway, a cook, was captured early in the war near Winchester, Va., and held until the end of the war.[76] Eli Dempsey of the 1st
North Carolina Artillery was captured in 1862 and held as a regular soldier until 1864.[77] Another servant said "I am proud of my war record."
He had been taken prisoner on two occasions, escaped, and returned to
his regiment with valuables that had been given to him for safekeeping.[78]
Robin, captured with his master during Morgan's raid into Ohio, was
imprisoned apart from him. Robin was offered his liberty several times
in exchange for taking an Oath of Loyalty. He refused, saying "I will
never disgrace my family by such an oath."[79] A number of servants captured at Vicksburg were offered their freedom with Federal protection,
but rejected the offers and chose instead to be sent to Northern prisons
with those they served.[80]

Since they were a part of the army, they were often drawn into battle.
Pompey Tucker was helping a doctor at Second Manassas when "a shell
blew off the head of the horse we were driving. Shrapnel from the same
shell wounded the doctor." They got separated, and Tucker searched for
the doctor while continuing to work with the wounded. A day and a half
later he found him as well as another white man from his home area,
both severely wounded. He found two horses, loaded them both in a
wagon and drove 15 miles to a railroad where he put them on a train

bound for Chimborazo Hospital in Richmond. Tucker went with the men, cared for them in the hospital and eventually helped the Confederate effort at home in Virginia, where "I helped the South by capturing six Yank guerrillas—three colored, three white—near Mortar Branch, hardly five miles from where I live now," he recalled.[81]

Occasionally the North's mistaken image of the black Southerner—that he could not possibly be expected to fight for the South—was used against them. A servant of Captain George Baylor of the 12th Virginia Cavalry lured an unsuspecting detachment of Yankees into a Confederate ambush.[82] Sam Collier had a similar experience. He had worked for his owner's nephew, and when Colonel Edwards was shot at Belmont in 1861 Collier took care of him. Decades later he remembered:

> When the Yankees came into Madison County, I hid Colonel Edwards' uniforms up in the attic. Then they came to our house that night, and Colonel Edwards told me to burn it up, so I slipped it out early the next morning before daylight and burned it up, so the Yankees could not see it, and find out that he had been in the Confederate Army.[83]

William Bibb had been a carriage driver and waiter for Algernon Bibb in Alabama. When Algernon organized a company in 1861, William went with him. In 1921 Algernon's widow testified that William "had screened his master from being captured by the Federals by joining with them and riding his master's horse for several hours and then made his escape back to Captain Bibb, riding a horse which had been presented his master by General Walker."[84] One black Southern woman was permitted because Northerners could not imagine a slave spying for the South, to frequently cross into Yankee territory. Called "Confederate Mary" by Northern troops, she secretly delivered messages for Confederate forces and smuggled medicine back into Southern lines.[85] Indeed, black spies were so common that U.S. Rear Admiral David Ammen noted that many of the slaves that had been driven away by Federal troops had returned to Confederate lines with accurate accounts of numbers and dispositions of National troops.[86]

Stories of servants caring for wounded masters abound. Anthony Watts of South Carolina stayed with his wounded master until he died, and then took the body home. Zack Brown was a servant of Robert Coleman, who was shot and taken to the hospital. Brown stayed with him as a nurse until they were captured. Jim Hampton summed up his experience and that of many black Confederates when he remembered that "Samuel Wilkes was killed in July (1862) and I came home with his body." When Captain Cothran of Orr's Rifles was wounded at Second Manassas, servant Wade Childs carried him on his back to the rear of the lines.[87] At Missionary Ridge a wounded 13th Tennessee private was carried by his body servant, Alf, four miles behind the lines. Alf took care of him for months, then returned to the war to work for his master's brother. Alf disappeared at the end of the war, but the three were reunited forty years later at a veteran's convention.[88] George Mills was at Big Bethel, Manassas, Seven Pines, Fair Oaks, Malvern Hill and Antietam with Captain William Bryson of Hendersonville, N.C. in Ransom's Brigade. Bryson was killed at Antietam. Mills put the body in a rough pine coffin and started off to North Carolina. In Fredericksburg, Va., he used some of the money Bryson had given him for safe keeping to ship the remains by rail to Greenville, Tennessee, where he hired a wagon and a white driver and finally reached home.[89] Henry Nelson told a similar story and added "that shows you I was a friend to the Southern army. I hid the meat from the yankees to keep them from taking everything we had."[90]

Alex Wharton served two brothers from Tennessee through the Atlanta campaign where both were wounded. Wharton took care of them and others at Chickamauga, Missionary Ridge, and Atlanta.[91]

Others actually took up arms and fought. When one white Confederate refused to go forward with his company at Mechanicsville, a servant named Westley came forward and asked permission to put on the deserted accouterments and took up the gun. He then went into action with the company "and though minie balls of the enemy were falling thick and fast about him, Westley never wavered, but brought down a Yankee at every fire," one of the men remembered.[92] A servant named Edward shot a Yankee soldier who had "made himself especially obnoxious" according to one Confederate Major.[93] Teen Blackburn, servant of Capt. Augustus Blackburn was at Manassas when the Captain got into trouble. Teen picked up a sword, fought off an oncoming Yankee, and thus saved his master's life.[94] One servant encountered a Federal soldier leading two horses; he shot the man, then led the horses into Confederate lines.[95] Another old vet remembered that his regiment's cooks "would not remain in camp, but marched out with the rest, and fought behind their masters." He remembered one man named Archie in particular, for he braved enemy fire to get water and ammunition on more than one occasion. The black Confederates, he recalled, "usually behaved like trumps."[96] It is recorded that at Seven Pines a cook and minister with an Alabama regiment got excited and in the midst of everything took up a rifle and went into battle. He was heard to yell at the regiment "De Lor' hab mercy on us all, boys, here dey comes agin! Dar it is," he exclaimed, as the Yankees fired over their heads, "just as I taught! Can't shoot worth

a bad five-cent piece. Now's de time, boys!" and as the Alabamians
returned a withering fire and mounted a furious charge, he was heard to
shout "Pitch in, White folks—Uncle Pomp's behind yer. Send all de Yankees to de 'ternal flames, whar dere's weeping and gnashing of-sail in
Alabama; stick 'em wid de bayonet, and send all de blue ornery cusses to
de state of eternal fire and brimstone!"[97]

Stories of servants actually fighting are numerous. One Confederate
officer recalled that his servant William, a strong 23-year-old and part
Indian, was six feet in height, and "when with me as bold as a lion,
having fought by my side in more than one affair."[98] Another officer
remembered that at Brandy Station "my negro servant Edmund, formed
the officers' servants and colored cooks in line immediately in the rear of
the regiment and flourishing an old saber over his head, took command
of them. As the troops moved into battle their servants went too, but
when the artillery shells started landing, they scattered in every direction."[99] At the same engagement, Tom and Overton, two servants in the
12th Virginia Cavalry, picked up rifles discarded by Northerners and
joined the 12th in a charge. They captured the black servant of a Union
officer and marched him back to camp at gunpoint, where they proceeded to hold him prisoner. For two months the Yankee servant waited
upon the Southerners.[100] Servant Levin Graham refused to stay behind
in camp when the time for battle came, instead grabbing a musket, he
"fought manfully" and "killed four of the Yankees."[101]

Even the cooks got into the action. Perhaps some of their enthusiasm comes through in the story related in terms common to the Civil
War era if not to ours. One veteran remembered that the cooks of his
company often joined in the fight:

> You might as well endeavor to keep ducks from water as to attempt to
> hold in the cooks of our company, when firing or fighting is on hand. In
> fact, an order has been frequently issued to keep darkies in the rear in
> time of battle, but although I lectured my boy about it, I was surprised
> to find him behind me at Manassas, rifle in hand, shouting out: "Go In,
> Massa! Give it to 'em, boys! Now you've got me, and give em H-ll!"[102]

And of course, many black Confederate servants were killed or
wounded. One recalled that servants started looking for their masters as
soon as they heard they were wounded, whether the fighting had ended
or not. Alfred Brown, a Surgeon's Assistant from Georgia, was often close
to the lines of battle, and was "wounded twice in one day" at Chickamauga. "A ball was shot through his left thigh and he was wounded in
the right leg by a piece of a . . . shell."[103] Hutson Longstreet, a servant for

four years, caught a bullet in the neck at Granada, Mississippi,[104] while Wade Watkins of Tennessee was shot in the right leg yet continued to serve the 48th Tennessee Cavalry throughout the rest of the war.[105] J. K. Knight of South Carolina was wounded at Petersburg, and Spencer Copeland had a foot amputated after injuring it while digging barefoot on the breastworks at Charleston.[106] Monroe Jones of the First Mississippi Light Artillery lost both legs at Snyder's Bluff near Vicksburg when a shell exploded.[107]

While body servants, cooks and others found their way into combat as circumstances dictated, other black Southerners enlisted, some officially and some surreptitiously, in regular units as individuals. Any estimate of the numbers involved will be merely a guess, though one reliable historian believes there were 3,000 from Louisiana alone.[108]

Perhaps the most numerous were the nameless individuals who took up the Southern cause. The first Northern officer killed in battle was Major Theodore Winthrop, member of an old, distinguished New England abolitionist family, shot by an unnamed black sniper at Big Bethel. He was a member of the Wythe Rifles of Hampton, Virginia, whose Captain had told him that the "Yankees would take you to Cuba and sell you. If you wish to stay with your wife and children, drive them out of Virginia."[109] General George H. Gordon, the man who ordered the charge at Battery Wagner, noted that "there was sharp picket firing from Wagner, in which many men from my command were killed, and strange stories were bruited about of the fatal precision and fire of a Negro marksman, a Rebel."[110] The Sheriff of Henderson County, North Carolina wrote a letter to a militia commander of his state asking him to bring all free blacks in his company in to check their papers.[111] A black artilleryman fired the last cannon shot at Federal forces as the Confederates abandoned the breastworks (built by slaves) at Yorktown in 1862.[112] William H. Dove and at least two others in the 5th North Carolina Cavalry was officially listed on the muster-rolls as "a free Negro—has no home."[113]

Numerous black Confederates enlisted and served as musicians. Henry Brown of Camden, South Carolina is probably a representative example. While his status at birth in 1830 is unclear, by 1861 he was a highly respected free Negro brickmason who joined a local defense unit, the Darlington Guards, as a drummer. He went with them to Charleston in 1861. After that unit disbanded he went to Virginia with Capt. W. H. Evans' company of the 8th South Carolina Infantry and later transferred to Capt. S. H. Wilds' company of the 21st South Carolina Infantry.[114] General John B. Gordon had Josepheus Black and two other musicians in his entourage,[115] and Charles McCuller served as a drummer in the 7th North

Carolina Cavalry ("Claiborne's Partisan Rangers") in 1864.[116] Another, "Old Dick" Slate, was a veteran of the Mexican War who enlisted as a drummer with the 18th Virginia Infantry in 1861. Along with fellow drummer George Price and fifer Austin Dix, all were listed as "free men of color." One Northerner who managed to observe Confederate troops on the march noted that "the only real music in their column today was from a bugle blown by a Negro. Drummers and fifers of the same color abound in their ranks."[117] James Clark, a free Negro born in Georgia enlisted at the age of 57 in Co. K, 28th Georgia Infantry and served as a fifer until 1865. Several members of his company testified that Clark had not been actually mustered in service but had joined on his own account and was paid by the members of the company for his services.[118] Charles Binger, a veteran of the Seminole War, signed on as a Fifer with the 2nd Georgia Infantry Battalion in May 1861 and served through the Seven Days and at Malvern Hill before being discharged in July 1862 at the age of 68![119] Indeed black musicians were so common that the Confederate Congress passed an act in 1862 providing that "whenever colored persons are employed as musicians in any regiment or company, they shall be entitled to the same pay now allowed by law to musicians regularly enlisted."[120]

Perhaps typical of the many who found their way into the army as individuals was Primus Kelly of Texas. Born a slave in North Carolina, Kelly moved to Texas before the war with the John W. S. West family. They settled in Grimes County, and became successful cotton planters. Kelly grew up with West's three sons, Robert, Richard, and John Jr. When the war came the three sons joined the 8th Texas Cavalry, part of Terry's Texas Rangers. On the day the regiment boarded a train in Houston to head East, Kelly showed up on his own and went with them. Being black, Kelly was prohibited from officially joining, and no official records carry his name. Yet he donned a gray uniform and carried a gun. Richard was wounded twice in battle, and each time Kelly carried him home to Texas. And each time when Richard returned to the war, Kelly went with him. At Woodsonville, Shiloh, Bardstown, Perryville, Murfreesboro, Chickamauga and Knoxville, all four members of the West family fought, black alongside white. After the war Primus Kelly returned to Texas, bought a small farm near his "brothers," and lived quietly until his death in 1890.[121]

In Sumter County, South Carolina, John Wilson Buckner grew up a free Negro, the son of a mulatto mother and black father. He was also the grandson of William Ellison, one of the most successful free blacks in antebellum America.[122] Ellison had been born a slave in 1791, probably the son of a black mother and white plantation owner. Ellison was trained as an artisan, making and repairing cotton gins. He was emancipated in

1816, and quickly went into business for himself. Between then and 1860 he developed a very successful cotton gin manufacturing and repair business and diversified into cotton planting. He eventually owned around 100 slaves and his family became a central part of a larger group of black slaveowners in and around Charleston. His two sons tried to join the Confederate service but were rejected, apparently on account of race. They did not, however, shrink from serving the South in other ways. Their chroniclers note that

> few planter families compiled a better war record than the Ellisons. They more than fulfilled every obligation the government imposed. As soon as the call went out, they quit growing cotton and began producing food crops. They supplied their neighbors and the rebel armies with provisions. They hired out their skilled slaves, apparently for war-related work. They paid all their taxes on time and invested their profits in government notes. Rather than slackers, the Ellisons were model Confederates.[123]

Despite being black, John Wilson Buckner joined the 1st South Carolina Artillery in March of 1863. He was wounded in action on July 12, 1863, at Battery Wagner, in the campaign that involved the 54th Massachusetts. His obituary noted that "he was always a freeman and at the breaking out of the war enlisted as a regular soldier in Capt. P. O. Gaillard's company. He served subsequently in Capt. Boykin's company and later as a scout. He was a faithful soldier . . ."[124]

There were many black Confederates in Louisiana, including one who fought at Gettysburg. For the story of Charles F. Lutz and the other black Confederates in Louisiana, see Arthur Bergeron's essay [reproduced in this volume on pages 361–68].

Blacks took part in every area of fighting. Hattie Carter was a female free Negro who served as an ammunition runner in Richmond throughout the war.[125] In Mississippi in 1861 or 1862, Elias, a slave belonging to Mr. Baber killed another named Jim. Elias was condemned to be hung. Instead he was given the option to go into the army and fight for the Confederacy. He was released and went into the army.[126] James Young enlisted in Company K, 29th Alabama as a Private in 1862 and stayed in the army until May of 1865, throughout the Atlanta campaign and at Bentonville, despite suffering from frostbitten feet. He was given a pension in 1902, but it was challenged in 1912 by the State Board of Pension Examiners because he was a Negro. In Young's favor a Judge wrote that Young had served in the 29th Alabama and that "he not only deserves the pension for actual fighting service rendered, but as he is now almost eighty years old, he deserves to be advanced into a higher class."[127]

Numerous other blacks in Alabama also receive pensions for their service.[128] Similarly Tom Bing served as a private in Colcock's Regiment of
South Carolina troops under Capt. Bill Peeples for the entire war.[129] Phil
Reese and George Dance served in the 18th Tennessee and "remained
with the Army until the surrender."[130]

Some black Confederates seemed to have a felicity for use of the rifle.
Several accounts of black Confederate sharpshooters exist. The appearance
of one during the Peninsula Campaign in 1862, firing at members of
Hiram Berdan's First U.S. Sharpshooters caught the imagination of the
unit's historian. His account deserves extensive quotation:

> For a considerable time during the siege the enemy had a Negro rifle
> shooter in their front who kept up a close fire on our men, and,
> although the distance was great, yet he caused more or less annoyance
> by his persistent shooting. On one occasion while at the advanced posts
> with a detail, the writer with his squad had an opportunity to note the
> skill of this determined darky with his well aimed rifle. Being stationed
> at a pit on the edge of a wood fronting the treeless stretch of ground
> around the opposing works, with sand bags piled up for cover, during
> the forenoon this rebellious black made his appearance by the side of an
> officer and under his direction commenced firing at us. For a long time
> this chance shooting was kept up, the black standing out in plain view
> and cool drawing bead, but failed to elicit any response, our orders
> being to lie quiet and not be seen. So the Negro had the shooting all to
> himself, his pop, pop, against the sand bags on the edge of the pit often
> occurring, while other close shots among the trees showed plainly that
> he was a good shot at long range. He became pretty well known among
> the scouts and pickets, and had established quite a reputation for marks-
> manship, before he came to grief. Emboldened by his having pretty
> much all this promiscuous shooting unopposed, the pickets rarely firing
> at him, he began to work at shorter distance, taking advantage of the
> ground and scattering trees. This was what our men wanted, to get him
> within more reasonable range, not caring to waste ammunition trying
> to cripple him at the long distance he had at first been showing himself.
> They wanted to make sure of him. In the meantime our boys would
> when opportunity offered, without being seen, post a man forward to
> await in concealment for the adventurous darky. The scheme succeeded
> and his fate was sealed. A scouting party was sent out, cornered the black
> sharpshooter in a chimney top a quarter of a mile in front of their lines,
> and shot him.[131]

A similar account around the same time claims that another black
sharpshooter "had done more injury to our men than any dozen of his
white peers . . ." He perched in a big tree, behind its trunk and shot at

Yankees in front of Yorktown. At one point he was nearly surrounded, and a Federal supposedly shouted at him: "I say, big nigger, you better come down from there." When told that he had been captured he replied "not as this chile knows of" and resumed firing, whereupon he was quickly shot through the head.

Finally, black Confederates served in the Navy as well as the Army. When the CSS *Shenandoah* arrived in Liverpool in November of 1865, one black seaman, Edward Weeks, was on board, and thus became one of the last Confederates of any color to cease fighting. At least two seamen were carried on the rolls as "Private(col'd)."[132] In one of the three photographs of the CSS *Alabama* a black crewman can be seen peering out at the camera from behind and between two officers.[133] At least three free blacks served as sailors aboard the CSS *Chicora* under Commander Ingraham in the defense of Charleston.[134] The Savannah squadron apparently had several black seamen, the most famous of which was Moses Dallas. He joined the Federal army for a short period but soon deserted and joined the Savannah squadron where he became "the best inland pilot on the coast," and drew praise and pay increases because of his effectiveness. On the night of June 2–3, 1864, he led a party of 132 Confederates on an attack that succeeded in sinking a Federal gunboat in Ossabaw Sound at the mouth of the Ogeechee River. He guided the raiders up to the USS *Water Witch*, and in the ensuing battle apparently was killed, or so it was officially reported. Three months later he quietly reappeared in a blue uniform. He ended up as a Corporal in the 128th U.S. Colored Infantry.[135]

Black Southerners supported the Confederate war effort not only as servants, as individuals in regularly enlisted white units, but also in units that were composed entirely, or almost entirely, of blacks, both free and bonded. These fall naturally into three categories. The first category are units for which our knowledge is exclusively anecdotal. The second category are units of regularly-enlisted black Southerners who were usually free. The all-black units of slaves raised by the Confederate government in March and April 1865 make up a third category.

At least three units of black Confederates were seen during the war, far enough apart in space and time that they cannot be confused with one another. In August of 1861 a Federal officer observed a group he called the "Richmond Howitzer Battery" new Newport News, Virginia that was manned by blacks.[136] A correspondent from the *New York Times* riding with Ulysses S. Grant reported in 1863 on a black artillery crew in Tennessee. "The guns of the rebel battery were manned almost wholly by Negroes," he noted, with "a single white man, or perhaps two, directing operations."[137] An Indiana soldier wrote a letter to his hometown newspaper about an exchange of fire with a group of black Confederates in the Fall of 1861. The story which was then reprinted all over the North:

> . . . a body of seven hundred Negro infantry opened fire on our men, wounding two lieutenants and two privates. The wounded men testify positively that they were shot by Negroes, and that not less than seven hundred were present, armed with muskets. This is, indeed, a new feature in the war. We have heard of a regiment of Negroes and Manassas, and another at Memphis, and still another at New Orleans, but did not believe it till it came so near home and attacked our men . . . One of the lieutenants was shot in the back of the neck and is not expected to live.[138]

These units could have been free or bonded men, like those described by John Parker, a slave who was pressed into service as an artilleryman at First Manassas. He had been a fieldhand on a large plantation. The master went off to war in 1861, followed soon by the overseer. He had been sent to work on earthworks around Fredericksburg, Winchester, and Richmond. He records the black population's excitement grew as the battle neared, when "all the colored people" were sent off to the front lines to fight. "I arrived at the Junction two days before the action commenced," he recalled.

> They immediately placed me in one of the batteries. There were four colored men in our battery, I don't know how many there were in the others. We opened fire about ten o'clock in the morning of Sunday the 21st; couldn't see the Yankees at all and only fired at random. Sometimes they were concealed in the woods and then we guessed our aim . . . My work was to hand the balls and swab out the cannon; in this we took turns. The officers aimed this gun; we fired grape shot. The balls from the Yankee guns fell thick all around. In one battery a shell burst and killed twenty, the rest ran. I felt bad all the time, and thought every minute my time would come; I felt so excited that I hardly knew what I was about, and felt worse than dead.[139]

Perhaps more noteworthy, and certainly more well-known to historians, were the units of free blacks who enlisted together. As we have already seen, black Confederate musicians abounded throughout the Southern armies, and at least one Confederate brigade had an all-black or predominantly black band. McCreary's 1st South Carolina Infantry had such a group, for we are able even now to name 14 of its members. All were listed as "free persons of color" except one, William Rose, a slave who apparently ran away from his master to join the Confederate army.[140] They were listed on the muster-rolls of each company, apparently serving the company as drummers and fifers, then switching to other instruments as appropriate for regimental and brigade-level occasions. Two of the men who enlisted in this group were blind, and one served six months before he dropped out.[141] The band served as the regimental band for McGowan's brigade, a unit that fought through the entire war with the Army of Northern Virginia, including Gettysburg.[142]

The Sixth Louisiana Cavalry had at least nine blacks in its ranks, and probably many more. Most of what we know comes from pension records filled out decades after the war ended. The men were all from the area around Campti, in Bossier Parish, and apparently joined Capt. Thomas W. Fuller's Bossier Cavalry company in April, 1862, soon becoming Company H, Sixth Louisiana. There were mulattos who "lived white, in almost all respects," recalled one descendant. There was "hardly any aspects of Campti life or society . . ." in which they "were not freely accepted. Almost all of the old [white] Campti families were their relatives and freely acknowledged it."[143]

The free black residents of New Orleans had a large, vibrant subculture, one with a long history of military service to their colony and state. Blacks had been a part of the Louisiana militia since the 1720s. They had fought against pirates in 1727, and later both slaves and free blacks had helped the French against the Choctaw Indians and in other wars. When the Spanish took over the area in the 1760s they continued to depend upon black militia. Don Bernando de Galvez marched them against the English forts at Natchez and Baton Rouge in 1779 and even more slaves and free blacks joined Galvez's army when it captured Pensacola in 1780. After the U.S. purchase in 1803 blacks still served in Louisiana, it being the only state where black participation was permitted it the early part of the century. They helped suppress a slave revolt in 1811 and at least two companies were with Andrew Jackson in the Battle of New Orleans.[144] Another source lists several units of "free men of color" in the Louisiana militia in the War of 1812.[145]

The Louisiana Native Guards were a direct result of the "monster rally" of free people of color in April of 1861. On May 12 Governor Thomas O. Moore issued a proclamation providing for the enrollment of free blacks in an all-black regiment with some black officers. Their mission was the defense of New Orleans and by early 1862 approximately 3,000 men had joined this regiment and assorted other units in and around New Orleans. Their officers were skilled tradesmen, craftsmen, and even a few slaveowners. While the exact racial heritage of all officers is not known, the majority were apparently mulattos with substantial influence in the community. Capt. Noel Bachus, 40, was a carpenter and landowner; Capt. Michael Duphart was a 62-year-old wealthy shoemaker, and Lt. André Callioux was a cigarmaker, a boxer, and had the reputation of being "the blackest man in New Orleans." (He joined the Union forces after the surrender of New Orleans and was killed leading a charge at Milliken's Bend). There were several sets of fathers and sons and also sets of brothers in the regiment, and all the males in the large Duphart family were members. Like most Southern militia regiments early in the war they provided all their own uniforms and equipment.[146]

However, they apparently weren't well provided for. One of the few existing documents, a morning report for January 10, 1862, records many absences due to lack of uniforms.[147] On the other hand, there are several accounts of them on parade in New Orleans fully armed and in complete, gray uniforms. "We must pay a deserved compliment to the companies of free colored men, all very well drilled, and comfortably uniformed," said the *New Orleans Picayune*. "Most of these companies, quite unaided by the administration, have supplied themselves with arms without regard to cost or trouble. One of these companies, commanded by the well-known veteran, Capt. Jordan, was presented, a little before the parade, with a fine war flag of the new style."[148]

The rolls in the National Archives list 1,307 men, including officers.[149] While their service was mostly relegated to guard duty in New Orleans, including serving as Provost Guards,[150] there is some indication that at least part of the regiment saw action at Fort Jackson during the New Orleans campaign.[151] As Federal troops approached and captured New Orleans in 1862, the Native Guards refused to abandon the city and surrendered. No parole or surrender documentation is available.

A community of free blacks was founded in the early 18th century in the area southeast of Natchitoches, Louisiana, between the Cane and Red Rivers.[152] The area is known as the Isle Brevelle, and has some of the richest farm land in the South. The forebearer was a mulatto woman who had been a lover of a white plantation owner and was given her freedom in the mid-18th Century. By the Civil War her descendants had grown to several hundred people in several families, with the Metoyer family as more or less the pole around which the rest clustered. These hard-working, industrious people had built several fine mansions along the rivers and had developed large cotton plantations totaling some 15,000 acres. Owners of nearly four hundred slaves, they hired private tutors for their children and built a Catholic Church which served the community. On a Sunday one could attend the church and witness black people sitting in the front pews with whites in the rear. They were a quiet, soft-spoken people and visitors often commented on their "gentlemanly manners," describing them as "honest and industrious, and . . . good citizens in all respects." By 1860 they felt themselves separated from their slaves by class, economics, education, religion and even race. They regarded themselves as a "third race," neither white nor black. When the war came they concluded that a Northern victory would be a disaster for them, and would probably bring the end of their status and destroy their property and prosperity. They felt no special kinship nor feelings for their slaves, and indeed actively opposed abolitionism.

When the news of Fort Sumter came they were elated and loudly proclaimed their Confederate patriotism. Throughout the war they provided Southern troops with tons of forage and sent many of their slaves off to build earthworks for defense of the Red River. They quickly organized their own local defense force, including two companies of all black men. The Augustin Guards, named for a patriarch, Augustin Metoyer, had one white officer. Like the Native Guards, they too supplied their own horses, uniforms, and arms. The Monet Guards, a company of infantry, were named after another family in the Isle. Unfortunately no official documentation of these groups has survived, so we know neither the names of all the men nor their exact number. However, if the best estimate of the historian most knowledgeable about them is correct, the two companies enrolled about 150 men, which was virtually the entire adult male population of the community.[153]

They took their work seriously, and apparently became good cavalrymen. An observer from a local newspaper noted:

> The squadron of cavalry, so skillfully trained by Dr. Bordin, their uniformity and precision were admirable. The firm commands and good cadence of the captain [*sic*], also that of the officers, the intelligent enthusiasm produced by all the soldiers; the excellent horsemanship by the squadron; all contributed to amaze the public who had come to attend these maneuvers. For us who have often attended cavalry drills in Europe, we wonder how, in so little time, these men have been able to attain this degree of perfection. The company of infantry, newly formed, has need of practice, but we are convinced that having a little, their drills will be executed with as much precision as in the cavalry.[154]

The writer also reported that the cavalry drilled by setting up a dummy with the name "Abe Lincoln" on its chest and attacking it with sabers.

The Augustin Guards volunteered their services to the Confederacy but were rejected because of their race. They continued to drill and in May 1862 were making plans to help defend New Orleans when it was captured. They kept together until early 1864 but apparently saw no combat. Their white officer died just before the Union began its Red River campaign, and the Guards never reorganized. When Banks moved up the river the Guards came together one night, but, due to squabbles amongst themselves, were not able to offer any resistance. The Union troops noticed the existence of a people they thought were peculiar—quiet and reserved—and burned their plantations and crops anyway.[155]

In May of 1861 the free Negro planters of the area around Point Coupee, Louisiana, organized a volunteer home guard quite similar to those of Natchitoches, and elected Colonel F. L. Claiborne as their commanding officer. Their company numbered 80 men, "the flower of that description in the state." Claiborne spoke highly of them, calling them my "dragoon company of brave quadroons."[156]

Black Southerners in Mobile, Alabama, also took part in the defense of that city. As early as 1862 a citizen had written to the Government that he felt he could organize a regiment of "creoles"—the term for people of mixed-blood. He noted that:

> all of them are free under the treaty with France by which Louisiana was acquired. They are mostly property-holders, owning slaves, and a peacable, orderly class, and capable of doing good service. They are as true to the South as the pure white race. As yet none of them have gone to war, but have been anxious to do so. If such a battalion or regiment can be received, I can raise it in a few days.[157]

In fact, by 1862 black Confederates were already organized and working actively on the defenses. In April of that year the *Mobile Evening News* carried the following notice:

> Creole Guards—Attention:
>   Attend a drill of your Company this evening at 7½ O'clock.
>   —By Order
>   Jerome Barnard, O.S.(PA)[158]

In November 1862 the state of legislature of Alabama passed an act authorizing the raising of troops of "mixed blood . . . commonly known as creoles" for the defense of the city and county of Mobile.[159] They were to have white officers.[160] Major General Dabney H. Maury had written to Adjutant General and Inspector General Samuel Cooper, the Confederacy's senior officer, asking to enlist creoles in Confederate service as artillerymen in defense of Mobile. He noted that "they were very anxious to enter Confederate service" and that he believed they were "admirably qualified" to be artillerymen. Cooper sent the letter to the Secretary of War James A. Seddon. Seddon, in a sort of written wink, indicated the problems involved and how to get around them. "Our position with the North and before the world will not allow the employment as armed soldiers of Negroes," he wrote, However, "If these creoles can be naturally and properly discriminated from Negroes, the authority may be considered as conferred; otherwise not, unless you can enlist them as 'navvies' (to use the English term) or for subordinate working purposes."[161] In other words, if Cooper could call them something other than blacks, he could go ahead. Apparently, he did, because in August of 1864 the Confederate commander of Mobile formed a special unit of cavalry with some blacks in it, and in October he ordered the city to enlist creoles and free blacks. An artillery unit was formed in 1864 and another in the Spring of 1865. At least one company of Native Guards was formed in the Spring of 1865. The commander was the Assistant Chief of Police and the other officers were Creoles.[162] Thus it appears that at least five different units of black troops were active in Mobile.

In March of 1865, after several months of official debate, the Confederate government finally began actively recruiting and enlisting black soldiers. The Confederacy had steadfastly opposed enrolling blacks in the armed services except as servants and laborers. In addition to the race question, early in the war it was felt that there were more than enough white Southerners to whip the Yankees. By the middle of the war, as the clamor grew, Jefferson Davis and others believed, as Seddon had said, that the foundation of the Southern theory of the racial superiority of whites would crumble if blacks were allowed to enlist. As Howell Cobb, a powerful Georgia planter and politician, and perhaps the richest man in his state, said, "If slaves will make good soldiers our whole theory of slavery is wrong . . ."[163]

But as the bloodbath of 1864 dragged on and Southern troops melted away from desertion as well as the fighting, more white voices were heard in favor of black Confederates.[164] In early 1865 Robert E. Lee himself publicly advocated the enlistment of black troops, and in March the Confederate Congress authorized the Administration to raise 300,000 new troops "irrespective of color." General Ordinance No. 14 went on the say that "no slave will be accepted as a recruit unless with his own consent and with the approbation of his master by a written instrument conferring, as far as he may, the rights of freedom . . ."[165] In the end, even Howell Cobb changed his mind and came out in favor of black Confederates. His son offered to raise a company from the family's plantations and even send a white overseer along as an officer.[166]

Several messages were sent out authorizing individuals to begin raising black troops,[167] and soon drilling was taking place. Indeed, on the day that the act was passed, "two companies [of black Confederate] were seen parading with a battalion . . ." Another witness recorded that "the streets of Richmond were filled with 10,000 Negroes who had been gathered at Camp Lee on the outskirts of Richmond. Negroes were armed and placed in trenches near Richmond."[168] A Camp of Instruction was established near the Alabama River,[169] and two blacks in Confederate uniform were arrested in Richmond and held until a white officer secured their release.[170]

As pointed out previously, some black Southerners had spent the entire war supporting the Confederacy in numerous laboring roles in the infrastructure, and now they began to make the transition from support to combat. Thomas Morris Chester, a black newspaper correspondent from Philadelphia, was near Richmond at this time and interviewed several blacks soon after the fall of the city. He recorded that they were abuzz with a discussion of how they should react to the call to arms, and that "after a cordial exchange of opinions it was decided with great unanimity, and finally ratified by all the auxiliary associations everywhere, that black men should promptly respond to the call of the rebel chiefs, whenever it should be made, for them to take up arms."[171] Richmond's vast hospitals were a prime source of recruits. One writer observed that "the Battalion from Camps Winder and Jackson, under the command of Dr. Chambliss, will parade on the square on Wednesday evening at 4½ O'clock. This is the first company of Negro Troops raised in Virginia," he noted. "It was organized about a month since, by Dr. Chambliss, from the employees of the hospitals and served on the lines during the recent Sheridan raid."[172] Another company raised by Major J. W. Turner was drilled daily in Richmond by Lt. Virginius Bossieux. On March 27 the *Richmond Examiner* reported that the company numbered 35 men, with new members coming in every day. The men were busily recruiting their friends, and it seemed that "the knowledge of the military art they already exhibit was something remarkable. They moved with evident pride and satisfaction to themselves. Their quarters in the rendezvous are neat, clean, warm and comfortable. Their rations are cooked in Libby Prison."[173]

Thus a few black Southerners finally saw combat in authorized Confederate units in 1865. Not only did Chambliss' regiment fight against Sheridan, but other units were noted at various points in the retreat to Appomattox. A Lieutenant in this regiment noted that "my men acted with the utmost promptness and good will . . . Allow me to state, Sir, that they behaved in an extraordinary suitable manner."[174] A Virginia private watched as one unit guarded a wagon train during the retreat. They were attacked by Yankee cavalry, but fired their rifles rapidly and successfully fought them off. The blue horsemen retreated and reformed on a nearby hillside, then proceeded to charge down on the wagon train, overrun, and capture the black Confederates.[175] A courier reported that on April 4 he saw black Confederates working on breastworks. "All wore good gray uniforms and I was informed that they belonged to the only company of colored troops in the Confederate service, having been enlisted by Major Turner in Richmond. Their muskets were stacked, and it was evident that they regarded their present employment in no very favorable light."[176]

In an action on April 7 the 108th New York Infantry captured an armed black Confederate. His name was Tom Brophy, and the Northern soldiers, rather than sending him to prison, made him their servant. He stayed with them until the regiment was disbanded, and then went North with them. He became a well-known resident of a small town in New York, where he died in 1888.[177]

The Southern armies that marched into Pennsylvania in 1863 and retreated to Atlanta in 1864 contained a good many black Southerners, marching as servants, as individual soldiers, and in black units. As C. Vann Woodward said, it is impossible to imagine any aspect of Southern society without them, and quite futile to try. Others have understood this, including British Colonel Arthur Fremantle. He traveled with the Army of Northern Virginia in 1863, and a comment he made might provide a fitting conclusion to this story. One does not have to agree with his reading of the motivations of black Southerners or the nature of their relationships with whites to appreciate his observations about their combat potential and the resistance of those in power in the Confederate government. From what he had seen of black Southerners,

> I am of the opinion that the Confederates could, if they chose, convert a great number into soldiers; and from the affection which undoubtably exists as a general rule between the slaves and their masters, I think that they would prove more efficient than black troops under any other circumstances. But I do not imagine such an experiment will be tried, except as a very last resort.[178]

Fremantle had correctly foreseen the future. As Lee retreated to Appomattox, and Johnston to North Carolina, their wagons were driven by blacks, and in them black Southerners rode as servants, caring for wounded white, and black, Confederate soldiers.

CHAPTER 26

General Patrick Cleburne's Proposal
to Arm Southern Slaves

Barbara C. Ruby

MAJOR GENERAL PATRICK RONAYNE CLEBURNE of the Army of the Confederate States of America was among the first to cogently suggest the use of slaves as soldiers in the armed forces of the South. Cleburne was one of the most respected military leaders of the Civil War, and his contemporaries would undoubtedly be shocked to discover that historians have virtually ignored him. While only touching upon his brilliant military career, this paper will examine General Cleburne's plan to recruit slaves into the Southern armed forces and his motivations to present such a plan, for both Cleburne's ideas and the reactions of others to them reveal much about what individuals in the South were fighting for and much about people's conceptions of the Negro at that time.

Pat Cleburne was born on March 17, 1828, just outside the city of Cork, Ireland. The son of a doctor, he became apprenticed to a druggist but failed the language exams for Apothecaries' Hall, Trinity College in Dublin. Cleburne was so ashamed of his failure that he left home and enlisted in the 41st Regiment of the Irish Infantry, his family and friends having no idea of his whereabouts for over a year. In 1849, three years after his enlistment, Cleburne purchased his discharge and migrated to America with a sister and two half-brothers. After six months in Cincinnati as a druggist's clerk, Cleburne moved to Helena, Arkansas, where he held a similar position. The owner of the drug store, Dr. Charles E. Nash, who became a close friend of the young clerk, and soon made him a business partner, recalled. "Cleburne was one of the most fastidious young men I ever knew. When a lady would come into the store to purchase an article, he would blush up to his eyelashes."[1] Despite this "social handicap," Cleburne became an extremely popular citizen of Helena, and there are several emotion-filled stories of his nursing the sick during a yellow fever epidemic and of being gravely wounded in a street fight while trying to aid a friend, Thomas C. Hindman.[2] (Hindman also became a Confederate general, and his connection with Cleburne's proposal for the arming of slaves will be pointed out later. It is interesting to note that the town of Helena contributed seven generals to the Confederate cause.)

Cleburne read law in his spare time and was admitted to the bar in 1856. He was a strong Whig supporter upon arriving in Helena, but became a Democrat after the Whigs went over to the Know-Nothings, with their anti-foreign persuasions.[3] In the summer of 1860, Cleburne joined a military company formed in Helena called the Yell Rifles and participated in the seizure of the United States arsenal at Little Rock in January 1861. When the Arkansas Military Board called for troops in the spring of 1861, Cleburne entered the state's service as a private. He was soon made a captain and, in May of 1861, was chosen colonel of the 15th Arkansas Regiment of Infantry.

Two letters written to his half-brother Robert indicate why Pat Cleburne joined the Southern military forces. Cleburne made it clear that he was not battling for the preservation of slavery, but for what he understood to be the rights of states as guaranteed by the Constitution. In the first letter, probably written in April 1861, Cleburne remarked that tensions were so high that the "first blood shed on Southern soil in a collision between the Federal troops and the State authorities of any Southern State will be the signal for a civil war which must ultimately array the fifteen Southern states against the Northern states." "As to my own position," he continued,

> I hope to see the Union preserved by granting to the South the full measure of her constitutional rights. If this cannot be done I hope to see all the Southern states united in a new confederation and that we can effect a peaceable separation. If bother these are denied us, I am with Arkansas in weal or in woe.[4]

In a letter dated May 7, 1861, Cleburne exclaimed, "I am with the South in life or in death, in victory or in defeat. I never owned a negro and care nothing of them, but these people have been my friends and have stood by me on all occasions."[5]

Cleburne served as a division commander under General W. J. Hardee's corps of the Army of Tennessee from late 1861 until the fall of 1864, and the historian Thomas Hay has concluded that by the time Cleburne issued his memorial on the recruitment of slaves in January of 1864, he "had acquired an enviable reputation as an efficient and capable officer and as a gallant and daring leader."[6] The *Dictionary of American Biography* summarizes his military career up to that time as follows:

> Early in 1862 he was made a brigadier-general. At Shiloh he won commendation for his valor and skill. He was wounded while leading his men in a fierce charge at Richmond, Ky., but was nevertheless able to participate in the battle of Perryville. On Dec. 12, 1862, he was made a major-general and a few days later showed at Murfreesboro that the confidence of his superiors had not been misplaced. But his most distinguished service was during the fighting around Chattanooga; at Chickamauga his men captured and held a position which had resisted several other attacks, and at Missionary Ridge he repulsed Sherman. At Ringgold Gap, at his own peril, he saved Bragg's artillery and wagon train from capture by pursuing the enemy for which he received a vote of thanks from the Confederate Congress.[7]

Only words of praise have been used to describe General Cleburne's accomplishments as a military leader. Jefferson Davis labeled him the "Stonewall Jackson of the West" and Colonel James Cooper Nisbet, in his memoirs, repeatedly referred to Cleburne as the "Wizard of War." Thomas Hay has remarked that Cleburne "made his division what it was, a well drilled and well disciplined force, able and willing at all times and under all conditions and circumstances, to carry out the directives of its commander."[8] General Basil W. Duke recalled:

> I cannot remember that I ever saw an officer who was so industrious and persistent in his efforts properly to drill and instruct the men under his command. He took great interest in everything connected with tactics, and personally taught it all, and was occupied from morning until night in superintending . . . everything mentioned in the books or that he could conceive of. I have seen him during the hottest hours of the hottest days in August instruct squad after squad in the bayonet exercise until I wondered how any human frame could endure the fatigue that his exertions must have induced.[9]

The historian Ella Lonn has noted that the:

> verdict of military authorities seems to be that as a division commander he had no superior. His officers and men alike had implicit confidence in him, and therefore his orders were obeyed promptly and unquestioningly, a

factor which was one of the elements in his success. That success was so uniform that as the war dragged on friend and foe learned to look for the position in battle of his distinctive blue and white battle flag. "Cleburne is here!" meant to the Confederates that all was well.[10]

The humiliating defeat of Confederate forces at Missionary Ridge in the Chattanooga campaign of late November 1863 was followed by General Cleburne's courageous stand at Ringgold Gap and the retreat of the bulk of the army to Dalton, Georgia, where winter headquarters were set up. Cleburne's division was stationed several miles north at Tunnel Hill on outpost. While in winter quarters, Cleburne, "ever alive to the necessity of improving the discipline and efficiency of his command," built a log hut to serve as a school where he could instruct his brigade commanders in warfare and they, in turn, could teach regimental and company commanders.[11]

Cleburne was well aware of the serious depletion of the Confederate ranks, a depletion which was worsening as the enlistment terms of the three-year men began to expire. Most of Cleburne's division were residents of Arkansas and Texas, from where no communications could be received because of the Federal gunboats that patrolled the Mississippi. As General W. H. Hardee related:

> Many of these men had not heard from their homes and wives and little ones for three years. To add to this, the occasional reports received from the Trans-Mississippi were but repeated narratives of the waste and ravages of their homes by the Federal soldiery. No husband could know that his wife was not homeless, no father that his children were not starving. Every instinct that appeals most powerfully and most sacredly to manhood called upon these men to return to their homes as soon as they could do so honorably. Cleburne was a man of warm sympathies, and he felt profoundly the extent of the sacrifice his men were called upon to make; but . . . he set high above all other earthly considerations the achievement of Southern independence. He adapted himself to the peculiar conditions of a volunteer soldiery, and, laying aside the commander, he appealed to his men as a comrade to give up everything else and stand by the cause and the country. He succeeded in inspiring them with his own high purposes and exalted patriotism. . . . [12]

Cleburne persuaded about ninety percent of his men to re-enlist, but few other divisions were as successful.

This was not the first time that Cleburne had shown a deep concern about the depletion of the Confederate army. He was one of eighteen generals who signed a memorial sent to General Samuel Cooper, Confederate

Adjutant and Inspector General, on July 25, 1863. The signers stated they were "deeply impressed with the belief that unless the ranks are speedily replenished our cause will be lost," and asked President Davis to step up recruitment either by enlarging state quotas or by having the Confederate Congress reduce draft exemptions. They pointedly remarked that "in the vain hope of saving the people at home from transient annoyances and privations we are endangering the liberties of the country."[13]

It was this same "conscientious, almost fanatical devotion"[14] to duty and to the South which led Pat Cleburne to compose, in December of 1863, his memorial, later described by his friend and biographer Captain Irving A. Buck as "one of the most remarkable documents of the war."[15] Before discussing the opinions of Cleburne's contemporaries regarding his memorial on arming the slaves, it would be well to examine the ideas presented in the document.

Cleburne first noted that three years of bloody warfare had left the South "nothing but long lists of dead and mangled," and that the Confederate soldiers were now "sinking into a fatal apathy."[16] He tried to convey just what the apparently-impending defeat of the South would bring.

> It means that the history of this heroic struggle will be written by the enemy; that our youth will be trained by Northern school teachers; will learn from Northern school books their version of the war; will be impressed by all the influences of history and education to regard our gallant dead as traitors, our maimed veterans as fit objects for derision.[17]

Cleburne felt there were three factors contributing toward the downfall of the South. The first was "the inferiority of our armies to those of the enemy in point of numbers."[18] Not only was the United States drafting more and more whites, but it was "'training an army of 100,000 negroes as good as any troops'" and gaining more potential Negro forces with each piece of Southern land that was conquered. This was related to the second factor which Cleburne saw leading to a Southern defeat: "the poverty of our single source of supply in comparison with his several sources."[19] While the South could turn only to those fit white men who were not already serving, the enemy had "First, his own motley population; secondly, our slaves; and thirdly, Europeans whose hearts are fired into a crusade against us by fictitious pictures of the atrocities of slavery, and who meet no hindrance from their Governments in such enterprise, because these Governments are equally antagonistic to the institution."[20] This, in turn, was related to the third significant factor, "the fact that slavery, from being one of our chief sources of strength at the commencement of the war, has now become, in a military point of view, one of our chief sources of weakness."[21] Not only did slavery alienate potentially friendly European nations, but

> wherever slavery is once seriously disturbed, whether by the actual presence of the approach of the enemy, or even by a cavalry raid, the whites can no longer with safety to their property openly sympathize with our cause. The fear of their slaves is continually haunting them, and from silence an apprehension many of these soon learn to wish the war stopped on any terms.[22]

Cleburne commented that any area with a slave to be set free was a vulnerable area of the South. He noted the value of slaves to the North as a source of information, describing slavery as "an omnipresent spy system."[23]

President Davis had realized that insufficient military forces were contributing to Southern defeats and incomplete successes, and on December 8, 1863, had ordered that the armed forces be supplemented by "restoring to the army all who are improperly absent, putting an end to substitution, modifying the exemption in law, restricting details, and placing in the ranks such of the able-bodied men now employed as wagoners, nurses, cooks, and other employees, as are doing service for which the negroes may be found competent."[24] While this seemed to be a positive response to the memorial requesting more manpower which Cleburne had signed in July of 1863, in this December memorial, Cleburne rejected Davis' plan as providing only a temporary source of relief.

General Cleburne then suggested that to

> adequately . . . meet the causes which are now threatening ruin to our country, we propose, in addition to a modification of the President's plans, that we retain in service for the war all troops now in service, and that we immediately commence training a large reserve of the most courageous of our slaves, and further that we guarantee freedom within a reasonable time to every slave in the South who shall remain true to the Confederacy in this war. As between the loss of independence and the loss of slavery, we assume that every patriot will freely give up the latter—give up the negro slave rather than be a slave himself. If we are correct in this assumption it only remains to show how this great national sacrifice is, in all human probabilities, to change the current of success and sweep the invader from our country.[25]

Cleburne then proceeded to discuss the advantage he felt would accrue from this plan to recruit slaves and to free those loyal to the South. Among the results he foresaw were a growing sympathy of the nations of the world for the South and moral and material support from Britain and

France, support which he felt had previously been withheld because it would have appeared these nations were backing slavery. Cleburne felt that if the United States continued to wage war against the South after this offer of emancipation, foreigners would see the war as an attempt to repress a movement for independence and not as a philanthropic effort to emancipate the slave; these aliens would no longer see any reason to fight for the North. Nor would the Negro in the North or the South have any reason to aid the Northern war effort.[26] To quote Cleburne:

> The chronic irritation of hope deferred would be joyfully ended with the negro, and the sympathies of his whole race would be due to his native South. It would restore confidence in an early termination of the war with all its inspiring consequences, and even if contrary to all expectations the enemy should succeed in over-running the South, instead of finding a cheap, ready-made means of holding it down, he would find a common hatred and thirst for vengeance, which would break into acts at every favorable opportunity, would prevent him from settling on our lands, and render the South a very unprofitable conquest. It would remove forever all selfish taint from our cause and place independence above every question of property. The very magnitude of the sacrifice itself, such as no nation has ever voluntarily made before, would appal [*sic*] our enemies, destroy his spirit and his finances, and fill our hearts with a pride and singleness of purpose which would clothe us with new strength in battle.[27]

Besides, Cleburne pointed out, more men were desperately needed, and only by arming the Negro could a sufficient number of men be obtained; and if the slave were to fight for the South, it was only right that his race be freed. "It is a first principle with mankind that he who offers his life in defense of the State should receive from her in return his freedom and his happiness, and we believe in the acknowledgement of this principle"[28]

General Cleburne also tried to counter several arguments he foresaw arising against his plan of emancipation. To those who held that slavery was essential to a republican form of government, he held that he preferred any form of government, created by the South, to "one forced upon us by a conqueror."[29] Replying to the idea that the Negroes were needed to work the fields, he stated, "it would be better to take half the able bodied men off a plantation than to take the one master mind that economically regulated its operations."[30] Cleburne also interestingly remarked that after the war, slaves would be compelled to work for a living through "necessity and a wise legislation."[31] Continued Cleburne, "It is said slavery is all we are fighting for, and if we give it up we give up all. Even if this were true, which we deny, slavery is not all our enemies are fighting for. It is merely the pretense to establish sectional superiority and a more central-ized form of government, and to deprive us of our rights and liberties."[32] Cleburne made it quite clear in his memorial that it was time for the South to choose between independence and slavery, and prophetically ended his paper with the statement, "there is danger that this concession to common sense may come too late."[33]

Few people who had contact with Cleburne while he was preparing his manuscript have written about the subject. Colonel Irving Buck wrote that in December 1863, he "noticed that General Cleburne was for several days deeply preoccupied and engaged in writing."[34] Cleburne gave Buck the completed manuscript to read and asked him what he thought of its proposals. In 1904 Buck recalled having warned Cleburne that although men were certainly needed in the army, and Cleburne had presented a forceful argument for the enlistment of Negroes, "I doubted the expedi-ency at that time, of his formulating these views." Reasoned Buck, "the slaveholders . . . were totally unprepared to consider such a radical mea-sure, and many, not being in our service, could not properly appreciate that it had become a matter of self-preservation . . .—consequently, it would raise a storm of indignation against him."[35] Buck also remembered pointing out that the corps had a vacancy in the rank of lieutenant general, and that Cleburne's achievement at Ringgold Gap made it likely the major general would be promoted. However, Buck warned, "I felt assured the publicity of this paper would be used detrimentally to him, and his chances of promotion destroyed." Buck recalled:

> To that he answered that a crisis was upon the South, the danger of which he was convinced could most quickly be averted in the way out-lined, and feeling it to be his duty to bring this before the authorities, he would try to do so, irrespective of any personal result.[36]

Captain Thomas J. Key, in the entry of his diary for December 28, 1863, reported having called upon Cleburne that day and being con-fronted with this plan to arm the slaves. Key stated that Cleburne said the idea was not just his own, "but that it represented the views of Gen-eral Hindman, Colonel Govan, General Polk, General Hardee, and Gen-eral Breckinridge, though the latter thought the period had not yet arrived for calling into the army the negro force."[37] Cleburne wanted the social rights of the slaves to be immediately increased so that they could see that the promise of emancipation was valid. And, said Key, "he assumed the position that Confederate acceptance of the Emancipation Act would turn it to our advantage whereas the Lincoln Government was now using it to injure us."[38] Key's general impression that day was that Cleburne had posed one of the "weightiest questions" that had been brought forth since the beginning of this revolution. "It will make or ruin the South. It will conclude the war speedily or cause blood to flow more freely than heretofore."[39]

Two days later, on December 30, Key told a Captain Swett about Cleburne's proposal. Swett said he preferred "his negro women to keep his wife from the wash tub. Nevertheless, to close the war and give us liberty he was ready to free his negroes, as he did not value them above a 'dime each.'"[40] Key commented in his diary that:

> The idea of abolishing the institution at first startles everyone, but when it is viewed as the means of giving us victory or closing the war, every person with whom I have conversed readily concurs that liberty and peace are the paramount questions and is willing to sacrifice everything to obtain them. All, however, believe the institution to be a wise one and sanctioned by God.[41]

In the light of the government's suppression of Cleburne's proposal just days after this diary entry, one must remark that Captain Key must have had a group of unusually liberal friends, friends Cleburne would have loved to have seen in some high governmental positions.

General Cleburne first read his paper to the members of his staff, one of whom, Major Calhoun Benham, "strongly dissented" and obtained a copy of the paper so that he could write a dissenting reply to be presented later. Cleburne next called together his four division brigadiers (Polk, Lowery, Govan, and Granberry) who, upon hearing it, all said they approved of the major general's plan. An invitation was finally sent to all the general officers of the Army of Tennessee including the commanding general, Joseph E. Johnston, to meet on the evening of January 2, 1864, at army headquarters in Dalton. At this meeting Major Benham read his letter of protest. Cleburne's plan met with great disapproval from this assemblage, with only Generals Hardee and Johnston appearing to assent silently to the plan. Johnston, however, "declined to forward it to the War Department, on the ground that it was more political than military in tenor."[42]

Cleburne was disappointed that he would not get to bring his plan to the attention of President Davis, but as luck (or a lack of luck) would have it, one of the officers at the January 2nd meeting, Major General W. H. T. Walker, sent Cleburne a note on the 3rd, stating that he felt the plan was so "incendiary" that he felt duty-bound to report it to the president.[43] Cleburne supplied Walker with a copy, signed by himself and thirteen other officers and avowed himself the author. A letter, dated January 9th, was sent by Major General Walker to Major General T. C. Hindman, who was at the January 2nd meeting, in which Walker related his intentions of forwarding the plan to the War Department. Walker continued: "Will you please inform me whether you favor the proposition and sentiments of the document in any form. A similar letter to this I shall address to each of the gentlemen who were at the meeting, and their answer will be sent with this document, for I don't like to misrepresent any one."[44] None of these other letters has been found. Only Hindman's rather biting reply is in evidence today. Said Hindman in a letter also dated the ninth:

> I have the honor to acknowledge the receipt of your note of this date, and to decline complying with your request. Whenever my proper superiors see fit to propound any interrogatories to me touching matters as to which they are entitled to inquire, it will be my duty to answer directly, and I shall do so. I have no opinions to conceal and will evade no responsibility that belongs to me. But I do not choose to admit any inquisitorial rights in you. Permit me also to say that, according to my understanding, the course you proposed to take conflicts with a distinct agreement of privacy among the officers consulted by General Cleburne which agreement none of them can waive without the consent of all.[45]

On January 12, 1864, Walker wrote to Jefferson Davis explaining that he was sending the president this document because General Johnston had declined to send it through proper official channels. Continued Walker, "The gravity of the subject, the magnitude of the issues involved, my strong convictions that the further agitation of such sentiments and propositions would ruin the efficacy of our Army and involve our cause in ruin and disgrace constitute my reasons for bringing the document before the Executive."[46]

The very next day, President Davis, evidently not realizing the South's desperate military situation, sent a reply to Walker thanking him for sending the document and informing him of the conclusion that had been reached concerning the paper's contents.

> Deeming it to be injurious to the public service that such a subject should be mooted, or even known to be entertained by persons possessed of the confidence and respect of the people, I have concluded that the best policy under the circumstances will be to avoid all publicity, and the Secretary of War has therefore written to General Johnston requesting him to convey to those concerned my desire that it should be kept private. If it be kept out of the public journals its ill effect will be much lessened.[47]

On January 24th, Secretary of War James Seddon wrote to General Johnston who, one week later, informed Cleburne and the other general officers of the Army of Tennessee of the decision of the Confederate government. Seddon's letter is most interesting and much of it is quoted below:

> He [Davis] is gratified to infer, from your declining to forward officially General Walker's communication of the memorial, that you neither approved the views advocated in it, nor deemed it expedient that, after meeting as they happily did the disapproval of the council, they should have further dissimination or publicity. The motives of zeal and patriotism which have prompted General Walker's action are, however, fully appreciated, and that action is probably fortunate, as it affords an appropriate occasion to express the earnest conviction of the President that the dissemination or even promulgation of such opinions under the present circumstances of the Confederacy . . . can be productive only of discouragement, distraction, and dissension. The agitation and controversy which must spring from the presentation of such views by officers high in public confidence are to be deeply deprecated, and while no doubt or mistrust is for a moment entertained of the patriotic intents of the gallant author . . . and . . . his brother officers as may have favored his opinions, it is requested you will communicate to them, as well as all others present on the occasion, the opinions . . . of the President, and urge on them the suppresion, not only of the memorial itself, but likewise of all discussion and controversy respecting or growing out of it. . . . the measures advocated in the memorial are considered to be little appropriate for consideration in military circles, and indeed in their scope pass beyond the bounds of Confederate action, and could under our constitutional system neither be recommended by the Executive to Congress nor be entertained by that body. Such views can only jeopard among the States and people unity and harmony, when for successful co-operation and the achievement of independence both are essential.[48]

Davis returned to Cleburne the copy of the memorial Walker had sent to him, and Cleburne ordered all copies of the memorial destroyed, with the exception of the one returned from Richmond. It was placed in Colonel Buck's desk and subsequently destroyed with the desk by Federal troops during the Atlanta campaign. It was not until approximately thirty years later that a copy of Cleburne's memorial was ever found: it turned up in California in the papers of the late Major Benham, and was the copy Benham had used to write his dissenting reply.[49]

There were a few letters and accounts written between the January 2nd meeting and the decision of the Confederate government which added another perspective to the issue raised by Cleburne. What fun it would have been to have seen the horrified General Patton Anderson during the days following the meeting on the 2nd. On the 14th he wrote a troubled letter to General Leonidas Polk about the "monstrous proposition." Exclaimed Anderson:

> I will not attempt to describe my feelings on being confronted by a project so startling in its character—may I say so revolting to Southern sentiment, Southern pride, and Southern honor. . . . do you believe . . . [the] South will now listen to the . . . proposition which heretofore our insolent foes themselves have not even dared to make in terms so bold and undisguised? What are we to do?[50]

Unfortunately Polk's reply has never been found, but, hopefully the Confederate government's decision to suppress the memorial tranquilized poor General Anderson enough so that he might continue the war with normal blood pressure.

In his memoirs, Colonel James C. Nisbet recorded an absolutely fascinating conversation between himself and Brigadier General Clement H. Stevens, who had arrived in Dalton to hear Cleburne's paper read on the 2nd. Nisbet was curious as to why Stevens was in Dalton and pressured him to reveal why he had come. After receiving assurances that anything revealed would be kept strictly confidential, Stevens told Nisbet about the plan Cleburne had presented. Stevens called Cleburne a "skilled army officer" but felt that the Irishman's "being foreign born" gave him an incorrect conception of the Negro. Exclaimed Stevens, "I do not want independence, if it is to be won by the help of negroes."[51] Nisbet replied that he favored using every Negro that could be "properly armed, equipped and fed, who is physically fit and will volunteer."[52] Stormed Stevens, sounding a bit like General Anderson, "I am astonished at you! You are demoralized! We can, and will whip the fight as it is. Who would command negro Regiments and Brigades?"

> Colonel Nisbet: I will; and there are others who, like me, place the success of our cause above all things! I am for using any and all fair means. The war has progressed too far for us to fail now, if disaster can be averted by wise foresight. Negroes will do better under Southern men who understand them; as they do us. Their sympathies are strongly Southern. If freed they will be proud to fight under their old masters. It will soon become with them a fight for home and fireside, as with us. . . .

> General Stevens: I contend that slavery was the irritating cause of this war, brought on by the abolition leaders, and that the cry of Union and rebellion are only a subterfuge to enlist the masses in a crusade against slavery. The negro is in his right place, producing under the direction of the white man. If slavery is to be abolished then I take no more interest

in our fight. The *justification* of slavery in the South is the *inferiority* of the negro. If we make him a soldier, we concede the whole question.[53]

Nisbet concluded the conversation by admitting that the Negro was incapable of making progress by himself but chastized Stevens for failing to admit that under American slavery, the Negro had attained his highest form of civilization ever—he had become a faithful and strong laborer, not rebellious as "laborers of the Latin race or the Slavs. . . . General, you are familiar with the coast Negroes of South Carolina and Georgia who with a few exceptions are but little better than the native African. It is from the upcountry we would recruit our Negro soldiers. They have been used to associate with white folks."[54]

Fortunately there is a letter in existence written by someone who spoke to Cleburne during the period in which the general was waiting for Davis' decision. Its contents may show the reader the Cleburne was not quite as "liberal" in his views on race relations as one might be tempted to believe. The letter is from Colonel A. S. Colyar, a member of the Confederate Congress from Tennessee, to his cousin Colonel A. S. Marks. Colyar reported:

> I was very much surprised to hear him [Cleburne] say that he considered slavery at an end. That we ought to put many of the negroes in the service, but that we could not risk them and the consequences without first changing our relation to them, . . . not by military law, but by the action of the States. . . . That if we take this step now, we can mould the relations, for all time to come, between the white and colored races; and we can control the negroes, and that they will still be our laborers as much as they now are, and . . . will be our servants, at less cost than now. His great argument is that if the Yankees succeed in abolishing slavery, equality and amalgamation will finally take place.[55]

However, twentieth-century America's idea of liberality differs greatly from that of the nineteenth century, and in the months after Cleburne suggested "freeing" and arming the slaves, he undoubtedly saw that the people in command felt his views were much too liberal. In the eight months following the suppression of Cleburne's plan, there were three vacancies in the next rank in the Army of Tennessee, and all three went to soldiers of lower rank and with less successful military records than Cleburne had.[56] Although Cleburne had alienated Generals Hood and Braxton Bragg by questioning their leadership abilities, most of Cleburne's contemporaries and many later historians have held that President Davis' disapproval of Cleburne's memorial was the main factor preventing the major general's promotion.

In 1864 Cleburne fought under General Hood for Atlanta and retreated with the army to Tennessee. Cleburne died on the battlefield at Franklin on November 30, 1864, and was mourned throughout the South, some people avowing that only the loss of Stonewall Jackson had hurt the Southern cause more. Three months after Cleburne's death, the Confederate Congress, with the urging of Robert E. Lee, passed a bill authorizing the arming of slaves, but as Cleburne had predicted, this concession came too late to be of help to the Souther war effort.

Unfortunately, the few sources about Cleburne available to the historian are rather superficial tales of his heroism and kind-heartedness in which it is difficult to separate the idealization of his contemporaries from factual data. At any rate, this writer must conclude from available research materials that even when not studying Patrick Cleburne's achievements on the battlefield, the man can be understood only if seen as a duty-bound soldier with a deep love for the South. In 1863 he saw that more troops were needed in the Confederate army and recognized the Negro as the only potentially sizeable source to supply the necessary men. Although the fact that he had no capital invested in slaves may have made it easier for him than for any equally dedicated soldiers to suggest giving the slaves freedom, regardless of how limited his conception of freedom was, he admittedly risked his career by even writing the memorial. When this risk was pointed out to him, he commented that the worst that could happen to him would be a court-martial and cashiering, upon which he would simply "enlist in his old regiment, the 15th Arkansas . . . [so that] he could at least do his duty in the ranks."[57] Being a dutiful soldier, he immediately complied with the order of his superiors to suppress his memorial and was never reported to have advocated its measure again. One must conclude with Dr. Charles Nash: "He seemed utterly unconscious of the petty ambitions and rivalries which so disturb the happiness of others, but moved straight forward in the path of duty, without any concern for himself."[58]

Notes

Chapter 1: Frederick Douglass and the American Apocalypse

1. Robert Penn Warren, *The Legacy of the Civil War* (Cambridge, Mass.: Harvard University Press, 1961), 108.
2. "The War and How to End It," speech delivered by Douglass at Corinthian Hall, Rochester, March 25, 1862, in *Douglass Monthly* (hereafter cited as *DM*), April 1862.
3. Roy P. Basler, ed., *The Collected Works of Abraham Lincoln* (Westport, Conn.: Greenwood Press, 1974), 7:332–33. For analysis of Howe's "Battle Hymn," see Edmund Wilson, *Patriotic Gore: Studies in the Literature of the American Civil War* (New York: Oxford University Press, 1962; rpt. Boston: Northeastern University Press, 1984), 92–97; Ernest Tuveson, *Redeemer Nation: The Idea of America's Millennial Role* (Chicago: University of Chicago Press, 1968), 197–202; and James H. Moorhead, *American Apocalypse: Yankee Protestants and the Civil War, 1860–1869* (New Haven: Yale University Press, 1978), 79–80.
4. Gordon Wood, in *The Creation of the American Republic, 1776–1787* (New York: Norton, 1969), 117, uses the term "millennial tone" to describe the rhetoric of both clergy and laymen on the eve of the Revolution. The literature on millennialism is extensive. Most helpful to me have been Moorhead, *American Apocalypse*, 1–128; James H. Moorhead, "Between Progress and Apocalypse: A Reassessment of Millennialism in American Religious Thought, 1800–1880," *Journal of American History* 71 (December 1984): 524–42; Tuveson, *Redeemer Nation*, 1–90 and 187–214; Ira Brown, "Watchers for the Second Coming: The Millennial Tradition in America," *Mississippi Valley Historical Review* 39 (December 1952): 441–58; David E. Smith, "Millennial Scholarship in America," *American Quarterly* 17 (Fall 1965): 535–49; Conrad Cherry, ed., *God's New Israel: Religious Interpretations of American Destiny* (Englewood Cliffs, N.J.: Prentice-Hall, 1971); Rush Welter, *The Mind of America, 1810–1860* (New York: Columbia University Press, 1975), 19–21, and 260–61; J. F. Maclear, "The Republic and the Millennium," in Elwyn A. Smith, ed., *The Religion of the Republic* (Philadelphia: Fortress Press, 1971), 183–216; and George M. Fredrickson, *The Inner Civil War: Northern Intellectuals and the Crisis of the Union* (New York: Harper and Row, 1965), 7, 68–69, 118–19; and Wilson, *Patriotic Gore,* 91–106; see R. W. B. Lewis, *The American Adam: Innocence, Tragedy, and Tradition in the Nineteenth Century* (Chicago: University of Chicago Press, 1955). For a discussion of the idea of America on the brink of disaster in the 1850s, see Moorhead, *American Apocalypse*, 18–22.
5. See, for example, Amos 5:18, Isa. 1–2, and Rev. 19:11–21. For apocalyptic references see Moorhead, *American Apocalypse*, 9–10; and George M. Marsden, *The Evangelical Mind and the New School Presbyterian Experience: A Case Study of Thought and Theology in Nineteenth-Century America* (New Haven: Yale University Press, 1970), 197, In antebellum America, a distinction arose between what has been termed pre- and postmillennialism. Premillennialists held to the traditional

notion that Christ must return to earth in the flesh *before* the new kingdom could occur. The evils of the present day, premillennialists maintained, betokened God's imminent decision to impose his judgment on the world. By far the more prevalent position in America, though was postmillennialism. It taught that Christ would return to earth *after* the millennium. Postmillennialists believed they already lived in the millennial age; their world already exhibited triumphs of reform, progress, and human potential. For the differences between the two positions and the problems of ambiguity, see Moorhead, *American Apocalypse*, 6–41; Lewis Perry, *Radical Aboli- tionism: Anarchy and the Government of God in Antislavery Thought* (Ithaca: Cornell University Press, 1973), 37–46; and Welter, *Mind of America*, 19–21, 260–61.

6. As the companion concept to millennialism, and frequently considered synony- mous, apocalypticism commands a careful definition as well. For my working defin- ition I have relied upon George A. Buttrick, ed., *The Interpreter's Dictionary of the Bible* (Nashville: Abingdon Press, 1962), 1:157–61, and Martin Rist, "Revelation," in *The Interpreter's Bible* (Nashville: Abingdon Press, 1957), 12:347–51. Rist defines apocalypticism as follows: "the eschatological belief that the power of evil (Satan), who is now in control of this temporal and hopelessly evil age of human history in which the righteous are afflicted by his demonic and human agents, is soon to be overcome and his evil rule ended by the direct intervention of God, who is the power of good, and who thereupon will create an entirely new, perfect, and eternal age under his immediate control for the everlasting enjoyment of his righteous followers from among the living and the resurrected dead" (347). On the hold that the apocalyptic outlook had on the Northern mind at the time of the Civil War, see Wilson, *Patriotic Gore*, 91, 106. This "vision of judgment," writes Wilson, was the myth that "possessed the minds of the publicists, the soldiers, and the politicians to an extent of which the talk about 'Armageddon' at the time of the first World War can give only a feeble idea, and the literature of the time was full of it" (91). Also see Moorhead, "Between Progress and Apocalypse," 524–42; and Robert M. Albrecht, "The Theological Response of the Transcendentalists to the Civil War," *New England Quarterly* 38 (March 1965): 21–34.

7. See Moorhead, *American Apocalypse*, 82–83; Tuveson, *Redeemer Nation*, espe- cially 187–214. On the reaction to the Civil War among Northern Protestants, see Sydney Ahlstrom, *A Religious History of the American People* (New Haven: Yale University Press, 1972), 670–97; and William A. Clebsch, "Christian Interpreta- tions of the Civil War," *Church History* 30 (June 1961): 212–22.

8. Robert N. Bellah, "Civil Religion in America," *Daedalus* (Winter 1969), 1–21. An excellent collection of the writings on civil religion is Russell E. Richey and Donald G. Jones, eds., *American Civil Religion* (New York: Harper and Row, 1974). Also helpful in understanding the varied sources and uses of civil religion are Tuveson, *Redeemer Nation;* Cherry, ed., *God's New Israel*, 8–21; and Nathan O. Hatch, "The Origins of Civil Millennialism in America: New England Clergymen, the War with France, and the Revolution," *William and Mary Quar- terly* 31 (July 1974): 407–30. Numerous scholars have analyzed the role of myth in American cultural and political history, but none more succinctly than Sacvan Bercovitch, when he wrote that "myth may clothe history as fiction, but it per- suades in proportion to its capacity to help people act in history." See Sacvan Bercovitch, *The American Jeremiad* (Madison: University of Wisconsin Press, 1978), xi. Civil religion has served precisely this function.

9. Perry Miller first analyzed this rhetorical device as the earliest American genre of literature. The seventeenth-century New England clergy vented their outrage over the waning zeal of their parishioners, chastizing them in an "unending, monotonous wail" for their part in the failure of the Puritan "errand." See Perry Miller, "Errand into the Wilderness," in *Errand into the Wilderness* (Cambridge, Mass.: Belknap Press, 1958), 8; and Perry Miller, *The New England Mind: From Colony to Providence* (Boston: Beacon Press, 1953), 27–39. Sacvan Bercovitch has broadened the definition of the jeremiad, emphasizing especially the optimistic aspects of the American sense of mission. For his analysis of the nineteenth century, see Bercovitch, *The American Jeremiad,* 148–210. James Moorhead has followed Miller's model in characterizing the jeremiad for the nineteenth century as a "theological rationale for the sufferings of a chosen people," and demonstrated how the Civil War reinvigorated its use. See Moorhead, *American Apocalypse,* 43–49.

10. On the Boston jubilee meeting, see *Life and Times of Frederick Douglass, Written by Himself* (New York: Collier, 1962), 351–54; Benjamin Quarles, *Frederick Douglass* (1948; rpt. New York: Atheneum, 1968), 199–202; and Benjamin Quarles, *Lincoln and the Negro* (New York: Oxford University Press, 1962), 143–46. For a thorough reporting of the jubilee meetings held all over the North see *DM,* February 1863. For an overview of the Christian interpretations of the Civil War, see Clebsch, "Christian Interpretations."

11. *Life and Times,* 353. On Douglass's millennialism, see Waldo E. Martin, *The Mind of Frederick Douglass* (Chapel Hill: University of North Carolina Press, 1984), 173–74.

12. See William L. Andrews, "Frederick Douglass, Preacher," *American Literature* 54 (December 1982): 592–97. Douglass made this claim in a letter written in 1894, solicited by one of the AMEZ church's early historians, James W. Hood. In his article, Andrews reprints that letter in full. Douglass declared that his connection with the church began in 1838 and that "as early as 1839 I obtained a license from the Quarterly Conference as a local preacher, and often occupied the pulpit by request of the preacher in charge" (596). Testimony to Douglass's formal associations with the AMEZ church throughout his life are also found in David Henry Bradley Jr., *A History of the A.M.E. Zion Church* (1796–1872), pt. 1 (Nashville: Abingdon Press, 1956), 111–12. On Douglass the preacher, also see Robert G. O'Meally, "Frederick Douglass' 1845 Narrative: The Text Was Meant to be Preached," in Dexter Fisher and Robert B. Stepto, eds., *Afro-American Literature* (New York: Modern Language Assoc., 1978), 192–211. Douglass's writing style has often been described as oratorical or suited for the platform. But O'Meally's argument, as reflected in his title, also goes a long way in explaining the motivations behind Douglass's writings, in editorials as well as the autobiographies. On Douglass's religion, see William L. Van Deburg, "Rejected of Men: The Changing Religious Views of William Lloyd Garrison and Frederick Douglass" (Ph.D. diss., Michigan State University, 1973).

13. Frederick Douglass, *My Bondage and My Freedom* (1855; rpt. New York: Dover, 1969), 166–67.

14. Ibid., 168–69. On the influence of Uncle Lawson, see Dickson J. Preston, *Young Frederick Douglass: The Maryland Years* (Baltimore: Johns Hopkins University Press, 1980), 97–98; and Andrews, "Frederick Douglass, Preacher," 592–93. On the changes in Douglass's religious outlook, beginning in the 1850s, see Martin, *Mind,* 173–82. Martin charts a course for Douglass from "divine determinism" to religious

"liberalism" and "humanism," According to Martin, this process had already begun in the mid-1850s as Douglass became involved in political abolitionism and emphasized human will over religious faith. While Martin's analysis of the "demystification" of Douglass's religion is very interesting, he underestimates the significance of millennialism in the black thinker's mind. From my reading of the sources, Douglass did not abandon a "sacred world view" and develop a "supremely rational view" as early as Martin indicates. Human will and divine power were equal forces in much of nineteenth-century millennial thought. The reformist-activistic aspects of millennialism (its secular dimensions) are crucial to understanding the growth of Douglass's thought throughout the Civil War era. Douglass's brand of millennialism was never without emphasis on divine *and* human power. Overt expression of religious millennialism waned in the wake of the Civil War throughout American society. Douglass's full espousal of religious liberalism by the 1870s was merely part of that inevitable postwar pattern. Much recent scholarship has stressed this ambiguity and dualism in millennialism. See especially Moorhead, "Between Progress and Apocalypse," 524–33. On the growth of Douglass's religious liberalism, also see William L. Van Deburg, "Frederick Douglass: Maryland Slave to Religious Liberal," *Maryland Historical Magazine* 69 (Spring 1974): 27–43.

15. Douglass, *My Bondage and Freedom,* 169: "The Proclamation and the Negro Army," speech delivered at Cooper Institute, New York, February 1863, *DM,* March 1863, in Philip S. Foner, ed., *The Life and Writings of Frederick Douglass* (New York: International Publishers, 1952), 3:326. For another of Douglass's comparisons of history to the "changeless laws of the universe," see "The War and How to End It," *DM,* April 1862.

16. Douglass to Samuel J. May, Rochester, August 30, 1861, in Foner, *Life and Writings* 3:159; "Signs of the Times," column in response to letter from S. Dutton, Meredith, N.Y., October 14, 1861, *DM,* November 1861, in Foner, *Life and Writings* 3:170–73. Douglass's discussion of the importance of events was varied and frequent. In a November 1861 editorial on the Frémont affair (General John C. Frémont's attempt to free slaves in Missouri and Lincoln's controversial overturning of the order), in which Douglass used such terms as the "voice of history" to describe the significance of Frémont's actions, he contended that "truth consults no man's taste, and events enter without begging any man's permission." See "Frémont and Freedom—Lincoln and Slavery," *DM,* November 1861, in Foner *Life and Writings* 3:174–75.

17. "The War and How to End It," *DM,* April 1862; Douglass to Charles Sumner, April 8, 1862, in Foner, *Life and Writings* 3:233. Also see, "A Change of Attitude," *DM,* June 1861, in Foner, *Life and Writings* 3:110, where Douglass wrote that "events are more potent than arguments."

18. "Emancipation Proclaimed," *DM,* October 1862, in Foner, *Life and Writings* 3:274; "January First, 1863," *DM,* January 1863 in Foner, *Life and Writings* 3:306.

19. "A Lecture on John Brown," 6, in Frederick Douglass Papers (hereafter cited as FD Papers), Library of Congress, reel 14. The index for the FD Papers at the Library of Congress dates this speech as 1860. It was first delivered in 1860, but the collection's version must be dated at least 1880. On page 11, Douglass stated that "more than 20 years have passed" since Brown's Harpers Ferry raid.

20. Frémont and his Proclamation," *DM,* December 1861, in Foner, *Life and Writings* 3:182–83.

21. For the way in which diverse Northern intellectuals shared in this millennial enthusiasm and used its language, see Fredrickson, *Inner Civil War,* 118–19; Tuveson, *Redeemer Nation,* 187–214; Moorhead, *American Apocalypse,* 23–104.

22. West Indian Emancipation," speech delivered at Canandaigua, N.Y., August 4, 1857, pub. as pamphlet (Rochester, 1857), in FD Papers, reel 14. On Douglass's liberation through language—his "quest for being" through autobiography—see Houston A. Baker, *The Journey Back: Issues in Black Literature and Criticism* (Chicago: University of Chicago Press, 1980), 23–46.

23. "The Wicked Flee When No Man Pursueth," *DM,* April 1861.

24. "Decision of the Hour," lecture delivered at Zion church, Rochester, June 16, 1861, in Foner, *Life and Writings* 3:119.

25. "Of the War" and "A Report of Progress," *DM,* May 1862; "Abraham Lincoln—A Speech," FD Papers, reel 14, 2.

26. See Clebsch, "Christian Interpretation," 216–17; Moorhead, *American Apocalypse,* 14–18; Fredrickson, *Inner Civil War,* 184–89; Tuveson, *Redeemer Nation,* especially chapters 4–5; Paul C. Nagel, *One Nation Indivisible: The Union in American Thought, 1776–1861* (New York: Oxford University Press, 1964), 147–76; and Maclear, "Republic and Millennium," in Smith, ed., *Religion of the Republic,* 203–5.

27. *New York Independent,* August 22, 1861, quoted in Moorhead, *American Apocalypse,* 40; "The Mission of the War," in Foner, *Life and Writings,* 3:390. On the notion of world significance, see Moorhead, *American Apocalypse,* 36–41, 56–65.

28. "The Reason for Our Troubles," speech delivered in National Hall, Philadelphia, January 14, 1862, in Foner, *Life and Writings* 3:197.

29. Horace Bushnell, "Reverses Needed: A Discourse delivered on the Sunday after the Disaster of Bull Run" (Hartford, Conn. 1861), quoted in Moorhead, *American Apocalypse,* 139–41. No American thinker exemplified this strain of thought better than Bushnell. "We are born into government as we are into the atmosphere," he contended. Men could not make governments, they only "sketched them" he argued, "and God put them in us to be sketched." Bushnell believed the American republic to be only a fiction until tested. That testing and suffering could not occur "without the shedding of blood." On Bushnell, also see Cherry, ed., *God's New Israel,* 60; Clebsch, "Christian Interpretations," 215–18; Maclear, "Republic and Millennium," 203–5; and Lewis, *American Adam,* 66–73.

30. "The Slaves' Appeal to Great Britain," *Independent,* November 20, 1862, in Foner, *Life and Writings* 3:301. There are many examples of Douglass's use of the "nations and individuals" analogy. In a letter to a French newspaper in November 1865, he gave a summation of the meaning of the war: "The doctrine that one race can raise itself by degrading another has met with powerful refutation in the terrible war that has just ended in our country. That war has taught us that nations like individuals, must respect the rights of human nature. The chain around the ankle of the slave is attached to the neck of the oppressor." Douglass to *Beacon of the Loire,* November 1865, in Douglass Collections, Moorland-Spingarn Research Center, Howard University, Washington, D.C.

31. "The Reasons for Our Troubles," speech delivered at Philadelphia, January 14, 1862, in Foner *Life and Writings* 3:197–99. Douglass frequently discussed the notion of a national soul. The following is typical of these expressions: "It is the *soul* that makes the nation great or small, noble or ignoble, weak or strong. It is the

Soul that exalts it to happiness or sinks it to misery." See *Quotations and Acrostics From Speeches by Frederick Douglass,* a collection begun by Douglass's oldest daughter, Rosetta Sprague Douglass, and completed by her daughters, in Douglass Collections, Moorland-Spingarn Research Center. Douglass's biblical reference here is Isa. 1:5. Douglass's conception of the war as a rite of passage for the youthful nation is very similar to numerous other Northern intellectuals. Emerson, for example, believed the war meant that America was "just passing through a great crisis in its history, as necessary as . . . puberty to the human individual . . . settling for ourselves and our descendents questions which . . . will make the peace and prosperity or the calamity of the next ages." Emerson is quoted in Bercovitch, *American Jeremiad,* 201.

32. Do Not Forget Truth and Justice," *DM,* April 1863, in Foner, *Life and Writings* 3:338–39.

33. Clebsch, "Christian Interpretations," 218. A prime example of this attitude is Henry Ward Beecher who, on the day after the surrender of Fort Sumter, said: "Give me war redder than blood, and fiercer than fire; if this terrific infliction is necessary that I may maintain my faith . . . in this land as the appointed abode and chosen refuge of liberty for all the earth." See Henry Ward Beecher, "The Battle Set in Array," sermon, April 14, 1861, Plymouth Church, Brooklyn, N.Y., in Cherry, ed., *God's New Israel,* 172–73. An excellent example from the end of the war is Horace Bushnell, "Our Obligations to the Dead," commencement address, Yale College, July 26, 1865, in Cherry, ed., *God's New Israel,* 199. On this question generally, see also Fredrickson, *Inner Civil War,* 82–83. Much of Douglass's rhetoric was in this same style.

34. Antislavery Progress," *DM,* September 1862, in Foner, *Life and Writings* 3:271. For strikingly similar expressions of this idea, see Bushnell, "Our Obligations to the Dead," in Cherry, ed., *God's New Israel,* 201.

35. The Slaves' Appeal," *Independent,* November 20, 1862, in Foner, *Life and Writings* 3:305; and "The Proclamation and the Negro Army," speech at Cooper Institute, N.Y., February, 1862, in Foner, *Life and Writings,* 3:322; Wilson J. Moses, *The Golden Age of Black Nationalism* (Hamden, Conn.: Archon Books, 1978), 38–44, 46, 50–55. With insight, Moses argues that Douglass "belonged to that tradition of black nationalists who militantly asserted their right to American citizenship." A rigid distinction between nationalism and emigrationism is not very useful in understanding black nationalism in the Civil War era. We can best understand Douglass's black nationalism as a mixture of assimilation and pragmatic separatism. On the nature of mid-nineteenth-century black nationalism as a direct product of American "civil religion," see Wilson J. Moses, *Black Messiahs and Uncle Toms: Social and Literary Manipulations of a Religious Myth* (University Park, Pa: Pennsylvania State University Press, 1982), 28–29; and Leonard I. Sweet, *Black Images of America, 1784–1870* (New York: Norton, 1976), 5.

36. Clebsch, "Christian Interpretations," 216–17; "Our Work is Not Done," speech at thirtieth anniversary celebration of the American Anti-Slavery Society, Philadelphia, December 3, 1863, in Foner, *Life and Writings* 3:385–86.

37. Address for the Promotion of Colored Enlistments," Philadelphia, July 6, 1863, *DM,* August 1863, in Foner, *Life and Writings* 3:364.

38. Moses, *Black Messiahs and Uncle Toms,* 30–31. But also see the whole of chapter 3, which concentrates on the thought of David Walker. Surprisingly, Moses does not include Douglass in his analysis, and considers the black jeremiad largely a pre-Civil

War phenomenon. But in words that could accurately describe Douglass's use of the jeremiad, Moses argues that the black adaptation of this tradition "revealed a conception of themselves as a chosen people, but it also showed a clever ability to play on the belief that America as a whole was a chosen nation with a convenantal duty to deal justly with the blacks." One of my goals in this essay has been to place Douglass at the head of the black adaptation of this tradition in the nineteenth century.

39. "The True Issue," and "The President's Address," *DM,* January 1859. For good examples of how Douglass's jeremiads took aim at the indifference (declension) of his own people, see Douglass, "drag along in a state of indifference . . . with about the same resignation experienced by a drove of cattle when driven out of an excellent pasture . . . . They are wrapt in a mental midnight," he concluded, "and we are asleep."

40. *DM,* July 1859. For one of Douglass's bitterest attacks on America see "American Civilization," *DM,* October 1859.

41. "Nemesis," *DM,* May, 1861, in Foner, *Life and Writings* 3:98–99.

42. "Our National Fast," *DM,* October 1861, Isa. 1:4–5.

43. Bercovitch, *American Jeremiad,* 180.

44. "Our National Fast," *DM,* October 1861.

45. "The Mission of the War," speech delivered in New York, February 13, 1864, in Foner, *Life and Writings* 3:397, 399–400, 401.

Chapter 2: African Americans, the British Working Class and the American Civil War

1. Quoted in Mary Ellison, *Support for Secession, Lancashire and the American Civil War* (Chicago, 1972), p. 5.

2. *Ashton and Stalybridge Reporter,* 16 August 1862.

3. Samuel Fielden, "Autobiography of Samuel Fielden," in Philip S. Foner, ed., *The Autobiographies of the Haymarket Martyrs* (New York: 1969), pp. 142–3.

4. See Ephraim Douglas Adams, *Great Britain and the American Civil War,* 2 vols. (London, 1925) a still valuable interpretation of events; Mary Ellison, *Support for Secession.*

5. Donaldson Jordan and Edwin J. Pratt, *Europe and the Americas,* p. 178; Benjamin Quarles, *Black Abolitionists* (New York, 1969), p. 141

6. W. O. Henderson, *The Lancashire Cotton Famine, 1861–1865* (Manchester, 1934), p. 1; Frank L. Owsley, *King Cotton Diplomacy* (Chicago, 1959), pp. 7–8; Neville Kirk, *The Growth of Working Class Reform in Mid-Victorian England* (Urbana, 1985), p. 33.

7. *Newcastle Guardian,* 11 November 1861; for Douglass' views *Douglass Monthly,* April 1860; See Douglas A. Lorimer, *Color, Class and the Victorians. English Attitudes to the Negro in Mid 19th Century* (Leicester, 1978) for the emergence of British racism.

8. *Morning Star,* 11 November 1862, 21 January 1865; Nigel Todd, "Black-on-Tyne: The Black Presence on Tyneside in the 1860s," *Bulletin of the North East Labour History Society,* No. 21, 1987, p. 18.

9. Chamerovozow to Dear Sir, London, 5 July 1865, American Missionary Association Papers, New Orleans; *Anti Slavery Reporter,* 2 May 1864; *Cardiff Times,* 14 and 21 October 1864.

10. *Bradford Review,* 19 November 1863; *New York Tribune,* 24 May 1862; *Harpers Weekly,* 7 June 1862; *Rochdale Observer,* 22 October 1864; *Halifax Courier,* 3

October 1863; *Halifax Guardian,* 18 May 1861; *Stockton Herald,* 11 and 18 October 1861; *Staffordshire Advertiser,* 30 August 1862.

11. Fielden, "Autobiography of Samuel Fielden," p. 142; *Leigh Chronicle,* 11 January 1862; *Staffordshire Advertiser,* 30 August 1862; *Stockton Herald,* 11 October 1861; *Leeds Mercury,* 17 March 1864.

12. *Leicester Mercury,* 5, 12 and 19 December 1863; *Gloucester Mercury,* 27 February 1864, 5 and 26 March 1864; *Bradford Review,* 12 March 1863; *Morning Star,* 20 October 1863, 29 November 1863.

13. *Todmorden Times,* 26 September 1863; *Liverpool Mercury,* 22 February 1862.

14. *Midland Counties Herald,* 12 December 1861; *Halifax Courier,* 22 October 1864; *Rochdale Pilot,* 15 October 1864; *Rochdale Observer,* 22 October 1864; *Leicester Mercury,* 21 and 28 June 1862; *Sunderland Times,* 11 May 1861; *Todmorden Times,* 26 September 1863.

15. *Midlands Counties Herald,* 19 December 1861; *Sunderland Times,* 11 May 1861; *Leicester Mercury,* 21 and 28 June 1862; *Rochdale Observer,* 22 October 1864; *Halifax Courier,* 10 January 1863; *Huddersfield Examiner,* 10 January 1863; *Ashton and Stalybridge Reporter,* 30 January 1864.

16. *Todmorden Times,* 29 August 1863, 12 September 1863.

17. *Preston Herald,* 12 July 1862.

18. *Stockport and Cheshire County News,* 12 July 1862; Hotze to Decretary of State, London, 25 April 1862, Hotze Papers, Library of Congress; Spence to Mason, Liverpool, 28 April 1862, Mason Papers, Library of Congress.

19. Julian Karel Wierzbicki, "Bury, Poverty and the Cotton Famine, 1861–1865," pp. 2–4 (transcript, Bury Public Library); *Bury Times,* 23 and 30 August 1862.

20. *Bury Times,* 7 and 14 February 1863, 23 May 1863; *Bury Guardian,* 14 February 1863.

21. *Bury Times,* 21 February 1863.

22. Douglas Maynard, "Civil War 'Care': The Mission of the George Griswold," *New England Quarterly,* Vol. 34, No. 3, September 1961, pp. 310–2; *Reynolds's Newspaper,* 15 February 1863.

23. *Bury Times,* 9 May 1863, 4 April 1863.

24. *Bury Times,* 5 May 1863.

25. *Bury Times,* 30 May 1863; *Bury Guardian,* 30 May 1863.

26. *Bury Guardian,* 30 May 1863; *Bury Times,* 13 June 1863.

27. *Bury Times,* 13 June 1863; *Bury Guardian,* 13 June 1863.

28. *Bury Guardian,* 20 June 1863; *Bury Times,* 20 June 1863.

29. *Bury Times,* 7 and 21 November, 13 February 1864, 5 March 1864; *Bury Guardian,* 7 November 1863.

30. *Bee Hive,* 2 January 1864.

31. Index, 19 November 1863.

Chapter 4: Abraham Lincoln and the Recruitment of Black Soldiers

1. Cf. Fredrick Douglass's perceptive comment: "Any man can say things that are true of Abraham Lincoln, but no man can say anything that is new of Abraham Lincoln. . . . He was a mystery to no man who saw him and heard him," *Life and Times of Frederick Douglass, Written By Himself* (Hartford, Conn.: Park Publishing

Co., 1882), p. 541. The quoted words are from Douglass's magnificent oration "on the occasion of the unveiling of the Freedmen's Monument, in memory of Abraham Lincoln, in Lincoln Park, Washington, D.C., April 14, 1876."

2. When Douglass remarked that Lincoln "shared the prejudices common to his countrymen towards the colored race," he was speaking in the context of public policy. Note also his moving description of Lincoln's Second Inaugural and subsequent conversation with the President (ibid., pp. 364–66, 402–07, 488). In a letter to Joshua Speed, August 24, 1855, Lincoln wrote: "As a nation, we begin by declaring that *'All men are created equal.'* We now practically read it 'all men are created equal, *except negroes.'* When the Know-Nothings get control, it will read 'all men are created equal, except negroes, *and foreigners, and catholics.'* When it comes to this I should prefer emigrating to some country where they make no pretence of loving liberty—to Russia for instance, where despotism can be taken pure, and without the base alloy of hypocracy." Roy P. Basler, ed., Marion Dolores Pratt and Lloyd A. Dunlap, asst. eds., *The Collected Works of Abraham Lincoln* (New Brunswick, N.J.: Rutgers University Press, 1853–1955), 2:323 (hereafter cited as *Collected Works*).

3. Dudley Taylor Cornish, *The Sable Arm: Negro Troops in the Union Army, 1861–1865* (New York: Longmans, Green and Co., 1956), pp. 1–12.

4. See, for example, Ulysses S. Grant to his father, Jesse Root Grant, May 6, 1861, in John Y. Simon, ed., *The Papers of Ulysses S. Grant, Vol.2: April-September, 1861* (Carbondale: Southern Illinois University Press, 1969), pp. 20–22: "A Northern army may be required in the next ninety days to go south to suppress a negro insurrection."

5. Allan Nevins, *The War for the Union: Vol. 2, War Becomes Revolution* (New York: Charles Scribner's Sons, 1960), p. 513; Benjamin Quarles, *Lincoln and the Negro* (New York: Oxford University Press, 1962), pp. 163–66; J. G. Randall, *Lincoln the President: Springfield to Gettysburg* (New York: Dodd, Mead & Co., 1946), 2, 1–16.

6. Cornish, pp. 17–18.

7. Ibid., pp. 18–24; Randall, pp. 54–61; Benjamin P. Thomas and Harold M. Hyman, *Stanton: The Life and Times of Lincoln's Secretary of War* (New York: Knopf, 1962), pp. 131–37.

8. Thomas and Hyman, pp. 234–37; Cornish, pp. 43–46.

9. Cornish, pp. 50–52; Nevins, pp. 231–33.

10. Cornish, pp. 52–55, 80 (Adams's remark is on p. 55).

11. Ibid., pp. 56–78; Quarles, pp. 155–56.

12. Cornish, p. 100.

13. Ibid., pp. 101–06.

14. Richard H. Abbott, "Massachusetts and the Recruitment of Negro Soldiers, 1863–1865," *Civil War History,* 14 (1968), 197–210.

15. Cornish, pp. 111–31, contains an excellent account of Thomas's recruiting efforts. The reference to Eaton is in John Eaton, *Grant, Lincoln and the Freedmen* (New York: Longmans, Green, and Co., 1907), pp. 9–15. Grant's exchanges with Hallack are in Simon, *Papers of Ulysses S. Grant,* Vol. 8 (1979), 90–94.

16. Lincoln to James C. Conkling, August 26, 1863, in *Collected Works,* 6:409.

17. Lincoln to Grant, August 9, 1863, ibid., p. 374.

18. Lincoln to Conkling, August 26, 1863, ibid., pp. 408–10. This letter was intended to be a campaign document for the fall elections in Illinois and a public statement on his policy regarding blacks.

19. Quarles, pp. 163–65; Lincoln to Albert G. Hodges, April 4, 1864, *Collected Works,*
    7:281–83.
20. *Life and Times of Frederick Douglass,* pp. 541–42.

Chapter 5: Massachusetts and the
Recruitment of Southern Negroes

1. Douglass quoted in Dudley Taylor Cornish, *The Sable Arm: Negro Troops in the
   Union Army, 1861–1865* (New York, 1956), pp. 109–110. I am grateful to
   Richard D. Goff for a critical reading of this paper.
2. *United States Census, 1860: Manufactures* (Washington, 1865), p. 729; ibid., *Population* (Washginton, 1864), pp. 592–593; Emerson D. Fite, *Social and Industrial
   Conditions in the North During the Civil War* (New York, 1910), pp. 84, 86, 91.
3. Henry Greenleaf Pearson, *An American Railroad Builder: John Murray Forbes*
   (Boston, 1911).
4. Frank P. Stearns, *The Life and Public Service of George Luther Stearns* (Philadelphia,
   1907), p. 330.
5. Edward Atkinson to Henry D. Hyde, December 22, 1863, Atkinson Papers,
   Massachusetts Historical Society (hereafter cited as MHS); Amos Lawrence to John
   Murray Forbes, December 1, 1863, Lawrence letterbooks, MHS; John Murray
   Forbes to Zachariah Chandler, December 28, 1863, Zachariah Chandler Papers,
   Library of Congress; Boston *Commonwealth,* August 28, 1863.
6. Pearson, *Forbes,* pp. 134–136; Forbes to Abraham Lincoln (copy), August 24,
   1863, John A. Andrew Papers, MHS; Forbes to Edwin M. Stanton, October 21,
   1863, clipping dated August 3, 1863, from George L. Stearns to Amos Lawrence,
   and clipping dated August 13, 1863, titled "Realative to organizing of colored
   troops in the state of Massachusetts," all in Bureau for Colored Troops, Folder F-
   35, National Archives; Mrs. W. S. Robinson, ed., *Warrington Pen-Portraits*
   (Boston, 1877), pp. 298–299; clipping from Boston *Daily Advertiser,* August 24,
   1863, in Publications of New England Loyal Publication Society, vol. 1, p. 123,
   rare book room, Boston Public Library (hereafter cited as NELPS).
7. Forbes to Zachariah Chandler, January 26, 1863, Zachariah Chandler Papers.
8. Harold Hyman and Benjamin P. Thomas, *Stanton: The Life and Times of Lincoln's
   Secretary of War* (New York, 1962), p. 263.
9. Cornish, *Sable Arm,* pp. 83–85, 95–96, 99, 113, 123–125.
10. Amos Lawrence to Henry Wilson, August 10, 1863, Lawrence letterbooks, MHS;
    circular of Boston Businessmen's Committee, August 29, 1863, in Bureau for Col-
    ored Troops, Folder F-35, National Archives; Henry Wilson to Abraham Lincoln,
    October 25, 1863, Robert Todd Lincoln Papers, Library of Congress. See also
    draft of letter from executive committee of same businessman's group, dated 1863,
    in Lawrence Papers, MHS.
11. Forbes to Amos Lawrence, September 1, 1863, Lawrence Papers, MHS; Forbes to
    John A. Andrew, November 18, 21, 24, 25, 1863, Andrew Papers, MHS.
12. Forbes to John A. Andrew, November 29, 1863, *ibid.*
13. *Congressional Globe,* 38 Cong., 1 sess., 85–86.
14. Forbes to Charles Eliot Norton, December 29, 1863, manuscript in NELPS.
15. See newspaper clippings and editorials in NELPS, 2:180, 187; Forbes to Samuel
    Hooper, December, 1863; to Edwin M. Stanton, December 10, 1863; to Henry

Ward Beecher, December 28, 1863; and to Rev. William G. Eliot, February 4, 1864, in Sarah Forbes Hughes, ed., *Letters of John Murray Forbes* (supplementary edition, Boston, 1905), 2:176–177, 179–182, 191–192, 206–207.

16. Clipping dated December 22, 1863, NELPS, 2:176; Springfield *Republican,* quoted in Boston *Commonwealth,* January 8, 1864.

17. *Congressional Globe,* 38 Cong., 1 sess., 240–247; Forbes to John A. Andrew, November 29, 1863 and February 26, 1864, Andrew Papers, MHS.

18. *Congressional Globe,* 38 Cong., 1 sess., 845–846, 3383. There was no clear sectional division in voting on the bill.

19. Bird to Charles Sumner, February 27, 1864, Sumner Papers, Houghton Library, Havard University; Amos Lawrence to wife, March 17, 1864, Lawrence letterbooks, MHS; Forbes to F. G. Shaw, March 16, 1864, in Hughes, ed., *Letters,* 2:231–232; Forbes to John A. Andrew, March 20, March 25, April 7, 1864, Andrew Papers MHS.

20. *Congressional Globe,* 38 Cong., 1 sess., 1403–1405.

21. Ibid., 2025, 2222; NELPS, 2:215, 219, 232, 237.

22. *Congressional Globe,* 38 Cong., 1 sess., 2367–2379, 3317, 3357. On bargain over commutation, see ibid., 3435, and Boston *Commonwealth,* July 15, 1864.

23. Forbes to Henry Wilson, April 26, June 25, 1864, in Hughes, ed., *Letters,* 2:238, 266; Forbes to Charles Eliot Norton, June 28, 1864, manuscript in NELPS.

24. *Congressional Globe,* 38 Cong., 1 sess., 3381–3382.

25. Ibid., 3383–3386.

26. Ibid., 3432–3435, 3465.

27. Ibid., 3488–3490.

28. Forbes to John A. Andrew, July 7, 1864, Andrew Papers, MHS; Forbes to Gen. Francis C. Barlow, July 19, 1864, in Hughes, ed., *Letters,* 2:277–279.

29. William T. Sherman, *Memoirs of William T. Sherman* (New York, 1875), 2:246,249; Lloyd Lewis, *Sherman: Fighting Prophet* (New York, 1932), pp. 391–394. On Sherman's protests to Gen. Halleck, see Roy P. Basler, ed., *The Collected Works of Abraham Lincoln* (Brunswick, N.J., 1953–1955), 8:450n. Lincoln told Sherman: "To be candid, I was for passage of the law, not apprehending at the time that it would prove such inconvenience to the armies in the field, as you now cause me to fear. Many of the States were very anxious for it. . . . I still hope advantage from the law." Lincoln to Sherman, July 18, 1864, in Basler, ed., *Collected Works,* 7:449–450.

30. Tyler Dennett, ed., *Lincoln and the Civil War in the Diaries of John Hay* (New York, 1939), pp. 241–242 (entry for November 16, 1864); Lorenzo Thomas to Edwin M. Stanton, September 5, 1864, U.S. War Dept, *The War of the Rebellion: A Compilation of the Official Records of the Union and Confederate Armies* (Washington, 1880–1901), ser. 3, 4, 694–695.

31. Carl Sandburg, *Abraham Lincoln: The War Years* (New York, 1939), 3:179; A. G. Browne to John Andrew, October 1, 1864, Andrew Papers, MHS.

32. *Congressional Globe,* 38 Cong., 2 sess., 183, 606–610.

33. Henry G. Pearson, *The Life of John A. Andrew* (Boston, 1904), 2:143–146; Bell I. Wiley, *Southern Negroes, 1861–1865* (New Haven, 1938), pp. 306–307; James L. Bowen, *Massachusetts in the War, 1861–1865* (Springfield, 1889), p. 75.

34. Fred A. Shannon, *Organization and Administration of the Union Army* (Cleveland, 1925), 2:113.

35. Cornish, *Sable Arm,* pp. 255–256.

Chapter 6: Raising the African Brigade

1. "Corporal" [Zenas T. Haines], *Letters from the Forty-fourth Regiment M.V.M.: A Record of the Experience of a Nine Months' Regiment in the Department of North Carolina in 1862–3* (Boston: Herald Job Office, 1863), 109.
2. William P. Derby, *Bearing Arms in the Twenty-seventh Massachusetts Regiment of Volunteer Infantry during the Civil War, 1861–1865* (Boston: Wright and Potter Printing Co., 1883), 192.
3. *The War of the Rebellion: A Compilation of the Official Records of the Union and Confederate Armies,* ser. 3, 5:138. The relatively small number from North Carolina, estimated as 8 percent of the 1860 population of black men ages eighteen to forty-five, reflected both the limited area in the east under Union control and the practice of Confederate planters of removing most of their slaves to the interior, where escape to the Union lines was much more difficult.
4. Joseph T. Glatthaar, *Forged in Battle: The Civil War Alliance of Black Soldiers and White Officers* (New York: Free Press, 1990), 61–66, 76.
5. Howard C. Westwood, "Generals David Hunter and Rufus Saxton and Black Soldiers," *South Carolina Historical Magazine* 86 (July 1985): 168–171; Willie Lee Rose, *Rehearsal for Reconstruction: The Port Royal Experiment* (Indianapolis, Ind.: Bobbs-Merrill Co., 1964), 146–148.
6. Howard C. Westwood, "The Cause and Consequence of a Union Black Soldier's Mutiny and Execution," *Civil War History* 31 (September 1985): 225–232.
7. Ira Berlin, Joseph P. Reidy, and Leslie S. Rowland, eds., *The Black Military Experience,* ser. 2 of *Freedom: A Documentary History of Emancipation, 1861–1867* (New York: Cambridge University Press, 1982), 121.
8. A critical factor in Butler's decision in the summer of 1862 was the small size of his command and his belief that the Confederates presented a very real threat to continued Union occupation of New Orleans. Recognition that Louisiana's free black militia, even with the addition of some newly freed slaves, represented a unique case is seen in the fact that the black militia officers were given line commissions, something that occurred nowhere else. Howard C. Westwood, "Benjamin Butler's Enlistment of Black Troops in New Orleans in 1862," *Louisiana History* 26 (Winter 1985):5–22.
9. *Official Records,* ser. 3, 3:36, 46–47; Berlin, Reidy, and Rowland, *Black Military Experience,* 6, 9, 75–76.
10. Berlin, Reidy, and Rowland, *Black Military Experience,* 9, 75.
11. *Official Records,* ser. 3, 3:109–110.
12. *Official Records,* ser. 3, 3:110.
13. Russell Duncan, ed., *Blue-Eyed Child of Fortune: The Civil War Letters of Colonel Robert Gould Shaw* (Athens: University of Georgia Press, 1992), 320.
14. Henry A. Clapp to "Dear Willie," February 27, 1863; Henry A. Clapp to "Dear Father," March 1, 1863; Henry A. Clapp to "Dear Mother," March 14, 1863, all in Henry A. Clapp Letter Book, Collections Branch, Tryon Palace Historic Sites and Gardens, New Bern.
15. In the town and outskirts there were 5,962 persons, while the three camps contained, "by the best estimate, about twenty-five hundred souls." Henry A. Clapp to Helen Clapp, March 20, 1863; Henry A. Clapp to Louise Clapp, March 26, 1863, both in Clapp Letter Book.

16. *Official Records,* ser. 3, 3:110.

17. Andrew wished to reserve the Fifty-fourth Massachusetts to serve in an active theater where it could demonstrate in battle the qualities that would make white Americans appreciate the value of black soldiers. *Official Records,* ser. 3, 3:110.

18. Duncan, *Blue-Eyed Child of Fortune,* 320, 321, 322.

19. Duncan, *Blue-Eyed Child of Fortune,* 333.

20. Edward Stanly to Hon. Edwin Stanton, June 12, 1862, *Official Records,* ser. 1, 9:400. Stanly allowed a slaveholder to enter Union lines to search for slaves freed by "a rude soldier" but advised the owner "to use mildness and persuasion." The provisional governor was pleased to see one slave "returned to the home of a kindly master."

21. Ira Berlin et al., eds., *The Destruction of Slavery,* ser. 1 of *Freedom: A Documentary History of Emancipation, 1861–1867* (New York: Cambridge University Press, 1985), 87–88.

22. Berlin, Reidy, and Rowland, *Black Military Experience,* 132.

23. John G. Barrett, *The Civil War in North Carolina* (Chapel Hill: University of North Carolina Press, 1963), 131.

24. "Corporal," *Letters from the Forty-fourth,* 35, 45, 91; Derby, *Bearing Arms in the Twenty-seventh,* 192; Barrett, *Civil War in North Carolina,* 87, 106; Stephen V. Ash, *Middle Tennessee Society Transformed, 1860–1870* (Baton Rouge: Louisiana State University Press, 1988), 106–107; Joseph T. Glatthaar, *The March to the Sea and Beyond: Sherman's Troops in the Savannah and Carolinas Campaigns* (New York: New York University Press, 1985), 53, 59–65.

25. "Corporal," *Letters from the Forty-fourth,* 35; Wayne K. Durrill, *War of Another Kind: A Southern Community in the Great Rebellion* (New York: Oxford University Press, 1990), 108.

26. William F. Draper to "Father," August 1, 1862, William Franklin Draper Papers, Manuscript Division, Library of Congress, Washington, D.C.

27. Thomas J. Jennings to "Eternal Friend," February 25, 1863, Thomas J. Jennings Letters, Southern Historical Collection, University of North Carolina Library, Chapel Hill.

28. Spruill Memorandum, July 19, 1862, Pettigrew Family Papers, Southern Historical Collection, cited in Durrill, *War of Another Kind,* 119.

29. Vincent Colyer, *Brief Report of the Services Rendered by the Freed People to the United States Army in North Carolina in the Spring of 1862, after the Battle of Newbern* (New York: Vincent Colyer, 1864), 9.

30. Beth G. Crabtree and James W. Patton, eds., *"Journal of a Secesh Lady": The Diary of Catherine Ann Devereux Edmondston, 1860–1866* (Raleigh: Division of Archives and History, Department of Cultural Resources, 1979), 226–227.

31. Barrett, *Civil War in North Carolina,* 127.

32. B.F.B. to D. W. Bell, January 28, 1863, George Holland Collection, Private Collections, State Archives, Division of Archives and History, Raleigh.

33. Henry A. Clapp to Willie Clapp, April 10, 1863, Clapp Letter Book.

34. In total Hill had about fourteen thousand men. Although his prime goal was to secure and ensure supplies from eastern North Carolina, he was also to "make a diversion" upon the Union-held towns. Barrett, *Civil War in North Carolina,* 150–151.

35. H. G. Spruill to Josiah Collins, March 16, 1863. Josiah Collins Papers, Private Collections, State Archives, cited in Durrill, *War of Another Kind,* 173.

36. Derby, *Bearing Arms in the Twenty-seventh,* 168.

37. Derby, *Bearing Arms in the Twenty-seventh,* 168–169.

38. "Corporal," *Letters from the Forty-fourth,* 95.

39. *Official Records,* ser. 3, 3:122. Wild's relationship with Andrew was such that in June, 1861, as the junior captain in the First Massachusetts Volunteers, he wrote to persuade the governor to take steps to replace the regiment's colonel with the lieutenant colonel. Wild concluded that, as the junior captain, he would not be seen to be acting out of any hope of promotion. E. A. Wild to Governor Andrew, June 7, 1861, Edward A. Wild Correspondence, Massachusetts MOLLUS Collection, United States Army Military History Institute, Carlisle Barracks, Pa.

40. *Official Records,* ser. 3, 3:110. Barlow, still recuperating from wounds he suffered at the Battle of Antietam, instead accepted command of a brigade in the Second Division, Eleventh Corps, Army of the Potomac.

41. Bradford Kingman, "General Edward Augustus Wild," *New England Historical and Genealogical Register* 49 (October 1895): 405–408; *Address of Martin P. Kennard* ([Brookline, Mass]: printed for the town, 1894), 7–8, 13; "The Military Life of Edward A. Wild," Massachusetts MOLLUS Collection; Papers in Regards to Brookline in the Civil War, 1861–1865, Brookline Cadet Records, Gen. E. A. Wild Civil War Papers, Public Library, Brookline, Mass.; Assistant Adjutant General to the War Department, July 6, 1878, Letters Received by the Commission Branch, Records of the Adjutant General's Office, Record Group 94, National Archives, Washington, D.C., *Official Records,* ser. 3, 3:363, 438.

42. E. A. Wild to Calvin Cutter, March 13, 1863, Wild Correspondence, Massachusetts MOLLUS Collection.

43. Gen. E. A. Wild to Sen. Henry Wilson, May 10, 1865, Wild Correspondence, Massachusetts MOLLUS Collection.

44. Duncan, *Blue-Eyed Child of Fortune,* 323.

45. In contrast, both Capt. Thomas Wentworth Higginson, when raising South Carolina's first black regiment, and Brig. Gen. Daniel Ullmann, organizing the Corps d'Afrique in Louisiana, wanted men of good character but were not concerned about previous military service. Adj. Gen. Lorenzo Thomas, on the other hand, sought officers for his black regiments entirely within the military structure and accepted at face value assurances of concern for African Americans. Glatthaar, *Forged in Battle,* 35–39.

46. In February 1863 Andrew had asked Stanton to withdraw his prohibition of commissioning black officers "so far as concerns line officers, assistant surgeons, and chaplains." *Official Records,* ser. 3, 3:36.

47. "Appointment of Col. Edward A. Wild," Personnel File, RG 94. Twenty-six officers were appointed on April 28, 1863, although the colonel and lieutenant colonel were not appointed until June 1, perhaps reflecting Wild's unsuccessful search for senior Massachusetts officers. "Roster, First North Carolina African Volunteers," Massachusetts MOLLUS Collection.

48. E. A. Wild to Maj. Thomas M. Vincent, September 4, 1863, Wild Correspondence, Massachusetts MOLLUS Collection.

49. E. A. Wild to Maj. Thomas M. Vincent, September 4, 1863, Wild Correspondence, Massachusetts MOLLUS Collection.

50. Thirteen officers came directly from Massachusetts units, while eighteen others were residents of that state. "North Carolina Volunteers, Wild's African Brigade," Letters Received, Colored Troops Division, RG 94.

51. Edward W. Kinsley to E. A. Wild, September 9, 1863, Wild Correspondence, Massachusetts MOLLUS Collection.
52. W. H. R. Brown to E. A. Wild, August 9, 1863, Wild Correspondence, Massachusetts MOLLUS Collection.
53. Glatthaar, *Forged in Battle,* 240–241.
54. The official military records do not indicate that Reed was not white, but other records do. In late 1863 Surgeon Horace R. Wirtz claimed that Reed was a "mulatto," while years later George W. Williams wrote that Reed was reportedly "bound to both races by the ties of consanguinity." H. R. Wirtz to ——, September 29, 1863, Personal Papers of Medical Officers and Physicians, RG 94; George W. Williams, *A History of the Negro Troops in the War of the Rebellion, 1861–1865* (New York: Harper and Brothers, 1888), 207–208. If Reed was not a mulatto, the rumors may have resulted from the fact that he was a constant supporter of black soldiers in the face of white prejudice.
55. *North Star* (Rochester, N.Y.), June 8, 1849; *Frederick Douglass' Paper* (Rochester, N.Y.), September 22, 1854.
56. Asst. Surgeon John De Grasse, Proceedings of General Courts-Martial, Records of the Judge Advocate General's Office, Record Group 153, National Archives.
57. E. A. Wilde to Maj. Thomas M. Vincent, May 21, 1863, Letters Received, Colored Troops Division, RG 94.
58. John N. Mars, Compiled Military Service Records, RG 94.
59. Thomas Hale to "Dear Mother," May 19, 1863, Eben Thomas Hale Papers, Southern Historical Collection.
60. *Wilmington Journal,* May 23, 1863.
61. *Wilmington Journal,* May 23, 1863.
62. Dudley T. Cornish, *The Sable Arm: Negro Troops in the Union Army, 1861–1865* (New York: Longmans, Green and Co., 1956), 168.
63. *Memorandum and Journal of Samuel Chapin of South Wilbraham, Massachusetts, Company 1, 46th Regt. M.V.M.* (n.p.: Historical Society of the Town of Hampden, 1987), 109.
64. One of the soldiers questioned, Sgt. William R. Sessions, prided himself that the Confederate "found out but little that he wished to know," even though Sessions had told him that he "knew nothing of the Negroes but believed that a Bat. Was forming at N——." *Diary of Sgt. William R. Sessions of South Wilbraham, Massachusetts, Company 1, 46th Regt. M.V.M.* (n.p.: Historical Society of the Town of Hampden, 1987),8.
65 This information and the subsequent data in the paragraph are drawn from the Descriptive Books, Thirty-fifth Regiment United States Colored Troops (USCT), RG 94.
66. Henry A. Clapp to "Dear Mother," May 25, 1863, Clapp Letter Book.
67. Alfred S. Roe, *The Fifth Regiment Massachusetts Volunteer Infantry in Its Three Tours of Duty, 1861, 162–'63, 1864* (Boston: Fifth Regiment Veteran Association, 1911), 244.
68. *Official Records,* ser. 3, 3:684. By the next year agents bringing in recruits to the Third NCCV received two dollars, while the enlisting men got a small bounty of ten dollars. Wild may have been using his own money for that type of payment.
69. Albert W. Mann, *History of the Forty-fifth Regiment Massachusetts Volunteer Militia* (Boston: W. Spooner, 1908), 301–302, 446–449.
70. Edward A. Wilde to Edward W. Kinsley, November 30, 1863, Edward Wilkinson Kinsley Papers, Special Collections Department, Duke University Library, Durham. Galloway, who was politically active in New Bern and Wilmington during Reconstruction,

managed at this time to get his mother out of Wilmington, where she was a slave, and arrange for her transportation to the North.

71. Williams had acquired a reputation as an antislavery speaker in parts of the North. Edwin S. Redkey, ed., *A Grand Army of Black Men: Letters from African-American Soldiers in the Union Army, 1861–1865* (New York: Cambridge University Press, 1992), 90.

72. Edward A. Wild to Edward W. Kinsley, July 28, 1863; Joseph E. Williams to Edward W. Kinsley, August 19, 1863, both in Kinsley Papers.

73. General Order No. 103, entry 44, Orders and Circulars, 1797–1910, Eighteenth Army Corps, RG 94.

74. "Military Life of Edward A. Wild," Massachusetts MOLLUS Collection.

75. Oscar Doolittle to J. W. Sullivan, July 22, 1863, Kinsley Papers.

76. Edward A. Wild to Edward W. Kinsley, July 28, 1863, Kinsley Papers; *Official Records*, ser. 1, 29, pt. 2:166; Joe A. Mobley, *James City: A Black Community in North Carolina, 1863–1900* (Raleigh: Division of Archives and History, Department of Cultural Resources, 1981), 4, 21.

77. Although needy freedmen in North Carolina received rations just sufficient "to prevent positive suffering," the families of the soldiers automatically received full rations. Stephen Edward Reilly, "Reconstruction through Regeneration: Horace James' Work with the Blacks for Social Reform in North Carolina, 1863–1867" (Ph.D. diss., Duke University, 1983), 45–46.

78. Derby, *Bearing Arms in the Twenty-seventh*, 192.

79. That enlistment, in late April or early May 1865, added 118 soldiers to the regiment, or 10.8 percent of all the men on the regimental books.

80. Muster Rolls, Thirty-fifth Regiment USCT, Duke Special Collections.

81. Sgt. Richard Etheredge and Wm. Benson to General Howard [May or June 1865], Unregistered Letters Received, Records of the Bureau of Refugees, Freedmen, and Abandoned Lands for North Carolina, Record Group 105, National Archives; Frank James to Gen. A. G. Draper, June 4, 1865, and Endorsements, Unregistered Letters Received, RG 105, both printed in Berlin, Reidy, and Rowland, *Black Military Experience*, 729–730.

82. The imprecision of this assessment is aggravated by the fact that in some units, such as Company B, all men were listed as "dark," while in others men were described as "black" and "dark" or as "dark" and "brown." In this study only those listed as "light" are considered mulattoes, and therefore the figure 7.5 percent represents only a minimum number. An added complication arises from the fact that a large number of the men described as "light" were recruited in Virginia after September 1863.

83. By late in 1864, if not earlier, Monroe had taken over witnessing of the clothing issuing, a function previously handled by 2d Lt. George P. Guerrier. "Returns of Clothing, Camp, and Garrison Equipment," November 1863, October 1864, Clarke H. Remick Papers, Duke Special Collections.

84. *The History of a Gallant Regiment* (Boston: New England Loyal Publication Society, 1864), broadside (copy in Massachusetts MOLLUS Collection).

85. *History of a Gallant Regiment*.

86. *History of a Gallant Regiment*.

87. The quartermaster returns are part of the Remick Papers.

88. Maj. A. Bogle to Lieutenant Robinson, December 30, 1863, Order Book, Thirty-fifth Regiment USCT, RG 94.

89. Muster Rolls, February 1864, Company I, Thirty-fifth Regiment USCT, RG 94.

90. *Official Records,* ser. 1, 28, pt. 2:73; Cornish, *Sable Arm,* 95–96; E. A. Wild to Maj. T. M. Vincent, June 25, 1863, Letters Received, Colored Troops Division, RG 94.

91. The ranks of these men are not cited to suggest that they were unlikely officer material. Certainly one of the men Wild requested, Pvt. Hiram W. Allen of the First Massachusetts Volunteers, had already been recommended for a commission as adjutant by several individuals, including Gen. Henry M. Naglee. E. A. Wild to Maj. T. M. Vincent, June 25, 1863, Letters Received, Color Troops Division, RG 94.

92. "Roster, Wild's African Brigade," 1863, Letters Received, Colored Troops Division, RG 94.

93. E. A. Wild to Maj. Thomas M. Vincent, September 4, 1863, Letters Received, Colored Troops Division, RG 94.

94. "Roster, 2nd North Carolina African Volunteers," Massachusetts MOLLUS Collection.

95. Company A's men averaged 26.8 years of age, while Company B's soldiers were significantly younger at an average of 23.7 years old. Descriptive Books, Thirty-sixth Regiment USCT, RG 94.

96. *New Era* (Washington, N.C.), June 25, 1863.

97. *Official Records,* ser. 1, 27, pt. 2:863.

98. Redkey, *Grand Army of Black Men,* 92.

99. *Wilmington Journal,* July 9, 1863.

100. *Wilmington Journal,* July 30, 1863.

101. *Wilmington Journal,* July 30, 1863. The man involved was almost certainly James H. Jackson, a mason from New Hanover County who had enlisted at age thirty-eight as a bugler in First Company C, Second Regiment North Carolina Artillery. He was discharged for medical reasons in January 1864. Louis H. Manarin and Weymorth T. Jordan Jr., comps., *North Carolina Troops, 1861–1865: A Roster,* 12 vols. to date (Raleigh: Division of Archives and History, Department of Cultural Resources, 1966–), 1:222, 572.

102. Maj. George L. Stearns to Hon. Edwin M. Stanton, August 17, 1863, Letters Received, Colored Troops Division, RG 94, printed in Berlin, Reidy, and Rowland, *Black Military Experience,* 100–101. Stearns indicated that impressment spread the same sense of fear throughout the black community whether the men were drafted as laborers or as soldiers.

103. At that time Maj. Gen. John Peck had complained that the high wages made it "impossible to make much headway with recruiting." Peck to Brig. Gen. I. Thomas, November 16, 1863, enclosing Capt. R. C. Webster, "Report of Negroes employed by the Quartermaster's Department at Newberne N.C.," [November 2, 1863], Letters Received, Colored Troops Division, RG 94, printed in Berlin, Reidy, and Rowland, *Black Military Experience,* 133–134.

104. E. A. Wild to Maj. Thomas M. Vincent, September 4, 1863, Letters Received, Colored Troops Division, RG 94.

105. The delay may have been the result of Stanton's unsuccessful suggestion to Governor Andrew that the Fifty-fifth Massachusetts be part of the force used in "relieving the troops at New Orleans and substituting for them troops of African descent." *Official Records,* ser.3, 3:483.

106. *Official Records,* ser. 1, 28, pt. 2:30; "Military Life of Edward A. Wild," Massachusetts MOLLUS Collection.

107. *Official Records,* ser. 1, 28, pt. 2:96.

108. Maj. A. Bogle to F. W. Taggart, January 10, 1864, Descriptive Book, Thirty-sixth Regiment USCT, RG 94.

109. General Order No. 6, July 30, 1863, Order Book, Thirty-fifth Regiment USCT, RG 94.

110. Alonzo G. Draper, Compiled Military Service Records, RG 94.

111. Alonzo G. Draper, Compiled Military Service Records, RG 94; *Official Records,* ser. 1, 28, pt. 2:290, 412.

112. The first company of the First Regiment Heavy Artillery (African Descent) was mustered in at New Bern in March 1864, while the last company was completed in April 1865, by which time the regiment bore the name Fourteenth United States Colored Heavy Artillery. Throughout that period a swarm of out-of-state recruiters attempted to raise at least nine different regiments. *Official Records,* ser. 1, 33:870–871; Frederick H. Dyer, *A Compendium of the War of the Rebellion* (Des Moines, Iowa: Dyer Publishing Co., 1908; New York: Thomas Yoseloff, 1959), 1722.

113. *Official Records,* ser. 1, 29, pt. 2:36, 81–82.

114. General Order No. 8, August 28, 1863; Major General Peck to Colonel Draper, August 29, 1863; Asst. Adj. Gen. J. A. Judson to Colonel Draper, August 29, 1863, all in Letter, Endorsement, and Order Book, Thirty-sixth Regiment USCT, RG 94.

115. Gen. John G. Foster had assumed command of the Department of Virginia and North Carolina. *Official Records,* ser. 1, 29, pt. 2:87–88, 99.

116. *Official Records,* ser. 1, 29, pt. 2:165.

117. Also attached to the brigade was an independent company under Capt. John Wilder, which was briefly attributed to the Third NCCV. *Official Records,* ser. 1, 28, pt. 2:75.

118. *Official Records,* ser. 1, 29, pt. 2:619. At this time the Fifty-fourth Massachusetts and the First NCCV were still stationed at Folly Island, soon to be sent to Florida.

119. Dyer, *Compendium of the War of the Rebellion,* 1729–1730.

120. Gen. E. A. Wild to Maj. Thomas M. Vincent, June 25, 1863, Letters Received, Colored Troops Division, RG 94.

121. By contrast, the white Union troops raised in North Carolina retained their state designation. It is true that the Federal government, as the war progressed, tried to move toward the direct Federal enlistment of volunteers in other areas such as the Veteran Reserve Corps. Nevertheless, the difference in treatment of the white and black North Carolina regiments is very revealing. For a discussion of Federal attitudes on this issue see Russell F. Weigley, *History of the United States Army* (New York: Macmillan, 1967; Bloomington: Indiana University Press, 1984), 213–216.

122. Col. James Beecher to Gen. E. A. Wild, September 13, 1863, Letters Received, Thirty-fifth Regiment USCT, RG 94; General Order No. 105, November 25, 1863, Letters Received, Department of the South, RG 64, both printed in Berlin, Reidy, and Rowland, *Black Military Experience,* 493–494.

123. Colonel Beecher to Lieutenant Colonel Reed, October 29, 1863; Captain Henry to Colonel Beecher, October 29, 1863; Special Order No. 48, October 21, 1863, all in Order and Letter Book, Thirty-fifth Regiement USCT, RG 94.

124. H. R. Wirtz to ——, September 29, 1863, Personal Papers of Medical Officers and Physicians, RG 94.

125. H. R. Wirtz to ——, September 29, 1863, Personal Papers of Medical Officers and Physicians, RG 94.

126. While evidence from the court-martial indicated that De Grasse probably had a dependence on alcohol, it was also clear that some of the charges were radically

motivated. Asst. Surgeon John De Grasse, Proceedings of General Gourts-Martial, RG 153.

127. Col. James Beecher to Col. C. W. Foster, March 14, 1864, Descriptive and Letter Book, Thirty-fifth Regiment USCT, RG 94.

128. These men included Hospital Steward Delos Barber, formerly of the Eighty-fifth New York Volunteers, Sgt. Maj. James Elmsly, formerly corporal in the 132d New York Volunteers, and Commissary Sgt. Charles A. Clark of Brooklyn, N.Y. Order Book, Thirty-fifth Regiment USCT, RG 94.

129. At the time these orders were issued, it may not have been known just how much time company officials would have to spend, often on detached duty, recruiting new troops. General Order No. 1, June 5, 1963, Order Book, Thirty-fifth Regiment USCT, RG 94,

130. Seven of these men received commissions and two, Samuel D. Edgar and Charles Drayton, were brevetted captain for "faithful and meritorious service during the war." A third man, James J. Sullivan, originally the first sergeant in Company C, was ultimately brevetted major. Descriptive Book, Thirty-seventh Regiment USCT, RG 94; "Detachment Received by the 3rd NCCV," Muster Rolls and Records, Thirty-seventh Regiment USCT, RG 94; "Detachment Received by the 3rd NCCV," Muster, Rolls and Records, Thirty-seventh Regiment USCT, RG 94; *Official Army Register of the Volunteer Forces of the U.S, Army for the Years 1861–1865* (Washington: Government Printing Office, 1865), 209.

131. Reilly, "Reconstruction through Regeneration," 45.

132. "Request of the Men of the 36th USCT," William A. Green, Compiled Military Service Records, RG 94.

133. Berlin, Reidy, and Rowland, *Black Military Experience*, 729.

134. Hadley had served as a private in Company D, Thirty-seventh USCT. Another private from that same regiment, William Brewer, described his old unit to the enumerator compiling the 1890 census of Civil War veterans as the "37 Boston Col. Inf." Sandra Lee Almasy, comp., *North Carolina 1890 Civil War Veterans Census* (Joliet, Ill.: Kensington Glen Publishing, 1990), 95, 99.

Chapter 7: Terrible Dilemmas

1. Ira Berlin, Joseph Reidy, and Leslie Rowland, eds., *Freedom: A Documentary History of Emancipation: Series II—The Black Military Experience* (New York, 1982), p. 12.

2. Ibid., p. 12.

3. Leon Litwack, *Been in the Storm So Long: The Aftermath of Slavery* (New York, 1979), p. 75.

4. See, for example, Joseph Glatthaar, *Forged in Battle: The Civil War Alliance of Black Soldiers and White Officers* (New York, 1990), who writes, "In the North, recruiting blacks was not a difficult chore" p. 71; and Benjamin Quarles, *The Negro in the Civil War* (Boston, 1953), pp. 183–98.

5. James Henry Gooding, *On the Altar of Freedom: A Black Soldier's Civil War Letters from the Front,* ed. Virginia M. Adams (New York, 1992), p. 105.

6. Litwack, *Been in the Storm So Long,* p. 27.

7. *Anglo-African,* 17 August 1861.

8. Ibid., 9 November 1861; see James McPherson, *The Negro's Civil War: How American Negroes Felt and Acted During the War for the Union* (New York, 1965),

pp. 20–36, for an excellent summary of Northern blacks' response to the outbreak of war; also Berlin et al., *The Black Military Experience,* chap. 2; Herbert Aptheker, ed., *A Documentary History of the Negro People in the United States,* chap. 4; John Blassingame, ed., *The Frederick Douglass Papers,* ser. 1, vol. 3, 1855–63 (New Haven, 1985); Philip Foner, ed., *The Life and Writings of Frederick Douglass,* vol. 3, *The Civil War* (New York, 1952).

9. McPherson, *The Negro's Civil War,* p. 22; for a full discussion of this issue, see Mary Frances Berry, *Military Necessity and Civil Rights Policy* (New York, 1977), chap. 3.

10. Berlin et al., *The Black Military Experience,* doc. 25.

11. Reid Mitchell, *Civil War Soldiers* (New York: 1988), p. 195.

12. Berry, *Military Necessity,* p. 56.

13. Berlin et al., *The Black Military Experience,* p. 39.

14. Thomas Wentworth Higginson, *Army Life in a Black a Regiment* (Boston, 1962), p. 40.

15. Berlin et al., *The Black Military Experience,* Doc. 127.

16. Ibid., p. 45.

17. For the story of Governor Andrew of Massachusetts and his efforts to form regiments of black soldiers, see James McPherson, *The Struggle for Equality: Abolitionists and the Negro in the Civil War and Reconstruction* (Princeton, 1964), pp. 202–7.

18. Berlin et al., *The Black Military Experience,* p. 113.

19. *Christian Recorder,* 11 July 1863.

20. *Anglo-African,* 14 September 1861.

21. William Wells Brown was one of the few prominent blacks to speak out against enlistment at the beginning of the war. However, by 1863 he had changed his mind and opened a recruiting office in New York. *Anglo-African,* 4 May 1861; *Christian Recorder,* 28 March 1863.

22. At the National Convention for Colored Men held in Syracuse in October 1864, the black elite drew attention to the sacrifices made by black soldiers in defense of the Union to lobby for equal treatment for soldiers and increased political rights for all blacks. Howard Bell, ed., *Minutes of the Proceedings of the National Negro Conventions 1830–1864* (New York, 1969), p. 33.

23. John Blassingame, "The Recruitment of Colored Troops in Kentucky, Maryland and Missouri," *The Historian* 29 (1967), p. 544; Litwack, *Been in the Storm So Long,* p. 79.

24. Berlin et al., *The Black Military Experience,* Doc. 28; Howard Westwood, "The Cause and Consequences of a Union Black Soldier's Mutiny and Execution," *Civil War History* vol. 31 (1985), p. 233; Herman Belz, "Law, Politics, and Race in the Struggle for Equal Pay During the Civil War," *Civil War History,* 22 (1976), p. 198.

25. Berlin et al., *The Black Military Experience,* p. 362.

26. McPherson, *The Negro's Civil War,* p. 197.

27. Gooding, *On the Altar of Freedom,* p. 49.

28. *Christian Recorder,* 2 April 1864.

29. See Westwood, "The Cause and Consequences," for the full details of Sergeant Walker of the 3rd South Carolina Colored Infantry who urged the men under his command to stack arms and declared he "would not do duty any longer for $7 a month." For this he was court-martialed and executed.

30. Berlin et al., *The Black Military Experience,* docs. 149, 68.

31. *Christian Recorder,* 14 February 1863.

32. Ibid., 21 May 1864.
33. Blassingame, *The Frederick Douglass Papers,* pp. 590–598.
34. *Christian Recorder,* 18 July 1863.
35. See Victor Ullman, *Martin R. Delany: The Beginnings of Black Nationalism* (Boston, 1979), p. 279; McPherson, *The Struggle for Equality,* p. 203; and Litwack, *Been in the Storm So Long,* p. 79.
36. Lorenzo Green and Carter Woodson, *The Negro Wage Earner* (New York, 1969), p. 22.
37. Philip Foner and Ronald Lewis, eds., *The Black Worker to 1869: A Documentary History* (Philadelphia, 1969), p. 22.
38. Berlin et al., *The Black Military Experience,* docs. 45, 68.
39. *Liberator,* 12 December 1862.
40. See Edwin Redkey, "Black Chaplains in the Union Army," *Civil War History,* 33 (1987).
41. Howard Westwood, *Black Troops, White Commanders and Freedmen During the Civil War* (Edwardsville, 1992), p. 146.
42. *Christian Recorder,* 5 September 1863; 12 December 1863.
43. Berlin et al., *The Black Military Experience,* doc. 35.
44. *The War of the Rebellion; A Compilation of Official Records of the Union and Confederate Armies* [hereafter *COR*] (Washington: 1880–1901), ser. 3, vol. 4 pp. 559, 694.
45. *Christian Recorder,* 23 May 1863.
46. Ibid., 13 February 1864; See Litwack, *Been in the Storm So Long,* pp. 80–81 for a discussion of the Delany accusations.
47. Dudley Cornish, *The Sable Arm: Negro Troops in the Union Army, 1861–1865* (New York, 1956), p. 183; and Berlin et al., *The Black Military Experience,* pp. 363–8.
48. Higginson, *Army Life,* p. 212.
49. Ira Berlin, Joseph Reidy, Leslie Rowland, and Thavolia Glymph, eds., *Freedom: A Documentary History of Emancipation 1861–1867,* ser. 1, vol. 1: *The Destruction of Slavery* (New York, 1985), doc. 237.
50. Ira Berlin, Joseph Reidy, Leslie Rowland, Thavolia Glymph, Steven Miller and Judy Saville, eds., *Freedom: A Documentary of Emancipation, 1861–1867,* ser. 1, vol. 3: *The Wartime Genesis of Free Labour: The Lower South* (New York, 1990), p. 64.
51. Berlin et al., *The Black Military Experience,* doc. 107.
52. Victor Howard, "The Civil War in Kentucky: The Slave Claims His Freedom," *Journal of Negro History,* 67 (1982), p. 251.
53. Berlin et al., *The Black Military Experience,* p. 659; Berlin et al., *The Destruction of Slavery,* p. 39.
54. Gerald Linderman, *Embattled Courage: The Experience of Combat in the American Civil War* (New York, 1987), p. 8.
55. Glatthaar, *Forged in Battle,* p. 74.
56. Berlin et al., *The Black Military Experience,* p. 30.
57. *Liberator,* 13 March 1863.
58. *Anglo-African,* 14 September 1861.
59. McPherson, *The Negro's Civil War,* p. 169; *Christian Recorder,* 11 July 1863.
60. Glatthaar, *Forged in Battle,* p. 79.
61. *Christian Recorder,* 30 January 1864.
62. Litwack, *Been in the Storm So Long,* p. 64.
63. *Christian Recorder,* 2 April 1864.

64. Berlin et al., *The Black Military Experience,* doc. 46.

65. Cornish, *The Sable Arm,* p. 232.

66. *Christian Recorder,* 7 February 1864.

67. Litwack, *Been in the Storm So Long,* p. 75.

68. Richard Abbot, "Massachusetts and the Recruitment of Southern Negros, 1863–1865," *Civil War History,* 14 (1968), p. 208.

69. Peter Ripley, *Slaves and Freedmen in Civil War Virginia* (Baton Rouge, 1976), p. 107; Berlin et al., *The Black Military Experience,* p. 118.

70. Berlin et al., *The Black Military Experience,* doc. 47b.

71. *Christian Recorder,* 18 July 1863.

72. Glatthaar, *Forged in Battle,* p. 74.

73. A recent study of black soldiers in Civil War Virginia supports this conclusion. "When the 19th United States Colored Infantry was sent from Harper's Ferry to recruit blacks in the Shenandoah Valley in 1864 it was assumed that the sight of blacks in uniform would entice volunteers. After two weeks the regiment returned in failure; fearing conscription and mistreatment, Afro-Virginians not only refused to join but hid themselves." Ervin L. Jordan Jr., *Black Confederates and Afro-Yankees in Civil War Virginia* (Charlottesville, 1955), p. 269.

74. Berry, *Military Necessity,* p. 66.

75. *COR,* ser. 3, vol. 4, p. 132.

76. Eugene Murdock, *One Million Men: The Civil War Draft in the North* (Worcester, 1971), p. 289.

77. *Liberator,* 22 May 1863.

78. *Anglo-African,* 28 September 1861; 5 October 1861. It was common policy in the early part of the war for Union military commanders to return escaped slaves to their Confederate and border state masters.

79. *Christian Recorder,* 23 May 1863.

80. All black officers who served in the Civil War are listed in Berlin et al., *The Black Military Experience,* pp. 310–11. There were just over a hundred officers, three quarters of whom served with the Louisiana Native Guards. All of the officers from this unit were forced to resign.

81. Glatthaar, *Forged in Battle,* p. 41. See chapter 3 in this book for a full discussion of the officers who commanded black regiments.

82. Ibid., p. 109.

83. *Christian Recorder,* 30 July 1864.

84. Robert Alotta, *Civil War Justice: Union Army Executions Under Lincoln* (Shippensburg, 1989), pp. 53, 26, 30. See appendix 2 for a complete listing of the black soldiers executed to the end of 1865.

85. *Christian Recorder,* 9 April 1864; *Liberator,* 7 October 1864.

86. See for example, the *Christian Recorder,* 20 June 1863 for accounts of assaults on black soldiers in Washington D.C. and the *Liberator,* 8 May 1863 for a report of the attempted murder of Dr. Alexander Augusta, one of the few black officers, by a Baltimore mob.

87. Blassingame, *The Frederick Douglass Papers,* p. 597; McPherson, *The Negro's Civil War,* p. 178—cited in *Douglass Monthly* 5 (March 1863), p. 802.

88. Berlin et al., *The Black Military Experience,* pp. 304, 307 and doc. 133, 137.

89. Ibid., doc. 146c.

90. Ibid., p. 483.

91. *Liberator,* 17 July 1863.
92. *COR,* ser. 3, vol. 4, p. 431.
93. Berlin et al., *The Black Military Experience,* doc. 212a.
94. Howard Westwood, "Captive Black Soldiers in Charleston—What to Do?" *Civil War History,* 28 (1982), p. 34.
95. *Christian Recorder,* 13 June 1863.
96. Leon Litwack, "Free at Last" in Tamara Hareven, ed., *Anonymous Americans* (New Jersey, 1971), p. 136.
97. Berlin et al., *The Destruction of Slavery,* doc. 319.
98. Berlin et al., *The Black Military Experience,* doc. 100.
99. Glatthaar, *Forged in Battle,* p. 69.
100. For accounts of Fort Pillow, see Berlin et al., *The Black Military Experience,* Docs. 214a, 214b and 214c; also Albert Castel, "The Fort Pillow Massacre: A Fresh Examination of the Evidence," *Civil War History* 51, 1 (1958).
101. Cornish, *The Sable Arm,* 177.
102. *COR,* ser. 2, vol. 5, pp. 795–7.
103. Ibid., ser. 5, vol. 2, p. 455.
104. Ibid., ser. 2, vol. 5, p. 844.
105. William Hesseltine, *Civil War Prisons* (New York, 1930), p. 104.
106. Gooding, *On the Altar of Freedom,* p. 24; Higginson, *Army Life,* p. 150.
107. For reproductions of recruiting posters see Berlin et al., *The Black Military Experience,* doc. 37; and Glatthaar, *Forged in Battle,* p. 243.
108. Blassingame, "The Recruitment of Colored Troops," p. 545; Berlin et al., *The Black Military Experience,* p. 186.
109. *COR,* ser. 4, vol. 4, pp. 1219, 1228; Berlin et al., *The Black Military Experience,* p. 197.
110. Bobby Lovett, "The Negro's Civil War in Tennessee, 1861–1865" *Journal of Negro History,* vol. 61 (1967), p. 49.
111. *Christian Recorder,* 27 June 1863.
112. Foner, *The Life and Writings of Frederick Douglass,* p. 344.
113. Edwin Redkey, *A Grand Army of Black Men: Letters from African-American Soldiers in the Union Army, 1861–1865* (Cambridge, 1992), p. xv.
114. *Liberator,* 12 June 1863.
115. *Christian Recorder,* 2 April 1864.
116. *Liberator,* 24 July 1863; Blassingame, *The Frederick Douglass Papers,* p. 596.
117. Gooding, *On the Altar of Freedom,* p. 4.
118. Higginson, *Army Life,* p. 22.
119. Berlin et al., *The Black Military Experience,* p. 17.
120. Litwack, *Been in the Storm So Long,* pp. 94, 100.
121. Gooding, *On the Altar of Freedom,* p. 6.
122. McPherson, *The Negro's Civil War,* p. 175—cited in *Douglass' Monthly,* 5 (March 1863), p. 804.
123. Berlin et al., *The Black Military Experience,* p. 570.

Chapter 8: In the Service of the United States

1. Dudley Taylor Cornish, *The Sable Arm: Black Troops in the Union Army, 1861–1865* (Dudley Taylor Cornish, 1956; reprint, Lawrence, Kansas, 1987); Benjamin Quarles,

The Negro in the Civil War (Benjamin Quarles, 1953; New York: Da Capo Press Inc., 1989); James M. McPherson, *The Negro's Civil War: How American Blacks Felt and Acted During the War for the Union* (James M. McPherson, 1965; reprint, New York, 1991); Joseph T. Glatthaar, *Forged in Battle: The Civil War Alliance of Black Soldiers and White Officers* (New York, 1991); Hondon B. Hargrove, *Black Union Soldiers in the Civil War* (Jefferson: McFarland & Co. Inc., 1988); Ira Berlin ed., *Freedom a Documentary History 1861–1867; Selected from the Holdings of the National Archives of the United States, Series 2: The Black Military Experience* (Cambridge, 1982); Herbert Aptheker, "Negro Casualties in the Civil War," *Journal of Negro History* 32 (January, 1947): 10–80; Herbert Aptheker, "The Negro in the Union Navy," *Journal of Negro History* 32 (April, 1947): 169–200; Warren B. Armstrong, "Union Chaplains and the Education of the Freedman," *Journal of Negro History* 52 (January, 1967): 104–115; Martha M. Bigelow, "The Significance of Millikin's Bend in the Civil War," *Journal of Negro History* 45 (July, 1960): 156–163, Frederick M. Binder, "Pennsylvania Negro Regiments in the Civil War," *Journal of Negro History* 37 (October, 1952): 383–417; Albert Castel, "Civil War Kansas and the Negro," *Journal of Negro History* 51 (January, 1966): 125–138; Dudley T. Cornish, "The Union Army As a School for Negroes," *Journal of Negro History* 37 (October, 1952): 368–382; Brainerd Dyer, "The Treatment of Colored Union Troops by the Confederates, 1861–1865," *Journal of Negro History* 20 (January, 1935): 273–286; Fred Harvey Harrington, "The Fort Jackson Mutiny," *Journal of Negro History* 27 (July, 1942): 420–431; Fred A. Shannon, "The Federal Government and the Negro Soldier, 1861–1865," *Journal of Negro History* 11 (October, 1926): 563–583; Edgar A. Toppin, "Humbly They Served: The Black Brigade in the Defense of Cincinnati," *Journal of Negro History* 48 (April, 1963): 75–97.

2. (Baton Rouge, 1971), 124–125; Berlin ed., *Freedom*, 633–655.

3. United States Surgeon General's Office, *The Medical and Surgical History of the War of the Rebellion* (Washington D.C.: United States Government Printing Office, 1888), pt. 3, volume 1, 2 (hereafter referred to as *Medical and Surgical History,* 3:1).

4. United States Surgeon General's Office, *Circular No. 6: Reports on the Extent of the Materials Available for the Preparation of a Medical and Surgical History of the Rebellion* (Philadelphia: J. B. Lippincott & Co., 1865) 96 (hereafter referred to as *Circular No. 6*); *Medical and Surgical History,* 3:1, table facing page 24.

5. United States Surgeon General's Office, *The Medical and Surgical History of the War of the Rebellion (1861–1865)* (Washington D.C.: United States Government Printing Office, 1870), pt. 1, vol. 1, xx–xxi (hereafter referred to as *Medical and Surgical History,* 1:1).

6. Bennet M. D., *Tableau of the Yellow Fever of 1853, With Topographical Chronological and Historical Sketches of the Epidemics of New Orleans Since Their Origin in 1793 Illustrative of the Quarantine Question* (New Orleans, Printed at the Office of the Picayune, 66 Camp Street, 1854).

7. *Annual Reports of the Visitors and the Board of Examiners of the Natchez Institute* (Natchez: Printed at The Daily Courier Book and Job Office, 1854), 6.

8. *Medical And Surgical History,* 3:1, 85.

9. See Peter H. Wood, *Black Majority: Negroes in Colonial South Carolina from 1670 Through the Stono Rebellion* (New York: W. W. Norton & Company, 1974), 63–91

and William H. Freehling, *Prelude to the Civil War: The Nullification Controversy in South Carolina 1816–1836* (New York: Harper & Row, 1966), 7–86, *Medical and Surgical History*, 3:1, 18.

10. Walter D. Glanze, Kenneth N. Anderson, Lois E. Anderson, ed., *Mosby's Medical Nursing and Allied Health Dictionary*, 3d ed. (St. Louis, 1990); Kenneth M. Stampp, *America in 1857: A Nation on the Brink* (New York, 1990), 60, 63, 68.

11. United States Surgeon General's Office, *The Medical and Surgical History of the War of Rebellion* (Washington D.C.: United States Government Printing Office, 1879), pt. 2, vol. 1, 1 (hereafter referred to as *Medical and Surgical History*, 2:1).

12. *Medical and Surgical History*, 1:1, 710–711.

13. The Picura is a part of the lining of the lungs and thorax.

14. Edward Montgomery, "A Few Remarks on the Typhus Fever, Commonly Called Winter Fever," *New Orleans Medical Journal* 2 (July 1945), 21–34; John Duffy, "The Impact of Malaria on the South," in *Disease and Distinctiveness in the American South*, ed. Todd L. Savitt and James Harvey Young (Knoxville, Tenn., 1988), 33; Different varieties of malaria occur in distinct patterns. If the cycle of attacks is daily it is known as quotidian malaria; every other day as tertian malaria; every third day as quartan malaria. Benjamin F. Miller MD and Claire Brackman Keane, RN, BS, MED, *Encyclopedia and Dictionary of Medicine, Nursing, and Allied Health* (Philadelphia: W. B. Saunders Company, 1987), 735–736, 1046; *Medical and Surgical History*, 1:1, 710–711.

15. Dale C. Smith, "The Rise and Fall of Typhomalarial Fever: I. Origins," *Journal of the History of Medicine* (April 1982): 182–220.

16. Ibid., 187.

17. Stewart Brooks, *Civil War Medicine* (Springfield, 1966), 119.

18. This important topic remains without a comprehensive treatment.

19. Todd L. Savitt, "Slave Health and Southern Distinctiveness," in *Disease and Distinctiveness in the American South*, ed. Todd L. Savitt and James Harvey Young (Knoxville, Tenn., 1988), 134.

20. Eugene Genovese, "The Medical and Insurance Costs of Slaveholding in the Cotton South," *Journal of Negro History* 45 (July 1960): 141–155.

21. *Medical and Surgical History*, 3:1, 89.

22. *House Executive Document No. 83*, 38th Cong., 2nd session, Serial No. 1249, 29.

23. Ibid., 29.

24. Ibid.

25. Thomas Wentworth Higginson, *Army Life in a Black Regiment* (Thomas Wentworth Higginson, 1869; reprint New York, 1984), 246.

26. *House Executive Document No. 83*, 89.

27. Aptheker, "Negro Casualties in the Civil War," 20.

28. *Medical and Surgical History*, 1, xv.

29. Peter H. Wood, *Black Majority: Negroes in Colonial South Carolina from 1670 Through the Stono Rebellion* (New York, 1974), 63–91.

Chapter 9: "To Come Forward and Aid in Putting Down This Unholy Rebellion"

The authors would like to acknowledge the assistance of Sara Dunlap Jackson of the National Archives and Edna Medford of the University of Maryland in locating service

records and pension files at the National Archives, Washington, D.C. Thanks are also
due to Ira Berlin and Leslie S. Rowland of the Freedmen and Southern Society Project
at the University of Maryland for their comments on early drafts of this essay.

1. Ira Berlin, *Slaves Without Masters: The Free Negro in the Antebellum South* (New York,
   1974) 108–30: H. E. Sterks, *The Free Negro in Ante-Bellum Louisiana* (Rutherford,
   N.J., 1972): John W. Blassingame, *Black New Orleans 1860–1880* (Chicago, 1973):
   Laura Foner, "The Free People of Color in Louisiana and St. Dominique: A Compar-
   ative Portrait of Two Three-Caste Slave Societies, " *Journal of Social History 3*
   (Summer 1970): 406–30: David C. Rankin, The Orgins of Black Leadership in New
   Orleans During Reconstruction," *Journal of Southern History* 40 (August 1974):
   417–40: Rankin, "The Impact of the Civil War on the Free Colored Community of
   New Orleans, *Perspectives in American History* 11 (1977–78): 379–416, esp. 382–83.
   See also David W. Cohen and Jack P. Greene, eds., *Neither Slave Nor Free: The Freedmen of African Descent in the Slave Societies of the New World* (Baltimore, 1972).
2. George W. Williams, *A History of the Negro Troops in the War of the Rebellion
   1861–1865* (New York, 1888: rep. 1969), 55–57; Joseph T. Wilson, *The Black Phalanx: A History of the Negro Soldiers of the United States in the Wars of 1775–1812,
   1861–65* (New York, 1890: rep. 1968), 72–88; Roland C. McConnell, *Negro Troops
   of Antebellum Louisiana: A History of the Battalion of Free Men of Color* (Baton
   Rouge, 1968): and Mary F. Berry, "Negro Troops in Blue and Gray: The Louisiana
   Native Guards, 1861–63," *Louisiana History* 8 (Spring 1967): 165–90. The service
   of the free blacks with General Jackson generated a legacy that blacks throughout the
   country drew upon during the antebellum years. See especially the references in the
   proceedings of various state conventions of blacks. Philip S. Foner and George E.
   Walker, *Proceedings of the Antebellum Black State Conventions,* 2 vols. (Philadelphia,
   1979), 1:41, 192, 271, 301–2, 324,
3. McConnell, *Negro Troops,* pp. 108–11: see also Antoine Remy, Barthelemy Populus
   and P. Monette to Major General Butler [1862], P-1 1862. Letters Received, Dept.
   of the Gulf, Records of U.S. Army Continental Commands, Record Group (RG)
   393 pt. 1. National Archives, Washington, D.C. (hereafter all record group citations
   will be to documents in the National Archives): and Mt. Moreau et al. to the Senate
   and House of Representatives of the State of Louisiana [undated], printed copy filed
   with Letters Received. Bureau of Civil Affairs, Dept. of the Gulf, RG 393 pt. 1.
4. General Butler's free black translator later explained why freemen chose to serve the
   Confederacy: "If we had not volunteered, they would have forced us into the ranks,
   and we should have been suspected. We have property and rights here, and there is
   every reason why we should take care of ourselves." Quoted in testimony of Benjamin F. Butler before the American Freedmen's Inquiry Commission, 1 May 1863,
   filed with 0–328 1863. Letters Received, Records of the Adjutant General's Office,
   RG 94. A Native Guard officer reported that Confederates threatened injury and
   even death to anyone who refused to cooperate. Testimony of Charles W. Gibbons,
   New Orleans Riots, U.S. Congress, House, Report No. 16, 39th Cong., 2nd Sess.,
   pp. 124–26.
5. Muster rolls, 1st Louisiana Native Guards, Regimental Records. War Department Collection of Confederate Records, RG 109. Rodolphe Lucien Desdumes, *Our People
   and Our History,* ed. and tr., Sister Dorothea Olga McCants (Baton Rouge, 1973),
   pp. 120–21.

6. R. H. Isabelle to Brig. Genl. Ullman, 12 June 1863, Isabelle's compiled service record, 74th U.S. Colored Infantry (hereafter USCI), RG 94.

7. U.S. War Department, *The War of the Rebellion: A Compilation of the Official Records of the Union and Confederate Armies* 128 vols. (Washington, 1880–1901), ser. 1, vol. 15, p. 442; testimony of Butler, 1 May 1863, filed with 0–328 1863. Letters Received, RG 94; Desdunes, *Our People*, pp. 119–20.

8. *Official Records,* ser. 1, vol. 15, p. 535.

9. No other black achieved the field rank of major until the closing months of the war, when Martin R. Delany was appointed major of the 104th USCI. U.S. Adjutant General's Office, *Official Army Register of the Volunteer Force of the United States Army . . .* (Washington, 1865), pt. 8, p. 285.

10. See "The Negro in the Military Service of the United States, 1639–1886," pp. 946–50. Colored Troops Division, RG 94.

11. Joseph G. Parker to E. M. Stanton, 30 May 1863, P-26 1863. Letters Received, Colored Troops Division, RG 94.

12. J. A. Gla et al. to Maj. Gen. N. P. Banks, 19 February 1863, compiled service record of Leon G. Forstall, 75th USCI, RG 94.

13. For hostile views of superior officers, see, for example, the endorsements of Colonel John A. Nelson, commander of the 3rd Native Guard Regiment, upon the resignations of two officers in his regiment, characterizing each as "of no use to the Service And entirely unfit for [command] having no military Knowledge or any Controls over his command." (Capt. Samuel Laurence to Maj. Gen. Nathaniel P. Banks, 4 February 1863, compiled service record of Samuel Laurence, 75th USCI, RG 94; Lt. Ernest Longpre Jr. to Maj. Gen. N. P. Banks, 5 February 1863, Compiled Service Record of Ernest Longpre Jr., 75th USCI, RG 94.) For Banks's view, see the endorsement of his adjutant, Richd. B. Irwin, 25 November 1863, on Joseph G. Parker to E. M. Stanton, 30 May 1863, P-26, 1863. Letter Received, Colored Troops Division, RG 94. The officers' complaints are neatly summarized in Capt. P. B. S. Pinchback et al. to Major Genl. N. P. Banks, 2 March 1863. Letters Received, 6th USCI. Regimental Records U.S. Colored Troops (USCT), RG 94.

14. R. H. Isabelle to Wickham Hoffman, 3 March 1863, compiled service record of Robert H. Isabelle, 74th USCI, RG 94: see also resignations of Arnold Bertonneau to Wickham Hoffman, 2 March 1863. Ernest Morphy to Hoffman, 3 March 1863, and Octave Rey to Hoffman, 2 March 1863, in their respective compiled service records, 74th USCI, RG 94.

15. S. W. Ringgold to Maj. Genl. N. P. Banks, 7 July 1863, and Samuel J. Wilkinson to Banks, 6 July 1863, in their respective compiled service records, 74th USCI, RG 94. The officers protested the composition of the board in Capt. P. B. S. Pinchback et al. to Maj. Genl. N. P. Banks, 31 March 1863, Letters Received, 6th USCI, Regimental Records USCI, RG 94.

16. Joseph Follin to George B. Drake, 18 February 1864, compiled service record, RG 94.

17. Adolph J. Gia et al. to Majr. Genl. Banks, 7 April 1863, G-35 1863, Letters Received, Civil Affairs, Dept. of the Gulf, RG 393 pt. 1.

18. Joseph G. Parker Jr. to Brig. Gen. Daniel Ullmann, 22 May 1863, compiled service record, RG 94. Later Banks's authorized Pinchback to recruit a company of cavalry but subsequently revoked the approval. William J. Simmons, *Men of Mark: Eminent, Progressive and Rising* (New York, 1887: rep. 1968), pp. 759–81: James Haskins, *Pinckney Benton Stewart Pinchback* (New York, 1973), 27–29.

19. Unlike other high ranking officers in the Department of the Gulf, Ullmann seems to have only reluctantly cooperated with Banks's purge of the free black officers. As a rule, he forwarded letters of resignation without comment while other commanders, including General George L. Andrews, vigorously approved the resignations. Cf. the comments of General George Andrews on the resignation of Joseph Follin, cited in n. 17.

20. R. H. Isabelle to Brig. Genl. Ullmann, 12 June 1863. Isabelle's compiled service record, 74th USCI, RG 94.

21. *Official Army Register,* pt. 8, pp. 317–18. Gibbons's testimony, "New Orleans Riots," p. 125.

22. Pension file of Jordan B. Noble, RG 15; McConnell, *Negro Troops,* pp. 114–15.

23. Capt. Sheldon Sturgeon to Maj. Geo. B. Drake, 18 November 1864, enclosing Major Geo. B. Drake to Mr. James Lewis, 1 and 16 November 1864, service record of James Lewis, 73rd USCI, RG 94. The letter from Sturgeon to Lewis of 1 November is a printed authorization to recruit with Lewis's name inserted in manuscript. A list of names of all the black officers who served in the Louisiana Native Guard appears in Ira Berlin, Joseph P. Reidy, and Leslie S. Rowland, eds., *Freedom: A Documentary History of Emancipation, 1861–1867, Series 2: The Black Military Experience* (New York, 1982), p. 310n. That volume also contains transcripts of many of the documents cited in this essay. The names of black officers who served in the two sixty-day regiments raised during the summer of 1863 appear in Adjutant General's Office, *Official Army Register,* pt. 8, pp. 317–18.

24. Lt. Col. C. J. Bassett to Capt. G. B. Halsted, 8 October 1863. Applications for Commissions, Records of Boards of Examination for Commission. Dept. of the Gulf, RG 393 pt. 1.

25. *Official Records,* ser. 1, vol. 15, pp. 556–57.

26. Herman Belz, "Law, Politics, and Race in the Struggle for Equal Pay During the Civil War," *Civil War History* 22 (September 1976): 197–222; James M. McPherson, *The Negro's Civil War: How American Negroes Thought and Acted during the War for the Union* (New York, 1965), pp. 193–203.

27. Capt. P. B. S. Pinchback et al. to Maj. Genl. Banks, 3 March 1863. Letters Received, 6th USCI. Regimental Books & Papers, USCI, RG 94: Capt. P. B. S. Pinchback et al. to Edwin M. Stanton, (October 1863). G-104 1863. Letters Received, Colored Troops Division, RG 94. See also Addl. Paymaster H. O. Brigham to Col. T. P. Andrews, 14 July 1863. #632/20. Letters Received. Records of the Paymaster General of the Army. RG 99, for Banks's earlier determination to pay blacks and whites equally.

28. Williams, *History of the Negro Troops,* pp. 214–23: Wilson, *Black Phalanx,* pp. 207–11 and chap. 5 in general. See also the remarks of P. B. S. Pinchback in undated fragments of speeches. "The Negro as a Soldier," and "The Negro in the Civil War." Pinchback Papers, Moorland-Spingarn Collection, Howard University, Washington, D.C.

29. Adolph J. Gla et al. to Majr. Genl. Banks, 7 April 1863, G-35 1863. Letters Received, ser. 1920, Civil Affairs, Dept. of the Gulf, RG 393 pt. 1.

30. Rich J. Evans to Brig. Gen. Bowen, 21 July 1863. Letters Received. Provost Marshal, Dept. of the Gulf, RG 393 pt. 1.

31. Roger A. Fischer, "A Pioneer Protest: The New Orleans Street-Car Controversy of 1867," *Journal of Negro History* 53 (January 1968): 219–33.

32. J. B. Roudanez and Arnold Bertonneau to A. Lincoln, the Senate and the House of Representatives of the United States, 5 January 1864, HR38A-G25.6. Petitions & Memorials, 38th Cong., Records of the House of Representatives. RG 233: Donald E. Everett, "Demands of the New Orleans Free Colored Population for Political Equality, 1862–1865." *Louisiana Historical Quarterly* 38 (April 1955): 43–64; C. Peter Ripley, *Slaves and Freedmen in Civil War Louisiana* (Baton Rouge, 1974), chap. 9; Peyton McCrary, *Abraham Lincoln and Reconstruction* (Princeton, 1979), chaps. 6–9: William P. O'Connor, "Reconstruction Rebels: The New Orleans Tribune in Post-War Louisiana," *Louisiana History* 21 (Spring 1980): 159–81; LaWanda Cox, *Lincoln and Black Freedom: A Study in Presidential Leadership* (Columbia, S.C., 1981), passim; Haskins, *Pinchback*, pp. 26–27.

33. Proceedings of the Louisiana State Equal Rights Convention, New Orleans *Tribune*, 10–15 January 1865. At the convention, the former officers put in another bid to regain their commissions. Ingraham had attended the Syracuse convention. "Proceedings of the National Convention of Colored Men . . . 1864," p. 5, in Howard H. Bell, ed., *Minutes of the Proceedings of the National Negro Conventions 1830–1864* (New York, 1969).

34. Capt. Hannibal Carter to Col. N. W. Daniels, 8 February 1863, filed with J. A. Pickens to Major General Banks, 5 January 1863. Letters Received. 6th USCI, Regimental Books & Papers USCT, RG 94.

35. James H. Ingraham and Dr. A. W. Lewis to Major General S. A. Hurlbut, 21 March 1865, I-5 1865. Letters Received. Civil Affairs, and M.G. S. A. Hurlbut to Ingraham and Lewis, 23 March 1865, vol. 9, pp. 327–30. Letters Sent, Dept. of the Gulf, RG 393 pt. 1.

36. S. W. Ringgold et al. to the Generals Commanding the District and Department of the Gulf [December 1864], filed with Capt. Geo. E. Smith to Major Geo. W. Durgin Jr., 2 January 1865. S-3 1865. Letters Received. ser. 760. Dist. of Baton Rouge & Port Hudson, RG 393 pt. 2 No. 13.

37. Rankin, "The Impact of the Civil War."

38. Rankin, "Origins of Black Leadership," 417–40; Joe Gray Taylor, *Louisiana Reconstructed, 1865–1877* (Baton Rouge, 1974), passim: Charles Vincent, *Black Legislators in Louisiana during Reconstruction* (Baton Rouge, 1976), passim; Haskins, *Pinchback*, chaps. 4–9.

39. Desdunes's *Our People* represents this trend quintessentially.

40. See especially, Louis B. Harlan, "Desegregation in New Orleans Public Schools During Reconstruction," *American Historical Review* 67 (April 1962): 663–75, and Roger A. Fischer, *The Segregation Struggle in Louisiana, 1863–77* (Urbana, Ill., 1974).

41. Otto H. Olsen, *The Thin Disguise: Turning Point in Negro History, Plessy v. Ferguson, A Documentary Presentation, 1864–1896* (New York, 1967): Haskins, *Pinchback*, pp. 253–55: and Desdunes, *Our People,* chap. 12: Fischer, *Segregation Struggle,* pp. 151–54. One of Desdunes's sons, Daniel, filed the first suit that resulted in the Plessy decision.

Chapter 10: A Brothers' Fight for Freedom

1. See, e.g., James M. McPherson, *Ordeal by Fire: The Civil War and Reconstruction* (New York: Alfred A. Knopf, Inc., 1982), pp. 149–62.

2. Ira Berlin, Joseph P. Reidy, and Leslie S. Rowland, eds., *Freedom: A Documentary History of Emancipation, 1861–1867, Series 2: The Black Military Experience* (Cambridge: Cambridge University Press, 1982), pp. 656–61.

3. Barbara J. Fields, *Slavery and Freedom on the Middle Ground: Maryland during the Nineteenth Century* (New Haven: Yale University Press, 1985), p. 27.

4. State of Maryland, General Assembly, *History and Roster of the Maryland Volunteers, War 1861–1865* (2 vols.; Baltimore, 1899), 2:198–205.

5. Details of the Pinkett brothers' military service were obtained mainly from Record Group 94. Records of the Adjutant-General's Office, National Archives, Washington, D.C. These records, arranged according to military organization, show the name, rank, and unit of individual soldiers and provide information about them based on original muster rolls, returns, hospital rolls, and descriptive books.

6. Joseph M. Califf, *Record of the Services of the Seventh Regiment, U.S. Colored Troops* (Providence, R.I.; R. L. Freeman & Co., 1878; repr. 1971), pp. 18–19. Califf served as a 2d lieutenant in Company F of the regiment. His unique and valuable eyewitness account mentions many experiences that this unit shared with its Maryland counterpart, the 9th Regiment, U.S.C.T.

7. Birney to Maj. C. W. Foster, 12 April 1864, printed in *The War of the Rebellion: A Compilation of the Official Records of the Union and Confederate Armies* (127 vols.; Washington: Government Printing Office, 1880–1901), series 3, 4:226.

8. *History and Roster of the Maryland Volunteers*, 2:156. See also Califf, *Services of the Seventh Regiment*, p. 28.

9. Califf, *Services of the Seventh Regiment*, p. 30.

10. Dispatch of 18 August 1864 in R. J. M. Blackett, ed., *Thomas Morris Chester, Black Civil War Correspondent: His Dispatches from the Virginia Front* (Baton Rouge: Louisiana State University Press, 1989), p. 104.

11. Califf, *Services of the Seventh Regiment*, pp. 45–46.

12. Ibid., p. 63.

13. Blackett, *Thomas Morris Chester*, p. 230.

14. Ibid., p. 277.

15. Califf, *Services of the Seventh Regiment*, p. 68.

16. Blackett, *Thomas Morris Chester*, p. 3.

17. Ibid., p. 313.

18. Califf, *Services of the Seventh Regiment*, p. 86.

19. Berlin, Reidy, and Rowland, *Freedom*, pp. 733–736. See also Joseph T. Glatthaar, *Forged in Battle: The Civil War Alliance of Black Soldiers and White Officers* (New York: The Free Press, 1990), pp. 210, 218.

20. Califf, *Services of the Seventh Regiments*, p. 86.

Chapter 11: Negro Troop Activity in Indian Territory, 1863–1865

1. Williams to Phillips, July –, 1863, U.S. War Department, *War of the Rebellion; A Compilation of the Official Records of the Union and Confederate Armies* (70 vols., 128 books in U.S. Serial Set, Washington; Government Printing Office, 1880–1901), 1, 22, pt. 1, pp. 379–380. Hereinafter cited as *Official Records*. Blunt to Curtis, July 13, 1863, ibid., pt. 2, p. 367; Lary C. Rampp, "The Twilight of the Confederacy in Indian Territory, 1863–1865" (Unpublished Master of Arts Thesis, Oklahoma State University, Stillwater, Oklahoma, 1968), pp. 28–29; Worten

Manson Hathaway, "Brigadier General Stand Watie, Confederate Guerrilla" (Unpublished Master of Arts Thesis, Oklahoma State University, Stillwater, Oklahoma, 1966), pp. 51–59; Barney King Neal Jr., "Federal Ascendancy in Indian Territory, 1862–1863" (Unpublished Master of Arts Thesis, Oklahoma State University, Stillwater, Oklahoma, 1966), pp. 83–87, 95–103; Sharon Dixon Wyant, "Colonel William A. Phillips and the Civil War in Indian Territory" (Unpublished Master of Arts Thesis, Oklahoma State University, Stillwater, Oklahoma, 1967), pp. 41–42, 46–53; Annie Rosser Cubage, "Engagement at Cabin Creek, Indian Territory," *Chronicles of Oklahoma*, X (March 1932), pp. 44–51; James G. Blunt, "General Blunt's Account of His Civil War Experiences," *Kansas Historical Quarterly*, I (May, 1932), pp. 243–245; Wiley Britton, *Memoirs of the Rebellion on the Border, 1863* (Chicago: Cushing, Thomas and Co., 1882), pp. 342–343; Charles R. Freeman, "The Battle of Honey Springs," *Chronicles of Oklahoma*, 8 (June, 1935), p. 154.

2. Rampp, "The Twilight of the Confederacy in Indian Territory, 1863–1865," pp. 28–29; Cubage, "Engagement at Cabin Creek, Indian Territory," *Chronicles of Oklahoma*, 10, pp. 46–47; Williams to Phillips, July –, 1863, *Official Records*, 1, 22, pt. 1, p. 380.

3. Ibid.

4. Ibid., pp. 380–381.

5. Thomas J. Boyd, "The use of Negro Troops by Kansas During the Civil War" (Unpublished Master of Arts Thesis, Kansas State Teachers College, Pittsburg, Kansas, 1950), pp. 1–2.

6. Ibid., pp. 2–4.

7. Ibid., p. 11.

8. Ibid., pp. 14–15.

9. Ibid., p. 15.

10. Ibid., pp. 16, 17, 20–21

11. The Texas Road was also knows as the "Military Road" though the former name was by far the more familiar. The Texas Road ran roughly in a north-south direction bisecting the eastern part of Indian Territory, Rampp, "The Twilight of the Confederacy in Indian Territory, 1863–1865," p. 45.

12. Phillips to Blunt, July 7, 1863, *Official Records*, 1, 22, pt. 1, pp. 378–379; Cubage, "Engagement at Cabin Creek, Indian Territory," *Chronicles of Oklahoma*, 10, pp. 47–48.

13. Wiley Britton, *The Union Indian Brigade in the Civil War* (Kansas City, Missouri: Franklin Hudson Publishing Co., 1922), pp. 258–262; Phillips to Blunt, July 7, 1863, Williams to Phillips, July –, 1863, Foreman to Phillips, July 5, 1863, *Official Records*, 1, 22, pt. 1, pp. 378–379, 380–381, 382.

14. Britton, *The Union Indian Brigade in the Civil War*, pp. 261–263; Williams to Phillips, July –, 1863, Foreman to Phillips, July 5, 1863, *Official Records*, 1, 22, pt. 1, pp. 380, 382.

15. Williams to Phillips, July –, 1863, *Official Records*, 1, 22, pt. 1, p. 380.

16. Ibid., pp. 380–381.

17. Neal, "Federal Ascendancy in Indian Territory, 1862–1863," pp. 102–103; Phillips to Blunt, July 7, 1863, Williams to Phillips, July –, 1863, *Official Records*, 1, 22, pt. 1, pp. 379, 380–381.

18. Britton, *The Union Indian Brigade in the Civil War*, p. 273.

19. Blunt to Schofield, July 26, 1863, Phillips to Blunt, July 7, 1863, General Report, Brigadier General W. L. Cabell, December 7, 1863, *Official Records,* 1, 22, pt. 1, pp. 447, 379, 604; Blunt to Curtis, July 13, 1863, ibid., pt. 2, p. 367; Wiley Britton, *The Civil War on the Border,* 2 vols. (New York: G. P. Putnam's Sons, 1899–1904), 2:100, 115–116; Rampp, "The Twilight of the Confederacy in Indian Territory, 1863–1865," pp. 29–30.

20. Cabell to Duvall, December 7, 1863, Blunt to Schofield, July 26, 1863, *Official Records,* 1, 22, pt. 1, pp. 604, 447; Phillips to Blunt, July –, 1863, ibid., pt. 2, pp. 355–356; Britton, *The Civil War on the Border,* 2:115–119; Britton, *The Union Indian Brigade in the Civil War,* p. 273; Neal, "Federal Ascendancy in Indian Territory, 1862–1863," p. 106; Wyant, "Colonel William A. Phillips and the Civil War in Indian Territory," p. 54; Charles R. Freeman, "The Battle of Honey Springs," *Chronicles of Oklahoma,* 23 (June, 1935), p. 163.

21. Bowles to Judson, July 20, 1863, *Official Records,* 1, 22, pt. 1, p. 449.

22. Ibid., p. 450.

23. Ibid.; Neal, "Federal Ascendancy in Indian Territory, 1862–1863," pp. 107–109; Rampp, "The Twilight of the Confederacy in Indian Territory, 1863–1865," pp. 31–32.

24. Britton, *The Union Indian Brigade in the Civil War,* pp. 282–283.

25. Blunt to Schofield, July 26, 1863, *Official Records,* 1, 22, pt. 1, p. 448; Neal, "Federal Ascendancy in Indian Territory, 1862–1863," pp. 109–110.

26. Joseph Thomas Wilson, *The Black Phalanx: A History of the Negro Soldiers of the United States in the Wars of 1775–1812, 1861–1865* (Hartford, Connecticut: The American Publishing Company, 1888), p. 234; Boyd, "The use of Negro Troops by Kansas During the Civil War," p. 36.

27. Authorization to raise a second regiment of Negro troops came from the War Department in June, 1863. The completion of this second regiment, the Kansas Second Colored Volunteers Regiment, was reached in November, 1863, having ten infantry companies. Boyd, "The Use of Negro Troops by Kansas During the Civil War," pp. 31–36, passim.

28. Wilson, *The Black Phalanx: A History of the Negro Soldiers of the United States in the Wars of 1775–1812, 1861–1865,* pp. 234–240.

29. Maxey to Kirby-Smith, January 15, 1864, Samuel Bell Maxey Papers, Thomas Gilcrease Institute of American History and Art, Tulsa, Oklahoma; Phillips to Curtis, March 7, 1864, *Official Records,* 1, 34, pt. 2, pp. 524–525; Cooper to Scott, June 17, 1864, Watie to Cooper, June 17, 1864, Watie to Cooper, June 27, 1864, ibid., pt. 1, pp. 1011–1012, 1013; Thayer to Steele, May 23, 1864, Thayer to Rosecrans, May 26, 1864, Durbin to Heiston, June 14, 1864, ibid., pt. 4, pp. 11, 50, 687; Civil War Claims, Foreman papers Indian Archives Division, Oklahoma historical Society, Oklahoma City, Oklahoma; James D. Morrison, "Capture of J. R. Williams," *Chronicles of Oklahoma,* 42 (Summer, 1964), pp. 107–108; Britton, *The Union Indian Brigade in the Civil War,* p. 401; Joseph B. Thoburn and Muriel H. Wright, *Oklahoma: A History of the State and Its People* (4 vols., New York: Lewis Historical Publishing Company, Inc., 1929), 1:361–362; Joseph B. Thoburn, *A Standard History of Oklahoma,* I (5 Vols., Chicago: The American Historical Society, 1916), pp. 326–327.

30. Cooper to Steele, June 17, 1864, *Official Records,* 1, 34, pt. 1, p. 1012; Thayer to Steele, June 22, 1864, Maxey to Boggs, June 20, 1864, ibid., pt. 4, pp. 504, 686; Special Orders Number 171, Adjutant and Inspector General's Office, July 21,

1864, ibid., 41, pt. 2, p. 1019; Rampp, "The Twilight of the Confederacy in Indian Territory, 1863–1865," pp. 93–96.

31. Watie to Cooper, June 27, 1864, Watie to Cooper, June 17, 1864, *Official Records,* 1, 34, pt. 1, pp. 1013, 1012; Hathaway, "Brigadier General Stand Watie, Confederate Guerrilla," p. 74; Rampp, "The Twilight of the Confederacy in Indian Territory, 1863–1865," pp. 94–95.

32. Organization of the Army of the Trans-Mississippi Department, Kirby-Smith, C.S. Army, commanding, September 30, 1864, Gano to Cooper, September 29, 1864, Watie to Heiston, October 3, 1864, Johnson to Hoyt, September 25, 1864, Maxey to Boggs, October 7, 1864, Maxey to Boggs, September 16, 1864, *Official Records,* 1, 41, pt. 1, pp. 967, 788–789, 785, 775–776, 780, 777; Hathaway, "Brigadier General Stand Watie, Confederate Guerrilla," p. 77–78. Flat Rock is located on the prairie near the mouth of Flat Rock Creek on the west side of Grand River about five miles northeast of present-day Wagoner, in Wagoner County; Muriel H. Wright and LeRoy H. Fischer, "Civil War Sites in Oklahoma," *Chronicles of Oklahoma,* 44 (Summer, 1966), p. 212; Britton, *The Union Indian Brigade in the Civil War,* pp. 437–440, 428–429, 434–435; Norman P. Morrow, "Prices' Missouri Expedition, 1864" (Unpublished Master of Arts Thesis, University of Texas, Austin, Texas, 1949), pp. 138–158.

33. Baker to Adjutant General, September 20, 1864, *Official Records,* 1, 41, pt. 1, pp. 771–772; Britton, *The Union Brigade in the Civil War,* p. 438; Hathaway, "Brigadier General Stand Watie, Confederate Guerrilla," p. 78; Rampp, "The Twilight of the Confederacy in Indian Territory, 1863–1865," pp. 118–119.

34. For further information on the treatment of the Negro soldier by Confederate forces in Indian Territory and the trans-Mississippi Department, see Britton, *The Union Indian Brigade in the Civil War,* pp. 359–373, 435–439 and Dudley Taylor Cornish, *The Sable Arm: Negro Troops in the Union Army* (New York: Longman, Green and Co., 1956), pp. 145–147.

35. Watie to Cooper, September 23, 1864, Gano to Cooper, September 29, 1864, Watie to Heiston, October 3, 1864, Baker to Adjutant General, September 20, 1864, *Official Records,* 1, 41, pt. 1, pp. 784, 788–789, 785, 771–772; Hathaway, "Brigadier General Stand Watie, Confederate Guerrilla," p. 78; Rampp, "The Twilight of the Confederacy in Indian Territory, 1863–1865," pp. 119–120; Britton, *The Union Indian Brigade in the Civil War,* p. 438.

36. Ibid., pp. 439–440; Maxey to Boggs, October 7, 1864, Cooper to Scott, September 14, 1864, Cooper to Scott, September 24, 1864, *Official Records,* 1, 41, pt. 1, pp. 780, 781, 782.

37. Thayer to Steele, September 8, 1864, Thayer to Wattles, September 14, 1864, Thayer to Wattles, September 18, 1864, ibid., pt. 3, pp. 105–106, 187–188, 238–239.

38. Report of Hopkins, September 22, 1864, Gano to Cooper, September 28, 1864, Watie to Heiston, October 3, 1864, Jennison to Hampton, September 22, 1864, ibid., pt. 1 pp. 766–767, 789–790, 786, 772–773; Britton, *The Union Indian Brigade in the Civil War,* p. 441.

39. Marvin J. Hancock, "The Second Battle of Cabin Creek, 1864," *Chronicles of Oklahoma,* 39 (Winter, 1961–62), pp. 415–418, 420; Report of Hopkins, September 22, 1864, Watie to Heiston, October 3, 1864, Gano to Cooper, September 29, 1864, Jennison to Hampton, September 22, 1864, Watie to Cooper, September 23, 1864, Return of casualties in Gano's brigade, September 19, 1864, Hopkins to Thomas,

September 25, 1864, Sykes to Charlot, September 25, 1864, Oliver to Bell, September 25, 1864, Hildebrand to Cooper, September 26, 1864, Maxey to Boggs, October 8, 1864, *Official Records*, 1, 41, pt. 1, pp. 767, 786, 789, 778, 784, 792, 770–771, 764–765, 778, 779, 780; Rampp, "The Twilight of the Confederacy in Indian Territory, 1863–1865," pp. 129–136; Hathaway, "Brigadier General Stand Watie, Confederate Guerrilla," pp. 78–81.

40. Williams to Blair, September 20, 1864, Gano to Cooper, September 29, 1864, Hildebrand to Cooper, September 26, 1864, Maxey to Boggs, September 30, 1864, Cooper to Scott, September 24, 1864, Cooper to Scott, September 27, 1864, Cooper to Scott, October 1, 1864, Watie to Cooper, September 23, 1864, Watie to Heiston, October 3, 1864, *Official Records*, 1, 41, pt. 1, pp. 765, 790–791, 779, 782, 783, 778, 784, 787–788; Hancock; "Second Battle of Cabin Creek, 1864," *Chronicles of Oklahoma*, 39, pp. 421–423; Hathaway, "Brigadier General Stand Watie, Confederate Guerrilla," p. 80; Rampp, "The Twilight of the Confederacy in Indian Territory, 1863–1865," pp. 137–138.

41. Wilson, *The Black Phalanx: A History of the Negro Soldiers of the United States in the Wars of 1775–1812, 1861–1865*, p. 240.

42. Boyd, "The Use of Negro Troops by Kansas During the Civil War," pp. 47–48.

43. Ibid., p. 48.

44. Dudley Taylor Cornish, "Negro Troops in the Union Army, 1861–1865," (Unpublished Doctoral Dissertation, University of Colorado, Boulder, Colorado, 1949), p. 423.

Chapter 12: Black Chaplains in the Union Army

1. For a concise review of the efforts of blacks to serve as army officers, see Ira Berlin, ed., *The Black Military Experience (Freedom: A Documentary History of Emancipation, 1861–1867; Ser. 2)* (Cambridge: Cambridge University Press, 1982), 303–12. See also John Blassingame, "Negro Chaplains in the Civil war," *Negro History Bulletin* 27 (1963): 23–24.

2. Dudley T. Cornish, *The Sable Arm: Negro Troops in the Union Army, 1861–1865* (New York: Norton, 1966), 129–31; these numbers are derived from the lists of officers who served with the black units, as found in *The Official Army Register of the Volunteer Force of the United States Army for the Years 1861, '62, '63, '64, '65* (Washington, D.C.: Adjutant General's Office, 1865–67).

3. Elon A. Woodward, ed., *The Negro in the Military Service of the United States, 1639–1886*, National Archives Microfilm M858, RG 94, 1087.

4. Governor John A. Andrew, "Special Order," 23 March 1863, in "Letters Official, 1861–1866," 28:322, in Massachusetts State Archives (hereafter cited as MA); W. Jackson to J. A. Andrew, 9 July 1863, "Executive Letters Received 1861–1867," 60:190, MA.

5. *War of the Rebellion: A Compilation of the Official Records of the Union and Confederate Armies*, 128 vols. (Washington, D.C.: GPO, 1880–1901), ser. 3, vol. 1, 154 (hereafter cited as *OR*).

6. David B. Sabine, "The Fifth Wheel," *Civil War Times Illustrated* 19 (1980):21.

7. Rollin W. Quimby, "The Chaplain's Predicament," *Civil War History* 8 (March 1962): 25. See also Quimby, "Congress and the Civil War Chaplaincy," *Civil War History* 10 (September 1964): 246–59. Bell I. Wiley, "'Holy Joes' of the Sixties: A Study of Civil

War Chaplains," *Huntington Library Quarterly* 16 (1952–53):287–304. Charles B. Pfab, "American Hospital Chaplains during the Civil War, 1861–1865" (Master's thesis, Catholic University of America, 1955). Roy J. Honeywell, *Chaplains of the United States Army* (Washington, D.C.: Department of the Army, 1958), 126–51. Sabine, "The Fifth Wheel," 14–23.

8. *Washington Star,* 10 June 1863. *Christian Recorder,* 30 May 1863 (hereafter cited as *CR*). H. M. Turner to E. M. Stanton, 1 August 1863, Letters Received, ser. 360 (Colored Troops Division) T-18, 1863, RG 94, National Archives (hereafter cited as NA).

9. H. M. Turner to E. M. Stanton, 1 and 24 August 1863 and S. P. Chase and O. Lovejoy to E. M. Stanton, 4 September 1863, in Letters Received, ser. 360, T-18, 1863, RG 94, NA; Col. J. H. Holman to Asst. Adjutnat General, 13 October 1863, Adjutant General's Office (AGO) Letters Received 1863, H-138, RG 94, NA. H. M. Turner Service Record, RG 94, NA.

10. W. M. Walker to W. M. Crane, 6 April 1863, Executive Letters Received, 1861–63, 21b:62, MA; A. Stearns to M. Stansfield, 27 May 1863, Governor's Letters Received, new no. 84:171, MA; Dennis Dickerson, "Reverend Samuel Harrison: A Nineteenth Century Black Clergyman," in David W. Wills and Richard Newman, eds. *Black Apostles at Home and Abroad* (Boston: G. K. Hall, 1982), 149–50.

11. J. A. Andrew to Col. R. G. Shaw, 8 July 1863, E. N. Hallowell to J. A. Andrew, 22 August 1863, and Muster Roll, 12 November 1863, all in S. Harrison Service Record, RG 94, NA; Samuel Harrison, *Rev. Samuel Harrison: His Life Story Told by Himself* (Pittsfield, Mass.: privately printed, 1899), 23–28; L. F. Emilio, *A Brave Black Regiment: History of the Fifty-Fourth Massachusetts Volunteer Infantry, 1863–1865* (Boston: Boston Book Co., 1894), 67–104–118.

12. W. J. Hodges to Editor, *Weekly Anglo-African,* 13 February 1864; Dr. T. S. Bell, medical report in F. A. Boyd Service Record, RG 94,NA; Company Muster Roll, November/December 1864, F. A. Boyd Service Record, RG 94, NA; F. A. Boyd to Gen. B. Butler, 5 January 1865, F. A. Boyd Service Record, RG 94, NA, F. A. Boyd to President Andrew Johnson, 12 May 1865, in Berlin, *The Black Military Experience,* 353.

13. G. H. White to Stanton, 7 May 1862, in Berlin, *The Black Military Experience,* 82–3; H. W. Pierson to Charles Sumner, 1 May 1863, Executive Department Letters Received, 1861–1863, 21b:104, MA; G. H. White to W. H. Seward, 27 April 1863, in C. Peter Ripley et al., eds., *Black Abolitionist Papers,* (microfilm edition [New York, Microfilming Corp. of America, 1981–83]), roll 14, frame 0826; G. H. White to W. H. Seward, 18 May 1864 and Col. C. S. Russell to Adjutant General, 1 September 1864, both in G. H. White Service Record, RG 94 NA.

14. Pfab, "American Hospital Chaplains," 13.

15. G. W. LeVere to Christianson, 10 June 1865, G. W. LeVere Service Record, RG 94, NA; J. Asher to AGO, 13 June 1864, AGO Letters Received 1864, microfilm M619, roll 233, frame 0459, A754, NA; H. M. Turner to Editor, 11 February 1865, *CR*, 4 March 1865.

16. D. Stevens to Adjutant General, 20 April 1864, with endorsement on reverse by Gen. B. Butler, D. Stevens Service Record, RG 94, NA; "Harrisburg, Penna., Celebrates Emancipation," *Weekly Anglo-African,* 14 February 1863; H. M. Turner Service Record, RG 94, NA; H. M. Turner to Commissioner of Pensions, 13 June 1901, Turner Pension Record, RG 15, NA; *Official Army Register,* 8:175.

17. H. M. Turner to Editor, 29 February 1865. *CR*, 25 March 1865; H. M. Turner to Editor, 23 June 1865, *CR*, 1 July 1865.

18. Rollin W. Quimby, "Recurrent Themes and Purposes in the Sermons of the Union Army Chaplains," *Speech Monographs* 31 (1964): 425–36.

19. G. H. White to AGO, 30 August 1865, AGO Letters Received, M619, 440, 0238, W1871, NA; C. Leonard to AGO, 30 April 1865, in Berlin, *The Black Military Experience*, 653; B. F. Randolph to AGO, 31 May 1865, in Berlin, *The Black Military Experience*, 420; H. M. Turner to Editor, 18 September 1864, *CR*, 24 September 1864.

20. Ward," 4th USCT to Editor, 26 November 1863, *CR*, 12 December 1863.

21. "Observer J.P." to Editor, 1 September 1864, *CR*, 1 October 1864.

22. G. H. White to Editor, 8 August 1864, *CR*, 20 August 1864; G. H. White to AGO, 30 August 1865, AGO Letters Received, M619, 440, 0238, W1871, NA; B. F. Randolph to AGO, 31 May 1865, in Berlin, *The Black Military Experience*, 420.

23. G. H. White to AGO, 30 August 1865, AGO Letters Received, M619, 440, 0238, W1871, NA; B. F. Randolph to AGO, 31 May 1865, in Berlin, *The Black Military Experience*, 420–21.

24. G. H. White to AGO, 30 August 1865, AGO Letters Received, M619, 440, 0238, W1871, NA. The certificate of a marriage performed by H. M. Turner is reproduced in Berlin, *The Black Military Experience*, 662. G. H. White to AGO, 30 August 1865, AGO Letters Received, M619, 440, W1871, NA.

25. J. Asher to AGO, 13 July 1864, AGO Letters Received, M619, 233, 0459, A754, NA.

26. H. M. Turner to AGO, 6 June 1864, AGO Letters Received, M619, 312 0037, T302, NA; H. M. Turner to AGO, 29 June 1865, AGO Letters Received, M619, 425, 736, NA.

27. G. H. White to AGO, 30 August 1865, AGO Letters Received, M619, 440, 0238, W1871, NA; H. M. Turner to Editor, 23, June 1865, *CR*, 1 July 1865.

28. Cornish, *The Sable Arm*, 288; G. H. White to Editor, 13 June 1864, *CR*, 23 October 1865; H. M. Turner to Editor, 29 February 1864, *CR*, 25 March 1865.

29. G. LeVere to Editor, 1 December 1864, *CR*, 31 December 1864; G. H. White to Editor, 20 April 1865, *CR*, 6 May 1865.

30. Pfab, "American Hospital Chaplains," 1–16.

31. C. Leonard to AGO, 30 April 1865, in Berlin, *The Black Military Experience*, 652–53. Miles Mark Fisher, "The Negro Baptists and Foreign Missions" (B.D. thesis, Northern Baptist Theological Seminary, 1922), 74–76.

32. Letter from Virginia" by "Look In," 2 July 1864, *CR*, 9 July 1864; "Look In" to Editor, 11 July 1864. *CR*, 16 July 1864; J. Asher to AGO, 14 September 1864, AGO Letters Received, M619, 234, A1000, NA.

33. Wiley, "Holy Joes," 289; H. M. Turner to E. M. Stanton, 30 June 1864, in Berlin, *The Black Military Experience*, 359.

34. Cornish, *The Sable Arm*, 232–39. Berlin, *The Black Military Experience*, 9–17, 37–279. John Hope Franklin, ed., *The Diary of James T. Ayres, Civil War Recruiter* (Springfield, Ill., State of Illinois, 1947). John Blassingame, "The Recruitment of Colored Troops in Kentucky, Maryland, and Missouri, 1863–1865," *Historian* 29 (1967): 533–45. Richard H. Abbott, "Massachusetts and the Recruitment of Southern Negroes, 1863–1865," *Civil War History* 14 (1968): 197–210; H. M. Turner to E. M. Stanton, 3 April 1865, Letters Received, ser. 360, T-18, 1865, RG 94, NA.

35. Cornish, *The Sable Arm*, 216–17. For Waring, see *The Official Army Register*, 8:283–85; H. M. Turner to E. M. Stanton, 3 April 1865, Letters Received, ser. 360, T-18, 1865; RG 94, NA. Emphasis in the original handwritten letter.

36. Chester F. Dunham, *The Attitude of the Northern Clergy toward the South, 1860–1865* (Toledo: Gray Co., 1942), 95–100; Warren B. Armstrong, "Union Chaplains and the Education of the Freedmen," *Journal of Negro History* 52 (1967): 104–15; Dudley T. Cornish, "The Union Army as a School for Negroes," *Journal of Negro History* 37 (1952): 368–82; John Blassingame, "The Union Army as an Educational Institution for Negroes, 1862–1865," *Journal of Negro Education* 34 (1965): 153–166; H. M. Turner to Editor, 7 July 1865, *CR*, 22 July 1865.

37. F. A. Boyd to AGO, 31 December 1864, AGO Letters Received, M619, 244, 0137, B1861, NA; H. M. Turner to Editor, 28 November 1864, *CR*, 17 December 1864.

38. C. Leonard to Surgeon General's Office, 30 November 1864, quoted in Pfab, "American Hospital Chaplains," 37; F. A. Boyd to Ago, 31, December 1864, AGO Letters Received, M619, 244, 0137, B1861, NA; E. S. Wheeler to Gen. D. Ullmann, 8 April 1864, in Berlin, *The Black Military Experience*, 618.

39. H. M. Turner to Editor, 7 July 1865, *CR*, 22 July 1865; H. M. Turner to AGO, 14 August 1865, AGO Letters Received, M619, 424,591, NA.

40. H. M. Turner to AGO, 29 June 1865, AGO Letters Received, M619, 425, 736, NA; H. M. Turner to AGO, 14 August 1865, Ago Letters Received, M619, 424, 591, NA.

41. G. H. White to AGO, 1 October 1865, AGO Letters Received, M619, 441, 0018, W2015, NA; H. M. Turner to AGO, 31 August 1865, AGO Letters Received, M619, 425, 695, NA: Trotter is quoted in Joseph T. Wilson, *The Black Phalanx: A History of the Negro Soldiers of the United States* (Hartford: American, 1890), 507.

42. John H. Jenkins to Mrs. Amanda Jenkins (written by John H. Bowles, Chaplain), 22 January 1865, in "Miscellaneous Letters and Papers belonging to the 55th Mass. Volunteer Infantry—Civil War Service" (outer label reads: Prescriptions—36th-40th & 54th-62d Regiments, Vol. 11), Massachusetts War Records Office.

43. G. H. White to Editor, 8 August 1864, *CR*, 20 August 1864; H. M. Turner to Editor, 29 February 1865, *CR*, 25 March 1865.

44. Dickerson, "Reverend Samuel Harrison," 150–57; Jesse B. Barber, *Climbing Jacob's Ladder: The Story of the Work of the Presbyterian Church, U.S.A., among the Negroes* (New York: Board of National Missions of the Presbyterian Church in the U.S.A., 1952), 38; Clifford M. Drury, *Presbyterian Panorama: One Hundred Years of National Missions History* (Philadelphia: Westminster, 1952), 134–35; C. G. Woodson, "The Waring Family," *Negro History Bulletin* 12 (February 1948): 99–107; Thomas Holt, *Black over White: Negro Political Leadership in South Carolina During Reconstruction* (Urbana: University of Illinois Press, 1979), 105, 141; Edwin S. Redkey, *Black Exodus: Black Nationalist and Back-to-Africa Movements, 1890–1910* (New Haven: Yale University Press, 1969), 24–31, passim; Edwin S. Redkey, *Respect Black! The Writings and Speeches of Henry McNeal Turner* (New York: Arno, 1971).

Chapter 13: Occupying the Middle Ground

1. The idea of a red, white, and black cultural equation being of central importance is an understanding of American History is most forcefully brought out in Gary D. Nash, *Red, Black, and White: The Peoples of Early North America* (Englewood Cliffs, New Jersey: Prentice Hall, 1992). Murray Wickett applied the same idea in this dissertation, "Contested Territory: Whites, Native Americans and African

Americans in Oklahoma, 1865–1907," (Ph.D. diss., University of Toronto, 1996). Richard White coined the term "middle ground" in *The Middle Ground: Indians, Empires, and the Republics in the Great Lakes Region, 1650–1815* (Cambridge: Cambridge University Press, 1991).

2. Daniel F. Littlefield, *Africans and Creeks: From the Colonial Period to the Civil War* (Westport, Connecticut: Greenwood Press, 1979), 151; Angie Debo, *The Road to Disappearance: A History of the Creek Indians* (Norman: University of Oklahoma Press, 1941), 127.

3. T. Lindsay Baker and Julie P. Baker, *The WPA Oklahoma Slave Narratives* (Norman: University of Oklahoma Press, 1996), 225–226, 172–173; Claim 91–Jacob Perryman, Records Relating to the Loyal Creek Claims, Record Group (RG) 75, National Archives (NA), Washington, D.C. (hereafter cited as Loyal Creek Claims, claim number, and name).

4. Littlefield, *Africans and Creeks,* 151; Interview with George McIntosh, "Indian-Pioneer History Collection," ed. Grant Foreman (112 vol., unpublished manuscript), 7:73, Archives and Manuscripts Division, Oklahoma Historical Society, Oklahoma City (hereafter cited as "I-PH," AMD OHS); Claim 519–David Barnwell, Claim 143–Thomas Bruner, Claim 55–Joseph Cooney, Loyal Creek Claims, NA.

5. Sigmund Sameth, "Creek Negroes: A Study of Race Relations" (M.A. thesis, University of Oklahoma, 1941), 20–23; Interview with Siegal McIntosh, "I-PH," 35:236–237, AMD OHS.

6. Baker and Baker, *Slave Narratives,* 30, 172, 109; Interview with Ned Thompson, "I-PH," 112:279, AMD OHS.

7. William Capers, "Report before the Bishops and South Carolina Conference of the Methodist Episcopal Church: February 21, 1822" (Georgetown: Wiayan Intelligencer, 1822), 3, and "Second Annual Report of the Missionary Commission of the South Carolina Conference: February 26, 1823" (Midgeville, Georgia: Grantland and Ormer, 1823), 6, Gilcrease-Hargrett Collection, Manuscripts Division, Thomas Gilcrease Institute of American Art and History, Tulsa, Oklahoma (hereafter cited as GH); James S. Buchanan, Research, "I-PH," 89: 298–308, AMD OHS; Isaac McCoy, *Periodical Account of the Baptist Missions Within the Indian Territory* (Shawnee Mission, Indian Territory: Isaac McCoy, 1836), 40, Special Collections, Mullins Library, University of Arkansas-Fayetteville; Isaac McCoy, *Annual Register of Indian Affairs Within the Indian Territory: 1835* (Shawnee Mission, Indian Territory: Isaac McCoy, 1835–1838), 14, *1836,* 15, *1837,* 19, *1838,* 52, in "Western Americana: History of the Trans-Mississippi West, 1500–1900" (New Haven, Connecticut: Research Publications, 1975), Entry 177, Reel 12; Carolyn T. Foreman, "North Fork Town," *The Chronicles of Oklahoma,* 29 (Spring, 1951): 81–*83,* 95.

8. Sameth, "Creek Negroes," 38; Ethan Allen Hitchcock, *A Traveler in the Indian Territory,* ed. Grant Foreman (Cedar Rapids, Iowa: Torch Press, 1930), 95 n56; Littlefield, *African and Creeks,* 139–140; Baker and Baker, *Slave Narratives,* 111–112.

9. Creek Nation, *Laws of the Creek Nation,* Laws 110–111, Grant Foreman Collection, AMD OHS (hereafter cited as *Creek Laws* and law number); United States Census Bureau, *Population Schedules of the Eighth Census of the U.S. 1860: Arkansas and Indian Lands,* "Non-Citizens, Creek Nation," M653, Reel 52, passim, NA (hereafter cited as *Eighth Census*); Littlefield, *Africans and Creeks,* 154.

10. *Creek Laws,* 124–133; Althea Bass, *The Story of Tullahassee* (Oklahoma City, Oklahoma: Semco Color Press, 1960), 90; Debo, *Road to Disappearance,* 142–146.

11. Littlefield, *Africans and Creeks,* 235–236; Christine Schultz White and Benton R. White, *Now the Wolf Has Come: The Creek Nation in the Civil War* (College Station: Texas A&M University Press, 1996), 9–10; Debo, *Road to Disappearance,* 142–147: Kenneth W. Porter, "Billy Bowlegs (Holuta Micco) in the Civil War: Part 2," *Florida Historical Quarterly,* 45 (April, 1967), 391.

12. United States War Department, *War of the Rebellion: Compilation of the Records of the Union and Confederate Armies,* 70 vols. In 128 books and index (Washington, D.C., 1890–1901), ser. 1, vol. 8: 5 (hereafter cited as *OR* and series, volume, part, and page numbers).

13. Baker and Baker, *Slave Narratives,* 31, 173; Littlefield, *Africans and Creeks,* 236.

14. Enrollment Card 357–Simon Brown, Enrollment Cards for the Five Civilized Tribes: Creek Freedom, M1186, Reel 85, NA; Bass, *Story of Tullahassee,* 131; William S. Robertson to Parens, October 22, 1848, Box 2, File 7, and William Robertson to Unidentified, ca. September, 1850, Box 3, File 8, Alice Robertson Collection, AMD OHS.

15. James L. DeGroot, "Old Timer Article," n.d., ser. 1, Box 1, File 3, Alice Robertson Collection, McFarlin Library, Special Collections, University of Tulsa, Oklahoma.

16. Claim 58–Simon Brown, Loyal Creek Claims, NA.

17. Frist Indian Home Guard Muster Roll, Company H, October-December, 1862, Records of the Adjutant General's Office, United States War Department, RG 94, NA (hereafter cited as Muster Roll(s), company designation, and date).

18. J. P. Evans to his wife, December 5, 1861, John Drew Collection, Folder 309, GI.

19. House, *Report of the Secretary of the Interior: Commissioner of Indian Affairs Report 1862,* 37th Cong., 3d sess., H. Ex. Doc. 1, 286–287, 295, NA (hereafter cited as *COIA* and year); William Kile to William Dole, February 21, 1862, Letters Received by the Office of Indian Affairs: 1824–1880, M234, Roll 834, Frame 1548, NA (hereafter cited as LROIA and roll and frame numbers).

20. Sameth, 23; *COIA, 1862,* 298, NA; Kile to Dole, February 21, 1862, LROIA, Roll 834, Frame 1548, NA.

21. A. G. Lorenzo Thomas to Col. Robert W. Furnas, April 2, 1862, Records of the United States Army Adjutant General's Office, First Indian Home Guard Regimental Order Book, 1, NA (hereafter cited as Order Book); *Emporia* (Kansas) *News,* February 8, 1862.

22. Muster Rolls, Companies A, C, E, G, H, and I, NA; First Indian Home Guard Descriptive Book, Records of the Adjutant General's Office, War Department, passim, BG 94, NA (hereafter cited as Descriptive Book).

23. Robert C. Farb, "The Military Career of Robert W. Furnas," *Nebraska History,* 32 (March, 1951): 19–20.

24. Albert Chapman Ellithorpe, "Biographical material 1897–1907," Ellithorpe Family Papers, Box 1, Folder 4, Manuscript Collections, Kansas State Historical Society (KSHS), Topeka; Annie Heloise Abel, *The American Indian in the Civil War: 1862–1865* (1919; Lincoln: University of Nebraska Press, 1992), 126 n135.

25. *OR,* 1, 13: 452.

26. *COIA, 1862,* 306–308, NA.

27. A. C. Ellithorpe, July 12, 14, 1862, Diary of A. C. Ellithorpe, private collection of Dr. Tom Sweeney and on display at General Sweeney's: A Museum of Civil War

History, Republic, Missouri; *OR*, 1, 13: 181–183; Furnas to Stanton, September 7, 1862, Robert W. Furnas Papers, Roll 11, Frames 11324–11327, Archives and Manuscripts Division, Nebraska Historical Society, Lincoln.

28. Ellithorpe Diary, July 12, 14, 1862, Sweeney Collection; *OR* I, 13: 181–183.
29. Cutler to Coffin, August 13, 1862, LROIA, Roll 834, Frames 1263–1265, NA.
30. Abel, *American Indian in the Civil War,* 195, 203; Muster Rolls, Companies A, B, C, E, F, G, H, I, and K, August-October, 1862, and October-December, 1862.
31. Order Book, 7, NA; Blunt to Smith, November 21, 1862, LROIA, Roll 834, Frame 1532, NA.
32. Muster Rolls, Companies A, C, E, G, and I, NA.
33. Edwin C. Manning, *Biographical, Historical and Miscellaneous Selections* (Cedar Rapids, Iowa: privately printed, 1911), 48–49; John Howard Kitts, "The Civil War Diary of John Howard Kitts," *Kansas State Historical Society Collections,* 14 (1918): 324.
34. John Bartlett Meserve, "The Perryman's," *The Chronicles of Oklahoma,* 15 (March, 1937): 177–178.
35. Interview with Richard Atkins, "I-PH," 12: 128–129, AMD OHS.
36. Baker and Baker, *Slave Narratives,* 31, 172–174.
37. Claims 48, 91, 96, 97, 98, 100, 119, 135, 198, Loyal Creek Claims, NA.
38. R. C. Parks, November 9, 1862, Day Book, First Cherokee Regiment (Confederate), Military History Collection, KSHS.
39. Luman Harris Tenney, *War Diary of Luman Harris Tenney: 1861–1865* (Cleveland, Ohio: Evangelical Publishing House, 1914), 44.
40. Muster Rolls, Companies C and H, October-December, 1862, NA; Descriptive Book, Company D, NA.
41. Ellithorpe Diary, November 17, 18, 1862, Sweeney Collection; Muster Rolls, Companies C and I, October-December, 1862, NA.
42. Ellithorpe to Chipman, November 21, 1862, Ellithorpe to Coffin and Creek Chiefs and Soldiers, November 7, 1862, Ellithorpe Collection, KSHS; Ellithorpe Diary, November 17, 1862, Sweeney Collection.
43. Case MM377–Lieutenant George H. Dobler, Records of the Unites States Army Judge Advocate, Court-Martial Case Files, 4, RG 153, NA (hereafter cited as JA with case number, name, and page number).
44. Manning, *Selections,* 48.
45. Ibid., 48; Ellithorpe Diary, November 29, 1862, Sweeney Collection; *OR,* 1, 22, pt. 1: 48.
46. Muster Rolls, Companies A, C, E, G, H, and I, October-December, 1862, NA; Descriptive Book, passim, NA.
47. *Arkansas Gazette,* December 27, 1862; *San Antonio Herald,* January 10, 1863, based on transcription generously provided by Michael E. Banasik, Wentzville, Missouri.
48. Muster Rolls, Companies C and I, October-December, 1862, NA; *OR,* 1, 22, pt. 1: 168, 873–874.
49. *Chicago Evening Journal,* January 8, 29, 1863, taken from transcriptions, Sweeney Collection.
50. Ibid., January 29, 1863.
51. Baker and Baker, *Slave Narratives,* 176.
52. Interview with Ellen Rentie Bruner, "I-PH," 89: 262, AMD OHS; Muster Rolls, Companies B, C, G, and I, December, 1862–February, 1863, NA; Descriptive Book, Company D, NA.

53. Long John to Lincoln, March 10, 1864, LROIA, Roll 803, S 21; *OR*, 1, 22, pt. 2: 162–163, 165–167, 282–283.
54. Order Book, passim, NA.
55. Wiley Britton, *Memoirs of the Rebellion on the Border* (1882; Lincoln: University of Nebraska Press, 1993), 141–142; Wiley Britton, *The Civil War on the Border: Volume 2* (1899; Ottawa: Kansas Heritage Press, 1994), 24–25.
56. *COIA, 1863,* 307, *1864,* 452, NA.
57. Interview with Jake Simmons, "I-PH," 9:355, AMD OHS; Wiley Britton, *The Union Indian Brigade in the Civil War* (1922; Ottawa: Kansas Heritage Press, n.d.), 273.
58. Order Book, "Special Order 36, August 8, 1863," 19, NA.
59. Muster Rolls, various companies, April, 1863–May, 1865, NA; Order Book, passim, NA. From early 1863 until the unit was mustered out of service in May, 1865, an overwhelming number of the orders issued in the First Indian involved assignments and reassignments for the African Creek soldiers.
60. Bruner interview, 89: 262.
61. Baker and Baker, *Slave Narratives,* 32.
62. *COIA, 1863,* 338–339, 341, NA.
63. *OR*, 1, 22, pt. 1: 689, 701; Muster Rolls, Company C, August-October, 1863, NA; Descriptive Book, Company D, NA.
64. Muster Roll, Company H, August-October, 1863, NA.
65. Abel, *American Indian in the Civil War,* 322–323; *OR*, 1, 34, pt. 2: 272.
66. Descriptive Book, passim, NA; Muster Rolls, Companies D, E, and I, August-October and October-December, 1863, NA.
67. Muster Roll, Company H, January, 1864–May, 1865, NA; Order Book, "Special Order 88," May 3, 1864, 35, NA.
68. *COIA, 1864,* 476, NA.
69. Muster Rolls, various companies, June-September, 1864, NA.
70. D. D. Hitchcock to Anna Eliza W. Robertson, March 24, 1864, June 2, 1864, Box 18, Folder 1, Alice Robertson Collection, McFarlin Library, Special Collections, University of Tulsa.
71. Descriptive Book, Companies B, D, E, G, and H, NA.
72. Court Martial Files, NN3397–Tas-he-hia-e-ha, and NN3157–Sul-lik-koh-hih, passim, JA.
73. Muster Rolls, various companies, June, 1864–April, 1865, NA; *OR*, 1, 48, pt. 1: 143–145, 543–544, 1193; pt 2: 89.
74. Abel, *The American Indian and the End of the Confederacy: 1863–1865* (1925; Lincoln: University of Nebraska Press, 1994), 97. In chapter three, "Cattle Driving in the Indian Country," 73–97, Abel provides a thorough look at the complexities and the scope of the rustling activities.
75. Claim 91–Jacob Perryman, Loyal Creek Claims, NA; Daniel Childress Affidavit, LROIA, Roll 836, Frame 1077, NA; Oc-ta-has-as-har-jo to Commissioner Dole, January 11, 1865, Roll 231, Frames 41–42, NA; Fred Crafts Affidavit, LROIA, Roll 836, Frames 1090–1091, NA.
76. *OR*, 1, 41, pt. 1: 605–606; *COIA, 1865,* 436–437, 447, 450–452, 455–456, NA.
77. Muster Rolls, Companies A, E, and I, December, 1864–April, 1865, NA; Phillips to Dole, February 27, 1865, LROIA, Roll 231, Frames 47–48, NA; *OR*, 1, 48, pt. 2: 27, 136.

78. *OR*, 1, 48, pt. 2: 27, 136; Muster Rolls, Companies A, E, G, and I, February-April, 1865, NA.

79. Muster Roll, Company I, April-June, 1863, NA. Silas Jefferson, also known as "Tucker" in the African Creek community, later served in the House of Warriors and was one of Isparhecher's principal lieutenants. Debo, *Road to Disappearance,* 246, 268, 279. Tucker enlisted on May 27, 1863, at Fort Blunt (Gibson) in Company I.

80. The identified African Creek soldiers' graves at Fort Gibson National Cemetery include:

	Company	Grave Number	Section
Book	C	702	1
Peter Johnson	C	154	1
John Steadham	C	1239	2
George	D	538	1

Chapter 14: *"We Cannot Treat Negros . . . As Prisoners of War"*

1. April 18, 27, 1864, "Receipts" Book (Diary), Henry Merrell Papers, Southwest Arkansas Regional Archives, Washington, Arkansas; *Fort Smith New Era,* May 7, 21, 1864. For a recent overview of military operations in Arkansas that places the Poison Spring affair in context, see Mark K. Christ, ed., *Rugged and Sublime: The Civil War in Arkansas* (Fayetteville: University of Arkansas Press, 1994).

2. Jay S. Miller and Elwin Goolsby, *The Red River Campaign in Arkansas* (Little Rock: Arkansas State Parks, 1989), 1–4; *Arkansas Democrat Gazette,* September 11, 1994

3. Wiley Britton to his wife, "The Camden Expedition," June 1, 1864, pp. 1, 10, Wiley Britton Letters, J. N. Heiskell Historical Collection, H-4, 13, UALR Archives and Special Collections, UALR Library, University of Arkansas at Little Rock; Wiley Britton, *The Union Indain Brigade in the Civil War* (Kansas City, Mo.: Franklin Hudson, 1922), 346–47, 355–56; Dudley Taylor Cornish, "Kansas Negro Regiments in the Civil War," *Kansas Historical Quarterly* 21 (May 1953): 420–27; *Lafayette County (Ark) Democrat,* July 8, 1971; John M. Harrell, "Arkansas," in Clement A. Evans, ed., *Confederate Military History,* vol. 10 (Seacaucus, N.J.: Blue and Grey, 1975), 239; "An Abstract of Facts in Case of John Taylor, Co. C. 79th U.S.C. Troops," ca. 1891, Military File of John Taylor, Military Service Branch, National Archives, Washington, D.C.

4. Ludwell H. Johnson, *Red River Campaign: Politics and Cotton in the Civil War* (1958; reprint, Kent, Ohio: Kent State University Press, 1993), 46–48, 81, 85.

5. March 25, 1864, James A. Campbell Diary, J. N. Heiskell Historical Collection, H-16, box 1, file 4, UALR Archives and Special Collections; *The War of the Rebellion: A Compilation of the Official Records of the Union and Confederate Armies,* 128 vols. (Washington D.C.: GPO, 1880–1901), ser. 1, vol. 34, 1:660–63 (hereafter cited as *OR,* with all references to ser. 1, vol. 34, pt. 1, unless otherwise noted); Roman J. Zorn, ed., "Campaigning in Southern Arkansas: A memoir by C. T. Anderson," *Arkansas Historical Quarterly* 8 (Autumn 1949): 241–42; John N. Edwards, *Shelby and His Men; or, the War in the West* (Cincinnati: Miami Printing and Publishing, 1867), 263; Harrell, "Arkansas," 238–39.

6. Carl H. Moneyhon, *The Impact of the Civil War and Reconstruction on Arkansas: Persistence in the Midst of the Ruin* (Baton Rouge: Louisiana State University Press,

1994), 116, 129; Lenore Routon, "The Carrigans: Family History" (1945), p. 129, MsF# 326, Southwest Arkansas Regional Archives, Washington, Arkansas; George Boddie to Mary E. Boddie, Feb. 2, 1864, and George Boddie to Mary E. Boddie, Feb. 12, 1864, in Sarah M. Fountain, ed., *Sister, Seeds, & Cedars: Rediscovering Nineteenth-Century Life through Correspondence from Rural Arkansas and Alabama* (Conway: University of Central Arkansas Press, 1995), 174–75; April 20, 1864, John W. Brown Diary, Arkansas History Commission, Little Rock; *OR,* 661, 679–80; April 15, 1864, Campbell Diary: A. W. M. Petty, *A History of the Third Missouri Cavalry from Its Organization at Palmyra, Missouri, 1861, up to November Sixth, 1864: With an Appendix and Recapitulation* (Little Rock: J. William Denby, 1865), 67–68; April 23, 1864, Merrell Diary; Britton, *Union Indian Brigade,* 360–61.

7. *OR,* 743–44, 746; Britton, *Union Indian Brigade,* 362–63; Glenn L. Carle, "The First Kansas Colored," *American Heritage,* February-March 1992, 79–80, 82–90.

8. *OR,* 680, 743–44, 819, 828, 848, 849.

9. Ibid., 819, 828, 848, 849; James L. Skinner III, ed., *The Autobiography of Henry Merrell: Industrial Missionary to the South* (Athens: University of Georgia Press, 1991), 352; Harrell, "Arkansas," 238–39.

10. *OR,* 745, 751–54, 792, 818–19, 842; *Fort Smith New Era,* May 21, 1864; Britton, *Union Indian Brigade,* 369; William M. Stafford, "Battery Journal," April 18, 1864, M. D. Hutcheson Papers, Camden, Arkansas.

11. *OR,* 745–46, 752–53, 755–56, 829; Britton, *Union Indian Brigade,* 370–72.

12. *Washington Telegraph,* May 25, 1864; April 18, 1864, Campbell Diary; April 18, 1864, Merrell Diary; *OR,* 746, 748, 754, 756; *Fort Smith New Era,* May 7, 21, 1864; Britton, *Union Indian Brigade,* 372–73.

13. *OR,* 746, 753; *Fort Smith New Era,* May 7, 28, 1864; Petty, *Third Missouri Cavalry,* 76.

14. Stafford "Battery Journal" April 18, 1864; John C. Wright, *Memoirs of Colonel John C. Wright* (Pine Bluff, Ark.: Rare Book Publishers, 1982), 142; J. T. Kidd, "The History of J. T. Kidd from March 18th, 1862, until May 28th, 1865," n.d., p. 12, SF# 101, Southwest Arkansas Regional Archives; "A Confederate Veteran's Story," in Charlean Moss Williams, ed., *The Old Town Speaks: Washington, Hempstead County, Arkansas* (Houston: Anson Jones Press, 1951), 91; *Lafayette County Democrat,* July 15, 1971; Ralph R. Rea, *Sterling Price: The Lee of the West* (Little Rock: Pioneer Press. 1959), 160; *Washington Telegraph,* May 11, 1864; Edmund Kirby Smith to his wife, April 20, 1864, Edmund Kirby Smith Papers, Southern Historical Collection, Manuscripts Department, Wilson Library, University of North Carolina, Chapel Hill; Skinner, *Autobiography of Henry Merrell,* 367–68.

15. Stafford, "Battery Journal," April 18, 1864; Zorn, "Campaigning in Southern Arkansas," 242–43; James McCall Dawson to "Dear Father Sister and Brothers," May 5, 1864, in James Reed Eison, ed., "'Stand We in Jeopardy Every Hour': A Confederate Letter, 1864," *Pulaski County Historical Review* 31 (Fall 1993): 52. For another account of the massacre by a different member of Dawson's regiment, see W. C. Braly to "My Dear Ma," May 7, 1864, Amanda Malvina Fitzallen; McClellan Braly Papers, Special Collections Division, University of Arkansas Libraries, Fayetteville; Elizabeth Godbold Watts to John Comer Watts, May 9, 1864, in "Poison Springs Battle Recalled by 1864 Letter," *Ouachita County Historical Quarterly* 19 (September 1987): 14; *Fort Smith New Era,* May 21, 1864.

16. *Washington Telegraph,* May 11, 1864; Charles H. Lothrop, *A History of the First Regiment Iowa Cavalry Veteran Volunteers, from Its Organization in 1861 to Its Muster Out of the United States Service in 1866* (Lyons, Iowa: Beers and Eaton, 1890), 182; For more on the Choctaws' implacable hatred for black Union troops, see Henry Cathey, ed., "Extracts from the Memoirs of William Franklin Avera," *Arkansas Historical Quarterly* 22 (Summer 1963): 103, 107; Wright, *Memoirs,* 146; John Hallum, *Reminiscences of the Civil War,* vol. 1 (Little Rock: Yunnah and Pittard, 1903), 115–16, 315–16; *Fort Smith New Era,* May 28, 1864; *Washington Telegraph,* August 3, 1864, Skinner, *Autobiography of Henry Merrell,* 367–68; *OR,* 843, 849.

17. Hellice Gillespie Burton, *Arkansas' Role in the War between the States 1861–1865* (Houston: Privately printed, 1986) 12; Cathey, "Avera Memoirs," 107; May 2, 3, 1864, Mary Elizabeth Moore Carrigan Diary, SMF# 479, Southwest Arkansas Regional Archives; April 18, 1864, Merrell Diary; Artie Whiteside Vardy, "The Battle of Moscow: As It Was Told to Me by My Grandmother, Martha Holcomb," n.d., p. 2, SMF# 191, Southwest Arkansas Regional Archives.

18. *OR,* 781, 791–92, 820, 842–43, 847–49; For additional consideration of this point, see Ira Don Richards, "The Battle of Poison Spring: *Arkansas Historical Quarterly* 18 (Winter 1959): 349; Anne J. Bailey, "Was There a Massacre at Poison Spring?" *Military History of the Southwest* 20 (Fall 1990): 161.

19. *OR,* 847, Harrell, "Arkansas," 250; *Lafayette County Democrat,* July 15, 1971.

20. Aside from officers of the 1st Kansas, the Confederates may have murdered at least one white Federal soldier at Poison Spring. But the motive was racial even in this case, as the Unionist *Fort Smith New Era* reported: "An officer . . . saw a man who was wounded taken out of the ambulance by the rebels and asked what command he belonged to, he told them the 18th Iowa, they called him a *damned liar,* and said he belonged to the 12th Kansas, brigaded with the negroes and knocked his brain out with the butt of a gun." *OR,* 743–44; *Fort Smith New Era,* May 7. 1864.

21. *OR,* 744, 748; Britton *Union Indian Brigade,* 365; Burton, *Arkansas'Role,* 11.

22. Burton, *Arkansas' Role,* 12.

23. April 17, 24, 1864, Brown Diary; *Washington Telegraph. May* 25, 1864; United Confederate Veterans, Arkansas Division, *Confederate Women of Arkansas in the Civil War 1861–65: Memorial Reminiscences* (Little Rock; H. G. Pugh, 1907), 41, 49–52. See also "The Federal Occupation of Camden as Set Forth in the Diary of a Union Officer," *Arkansas Historical Quarterly* 9 (Autumn 1950): 216–17; Clara Dunlap to "Dear Dear Sister," July 24, 1864, Fred J. Herring Collection, Small Manuscripts Collection, Arkansas History Commission. For more on the depredations committed by Kansas cavalrymen in the Trans-Mississippi, see Stephen Z. Starr, *Jennison's Jayhawkers: A Civil War Cavalry Regiment and Its Commander* (Baton Rouge: Louisiana State University Press, 1973); Arabella Lanktree Wilson to William H. D. Wilson, November 2, 1863, in James W. Leslie, ed., "Arabella Lanktree Wilson's Civil War Letter," *Arkansas Historical Quarterly* 47 (Autumn 1988): 257–72.

24. Lonnie J., White, ed., "A Bluecoat's Account of the Camden Expedition," *Arkansas Historical Quarterly* 24 (Spring 1965): 84; Vardy, "Battle of Moscow," 2.

25. *Washington Telegraph,* May 25, 1864.

26. Vardy, "Battle of Moscow," 2; April 18, 1864, Merrell Diary; Skinner, *Autobiography of Henry Merrell,* 372–73; April 15, 17, 26, 1864, Brown Diary; Virginia Mc'Collum Stinson, "Memories," in Mrs. M. A. Elliott, comp., *The Garden on*

Memory: Stories of the Civil War as Told by Veterans and Daughters of the Confederacy (Camden, Ark.: Brown Printing, 1911), 33–34.

27. *OR*, 820, 826.

28. Robert Freeman Smith, "John R. Eakin: Confederate Propagandist," *Arkansas Historical Quarterly* 12 (Winter 1953): 316–26; *Washington Telegraph*, May 25, 1864.

29. *Washington Telegraph*, May 25, 1864, For more on the Confederate reaction to blacks in the Union army, see Joseph T. Glattharr, *Forged in Battle: The Civil War Alliance of Black Soldiers and White Officers* (New York: Free Press, 1990), 155–59; Dudley Taylor Cornish, *The Sable Arm: Black Troops in the Union Army, 1861–1865* (1956; reprint, Lawrence: University Press of Kansas, 1987), 157–80; Michael Fellman, *Inside War: The Guerrilla Conflict in Missouri during the American Civil War* (New York: Oxford University Press, 1989), 69–70.

30. Skinner, *Autobiography of Henry Merrell*, 24, 38–39, 44, 260; Wright, *Memoirs*, 266–67; Clara Dunlap to Clarissa Dickson, October 7, 1863, in Fountain, *Sisters, Seeds, & Cedars*, 152; *Washington Telegraph*, July 27, 1864, January 13, 1865; *Arkansas Gazette*, November 4, 1853, April 6, June 15, 1855.

31. *Washington Telegraph*, October 15, 1862, June 8, 1864; *Southern Shield* (Helena, Ark.), December 20, 1862; *Arkansas Gazette*, October 11, 1862; Moneyhon, *Civil War and Reconstruction*, 62, 81, 93–94.

32. *True Democrat*, April 22, 1863; *Arkansas Gazette*, October 11, 1862; *Washington Telegraph*, October 15, 1862.

33. *Washington Telegraph*, June 8, 1864.

34. Stinson, "Memories," 31; Elizabeth Godbold Watts to John Comer Watts, May 9, 1864, in "Poison Springs Letter," 14.

35. *OR*, ser. 2, vol. 6:21–22; James G. Hollandsworth Jr., "The Execution of White Officers from Black Units by Confederate Forces during the Civil War." *Louisiana History* 35 (Fall 1994); 475–89; Mrs. J. S. Adamson, "Personal Reminiscences of the Civil War," *Pulaski County Historical Society Review* 7 (March 1959): 2–3; *Fort Smith New Era*, April 9, 1864; Glatthaar, *Forged in Battle*, 69–70; Sheridan, "From Slavery in Missouri," 36; Michael Fellman, "Emancipation in Missouri," *Missouri Historical Review* 83 (October 1988): 50; excerpt from testimony of R. A. Watt, November 30, 1863, in Ira Berlin, Joseph P. Reidy, and Leslie S. Rowland, eds., *Freedom: A Documentary History of Emancipation, 1861–1867*, ser. 2; *The Black Military Experience* (Cambridge: Cambridge University Press, 1982), 235–36; Henry Orr to "Dear Sister," July 1, 1863, in John Q. Anderson, ed., *Campaigning with Parsons' Texas Cavalry Brigade, CSA: The War Journals and Letters of the Four Orr Brothers, 12th Texas Cavalry* (Hillsboro, Texas: Hill Junior College Press, 1967), 111–12; Junius N. Bragg to "My Dear Wife," July 1, 1863, in Mrs. T. J. Gaughan, ed., *Letters of a Confederate Surgeon 1861–1865* (Camden, Ark: Privately printed, 1960), 142–44; *OR*, ser.1, vol. 24, 2:450–66; Anne J. Bailey, "A Texas Cavalry Raid: Reaction to Black Soldiers and Contrabands," *Civil War History* 35 (June 1989): 138–52.

36. Britton, *Union Indian Brigade*, 176–77, 242; John R. Graton to "My Dear Wife," May 22, 1863; John R. Graton Papers, 1838–1910, Kansas State Historical Society, Topeka; Joseph T. Wilson, *The Black Phalanx* (Hartford, Conn.; American Publishing Company, 1890), 231–32; Cornish, "Kansas Negro Regiments," 425.

37. Charles DeMorse was the colonel of the 29th Texas at Honey Springs, and he took a bullet in the right arm in the first volley fired by the 1st Kansas Colored. Recovered

from his wound, DeMorse commanded a brigade at Poison Spring (consisting of the 29th, 30th, and 31st Texas Cavalry), which, as he put it, took "but few prisoners." *OR*, ser. 1, vol. 22, 1:447–52; Britton, *Union Indian Brigade*, 242, 277, 279–84, 367, 372–73; Cornish, "Kansas Negro Regiments," 425; *OR*, 848, Rea, *Sterling Price*, 105.

38. *OR*, 712–13; F. M. Drake, "Campaign of General Steele," in *War Sketches and Incidents as Related by Companions of the Iowa Commandery of the Loyal Legion of the United States*, vol. 1 (Des Moines: Press of P. C. Kenyon, 1893), 65–66, 68–69; Charles H. Lothrop, "The Fight at Marks' Mills," n.d., p.1, Civil War Manuscripts, State Hisroical Society of Iowa, Des Moines; Ira Don Richards, "The Engagement at Marks' Mills," *Arkansas Historical Quarterly* 19 (Spring 1960): 54–55.

39. *OR*, 713–15, 788–99; Harrell, "Arkansas," 255, 259; Richards, "Marks' Mills," 55–60; Elizabeth Titsworth, ed., "The Civil War Diary of a Logan County Soldier," *Wagon Wheels* 1 (Winter 1981); 19.

40. R. P. Marshall of Shelby's brigade defended the excesses committed by his comrades at Marks' Mills and other locations with these words: "People called us rough and Savages we had to be we had to lay aside the Golden Rule with the Federals and treat them just like they treat us. [A]nd as old David Haram said do it First." "Benjamin Pearson's War Diary" (pt. 5), *Annals of Iowa* 15 (October 1926): 441; *OR*, 714–15; Edwards, *Shelby and His Men*, 279; Rea, *Sterling Price*, 110; Lurton Dunham Ingersoll, *Iowa and the Rebellion: A History of the Troops Furnished by the State of Iowa to the Volunteer Armies of the Union, which Conquered the Great Southern Rebellion of 1861–5* (Philadelphia: J. B. Lippincott, 1866), 658; Cathey, "Avera Memoirs," 107; R. P. Marshall to W. L. Skaggs, February 1912, W. L. Skaggs Collection, Arkansas History Commission.

41. "Pearson's War Diary," 441; George Boddie to Mary E. Boddie, June 11, 1864, in Fountain, *Sisters, Seeds, & Cedars*, 179. For more on the problem of stolen Arkansas slaves being sold illegally to new owners in Texas, see John Hudson to Harris Flanagin, May 30, 1864, Kie Oldham Papers, Arkansas Historical Commission; John Hugh Reynolds, ed., "Official Orders of Governor Harris Flanagin, Commander in Chief of the Militia of Arkansas," in John Hugh Reynolds, ed., *Publications of the Arkansas Historical Association*, vol. 2 (Fayetteville: Arkansas Historical Association, 1908), 400–401.

42. *Washington Telegraph*, June 1, August 3, 1864; Elizabeth Godbold Watts to John Comer Watts, May 9, 1864, in "Poison Springs Letter," 14; Vardy, "Battle of Moscow," 2.

43. A. F. Sperry, *History of the 33rd Iowa Infantry Volunteer Regiment 1863–6* (Des Moines: Mills and Company, 1866), 94; Stinson, "Memories," 33–34; April 26, 1864, Brown Diary; Clara Dunlap to "Dear Sister," July 24, 1864; William Blain to "Dear Wife," June 1, 1864, in Dolly Bottens, comp., *Rouse Stevens Ancestry & Allied Families* (Carthage, Mo.; Privately printed, 1970), 110A; Samuel J. Crawford, *Kansas in the Sixties* (Chicago: A. C. McClurg, 1911), 117; *Washington Telegraph*, May 25, 1864.

44. The 2nd Kansas Colored was nicknamed the "Iron Clads" soon after its formation in 1863. *OR*, 697–98, 781, 813; *Unconditional Union*, May 13, 20, 1864; George Carr to "Dear Father," May 2, 1864, Eugene A. Carr Papers, Archives Branch, U.S. Army Military History Institute, Carlisle Barracks, Pennsylvania; John W. Long to "Sir," May 17, 1864, in "A Union Soldier's Personal Account of the Red

River Expedition and the Battle of Jenkins Ferry," *Grassroots* 8 (July 1988): 3; Crawford, *Kansas in the Sixties,* 124. 128; White, "Camden Expedition," 87–88; William E. McLean, *Forty-Third Regiment of Indiana Volunteers: An Historic Sketch of Its Career and Services* (Terre Haute, Ind., C. W. Brown, 1903), 26; Samuel J. Crawford to James T. Wilson, December 31, 1885, in Wilson, *Black Phalanx,* 242; *Fort Scott (Kans.) Union Monitor,* October 22, 1863; Skinner, *Autobiography of Henry Merrell,* 368.

45. Crawford, *Kansas in the Sixties,* 124; Milton P. Chambers to "Dear Brother," May 7, 1864, Milton P. Chambers Papers, Special Collections Division, University of Arkansas Libraries, Fayetteville.

46. Milton P. Chambers to "Dear Brother," May 7, 1864, Chambers Papers.

47. Crawford, *Kansas in the Sixties,* 131–32; *OR,* 759; Samuel J. Crawford to James T. Wilson, December 31, 1885, in Wilson, *Black Phalanx,* 245; William L. Nicholson, "The Engagement at Jenkins' Ferry," *Annals of Iowa* 11 (October 1941): 511.

48. Mamie Yeary, comp., *Reminiscences of the Boys in Gray, 1861–1865* (Dallas: Smith and Lamar, 1912), 437.

49. Edward W. Cade to "My dear Wife," May 6, 1864, Edward W. and Allie Cade Correspondence, John Q. Anderson Collection, Texas State Archives, Austin; James McCall Dawson to "Dear Father Sister and Brothers," May 5, 1864, in Eison, "'Stand We in Jeopardy,'" 52; Junius N. Bragg to Anna Josephine Goodard Bragg, May 5, 1864, in Gaughan, *Letters,* 230; *OR,* 817; Yeary, *Reminiscences of the Boys in Gray,* 390.

50. Yeary, *Reminiscences of the Boys in Gray,* 799.

51. Milton P. Chambers to "Dear Brother," May 7, 1864, Chambers Papers; *OR,* 671, 698; White, "Camden Expedition," 87; William Blain to "Dear Wife," May 17, 1864, in Bottens, *Rouse Stevens Ancestry,* 108B.

52. Nicholson's story was corroborated by two other captured Union officers, Lt. John Hayes of the 2nd Kansas Colored and Surgeon C. R. Stuckslager of the 12th Kansas Infantry, who were interviewed for the *Fort Smith New Era* following their release from prison camp. Nicholson, "Jenkins' Ferry," 509, 511–15, 519; *Fort Smith New Era,* June 16, August 6, 1864.

53. In another irony, Gano's brigade included three regiments that participated in the Poison Spring Massacre—the 29th, 30th, and 31st Texas Cavalry. Marvin J. Hancock, "The Second Battle of Cabin Creek," *Chronicles of Oklahoma* 39 (Winter 1961–62); 416–18; Lary C. Rampp, "Negro Troop Activity in Indian Territory," *Chronicles of Okalahoma* 47 (Spring 1969); 550–53; Britton, *Union Indian Brigade,* 437, 439–40; John R. Graton to "Dear Wife," September 29, 1864, Graton Papers.

54. Yeary, *Reminiscences of Boys in Gray,* 46, 352–53; 684, 812, 831; John R. Graton to "My Dear Wife," March 12, 1865, Graton Papers.

55. For balanced accounts of these and other anti-black atrocities committed in 1864, see Brian Steel Wills, *A Battle from the Start: The Life of Nathan Bedford Forrest* (New York: HarperCollins, 1992); Richard L. Fuchs, *An Unerring Fire: The Massacre at Fort Pillow* (Rutherford, Madison, and Teaneck, N.J.: Fairleigh Dickinson University Press, 1994); Michael A. Cavanaugh and William Marvel, *The Battle of the Crater: The "Horrid Pit," June 25–August 6, 1864* (Lynchburg, Va: H. E. Howard, 1989); Richard J. Sommers, *Richmond Redeemed: The Siege at Petersburg* (Garden City, N.Y.; Doubleday, 1981).

56. For more on the role of racial violence in Reconstruction and the "Jim Crow" South, see George C. Rable, *But There Was No Peace: The Role of Violence in the Politics of Reconstruction* (Athens: University of Georgia Press, 1984); Eric Foner, *Reconstruction: America's Unfinished Revolution 1863–1877* (New York: Harper and Row, 1988); Nell Irvin Painter, *Exodusters: Black Migration to Kansas after Reconstruction* (1977; reprint, Lawrence; University Press of Kansas, 1986).

Chapter 15: Black Experience in the Union Army: The Other Civil War

1. James Turner Johnson, *Just War Tradition and the Restraint of War* (Princeton, 1981), 49.
2. Gerald F. Lindeman, *Embattled Courage: The Experience of Combat in the American Civil War* (New York, 1987), 71; James I. Robertson Jr., *Soldiers Blue and Gray* (Columbia, 1987).
3. Given the size of Civil War historiography, there is only a limited amount which deals with black involvement in the war. Relevant books include George W. Williams, *A History of the Negro Troops in the War of the Rebellion, 1981–1865* (New York, 1888); Joseph T. Wilson, *The Black Phalanx: A History of the Negro Soldiers of the United States* (Hartford, 1890); Benjamin Quarles, *The Negro in the Civil War* (Boston, 1955); Dudley Taylor Cornish, *The Sable Arm: Negro Troops in the Union Army, 1861–1865* (New York, 1956); James M. McPherson, *The Negro's Civil War* (New York, 1965); Ira Berlin, *Freedom: A Documentary History of Emancipation, 1861–1867: Series 2, The Black Military Experience* (Cambridge, 1982); Thomas Wentworth Higginson, *Army Life in a Black Regiment* (East Lansing, 1960); Luis F. Emilio, *History of the Fifty-Fourth Regiment of Massachusetts Volunteer Infantry* (Boston, 1894); William Wells Brown, *The Negro in the American Rebellion: His Heroism and His Fidelity* (Boston, 1867); Joe H. Mays, *Black Americans and Their Contributions towards Union Victory in the American Civil War, 1861–1865* (Lanham, 1984); Charles H. Wesley and Patricia W. Romero, *Negro Americans in the Civil War: From Slavery to Citizenship* (New York, Publishers Company "under auspices of the Association for the Study of Negro Life and History," 1968).
4. James M. McPherson, *Battle Cry of Freedom* (Oxford, 1988), 563.
5. R. W. Scott et al., eds., *War of the Rebellion: A Compilation of the Official Records of the Union and Confederate Armies* (Washington, 1880–1901) [*ORA*], ser. 1, vol. 6, 263–264.
6. Berlin, 6–7, 41–43.
7. McPherson, 565.
8. Governor Andrew once again had played an important role, lobbying Secretary of War Stanton on Wild's behalf. See Governor Andrew to Major General Foster, May 14, 1863, Wild Papers; Military History Institute [MHI], Carlisle Barracks, Carlisle; *ORA* ser. 1, vol. 26, pt. 2, 294; ser. 3, vol. 3, 122.
9. Berlin, 56.
10. Berlin, 421.
11. Fred Albert Shannon, *The Organization and Administration of Union Army, 1861–1865* (Cleveland, 1928), vol. 2, 160. Of the 186,017 blacks who served in the Union Army, 104,387 were recruited in the Confederate states.

12. Howard C. Westwood, "The Causes and Consequences of a Union Black Soldier's Mutiny and Execution," *Civil War History* 31 (1985), 224–226.

13. Ibid., 226–236. The sad postscript to the affair was that it was ultimately decided that Walker's execution had been illegal. He was one of the fourteen black compared to five white Union soldiers who were executed for mutiny during the Civil War.

14. A few blacks were commissioned as chaplains or assistant surgeons, positions outside the normal chain of command. For an analysis of the fourteen black chaplains who served in the Civil War see Edwin S. Redkey, "Black Chaplains in the Union Army," *Civil War History* 33 (1988), 331–350.

15. Berlin, 303–312,

16. Wild to Major T. M. Vincent, Assistant Adjutant-General, June 25, 1863, Records of the Adjutant-General's Office. Letters Received, Colored Troops Branch [CTB], National Archives, Washington.

17. Description Lists of Companies of the 35th, 36th and 37th United States Colored Troops, RG94, Records of the Adjutant-General's Office, National Archives, Washington.

18. Proposed Roster of 1st Regiment, April 27, 1863; 3rd NCCV Regiment, Proposed Roster, September 4, 1863, CTB.

19. *ORA,* ser. 2, vol. 4, 945–946, 954.

20. *ORA,* ser. 2, vol. 4, 857.

21. For a full discussion of the attempt by the Confederate authorities to handle captured black soldiers, see Howard C. Westwood, "Captive Black Union Soldiers in Charleston: What to Do?" *Civil War History,* 28 (1982), 28–44. An attempt to establish separate policies for ex-slaves and free blacks, which varied with their state of origin and the location of any owner, was impossibly difficult. The Union threat to retaliate effectively paralyzed official sanctions to execute prisoners of war.

22. In April 1863 two captured Massachusetts blacks were sold into slavery and transported to Texas. *ORA,* ser. 2, vol. 5, 455, 456, 469–470.

23. As first drafted, the Confederate would be executed if the Union soldier were enslaved. Mary Frances Berry, *Military Necessity and Civil War Policy* (Port Washington, 1977), 62–63.

24. Berlin, 578.

25. Berlin, 585.

26. Ibid.

27. *ORA,* ser. 2, vol. 6, 960–961.

28. *Private and Official Correspondence of Gen. Benjamin F. Butler* (Privately Issued, 1917), vol. 3, 310–316.

29. Report of General Wild, January 10, 1864, E. A. Wild Papers, Southern Historical Collection [hereafter SHC], Chapel Hill, North Carolina.

30. Report of the Special Committee, February 17, 1864, Confederate States of America, Library of Congress.

31. *ORA,* ser. 1, vol. 24, pt. 2, 446–448.

32. Report of the Military Services of Edward A. Wild, July, 1863, Wild Papers, MHI; *ORA,* ser. 1, vol. 33, 957.

33. For a discussion of the nature of the Fort Pillow battle, see Albert Castel, "The Fort Pillow Massacre: A Fresh Examination of the Evidence," *Civil War History,* 4 (1958), 37–50; John Cimprick and Robert C. Mainfort Jr., "Fort Pillow Revisited: New Evidence about an Old Controversy," *Civil War History,* 28 (1982), 293–306.

34. Cimprick and Mainfort, 299.
35. Ibid., 295.
36. McPherson, 748.
37. *ORA,* ser. 1, vol. 42, pt. 2, 653.
38. Joseph T. Glatthaar, *The March to the Sea and Beyond,* (New York, 1985), 64–65.
39. Ibid. Davis had done the same thing at Bear Creek two weeks earlier.
40. Hinks to Wild, May 11, 1864, Wild Papers, MHI.
41. Wild to Major Davis, May 12, 1864, Wild Papers, MHI.
42. Berlin, 715–718.
43. Ibid., 720.
44. Wild to Major T. M. Vincent, September 4, 1863, CTB. *ORA,* ser. 1, vol. 29, pt. 2, 290.
45. Berlin, 207.
46. Brigadier-General W. A. Pile to Major O. D. Green, February 11, 1864, Letters Received, Department of the Mastering Officer [DMO], National Archives of the U.S. Government.
47. Lieutenant J. A. Mayhall to Brigadier-General W. A. Pile, February 4, 1864, Letters Received, DMO.
48. Capt. Hiram Cornell to Col. J. P. Sanderson, March 28, 1864, Letters Received, DMO.
49. Mays, 27–28.
50. Gary Scharnhorst, "From Soldier to Saint: Robert Gould Shaw and the Rhetoric of Racial Justice," *Civil War History* 34 (1988), 308–322.
51. *ORA,* ser. 1, vol. 46, pt. 2, 212, 336; Edward G. Longacre, "Black Troops in the Army of the James, 1863–65," *Military Affairs* 44 (1981), 4.
52. Wild to Wilson, May 10, 1865, Wild Papers, MHI.
53. *ORA,* ser. 1, vol. 29, pt. 2, 262.
54. Ibid., 142; ser. 1, vol. 33, 485.

Chapter 16: Captive Black Union Soldiers in Charleston

1. *Official Records of the Union and Confederate Armies,* ser. 2, 6:123; Papers of F. W. Pickens and M. L. Bonham, Library of Congress, 3:519. Hereafter, citation to the *ORA* will be to series 2 except where otherwise indicated, and citation to the Pickens/Bonham Papers will be to volume 3.
2. *ORA,* 6:124.
3. Bonham Papers, p. 519; *ORA,* 6:125.
4. *ORA,* 5:795–97. In his message of January 12, 1863, opening the third session of the First Confederate Congress, President Davis said that he would treat the "enlisted soldiers" (meaning whites) as "unwilling instruments" of crime and would release them on parole. James D. Richardson, *Messages and Papers of the Confederacy,* 2 vols. (Nashville, 1905), 1:290–91.
5. *ORA,* 4:945–46, 954.
6. *ORA,* 5:970.
7. It is virtually certain that the captives in the Beaufort jail were the Confederate soldiers, captured by the Union army, whose custody as hostages Hunter had demanded of Admiral DuPont, naval commander in the area, of Secretary of Navy Welles, and of President Lincoln. *ORA,* 5:646–47, 659, 666, 697, 698, 708, 711–13. Hence, I infer that Hunter's demand had been met.

8. *ORA*, 5:770.

9. *ORA*, ser. 1, 14:448–49, 599; *Charleston Mercury*, June 9, 1863.

10. *Charleston Mercury*, June 9, 13, 1863.

11. *ORA*, 6:136; William Best Hesseltine, *Civil War Prisons* (1930; reprinted ed., New York, 1964), pp. 87–89, 112–13, 186–88, 216–30.

12. Bonham Papers, p. 251.

13. *Charleston Mercury*, August 15, 1863.

14. Edward McCrady Jr. and Samuel A. Ashe, *Cyclopedia of Eminent and Representative Men of the Carolinas,* 2 vols. (Madison, Wis., 1892), 1:88–90; Charles Edward Cauthen, *South Carolina Goes to War* (Chapel Hill, 1950), p. 166.

15. *ORA*, 6:134.

16. *ORA*, 6:139–40, 145–46; Bonham Papers, p.523.

17. *ORA*, 6:139, 145.

18. *Charleston Mercury*, August 15, 1863.

19. *ORA*, 5:940–41.

20. *Charleston Mercury*, August 13, 15, 20, 1863; commitment to jail of Alfred Whiting and other Negro soldiers, S.C. Archives, Commitments, 1863, 1864, penal system papers, 1860–65, 7:238, dr. 3.

21. *ORA*, 6:190–91.

22. *ORA*, 5:940–41.

23. *ORA*, 6:193–94; Bonham Papers, p. 535.

24. *Charleston Courier*, July 17, 20, 22, August 1, 1863; *Charleston Mercury*, August 15, 1863.

25. *Charleston Mercury*, August 11, 12, 1863.

26. Ibid., August 13, 15, 1863; Bonham Papers, p. 536.

27. Bonham Papers, pp. 540–41. In the Bonham Papers, pp. 542–49, immediately following the commission's report, are notes of interviews with each of the 24 blacks; legibility is difficult. (At that time, there were twenty-odd hospitalized wounded black captives in addition to those held in Castle Pinckney; see *ORA*, 6:187–88; *Charleston Courier*, August 11, 1863.) The professed disillusionment of the blacks probably was not feigned. Early in 1863, Governor Andrew of Massachusetts secured authority from the War Department to raise and organize black troops; thus was created the Fifty-fourth Massachusetts. But there were few blacks in Massachusetts or even in all of New England. An intensive recruiting drive was launched throughout much of the North. Unquestionably, recruiters offered strong inducements. The failure to make good on promised compensation is a familiar story. Familiar too is the fact that Col. Robert Gould Shaw, commanding the Fifty-fourth, sought and secured a lead spot in opening assaults in the Fort Wagner operation; see Dudley Taylor Cornish, *The Sable Arm* (New York, 1966), pp. 105–10, 150–56, 184–96. Interestingly, though the preliminary Emancipation Proclamation had not referred to blacks' becoming soldiers, the final proclamation had announced that the freed slaves would be received into the armed service "to garrison forts, positions, stations, and other places and to man vessels"; see James D. Richardson, *Messages and Papers of the Presidents*, U.S. Congress, House Misc. Doc. 210 (1897) 53d Cong., 2d sess., pt. 6, pp. 96–99, 157–59. When general recruitment of blacks began in early 1863, many had the impression that they would be assigned to garrison and fatigue duty; see Cornish, *Sable Arm*, p. 240.

28. *ORA*, 6:202.

29. Bonham Papers, p. 553.

30. Ibid., p. 560.
31. *ORA,* 7:673. The attorney general's co-counsel was Mr. A. P. Aldrich, who had been a member of the examining commission subscribing to the report to the governor. Bonham Papers, p. 541.
32. *Charleston Courier,* August 26, 1863.
33. Bonham Papers, pp. 568–72. This citation is to report on the trial made to the governor by what appears to have been the five members of the tribunal conducting it. The report refers to the court as "the provost-marshal's court for Charleston district." *ORA,* 7:673; see also Bonham Papers, pp. 536, 597; and *Charleston Courier,* August 26, 1863. The court had been recently created. Its creation and powers are recounted in a letter to the author of October 21, 1980, from Mr. William L. McDowell, deputy director, South Carolina Department of Archives and History.
34. *ORA,* 6:245–46; Bonham Papers, pp. 561–64.
35. *ORA,* 5:960, 966–67.
36. *ORA,* 6:21–22.
37. *ORA,* 6:115. It seems that a little later Seddon wrote Smith suggesting that captured white officers "be dealt with red-handed in the field, or immediately thereafter." Herbert Aptheker, *To Be Free—Studies in American Negro History,* 2d ed., (New York, 1968), p. 94.
38. *ORA,* 6:163; *Charleston Mercury,* August 10, 1863.
39. *ORA,* 6:193–94.
40. *ORA,* 6:245–46, 194; Bonham Papers, pp. 561–64. The South was keenly aware of the threat of retaliation; *Charleston Courier,* October 2, 1863.
41. *ORA,* 6:225–26.
42. Bonham Papers, pp. 568–72.
43. Herbert Aptheker, "The Negro in the Union Navy," *Journal of Negro History* 32 (April 1947): 169, 170–74, 179.
44. *ORA,* ser. 1, 14:199–202; *ORA,* 5:708, 823–27; *ORA,* 6:171–72, 188.
45. Elon A. Woodward, *The Negro in the Military Service of the United States—A Compilation* (1888), National Archives, microcopy M-858, roll 5, p. 4224.
46. Luis F. Emilio, *History of the Fifty-Fourth Regiment of Massachusetts Volunteer Infantry, 1863–1865,* 2d ed. rev. (Boston, 1894), p. 413. Emilio's history, though based on painstaking research, including interviews with survivors, was written before records were fully organized and has some errors, including on pp. 97 and 406, a mistaken identification of the prisoners tried by the Charleston court.
47. Each defense counsel, Nelson Mitchell and Edward McCrady, had been prominent members of the state legislature in prewar days and were leaders of the Charleston bar. *Biographical Directory of the South Carolina House of Representatives,* 3 vols. to date (Columbia, 1974) 1:356, 360, 364, 369, 373, 376; Mary C. Simms Oliphant and T. C. Duncan Eaves, eds., *The Letters of William Gilmore Simms,* 5 vols. (Columbia, 1954), 3:221, n. 250; obituary, *Columbia Daily Southern Guardian,* April 21, 1864 (Mitchell); *Biographical Directory,* supra, pp. 364, 369, 373, 376; McGrady and Ashe, *Cyclopedia,* 1:51–58 (McCrady). In Emilio, *History of the Fifty-Fourth,* pp. 97, 406–8, it is said that Mitchell suffered obloquy and poverty as a result of his representation of the defendants. The statement is based on hearsay, principally an unsigned letter appearing in *Harpers Weekly* of April 8, 1865. Quite inconsistent with any such statement is the fact that both Mitchell and McCrady were selected as members of a citi-

zens' committee to welcome President Davis on his visit to Charleston in November 1863, several weeks after the trial; see *Charleston Courier,* October 30, 31, November 2, 1863. Inconsistent too, is the highly commendatory obituary published after Mitchell's death in February 1864; see *Southern Guardian,* supra; Henry A. DeSaussure, "Death Records," *South Carolina Historical Magazine* 59 (April 1958): 116. It is notable also that McCrady again was elected to the state legislature in 1864. McCrady, incidentally, had been a member of the state convention of December 1860 and had voted for secession. *Biographical Directory,* p. 392; McCrady and Ashe, *Cyclopedia,* pp. 151–58; Cauthen, *South Carolina Goes to War,* pp. 65–66.

48. *ORA,* 6:1081–82; *ORA,* 7–673.

49. Brainerd Dyer, "The Treatment of Colored Union Troops by the Confederates, 1861–1865," *Journal of Negro History* 20 (July 1935): 273, 282; Aptheker, *To Be Free,* pp. 94–95.

50. *ORA,* 7:409.

51. *ORA,* 7:673.

52. Bonham Papers, pp. 597–98.

53. *ORA,* 7:703.

54. *Public Laws of the Confederate States of America—First Congress 2d Sess.,* ed. James M. Matthews (Richmond, 1862), pp. 89–90; *Journal of the Congress of the Confederate States of America,* 58th Cong., 2d Sess., Sen. Doc. 234 (1904), 5:537–38.

55. *ORA,* 7:538; Dyer, "Treatment of Colored Union Troops," pp. 275–77.

56. *ORA,* 7:990–93, 1010–12. Grant's reply to Lee refused to discuss "the slavery question," adhering to the position that all captured Union soldiers "regardless of color . . . must be treated as prisoners of war." *ORA,* 7:1018–19, 1029–30.

57. The Charleston court's report to the governor identified the Missourians as Henry Kirk and William Harrison, the Virginians as George Council and Henry Worthington. Evidence conflicted, it said, as to whether Worthington was a slave; see Bonham Papers, pp. 568–72. The descriptive roll of Co. B, Fifty-fourth Massachusetts (Colored), RG 94, National Archives, Washington, D.C., shows George Counsel—not "Council." The roll of Co. H shows the other three. The rolls show the residence of each. Worthington is shown as from Ohio, where, according to his Compiled Military Service Record (also RG 94), he was born. There were two men in Co. H named William H. Harrison, one shown as "1st," the other as "2d." The Compiled Military Service Record for each shows the "1st" as having been captured and the "2d" as killed at Fort Wagner in July 1863.

58. *ORA,* 7:673.

59. Emilio, *History of the Fifty-Fourth,* pp. 402–3, 414–15.

60. Ibid., pp. 218, 395, 411–13; Compiled Military Service Records for Henry Kirk, William H. Harrison "1st," and Henry W. Worthington, of Co. H, Fifty-fourth Mass., RG 94, National Archives.

61. Emilio, *History of the Fifty-Fourth,* pp. 419–22, 431. Worthington died on January 12, Harrison on January 26, both at Florence, according to their Compiled Military Service Records.

62. *ORA,* 8:96.

63. Emilio, *History of the Fifty-Fourth,* pp. 422–23.

64. *ORA,* 8:197; *Journal of the Confederate Congress,* 4:501, 503, 507, 510, 520, 545; 7:521, 528.

65. Emilio, *History of the Fifty-Fourth,* pp. 422–23; Compiled Military Service Records for George Counsel, Co. B, Fifty-fourth Mass., and for Henry Kirk, Co. H, Fifty-fourth Mass., RG 94, National Archives.

Chapter 17: The Execution of White Officers from Black Units by Confederate Forces During the Civil War

1. Dudley Taylor Cornish, *The Sable Arm: Negro Troops in the Union Army, 1861–1865* (1956; reprint ed., New York, 1966), 161–68, 224.

2. *Official Army Register of the Volunteer Forces of the U.S. Army, 1861–1865* (1865; reprint ed., Gaithersburg, Md., 1987). Deaths after May 26, 1865, were not included, although several white officers from black units were killed after the collapse of the Confederate government. These incidents can not be viewed as official acts of a deceased government, although the sentiments that provided the impetus for the resolution in the first place may have survived.

3. For the identities of the civilians involved with these murders, see *War of the Rebellion: A Compilation of the Official Records of the Union and Confederate Armies,* 70 vols., in 127 parts (Washington, D.C., 1880–1901), ser. 1, 29, pt. 2, p. 364; ser. 2, 6:106, 157, 187, 216, 323, 360; hereafter cited as *OR.*

4. It is likely that Orillion was black, one of the free men of color to receive a commission in the 1st Regiment of Butler's Native Guards (later the 73rd Infantry, USCT) when it was organized. Orillion's name appears on the list of officers dated September 27, 1862, in Box 44 (69–75th U.S.C. Infantry), Regimental Papers, Record Group 94, National Archives, Washington, D.C.

5. *OR,* ser. 2, 6:244, 258–59, 289, 960–61.

6. William F. Perkins to C. T. Hamblen, January 23, 1868, in a compiled military service and pension record for William B. Hamblen, National Archives, Washington, D.C. The advertisement alleged that the 2nd Louisiana Cavalry had been responsible for Hamblen's capture. The author was unable to verify that Crouch served in the 173rd New York Infantry. That name does not appear in the compiled military service index for that regiment.

7. Affidavit of R. M. McClermont, January 21, 1868, in compiled military service and pension record for William B. Hamblen, National Archives, Washington, D.C.

8. Compiled military service and pension record for Robert McClermont, National Archives, Washington, D.C.

9. *OR,* ser. 1, 24, pt. 3, pp. 425–26; 443–44; 469, 537, 590; ser. 2, 6:394; Cyrus Sears, *The Battle of Milliken's Bend* (Columbus, 1909), 15; Affidavit of Herman Lieb, January 9, 1873, in pension record for Corydon Heath, National Archives, Washington, D.C.

10. *OR,* ser. 1, 34, pt.2, p. 450, 466. The *Official Army Register* indicates that four officers were captured by Parsons' troops, which is confirmed in a letter written by one of the Confederate soldiers shortly after the incident (see John Q. Anderson, ed., *Campaigning with Parsons' Texas Cavalry Brigade, CSA: The War Journals and Letters of the Four Orr Brothers, 12th Texas Cavalry Regiment* [Hillsboro, Tex., 1967],111–12). The reports in the *OR,* however, refer to only three. A more recent study of Parsons' brigade also accepts three as the correct number. See Anne J. Bailey, *Between the Enemy and Texas: Parsons Cavalry in the Civil War* (Fort Worth, Tex., 1989), 240. The evidence suggests that East was the only officer serving in a black unit who was held at Camp Ford. "List of Officers, Prisoners, of War at Camp Ford,"

The Old Flag, 1864. Fiftieth Anniversary, 1914. First Published by Union Prisoners at Camp Ford, Tyler, Texas, 1864 (Bridgeport, 1914). There were several exchanges of prisoners from Camp Ford after East was captured, but he did not gain his release until two days after Gen. Buckner surrendered the Department of Trans-Mississippi to Gen. Canby in New Orleans. East lived to start drawing his pension in 1883. Pension record, National Archives, Washington, D.C.

11. *Official Army Register*, 6:122, 8:219; *OR,* ser. 1, 24, pt. 3, p. 590; ser. 2, 6:394; M. W. Sims's Application for Pardon dated April 20, 1866, and granted April 23, 1866, in pardon records, National Archives, Washington, D.C.

12. *OR,* ser. 2, 8:19–20.

13. *OR,* ser. 1, 45, pt. 2, pp. 578–79; also 45, pt. 1, p. 546.

14. *OR,* ser. 2, 6:213, 264; Albert Allen to George B. Drake, August 6, 1864, Charles E. Page to George B. Drake, July 26, 1864, both letters in the compiled military service records for Allen and Page, National Archives, Washington, D.C.

15. *OR,* ser. 2, 7:6, 198, 540, 956; *Official Army Register,* 8:174, 179, 190, 194, 201, 202; John L. Ransom, *Andersonville Diary, Escape, and List of Dead with Name, Co., Regiment, Date of Death and No. of Grave in Cemetery* (Auburn, N.Y., 1881); Individual compiled military service records in the National Archives, Washington, D.C.

16. For Lincoln's response to the Confederate resolution, see *OR,* ser. 2, 6:163; ser. 3, 3:148–64. For examples of general correspondence, see *OR,* ser. 2, 5:737, 6:33, 73, 115, 185, 226, 230, 244, 248, 349, 594–97.

17. *OR,* ser. 2, 6:244.

18. *OR,* ser. 2, 6:21–22

19. *OR,* ser. 1, 24, pt. 1, p. 102; 26, pt. 2, p. 478; 24, pt. 1, pp. 746, 753, 792; ser. 2, 6:817–18; ser. 3, 3:452–53; William Wells Brown, *The Negro in the American Rebellion: His Heroism and His Fidelity* (1867; reprint, New York, 1968), 232; Joseph T. Glatthaar, *Forged in Battle: The Civil War Alliance of Black Soldiers and White Officers* (New York, 1990), 156, 159–62; Randall C. Jimerson, *The Private Civil War: Popular Thought During the Sectional Conflict* (Baton Rouge, 1988), 113–15; Ira Don Richards, "The Battle of Poison Spring," *Arkansas Historical Quarterly,* 18 (1959): 348–49; Sears, *Battle of Milliken's Bend,* 13. When Confederate troops failed to overrun a position held by black troops, the ratio of killed to wounded in black and white units was comparable.

20. Rosella Debergue Orillion [*sic*] to "General," September 20, 1864, in compiled military service and pension record for Oscar Orillion, National Archives, Washington, D.C.

21. All units are United States Colored Troops unless otherwise indicated.

22. HA indicates Heavy Artillery.

23. All units are United States Colored Troops unless otherwise indicated.

24. Cd'A indicates Corps d'Afrique, HA for Heavy Artillery, and NG signifies Native Guard.

Chapter 19: The Jacksonville Mutiny

1. In 1882, three Indian Scouts (Sgt. Jim Dandy, Corp. Skippy, and Sgt. Dead Shot), who were attached to the 6th U.S. Cavalry, were executed on the charge of mutiny. These individuals were in the auxiliary status as scouts, and the offense for which they were convicted should have been charged as murder. These scouts joined with

a party of hostile Indians in a firefight that resulted in the death of an officer and six soldiers. See General Court Martial Order 12 of 1882.

2. Steven A. Channing, *Confederate Ordeal* (New York: Time-Life Books, 1984), 145.

3. Late in the war, several blacks were commissioned as officers to serve in black regiments. Additionally, several regiments of free blacks raised early in the war by General Butler and Sen. Jim Lane were officered by blacks. These officers, however, were replaced with whites.

4. Military Service Record, John L. Brower, National Archives, Washington, D.C. (hereafter cited as NA).

5. RHB to the editor, *A.M.E. The Christian Recorder,* August 6, 1864.

6. Joseph Glatthaar, *Forged in Battle: The Civil War Alliance of Black Soldiers and White Officers* (New York: Free Press, 1989), 84.

7. Ibid., 86.

8. Thomas W. Higginson, *Army Life in a Black Regiment* (Williamstown, Mass.: Corner House, 1971), 259.

9. The punishment of tying up by the thumbs, while not prohibited, was looked upon with great disfavor by most commanders. A number of departmental commanders had banned the practice at the time of the incident. The punishment called for the offender to be stripped by the waist and strung up by the thumbs for several hours so that only his toes were touching the ground. This obviously was a painful punishment that could easily result in dislocated thumbs.

10. Transcript of General Court-Martial of Pvt. Richard Lee, 001477, Record Group 153, NA.

11. Transcript of General Court-Martial of Pvt. Jacob Plowden, ibid.

12. Transcript of General Court-Martial of Pvt. Jonathan Miller, ibid.

13. Ibid.

14. Transcript of General Court-Martial of Pvt. Thomas Howard, ibid.

15. Transcript of General Court-Martial of Pvt. Joseph Nathaniel, ibid.

16. Transcript of General Court-Martial of Pvt. Calvin Dowrey, ibid.

17. Transcript of General Court-Martial of Pvt. James Allen, ibid.

18. Transcript of General Court-Martial of Pvt. Richard Lee, ibid.

19. Transcript of General Court-Martial of Pvt. Joseph Green, ibid.

20. Transcript of General Court-Martial of Pvt. James Thomas, ibid.

21. Special Order 189, District of East Florida, 1st Separate Brigade, October 30, 1865, ibid.

22. Du Chanel, "How Soldiers Were Tried," *Civil War Times Illustrated,* February 1969, p. 11.

23. William Winthrop, *Military Law and Precedents* (Washington, D.C.: GPO, 1868), 79.

24. Ibid., 578.

25. General Court-Martial Transcript of Pvt. Archibald Roberts, 001477, RG 153, NA.

26. Du Chanel, *How Soldiers Were Tried,* 12.

27. Winthrop, *Military Law and Precedents,* Article 65, p. 618.

28. Glatthaar, *Forged in Battle,* 199.

29. Winthrop, *Military Law and Precedents,* Article 65, p. 618.

30. Transcript of General Court-Martial of Pvt. Joseph Nathaniel, 001477, RG 153, NA.

31. Transcript of General Court-Martial of Pvt. Sam Harley, 001477, RG 153, NA.

32. Transcript of General Court-Martial of Pvt. Joseph Green, ibid.

33. Winthrop, *Military Law and Precedents,* Article 35, p. 592.

34. General Orders 39, Dept. of Florida, November 13, 1865, 001477, RG 153, NA.
35. Foster had earlier risen to prominence as an officer in the besieged garrison of Fort Sumter in April 1861.
36. Transcript of General Court-Martial of Pvt. Thomas Waters, 001477, RG 153, NA.
37. This was the same infamous prison where the alleged Lincoln conspirators, Dr. Samuel Mudd and Michael O'Laughlin, were incarcerated.
38. H. C. Marehand to Sen. Edgar Cowan, December 10, 1865, Military Service Record of Pvt. David Craig, NA.
39. Gen. John Foster to Col. J. A. Hardie, December 16, 1865, Military Service Record of Pvt. David Craig, NA.
40. Monthly Returns from Fort Jefferson, Florida, File 10–27–1, Returns from Army Posts (National Archives Microfilm Publication M617, Roll 542), NA.
41. Military Service Records, Cyrus W. Brown, NA.
42. Military Service Records, Sherman Conant, NA.
43. Robert I. Alotta, *Civil War Justice: Union Army Executions under Lincoln* (Shippensburg, Penn.: White Mane, 1989), 26.

Chapter 20: "Remember Poison Spring"

1. Mike Fisher, "The Camden Expedition" (unpublished Master's thesis, Pittsburg State University, Pittsburg, Kansas, 1976), 1:130. Also see Ludwell H. Johnson, *Red River Campaign Politics and Cotton in the Civil War* (Baltimore, Md., 1958) and Edwin C. Bearss, *Steele's Retreat from Camden and the Battle of Jenkins' Ferry* (Little Rock, Ark., 1967).
2. *The War of the Rebellion: A Compilation of the Official Records of the Union and Confederate Armies* (Washington, D.C., 1880–1902), ser. 1, vol. 34, pt. 1, 829. Hereafter cited as OR; all citations are to ser. 1, vol. 34, pt. 1. Bearss, *Steele's Retreat*, 115–117. The Federals were shortening their lines as the Confederates struck. *OR*, 689, 702, 724, 782, 799–800.
3. John M. Harrell, "Arkansas," in Clement A. Evans, ed., *Confederate Military History* (Atlanta, Ga., 1899), 10:265; *OR*, 782, 802, 809, 815, 817; Andrew F. Sperry, *History of the 33rd Iowa Volunteer Regiment* (Des Moines, 1866), 90–91.
4. Ibid., 88–89; *OR*, 677, 689, 829.
5. Ibid., 689, 702, 829; Bearss, *Steele's Retreat*, 117.
6. *OR*, 698, 702, 721; Bearss, *Steele's Retreat*, 117.
7. *OR*, 830.
8. Samuel J. Crawford, *Kansas in the Sixties* (Chicago, 1911), 120; *OR*, 757–758.
9. Crawford, *Kansas in the Sixties*. In his book, Colonel Crawford, who later became governor of Kansas, refers to his regiment as the 83rd United States Colored Troops.
10. Ibid., *OR*, 757–758.
11. Crawford, *Kansas in the Sixties*, 120–121; Bearss, *Steele's Retreat*, 133.
12. Crawford, *Kansas in the Sixties*, 107; Dudley T. Cornish, *The Sable Arm, Negro Troops in the Union Army* (New York, 1966). Cornish's history is the definitive work on black involvement in the Union cause.
13. Crawford, *Kansas in the Sixties*, 109.
14. Ibid., 117.
15. *OR*, 801; Bearss, *Steele's Retreat*, 119–121.
16. *OR*, 801–804; Bearss, *Steele's Retreat*, 121–122.

17. Ibid., 125; *OR,* 800, 802.
18. Ibid., The Confederates had made the mistake of committing their units piece-meal. See Bearss, *Steele's Retreat,* 126.
19. Ibid., 137; *OR,* 806.
20. *OR,* 809, 811, 813; Bearss, *Steele's Retreat,* 136, 138, 139.
21. Ibid., 136–137; *OR,* 809.
22. Ibid., 800, 802, 809–810; Bearss *Steele's Retreat,* 137.
23. Ibid., 138; *OR,* 810.
24. Ibid., 689; Bearss, *Steele's Retreat,* 140.
25. Ibid.; *OR,* 689, 810.
26. Ibid., 690; Bearss, *Steele's Retreat,* 138.
27. Ibid., 141; *OR,* 725, 808.
28. Ibid., 697; Bearss, *Steele's Retreat,* 139.
29. *OR,* 697. Ruffner's Battery of Parsons' Missouri Division. Lieutenant John O. Lockhart commanded the section. See *OR,* 812–813.
30. Ibid., 697–698, 758, 811, 813; Crawford, *Kansas in the Sixties,* 122.
31. Ibid., 122–123.
32. Ibid., 123–124.
33. *OR,* 690–691, 698. The cheering signaled a Confederate rather than a Federal advance as Rice had planned. Shortly thereafter, Rice was wounded and moved to Little Rock where his foot was amputated. He died the following August when the wound failed to respond to treatment.
34. Crawford, *Kansas in the Sixties,* 124.
35. *OR,* 758.
36. Ibid., 806; Crawford, *Kansas in the Sixties,* 124.
37. *OR,* 758.
38. Crawford, *Kansas in the Sixties,* 124.
39. Ibid., 126; See Bearss, *Steele's Retreat,* 35–37, 143–144.
40. Crawford, *Kansas in the Sixties,* 126–127. For a detailed account of the engagement at Poison Spring, see Mike Fisher, "The First Kansas Colored-Massacre at Poison Spring," *Kansas History, A Journal of the Central Plains,* 2 (Summer, 1979), 121–129.
41. Crawford, *Kansas in the Sixties,* 129; *OR,* 697–698, 758, 811, 813; Bearss, *Steele's Retreat.* Confederates claimed members of the Second Kansas Colored bayonetted and killed three prisoners in capturing Lockhart's guns.
42. Joseph B. Blessington, *The Campaigns of Walker's Texas Division* (New York, 1875), 219–250.
43. *OR,* 670; Bearss, *Steele's Retreat,* 156.
44. Blessington, *Walker's Texas Division,* 249–250; Bearss, *Steele's Retreat,* 149. Major General John C. Walker commanded the Texas Division.
45. *OR,* 785, 817. The composition of the brigade is not recorded. Bearss, *Steele's Retreat,* 149.
46. Ibid., 149–150; *OR,* 817
47. Ibid., 817; Bearss, *Steele's Retreat,* 149–150.
48. *OR,* 817; Bearss, *Steele's Retreat,* 153–155; Fisher, "The Camden Expedition," 211–212.
49. *OR,* 741, 817; Bearss, *Steele's Retreat,* 154–155.
50. Blessington, *Walker's Texan Division,* 251; Sperry, *33rd Iowa,* 91.
51. *OR,* 817. Both Confederate leaders died following the battle. Blessington, *Walker's Texas Division,* 250; Bearss, *Steele's Retreat,* 152.

52. Ibid., 155; *OR*, 817.

53. Blessington, *Walker's Texas Division*, 251.

54. Harrell, "Arkansas," 266.

55. *OR*, 817; Bearss, *Steele's Retreat*, 153.

56. *OR*, 818.

57. Ibid., 691.

58. Ibid., 690; Bearss, *Steele's Retreat*, 155–156.

59. *OR*, 690.

60. Sperry, *33rd Iowa*, 92.

61. Crawford, *Kansas in the Sixties*, 131.

62. Ibid., Official records conflict showing 15 killed, 55 wounded and three missing. Bears, *Steele's Retreat*, 169.

63. Crawford, *Kansas in the Sixties*. General Henry W. Halleck had sent Steele the bridge two years earlier. See *OR*, 670, 677; Bearss, *Steele's Retreat*, 157–158.

64. Ibid., 158.

65. *OR*, 790; Bearss, *Steele's Retreat*, 160–161, 165; Blessington, *Walker's Texas Division*, 253. Many Confederates criticized Fagan's tardy arrival.

66. *OR*, 691.

67. Crawford, *Kansas in the Sixties*, 131. Offiial reports list 594 dead, wounded and missing. Bearss estimates the total at over 700. Bearss, *Steele's Retreat*, 161.

68. *OR*, 788; Estimates place Confederate casualties at 1,000 of 6,000 men on the field.

69. Ibid., 671; Bearss, *Steele's Retreat*, 158.

70. Ibid., 158–159.

Chapter 21: The Southern Side of "Glory"

1. Widow's Pension File, Henry Clark, United States Colored Troops, Cavalry, A Company, 3rd. Regiment, National Archives and Records Administration (NARA), Washington, DC.

2. Eaton, John, *Grant, Lincoln, and the Freedmen: Reminiscences of the Civil War* (New York: Lonmans, Green, and Co. 1907), p. 83.

3. W. T. Sherman to Major General Halleck, 29 February 1864, letter in *The War of the Rebellion: A Compilation of the Official Records of the Union and Confederate Armies* (Washington, DC: Government Printing Office, 1880–1901), ser. 1, vol. 58, p. 498.

4. Widow's Pension File, Brown, John, Heavy Artillery, (USCHA), G, 5, Regiment, 387.412, NARA, Washington DC.

5. Widow's Pension File, Richard Roberts (USCHA), A, 5, 317.426, NARA, Washington, DC.

6. Widow's Pension File, Richard Sled (USCHA), I, 5, 394.755, 389.853, NARA, Washington, DC.

7. William Thirds to Mr. Whipple, 19 November 1863, American Missionary Association, Mississippi, 71570.

8. Samuel Thomas, letter, Register of Letters, Office of the General Superintendent of Freedmen, Mississippi, BRFAL, Record Group, 105, NARA, Washington, DC and Samuel Thomas, letter, Register of Letters Received, Office of the General Superintendent of Freedmen, Mississippi, BRFAL, Record Group, 105, NARA, Washington, DC.

9. Widow's Pension File, John Brown (USCHA), G, 5, 387.412, NARA, Washington, DC.

10. Widow's Pension File, Hubbard Reynolds (USCHA), G, 5, 163.950, 741.430, NARA, Washington, DC.

11. Widow's Pension File, Richard Roberts (USCHA), A, 5, 317.426, NARA, Washington, DC.

12. Widow's Pension File, Elick Westbrooks (USCHA), F, 5, 171.128, 309.238, NARA, Washington, DC.

13. Widow's Pension File, Nathaniel Foreman (USCHA), C, 5, 1211.340, 177.645, NARA, Washington, DC.

14. Widow's Pension File, Elick Westbrooks (USCHA), F, 5, 171.128, 309.238, NARA, Washington, DC.

15. Widow's Pension File, Richard Sled (USCHA), I, 5, 394.755, 389.853, NARA, Washington, DC.

16. Widow's Pension File, Louis Caston (USCHA), K, 5, 388.190, 384.190, NARA, Washington, DC.

17. Widow's Pension File, Tod Welcome (USCHA), I, 5, 397.384, 440.081; Samuel Taylor (USCHA), H, 5, 210.144, NARA, Washington, DC.

18. Widow's Pension File, Gordan Fulgert (USCINF), E. 53, 320.012, 266,793, NARA, Washington, DC.

19. Widow's Pension File, Hannibal Wallace (USCHA), K, 5, 375.899, NARA, Washington, DC.

20. Widow's Pension File, Benjamin Lee (USCHA), L, 5, 380.960, NARA, Washington, DC.

21. Samuel Thomas, letter, Register of Letters Received, Office of the General Superintendent of Freedmen, Mississippi, BRFAL, Record Group 105, NARA, Washington, DC, M826–14.

22. Leon F. Litwack, *Been in the Storm So Long: The Aftermath of Slavery* (New York: A. Knopf, 1979) p. 129; Jacqueline Jones, *Labor of Love, Labor of Sorrow: Black Women, Work and the Family, from Slavery to the Present* (New York: Vintage Books, 1986), pp. 50–51, and Joseph T. Glatthaar, *Forged in Battle: The Civil War Alliance of Black Soldiers and White Officers* (New York: The Free Press, 1990), p. 91.

23. S. G. Wright to Rev. George Whipple, 7 April 1864, American Missionary Association, Mississippi, 71635; Herbert G. Gutman, *The Black Family in Slavery and Freedom, 1750–1925* (New York: Vintage Books, 1977), pp. 23–24.

24. A. W. Brobet to A. S. Mitchell, 18 March 1865, Natchez: Unregistered Letters Received, Office of the Assistant Commissioner, Mississippi, BRFAL, Record Group 195, NARA, Washington, DC.

25. Widow's Pension File, Samuel Williams (USCHA), G, 5, 168.903, 175.358, NARA, Washington, DC.

26. Widow's Pension File, Gordan Fulgert (USCINF), E, 53, 320.012, 266.793, NARA, Washington, DC.

27. Widow's Pension File, William Washington (USCHA), I, 5, 687.674, J 512.928, NARA, Washington, DC.

28. Widow's Pension File, Richard Roberts (USCHA), A, 5, 317.426 also Widow's Pension File; Hubbard McReynolds (USCHA), G, 5, 163.950, 741.430, NARA, Washington, DC.

29. Widow's Pension File, Benjamin Lee (USCHA), L, 5, 380.960, NARA, Washington, DC.

30. Widow's Pension File, Moses Wilson (USCHA), G, 5, 315.778, 273.769, NARA, Washington, DC.
31. Widow's Pension File, Allen Alexander (USCINF) A, 58, 145.205, 97.533, NARA, Washington, DC.
32. Widow's Pension File, Richard Robert (USCHA), A, 5, 317.426; Widow's Pension File, Richard Sled (USCHA), I, 5, 394.755, 389.853, NARA, Washington, DC.

Chapter 22: Presence and Precedents

1. *Official Records of the Union and Confederate Navies in the War of the Rebellion*, 30 vols. (Washington, D.C.: GPO, 1894–1922), ser. 2, 1:189 (hereafter cited as *ORN*); U.S. Naval History Division, *Dictionary of American Naval Fighting Ships*, 8 vols. (Washington, D.C.; GPO, 1959–).6:51–52, 2:560–61 (hereafter cited as *DANFS*). Length: 256 feet; draft: 8 feet (fully loaded); tonnage: 786; top speed: 8–9 knots upstream. This data concerns the fully converted Red Rover, especially when listing the number of boilers (five).
2. *ORN*, ser. 2, 1:513, 431; "History of U.S. Navy Hospital Ship Red Rover," 1, Ship's History Section, Navy Department, Washington, D.C. (Hereafter cited as "Ship's History"); *ORN*, ser. 1, 22:800.
3. *ORN*, ser. 1, 22:746; "Ship's History," 1: James C. Tily, *The Uniforms of the United States Navy* (South Brunswick: Thomas Yosecloff, 1964). Tily describes how volunteers supplemented the federal navy: "Militia units were brought into Federal service, [with] no similar provision to supplement the Navy. Congress on July 24, 1861 authorized appointment of officers in an acting capacity and . . . [provided] for the recruitment of seamen. [They] were volunteers, [with] no previous commitment to serve in an emergency as did the . . . militia. After the war, this volunteer force was released, except for a limited number of officers who transfer[red] to the regular Navy" (180), *ORN*, ser. 1, 22:725.
4. *ORN*, ser. 1, 23:89–90, 91–92, 105–7: William M. Fowler, "Relief on the River: The *Red Rover*," *Naval History* 5 (Fall 1991): 16–17; Edward C. Kennedy, "From the Log of the *Red Rover*, 1862–1865: A History of the First U.S. Navy Hospital Ship." *Missouri Historical Review* 40 (October 1965):32.
5. *ORN*, ser. 1, 3:148–49; Kennedy, "From the Log," 32; Dennis M. Davidson, "*Red Rover*—The U.S. Navy's First Hospital Ship" (Unpublished paper, Annapolis: U.S. Naval Academy, 1960); 5; Fowler, "Relief on the River." 19.
6. *ORN*, ser. 1, 23:153–54; *DANFS* 6:51.
7. *ORN*, ser. 1, 23:148–49; 153–54
8. "Report of Persons and Articles Employed and Hired by Quartermaster George D. Wise." RG 92, National Archives, Washington, D.C.; *ORN*, ser. 1, 23:177–78.
9. Sister Mary Denis Maher, *To Bind up the Wounds: Catholic Sister Nurses in the U.S. Civil War* (New York: Greenwood Press, 1989), 37; Ann Leonard, "*Red Rover*, the Civil War and the Nuns," *Lincoln Herald* 93 (Winter 1991): 139; "Complete Descriptive List or Muster Roll of the Crew of the U.S. Naval Hospital 'Red Rover.' October 1, 1863 through August 15, 1865." RG 24; "Hospital Ship Red Rover, October 17, 1862 to August 31, 1865." Records of the General Accounting Office, RG 217, entry 818, book 2622; Sister Mary Elenore, *On the King's Highway: A History of the Sisters of the Holy Cross of St. Mary of the Immaculate Conception* (New York: D. Appleton, 1931), 234.

10. December 27, 1862–Dec 30, 1863; February 2, 1863, and January 1, 1864–January, 1865, "Deck Log of the U.S.S. Red Rover," 2 vols. RG 24: February 2, 1863; "Muster Roll," RG 24; *Divided Waters: The Naval History of the Civil War* (New York: Harper Collins, 1995), 57, 181.

11. "Report of Persons & Articles," RG 92; "Register of Sick & Wounded & c. 'U.S.S. Red Rover' during the year 1862." RG 52, Watson's entry reads: "Re'cd of Dr. Geo. H. Bixby the sum of $7.50 amt. of wages due me for half month. As Laundress on board the Aforesaid Boat [*Red Rover*], Sarah X [her mark] Watson."

12. Robert Underwood Johnson and Clarence Clough Buel, eds. *Battles and Leaders of the Civil War*, 4 vols. (New York: Century, 1887–88), 150. Monthly pay for white Union privates: calvary, twelve dollars, artillery and infantry, eleven dollars. From August 6, 1861, thirteen dollars for all arms; and from May 1 1864, sixteen dollars. The naval rate of landsmen received twelve dollars per month. The "hellish rate of 'coal heaver' . . . eighteen dollars per month. Many black recruits served as coal heavers, drawing nearly double the pay they could get in the army. Boys at thirteen, were permitted to enlist with the consent of parents or guardians, and were rated 'boy,' third class, with a monthly pay of eight dollars." Musicant, *Divided Waters*, 57.

13. "Correspondence of C. H. Davis," RG 45, entry 395, subsection E54.

14. "Report of Persons & Articles," RG 92; *ORN*, ser. 1, 23:110–11: "Register: Sick and Wounded," RG 52; "Correspondence of C. H. Davis," RG 45.

15. "Deck Log," vols. 1, 2, RG 24.

16. Johnson and and Buel, *Battles and Leaders*, 3:553–53; *ORN*, ser. 1, 23:177–78; "Correspondence of C. H. Davis," RG 45.

17. "Correspondence of C. H. Davis," RG 45; Louis H. Roddis, "The U.S. Hospital Ship *Red Rover*," Military Surgeon 87 (1935);94.

18. *ORN*, ser.1, 23:182–83; 229–30, 252: Davidson, "*Red Rover*," 6; *ORN*, ser. 1, 18:729–53.

19. *ORN*, ser. 1, 23:683–88; Harper Allen Gosnell, *Guns on the Western Waters: The Story of the River Gunboats in the Civil War* (Baton Rouge: Louisiana State University Press, 1949), chapt. 9, 10; Fowler "Relief on the River," 18; *ORN*, ser. 1, 23:677–75.

20. "Civil War Hospital Ship," *All Hands* no. 541 (February 1962); 60; Dudley W. Knox, "*U.S.S. Red Rover* (Hospital Ship)," *Steamboat Bill of Facts: The Official Journal of the Steamship Historical Society of America* 13 (December 1944): 270; William T. Adams, "Red Rover: First Hospital Ship of the U.S. Navy," *United States Naval Institute Proceedings* 94 (November 1968): 150–52; Fowler, "Relief on the River," 18; Roddis, "U.S. Hospital Ship," 94–95; Musicant, *Divided Waters*, 179–82, 259–60.

21. *ORN*, ser, 1, 23:363–64, 376; "Correspondence of C. H. Davis," RG 45; Roddis, "U.S. Hospital Ship," 94–95; "Ship's History," 7.

22. "U.S.S. Red Rover," *ORN*, ser, 2, 1:189; "Deck Log," vol. 1, RG 24.

23. December 27, 1862, "Deck Log," vol. 1, RG 24; "Register, Sick and Wounded," RG 52; "Hospital Ship Red Rover," GAO, RG 217; *ORN*, ser. 1, 24:91–92.

24. "Medical Journal, U.S.S. Red Rover, From January 1st 1863 to March 31st 1865, Inclusive. N. Pinkney—Surgeon of the Fleet. Geo H. Bixby—Senr Medical Officer," p. 85, RG 52.

25. December 29–31, 1862, January 1, 1863, "Deck Log," vol. 1, RG 24.

26. January 1, 1863, ibid.

27. Gosnell describes the armor of various Civil War naval craft: "Bales of cotton and hay were favorite articles of protection for . . . some of the flimsy . . . craft. Boats 'armored'

in such ways were described . . . as 'cotton-clad' and 'hay-plated.' The . . . 'tinclads' were protected by thin iron, . . . safe against musketry where covered by . . . plates of, say, ¼-inch thickness. Heavy ropes were often wound around the pilothouse. Anchor chains were frequently hung along the sides of . . . ships when about to fight in smooth water as was usually the case in this war" (19). For additional discussion of various types of vessels engaged on the western waters, see also Tony Gibbon's *War-ships and Naval Battles of the Civil War* (New York: Gallery Books, 1989). January 2–15, 1863. "Deck Log," vol. 1, RG 24; *ORN*, ser. 1, 24:100.

28. January 11–19, 1863, and multiple entries, "Deck Log," vol. 1, RG 24.
29. January 21, 1863, ibid.
30. January 23–April 25, 1863, ibid; *ORN*, ser. 1, 24:190, 323–24, 428–30, 508–10, 532.
31. "Ship's History," 10; "Civil War Hospital Ship," 62.
32. "Ship's History," 10–11; April 16, 1863 "Deck Log," vol. 1, RG 24.
33. April 26–May 31, 1863, "Deck Log," vol. 1, RG 24; "The Naval Hospital Boat 'Red Rover,'" *Harper's Weekly* 7 (May 9, 1863): 299–300.
34. May 20–June 8, 1863, and multiple entries, "Deck Log," vols. 1, 2, RG 24.
35. June 20–21, 29, 1863, ibid., vol. 1; *ORN*, ser. 2, 25:91–92; "Medical Journal," RG 52.
36. May 20–July 30, 1863, "Deck Log," vol. 1, RG 24.
37. July 4, 14–28, 1863, ibid., Gosnell, *Guns on the Western Waters,* 246; Davidson, "*Red Rover,*" 8.
38. July 27–August 14, 1863, "Deck Log," vol. 1, RG 24; Eleanore, *On the King's High-way,* 234.
39. *ORN*, ser. 1, 25:336–37, 379–80, 427, 507, 562; August 15–November 19, 1863, "Deck Log," vol. 1. RG 24.
40. October 8, November 20–December 31, 1863 "Deck Log," vol. 1, RG 24; January 1–April 13, 1864, ibid., vol. 2; *ORN*, ser. 1, 25:609–10, 637–38, 691–92, 753–54, 26:224–26; "Abstract of Patients treated in the U.S. Naval Hospital Ship Red Rover," RG 52; Robley Dunglison, *A Dictionary of Medical Science* (Philadelphia: Henry C. Lea, 1874), 934.
41. May 3–24, 1864, January 1, 1865, "Deck Log," vol. 2, RG 24. While the exact reasons for Wells's and others' detachment are unknown, possible answers may be found in *ORN*, ser. 1, 26:311–12, 316; "Register of the Commissioned, Warrant, and Volunteer Officers of the Navy of the United States, Including Officers of the Marine Corps and Others, to January 1, 1865" (Washington, D.C., 1865), 275.
42. "Ship's History," 12; *ORN*, ser. 1, 26:317–18.
43. May 25–August 4, 1864, "Deck Log," vol. 2, RG 24.
44. August 22–23, 1864, ibid., *ORN*, ser. 1, 26:517–18.
45. "Deck Log," vol. 2, December 4–12, 1864; *ORN*, ser. 1, 27:54–57, 76–79, 99–102, 126–30, 143–46, 172–75.
46. "Ship's History," 13; Robert E. Denney, *The Civil War Years: A Day-By-Day Chroni-cle of the Life of a Nation* (New York: Sterling Publishing, 1992), 557–75; *Civil War Naval Chronology: 1861–1865* (Washington, D.C., Navy Department, 1971), 81–104; *ORN*, ser. 1, 27:185, 205–7, 210–12, 217–18, 249–54, 257–67, 274–75, 277–78, 281–83, 285–86, 288–89, 291–93, 298, 301, 309–15, 312–13, 318, 329, 332–33, 335–36, 342, 344; November 17, 1865, "Register, Sick and Wounded," RG 52; "Abstract of Patients," RG 52; Gibbons, *Warships and Naval Battles,* 163, 172.

47. "Medical Journal," 141; "Report of Persons and Articles," book 2, p.51, RG 92. This records Eliza Jenkins's death as occurring on September 28.

48. "Muster Roll," RG 24; Hospital Ship Red Rover," GAO, RG 217; "Report of Persons and Articles," RG 92; "Register, Sick and Wounded," RG 52; "Ship's History," 14.

49. ORN, ser. 1, 27:185, 205–7, 210–12, 217–18, 249–54, 257–67, 274–75, 277–78, 281–83, 285–86, 288–89, 291–93, 298, 301, 309–15, 312–13, 318, 329, 332–33, 335–36, 342, 344; ser. 2, 1:189; "Ship's History," 14.

50. Frederick S. Harrod, *Manning the New Navy: The Development of a Modern Naval Enlisted Force, 1899–1940* (Westport, Conn.: Greenwood Press, 1978), 65.

51. Eleanore, *On the King's Highway*, 233–34; Leonard, "*Red Rover,* the Civil War and the Nuns," 137; Maher, *To Bind Up the Wounds*, 82. "Muster Roll," RG 24, "Reports—Deaths—Invoices &c., U.S.S. 'Red Rover,'" RG 52.

52. "Muster Roll," RG 24; "Medical Records of Nurses (Hospital Muster Rolls)," RG 94, entry 535, 44 boxes; "*supernumerary:* Exceeding a fixed or prescribed number; extra. One that is in excess of the regular, necessary, or the usual number" (*American Heritage* [1983]).

53. Hospital Ship Red Rover, GAO, RG 217.

54. "Deck Log," vol. 1, RG 24.

55. Maher, *To Bind Up the Wounds*, 51.

56. "General Index to Pension Files, 1861–1934," RG 15, T 288 (microfilm), 544 rolls, roll 455; "Deck Log," vol. 1, RG 24.

57. January 2, 27, 29, 1863, "Deck Log," vol. 1, RG 24; "Reports—Deaths—Invoices &c." RG 52; "Hospital Ship Red Rover," GAO RG 217.

58. The participation by African Americans in the Western Gunboat Flotilla and Mississippi Squadron is the current focus of my research.

Chapter 23: Sojourner Truth and President Lincoln

1. See my "Sojourner Truth, Bold Prophet: Why Did She Never Learn to Read?" *New York History* 69 (January 1988): 55–77.

2. Oliver Johnson, in the Orange, N.J., *Journal,* 29 July 1876. For a recent similar claim, see *Dictionary of Black Culture* (New York: Philosophical Library, 1973), p. 439.

3. Marie Harlowe, "Sojourner Truth: The First Sit-In," *Negro History Bulletin* 29 (Fall 1966): 173.

4. Lucy N. Colman, letter to editor, 1 November, *Rochester Evening Express,* 10 November 1864: Colman, *Reminiscences* (Buffalo, 1891) pp. 66–67. Dorothy Porter, "Sojourner Truth Calls Upon the President: An 1864 Letter," *Massachusetts Review* 13 (Winter-Spring 1972): 279–99, is mistaken on who accompanied Sojourner on her visit to Lincoln, as on other matters.

5. Mary Derby, "Sojourner Truth," *Opportunity* 18 (June 1940): 169.

6. Colman, *Reminiscences,* pp. 52, 65; Fred Tomkins, *Jewels in Ebony* (London, 1866[?]), pp. 1–2.

7. *Narrative of Sojourner Truth* (Boston, 1875), p. 178.

8. C. Euphemia Cochrane, in Detroit *Advertiser and Tribune,* 11 January 1869; Seth Hunt, in Northampton *Hampshire Gazette,* quoted in *National Anti-Slavery Standard* (hereafter called *Standard*), 4 March 1871.

9. *Narrative,* p. xi; Chicago *Daily Inter-Ocean,* 13 August 1879. For a later example, see *Webster's American Biographies* (Springfield, Mass.: Merriam-Webster, 1974).

10. *Narrative,* pp. 181–83.

11. Sojourner Truth to Oliver Johnson, 3 February, in *Standard,* 13 February 1864; Sojourner Truth to Mary K. Gale, 25 February 1864, Sojourner Truth Papers, Library of Congress, Washington, D.C.

12. Sojourner Truth to Amy Post, 3 November 1864, Amy Post Papers, University of Rochester, Captain G. B. Carse, in *Standard,* 17 December 1864; Colman, *Reminiscences,* pp. 65–67; Tomkins, *Jewels in Ebony,* pp.1–4.

13. Nellie Browne Duff, "Sojourner Truth," *American Motorist,* October 1929, p. 33.

14. Oliver Johnson, in Orange, N.J., *Journal,* 29 July 1876.

15. Anonymous letter from Battle Creek, in *Standard,* 4 July 1863.

16. Merl R. Eppse, *The Negro, Too, in American History* (Nashville: National Publication Co., 1943), pp. 174–75; Walter White, "Sojourner Truth: Friend of Freedom," *New Republic,* 24 May 1948, p.17. See also, e.g., *My Black Freedom: The Nonviolent Abolitionists* (New York: Macmillan, 1970), p. 337, and Wendy Martin, *The American Sisterhood: Writings of the Feminist Movement* (New York: Harper and Row, 1972), p. 102.

17. *Standard,* 27 June and 4 July 1863.

18. Detroit *Post,* 12 January 1869.

19. *Narrative,* p. 178. Sojourner continued to tell the story; see *New York Herald,* 16 December 1878, Chicago *Daily Inter-Ocean,* 13 August 1879. For a recent retelling, see Victoria Ortiz, *Sojourner Truth: A Self-Made Woman* (Philadelphia: Lippincott, 1974), pp. 109–10.

20. Richard Cordley, "Sojourner Truth," *Congregationalist,* 3 March 1880, p. 65.

21. Calvin Fairbank, *Rev. Calvin Fairbank During Slavery Times* (1890; reprinted New York: Negro Universities Press, 1969), pp. 177–78. Arthur Huff Fauset, *Sojourner Truth, God's Faithful Pilgrim* (Chapel Hill: University of North Carolina, 1938), pp. 149–50, recounts but is skeptical about the story.

22. Woonsocket, R.I., *Patriot,* 5 August 1870; Sojourner, in *Narrative,* p. 275.

23. New York *Daily Tribune,* 6 June 1851.

Chapter 24: Free Men of Color in Gray

1. George W. Williams, *A History of the Negro Troops in the War of the Rebellion, 1861–1865* (New York: Harper & Bros., 1888); Joseph T. Wilson, *The Black Phalanx: A History of the Negro Soldiers of the United States* (Hartford, Conn.: American Publishing Co., 1890); Benjamin Quarles, *The Negro in the Civil War* (Boston: Little, Brown & Co., 1955); Dudley Taylor Cornish, *The Sable Arm: Negro Troops in the Union Army, 1861–1865* (New York: Longmans, Green & Co., 1956); James M. McPherson, *The Negro's Civil War* (New York: Pantheon Books, 1965).

2. Williams, *History of the Negro Troops,* 82; Mary Frances Berry, *Military Necessity and Civil Rights Policy: Black Citizenship and the Constitution, 1861–1868* (Port Washington, N.Y.: Kennikat Press, 1977) 116 n. 12; *War of the Rebellion: A Compilation of the Official Records of the Union and Confederate Armies* (Washington, D.C.: GPO, 1880–1901), ser. 4, 1:1095, 1111, 2:941; General S. Cooper to Major General Dabney H. Maury, September 28, 1863, Letters and Telegrams Sent by the Confederate Adjutant and Inspector General, 1861–65, chap. 1, vol. 38, p. 458, Record Group 109, War Department Collection of Confederate Records, National Archives.

3. Charles H. Wesley, "The Employment of Negroes as Soldiers in the Confederate Army," *Journal of Negro History* 4 (1919): 243; J. K. Obatala, "The Unlikely Story of Blacks Who Were Loyal to Dixie," *Smithsonian* 9 (1979): 94–101.

4. H. C. Blackerby, *Blacks in Blue and Gray: Afro-American Service in the Civil War* (Tuscaloosa, Ala.: Portals Press, 1979), 6; Robert E. Green, *Black Defenders of America, 1775–1973* (Chicago: Johnson Publishing Co., 1974), 53–102. Greene discusses sixty-six blacks who had applied for Confederat pensions after the war, but none of the men served as infantrymen.

5. Bell I. Wiley, *Southern Negroes, 1861–1865* (1938; rpt. Baton Rouge: Louisiana State University Press, 1974), 160–61.

6. John D. Winters, *The Civil War in Louisiana* (Baton Rouge: Louisiana State University Press, 1963), 21.

7. I owe a special debt of gratitude to Mrs. Jan Tate who assisted me in locating historical and genealogical information which identified these three men and two others whom I will discuss later.

8. Population Schedules, Eighth Census of the United States, St. Landry Parish, Louisiana, 1860, National Archives; Compiled Service Records of Confederate Soldiers Who Served in Volunteer Organizations from Louisiana, Microcopy 320, Roll 194, National Archives, hereafter cited as CSR; Application File of Charles F. Lutz, Confederate Pension Files, Louisiana State Archives and Record Service; Population Schedules, Tenth and Twelfth Censuses, Calcasieu Parish, 1880 and 1900.

9. Population Schedules, Seventh Census, 1850, St. Landry Parish; CSR, Roll 355; Notebook, J. W. Byran Papers, Louisiana Adjutant General's Library, Jackson Barracks, Chalmette; Return of Company I, Twenty-ninth Louisiana Infantry, March 1865; Bryan Papers; Clothing Issue Book, Company I, Twenty-ninth Louisiana Infantry, 1864–65, Bryan Papers; Population Schedules, Twelfth Census, 1900, Calcasieu Parish; Application File of Jean Baptiste Pierre-Auguste, Louisiana Confederate Pension Files.

10. Population Schedules, Eighth Census, 1860, St. Landry Parish; Rev. Donald J. Herbert, *Southwest Louisiana Record,* 31 vols. (Cecilia, La., privately published, 1974–83), 9:14; ibid., 3:691; CSR, Roll 273; *Opelousas Courier,* May 20, 1865; Population Schedules, Tenth Census, 1880, St. Landry Parish.

11. Population Schedules, Eighth Census, 1860, St. Landry Parish; *Opelousas Courier,* July 9, 1864; CSR, Roll 114.

12. Population Schedules, Eighth Census, 1860, Calcasieu Parish; Compiled Service Records of Confederate Soldiers Who Served in Volunteer Organizations from Texas, Microcopy 323, Roll 2310; Herbert, *Southwest Louisiana Records* 3:686.

13. Elizabeth Shown Mills to author, November 8, 1981. Mrs. Mills provided historical and genealogical information helping to establish the identities of these nine men.

14. Ibid.; CSR, Roll 22; Succession Book 25, Office of the Clerk of Court, Natchitoches Parish; Population Schedules, Eighth Census, 1860, Natchitoches Parish; CSR, Roll 22; Lieutenant J. Alphonse Prudhomme to Lieutenant [?] Goodwill, October 1, 1864, Letter Book, July 12, 1864–May 15, 1865, 51 J. A. Prudhomme Papers, Louisiana Adjutant General's Library.

15. Population Schedules, Eighth Census, 1860, Natchitoches Parish; Mills to author, November 8, 1981.

16. Records of Baptisms, 1851–73, Church of the Nativity, Campti, La., no. 1862–64 and no. 1863–15; Mills to author, November 8, 1981.

17. Records of Baptisms, 1851–73, Church of the Nativity, no. 1864–1; Joseph Galion Perot to Marie Terencine Lamather, Records of Burials and Marriages, 1851–1905, ibid., unnumbered page; Succession Book 21, Clerk of Court, Natchitoches, Succession of Marie Felonize Condet; Enrollment Book; Natchitoches Parish, La., 1864–65, Louisiana Historical Association Collection, Manuscripts Department, Special Collections Division, Tulane University Library.

18. Records of Burials and Marriages, 1851–1905, Church of the Nativity, 268; Mills to author, November 8, 1981.

19. Mills to author, November 8, 1981.

20. Enrollment Book, LHA Collection.

21. Prudhomme to Goodwill, October 1, 1864, Prudhomme Letter Book, 51.

22. Enrollment Book, LHA Collection; P. A. Morse to Col. Edmund G. Randolph, October 7, 1864, Prudhomme Papers; Endorsement by Randolph, October 8, 1864, on Morse to Randolph, October 7, 1864, ibid.; unnumbered order, Conscript District of Louisiana, October 8, 1864, ibid.; CSR, Roll 22.

23. Enrollment Book, LHA Collection.

24. David C. Rankin, "The Forgotten People: Free People of Color in New Orleans, 1850–1870" (unpublished doctoral dissertation, Johns Hopkins University, 1976), 166–67; Mary F. Berry, "Negro Troops in Blue and Gray: The Louisiana Native Guards, 1861–1863," *Louisiana History* 8 (1967): 172. See also Obatala, "The Unlikely Story," passim, and Roland C. McConnell, *Negro Troops in Antebellum Louisiana: A History of the Battalion of Free Men of Color* (Baton Rouge: Louisiana State University Press, 1968), passim.

25. Quarles, *The Negro in the Civil War,* 38; see also McPherson, *The Negro's Civil War,* 24.

26. Gary B. Mills, *The Forgotten People: Cane River's Creoles of Color* (Baton Rouge: Louisiana State University Press, 1977), 230, 244; Claude Oubre, "St. Landry's Gens de Couleur Libre: The Impact of War and Reconstruction," in Vaughan B. Baker and Jean T. Kreamer, *Louisiana Tapestry: The Ethnic Weave of St. Landry Parish* (Lafayette: Center for Louisiana Studies, 1982), 82; H. E. Sterkx, *The Free Negro in Ante-Bellum Louisiana* (Rutherford, N.J.: Fairleigh Dickinson University Press, 1972), 213.

27. Alexander S. Dupre to wife, September 29, October 2, 1864, Melrose Collection, Archives Division, Northwestern State University Library, Natchitoches.

28. Rankin, "The Forgotten People," 168; Wilson, *The Black Phalanx,* 483–84; Quarles, *The Negro in the Civil War,* 38–39; McPherson, *The Negro's Civil War,* 24.

29. Geraldine Mary McTigue, "Forms of Radical Interaction in Louisiana, 1860–1880" (unpublished doctoral dissertation, Yale University, 1975), 173, 174.

Chapter 25: Black Southerners in Gray

1. C. Vann Woodward, *American Counterpoint,* quoted in Eugene Genovese, *Roll, Jordan, Roll: The World the Slaves Made* (New York: Pantheon Books, 1974), preface.

2. Quoted in Michael P. Johnson and James L. Roark, *Black Masters: A Free Family of Color in the Old South* (New York: W. W. Norton, 1986), 293–295.

3. Charles Wesley, *The Collapse of the Confederacy* (New York: Russell and Russell, 1937), 153.

4. Quoted in Clarence Mohr, *On The Threshold: Master and Slaves in Civil War Georgia, 1861–1865* (Baton Rouge: Louisiana State University Press, 1986), 66.

5. Wesley, *Collapse,* 244.

6. J. K. Obatala, "The Unlikely Story of Negroes Who Were Loyal to Dixie," *Smithsonian* 9 (1979), 94.
7. Wesley, *Collapse,* 153.
8. Ibid.
9. *Memphis Avalanche* 3 September 1861.
10. H. C. Blackerby, *Blacks in Blue and Gray: Afro-American Service in the Civil War* (Tuscaloosa, Ala.: Portals Press, 1973), 18.
11. Charles H. Wesley, "The Employment of Negroes as Soldiers in the Confederate Army," *Journal of Negro History* 4 (1919), 242.
12. *Rebellion Record,* 46.
13. Ibid., 245.
14. Benjamin Quarles, *The Negro in the Civil War* (Boston: Little, Brown, 1955), 36.
15. Ibid., 37.
16. Obatala, "Unlikely," 94, and Quarles, *Negro,* 35.
17. *Charleston Evening News,* May 1, 1861.
18. *New Orleans Picayune,* 28 April 1861.
19. Quarles, *Negro,* 38.
20. E. Smith, "Negroes in the Confederacy," 13.
21. James H. Brewer, *The Confederate Negro: Virginia's Craftsmen and Military Laborers, 1861–1865* (Durham, N.C.: Duke University Press, 1969).
22. Wiley, *Southern Negro,* 112.
23. Patricia Brady, "Black Artists in Antebellum New Orleans," *Louisiana History* 32 (Winter, 1991), 5–28.
24. *Arkansas Historical Quarterly,* 3 (1944), 77.
25. Quarles, *Negro,* 37.
26. T. Conn Ryan, *Confederate Georgia* (Athens: University of Georgia Press, 1943), 133–134.
27. Mohr, *Threshold,* 286.
28. *Battlefields of the South* (New York: John Bradburn, 1865), 282.
29. *Clarion* (Mississippi) *Ledger,* 3 May 1984.
30. See the chapter on "The Landscape of the South: The Union Soldier Views The South" in Reid Mitchell, *Civil War Soldiers: Their Expectations and Their Experiences* (New York: Simon and Schuster, 1988).
31. See Mohr, *Threshold,* for this viewpoint.
32. Quoted in George P. Rawick, ed., *The American Slave: A Composite Autobiography Vol. I. From Sundown to Sunup: The Making of the Black Community* (Westport, Conn.: Greenwood Press, 1972), 136.
33. Ibid.
34. See for example Gary B. Mills' account of the free Negro community in North Louisiana in *The Forgotten People: Cane River's Creoles of Color* (Baton Rouge: Louisiana State University Press, 1977). It is the intention here to simply suggest motivational factors, not to discuss them in depth.
35. Wiley, *Southern Negro,* 12.
36. Quarles, *Negro,* 39.
37. Quoted in Blackerby, *Blue and Gray,* 34.
38. Washington Wills, quoted in Manly Wade Wellman, *Rebel Boast: First at Bethel-Last at Appomattox* (New York: Henry Holt and Company, 1956), 117.
39. Quoted in Blackerby, *Blue and Gray,* p. 34.

40. See the slave narratives in James Mellon, Ed., *Bullwhip Days: The Slaves Remember* (New York: Weidenfeld and Nicholson, 1988), and John Blassingame, *Slave Testimony: Two Centuries of Letters, Speeches, Interviews and Autobiographies* (Baton Rouge: Louisiana State University Press, 1977). These stories appeared from Virginia to Mississippi.

41. Mohr, *Threshold,* 94.

42. Ira Berlin, *Slaves Without Masters*. See especially the chapter on "Sources of Free Negro Identity."

43. Ibid., 272.

44. *New Orleans Picayune,* 30 June 1860.

45. Berlin, *Slaves Without Masters,* 343–346.

46. Loren Schweninger, "Prosperous Blacks in the South, 1790–1880," *American Historical Review,* February, 1990, 31–56. See also his longer work, *Black Property Owners in the South, 1790–1915* (Urbana: University of Illinois Press, 1986).

47. Schweninger, "Prosperous," 36.

48. Larry Koger, *Black Slaveowners: Free Black Slave Masters in South Carolina, 1790–1860* (Jefferson, N.C.: 1985). For other studies of black slaveowners, see Mills, *Forgotten People;* David O. Whitten, *Andrew Durnford: A Black Sugar Planter in Antebellum Louisiana* (Natchitoches, La.:, 1981); Michael P. Johnson and James L. Roark, *Black Masters: A Free Family of Color in the Old South* (New York:, 1984).

49. Walter Fleming, *Civil War and Reconstruction in Alabama* (New York: Columbia University Press, 1905), 208.

50. David Rankin, "The Impact of the Civil War on the Free Colored Community of New Orleans," *Perspectives in American History,* 11 (1977–1978), 379–418.

51. Wayne R. Austerman, "Virginia's Black Confederates," *Civil War Quarterly* 8 (1987), 52. See also Berlin, *Slaves Without Masters.*

52. Quoted in Wiley, *Southern Negro,* 141–142.

53. Blackerby, *Blue and Gray,* ii.

54. Genovese, *Roll, Jordan, Roll;* see the chapter on "Life in the Big House."

55. Quoted in Greene, *Black Defenders,* 85. See also Jay S. Hoar, "Black Glory: Our Afro-American Civil War Old Soldiery," *Gettysburg Magazine* January, 1990, 212.

56. Quoted in Isaac W. Heysinger, *Antietam and the Maryland and Virginia Campaigns of 1862* (New York: Neale Publishing Company, 1912), 122–123.

57. Quoted in Genovese, *Roll, Jordan, Roll,* p. 347.

58. Fleming, *Civil War and Reconstruction in Alabama.*

59. *Battlefields of the South,* 2:59.

60. Wiley, *Southern Negroes.*

61. *OR,* 4, 1, 1059.

62. *OR,* 4, 2, 86.

63. Robert Greene, ed., *Black Defenders of America.*

64. Austerman, *"Black Confederates,"* 51.

65. Scott E. Sallee, "Black Soldier of the Confederacy," *Blue and Gray,* 1990.

66. Pension record of Silas Young, Alabama State Archives, Montgomery.

67. Ibid.

68. Alexia J. Helsley, "Black Confederates," *South Carolina Historical Magazine* 74 (July, 1973), 186.

69. Austerman, "Black Soldiers," 47.

70. Leroy Jones, Pension Application, Tennessee State Archives, Nashville.
71. *Confederate Veteran,* May 1916, 216.
72. Blackerby, *Blue and Gray,* 1.
73. Walter Lord, Ed., *The Fremantle Diary, Being the Journal of Lieutenant Colonel James Arthur Lyon Fremantle, Coldstream Guards, on His Three Months in the Southern States* (Boston: Little, Brown, 1954), 225.
74. Bell Irvin Wiley, *The Life and Times of Johnny Reb* (Baton Rouge: Louisiana State University Press, 1978), 328.
75. *Battlesfields of the South,* I, 157–158.
76. Hiram Conaway, Pension Application, Virginia State Archives, Richmond.
77. Greene, *Black Defenders,* 64.
78. *Confederate Veteran,* September, 1912, 410.
79. *Richmond Whig,* January 27, 1864.
80. *OR,* 2, 6, 397–398.
81. Jay S. Hoar, *The South's Last Boys in Gray: An Epic Poem Elegy* (Bowling Green, Ohio: The Bowling Green State University Popular Press, 1986), 212–213.
82. Austerman, "Black Soldiers," 47.
83. Ibid., 62. Similar stories appear on p. 84.
84. William Bibb, Pension Application, Tennessee State Archives, Nashville.
85. Blackerby, *Blacks in Gray,* 36.
86. Daniel Ammen, *The Navy in the Civil War* (New York: Charles Scribner's Sons, 1883–1885), V.2, 43.
87. Helsley, "Black Confederates," 186.
88. *Confederate Veteran,* April 1927, 152–3.
89. Sam Collier, Pension Application, Tennessee State Archives, Nashville.
90. Henry Nelson, Pension Application, Tennessee State Archives, Nashville.
91. Alex Wharton, Pension Application, Tennessee State Archives, Nashville.
92. *Battlefields of the South,* 284.
93. Henry B. McClelland, *I Rode with Jeb Stuart,* ed. Burke Davis (Bloomington: Indiana University Press, 1958), 109.
94. Hoar, *South's Boys,* 462.
95. Wiley, *Southern Negro,* 139.
96. *Battlefields of the South,* 2:22–23.
97. Ibid, 253.
98. Capt. Thomas Nelson, *The Confederate Scout* (Washington, D.C.: The Neale Publishing Company, 1957), 122.
99. Blackerby, *Blue and Gray,* 13.
100. Austerman, "Black Soldiers," 47.
101. *New Orleans Crescent,* November 15, 1861.
102. *Battlefields,* 282.
103. Alfred Brown, Pension Application, Tennessee State Archives, Nashville.
104. Hutson Longstreet, Pension Application, Mississippi State Archives, Jackson.
105. Wade Watkins, Pension Application, Tennessee State Archives, Nashville.
106. Helsley, "Black Confederates," 186.
107. Monroe Jones, Pension Application, Tennessee State Archives, Nashville.
108. John D. Winters, *The Civil War in Louisiana* (Baton Rouge: Louisiana State University Press, 1963), 21.
109. Moore, *Civil War in Song and Story,* 481.

110. George H. Gordon, *A War Diary* (Boston: Little, Brown, 1882), 194.

111. Blackerby, *Blacks in Gray,* 29.

112. George Alfred Townsend, *Rustics in Rebellion: A Yankee Reporter on the Road to Richmond, 1861–1865* (Chapel Hill: The University of North Carolina Press, 1950), 52.

113. Greene, *Black Defenders,* pp. 65, 79, 89.

114. Greg Tyler, "Rebel Drummer Henry Brown," *Civil War Times Illustrated,* February, 1989, 22–23, See also Greg Tyler, "Article Brings Notice to a Unique Rebel," *Civil War Times Illustrated* May/June 1990, 57.

115. Obatala, "Unlikely," 98.

116. Blackerby, *Blacks in Gray,* 21.

117. Ibid., 16.

118. James Clark, Pension Application, Department of Archives and History, Atlanta, Georgia.

119. Mohr, *Threshold,* 286.

120. *OR,* 4, 1, 1059.

121. Carroll, "Dignity, Courage and Fidelity," 26–27.

122. Johnson and Roark, *Black Masters.*

123. Ibid, 306.

124. *Sumter Watchman and Southron,* August 28, 1895.

125. Jay Hoar, "Black Glory," 126.

126. William T. Lewis, *The Centennial History of Winston County, Mississippi* (Pasadena, Texas: The Globe Publishers, 1876), 77.

127. James Young, Pension Application, Alabama State Archives, Montgomery, Alabama. The Board rejected the claim, saying that "the board takes judicial knowledge of the fact that Negroes are not by law authorized to be enlisted in the Confederate State's Army or Navy and that as a matter of fact no Negroes were so enlisted in said army or navy. Therefore, the State Auditor is hereby directed to strike the name of the said James Young from the pension roll."

128. Letter from State of Alabama Department of Archives and History, February 6, 1991, in Young's application file.

129. Helsley, "Black Confederates," 187.

130. Major Henry B. Morgan, "The Birth of a County," *Moore County* [Tennessee] *News,* no date, p. 26.

131. Capt. C. A. Stevens, *Berdan's United States Sharpshooters in the Army of the Potomac, 1861–1865* (St. Paul, Minnesota: Price-McGill, 1892), 55–56.

132. Greene, *Black Defenders,* 79.

133. William C. Davis, *Images of the War,* 4:193.

134. William N. Still Jr., *Iron Afloat: The Story of the Confederate Armor Clads* (Columbia: The University of South Carolina Press, 1985), 114.

135. Mohr, *Threshold,* 289–290.

136. Austerman, "Virginia's Black Confederates," 50.

137. Obatala, "Unlikely," 99.

138. Quoted in Blackerby, *Blacks in Gray,* 5.

139. Quoted in James M. McPherson, *The Negro's Civil War: How American Negroes Felt and Acted During the War for the Union* (Chicago: University of Illinois Press, 1982), 22–23.

140. *South Carolina Troops in Confederate Service,* A. S. Salley Jr., comp. (Columbia: The R. L. Bryan Co., 1913), I, 218, n. 17. 219. It is nearly impossible to tell the length of these men's service. Most of the records are missing, and those available list many of

them as deserters. On the other hand, several of them list their service in their pension records as with "McCreary's Regiment." McCreary did not command the Regiment until early in 1864, therefore it is logical to assume that those who described their Regiment as McCreary's served as late as 1864.

141. See *Black Defenders.* Also Blackerby, *Blacks in Gray,* 18, and *South Carolina Troops.*

142. J. F. J. Caldwell, *The History of a Brigade of South Carolinians, known first as "Gregg's" and subsequently as "McGowan's" Brigade* (Dayton: Morningside, 1974).

143. Bergeron. "Free Men of Color," 251.

144. Mary Berry, "Negro Troops in Blue and Gray: The Louisiana Native Guards, 1861–1863," *Louisiana History* 8 (1967), 165–190.

145. Powell A. Casey, *Louisiana in the War of 1812* (Privately Printed, 1963).

146. Berry, "Negro Troops in Blue and Gray."

147. National Archives Microcopy 320–94.

148. *New Orleans Picayune,* 10 January 1862.

149. Microcopy 320–94, National Archives.

150. *OR,* 1, 6, 858.

151. Ibid, 852–858.

152. All of the information on this community is drawn from Gary B. Mills, *Forgotten People,* and Gary B. Mills, "Patriotism Frustrated: The Native Guards of Confederate Natchitoches," Louisiana History (Winter, 1977), 437–451.

153. Ibid., 441.

154. Ibid., 441–442.

155. Ibid.

156. Quoted in H. E. Strekx, *The Free Negro in Antebellum Louisiana* (Rutherford, N.J.: Fairleigh Dickinson University Press, 1972), 212.

157. *OR,* 4, 1, 1088.

158. *Mobile Evening News,* 14 April 1862.

159. "Creole" is frequently used to describe people of Spanish-English or French-English blood. Since these two groups were considered legally white, no governmental action would be needed for them to serve. Therefore, I conclude that the references cited here are to people of black and white mixed blood, but it remains possible that this is a reference to the other groups.

160. *OR,* 4, 2, 197.

161. *OR,* 4, 2, 941.

162. Arthur Bergeron, *Confederate Mobile, 1861–1865* (Oxford: The University of Mississippi Press, 1992).

163. *OR,* 4, 3, 1009.

164. Robert F. Durden, *The Gray and the Black* (Baton Rouge: Louisiana State University Press, 1972).

165. *OR,* 4, 3, 1161.

166. Mohr, *Threshold,* 285.

167. To Majors J. W. Pegram and Thomas P. Turner, *OR,* 4, 3, 1144. Several more can be found in the *OR.*

168. Quoted in Blackerby, *Blue and Gray,* 27.

169. *OR,* 1, 54 pt. 1, 818.

170. Richmond *Whig,* March 31, 1865.

171. Quoted in R. J. M. Blackett, Ed., *Thomas Morris Chester, Black Civil War Correspondent* (Baton Rouge: Louisiana State University Press, 1989), 248.

172. *Richmond Sentinel,* March 21, 1865.
173. *Richmond Examiner,* March 27, 1865.
174. Austerman, "Virginia's Black Confederates," 53.
175. *Confederate Veteran,* 1915, 404, 411.
176. Lt. Moses Purnell Handy, "The Fall of Richmond in 1865," *The American Magazine and Historical Chronicle* (Ann Arbor: Clements Library) Vol. I, No. 2, 1985–86, n.p.
177. George Washburn, *History and Record of the 108th Regiment of New York Volunteers* (Rochester: E. R. Andrews, 1894).
178. Walter Lord, Ed., *The Fremantle Diary, Being the Journal of Lieutenant Colonel James Arthur Lyon Fremantle, Coldstream Guards, on His Three Months in the Southern States* (Boston: Little, Brown, 1954), 225.

Chapter 26: General Patrick Clebume's Proposal to Arm Southern Slaves

1. Charles Edward Nash, *Biographical Sketches of Gen. Pat Cleburne and Gen. T. C. Hindman Together with Humorous Anecdotes and Reminiscences of the Late Civil War* (Little Rock, 1898), 15.
2. This street fight is described by Biscoe Hindman, General Hindman's son, in *Southern Historical Society Papers,* 31 (Richmond, 1903), 163–165.
3. Irving A. Buck, *Cleburne and His Command,* ed. By Thomas Robson Hay (Jackson, Tennessee, 1959), 20.
4. Ibid.
5. Ibid., 21.
6. Thomas Robson Hay, "The Question of Arming the Slaves," *Mississippi Valley Historical Review,* 6 (1919), 36.
7. Allen Johnson and Dumas Malone, eds., *Dictionary of American Biography* (New York, 1930), 4:190.
8. Buck, *Cleburne,* 40.
9. Basil W. Duke, *Reminiscences of General Basil W. Duke, C.S.A.* (Garden City, New York, 1911), 69.
10. Ella Lonn, *Foreigners in the Confederacy* (Chapel Hill, 1940), 444.
11. Buck, *Cleburne,* 187.
12. W. H. Hardee, "Biographical Sketch of Major-General P. R. Cleburne," *Southern Histoical Society Papers,* 31 (Richmond, 1903), 156–157.
13. *The War of the Rebellion: A Compilation of the Official Records of the Union and Confederate Armies* (70 vols. in 128, Washington, 1880–1901), ser. 4, vol. 2, 670–671. (Cited hereafter as *OR*)
14. Duke, *Reminiscences,* 68.
15. Buck, *Cleburne,* 188.
16. *OR,* ser. 1, vol. 52, pt. 2, 586.
17. Ibid., 587.
18. Ibid.
19. Ibid.
20. Ibid.
21. Ibid.
22. Ibid., 588.
23. Ibid.

24. Ibid.
25. Ibid., 589.
26. Ibid., 589–590.
27. Ibid., 590.
28. Ibid.
29. Ibid., 591.
30. Ibid.
31. Ibid.
32. Ibid., 592.
33. Ibid.
34. Irving A. Buck, "Negroes in Our Army," *Southern Historical Society Papers,* 31 (Richmond, 1903), 215.
35. Ibid., 215–216.
36. Ibid.
37. Wirt Armistead Cate, *Two Soldiers* (Chapel Hill, 1938), 16.
38. Ibid., 17.
39. Ibid., 17–18.
40. Ibid.
41. Ibid., 19.
42. Buck, "Negroes in Our Army." *Southern Historical Society Papers,* 31, 216.
43. Ibid., 217.
44. *OR,* ser. 1, vol. 52, pt. 2, 591.
45. Ibid., vol. 32, pt. 2, 537.
46. Ibid., vol. 52, pt. 2, 595.
47. Ibid., 596.
48. Ibid., 606. The Confederate Constitution prohibited the passage of a law "denying or impairing the right of property in negro slaves."
49. Buck, "Negroes in Our Army," Southern Historical Soceity Papers, 31, 217.
50. *OR* ser. 1, vol. 52, pt. 2, 598–599.
51. James Cooper Nisbet, *Four Years on the Firing Line,* ed. by Bell Irvin Wiley (Jackson, Tennessee, 1963), 172.
52. Ibid.
53. Ibid., 172–173.
54. Ibid., 173–174.
55. E. L. Drake, ed., *The Annuals of the Army of Tennessee and Early Western History,* I, No. 2 (May, 1878), 51.
56. Buck, *Cleburne,* 52.
57. Buck, "Negroes in Our Army," *Southern Historical Society Papers,* 31, 217.
58. Nash, *Biographical Sketches,* 196.

For Further Reading

Berlin, Ira et al., eds. *The Black Military Experience*. Series 2 of *Freedom: A Documentary History of Emancipation, 1861–1867*. New York: Cambridge University Press, 1982.

Blight, David W. *Frederick Douglass's Civil War: Keeping the Faith in Jubilee*. Baton Rouge: Louisiana State University Press, 1989.

Cornish, Dudley Taylor. *The Sable Arm: Negro Troops in the Union, 1861–1865*. New York: Longmans Green and Co., 1956.

Glatthaar, Joseph T. *Forged in Battle: The Civil War Alliance of Black Soldiers and White Officers*. New York: Free Press, 1990.

Gooding, Cpl. James Henry. *On the Altar of Freedom: A Black Soldier's Civil War Letters from the Front*. Edited by Virginia Adams. New York: Warner Books, 1991.

Hollandsworth, James G. *The Louisiana Native Guards: The Black Military Experience During the Civil War*. Baton Rouge: Louisiana State University Press, 1995.

McPherson, James M. *The Negro's Civil War: How American Negroes Felt and Acted During the War for the Union*. New York: Ballentine Books, 1991.

Quarles, Benjamin. *The Negro in the Civil War*. Boston: Little, Brown, 1953.

Redkey, Edwin S., ed. *A Grand Army of Black Men: Letters from African American Soldiers in the Union Army, 1861–1865*. New York: Cambridge University Press, 1992.

Taylor, Susie King. *Reminiscences of My Life in Camp*. Boston: Susie King Taylor, 1902. Reprint, *A Black Woman's Civil War Memoirs: Reminiscences of My Life in Camp with the 33rd U.S. Colored Troops, Late 1st South Carolina Volunteers*. Edited by Patricia Romero. New York: M. Wiener, 1988.

Trudeau, Noah Andre. *Like Men of War: Black Troops in the Civil War, 1862–1865*. Boston: Little, Brown, 1998.

Wise, Stephen R. *Gate of Hell: Campaign for Charleston Harbor, 1863*. Columbia: University of South Carolina Press, 1994.

Index